CONTEMPORARY AUDITING
REAL ISSUES AND CASES

Fourth Edition

Michael C. Knapp
University of Oklahoma

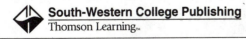
South-Western College Publishing
Thomson Learning™

Australia • Canada • Denmark • Japan • Mexico • New Zealand • Philippines
Puerto Rico • Singapore • South Africa • Spain • United Kingdom • United States

Contemporary Auditing: Real Issues and Cases, 4/e, by Michael C. Knapp
Team Director: David L. Shaut
Acquisitions Editor: Rochelle Kronzek
Production Editor: Deanna Quinn
Media Production Editor: Lora Craver
Marketing Manager: Jennifer Codner
Manufacturing Coordinator: Doug Wilke
Production House: Cover to Cover Publishing, Inc.
Cover Design: Paul Neff Design
Cover Image: © Chris Thomaidis/Tony Stone Images
Printer: West Group

Printed in the United States of America
1 2 3 4 5 03 02 01 00

For more information contact South-Western College Publishing, 5101 Madison Road, Cincinnati, Ohio, 45227 or find us on the Internet at http://www.swcollege.com

For permission to use material from this text or product, contact us by
• **telephone: 1-800-730-2214**
• **fax: 1-800-730-2215**
• **web: http://www.thomsonrights.com**

Library of Congress Cataloging-in-Publication Data

Knapp, Michael Chris
    Contemporary auditing : issues and cases / Michael C. Knapp. --
4th ed.
        p.   cm.
    Includes bibliographical references and index.
    ISBN 0-324-04861-0 (pbk. : alk. paper)
        1. Corporations--United States--Auditing--Case studies.
  2. Auditing--Corrupt practices--Case studies.   3. Auditors-
-Professional ethics--United States.   4. Auditing--Law and
legislation--United States--Cases.   I. Title.
    HF5686.C7K62 2001
    657'.95--dc21

This book is printed on acid-free paper.

DEDICATION

To Carol, Johnny, Lindsay, and Jessi

BRIEF CONTENTS

SECTION 7   PROFESSIONAL ISSUES   339

SECTION 8   CLASSIC LITIGATION CASES   393

CONTENTS

ix

Key Topics: identification of key management assertions, limitations of audit evidence, importance of candid predecessor-successor auditor communications, client confidentiality, and client-imposed audit scope limitations.

SECTION 2   AUDITS OF HIGH-RISK ACCOUNTS   147

SECTION 3   INTERNAL CONTROL ISSUES   191

SECTION 4   ETHICAL RESPONSIBILITIES
OF ACCOUNTANTS   243

SECTION 5   ETHICAL RESPONSIBILITIES OF INDEPENDENT AUDITORS   277

SECTION 6 PROFESSIONAL ROLES

311

SECTION 7 PROFESSIONAL ISSUES

339

SECTION 8   CLASSIC LITIGATION CASES   393

During the course of a consulting engagement, Yale Express's audit firm discovered that the company's prior year financial statements were materially in error, although the firm had issued an unqualified opinion on those statements.

In reviewing this case, the Supreme Court defined the degree of auditor misconduct that must be present before a client can recover damages from an auditor in a lawsuit filed under the Securities Exchange Act of 1934.

The huge Equity Funding scandal demonstrated the critical need for auditors to maintain a high level of skepticism when planning and carrying out an audit.

Two Big Eight accountants faced a long and grueling jury trial following their indictment on criminal fraud charges that stemmed from their audits of this once high-profile company.

PREFACE

Criticism of the accounting profession by regulatory authorities, the financial press, and the general public has forced the profession to reassess its societal purpose and future direction. One result of this reassessment has been a call for exploring ways of improving accounting education. Many parties suggest that accounting educators should employ a broader array of instructional resources, particularly experiential resources designed to stimulate active learning by students. In fact, a primary objective of the Accounting Education Change Commission was to encourage the development of those types of materials for use in accounting courses. The fourth edition of my casebook provides instructors with a source of such materials that can be used in both undergraduate and graduate auditing courses.

This casebook stresses the "people" aspect of independent audits. If you review a sample of recent "audit failures," I believe you will find that problem audits seldom result from inadequate audit technology. Instead, deficient audits typically result from the presence of one, or both, of the following two conditions: client personnel who intentionally subvert an audit and auditors who fail to carry out the responsibilities assigned to them. Exposing students to problem audits helps them recognize the red flags that often accompany potential audit failures. An ability to recognize these red flags and experience with discussing and dissecting problem audits should help students cope more effectively with the problematic situations they are certain to encounter in their own careers. In addition, this experiential approach allows students to more readily grasp the relevance of important auditing concepts and procedures.

The cases in this text also acquaint students with the work environment of auditors. After studying these cases, students will better understand how client pressure, peer pressure, time budgets, and related factors complicate the work roles of independent auditors. Also embedded in these cases are the ambiguity and lack of structure that auditors face each day. Missing documents, conflicting audit evidence, auditors' dual obligation to the client and to financial statement users, and the lack of definitive professional standards for many situations are additional aspects of the audit environment woven into these cases.

The fourth edition of this casebook features a new organizational structure. This edition contains eight sections of cases instead of the five sections found in the three earlier editions. The eight categories of cases include the following: Comprehensive Cases, Audits of High-Risk Accounts, Internal Control Issues, Ethical Responsibilities of Accountants, Ethical Responsibilities of Independent Auditors, Professional Roles, Professional Issues, and Classic Litigation Cases. This new organizational structure will help adopters more readily identify cases best suited for their particular needs.

Numerous cases appearing in earlier editions have been updated for new events and circumstances impacting those cases. For example, this edition updates the ongoing legal travails of Charles Keating (Lincoln Savings and Loan Association) and Eddie Antar (Crazy Eddie, Inc.). You probably will not be surprised to learn that Stanley Goldblum, former chief executive of Equity Funding, is associated with another headline-catching fraud. Other returning cases that contain new material include, but are not limited to, When Auditors Become Lobbyists, *Hopkins v. Price Waterhouse*, and The Fund of Funds, Ltd.

This edition of my casebook contains 13 new cases. These cases include Triton Energy Ltd., a case with an international angle that focuses on the Foreign Corrupt Practices Act. As you are probably aware, law enforcement authorities are once more "cracking down" on multinational companies that violate the anti-fraud and accounting provisions of that important federal statute. The Saks Fifth Avenue case introduces students to control issues relevant to a retail business. Saks' "zero tolerance" policy for employee theft typically sparks a lively debate among my students. In the Accuhealth, Inc., case, your students will find yet another scenario in which an accounting officer of a large firm faces an ethical dilemma. That officer must decide what to do when he discovers that his superiors are systematically "skimming" cash from the company's retail operations. A new comprehensive case appearing in this edition is Star Technologies, Inc. That case focuses on accounting and auditing issues pertinent to high-tech companies.

This casebook can be used in several different ways. Adopters can use the casebook as a supplemental text for the undergraduate auditing course or as a primary text for a graduate-level seminar in auditing. The instructor's manual contains a syllabus for a graduate auditing course organized around this text. Finally, this casebook can be used in the capstone professional practice course incorporated in many five-year accounting programs.

Listed next are brief descriptions of the eight groups of cases included in this casebook. The casebook's Table of Contents presents an annotated description of each case.

Comprehensive Cases

Most of these cases deal with highly publicized problem audits performed by large, international accounting firms. Among the clients involved in these audits are Mattel, ESM Government Securities, ZZZZ Best Company, and Lincoln Savings and Loan Association. These cases address a wide range of auditing, accounting, and ethical issues.

Audits of High-Risk Accounts

In contrast to the cases in the prior section, these cases typically highlight contentious accounting and auditing issues posed by a single account or group of accounts. For example, the Doughtie's Foods case focuses primarily on inventory audit procedures. The CapitalBanc case raises audit issues relevant to cash, while the Giant Stores case focuses on auditing accounts payable.

Internal Control Issues

Audit strategies increasingly emphasize the need for auditors to thoroughly understand their clients' internal control policies and procedures. The cases in this section introduce students to control issues in a variety of contexts. Goodner Brothers, Inc., raises control issues for a wholesaler, while both Saks Fifth Avenue and Howard Street Jewelers center on important control issues for retail businesses.

Ethical Responsibilities of Accountants

Integrating ethics into an auditing course requires much more than simply discussing the *AICPA Code of Professional Conduct*. This section presents actual situations in which accountants in private practice have faced perplexing ethical dilemmas. By requiring students to study real world contexts in which important ethical issues arise, they will be better prepared to cope with similar situations in their own professional careers. One of the cases in this section, Rocky Mount Undergarment Company, focuses on the accountants of a company who had to face the eternal question of whether the end justifies the mean. A new case in this edition, F&C International, profiles three corporate executives who had to decide whether to compromise their personal code of ethics in the face of a large scale fraud masterminded by their firm's chief executive.

Ethical Responsibilities of Independent Auditors

The cases in this section highlight common ethical dilemmas faced by independent auditors. An audit partner for the PTL Club maintained a check register for that organization, a check register through which Jim Bakker funneled various questionable disbursements. Was that an appropriate responsibility for an independent auditor to assume? Consider the dilemma faced by Michael Goodbread, an audit partner with a major accounting firm. His firm acquires a company in which he has a small but direct financial interest. What should he do? No doubt, any auditing textbook will provide the easy answer to that question. But, auditors in public practice don't always "go by the book."

Professional Roles

Cases in this section examine specific work roles in public accounting. These cases explore the responsibilities associated with these roles and related challenges that professionals in these roles encounter. Hopefully, introducing students to these roles in a meaningful way, that is, in a real world context, will better prepare them to transition successfully into these roles in the future. The Tommy O'Connell case involves a young auditor recently promoted to audit senior. Shortly following his promotion, Tommy finds himself assigned to supervise a small but difficult audit. Tommy's sole subordinate on that engagement happens to be a young man whose integrity and work ethic have been questioned by seniors he has worked for previously. Three cases in this section spotlight the staff accountant work role, the initial position typically assumed by recent college graduates who enter public accounting.

Professional Issues

The dynamic nature of the public accounting profession continually impacts the work environment of public accountants and the nature of the services they provide. The cases in this section explore this changing work environment. For example, the *Hopkins v. Price Waterhouse* case discusses the unique problems faced by women pursuing careers in public accounting. The Scott Fane and Stephen Gray cases focus on recent changes in the profession's ethics code that impact accounting practitioners. Both of these young practitioners became involved in legal disputes with their state boards. These disputes centered on the type of marketing efforts CPAs are allowed to use and the types of services CPAs are allowed to offer to clients, respectively.

Classic Litigation Cases

Auditing textbooks concentrate almost exclusively on the legal liability issues inherent in the classic audit litigation cases that have arisen over the past several decades. This text addresses the underlying auditing issues embedded in these cases in addition to the relevant legal liability issues. Cases in this section include Fred Stern & Company (Ultramares), 1136 Tenants, and First Securities Company of Chicago (Hochfelder).

Customize Your Own Casebook

To maximize the flexibility of using these cases, South-Western College Publishing has included *Contemporary Auditing, Issues and Cases* in its customized publishing program. Adopters have the option of creating a customized version of this casebook ideally suited for their specific needs. For more information on how to design your customized casebook, please contact your South-Western sales representative.

Acknowledgements

I greatly appreciate the insight and suggestions provided by the following reviewers of earlier editions of this text: Barbara Apostolou, Louisiana State University; Jane Baird, Mankato State University; Ed Blocher, University of North Carolina; Kurt Chaloupecky, Southwest Missouri State University; Ray Clay, University of North Texas; Mary Doucet, University of Georgia; Ruth Engle, Lafayette College; Laurence Johnson, Colorado State University; Donald McConnell, University of Texas at Arlington; Heidi Meier, Cleveland State University; Don Nichols, Texas Christian University; Marcia Niles, University of Idaho; Rajendra Srivastava, University of Kansas; and Jim Yardley, Virginia Polytechnic University. This project also benefited greatly from the editorial assistance of my sister, Paula Kay Conatser, and my wife, Carol Ann Knapp. Finally, I would like to acknowledge the contributions of my students, who have provided invaluable comments and suggestions on the content and use of these cases.

Section One
Comprehensive Cases

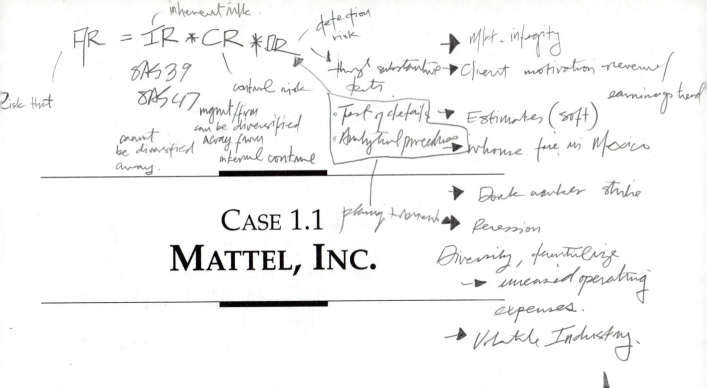

CASE 1.1
MATTEL, INC.

In 1945, Elliot and Ruth Handler, along with a friend, Harold Matson, founded a small toy company. Within a few months, Matson decided to pursue other interests and left Mattel, Inc., to the Handlers. For the next decade, the husband-and-wife team struggled to make their small company a success. Elliot Handler, an artist, designed the toys the company produced, while Ruth Handler managed the company's business affairs, concentrating much of her time on finding sales outlets for their products.

Mattel's net worth was a little more than $500,000 in 1955. That year, Ruth Handler took a daring step to expand the size of the company. She decided to advertise Mattel's toys on the popular children's television program, *The Mickey Mouse Club*. The advertising campaign cost several hundred thousand dollars and if unsuccessful could have bankrupted the small company. Ruth Handler's gamble paid off handsomely. Within a few months, Mattel's sales orders increased dramatically, and the company was on its way to establishing itself as a major player in the very competitive toy industry.

In 1959, Ruth Handler took a second gamble by introducing a full-figured, teenage doll. Ruth intended to christen the doll Babs, a pet name she used for her daughter Barbara. After discovering that "Babs" had been copyrighted by another toy maker, Ruth changed her doll's name to Barbie. Industry experts quickly dismissed the doll, insisting that it would not appeal to its target market of three- to eleven-year-old girls. The experts were wrong. Barbie was an instant success, with more than 350,000 sold the first year it was on the market. By Barbie's fortieth birthday, more than one billion dolls had been sold in 150 countries.

Ruth Handler, the youngest of 10 children of Polish immigrants, was never modest about explaining the success of Mattel. During an interview, she once noted matter-of-factly that she was "a marketing genius." A short and intensely competitive woman, Ruth Handler hated failure and refused to accept it. During the early 1970s, however, she and her company encountered a set of circumstances that would eventually drive Mattel to the verge of bankruptcy.

TRYING TIMES AT MATTEL

By 1971, financial analysts recognized Mattel as one of the premier growth companies in the United States. In that year, the company reported pretax profits of $34 million on sales approaching $275 million. Investors were so infatuated by the company and its prospects that Mattel common stock traded at an enormous price-earnings ratio, often exceeding 50 to 1. The Handlers and other key Mattel executives became fabulously wealthy as a result. By 1971, the Mattel stock controlled by Elliot and Ruth Handler had a market value approaching $300 million.

Despite the record earnings reported by Mattel for each successive year from 1967 through 1971, the company began experiencing serious problems in the early 1970s. Many of these problems could be traced to the Handlers' decision in the late 1960s to hire Seymour Rosenberg as the company's executive vice-president and chief financial officer. Rosenberg, formerly with Litton Industries, had earned a reputation for his skill in identifying and acquiring underperforming companies and making them financial successes. Shortly after joining Mattel, he convinced the Handlers to diversify into several industries and to overhaul the company's organizational structure, breaking its operations down into decentralized divisions. Unfortunately, four of the six companies acquired by Mattel on the recommendation of Rosenberg proved to be very poor investments, and his decentralization plan increased Mattel's operating costs tremendously.

Besides the problems created by Rosenberg, who was dismissed by the Handlers in late 1972, Mattel encountered a series of largely uncontrollable circumstances in the early 1970s that damaged the company's profitability. First, one of the company's large warehouses in Mexicali, Mexico, burned to the ground in 1970. The following year, a dockworkers' strike prevented the company from receiving any toy shipments from its large Hong Kong plant. Finally, the recession of the early 1970s cut sharply into the company's sales. These factors caused Mattel to register a loss of approximately $30 million in fiscal 1972, which ended January 29, 1972.

A large banking syndicate that had significant loans outstanding to Mattel persuaded the Handlers to dismiss Rosenberg. Following Rosenberg's departure, the Handlers named Albert Spear Mattel's executive vice-president and placed him in charge of the company's day-to-day operations. Spear soon discovered that Mattel's financial status had been grossly misrepresented to the public. Shortly before Spear accepted his new position in early 1973, Mattel issued a press release stating that the company had undergone a dramatic turnaround in fiscal 1973 compared with fiscal 1972. An intensive study of Mattel's financial records by Spear revealed that the company had actually suffered a huge loss in fiscal 1973—larger than the loss reported the previous year. When Spear released this information to the public, panicked investors dumped their Mattel stock. Angry stockholders and former stockholders quickly filed five class action lawsuits against Mattel and its executives. Spear's revelations also triggered an investigation of Mattel's financial affairs by the Securities and Exchange Commission (SEC).

In October 1975, Elliot and Ruth Handler resigned their positions with Mattel. One month later, Mattel's outside directors released a 500-page report that detailed a massive earnings manipulation scheme masterminded by the company's executive officers. According to the report, the Handlers and other key Mattel officials issued "financial statements that were deliberately false and misleading" to give an illusion of continued spectacular growth.[1] The lengthy report also focused on Arthur Andersen's audits of Mattel during the early 1970s. Price Waterhouse, which reviewed the Mattel audits, harshly criticized Arthur Andersen.

> In general, Price Waterhouse concluded that Arthur Andersen's audit procedures and tests weren't as comprehensive as they should have been in many areas and that certain information contained in the accountant's working papers should have been further pursued. If this had been done, the report said it could have led to the discovery of irregularities in the fiscal 1971 and 1972 financial statements.[2]

In March 1976, a federal judge approved an out-of-court settlement to the class action lawsuits filed by Mattel's stockholders. The $30 million settlement required multimillion-dollar payments by several former executives of Mattel, principally the Handlers and Rosenberg, as well as even larger payments by the executives' insurance companies. The only defendant that refused to participate in the settlement was Arthur Andersen, which maintained that it was not responsible for the huge losses suffered by Mattel's stockholders. Nevertheless, in April 1977, Arthur Andersen agreed to make a cash payment of approximately $900,000 to Mattel stockholders to resolve the matter.

In February 1978, a federal grand jury indicted Ruth Handler, Seymour Rosenberg, and four other former Mattel executives. The grand jury charged the executives with falsifying Mattel's financial statements for the period 1969 to 1974. In responding to the indictment, Ruth Handler proclaimed her innocence and maintained that she was "deeply offended" by the charges. Later that year, Handler submitted a plea of no contest to each of the ten counts of fraud filed against her. Handler's plea bargain agreement allowed her to escape a prison sentence but required her to perform 2,500 hours of community service and to pay a $57,000 fine. Rosenberg agreed to a similar plea bargain arrangement in the fall of 1978.[3]

ALLEGED DEFICIENCIES IN ARTHUR ANDERSEN'S AUDITS OF MATTEL

In June 1981, the SEC released the results of its lengthy investigation of Mattel's fraudulent earnings manipulation scheme and its report on Arthur Andersen's audits of Mattel. The SEC criticized Arthur Andersen's audits of Mattel, particu-

---

1. R. Lindsey, "A Million-Dollar Business from a Mastectomy," *The New York Times*, 19 June 1988, F3.

2. S. Sansweet, "Mattel Ex-Aides Tried Cover-Up, Report Asserts," *The Wall Street Journal*, 4 November 1975, 10.

3. Elliot Handler was never indicted for criminal fraud. The federal grand jury that investigated the Mattel earnings manipulation scheme apparently concluded that he was not involved in the fraud.

larly the 1971 and 1972 engagements. According to the SEC, numerous errors and oversights during those audits had prevented Arthur Andersen from discovering the fraudulent methods Mattel management used to manipulate the company's reported operating results. Mattel's illicit accounting methods and the related deficiencies in Arthur Andersen's audits are discussed in the following sections.

Improper Sales Cutoff at Year-End

For fiscal year 1971, which ended January 30, 1971, Mattel management faced the unpleasant prospect of informing stockholders that the company had failed for the first time in several years to post record sales and earnings. To inflate the company's reported earnings, Mattel's top executives instituted in January 1971 what became known as the "bill and hold" program. Mattel used this program to overstate its fiscal 1971 sales by almost $15 million and its pretax earnings by approximately $8 million. In simple terms, the bill and hold program involved billing customers for future sales and then recording the sales immediately. The SEC identified the following six reasons why the bill and hold sales should not have been recorded by Mattel in January 1971:

1. The merchandise was not shipped as of January 30, 1971.
2. The customer did not have to make any payments until the goods were received and accepted.
3. The merchandise was not physically segregated from Mattel's inventory nor labeled as the property of the customer.
4. The customer could cancel the order without penalty at any time prior to his receipt and acceptance of the merchandise.
5. The risks of ownership remained with Mattel, including the risk of loss due to damage, theft, or destruction of the merchandise.
6. In many instances, the invoices were prepared without prior consultation with, or participation by, the customer as to the content of the order.[4]

To provide documentary support for the bill and hold sales, Mattel prepared customer order forms, sales invoices, and bills of lading. Bills of lading required the signatures of a Mattel shipping employee and a representative of the common carrier transporting the goods. For the bogus bills of lading, Mattel shipping employees signed for both themselves and the common carrier.

The magnitude of the bill and hold program created tremendous confusion for Mattel accounting personnel. When the bill and hold sales were recorded in January 1971, the inventory quantities for the items allegedly sold were adjusted downward, although the goods were not segregated from the remaining inventory items. When the bill and hold goods were actually shipped, weeks or even months later, Mattel's inventory records became laced with errors resulting from employees recording the inventory shipments a second time. The end result was that Mattel's inventory records were unreliable.

To resolve the inventory control problems created by the bill and hold sales, Mattel executives reversed those sales in fiscal 1972. The first reversing entry was booked in May 1971 and involved $12 million in sales. Approximately one-half of

---

4. This information was taken from Securities and Exchange Commission, *Accounting Series Release No. 292*, 22 June 1981. All subsequent quotations, unless indicated otherwise, are reprinted from this source.

this total was for bill and hold sales recorded in fiscal 1971, while the other one-half was for bill and hold sales recorded near the end of the first quarter of fiscal 1972. The large reversing entry created another problem: the net sales for May 1971 was suddenly a negative figure. Mattel executives booked a fictitious $11 million sale in May to conceal the large impact of the reversing entry on the recorded sales for that month. The executives recorded this fictitious transaction only in the general ledger, not in the accounts receivable subsidiary ledger, which produced an unreconciled difference of $11 million between the two accounting records.

In August 1971, Mattel reversed the approximately $7 million of remaining bill and hold sales recorded in fiscal 1971. Then, in September, a month in which Mattel experiences a very high volume of sales, company management reversed the fictitious $11 million general ledger sales entry recorded in May of that year. This entry eliminated the large difference between the balance of the general ledger controlling account for receivables and the balance of the accounts receivable subsidiary ledger. The net effect of this series of bogus entries and correcting entries was that earnings and sales for fiscal 1972 were understated by approximately the same amounts that those items were overstated for fiscal 1971.

Arthur Andersen representatives insisted that their personnel were unaware of the fraudulent bill and hold sales until Mattel executives publicly revealed the scheme in 1974. However, the SEC pointed to several audit tests performed by Arthur Andersen during the 1971 and 1972 Mattel audits that should have uncovered the bill and hold sales. Among these audit tests were Arthur Andersen's receivables confirmation procedures.

Several of the accounts receivable confirmations mailed by Arthur Andersen during the 1971 audit were returned with discrepancies noted by Mattel's customers—discrepancies caused by bill and hold sales charged improperly to the customers' accounts as of January 30, 1971. In resolving these discrepancies, the Arthur Andersen auditors obtained copies of the bills of lading for the disputed charges to determine whether the goods had actually been shipped as of January 30, 1971. The SEC pointed out that although these bills of lading were clearly marked "bill and hold," the Arthur Andersen auditors apparently never asked client personnel to explain the significance of that phrase.[5]

The Arthur Andersen auditors also failed to notice that the bills of lading they obtained to clear the confirmation discrepancies conspicuously lacked the required routing or delivery instructions. Finally, the auditors failed to recognize that both required signatures on the bogus bills of lading were those of Mattel employees rather than one being the signature of a common carrier representative and the other being that of a Mattel employee. The auditors eventually cleared the confirmation discrepancies caused by the bill and hold sales with the following tickmark explanation: "Traced to Mattel invoice and bill of lading noting agreement of amount and that shipment made prior to 1/30/71."

Arthur Andersen tested Mattel's year-end sales cutoff for fiscal 1971 by selecting 82 large sales invoices processed near the end of that year. Twenty-six of these invoices involved bill and hold sales. Despite the phrase "bill and hold" written distinctly on the face of each of these invoices, and despite the earlier-noted prob-

---

5. However, an Arthur Andersen manager who reviewed the accounts receivable workpapers wrote a review comment addressed to an audit senior: "What does 'Bill and Hold' mean?" The audit senior apparently never cleared this review comment.

lems with the related bills of lading, Arthur Andersen failed to recognize that these 26 sales were fictitious.

During the internal control phase of the fiscal 1972 Mattel audit, Arthur Andersen selected the month of August 1971 to perform its tests of controls for the sales cycle. Ironically, August was the month that Mattel recorded one of the large reversing entries to eliminate a portion of the bill and hold sales booked in January 1971. This reversing entry of nearly $7 million caused the total of August's general ledger sales to be that much less than the corresponding monthly sales figure reported by a supplementary ledger maintained by Mattel, the sales invoice register. An Arthur Andersen staff person included in the audit workpapers the following explanation for this large difference—an explanation given to him by a Mattel employee:

> This amount is an offset to sales due to "invoicing errors" uncovered by client when comparing computer-prepared invoices to bills of lading. Client errors such as items not being shipped and wrong amount are the types found. At this time client does not know whether credit memos were issued or not. May create a cutoff problem for accounts receivable at year-end.

To his credit, the Arthur Andersen senior who reviewed this explanation noted that it was unsatisfactory and wrote the staff person the following note: "Need a better explanation. This looks like a big problem." The SEC could find no evidence in the audit workpapers that the problem had been further investigated.

Finally, the SEC criticized Arthur Andersen for not utilizing analytical procedures to evaluate the overall reasonableness of Mattel's monthly sales. If such tests had been performed, the Mattel auditors would have discovered that the client's monthly sales varied dramatically from 1970 through 1972. This volatility stemmed largely from the errors introduced into the accounting records by the bill and hold program and the subsequent errors created when the bill and hold sales were reversed.

Intentional Understatement of Inventory Obsolescence Reserve

The SEC determined that Mattel's management intentionally understated the company's reserve for inventory obsolescence by several million dollars over the two-year period 1971–1972. Inventory obsolescence is a major problem for toy manufacturers, given the inherent difficulty of predicting children's taste in toys. In fiscal 1971, Mattel executives confronted a huge and unexpected inventory buildup of Hot Wheels, traditionally one of the company's best-selling products. The following year, Mattel disposed of approximately 5.6 million of the Hot Wheels toys by selling them to a large oil company at a loss of more than $11 million.

In arriving at its year-end reserve for obsolete inventory, Mattel prepared weekly sales forecasts for the next several months for each toy considered an "excess inventory" item. A reserve for obsolescence was then recorded for those toys whose expected sales in the following months were less than the year-end inventory. In 1971 and 1972, the SEC found that Mattel inflated the projected future sales of several excess inventory items to justify not recording a reserve for obsolescence for those toys.

When auditing the reserve for inventory obsolescence, Arthur Andersen personnel compared the weekly sales forecasts for certain excess inventory toys to their actual sales for the first several weeks of the new fiscal year. Five of the eight toys selected for testing during the 1972 audit had no recorded sales in the first several weeks of the new year, while three others had negative net sales during that time. Mattel's weekly sales forecasts prepared at the end of fiscal 1972 had projected significant sales for each of these eight items. Despite the results of this audit test, Arthur Andersen did not challenge the sufficiency of Mattel's inventory obsolescence reserve.

Overstatement of Deferred Tooling Costs

Mattel incurs significant "tooling" costs during the developmental phase of each new product. These costs include expenditures to produce the molds and die casts needed for new products. Mattel defers such costs in an asset account and amortizes them over a new toy's estimated useful life. The proportion of the tooling costs amortized each year for a given toy equals the ratio of that year's sales for the toy to the total expected sales over the life of the toy. From 1970 through 1972, Mattel executives manipulated the company's deferred tooling costs to overstate Mattel's reported earnings. The SEC's investigation revealed the following abusive accounting methods Mattel used in 1971 to understate its amortization of deferred tooling costs by $3.7 million:

1. Reallocated tooling costs from various products with low forecasted sales to those with sizable forecasted sales.
2. Adjusted the ratio of various products' current sales to their forecasted sales.
3. Deferred all tooling costs incurred during the last three months of the year.
4. Deferred certain tooling costs twice.

Arthur Andersen's audit of Mattel's deferred tooling costs for 1971 involved obtaining and reviewing client-prepared schedules of these costs by product. The auditors then tested the propriety of the amortization amounts for a few products that had large deferrals. Among the most important of these audit tests were simple comparisons of actual current year sales to total forecasted sales for individual products to determine that the amount of tooling costs amortized during the year was reasonable. The SEC suggested that more extensive and rigorous audit tests should have been applied to Mattel's deferred tooling costs during the 1971 audit, given the large increase in those costs in 1971 and their subjective nature.

Arthur Andersen did uncover at least two instances of material overstatements of Mattel's deferred tooling costs. Arthur Andersen refused to accept certain of the revised sales forecasts Mattel used to justify reducing the amount of deferred tooling costs written off for several products. In 1971, Arthur Andersen's workpapers documented a $2 million overstatement of deferred tooling costs resulting from improper revisions of certain products' expected lifetime sales. Mattel subsequently adjusted the account balance by only $1.4 million. According to the SEC, Arthur Andersen's workpapers did not reveal how that figure was determined, nor did the workpapers provide any evidence suggesting that the $1.4 million adjustment remedied the noted problem.

Mattel's auditors also discovered during the 1972 audit that more than $1.2 million of tooling costs had been deferred twice. A senior member of the Arthur Andersen engagement team wrote a review comment instructing a subordinate to make sure that a proper adjusting entry was recorded. In responding to the review comment, the subordinate subsequently noted, "Tooling write-off adjusted for this fact." Despite this assertion, the SEC determined that the adjustment was never made.

Underpayment of Royalties

Mattel acquired the production rights to its popular Hot Wheels product from the gentleman who invented that toy. The contract between Mattel and the inventor called for him to begin receiving significant royalties on Hot Wheels sales when the product reached the break-even point. In 1970, the break-even point for the Hot Wheels toy was reached; however, to avoid paying royalties to the inventor, Mattel management fabricated an additional $4.4 million in expenses related to that product. These expenses consisted primarily of bogus advertising expenditures and increases in the operating losses allegedly incurred by the product in the first few years following its introduction. Because of these fraudulent expenses, Mattel avoided paying the inventor nearly $2 million in royalties that he had rightfully earned from 1970 through 1972.

The SEC charged that Arthur Andersen did not properly investigate the contractual arrangement between the inventor and Mattel and the related financial statement implications. Arthur Andersen failed to question the $4.4 million of fictitious expenses that Mattel added in 1970 to the schedule that summarized the operating results of the Hot Wheels product. Additionally, the auditors failed to obtain a copy of a computer-generated royalties report that disclosed the proper amount of royalties due the inventor.

Improper Computation of Business Interruption Insurance Claim

Mattel's large warehouse in Mexicali, Mexico, which was destroyed by a fire in September 1970, was fully insured, as were its contents. The company's insurance policy also included a business interruption clause providing up to $10 million in coverage for revenues lost as a result of damage to the facility. In its financial statements for the fiscal year ended January 30, 1971, Mattel included a $10 million receivable from its insurance company for a business interruption insurance claim. The SEC charged that neither Mattel nor Arthur Andersen should have expected the insurance company to pay the full amount of the claim. The federal agency argued that the method used by Mattel to compute the amount recoverable from the insurance company, a method approved by Arthur Andersen, was not credible. In fact, Mattel did not receive any payment from its insurance company until 1977 and then was paid only $4.4 million.

ADDITIONAL SEC CRITICISM OF ARTHUR ANDERSEN'S MATTEL AUDITS

Besides the specific criticisms of Arthur Andersen's Mattel audits already noted, the SEC also chastised the audit firm for other, more general deficiencies in those audits. First, the SEC criticized the Arthur Andersen auditors for failing to sufficiently investigate suspicious transactions and documents coming to their attention. An example noted earlier was the failure to adequately research Mattel's bill and hold sales. Second, the SEC maintained that Arthur Andersen neglected to "apply industry knowledge" during the Mattel audits. For example, if Arthur Andersen had been closely following its client's sales markets, the firm should have recognized that Mattel's large year-end inventory of Hot Wheels for 1970 required a significant write-down, given retailers' inability to sell their own inventories of that product. In commenting on this point, the SEC observed: "Auditors must acquire and apply sufficient knowledge of their clients' industries to enable them to intelligently audit their business operations and to evaluate the client's explanations of those operations."

The SEC also criticized Arthur Andersen for being overly willing to accept client representations as audit evidence "with little or no verification or documentation." As an example, the SEC noted the audit firm's acceptance of the spurious explanation given for the large discrepancy between the August 1971 sales reported by the general ledger controlling account and by the sales invoice register. Finally, the SEC charged that senior members of the Arthur Andersen engagement team had exhibited "insufficient control, coordination, and supervision" during the Mattel audits. In particular, the SEC expressed concern that Arthur Andersen's audit review process failed to ensure that important issues raised by staff auditors during the Mattel audits were resolved satisfactorily.

EPILOGUE

Under the leadership of new management, Mattel slowly recovered from its nearly disastrous experiences of the early 1970s. In 1994, Mattel overtook Hasbro as the nation's largest toy maker. Five years later, Mattel's annual revenues approached $5 billion, 40 percent of which was attributable to the Barbie product line. That product line included more than 100 different Barbie dolls. Among these dolls were Poodle Parade Barbie, Country Rose Barbie, Harley-Davidson Barbie, and the all-time best selling model, Totally Hair Barbie.[6]

Ruth Handler also staged a dramatic comeback following her traumatic experiences of the early 1970s. After her forced retirement from Mattel, she founded a company, Ruthton Corporation, that manufactures prosthetic devices for women who, like herself, have undergone mastectomies. Although a small company with a relatively small market, Ruthton Corporation quickly established itself and within a few years reported annual sales of several million dollars. In 1989, Ruth and Elliot Handler were recognized for their contributions to the toy industry by being inducted into the industry's hall of fame. Ten years later, Ruth Handler, at the age of 82, co-chaired, along with Rosie O'Donnell and Jackie Joyner-Kersee, a year-long educational program to commemorate Barbie's fortieth anniversary.

In 1981, the SEC censured Arthur Andersen for its alleged deficient audits of Mattel, Inc. The SEC apparently chose only to censure Arthur Andersen because

6. In 1995, a former Mattel executive charged that the company misrepresented its operating results in the early 1990s. The executive testified that Mattel improperly accounted for royalties and applied improper revenue recognition policies. An investigation supervised by Gary Lynch, the SEC's former chief of enforcement, cleared Mattel of those charges.

the audit firm demonstrated that it had implemented corrective measures to remedy the problems evident during the Mattel audits. Exhibit 1 contains the list of these corrective measures that was appended to the SEC enforcement release in which Arthur Andersen was censured.

EXHIBIT 1
Measures Taken by Arthur Andersen to Strengthen Its Audit Process Following the Mattel Audits

- **Consultation within the Firm.** In 1978, the firm's policies on intrafirm consultation regarding complex or unusual transactions were formalized and restated in a single source providing concise guidelines on specific practice problems where consultation is appropriate.
- **Rotation of Audit Partners.** In 1976, Arthur Andersen voluntarily adopted a policy requiring rotation of audit engagement partners every five years. A similar rule was adopted by the SEC Practice Section of the AICPA in 1977.
- **Second Partner Reviews.** In 1975, Arthur Andersen began requiring an extensive review of audit reports and supporting materials by a second partner not engaged in the audit. A similar requirement was subsequently adopted by the SEC Practice Section of the AICPA.
- **Personnel Training Programs.** In the early 1970s, Arthur Andersen opened a large training facility in St. Charles, Illinois, on a former college campus. This facility is used on a continuing basis to provide training for Arthur Andersen partners and professional employees.
- **Updating of Practice and Procedure Manuals.** Arthur Andersen updated all of its major practice and procedure manuals to provide a set of readily accessible guidelines to firm policy on financial reporting issues, accounting principles, auditing procedures, and ethical issues.
- **Public Review Board.** In 1974, Arthur Andersen established a Public Review Board, an independent body consisting of individuals from business, the professions, and government. The Board establishes its own program for reviewing the professional operations of the firm and has in each year of its existence focused on a different area of the firm's practice.

QUESTIONS

1. Identify the key "inherent risk" factors present during Arthur Andersen's 1971 and 1972 audits of Mattel.

2. The SEC noted six reasons why Mattel's bill and hold sales did not qualify as consummated sales transactions. Identify and discuss the general conditions for recognizing revenue from sales transactions. Also, identify circumstances in which revenue may be recognized on sales transactions even though one or more of these conditions are not met.

3. Identify and discuss the principal audit objectives associated with year-end sales cutoff tests. In general, is it appropriate to perform these tests at an interim date? Why or why not?

4. *SAS No. 31*, "Evidential Matter," identifies five key management assertions that underlie a set of financial statements. Identify the management assertions that would have been of primary concern to Arthur Andersen for the following items: the reserve for inventory obsolescence, royalty expense, and the receivable recorded by Mattel for the business interruption insurance claim. Why is it important for an auditor to identify the underlying management assertions for a client's major accounts?

5. In at least two instances, key issues raised during the review of Mattel's workpapers by Arthur Andersen personnel were not resolved satisfactorily prior to the completion of the audit. Which member of the audit engagement team has the primary responsibility for ensuring that such issues are properly resolved and documented in the audit workpapers? Defend your answer.

6. Assume that Arthur Andersen had compared Mattel's monthly sales during the early 1970s with the comparable monthly sales figures of prior years. What additional audit procedures should Arthur Andersen have performed once it discovered the extreme volatility in these monthly sales figures?

7. Arthur Andersen proposed a $2 million adjusting entry to the deferred tooling costs account during its 1971 Mattel audit. However, Mattel adjusted the balance of that account by only $1.4 million. Identify the conditions under which Arthur Andersen would have been justified in accepting this smaller adjusting entry.

①
Credit Risk   Audit Risk

$$ IR * CR * DR = AR $$

Internal Risk   TD   AP
                     (Analytical procedures)

(test of details)

② Revenue Recognition
 - Transaction exists
   → Risk of holding asset is transfered to buyer
 - Realizable / Realized + Earned

Exceptions:
 ○ Installment sale
 ○ % Complete
 ○ Production basis amt. — (Record mkt when complete)
   — guaranteed sale
     ○ Pork Bellies (futures market)
 ○ Cost Recovery Method (Only After 4 cover costs)

Completeness   Existence   → Objectives.

CASE 1.2
ESM GOVERNMENT SECURITIES, INC.

see AU Section 316

Cuban-born Jose Gomez emigrated to Miami in 1961. Only thirteen at the time and fatherless, Gomez obtained a job sacking groceries in a neighborhood supermarket to help his mother pay the bills. The young man's work ethic and cheerful personality made him a favorite of his superiors and the store's customers. A few years later, Gomez landed a job as a grocery buyer, a job that he used to finance an accounting degree at the University of Miami. Following graduation, Gomez entered public accounting with the hopes of becoming a partner of a major accounting firm.

On August 1, 1979, Jose Gomez achieved his long-sought goal when he was named a partner with Alexander Grant & Company, the tenth largest CPA firm in the United States at the time. Only 31 years old, Gomez was recognized by his fellow partners as an individual who would likely rise to the upper management ranks of Alexander Grant during his career. Gomez's bright future with Grant seemed even more assured when he was named the managing partner of the firm's Fort Lauderdale office while he was still in his early thirties. Unfortunately, Gomez never realized his potential. In March 1987, Gomez began serving a 12-year sentence in a federal prison in Tallahassee, Florida, after pleading guilty to forgery and fraud charges.

Ironically, Gomez's fate was sealed just a few days following his promotion to partner. During a lunch with Alan Novick, an officer of his largest audit client, Gomez was startled by Novick's admission that the client's audited financial statements for the prior two years contained material errors. The client, ESM Government Securities, Inc., a Fort Lauderdale brokerage firm specializing in government securities, had several million dollars in losses that Novick had concealed from Gomez and his subordinates on the ESM audit team. Novick reminded Gomez that he had personally authorized the unqualified opinions on

15

ESM's 1977 and 1978 financial statements. Disclosure of the large errors in those financial statements might jeopardize Gomez's career.

According to Gomez, Novick repeatedly goaded him with comments such as, "It's going to look terrible for you . . . and you just got promoted to partner."[1] Novick maintained that he could recoup the losses he had concealed from Alexander Grant if Gomez would not withdraw the audit opinions on ESM's 1977 and 1978 financial statements. If Gomez insisted on withdrawing the audit opinions, Novick warned him that ESM would fail and that several parties would suffer as a result, including Gomez and ESM's customers. Eventually, Gomez succumbed to Novick's persuasive arguments.[2]

When Novick made his startling confession to Gomez, he was aware that the audit partner was experiencing financial problems. Although Gomez earned a sizable salary as a partner of a major CPA firm, that salary was not sufficient to support his affluent lifestyle. After Gomez agreed to remain silent regarding the ESM fraud, Novick offered to help relieve Gomez's financial problems. In November 1979, Novick issued Gomez a $20,000 check to cover past-due credit card bills. The following year, after Gomez complained of his worsening financial condition, Novick gave him an additional $60,000. Court records document that during the seven-year ESM fraud, Gomez received approximately $200,000 from ESM officials. Gomez later acknowledged that his personal ambition and greed blinded him to the high ethical standards he had learned earlier in life.

> I was a young man in a hurry. I needed more money than I was making. I wanted nice clothes for my wife. I had to have a nice home, be seen at the right places. Take a trip to the Super Bowl. Do whatever was necessary to further my career. Use the plastic, the credit cards. When the plastic limit was reached, borrow and pay off the balances. Then use the plastic again.[3]

If Gomez actually believed, as he later alleged, that ignoring the misrepresentations in ESM's financial statements was the best alternative for all parties concerned, he was wrong. The relatively small unreported losses in the 1977 and 1978 ESM financial statements ballooned to collective losses of more than $300 million by the spring of 1985. Most financial scandals affect only the stockholders and creditors of one company. Not so with the ESM scandal. Public disclosure of the ESM fraud was the first domino to topple in a series of events that eventually rocked both the national and international financial markets.

ESM owed its largest customer, Home State Savings, an Ohio bank, approximately $145 million when the brokerage firm ceased operations in March 1985. Home State Savings happened to be the largest of the more than 70 banks in Ohio whose deposits were not insured by the Federal Deposit Insurance Corporation. These banks had formed their own private deposit insurance fund into which each paid annual premiums. Home State's collapse following ESM's closure caused panic-stricken depositors to trigger runs on the other privately insured Ohio banks. Within a matter of days, the governor of Ohio was forced to close all

---

1. M. Brannigan, "Auditor's Downfall Shows a Man Caught in Trap of His Own Making," *The Wall Street Journal*, 4 March 1987, 33.

2. Former colleagues at Alexander Grant maintain that Gomez's account of his involvement with Novick is not totally accurate. For instance, certain of Gomez's former colleagues suggest that he knew of the ESM fraud prior to 1979.

3. J. Russell, "Pride Led to Fall, ESM Auditor Says," *The Miami Herald*, 15 February 1987, 1A.

of the state's privately insured banks while state and federal regulatory authorities worked around the clock to contain the economic fallout from the ESM scandal. The closure of the Ohio banks and a growing loss of confidence in the government securities market destabilized all of the nation's capital markets. At the peak of the crisis, the U.S. dollar plunged 14 percent in value in the international markets in one day as foreign investors became concerned that the entire U.S. banking system might be jeopardized.

The impact of the ESM scandal was not restricted to the state of Ohio or the financial markets. Besides Home State Savings, ESM's major customers included municipalities scattered across the nation. Collectively, ESM owed these municipalities more than $100 million. When the news of the ESM insolvency broke, the credit ratings of these municipalities plummeted, and many were forced to take immediate and drastic measures to remain solvent. One example was the city of Beaumont, Texas, which laid off approximately 15 percent of its municipal employees following ESM's closure.

Among the parties most victimized by the ESM fraud were Gomez's colleagues, his fellow partners at Alexander Grant. A proud and respected firm nationwide, Alexander Grant suddenly became the focus of intense and adverse publicity. The poor judgment of one partner cost the firm much of the credibility and prestige it had earned over its 60-year history. Alexander Grant, its successor firm, Grant Thornton, and the company that provided the firms' malpractice insurance eventually absorbed $200 million of legal judgments and out-of-court settlements stemming from the ESM debacle.   #7

History of ESM Government Securities

Ronnie Ewton, Bobby Seneca, and George Mead founded ESM Government Securities, Inc., in November 1975 with a total capitalization of $75,000. ESM's principal line of business was buying and selling for customer accounts debt securities issued by the federal government and its various agencies. Ewton, who had a long and checkered career with several brokerage firms, was ESM's principal executive. Ewton hired a close friend, Steve Arky, to serve as the firm's legal   #6
counsel, and Alan Novick, a Wall Street investment banker who later corrupted Jose Gomez, to be the firm's principal securities trader.[4]

In the mid-1970s, the U.S. government securities market was subject to minimal regulatory oversight, although it was, and still is today, the world's largest securities market. The average daily dollar volume of U.S. treasury bills, notes, and bonds is typically several times larger than the daily sales volume of the New York Stock Exchange. Despite the enormous size of the government securities market, most private investors know very little about it. Until the mid-1970s, large brokerage firms accounted for nearly all of the daily sales volume of government securities. The tremendous growth in the national debt during the Carter and Reagan administrations forced the U.S. Treasury Department to begin working with so-called secondary dealers to raise the funds necessary to operate the federal government. Secondary dealers are generally small brokerage houses that

---

4. For an excellent and comprehensive history of the ESM scandal, see D.L. Maggin, *Bankers, Builders, Knaves and Thieves* (Chicago: Contemporary Books, 1989).

trade federal debt securities for the accounts of small to moderately sized banks and municipalities. Prior to legislation enacted in the late 1980s, such brokers were subject only to the regulatory oversight of state securities commissions. These state agencies tend to be severely underfunded and relatively ineffective as a result.

An intriguing aspect of the government securities markets is the degree of leverage available to investors. Margin requirements in securities transactions of publicly owned firms typically average 50 percent, meaning that an investor must put up at least one dollar for every two dollars in stock purchased. The federal government, because of the huge amount of funds it must raise, establishes much more liberal margin requirements for the government securities market. An investor who purchases government securities may be required to make a down payment equal to 5 percent, or even less, of the total cost of those securities. Because the market value of government securities may move 2 to 3 percent in any one day in response to fractional changes in market interest rates, an investor can easily have his or her initial cash investment in such securities wiped out in a few days. On the other hand, a lucky or skillful investor who accurately forecasts a change in interest rates may see the value of an initial investment in government securities double or triple over a short period of time.

Most of ESM's transactions were repurchase agreements, more commonly known as "repos." In a repo transaction, a government securities dealer sells a customer a block of federal securities and then simultaneously pledges to repurchase those securities at a later date at an agreed-upon price. The brokerage firm selling the securities hopes that their value will rise over the period of the repurchase agreement, which may be as short as 12 hours (overnight) or as long as 12 months. In substance, a repo transaction is a short-term loan from the customer to the securities dealer. ESM also engaged in a limited number of "reverse repos." In these transactions, ESM purchased government securities from a customer who simultaneously agreed to repurchase the securities at a later date at a predetermined price. Reverse repos were essentially loans made by ESM to another party.

In repo transactions, the purchaser should either take physical possession of the government securities or have a bonded third party assume physical possession. If the purchaser does not take physical possession of the securities, an unscrupulous broker could sell them to another customer. Unfortunately, many of the banks and municipalities with which ESM did business were not familiar with the government securities market. These customers naively relied on ESM to retain the securities or asked the brokerage firm to transfer the securities to a segregated account with a trust company for the term of the repurchase agreement. Even when instructed to transfer customer securities to a trust company, ESM often retained the securities, which allowed ESM officials to use the securities for whatever purpose they chose.

Besides making securities trades with customers, ESM also engaged in purely speculative transactions in which it attempted to predict and profit from future changes in market interest rates. Soon after joining ESM, Novick convinced Ewton that he could earn millions of dollars in profits for ESM in speculative securities trades. Novick intended to produce these profits by making effective use of the considerable leverage afforded by the small margin requirements in the government securities market. Unfortunately, Novick was less than proficient in predicting future movements of interest rates. Over a short period in 1980, Novick lost more than $80 million when interest rates leaped dramatically a few weeks after he had gambled that they would fall.

The trading losses suffered by Novick in 1980, when coupled with the much smaller pre-1980 trading losses he had rung up, easily wiped out the equity of ESM's three owners. At this point, the owners could either publicly admit that their firm was bankrupt or employ on a much larger scale a practice they had begun a few years earlier: using (stealing) customer securities for their own benefit. Sadly, Ewton and his colleagues chose the latter alternative.

Although ESM was insolvent by 1980, the firm managed to remain in business for several more years because of the huge sums of cash it acquired in repo transactions with customers. An accountant hired to reconstruct the history of the seven-year ESM scandal noted that cash flow, not profit, was the lifeblood of ESM: "The name of the game was cash flow. It had nothing to do with profit. As long as there was an ability to deliver enough cash, then whether or not the transactions made money was not relevant."[5] ESM could sell the same block of federal securities to several different customers, since most of its clients did not take physical possession of the securities. The positive cash flow produced by these and other fraudulent practices allowed Novick to continue "playing the market" in an increasingly desperate effort to recoup the millions he had gambled away on earlier trades.

ESM's Bookkeeping Scam

The most problematic aspect of the ESM fraud for Alan Novick, its principal architect, was concealing the fraud from the Alexander Grant auditors who annually examined ESM's financial records. Novick had developed a scheme to conceal the fraud from the auditors prior to informing Jose Gomez of ESM's unreported losses for 1977 and 1978. ESM Government Securities was just one of several companies controlled by Ewton and his associates. The other companies were "shells" with no express business purpose and were not audited by Alexander Grant. Novick used these nonoperating entities to hide ESM's huge trading losses.

Novick devised a bookkeeping scheme to transfer trading losses incurred by ESM to an affiliated company under the ESM corporate umbrella. Novick recorded a "mirror" intercompany transaction for each repo and reverse repo transaction of ESM. If the actual transaction with a customer was a repo, the mirror transaction would be a reverse repo, and vice versa. By covering both sides of each transaction, Novick could close out the "losing" side to the unaudited affiliate and close out the profitable side to ESM, ensuring that the latter appeared to be profitable. After this scam had gone on for several years, the cumulative trading losses transferred to the unaudited affiliate resulted in a huge receivable owed

5. Unless noted otherwise, this and subsequent quotations were taken from the following source: U.S. Congress, House, Subcommittee on Oversight and Investigations of the Committee on Energy and Commerce, *SEC and Corporate Audits, Part 2* (Washington, D.C.: U.S. Government Printing Office, 1985).

to ESM by that entity. This receivable did not appear explicitly on ESM's annual balance sheet.[6] The only reference to the mirror transactions was an oblique description of them in the footnotes accompanying the annual balance sheet. In 1984, the reference to these transactions was included in footnote D (see Exhibit 1).

EXHIBIT 1
ESM's 1984 Balance Sheet and Accompanying Footnotes

ESM Government Securities, Inc.
(a wholly-owned subsidiary of ESM Group, Inc.)
STATEMENT OF FINANCIAL CONDITION
December 31, 1984

ASSETS

Cash	$ 421,000
Deposits with clearing organizations and others (note B)	182,000
Receivable from brokers and dealers (note C)	3,643,000
Receivable from customers (note C)	73,050,000
Securities purchased under agreement to resell (notes A and D)	2,945,953,000
Accrued interest	406,000
Securities purchased not sold—at market (note A)	26,059,000
Due from parent	2,550,000
Other	61,000
	$3,052,325,000

LIABILITIES AND STOCKHOLDERS' EQUITY

Short-term bank loans (note E)	$ 47,258,000
Payable to brokers and dealers (note C)	12,266,000
Payable to customers	9,304,000
Securities sold under agreement to repurchase (notes A and D)	2,945,953,000
Accounts payable and accrued expenses	799,000
Commitments and contingencies (notes F and G)	
Stockholders' equity:	
Common stock—authorized, issued and outstanding; 1,000 shares, $1.00 par value	1,000
Additional contributed capital	4,160,000
Retained earnings	32,584,000
	$3,052,325,000

The accompanying notes are an integral part of this statement.

NOTES TO STATEMENT OF FINANCIAL CONDITION
December 31, 1984

NOTE A—SIGNIFICANT ACCOUNTING POLICIES
A summary of the significant accounting policies applied in the preparation of the financial statements follows.

Security Transactions. Security transactions are recorded on a settlement date basis, generally the first business day following the transaction date.

Purchases of securities under agreements to resell and sales of securities under agreements to repurchase are considered financing transactions and represent the amount of purchases and sales which will be resold or reacquired at amounts specified in the respective agreements.

---

6. Like many financial institutions, ESM issued only a balance sheet to external parties. ESM was not required by any regulatory body to issue a balance sheet but apparently chose to do so because many of its customers requested an audited balance sheet before they would transact business with the firm.

Securities Purchased, Not Sold. Securities inventory, which consists of marketable federal government or government agency securities, is carried at market value.

Furniture and Equipment. Furniture and equipment are stated at cost. Depreciation is provided in amounts sufficient to relate the cost of depreciable assets to operations over their estimated service lives, principally on a straight-line basis over five years.

Income Taxes. The company participates in the filing of a consolidated income tax return with its parent. Any tax liability of the affiliated group is allocated to each member company based on its contribution to taxable income.

NOTE B—DEPOSITS WITH CLEARING ORGANIZATIONS AND OTHERS
The company has deposits of cash and securities with commodity brokers to meet margin requirements. The company also has cash escrow deposits with its securities clearing agent.

NOTE C—BROKER, DEALER, AND CUSTOMER ACCOUNTS
Receivables from brokers, dealers, and customers at December 31, 1984, include outstanding securities failed to deliver. Payables to brokers, dealers, and customers at December 31, 1984, include outstanding securities failed to receive. "Fails," all of which have been outstanding less than 30 days, represent the contract value of securities which have not been received or delivered by settlement date. Fails to receive and fails to deliver from brokers and customers were $7,291,426 and $9,993,081 respectively at December 31, 1984.

NOTE D—SECURITY TRANSACTIONS
The company entered into repurchase and resale agreements with customers whereby specific securities are sold or purchased for short durations of time. These agreements cover securities, the rights to which are usually acquired through similar purchase/resale agreements. The company has agreements with an affiliated company for securities purchased under agreements to resell amounting to approximately $1,621,481,000 and securities sold under agreements to repurchase amounting to approximately $1,324,472,000 at December 31, 1984. Accrued interest receivable from and payable to the affiliated company at year-end were $11,174,000 and $64,410,000 respectively.

NOTE E—SHORT-TERM BANK LOANS
Short-term bank loans at December 31, 1984, are collateralized by securities purchased not sold.

NOTE F—RELATED PARTY TRANSACTIONS
Certain common expenses paid by the parent company, including depreciation, are allocated to the subsidiary companies based on transaction volume. The company paid a dividend of $10 million to its parent company as of December 31, 1984. The company occupies premises leased by the parent company from a partnership of which one of the officers is a partner. Rent expense paid the partnership amounted to $112,000 for the year ended December 31, 1984 (note G).

NOTE G—COMMITMENTS
The company conducts its operations in leased facilities under noncancellable operating leases expiring at various dates through 2010. The minimum lease payment for one location has been calculated based on current transaction volume (note F) under a 30-year lease. The minimum rental commitments under the operating lease are as follows:

Year ended December 31,	
1985	$ 162,900
1986	162,900
1987	141,900
1988	112,400
1989	112,400
1990 and thereafter	2,332,400
	$3,024,900

Rental expense charged to operations approximated $137,000 for the year ended December 31, 1984.

Novick also used the unaudited affiliate to conceal huge thefts of ESM funds. Novick diverted these funds to himself, his colleagues, and to co-conspirators who were officers or employees of ESM's major customers. Many of these co-conspirators established personal trading accounts with ESM, into which Novick dumped millions of dollars of profits from repo and reverse repo transactions. In return, when Novick needed additional government securities, these individuals would supply ESM with securities from their own firms' vaults.[7] Over the course of the ESM scam, Novick, his colleagues, and their co-conspirators were the beneficiaries of more than $100 million of ESM funds, funds stolen from the banks and municipalities that were ESM's major customers. When these thefts were added to the trading losses incurred by Novick and ESM's other investment losses, the net deficit for the corporate ESM group exceeded $300 million by the spring of 1985.

Two events in late 1984 proved to be the downfall of ESM. First, Novick collapsed and died at his desk of a massive heart attack in November 1984. Novick, in his early forties at the time, had been under immense stress for several years, since he had been responsible for the day-to-day operations of the ESM scam. Ewton and Steve Arky, ESM's legal counsel, tried to persuade Gomez to leave Alexander Grant and assume Novick's position. Gomez refused. Apparently concerned that the increasingly nervous Gomez might blow the whistle on the entire operation, Ewton transferred $100,000 to Gomez's personal ESM account to keep him on board.

The second event that led to ESM's undoing was a major customer's insistence in late 1984 that ESM turn over the securities the customer had purchased in a long-term repo transaction. ESM no longer had those securities. After stonewalling the customer for several months, Ewton resigned from the firm and retained the services of a criminal defense attorney. Within a short time, the ESM fraud made the headlines of metropolitan newspapers nationwide.

AUDIT ISSUES RAISED BY THE ESM DEBACLE

On February 28, 1985, Alexander Grant issued what would be its final audit opinion on financial statements of ESM Government Securities (see Exhibit 2). Less than 24 hours later, after Gomez admitted his involvement in the ESM fraud to fellow partners, Alexander Grant hastily withdrew the unqualified opinion and announced that the opinion should no longer be relied upon. After learning of Grant's withdrawal of its audit report, an attorney for Home State Savings (which was owed approximately $145 million by ESM) flew to Fort Lauderdale. This attorney demanded that ESM officials explain why the audit report had been rescinded. By this point, Ewton was nowhere to be found. Two of Ewton's subordinates referred the Home State attorney to a lawyer ESM had retained a few weeks earlier, following Steve Arky's resignation. The two attorneys then contacted a local accountant and asked him to meet them at ESM headquarters the following morning. By midmorning on March 2, 1985, only two hours after

7. These securities were allegedly collateral for loans that ESM had made earlier to these customers. Court records documented that these loans were grossly overcollateralized and that the true purpose of these transfers of securities was simply to perpetuate the ESM fraud.

EXHIBIT 2
**Alexander Grant's Audit
Report on ESM's 1984
Balance Sheet**

[Note: This audit report appeared on the letterhead of Alexander Grant & Company.]

Board of Directors

ESM Government Securities, Inc.

We have examined the statement of financial condition of ESM Government Securities, Inc. (a Florida corporation and wholly-owned subsidiary of ESM Group, Inc.) as of December 31, 1984. Our examination was made in accordance with generally accepted auditing standards and, accordingly, included such tests of the accounting records and such other auditing procedures as we considered necessary in the circumstances.

In our opinion, the statement referred to above presents fairly the financial condition of ESM Government Securities, Inc. at December 31, 1984 in conformity with generally accepted accounting principles applied on a basis consistent with that of the preceding year.

Alexander Grant & Company

[signed]

Fort Lauderdale, Florida

January 30, 1985

the accountant first obtained ESM's accounting records, he informed the attorneys that ESM was insolvent by at least $200 million.

The congressional subcommittee that investigated the ESM scandal was shocked that such a massive fraud could be detected in a matter of hours, when Alexander Grant failed for seven years to detect the scam. Members of the subcommittee insisted that at least some of Gomez's 40 colleagues and subordinates who worked on the ESM audits must have been aware of the fraudulent scheme. Nevertheless, state and federal prosecutors never indicted any other Alexander Grant auditors.[8] In a subsequent civil suit, Gomez testified that little effort had been required on his part to divert his subordinates away from the fraudulent sections of ESM's financial records: "I thought about when my own audit people would come up with questions that I wouldn't be able to answer without forcing me to lie extensively. That never happened."[9]

The accountant who uncovered the ESM fraud on March 2, 1985, did not unravel the thousands of intercompany transactions Novick used to conceal the firm's losses. Instead, the accountant happened to compare the firm's audited balance sheets with the consolidated corporate tax returns filed for the ESM corporate group. ESM executives did not want to pay income taxes on the "profitable" securities trades booked by Novick to offset the huge trading losses actually suffered by the company. So, the executives provided the firm's tax accountant from Alexander Grant with accurate financial data to prepare ESM's annual consolidated tax returns. These corporate tax returns clearly revealed that the collective ESM operation was consistently losing tens of millions of dollars each year. An attorney in the law firm appointed as ESM's receiver noted that the scam was

8. One individual on Alexander Grant's tax staff stumbled across a payment to Gomez entered in ESM's accounting records. Rather than bringing this matter to the attention of other partners, this individual took it directly to Gomez. Apparently, Gomez fabricated an explanation for the payment that satisfied the individual.

9. Maggin, *Bankers, Builders, Knaves and Thieves*, 215.

immediately obvious when the tax returns and audited balance sheets were compared: "It's incredible because it's so plain. It did not take detective work to find this. You just compare the reported balance sheets and the tax returns and you see the whole thing."[10]

Members of the congressional subcommittee queried expert witnesses in the ESM hearings at length regarding the complex maze of intercompany transactions Novick used to conceal the huge ESM deficits. Alexander Grant's apparent failure to audit these transactions thoroughly troubled the subcommittee.

MR. TEW [attorney for ESM receiver]: . . . it is critical that auditors inspect interrelated or affiliated transactions, because [in such cases] the client is booking entries with itself. If you can book an entry with yourself, you can commit a massive fraud.

CONGRESSMAN DINGELL: And control both entries?

MR. TEW: Yes, sir. You have it on both sides. You can do what you want. If this company [ESM Government Securities] lost money on a term repo, they would record a reverse repo or a mirror transaction, and move the loss up to the parent company.

Another issue raised by the congressional subcommittee was the failure of ESM's auditors and the auditors of ESM's customers to discover the constant shortage of securities that was a by-product of Novick's fraudulent scheme. Members of the subcommittee speculated that the most basic audit procedures should have uncovered this shortage.

MR. TEW: . . . the first thing you do, one of the first and simplest things, is to do a box count of the securities or confirm that the actual securities are in the possession of the custodian. *(Existence)*

CONGRESSMAN DINGELL: To make sure these securities and assets are (a) what they purport to be; and (b) are physically in the place that they are supposed to be; and (c) are in the custody of the people in whose custody they are supposed to be. Isn't that right? *Rights + Obligations*

MR. TEW: Correct on all counts. The fundamental confirmation technique is to cover all the issues you just raised.

Auditors of ESM's major customers testified that they had performed confirmation procedures. Unfortunately, they directed their confirmations to Jose Gomez. This testimony incensed Representative Ron Wyden, the most severe critic of the auditors involved in the ESM case.

The auditors tell us that they had no choice but to rely on second-party confirmations—in this case, the word of Mr. Gomez—that the collateral for these large loans did exist and did adequately secure their clients' interest. What disturbs me is that the system literally breeds this kind of buck-passing. If the auditors went as far as the system and the rules of their profession require in confirming the collateral, any reasonable person would conclude that once again the auditing system has failed . . . it is my view that the only watchdogs throughout this sorry spectacle were either asleep, forgot how to bark, or were taking handouts from the burglars.

---

10. J. Sterngold, "ESM's Auditor Is Sued," *The New York Times*, 16 March 1985, 30.

Several members of Congress also questioned the adequacy of Alexander Grant's audit review process. These members suggested that Grant's review procedures should have uncovered the flaws in the firm's ESM audits that prevented the auditors from discovering Novick's fraudulent activities.

CONGRESSMAN LUKEN: What is your [review] system?

MR. KLECKNER [managing partner of Grant Thornton, the successor firm to Alexander Grant & Company]: Every report that is issued by an office is required to receive what we call a basic review within that office. In certain circumstances, the report is required to receive what we call an in-depth review, and in other circumstances, a report is required to receive what we call a technical review, which normally involves people from outside that office.

CONGRESSMAN LUKEN: Would you say that the review system has broken down rather badly here since you say that Mr. Gomez passed the review system?

MR. KLECKNER: I think it's a key question.

CONGRESSMAN SIKORSKI: Can rendering an inaccurate audit opinion be the fault of only one person under your firm's quality control procedure?

MR. KLECKNER: I think it really depends upon the degree and the nature of the manipulation that was taking place.

CONGRESSMAN SIKORSKI: Well, your system allows that manipulation.

MR. KLECKNER: The system is based on a fundamental assumption. The fundamental assumption is that the audit partner is honest.

CONGRESSMAN SIKORSKI: That's right. What kind of system do you have set up to catch dishonest people?

MR. KLECKNER: I would have to admit that I don't think our system starts out to try to question the honesty and integrity of each partner.

In a subsequent court case, testimony obtained by a plaintiff attorney further disparaged Alexander Grant's audit review process. "Garcia-Pedrosa [plaintiff counsel] got a review partner to admit that he only made cursory investigations of Gomez's ESM workpapers from 1977 to 1982. And there was no refutation of Jose Gomez's testimony that another review partner said, 'I don't understand this s___ , so please tell me it's okay and I'll sign it.'"[11]

Congressman John Dingell asked the accountant retained by ESM's receiver to identify the key red flags that should have alerted Alexander Grant auditors that something was wrong at ESM. The first warning signal was the magnitude of the intercompany transactions between ESM and its unaudited affiliate. Even more important than the size of these transactions was the absence of an underlying business purpose for them. The inability of the auditors to follow these suspicious intercompany transactions from "cradle to grave," since the other party to the transactions was ESM's unaudited affiliate, could easily have been considered a material audit scope limitation. Ironically, the scheme used by Novick to hide the ESM losses was very similar to the bookkeeping scams used in several classic audit failures, including Continental Vending, Drysdale Securities, and Equity Funding.

---

11. Maggin, *Bankers, Builders, Knaves and Thieves*, 215.

Red Flag
#2

RED FLAG.
#3

Weak + incipient
SEC oversight

Another warning signal apparently overlooked by Alexander Grant auditors was the exorbitant lifestyles that ESM's key officers adopted and flaunted over the short history of their firm. As an example, Exhibit 3 lists the personal assets of Ewton that a bankruptcy judge froze following ESM's collapse.

Possibly the most important red flag disregarded by the Alexander Grant auditors was the personal background of ESM's chief executive, Ronnie Ewton. A thorough background investigation of Ewton would have revealed several suspicious incidents in his past. In 1973, the National Association of Securities Dealers censured Ewton. In that same case, prosecutors convicted two of Ewton's associates of falsifying financial records and using customer securities as collateral for personal loans. During the 12 months prior to forming ESM, Ewton had been employed by three different brokerage firms. Two of these firms had bilked investors out of millions of dollars. In each case, Ewton avoided prosecution, although several of his co-workers received jail terms.

The Securities and Exchange Commission (SEC) investigated Ewton shortly after he formed ESM. Although the SEC had no direct regulatory oversight over ESM, it filed suit against the firm, alleging that Ewton had attempted to swindle an SEC-registered bank holding company. The SEC report on this investigation included the following observation: "The staff believes that it may have uncovered the tip of an iceberg involving the fraudulent trading of Ginnie Mae's and

EXHIBIT 3
Personal Assets of Ronnie Ewton Frozen by Bankruptcy Court Order

Asset	Estimated Value (net of any mortgage balance)
Residence in Boca Raton, Fla.	$1,650,000
Residence in Greenwich, Conn.	330,000
5,600-acre horse farm in Aiken, S.C.	Unknown
Polo pony stable and 17 horses	700,000
House and two vacant lots in Boone, N.C.	Unknown
Boat slip in Key Largo, Fla.	Unknown
House and 57 acres in Aiken, S.C.	Unknown
One-fifteenth ownership interest in Hounds Lake Country Club in Aiken, S.C.	Unknown
Five lots in Elk River Country Club in Linville, N.C.	Unknown
One Aston Martin Laconda (automobile)	151,000
One 1984 Chevrolet Corvette	20,000
One Mercedes Benz, one Cadillac, one Toyota, and several jeeps and trucks	Unknown
70-foot yacht	1,350,000
Partnership interest in horse-breeding operation	Unknown
Account with Provident Securities	400,000
Letter of credit held by Provident Bank	200,000
Partnership interest in 5,600 acres of property in Jasper, Tenn.	Unknown
Partnership interest in Colee Hammock Building	200,000
Mortgages receivable	1,995,279
Partnership interest in Tampa Bay Bandits professional sports franchise	Unknown
Partnership interest in S-J Minerals Partnership	Unknown
Numerous partnership interests in oil and gas ventures and coal-mining projects	Unknown

other securities issued by the United States and its agencies."[12] Unfortunately for ESM's future customers, Steve Arky, ESM's skillful legal counsel, thwarted the SEC charges, and Ewton escaped unscathed once again.[13]

\# 6

EPILOGUE

The principal conspirators in the ESM scandal were convicted of various crimes and sentenced to jail. Ewton, for example, received a 24-year sentence and will apparently be required to serve 15 years before he is eligible for parole. Three months following ESM's collapse, Steve Arky committed suicide. Several months later, the accountant who maintained the fraudulent accounting records of ESM's bogus affiliate for Alan Novick committed suicide after being convicted and sentenced to prison.

Shortly after the ESM scandal began grabbing nationwide headlines, Alexander Grant & Company changed its name to Grant Thornton. In a negotiated settlement with the Florida Board of Accountancy in 1985, Grant received a 60-day suspension from accepting any new clients and agreed to submit to a peer review by a CPA firm selected by the state board.

QUESTIONS

1. In an interview following his admission of involvement in the ESM fraud, Jose Gomez reported that individuals recently promoted to partner in a major CPA firm are subject to considerable pressure from their superiors to attract and retain clients. What measures should audit firms take to ensure that such pressure does not become dysfunctional, as it did in the case of Jose Gomez?

Article

2. Note A to ESM's 1984 balance sheet (see Exhibit 1) discusses the consolidated tax return filed for the ESM corporate group. What responsibility, if any, do auditors have to review a client's corporate tax return? If tax and audit services are provided to a client by a CPA firm, what responsibility, if any, do the tax practitioners have to communicate to the audit team any information they discover that may have financial statement implications?

3. During his testimony before the congressional subcommittee, Grant Thornton's managing partner noted that his firm's audit review process is based on the fundamental assumption that the engagement audit partner is honest. Should CPA firms rethink their basic quality control strategies, given what happened in the ESM case?

Article

---

12. *Ibid.*, 75.

13. Ewton relied on Steve Arky's legal expertise on several occasions to bail ESM out of desperate straits. In 1980, the wife of Bobby Seneca, one of ESM's co-founders, sued him for divorce. To avoid a large divorce settlement, Seneca provided ESM's financial records, including those of the firm's affiliates, to the judge presiding over the divorce trial. These records clearly demonstrated that the ESM corporate entity was bankrupt. Steve Arky's law firm convinced the judge that ESM's insolvent condition should be kept confidential following the trial, ostensibly to allow ESM to liquidate in an orderly manner.

\#6

4. When Gomez informed his fellow partners of the ESM fraud, Alexander Grant immediately withdrew the audit opinion that had been issued on ESM's December 31, 1984, balance sheet. Was this the appropriate course of action to take in this set of circumstances? Did Alexander Grant have a responsibility to take any other actions?

5. During the ESM congressional hearings, the auditors of ESM's major customers were questioned regarding the confirmation procedures they used for their clients' transactions with ESM. What would be the key objective or objectives of an auditor's confirmation procedures when a client has engaged in (a) repo transactions with a government securities broker and (b) reverse repo transactions with a government securities broker?

6. Following his death, Steve Arky's law firm was sued by the ESM receiver on the grounds that Arky had an obligation to inform Alexander Grant that ESM was insolvent. Which party to this suit do you believe prevailed, and why?

7. Because of the concept of joint and several liability, each partner of Alexander Grant was held financially responsible for the malfeasance of Jose Gomez. Is it appropriate for society to impose joint and several liability on the partners of large professional firms? Why or why not?

8. Congressional testimony disclosed that ESM officers had several million dollars in outstanding loans from ESM. These loans were not shown separately on the 1984 ESM balance sheet. Do technical standards require that such loans be reported separately in a client's financial statements? If so, why?

CASE 1.3
UNITED STATES
SURGICAL CORPORATION

Leon Hirsch founded United States Surgical Corporation (USSC) in 1964 with very little capital, four employees, and one product: an unwieldy mechanical device that he intended to market as a surgical stapler. In his mid-thirties at the time and lacking a college degree, Hirsch had already tried several lines of business, including frozen foods, dry cleaning, and advertising, each with little success. In fact, the dry cleaning venture ended in bankruptcy. No doubt, few of Hirsch's friends and family members believed that USSC would become financially viable. Despite the long odds against him, by 1980 Hirsch had built the Connecticut-based USSC into a large and profitable public company whose stock was traded on a national exchange. More importantly, the surgical stapler that Hirsch invented revolutionized surgery techniques in the United States and abroad.

During the early years of its existence, USSC dominated the small surgical stapling industry that Hirsch established in the mid-1960s. By 1980, several companies were encroaching on USSC's domestic and foreign sales markets. USSC's principal competitor at the time was a company owned by Alan Blackman. Blackman's company sold its products primarily in foreign countries but was attempting to significantly expand its U.S. sales. Hirsch alleged that Blackman, who was a former friend and associate, had infringed on USSC's patents by "reverse-engineering" the company's products.

In the early 1980s, USSC began an aggressive counterattack to repel Blackman's intrusion into its markets. First, USSC adopted a worldwide litigation strategy to contest Blackman's right to manufacture and market his competing products. Second, the company embarked on a large research and development program to create a line of new products technologically superior to those being manufactured by Blackman. Each of these initiatives required multimillion-dollar commitments by USSC—commitments that threatened the company's steadily rising profits and Hirsch's ability to raise additional capital that USSC desperately needed to finance its rapid growth.

Hirsch overcame the major challenges facing his company in the early 1980s. USSC maintained its dominant position in the surgical stapling industry, while continuing to report record profits and sales each year. Ironically, those record profits and sales eventually spelled trouble for the company. Mounting suspicion that USSC's reported operating results were too good to be true prompted the Securities and Exchange Commission (SEC) to launch an investigation of the company's financial affairs. In 1983, the SEC leveled several charges of misconduct against key USSC officers, including Leon Hirsch. Within a short time, USSC's audit firm, Ernst & Whinney, resigned and withdrew the unqualified audit opinions it had issued on the company's 1980 and 1981 financial statements. In 1985, the SEC released a report on its lengthy investigation of USSC. The SEC ruled that the company had used a "variety of manipulative devices to overstate its earnings in its 1980 and 1981 financial statements."[1] (Exhibit 1 contains USSC's original balance sheets and income statements for the period 1979 to 1981.)

To settle the SEC charges, USSC officials signed an agreement with the federal agency that forced the company to reduce its previously reported earnings by $26 million. Additionally, senior executives of USSC agreed to return to the company large bonuses they had been paid during 1980 and 1981. Hirsch alone repaid more than $300,000 to USSC. Following the signing of the agreement with the SEC, Hirsch reported that the criticism of his company and his management decisions was undeserved. Hirsch implied that cost considerations motivated him to accept the SEC sanctions: "It was our opinion that the settlement [with the SEC] was preferable to long, costly and time-consuming litigation."[2]

USSC's Abusive Accounting Practices

The enforcement release that disclosed the key findings of the SEC's investigation of USSC charged the company with several abusive accounting and financial reporting practices. A focal point of the SEC's investigation was an elaborate scheme that USSC executives implemented to charge inventoriable production costs to a long-term asset account, molds and dies. This scheme, which required the cooperation of several of USSC's vendors, was deliberately concealed from the company's audit firm, Ernst & Whinney.[3]

The SEC investigation also revealed that USSC recorded inventory shipments to its sales force as consummated sales transactions. Until the mid-1970s, USSC had marketed its products through a network of independent dealers. Historically, inventory shipments to these dealers had been treated as arm's length transactions and thus reportable as revenue. By 1980, the company marketed its products almost exclusively through a sales staff consisting of full-time

---

1. This and subsequent quotations, unless indicated otherwise, were taken from Securities and Exchange Commission, *Accounting and Auditing Enforcement Release No. 109A*, 6 August 1986.

2. K.B. Noble, "U.S. Surgical Settlement to Restate Earnings," *The New York Times*, 28 February 1984, B2.

3. A subsequent section of this case discusses the details of this scheme, including the measures that USSC executives took to conceal it from Ernst & Whinney.

EXHIBIT 1
**United States Surgical
Corporation's
1979–1981 Financial
Statements**

U.S. Surgical Corporation
Consolidated Balance Sheets 1979–1981
(000s omitted)

	December 31, 1981	1980	1979
Current Assets			
Cash	$ 426	$ 1,243	$ 596
Receivables (net)	36,670	30,475	22,557
Inventories			
Finished Goods	29,216	9,860	5,685
Work in Process	5,105	2,667	1,153
Raw Materials	20,948	18,806	7,365
	55,269	31,333	14,203
Other Current Assets	7,914	1,567	1,820
Total Current Assets	100,279	64,618	39,176
Property, Plant, and Equipment			
Land	2,502	2,371	1,027
Buildings	32,416	18,511	13,019
Molds and Dies	32,082	15,963	8,777
Machinery and Equipment	40,227	23,762	12,362
	107,227	60,607	35,185
Allowance for Depreciation	(14,953)	(9,964)	(6,340)
	92,274	50,643	28,845
Other Assets	14,786	3,842	2,499
Total Assets	$ 207,339	$119,103	$70,520
Current Liabilities			
Accounts Payable	$ 12,278	$ 6,951	$ 6,271
Notes Payable	—	—	1,596
Income Taxes Payable	—	1,685	—
Current Portion of Long-Term Debt	724	666	401
Accrued Expenses	5,673	5,130	5,145
Total Current Liabilities	18,675	14,432	13,413
Long-Term Debt	80,642	47,569	33,497
Deferred Income Taxes	7,466	2,956	1,384
Stockholders' Equity			
Common Stock	1,081	930	379
Additional Paid-in Capital	72,594	34,932	10,736
Retained Earnings	32,665	20,881	13,189
Translation Allowance	(1,086)	—	—
Deferred Compensation—from Issuance of Restricted Stock	(4,698)	(2,597)	(2,078)
Total Stockholders' Equity	100,556	54,146	22,226
Total Liabilities and Stockholders' Equity	$ 207,339	$119,103	$70,520

(continued)

employees working on a commission basis. Everyone on the sales staff maintained an inventory of USSC products, which they transported from client to client. When USSC shipped products to a salesperson, the company recorded the

**EXHIBIT 1—continued
United States Surgical
Corporation's
1979–1981 Financial
Statements**

**U.S. Surgical Corporation
Consolidated Income Statements 1979–1981
(000s omitted)**

	December 31,		
	1981	**1980**	**1979**
Net Sales	$111,800	$86,214	$60,876
Costs and Expenses			
Cost of Products Sold	47,983	32,300	25,659
Selling, General, and Administrative*	45,015	37,740	23,935
Interest	5,898	4,063	3,403
	98,896	74,103	52,997
Income Before Income Taxes	12,904	12,111	7,879
Income Taxes			
Federal and Foreign	795	3,406	2,279
State and Local	325	820	471
	1,120	4,226	2,750
Net Income	$ 11,784	$ 7,885	$ 5,129
Net Income per common share and common share equivalent	$1.13	$.89	$.68
Average number of common shares and common share equivalents outstanding			
1981	10,403,392		
1980		8,816,986	
1979			7,555,710

* Included in these amounts are the following research and development expenses: 1981—$1,337, 1980—$3,020, 1979—$2,289.

inventory as having been sold, although employees could return unsold items for full credit.

In 1980 and 1981, USSC's management ordered that excessive amounts of inventory be shipped to salespeople to overstate the company's reported sales and profits. A former USSC sales manager later testified regarding this practice. "It was nothing to come home and find $3,000 worth of product sitting in a box on your front porch from UPS and a note saying, 'We thought you needed a little more product.'"[4] According to the SEC, USSC's policy of recognizing inventory shipments to its sales staff as consummated sales transactions overstated the company's 1980 and 1981 pretax profits by $1,150,000 and $750,000, respectively.

The SEC also charged that USSC abused the accounting rule that permits the capitalization of legal expenditures incurred to develop and successfully defend a patent. In 1980, the company capitalized less than $1 million of such expenditures; the following year, that figure leaped to $5.8 million. The SEC investigation disclosed that a significant portion of the 1981 litigation expenditures stemmed from Australian lawsuits filed against Alan Blackman and his company. Because USSC did not have any registered patents in Australia, these expenditures should

4. N.R. Kleinfeld, "U.S. Surgical's Checkered History," *The New York Times*, 13 May 1984, F4.

not have been deferred in an asset account but instead immediately charged to operations. Approximately $3.7 million of USSC's 1981 litigation expenditures involved efforts to defend the company's U.S. patents. However, USSC chose to amortize these costs over a 10-year period even though the 17-year legal life of most of the patents would expire in 1983 or 1984.

USSC leased, rather than sold, many of its surgical tools. The company's accounting staff recorded the cost of these assets in a subsidiary fixed asset ledger, leased and loaned assets. USSC periodically retired such assets and removed their accounts from the sub-ledger. However, SEC investigators discovered that the costs associated with these assets were often not removed from the sub-ledger but instead debited to the accounts of other assets still in service. In 1981, USSC also understated depreciation expense on several fixed assets and thus inflated the balance sheet values of those assets. These misstatements resulted from the company's accountants arbitrarily extending the useful lives of selected assets and establishing salvage values for the first time for other assets.

ALLEGATIONS OF AUDIT DEFICIENCIES

The SEC's investigation of USSC uncovered several alleged flaws in Ernst & Whinney's audits of the company, particularly the 1981 audit. An important risk factor present during the 1981 USSC audit that Ernst & Whinney may have overlooked was the company's strong incentive to reach targeted sales and profit goals. If those targeted figures were not reached, USSC would have had difficulty raising the additional capital needed for expansion purposes. A former USSC vice-president later revealed that Hirsch often made firm commitments to security analysts regarding the company's future sales and profits.[5] This individual maintained that many of USSC's abusive accounting practices sprang from Hirsch's efforts to deliver the promised sales and earnings figures. USSC's management bonus plan provided another incentive for USSC officials to misrepresent the company's financial data.

> Surgical's executive officers could earn bonuses ranging from 15% to 75% of their base salaries, if the earnings per share growth ranged from 15% to 30% over the previous year. Management therefore had powerful personal incentives to keep the earnings per share high.

The SEC also suggested that Ernst & Whinney failed to make proper use of analytical procedures during the planning phase of the 1981 audit. Ernst & Whinney apparently overlooked the important implications for its 1981 audit of several material changes in USSC account balances between December 31, 1980, and December 31, 1981. For example, the balance of the molds and dies account more than doubled from the end of 1980 to the end of 1981. According to the SEC, "This unusually large increase should have caused the auditors to scrutinize carefully the nature and source of the additions, and whether certain costs were properly identified and capitalized under GAAP."

Two other USSC accounts that reflected material changes between 1980 and 1981 were research and development expenses and patents. USSC reported a

---

5. *Ibid.*

greater than 50 percent decrease in research and development expenses in 1981 compared with the previous year. This decrease occurred even though USSC undertook a large product development campaign during 1981. USSC's accounting records for 1981 also reflected a significant increase in litigation expenditures that were deferred in its patents account. (USSC included the patents account in noncurrent "Other Assets" on its balance sheet. See Exhibit 1.) The SEC maintained that the unusually large changes in key USSC account balances between 1980 and 1981 should have placed Ernst & Whinney on alert that the 1981 USSC audit would have a higher-than-normal degree of risk associated with it: "The heightened audit attention was particularly important since the aggregate effect of the changes was material to Surgical's 1981 financial statements . . . [and] the changes all had the effect of increasing income."

The SEC ruled that Ernst & Whinney made three critical errors when considering the question of whether USSC should be allowed to record inventory shipments to its sales staff as valid sales transactions. First, the SEC pointed out that Ernst & Whinney failed to recognize that "sales" of inventory to employees generally do not qualify as arm's length transactions: "Because the potential for abuse is so great when a 'sale' transaction is between a company and its employee, the presumption is that no 'true' sale has taken place." Second, the SEC maintained that USSC's repurchase of significant amounts of inventory from its salespeople during 1981 should have alerted Ernst & Whinney that the original inventory shipments to these employees were not bona fide sales transactions. This oversight by Ernst & Whinney particularly troubled the SEC since the audit firm's 1980 and 1981 workpapers clearly documented these repurchases. Finally, the SEC criticized Ernst & Whinney for failing to investigate a client executive's assertion that USSC was not obligated to repurchase inventory from employees who resigned or were terminated. Ernst & Whinney's 1981 audit program included a procedure to obtain and review a copy of the employment contract signed by USSC's sales employees and to incorporate that contract in the permanent workpaper file. Although the Ernst & Whinney audit program indicated that this procedure had been completed, there was no evidence to this effect in the firm's 1981 workpapers. The SEC ruled that if the employment contract had been obtained and reviewed, Ernst & Whinney would have learned that USSC not only had a policy of repurchasing inventory from former employees but had a contractual obligation to do so.

The SEC reserved its harshest criticism of Ernst & Whinney for the firm's failure to prevent USSC from capitalizing a material amount of production expenses in the molds and dies account. During the last few months of 1980, USSC began systematically charging production costs to that noncurrent asset account, resulting in a significant overstatement of assets and a corresponding understatement of cost of goods sold. Company executives used several methods to conceal this illicit scheme. The most common of these methods was instructing the company's vendors, who did most of the production work on USSC's products, to describe generic production costs as capitalizable expenditures on invoices submitted for payment to USSC.

One of USSC's primary vendors was Lacey Manufacturing Company, a division of Barden Corporation—which also happened to be an Ernst & Whinney audit client. In late 1980, USSC officials instructed Barden Corporation to begin using the phrase "tooling modifications" to describe the work performed for USSC by Lacey Manufacturing. Previously, these invoices had described the expenditures incurred for USSC as generic production costs. This change in the description of the incurred costs was critical, since all tooling costs for new or redesigned products were capitalizable expenditures.

CHRONOLOGY OF USSC–ERNST & WHINNEY DISAGREEMENT REGARDING CAPITALIZATION OF ALLEGED TOOLING COSTS

For many years, accounting educators have maintained that the imbalance of power in the auditor-client relationship impairs the quality of audits.[6] This imbalance of power favors the client, largely because client executives retain and compensate their company's independent auditors. When technical disputes arise during an audit, client executives may use their leverage on auditors to extract important concessions from them.

A classic example of an audit conflict arose during Ernst & Whinney's 1981 audit of USSC. This conflict stemmed from USSC's illicit scheme to charge production costs to the noncurrent asset account molds and dies. The following chronology lists the key events in this dispute:

1/27/82	The Ernst & Whinney audit team completes its fieldwork on the USSC engagement.
2/2/82	Paul Yamont, senior vice-president and treasurer of Barden Corporation, makes an unsolicited telephone call to William Burke, the Ernst & Whinney audit engagement partner on the Barden audit. Yamont informs Burke that Barden accountants have discovered numerous USSC purchase orders and corresponding Barden invoices that do not accurately describe the work that Lacey Manufacturing (a division of Barden Corporation) has been performing for USSC. According to Yamont, these invoices and purchase orders, totaling approximately $1 million, indicate that the Lacey work for USSC has been for "tooling modifications." In fact, Lacey has simply been producing and assembling products for USSC. Burke immediately visits Barden to discuss this issue with Yamont.
2/3/82	Ernst & Whinney approves the issuance of a press release by USSC management that reports the company's sales and earnings for 1981. (At this point, Michael Hope, the USSC audit engagement partner, is unaware of the problem brought to William Burke's attention by Paul Yamont.)
2/5/82	Burke again visits Yamont to discuss the alleged mislabeled invoices.
2/8/82	Barden Corporation's board of directors votes to retain Ernst & Whinney to formally investigate the mislabeled invoices.
2/10/82	Burke contacts Norman Strauss, regional director of accounting and auditing for Ernst & Whinney's New York region, and informs him of Yamont's

---

6. A. Goldman and B. Barlev, "The Auditor–Firm Conflict of Interests: Its Implications for Independence," *Accounting Review* 49 (October 1974), 707–718; D.R. Nichols and K. Price, "The Auditor–Firm Conflict: An Analysis Using Concepts of Exchange Theory," *Accounting Review* 51 (April 1976), 335–346; M.C. Knapp and B.H. Ward, "An Integrative Analysis of Audit Conflict: Sources, Consequences and Resolution," *Advances in Accounting* 4 (1987), 267–286.

concerns. Strauss immediately informs Bruce Dixon, Ernst & Whinney partner in charge of the New York region, of the Barden situation. Shortly thereafter, Dixon calls Hope and instructs him not to sign off on the USSC audit until the questionable invoice charges have been fully investigated. Dixon also informs Robert Neary, Ernst & Whinney's chief technical partner, of the problem.

2/13/82   Burke sends an Ernst & Whinney audit manager to Barden Corporation to investigate the invoices and purchase orders in question.

2/15/82   Burke joins the Ernst & Whinney audit manager at Barden Corporation to tour the Lacey Manufacturing facility and to discuss the questionable invoices and purchase orders with Robert More, the Lacey general manager. More informs Burke that nearly all of the invoiced charges being reviewed were for generic production work performed for USSC rather than for tooling modifications.

2/18/82   Burke meets with the Barden board of directors and reports that the results of the Ernst & Whinney investigation demonstrate that the USSC purchase orders and the corresponding Barden invoices misrepresent the nature of the work performed by Lacey Manufacturing for USSC. The chairman of Barden's board of directors then reports that an independent investigation by an outside law firm has yielded the same conclusion. The Barden directors vote to require that all future work performed for USSC be properly described in invoices submitted for payment to the company.

2/20/82   Hope and Dixon are unsure how to proceed on the USSC audit, given the
(approx-   results of Burke's investigation. Because of confidentiality concerns, Hope
imately)   cannot raise the issue directly with USSC officers. Barden officers are concerned that if USSC perceives that Barden has brought the problem to the attention of Ernst & Whinney, USSC may terminate its relationship with Barden. Finally, Hope and Dixon decide to send a confirmation letter to Yamont and More that asks them to confirm that the disputed $1 million in charges were for tooling modifications. (Hope and Dixon realize that Yamont and More will refuse to sign the confirmation letter.)

2/25/82   Yamont contacts Hope and informs him that he cannot sign the confirmation letter since he is aware that the disputed charges are not for tooling modifications. Following the refusal of Yamont and, subsequently, More to sign the confirmation letter, Ernst & Whinney officials discuss the problem with the management of both USSC and Barden. Eventually, executives of each company agree to allow auditors from the two Ernst & Whinney teams to have mutual access to their company's accounting records.

3/3/82   Hope meets with top USSC executives and asks them to relate their understanding of the costs incurred by Lacey Manufacturing on behalf of USSC. The USSC officials inform Hope that in early 1981, they had instructed More, the Lacey general manager, to make certain tooling changes that would result in improved efficiency in the production of USSC products. The executives then provided an elaborate and confusing explanation as to why the tooling modifications were charged out on a per-unit basis. (Earlier, Ernst & Whinney representatives had noted that the disputed costs were billed to USSC based upon the number of units of product manufactured by Lacey. Intuitively, costs associated with tooling modifications should have been billed in one lump sum or in installments. The fact that the costs were billed on a per-unit basis suggested that they were production costs.)

Hope asks USSC's controller for purchase orders that the company had placed with outside contractors other than Barden (Lacey). Hope is looking for evidence of additional mislabeled costs. In the files that Hope is allowed to review, he finds charges billed to USSC that are similar to the disputed tooling modification costs billed to USSC by Barden. USSC officials assure Hope that the costs incurred on USSC's behalf by these vendors were, in fact, for tooling modifications.

3/5/82 Hope and Burke meet with senior USSC executives and More of Lacey Manufacturing. In More's presence, one of the USSC executives again explains that the disputed costs involved tooling changes requested by USSC in early 1981. More indicates that he agrees with that characterization of the costs. (Of course, More had previously maintained that the disputed amounts were production, not tooling, costs. More justifies his change in opinion by stating that earlier he "hadn't thought it through.")

3/10/82 Hope and Burke tour the Lacey Manufacturing facility to obtain a better understanding of the firm's production process. More is asked to act as a guide for the Ernst & Whinney partners on the tour. Shortly before the tour is scheduled to begin, a senior executive with USSC arrives unexpectedly at Lacey and asks permission to accompany the others on the tour. During the tour, More explains that production personnel charge their time to either tooling jobs or production jobs. He also notes that personnel often inadvertently charge tooling costs to production jobs.

3/11/82 During a conference call involving Hope, Burke, top technical partners of Ernst & Whinney, and the CPA firm's internal and external legal counsel, Hope explains the additional audit procedures performed to analyze the disputed tooling costs. He then reports his conclusion that the disputed costs involved tooling modifications, not generic production work. The other Ernst & Whinney personnel agree with Hope.

3/14/82 To support the conclusion that the disputed costs were for tooling modifi-
(approx-   cations, Hope is instructed to obtain a signed confirmation letter from
imately)   Yamont of Barden Corporation to that effect. When asked to sign the letter, Yamont refuses, as he had done in late February.

3/15/82 Hope decides not to investigate further the questionable tooling costs that he discovered on March 3—tooling costs charged to USSC by vendors other than Lacey Manufacturing. Regarding these items, Hope makes the following entry in the USSC workpapers: "Discussed with [other audit partner] on 3/15/82. Although explanations are incomplete, amounts are immaterial."

3/16/82 More signs the Ernst & Whinney confirmation letter regarding the tooling modification costs that Yamont had refused to sign.

3/17/82 Hope signs Ernst & Whinney's unqualified audit opinion on USSC's 1981 financial statements, which are issued shortly thereafter.

The SEC's investigation of USSC's 1981 financial statements and Ernst & Whinney's audit of those financial statements revealed that Hope and the other Ernst & Whinney auditors had been lied to extensively by USSC personnel. The mislabeled purchase orders and invoices that Ernst & Whinney uncovered were elements of a fraudulent scheme USSC's management had concocted to make production expenditures appear to be capitalizable tooling costs. Apparently, the scheme originated in 1980 when USSC executives tried to force several vendors to take back a significant amount of inventory that had been rendered obsolete by technological changes. When the vendors refused, the USSC executives devised a "compromise." The executives would inflate the amount of future purchase orders for production work to include the cost of the obsolete inventory and then label these purchase orders as being for tooling modifications rather than for production expenses. The USSC executives also instructed the vendors to describe these amounts on subsequent invoices as charges for tooling modifications. This agreement required USSC to pay for the obsolete inventory; however, the company benefitted since the cost of that inventory was not expensed immediately but rather capitalized in the molds and dies account and depreciated over several years.[7]

Although the SEC's investigation revealed that USSC officials had lied repeatedly to Michael Hope, the federal agency still censured the audit partner.[8] The SEC ruled that Ernst & Whinney, and Hope in particular, had sufficient opportunity to discover, and should have discovered, that USSC executives were misrepresenting their firm's financial condition and results of operations:

> The auditors failed to design proper audit procedures, test critical assertions, resolve material conflicts in the audit evidence, and reconcile with the other evidence what they should have recognized were implausible client representations, in violation of GAAS. The bulk of the evidence available to the auditors was so inconsistent with their client's position that the auditors should have realized the [disputed] billings were not properly capitalizable as tooling and that Surgical's representations were false and not made in good faith.

EPILOGUE

USSC recovered from the problems it experienced in the early 1980s. Impressive growth rates in revenues and earnings sent USSC's stock price spiraling upward during the latter part of that decade. By 1996, USSC reported a net income of $109 million on sales of $1.1 billion and total assets exceeding $1.5 billion. Leon Hirsch also recovered nicely from his close and unpleasant encounter with the SEC. Hirsch ranked as the third highest paid corporate executive in the nation in 1991, earning more than $23 million.[9] In September 1997, Hirsch's nearly five million shares of USSC stock had a market value surpassing $200 million.

Leon Hirsch made headlines once again in October 1997. In the midst of a takeover bid for a rival, Circon Corporation, Hirsch chastised certain executives of that company. Hirsch charged that the executives were not focusing sufficient attention on the economic interests of their stockholders and later attempted to

---

7. In some instances, the SEC found that USSC and its vendors simply fabricated phony purchase orders and invoices for tooling modifications to "convert" the obsolete inventory costs to capitalizable expenditures.

8. The SEC also filed a civil complaint against Barden Corporation and Robert More. The SEC alleged that Barden and More "provided substantial cooperation and assistance in furthering and concealing practices" that USSC employed to misrepresent its financial condition and results of operations. Barden and More settled the SEC complaint without admitting guilt or denying any wrongdoing by agreeing to abide by a court order that prohibited them from engaging in any future violations of federal securities laws.

9. "Executive Pay At New Highs," *The New York Times*, 11 May 1992, D5.

replace two of the company's directors with his own nominees to Circon's board. Hirsch justified his action by stating that his nominees "can make some of the other [Circon] directors understand their responsibilities to shareholders."[10] A leading stockholder rights activist was apparently not convinced that Hirsch, given his prior history, was motivated by a desire to improve Circon's corporate governance. This activist bluntly stated that Hirsch "is like the devil of corporate governance."[11]

USSC withdrew its takeover bid for Circon in mid-1998 after announcing that it had agreed to be acquired by Tyco International Ltd., a Bermuda-based company that manufactures fire and security systems. Analysts pegged the value of the takeover package at approximately $3.3 billion. Following the merger, Tyco executives reported that Leon Hirsch would continue to oversee USSC's operations.

QUESTIONS

1. Identify audit procedures that, if employed by Ernst & Whinney during the 1981 USSC audit, might have detected the overstatement of the leased and loaned assets account that resulted from the improper accounting for asset retirements.

2. In 1981, USSC extended the useful lives of several of its fixed assets and adopted salvage values for many of these same assets for the first time. Are these changes permissible under generally accepted accounting principles? Assuming these changes had a material effect on USSC's financial condition and results of operations, how should the changes have been disclosed in the company's financial statements? How should these changes have affected Ernst & Whinney's 1981 audit opinion? (Assume that the current audit reporting standards were in effect at the time.)

3. Prepare common-sized financial statements for USSC for the period 1979–1981. Also compute key liquidity, solvency, activity, and profitability ratios for 1980 and 1981. Given these data, identify what you believe were the high-risk financial statement items for the 1981 USSC audit.

4. What factors in the auditor-client relationship create a power imbalance in favor of the client? Discuss measures that the profession could take to minimize the negative consequences of this power imbalance.

5. Regarding the costs incurred for USSC by Barden, identify (a) the evidence Hope collected that supported USSC's claim that the costs involved tooling modifications and (b) the audit evidence that supported the position that the costs were generic production expenses. What do generally accepted auditing standards suggest are the key evaluative criteria that an auditor should consider when assessing audit evidence? Given these criteria, do you believe Hope was justified in deciding that the costs were for tooling modifications? Why or why not?

6. In your opinion, did Hope satisfactorily investigate the possibility that there were additional suspicious tooling charges being paid and recorded by USSC? If not, what additional steps should he have taken to further explore this possibility? If Hope believed there was some likelihood that his client had commit-

---

10. "U.S. Surgical's Rx for Circon: Corporate Governance," *The Wall Street Journal*, 6 October 1997, B4.

11. *Ibid.*

ted an illegal act, what additional audit procedures, if any, would have been appropriate?

7. When a CPA firm has two audit clients that transact business with each other, should the two audit teams be allowed to share information regarding their clients? Discuss the advantages and disadvantages of amending the client confidentiality rule to allow communication between audit teams under such circumstances.

CASE 1.4
ZZZZ BEST COMPANY, INC.

On May 19, 1987, a short article in *The Wall Street Journal* reported that ZZZZ Best Company, Inc., of Reseda, California, had signed a contract for a $13.8 million insurance restoration project. This project was just the most recent of a series of large restoration jobs obtained by ZZZZ Best (pronounced "zee best") Company. Located in the San Fernando Valley of southern California, ZZZZ Best had begun operations in the fall of 1982 as a small, door-to-door carpet cleaning operation. Under the direction of Barry Minkow, the ambitious 16-year-old who founded the company and initially operated it out of his parents' garage, ZZZZ Best experienced explosive growth in both revenues and profits during the first several years of its existence. In the three-year period from 1984 to 1987, the company's net income surged from less than $200,000 to more than $5 million on revenues of $50 million.

When ZZZZ Best went public in 1986, Minkow and several of his close associates became multimillionaires overnight. By the late spring of 1987, the market value of Minkow's stock in the company exceeded $100 million, and the total market value of ZZZZ Best surpassed $200 million. The youngest chief executive officer in the nation enjoyed the "good life," which included an elegant home in an exclusive suburb of Los Angeles and a fire-engine red Ferrari. Minkow's charm and entrepreneurial genius made him a sought-after commodity on the television talk show circuit and caused the print and visual media to tout him as an example of what America's youth could attain if they would only apply themselves. During an appearance on *The Oprah Winfrey Show* in April 1987, Minkow exhorted his peers with evangelistic zeal to "Think big, be big" and encouraged them to adopt his personal motto, "The sky is the limit."

Less than two years after his appearance on *The Oprah Winfrey Show*, Barry Minkow began serving a 25-year prison sentence. Tried and convicted on 57 counts of securities fraud, Minkow had been exposed as a fast-talking con artist who swindled his closest friends and Wall Street out of millions of dollars.

Federal prosecutors estimate that, at a minimum, Minkow cost investors and creditors $100 million. The company that Minkow founded was, in fact, an elaborate Ponzi scheme. The reported profits of the firm were nonexistent and the huge restoration contracts, imaginary. As one journalist reported, rather than building a corporation, Minkow created a hologram of a corporation. In July 1987, just three months after the company's stock reached a market value of $220 million, an auction of its assets netted only $62,000.

Unlike most financial frauds, the ZZZZ Best scam was perpetrated under the watchful eye of the Securities and Exchange Commission (SEC). The scrutiny of the SEC, one of the largest Wall Street brokerage houses, a large and reputable West Coast law firm that served as the company's general counsel, and an international public accounting firm failed to uncover Minkow's daring scheme. Ultimately, the persistence of an indignant homemaker who had been bilked out of a few hundred dollars by ZZZZ Best resulted in Minkow being exposed as a fraud.

How a teenage flimflam artist could make a mockery of the complex regulatory structure that oversees the U.S. securities markets was the central question posed by a congressional subcommittee that investigated the ZZZZ Best debacle. That subcommittee was headed by Representative John D. Dingell, chairman of the U.S. House Committee on Energy and Commerce. Throughout the investigation, Representative Dingell and his colleagues focused on the role the company's independent auditors played in the ZZZZ Best scandal.

> The ZZZZ Best prospectus told the public that revenues and earnings from insurance restoration contracts were skyrocketing but did not reveal that the contracts were completely fictitious. Where were the independent auditors and the others that are paid to alert the public to fraud and deceit?[1]

Like many other daring financial frauds, the ZZZZ Best scandal caused Congress to reexamine the maze of rules that regulate financial reporting and serve as the foundation of the U.S. system of corporate oversight. However, Daniel Akst, a reporter for *The Wall Street Journal* who documented the rise and fall of Barry Minkow, suggests that another ZZZZ Best is inevitable: "Changing the accounting rules and securities laws will help, but every now and then a Barry Minkow will come along, and ZZZZ Best will happen again. Such frauds are in the natural order of things, I suspect, as old and enduring as human needs."[2]

THE EARLY HISTORY OF ZZZZ BEST COMPANY

Barry Minkow was introduced to the carpet cleaning industry at the age of twelve by his mother, who helped make ends meet by working as a telephone solicitor for a small carpet cleaning firm. Although the great majority of companies in the carpet cleaning industry are legitimate, the nature of the business attracts a disproportionate number of shady characters. There are essentially no barriers to

---

1. This and all subsequent quotations, unless indicated otherwise, were taken from the following source: U.S. Congress, House, Subcommittee on Oversight and Investigations of the Committee on Energy and Commerce, *Failure of ZZZZ Best Co.* (Washington, D.C.: U.S. Government Printing Office, 1988).

2. D. Akst, *Wonder Boy, Barry Minkow—The Kid Who Swindled Wall Street* (New York: Scribner, 1990), 271.

entry: no licensing requirements, no apprenticeships to be served, and only a minimal amount of start-up capital needed. A 16-year-old youth with a driver's license can easily become what industry insiders refer to as a "rug sucker," which is exactly what Minkow did when he founded ZZZZ Best Company.

Minkow quickly recognized that carpet cleaning was a difficult way to earn a livelihood. Customer complaints, cutthroat competition, bad checks, and nagging vendors demanding payment complicated the young entrepreneur's life. Within months of striking out on his own, Minkow faced the ultimate nemesis of the small businessperson: a shortage of working capital. Because of his age and the fact that ZZZZ Best was only marginally profitable, local banks refused to loan him money. Ever resourceful, the brassy teenager came up with his own innovative ways to finance his business: check kiting, credit card forgeries, and the staging of thefts to fleece his insurance company. Minkow's age and personal charm allowed him to escape unscathed from his early brushes with the law that resulted from his creative financing methods. The ease with which the "system" could be beaten encouraged him to exploit it on a broader scale.

Throughout his short business career, Minkow realized the benefits of having an extensive social network of friends and acquaintances. Many of these relationships he developed and cultivated at a Los Angeles health club. Soon after becoming a friend of Tom Padgett, an insurance claims adjuster, Minkow devised a scheme to exploit that friendship. Minkow promised to pay Padgett $100 per week if he would simply confirm over the telephone to banks and any other interested third parties that ZZZZ Best was the recipient of occasional insurance restoration contracts. Ostensibly, Minkow had obtained these contracts to clean and do minor remodeling work on properties damaged by fire, storms, or other catastrophes. Minkow convinced the gullible Padgett that the sole purpose of the confirmations was to allow ZZZZ Best to circumvent much of the bureaucratic red tape in the insurance industry.

From this beginning, the ZZZZ Best fraud blossomed. Initially, Minkow used the insurance restoration work, which was totally fictitious, to generate paper profits and revenues needed to convince bankers to loan him money. Minkow's phony financial statements served their purpose, and he expanded his operations by opening several carpet cleaning outlets across the San Fernando Valley. Minkow soon realized that there was no need to tie his future to the cutthroat carpet cleaning industry when he could literally dictate the size and profitability of his insurance restoration "business." Within a short period of time, insurance restoration, rather than carpet cleaning, became the major source of revenue appearing on the ZZZZ Best income statements.

Minkow's "the sky is the limit" philosophy drove him to be even more innovative. The charming young entrepreneur began using his phony financial statements to entice wealthy individuals in his ever-expanding social network to invest in ZZZZ Best. Eventually, Minkow recognized that the ultimate scam would be to take his company public, a move that would allow him to tap the bank accounts of unsuspecting investors nationwide.

GOING PUBLIC WITH ZZZZ BEST

Minkow's decision to take ZZZZ Best public meant that he could no longer completely control his firm's financial disclosures. Registering with the SEC required auditors, investment bankers, and outside attorneys to peruse ZZZZ Best's financial statements.

ZZZZ Best was first subjected to a full-scope independent audit for the 12 months ended April 30, 1986. George Greenspan, the sole practitioner who performed that audit, confirmed the existence of ZZZZ Best's major insurance restoration contracts by contacting Tom Padgett. Padgett served as the principal officer of Interstate Appraisal Services, which reportedly contracted the jobs out to ZZZZ Best. By this time, Padgett was an active and willing participant in Minkow's fraudulent schemes. Minkow established Interstate Appraisal Services and Assured Property Management for the sole purpose of generating fake insurance restoration contracts for ZZZZ Best.

In testimony before the congressional subcommittee that investigated the ZZZZ Best scandal, Greenspan insisted that he properly audited Minkow's company. While planning the 1986 audit, Greenspan maintained that he performed various analytical procedures to identify any unusual relationships in ZZZZ Best's financial data. These analytical procedures allegedly included comparing ZZZZ Best's key financial ratios with industry norms. Regarding the insurance contracts, Greenspan testified that he not only confirmed their existence but also obtained and reviewed copies of all key documents regarding those jobs. However, Greenspan admitted that he did not inspect any of the insurance restoration sites.

CONGRESSMAN LENT: Mr. Greenspan, I am interested in the SEC Form S-1 that ZZZZ Best Company filed with the SEC. . . . You say in that report that you made your examination in accordance with generally accepted auditing standards and accordingly included such tests of the accounting records and other auditing procedures as we consider necessary in the circumstances. . . . You don't say in that statement that you made any personal on-site inspections.

MR. GREENSPAN: It's not required. Sometimes you do; sometimes you don't. I was satisfied that these jobs existed and I was satisfied from at least six different sources, including payment for the job. What could you want better than that?

CONGRESSMAN LENT: Your position is that you are an honest and reputable accountant.

MR. GREENSPAN: Yes, sir.

CONGRESSMAN LENT: You were as much a victim as some of the investors in this company?

MR. GREENSPAN: I was a victim all right. . . . I am as much aghast as anyone. And every night I sit down and say, why didn't I detect this damned fraud.

RETENTION OF ERNST & WHINNEY BY ZZZZ BEST

Shortly after Greenspan completed his audit of ZZZZ Best's April 30, 1986, financial statements, Minkow dismissed him and retained Ernst & Whinney to perform the following year's audit. Apparently, ZZZZ Best's investment broker insisted that Minkow obtain a Big Eight accounting firm to enhance the credibility of the company's financial statements. About the same time, and for the same reason, Minkow retained a high-profile Los Angeles law firm to represent ZZZZ Best as its legal counsel.

The congressional subcommittee asked Greenspan what information he provided to Ernst & Whinney regarding his former client. In particular, the subcommittee wanted to know whether Greenspan discussed the insurance restoration contracts with the new auditors.

CONGRESSMAN WYDEN: Mr. Greenspan, in September 1986, Ernst & Whinney came on as the new independent accountant for ZZZZ Best. What did you communicate to Ernst & Whinney with respect to the restoration contracts?

MR. GREENSPAN: Nothing. I did—there was nothing because they never got in touch with me. It's protocol for the new accountant to get in touch with the old accountant. They never got in touch with me, and it's still a mystery to me.

Representatives of Ernst & Whinney later testified that they did, in fact, communicate with Greenspan prior to accepting ZZZZ Best as an audit client. However, Ernst & Whinney's testimony did not disclose the nature or content of that communication, and Greenspan was not recalled to rebut Ernst & Whinney's testimony on this issue.

Exhibit 1 contains the engagement letter signed by Ernst & Whinney and Barry Minkow in September 1986. The engagement letter outlined four services that the audit firm intended to provide ZZZZ Best: a review of the company's financial statements for the three-month period ending July 31, 1986; assistance in the preparation of a registration statement to be filed with the SEC; a comfort letter to be submitted to ZZZZ Best's underwriters; and a full-scope audit for the fiscal year ending April 30, 1987. Ernst & Whinney completed the review, provided the comfort letter to ZZZZ Best's underwriters, and apparently assisted the company in preparing the registration statement for the SEC; however, Ernst & Whinney never completed the 1987 audit. The audit firm resigned on June 2, 1987, amid growing concerns that ZZZZ Best's financial statements were grossly misstated.

The congressional subcommittee investigating the ZZZZ Best fraud questioned Ernst & Whinney representatives at length regarding the bogus insurance restoration contracts—contracts that accounted for 90 percent of ZZZZ Best's reported profits. Congressional testimony disclosed that Ernst & Whinney repeatedly insisted on visiting several of the largest of these contract sites, and that Minkow and his associates attempted to discourage such visits. Eventually, Minkow realized that the auditors would not relent and agreed to allow them to visit certain of the restoration sites, knowing full well that none of the sites actually existed.

To convince Ernst & Whinney that the insurance restoration contracts were authentic, Minkow and his associates plotted and carried out a series of sting operations. In the late fall of 1986, Larry Gray, the engagement audit partner for ZZZZ Best, demanded to inspect a restoration site in Sacramento on which ZZZZ Best had reported obtaining a multimillion-dollar contract. Minkow sent two of his cohorts to Sacramento to find a large building under construction or renovation that would provide a plausible site for a restoration contract. Gray had visited Sacramento weeks earlier to search for the site that Minkow had refused to divulge. As chance would have it, the building chosen by the ZZZZ Best conspirators was the same one Gray had identified as the most likely site of the insurance restoration job.

EXHIBIT 1
Ernst & Whinney's ZZZZ
Best Engagement Letter

September 12, 1986

Mr. Barry Minkow
Chairman of the Board
ZZZZ Best Co., Inc.
7040 Darby Avenue
Reseda, California

Dear Mr. Minkow:

This letter is to confirm our understanding regarding our engagement as independent accountants of ZZZZ BEST CO., INC. (the Company) and the nature and limitations of the services we will provide.

We will perform the following services:

1. We will review the balance sheet of the Company as of July 31, 1986, and the related statements of income, retained earnings, and changes in financial position for the three months then ended, in accordance with standards established by the American Institute of Certified Public Accountants. We will not perform an audit of such financial statements, the objective of which is the expressing of an opinion regarding the financial statements taken as a whole, and, accordingly, we will not express an opinion on them. Our report on the financial statements is presently expected to read as follows:

"We have made a review of the condensed consolidated balance sheet of ZZZZ BEST CO., INC. and subsidiaries as of July 31, 1986, and the related condensed consolidated statements of income and changes in financial position for the three-month period ended July 31, 1986, in accordance with standards established by the American Institute of Certified Public Accountants. A review of the condensed consolidated financial statements for the comparative period of the prior year was not made.

　A review of financial information consists principally of obtaining an understanding of the system for the preparation of interim financial information, applying analytical review procedures to financial data, and making inquiries of persons responsible for financial and accounting matters.

　It is substantially less in scope than an examination in accordance with generally accepted auditing standards, which will be performed for the full year with the objective of expressing an opinion regarding the financial statements taken as a whole. Accordingly, we do not express such an opinion.

　Based on our review, we are not aware of any material modifications that should be made to the condensed consolidated interim financial statements referred to above for them to be in conformity with generally accepted accounting principles."

Our engagement cannot be relied upon to disclose errors, irregularities, or illegal acts, including fraud or defalcations, that may exist. However, we will inform you of any such matters that come to our attention.

2. We will assist in the preparation of a Registration Statement (Form S-1) under the Securities Act of 1933 including advice and counsel in conforming the financial statements and related information to Regulation S-X.

3. We will assist in resolving the accounting and financial reporting questions which will arise as a part of the preparation of the Registration Statement referred to above.

4. We will prepare a letter for the underwriters, if required (i.e., a Comfort Letter), bearing in mind the limited nature of the work we have done with respect to the financial data.

5. We will examine the consolidated financial statements of the Company as of April 30, 1987, and for the year then ended and issue our report in accordance with generally accepted auditing standards approved by the American Institute of Certified Public Accountants. These standards contemplate, among other things, that (1) we will study and evaluate the Company's internal control system as a basis for reliance on the accounting records and for determining the extent of our

EXHIBIT 1—continued
Ernst & Whinney's ZZZZ
Best Engagement Letter

audit tests; and (2) that we will be able to obtain sufficient evidential matter to afford a reasonable basis for our opinion on the financial statements. However, it should be understood that our reports will necessarily be governed by the findings developed in the course of our examination and that we could be required, depending upon the circumstances, to modify our reporting from the typical unqualified opinion. We will advise you, as our examination progresses, if any developments indicate that we will be unable to express an unqualified opinion. Because our examination will be performed generally on a test basis, it will not necessarily disclose irregularities, if any, that may exist. However, we will promptly report to you any irregularities which our examination does disclose.

Our fees will be derived from our customary rates for the various personnel involved plus out-of-pocket expenses. Certain factors can have an effect on the time incurred in the conduct of our work. Among these are the general condition of the accounting records, the amount of assistance received from your personnel in the accumulation of data, the size and transaction volume of business, any significant financial reporting issues that arise in connection with the SEC's review of the S-1, as well as unforeseen circumstances. Based upon our current understanding of the situation, the amount of our proposed billing for the various services which we will be providing are estimated to be:

Review of the July 31, 1986 financial statements	$ 5,000— $ 7,500
Assistance in the preparation of the Registration Statement	8,000— 30,000
Comfort Letter	4,000— 6,000
Audit of financial statements as of April 30, 1987	24,000— 29,000

We will invoice you each month for the time charges and expenses incurred in the previous month and such invoices are due and payable upon presentation.

Larry D. Gray, Partner, is the Client Service Executive assigned to the engagement. Peter Griffith, Audit Manager, and Michael McCormick, Tax Manager, have also been assigned.

We greatly appreciate your engagement of our firm; if you have any questions, we shall be pleased to discuss them with you. Please indicate your acceptance of the above arrangements by signing and returning the enclosed copy. This letter constitutes the full understanding of the terms of our engagement.

Very truly yours,

Ernst & Whinney

By Larry D. Gray, Partner

ACCEPTED:

ZZZZ BEST CO., INC.

Barry J. Minkow, Chairman of the Board

(signed)

9-16-86

Minkow's two confederates, while posing as leasing agents of a property management firm, convinced the supervisor of the construction site to provide the keys to the building one weekend on the pretext that a large prospective tenant wished to tour the facility. Prior to the arrival of Larry Gray and an attorney representing ZZZZ Best's law firm, Minkow's subordinates visited the site and placed placards on the walls at conspicuous locations indicating that ZZZZ Best was the contractor for the building renovation. No details were overlooked by Minkow's lieutenants. They even paid the building's security officer to greet the visitors and demonstrate that he was aware in advance of their tour of the site and its purpose. Although the building had not been damaged and instead was simply in the process of being completed, the sting operation went off as planned. Exhibit 2 presents the memorandum Gray wrote describing his tour of the building—a memorandum included in Ernst & Whinney's ZZZZ Best workpapers.

Congressional investigators quizzed Gray regarding the measures he took to confirm that ZZZZ Best actually had a restoration contract on the Sacramento building. They were particularly concerned that he never discovered the building had not suffered several million dollars in damages a few months earlier, as claimed by ZZZZ Best personnel.

CONGRESSMAN LENT: . . . did you check the building permit or construction permit?

MR. GRAY: No, sir. That wouldn't be necessary to accomplish what I was setting out to accomplish.

CONGRESSMAN LENT: And you did not check with the building's owners to see if an insurance claim had been filed?

MR. GRAY: Same answer. It wasn't necessary. I had seen the paperwork internally of our client, the support for a great amount of detail. So, I had no need to ask—to pursue that.

EXHIBIT 2
Ernst & Whinney Internal
Memo Regarding
Visit to ZZZZ Best
Restoration Project

TO: ZZZZ Best Co., Inc. File

FROM: Larry D. Gray

RE: Visit to Sacramento Job

At our request, the Company arranged for a tour of the job site in Sacramento on November 23rd [1986]. The site (not previously identified for us because of the confidentiality agreement with their customer) had been informally visited by me on October 27. I knew approximately where the job was, and was able to identify it through the construction activity going on.

On November 23, Mark Morse accompanied Mark Moskowitz of Hughes Hubbard & Reed and myself to Sacramento. We visited first the offices of the Building Manager, Mark Roddy of Assured Property Management, Inc. Roddy was hired by the insurance company (at Tom Padgett's suggestion according to Morse) to oversee the renovation activities and the leasing of the space. Roddy accompanied us to the building site.

We were informed that the damage occurred from the water storage on the roof of the building. The storage was for the sprinkler systems, but the water was somehow released in total, causing construction damage to floors 17 and 18, primarily in bathrooms which were directly under the water holding tower, then the water spread out and flooded floors 16 down through about 5 or 6, where it started to spread out even further and be held in pools.

We toured floor 17 briefly (it is currently occupied by a law firm) then visited floor 12 (which had a considerable amount of unoccupied space) and floor 7. Morse pointed out to us the carpet, painting and clean up work which had been ZZZZ Best's responsibility. We noted some work not done in some other areas (and in unoccupied tenant space). But per Mark, this was not ZZZZ Best's responsibility, rather was work being undertaken by tenants for their own purposes.

Per Morse (and Roddy) ZZZZ Best's work is substantially complete and has passed final inspection. Final sign-off is expected shortly, with final payment due to ZZZZ Best in early December.

Morse was well versed in the building history and in the work scope for ZZZZ Best. The tour was beneficial in gaining insight as to the scope of the damage that had occurred and the type of work that the Company can do.

CONGRESSMAN LENT: You understand that what you saw was not anything that was real in any sense of the word? . . . You are saying you were duped, are you not?

MR. GRAY: Absolutely.

Congressional testimony disclosed that one of the visitations by Ernst & Whinney forced ZZZZ Best to lease a partially completed building and to hire subcontractors to do a considerable amount of work on the site. In total, ZZZZ Best spent several million dollars for the sole purpose of deceiving its auditors.

The success of the bogus site visitations was due in large part to Minkow's insistence that Ernst & Whinney and ZZZZ Best's law firm sign confidentiality agreements before the visits were made. Exhibit 3 presents a copy of one such agreement. Members of the congressional subcommittee were troubled by the following stipulation of that confidentiality agreement: "We will not make any follow-up telephone calls to any contractors, insurance companies, the building owner, or other individuals involved in the restoration contract." This restriction effectively precluded the auditors and attorneys from corroborating the insurance restoration contracts with independent third parties.

RESIGNATION OF ERNST & WHINNEY

Ernst & Whinney resigned as ZZZZ Best's auditor on June 2, 1987, following a series of disturbing events that caused the firm to question the integrity of Minkow and his associates. First, Ernst & Whinney was alarmed by a *Los Angeles Times*

EXHIBIT 3
Ernst & Whinney's
Confidentiality Agreement
with ZZZZ Best
Regarding Visits to
Restoration Projects

Mr. Barry Minkow, President
ZZZZ Best Co., Inc.
7040 Darby Avenue
Reseda, California

Dear Barry:

In connection with the proposed public offering (the Offering) of Units consisting of common stock and warrants of ZZZZ Best Co., Inc. (the Company), we have requested a tour of the site of the Company's insurance restoration project in Sacramento, California, Contract No. 18886. Subject to the representations and warranties below, the Company has agreed to arrange such a tour, which will be conducted by a representative of Assured Property Management Inc. (the Representative), which company is unaffiliated with Interstate Appraisal Services. The undersigned, personally and on behalf of Ernst & Whinney, hereby represents and warrants that:

1. We will not disclose the location of such building, or any other information with respect to the project or the building, to any third parties or to any other members or employees of our firm;

2. We will not make any follow-up telephone calls to any contractors, insurance companies, the building owner, or other individuals involved in the restoration project;

3. We will obey all on-site safety and other rules and regulations established by the Company, Interstate Appraisal Services and the Representative;

4. The undersigned will be the only representative of this Firm present on the tour.

This Confidentiality Letter is also being furnished for the benefit of Interstate Appraisal Services, to the same extent as if it were furnished directly to such company.

article in mid-May 1987 that revealed Minkow had been involved in a string of credit card forgeries as a teenager. Second, on May 28, 1987, ZZZZ Best issued a press release, without consulting or notifying Ernst & Whinney, that reported record profits and revenues. Minkow intended this press release to restore investors' confidence in the company—confidence that had been shaken by the damaging *Los Angeles Times* story. Third, and most important, on May 29, Ernst & Whinney auditors discovered evidence supporting allegations made several weeks earlier by a third party informant that ZZZZ Best's insurance restoration business was fictitious. The informant had contacted Ernst & Whinney in April 1987 and asked for $25,000 in exchange for information proving that one of the firm's clients was engaging in a massive fraud. Ernst & Whinney refused to pay the sum, and the individual recanted shortly thereafter, but not until the firm determined that the allegation involved ZZZZ Best. (Congressional testimony disclosed that the individual recanted because of a bribe paid to him by Minkow.) Despite the retraction, Ernst & Whinney questioned Minkow and ZZZZ Best's board of directors regarding the matter, at which point Minkow denied knowing the individual who had made the allegation. On May 29, 1987, however, Ernst & Whinney auditors discovered several cancelled checks that Minkow had personally written to the informant several months earlier.

Because ZZZZ Best was a public company, the resignation of its independent auditor had to be reported to the SEC in an 8-K filing. This requirement alerts investors and creditors of the circumstances that may have led to the change in auditors. At the time, SEC registrants were allowed 15 days to file an 8-K auditor change announcement. After waiting the maximum permissible time, ZZZZ Best reported the change in auditors but, despite Ernst & Whinney's insistence, made no mention in the 8-K of the fraud allegation that had been subsequently recanted. The SEC requires a former audit firm to prepare a letter to be filed as an exhibit to its former client's 8-K auditor change announcement. That exhibit letter must comment on the 8-K's accuracy and completeness. In 1987, former audit firms had 30 days to file an exhibit letter, which was the length of time Ernst & Whinney waited before submitting its exhibit letter to the SEC. In that letter, Ernst & Whinney expressed concern that ZZZZ Best's insurance contracts might be fraudulent.

The congressional subcommittee was alarmed that 45 days passed before the charges of fraudulent misrepresentations in ZZZZ Best's financial statements were disclosed to the public. By the time the SEC released Ernst & Whinney's exhibit letter to the public, ZZZZ Best had filed for protection from its creditors under Chapter 11 of the federal bankruptcy code. During the period that elapsed between Ernst & Whinney's resignation and the public release of its 8-K exhibit letter, ZZZZ Best obtained significant financing from several parties, including $1 million from a close friend of Minkow's. These parties never recovered the funds invested in, or loaned to, ZZZZ Best. As a direct result of the ZZZZ Best debacle, the SEC shortened the length of time that registrants and their former auditors may wait before filing auditor change documents.

The congressional subcommittee also quizzed Ernst & Whinney representatives regarding the information they disclosed to Price Waterhouse, the audit firm Minkow retained to replace Ernst & Whinney.[3] Congressman Wyden wanted to

---

3. Price Waterhouse never issued an audit report on ZZZZ Best's financial statements because the company was liquidated less than two months after that audit firm was retained.

know whether Ernst & Whinney candidly discussed its concerns regarding Minkow's integrity with Price Waterhouse.

CONGRESSMAN WYDEN: I am going to insert into the record at this point a memo entitled "Discussion with successor auditor, written by Mr. Gray and dated June 9, 1987." Regarding a June 4 meeting, Mr. Gray, with Dan Lyle of Price Waterhouse concerning the integrity of ZZZZ Best's management, you stated that you had no reportable disagreements and no reservations about management integrity pending the results of a board of directors' investigation. Then you went on to say that you resigned because, and I quote here: "We came to a conclusion that we didn't want to become associated with the financial statements."

Is that correct?

MR. GRAY: That is correct.

MR. WYDEN: . . . Mr. Gray, you told the committee staff on May 29, 1987, that when you uncovered evidence to support allegations of fraud that you decided to pack up your workpapers and leave the ZZZZ Best audit site. How did your leaving without telling anybody except the ZZZZ Best management and board of directors the reasons for leaving help the public and investors?

Ernst & Whinney's reluctance to disclose its reservations concerning Minkow's integrity possibly stemmed from fear that such disclosures might provoke him to sue the audit firm.[4]

A final twist to the ZZZZ Best scandal was an anonymous letter Ernst & Whinney received exactly one week after the firm resigned as ZZZZ Best's auditors. On that date, no one other than Ernst & Whinney and ZZZZ Best's officers was aware of the firm's resignation. The letter, shown in Exhibit 4, contained several allegations suggesting that ZZZZ Best's financial statements were fraudulent. According to the congressional testimony, Ernst & Whinney forwarded this letter to the SEC on June 17, 1987.

COLLAPSE OF ZZZZ BEST

When the negative article regarding Minkow appeared in the *Los Angeles Times* in mid-May 1987, the collapse of ZZZZ Best was probably inevitable. Several years earlier, a homemaker had fallen victim to Minkow's credit card forgeries. Minkow had added a fraudulent charge to a credit charge slip the woman had used to make a payment on her account. Despite her persistence, Minkow avoided repaying the small amount. The woman never forgot the insult and industriously tracked down, and kept a record of, the individuals who had been similarly harmed by Minkow. At the urging of this individual, a reporter for the *Los Angeles Times* investigated her allegations. The woman's diary eventually became the basis for the *Los Angeles Times* article that, for the first time, cast doubt on the integrity of the "boy wonder" who was the talk of Wall Street.

---

4. For a discussion of this issue and related issues, see M.C. Knapp and F.M. Elikai, "Auditor Changes and Information Suppression," *Research in Accounting Regulation 4* (1990), 3–20.

EXHIBIT 4
Anonymous Letter
Received by
Ernst & Whinney
Regarding ZZZZ Best

June 9, 1987

Mr. Guy Wilson
Ernst & Whinney
515 South Flower
Los Angeles, California 90021

Dear Mr. Wilson:

I am an individual having certain confidential information regarding the financial condition of ZZZZ Best Co., Inc. I have read the prospectus and your Review Report dated October 3, 1986 and recognize you have not done an examination in accordance with generally accepted auditing standards, but that such audit will be forthcoming by you.

I wish to make you aware of the following material facts which require you to confirm or disaffirm:

1. The electric generators which appear on the balance sheet under Note 6 as being purchased for $1,970,000 were purchased for scrap for less than $100,000 thru intermediaries of ZZZZ Best and resold to ZZZZ Best at the inflated value. The sole purpose was to boost the assets on the balance sheet. These generators have never been used and have no utility to the company.

2. Note 5 of the balance sheet discusses joint ventures and two restoration contracts. These contracts are fictitious as are the bookkeeping entries to support their validity. Interstate Appraisal Service [sic] did not let such contracts although they confirm their existence. The same is true for the alleged $7,000,000 Sacramento contract and the $40–100 million contracts with Interstate.

3. Further, checks made and passed between ZZZZ Best, its joint venturers and some of its vendors are no more than transactions among conspirators to support the validity of these restoration contracts.

4. Earnings reported by ZZZZ Best are being reported as Billings in excess of costs and estimated earnings on restoration contracts. These contracts do not exist nor do the earnings. This can be confirmed directly by contacting the alleged insurance carriers as well as physical inspections as to the existence and extent of the contracts.

5. Billings and Earnings for 1985 and 1986 were fabricated by the company before being presented to other accountants for certification.

Confirmation of these allegations can be accomplished by a careful due diligence. Such due diligence on your behalf is imperative for your protection.

Very truly yours,

B. Cautious
(Signed)

The newspaper article triggered a chain of events that quickly spelled the end of ZZZZ Best. First, a small brokerage firm specializing in newly registered companies with suspicious earnings histories began short-selling ZZZZ Best stock, forcing the stock's price into a tailspin. Second, Ernst & Whinney, ZZZZ Best's law firm, and ZZZZ Best's brokers began giving more credence to the allegations and rumors of financial wrongdoing by Minkow and his associates. Third, and most important, the article panicked Minkow and compelled him to take several daring moves that cost him even more credibility. The most critical mistake was his issuance of the May 28, 1987, press release that boldly reported record profits and revenues for his firm.

EPILOGUE

Among the parties most criticized for their roles in the ZZZZ Best scandal was Ernst & Whinney. The congressional testimony into the ZZZZ Best fraud included a list of 10 "red flags" that the audit firm had allegedly overlooked while examining ZZZZ Best's financial statements (see Exhibit 5). In testifying before the subcommittee, Leroy Gardner, the West Coast director of accounting and auditing for Ernst & Whinney, maintained that when all the facts were revealed, his firm would be totally vindicated.

> The ZZZZ Best situation proves at least one thing: a well-orchestrated fraud will often succeed even against careful, honest, hard-working people. . . . The facts that have begun to emerge establish that Minkow along with confederates both inside and outside ZZZZ Best went to extraordinary lengths to deceive Ernst & Whinney. For example, Thomas Padgett, an alleged conspirator, revealed in a recent televised interview that Minkow spent $4 million to deceive Ernst & Whinney during a visit to one of ZZZZ Best's job sites. . . . Ernst & Whinney never misled investors about the reliability of ZZZZ Best's financial statements. Ernst & Whinney never even issued an audit opinion for ZZZZ Best. . . . We are not part of the problem in this case. We were part of the solution.

In one of the largest civil suits stemming from the ZZZZ Best fraud, Ernst & Whinney was found not liable to a large California bank that had extended ZZZZ Best a multimillion-dollar loan in 1986. The bank alleged that in granting the loan, it had relied upon the review report issued by Ernst & Whinney on ZZZZ Best's financial statements for the three-month period ending July 31, 1986. However, an appellate judge ruled that the bank was not justified in relying on the review report since Ernst & Whinney had expressly stated in the report that it was not issuing an opinion on the ZZZZ Best financial statements: "Ernst, because it issued only a review report, specifically declined to express an opinion on ZZZZ

EXHIBIT 5
Ten Red Flags that ZZZZ Best's Auditors Allegedly Overlooked

Has to file 8k.

30 days

1. The amounts called for by the insurance restoration contracts were unrealistically large.
2. The number of multimillion-dollar insurance restoration contracts reportedly obtained by ZZZZ Best exceeded the total number available nationwide during the relevant time period.
3. The purported contracts failed to identify the insured parties, the insurance companies, or the locations of the jobs.
4. The contracts consisted of a single page which failed to contain details and specifications of the work to be done, such as the square yardage of carpet to be replaced, which were usual and customary in the restoration business.
5. Virtually all of the insurance restoration contracts were with the same party.
6. A large proportion of the ZZZZ Best insurance restoration contracts occurred immediately, and opportunistically, prior to a planned offering of stock.
7. The purported contracts provided for payments to ZZZZ Best or Minkow alone rather than to the insured or jointly with ZZZZ Best and the insured, contrary to the practice of the industry.
8. The purported contracts provided for payments by the insurance adjustor contrary to normal practice in the industry under which payments are customarily made by the insurance company directly to its insured or jointly to its insured and the restorer.
9. ZZZZ Best's purported gross profit margins for its restoration business were greatly in excess of the normal profit margins for the restoration industry.
10. The internal controls at ZZZZ Best were grossly inadequate.

Best's financial statements. The report expressly disclaimed any right to rely on its content."[5]

In the late 1980s, ZZZZ Best's former stockholders filed a class action lawsuit against Ernst & Whinney, ZZZZ Best's former law firm, and ZZZZ Best's former brokers. An Internet publication reported in March 1996 that this lawsuit had been settled privately. The defendants reportedly paid the former ZZZZ Best stockholders $35 million. However, the contribution of each defendant to the settlement pool was not disclosed.[6]

In late 1994, Barry Minkow was released from prison. Minkow secured the reduction in his 25-year prison sentence for "good behavior and efforts to improve himself."[7] These efforts included earning by correspondence bachelor's and master's degrees in religion from Liberty University, the university founded by Jerry Falwell. Shortly after being paroled, Minkow married a young woman introduced to him by a fellow inmate. That inmate was a former subordinate of Charles Keating, the principal architect of the huge Lincoln Savings and Loan Association scandal.

Minkow began serving as the associate pastor of a large evangelical church in a community near his hometown of Reseda in early 1995. Two years later, Minkow was appointed the senior pastor of a large nondenominational church in San Diego. Besides his pastoral duties, Minkow presents lectures and seminars across the United States on how to prevent and detect financial fraud. Minkow has spoken to groups of CPAs, educational institutions and, most notably, the FBI Academy at Quantico, Virginia.

In his lectures, Minkow often chastises the accountants and auditors in his audience. In one case, Minkow noted that "CPAs are creatures of habit. You're interested in making tick marks and footnotes, not in thinking outside the box."[8] Minkow also chides auditors for being overly willing to accept weak forms of audit evidence, such as client representations: "Don't give up objectivity for convenience." Finally, Minkow often recalls how easily he deceived his auditors. He points out that during the 1980s the profit margin for companies in the insurance restoration industry typically ranged from 8 to 9 percent and that the average revenue on a restoration job was approximately $1,000. "We were reporting an average job of $3 million with margins of 30 to 40 percent . . . and we got three clean opinions."

QUESTIONS

1. Ernst & Whinney never issued an audit opinion on the financial statements of ZZZZ Best; however, Ernst & Whinney did issue a review report on the company's quarterly statements for the three months ending July 31, 1986. How does a review differ from an audit, particularly in terms of the level of assurance implied by the auditor's report?

---

5. "Ernst & Young Not Liable in ZZZZ Best Case," *Journal of Accountancy* 172 (July 1991), 22.

6. C. Byron, "$26 Million in the Hole," *Worth Online*, March 1996.

7. M. Matzer, "Barry Minkow," *Forbes*, 15 August 1994, 134.

8. T. Sickinger, "Ex-Con Artist Helps Find Fraud," *The Kansas City Star*, 18 October 1995, B1.

2. *SAS No. 31*, "Evidential Matter," identifies five key management assertions that underlie a set of financial statements. In the case of ZZZZ Best, the existence assertion was particularly critical with respect to the insurance restoration contracts. ZZZZ Best's auditors obtained third party confirmations to support the contracts, reviewed available documentation, performed analytical procedures to evaluate the reasonableness of the revenues recorded on the contracts, and visited selected restoration sites. Comment on the limitations of the evidence that these procedures provide with regard to the management assertion of existence.

3. Besides existence, what other management assertion or assertions should ZZZZ Best's auditors have considered corroborating for the insurance restoration contracts? What audit procedures would have been appropriate to substantiate these assertions?

4. In testimony before Congress, George Greenspan reported that one means he used to substantiate the insurance restoration contracts was to verify that his client actually received payment on those jobs. How can such apparently reliable evidence lead an auditor to an improper conclusion?

5. What is the purpose of predecessor-successor auditor communications? Which party, the predecessor or successor auditor, has the responsibility for initiating these communications? Briefly summarize the information that a successor auditor should obtain from the predecessor auditor.

6. Did the confidentiality agreement that Minkow required Ernst & Whinney to sign improperly limit the scope of the ZZZZ Best audit? Why or why not? Discuss general circumstances under which confidentiality concerns on the part of a client may properly affect audit planning decisions. At what point would these limitations be so significant as to affect the type of audit opinion issued?

7. What procedures, if any, do professional standards require auditors to perform when reviewing a client's pre-audit but post-year-end earnings press release?

CASE 1.5
LINCOLN SAVINGS
AND LOAN ASSOCIATION

"Deposits ensured by FDIC"

NOW — Negotiated on withdrawal
Acct.

• BATISTA
• ORTIZ
• HERMANSON

In 1978, Charles Keating, Jr., founded American Continental Corporation (ACC) in Ohio. Six years later, ACC acquired Lincoln Savings and Loan Association, which was headquartered in Phoenix, although its principal operations were in California. In his application to purchase Lincoln, Keating pledged to regulatory authorities that he would retain the Lincoln management team, not use brokered deposits to expand the size of the savings and loan, and continue residential home loans as Lincoln's principal line of business. After gaining control of Lincoln, Keating replaced the management team; began accepting large deposits from money brokers, which allowed him to nearly triple the size of the savings and loan in two years; and shifted the focus of Lincoln's lending activity from residential mortgage loans to land development projects.

On April 14, 1989, the Federal Home Loan Bank Board (FHLBB) seized control of Lincoln Savings and Loan, alleging that Lincoln was dissipating its assets by operating in an unsafe and unsound manner. On that date, Lincoln's balance sheet reported total assets of $5.3 billion, only 2.3 percent of which were investments in residential mortgage loans. Nearly two-thirds of Lincoln's asset portfolio was invested directly or indirectly in high-risk land ventures and other commercial development projects. At the time, federal authorities estimated that the closure of Lincoln Savings and Loan would eventually cost U.S. taxpayers at least $2.5 billion.

Congressional hearings into the collapse of Lincoln Savings and Loan initially focused on the methods Keating used to circumvent banking laws and on disclosures that five U.S. senators intervened on Keating's behalf with federal banking regulators. Eventually, the hearings centered on the failure of Lincoln's independent auditors to expose fraudulent real estate transactions that allowed the savings and loan to report millions of dollars of nonexistent profits. In summarizing the Lincoln debacle, U.S. Representative Jim Leach laid the blame for the costly savings and loan failure on a number of parties, including Lincoln's auditors and the accounting profession as a whole.

> I am stunned. As I look at these transactions, I am stunned at the conclusions of an independent auditing firm. I am stunned at the result. And let me just tell you, I think that this whole circumstance of a potential $2.5 billion cost to the United States taxpayers is a scandal for the United States Congress. It is a scandal for the Texas and California legislatures. It is a scandal for the Reagan administration regulators. And it is a scandal for the accounting profession.[1]

CREATIVE ACCOUNTING, INFLUENCE PEDDLING, AND OTHER ABUSES AT LINCOLN SAVINGS AND LOAN

Representative Henry Gonzalez, chairman of the U.S. House Committee on Banking, Finance and Urban Affairs, charged that over the five years Charles Keating owned Lincoln, he employed accounting schemes to divert the savings and loan's federally insured deposits into ACC's treasury. Keating was aware that he would be permitted to withdraw funds from Lincoln and invest them in ACC or use them for other purposes only to the extent that Lincoln reported after-tax profits. Consequently, he and his associates wove together complex real estate transactions involving Lincoln, ACC, and related third parties to manufacture paper profits for Lincoln. Kenneth Leventhal & Company, an accounting firm retained by regulatory authorities to analyze and report on Lincoln's accounting practices, used a few simple examples to explain the saving and loan's fraudulent schemes. Exhibit 1 contains a portion of the Leventhal firm's testimony before Representative Gonzalez's committee, which sponsored the lengthy congressional investigation of Lincoln Savings and Loan.

One of the most scrutinized of Lincoln's multimillion-dollar real estate deals was the large Hidden Valley transaction that took place in the spring of 1987. On March 30, 1987, Lincoln loaned $19.6 million to E.C. Garcia & Company. On that same day, Ernie Garcia, a close friend of Keating and the owner of the land development company bearing his name, extended a $3.5 million loan to Wescon, a mortgage real estate concern owned by Garcia's friend, Fernando Acosta. The following day, Wescon purchased 1,000 acres of unimproved desert land in central Arizona from Lincoln for $14 million, nearly twice the value established for the land by an independent appraiser one week earlier. Acosta used the loan from Garcia as the down payment on the tract of land and signed a nonrecourse note for the balance. Lincoln recorded a profit of $11.1 million on the transaction—profit that was never realized, since the savings and loan never received payment on the nonrecourse note.

In fact, Lincoln never expected to be paid the balance of the nonrecourse note. Lincoln executives arranged the loan simply to allow the savings and loan to book a large paper gain. Garcia later testified that he agreed to become involved in the deceptive Hidden Valley transaction only because he wanted the $19.6 mil-

1. This and all subsequent quotations, unless indicated otherwise, were taken from the following source: U.S. Congress, House, Committee on Banking, Finance and Urban Affairs; *Investigation of Lincoln Savings and Loan Association, Part 4* (Washington, D.C.: U.S. Government Printing Office, 1990).

To illustrate the accounting concepts Lincoln used, let me give you a few simple, hypothetical examples. Suppose you own a house that you paid $100,000 for, and against which you still owe $60,000. Now, suppose you could not find a buyer for your house. Therefore, you go out and find an individual who agrees to pay you the $200,000 you want for your house, but is only willing to give you one dollar in cash and a nonrecourse note for the balance of $199,999. A nonrecourse note means that you cannot get at him personally. If he defaults on the note, your only recourse is to take the house back.

So now you have one dollar in your pocket, and a note for the rest. You very likely have not parted company with your house in this situation, because your so-called buyer may be unable to pay you, or he may simply decide that he does not want to pay you. Economically, he has an option to stick to the deal if the price of the house appreciates, or he can walk away from it if it does not. That is not a sale.

Now, suppose you have the same house again. Your next-door neighbor has a different house, but it is worth the same as yours, and has the same outstanding mortgage balance. You then swap houses and mortgages with your neighbor.

You now have a house which is different, but very similar to the one that you did have. I think that you will agree, there is no profit realized on this exchange. By the accounting theory that Lincoln appears to have followed, you would be able to record a $100,000 profit, the difference between what you originally paid for your house and what you think your neighbor's house is worth.

Really, it could have been more, if you could have found an appraiser to tell you that your neighbor's house was worth $300,000. And it could have been still more if you and your neighbor had simply chosen to agree upon a stated price which was even in excess of these amounts.

As you can see, all sales of real estate are not created equal. Over the years, accountants have had to wrestle with what is economically a sale and what is not. The economic substance of a transaction should of course be the controlling consideration.

EXHIBIT 1
Congressional Testimony of Kenneth Leventhal & Company Regarding Lincoln's Real Estate Transactions

lion loan from Lincoln.[2] Recognizing a profit on the Hidden Valley transaction would have openly violated financial accounting standards if Garcia had acquired the property directly from Lincoln and used funds loaned to him by the savings and loan for his down payment. Acosta eventually admitted that his company, Wescon, which prior to the Hidden Valley transaction had total assets of $87,000 and a net worth of $30,000, was only a "straw buyer" of the Hidden Valley property. In a *Los Angeles Times* article, Acosta reported that Wescon "was too small to buy the property and that he signed the documents without reading them to help his friend, Ernie Garcia."[3] Exhibit 2 contains a letter that a worried Acosta wrote to Garcia in 1988 regarding the Hidden Valley transaction. In that letter, Acosta encourages Garcia to assume title to the property so that he can take it off Wescon's books.

Keating and his associates used bogus real estate transactions to produce enormous gains for Lincoln. In 1986 and 1987 alone, Lincoln recognized more than $135 million of profits on such transactions. That amount represented more than one-half of the savings and loan's total reported profits for the two-year period. The gains recorded by Lincoln on its real estate transactions allowed ACC to withdraw huge sums of cash from the savings and loan, funds that were actually federally insured deposits. When the "purchasers" of these tracts of land defaulted

---

2. K. Kerwin and C. Yang, "Everything Was Fine until I Met Charlie: The Rise and Stumble of Whiz Kid and Keating Crony Ernie Garcia," *Business Week*, 12 March 1990, 44, 46.

3. J. Granelli, "Firm Says It Was a 'Straw Man' in Lincoln Deal," *Los Angeles Times*, 3 January 1990, D1, D13.

EXHIBIT 2
Letter from Wescon to Ernie Garcia Regarding Hidden Valley Property

[This letter was addressed to Mr. E.C. Garcia, E.C. Garcia and Company, Inc., and appeared on Wescon letterhead.]

Re: Hidden Valley Project/Property

Dear Ernie:

The time when we should have been out of this project is well past.

For various reasons, our discomfort with continuation in the project is growing. Particularly of late, we have been concerned with how to report this to the IRS. We are convinced that all we can do is report as if the corporation were not the true/beneficial owner, but merely the nominal title holder, which is consistent with the facts and the reality of the situation. Correspondingly, it seems you should have, and report, the real tax burdens and benefits arising from this property.

Also, we are increasingly uncomfortable with showing this property on our company's financial statements (and explaining why it is there). We absolutely need to extract this item.

In order to expedite relief for us on this matter, in line with your repeated assurances, please arrange for the transfer of this property to its rightful owner as soon as possible.

Sincerely,

FRA/Wescon

Fernando R. Acosta

on their nonrecourse notes, Lincoln was forced to recognize losses—losses that the savings and loan offset with additional "profitable" real estate transactions. This recurring cycle of events ensured that Lincoln would eventually fail. However, since the Federal Savings and Loan Insurance Corporation (FSLIC) guaranteed Lincoln's liabilities (that is, its deposits), and since ACC had little equity capital invested in Lincoln, Keating was not overly concerned by the inevitable demise of his company's savings and loan subsidiary.

Lincoln's convoluted and contrived real estate transactions appalled members of Representative Gonzalez's congressional committee. One of the Leventhal partners who testified before the congressional committee provided the following overview of his firm's report on Lincoln's accounting schemes:

> Seldom in our experience have we encountered a more egregious example of misapplication of generally accepted accounting principles. This association [Lincoln] was made to function as an engine, designed to funnel insured deposits to its parent in tax allocation payments and dividends. To do this, it had to generate reportable earnings. It created profits by making loans. Many of these loans were bad. Lincoln was manufacturing profits by giving money away.

Critics chastised Charles Keating not only for employing creative accounting methods but for several other abusive practices as well. For example, in 1979, Keating signed a consent decree with the Securities and Exchange Commission (SEC) to settle conflict of interest charges the agency had filed against him. In 1985, Keating handpicked his 24-year-old son, Charles Keating III, to serve as Lincoln's president. Along with the impressive job title came an annual salary of $1 million. At the time, the young man's only prior work experience was reportedly as a busperson in a country club restaurant. Years later, the younger Keating testified that he did not understand many of the transactions he signed off on as Lincoln's president.

The elder Keating's gaudy lifestyle and ostentatious spending habits were legendary. U.S. taxpayers absorbed many of the outrageous expenses rung up by Keating, since he pawned them off as business expenses of Lincoln. The bill for a 1987 dinner Keating hosted at an upscale Washington, D.C., restaurant came to just slightly less than $2,500. One of the guests at that dinner was a former SEC commissioner. In another incident, after inadvertently scuffing a secretary's $30 shoes, Keating wrote her a check for $5,000 to replace them—and the rest of her wardrobe as well, apparently. Other Keating excesses documented by federal and state investigators included safaris, vacations in European castles, numerous trips to the south of France, and lavish parties for relatives and government officials.

The most serious charges leveled at Keating involved allegations of influence peddling. Keating contributed heavily to the election campaigns of five prominent senators, including John Glenn and John McCain. These five senators, who became known as the Keating Five, met with federal banking regulators and allegedly lobbied for favorable treatment for Lincoln Savings and Loan. The key issue in these lobbying efforts was the so-called direct investment rule adopted by the FHLBB in 1985. This rule limited the amount that savings and loans could invest directly in subsidiaries, development projects, and other commercial ventures to 10 percent of their total assets. Because such investments were central to Lincoln's operations, the direct investment rule imposed severe restrictions on Keating—restrictions that he repeatedly ignored.

In 1986, a close associate of Keating's was appointed to fill an unexpired term on the FHLBB. Shortly following his appointment, this individual proposed an amendment to the direct investment rule that would have exempted Lincoln from its requirements. The amendment failed to be seconded and thus was never adopted. Congressional testimony also disclosed that Keating loaned $250,000, with very favorable payback terms, to a former SEC commissioner, who then lobbied the SEC on Lincoln's behalf. Keating also hired Alan Greenspan to represent Lincoln before the FHLBB shortly before Greenspan was appointed to the powerful position of chairman of the Federal Reserve Board. In a legal brief submitted to the FHLBB, Greenspan reported that Lincoln's management team was "seasoned and expert" and that the savings and loan was a "financially strong" institution.

The charges of influence peddling failed to concern or distract Keating. In responding to these charges, Keating made the following remarks during a press conference: "One question, among the many raised in recent weeks, has to do with whether my financial support in any way influenced several political figures to take up my cause. I want to say in the most forceful way I can: I certainly hope so."[4]

Federal authorities eventually indicted Keating on various racketeering and securities fraud charges. He was also sued by the Resolution Trust Corporation, the federal agency created to manage the savings and loan crisis. That agency charged Keating with insider dealing, illegal loans, sham real estate and tax transactions, and the fraudulent sale of Lincoln securities.

---

4. D.J. Jefferson, "Keating of American Continental Corp. Comes Out Fighting," *The Wall Street Journal*, 18 April 1989, B2.

AUDIT HISTORY OF LINCOLN SAVINGS AND LOAN

Arthur Andersen served as Lincoln's independent auditor until 1985, when it resigned "to lessen its exposure to liability from savings and loan audits," according to a *New York Times* article.[5] That same article described the very competitive nature of the Phoenix audit market during the mid-1980s, when Lincoln was seeking a replacement auditor. Because of the large size of the Lincoln audit, several audit firms pursued the engagement, including Arthur Young & Company.[6] From 1978 through 1984, Arthur Young suffered a net loss of 63 clients nationwide.[7] Over the next five years, an intense marketing effort produced a net increase of more than 100 audit clients for the firm. During the 1980s, critics of the accounting profession suggested that the extremely competitive audit market induced many audit firms to accept high-risk clients, such as Lincoln, in exchange for large audit fees: "The savings industry crisis has revived questions repeatedly raised in the past about the profession's independence in auditing big corporate clients: whether the accounts need more controls and whether some firms are willing to sanction questionable financial statements in exchange for high fees, a practice called 'bottom fishing.'"[8]

Before pursuing Lincoln as an audit client, Jack Atchison, an Arthur Young partner in Phoenix, contacted the former Lincoln engagement partner at Arthur Andersen. The Arthur Andersen partner told Atchison that he had no reason to question the integrity of Lincoln's management and that no major disagreements preceded the resignation of his firm as Lincoln's auditor. At the time of Arthur Andersen's resignation, Lincoln was undergoing an intensive examination by FHLBB auditors, who were raising serious questions regarding Lincoln's financial records. Arthur Young was not informed of this investigation by Arthur Andersen. Years later, Arthur Andersen partners denied that they were aware of the examination when they resigned from the audit.

Shortly after accepting Lincoln as an audit client, Arthur Young learned of the FHLBB audit. Among the most serious charges of the FHLBB auditors was that Lincoln had provided interest-free loans to ACC—a violation of federal banking laws—and had falsified loan documents. Three years later, officials from the Office of Thrift Supervision testified before Congress that Arthur Andersen and Lincoln employees had engaged in so-called file-stuffing. These charges resulted in formal inquiries by the Federal Bureau of Investigation and the U.S. Justice Department.[9] Arthur Andersen officials denied involvement in any illegal activi-

---

5. E.N. Berg, "The Lapses by Lincoln's Auditors," *The New York Times*, 28 December 1989, D1, D6.

6. Arthur Andersen and, subsequently, Arthur Young audited both ACC and Lincoln, a wholly-owned subsidiary of ACC. However, the Lincoln audit was much more complex and required much more time to complete than the ACC audit. Reportedly, the ACC/Lincoln audit accounted for one-fifth of the annual audit revenues of Arthur Young's Phoenix office during 1986 and 1987.

7. L. Berton, "Spotlight on Arthur Young Is Likely to Intensify as Lincoln Hearings Resume," *The Wall Street Journal*, 21 November 1989, A20.

8. N.C. Nash, "Auditors of Lincoln on the Spot," *The New York Times*, 14 November 1989, D1, D19.

9. P. Thomas and B. Jackson, "Regulators Cite Delays and Phone Bugs in Examination, Seizure of Lincoln S&L," *The Wall Street Journal*, 27 October 1989, A4; Berg, "Lapses by Lincoln's Auditors," D1, D6.

ties but did acknowledge that employees of their firm had worked "under the direction of client [Lincoln] personnel to assist them in organizing certain [loan] files."[10] Later, a representative of Lincoln admitted that "memorialization" had been used for certain loan files.

Congressional testimony of several Arthur Young representatives revealed that the 1986 and 1987 Lincoln audits were very complex engagements. William Gladstone, the co-managing partner of Ernst & Young (the firm formed by the 1989 merger of Ernst & Whinney and Arthur Young), testified that the 1987 audit required 30,000 hours to complete. Despite concerns being raised by regulatory authorities, Arthur Young issued an unqualified opinion on Lincoln's financial statements in both 1986 and 1987. Critics contend that these clean opinions allowed Lincoln to continue engaging in illicit activities. Of particular concern to congressional investigators was that during this time Keating and his associates sold ACC's high-yield "junk" bonds in the lobbies of Lincoln's numerous branches. The sale of these bonds, which were destined to become totally worthless, raised more than $250 million for ACC. The marketing campaign for the bonds targeted retired individuals. Many of these retirees believed that the bonds were federally insured, since they were being sold on the premises of a savings and loan.

When called to testify before the U.S. House committee, SEC Commissioner Richard Breeden was asked to explain why his agency did not force ACC to stop selling the junk bonds in Lincoln's branches.

CONGRESSMAN HUBBARD: Didn't the SEC have not one, not two, but actually three or more opportunities to stop the sale of the ACC subordinated debt?

COMMISSIONER BREEDEN: We did not have any opportunity—the only way in which the SEC can stop the sale of securities is if we are able to prove those securities are being distributed based on false and misleading information. And we have to prove that in court. We cannot have reasons to be concerned about it, we cannot have suspicions, we cannot just have cause to be concerned; we have to be able to prove that in court.

And remember that this is a situation in which one of the Big Eight accounting firms is certifying that these accounts comply fully with generally accepted accounting principles, without caveat or limitation in any way. That is an important factor in that kind of decision. [Emphasis added.]

Following the completion of the 1987 Lincoln audit, the engagement audit partner, Jack Atchison, resigned from Arthur Young and accepted a position with ACC. Exhibit 3 contains the memorandum Atchison wrote to William Gladstone, who at the time was Arthur Young's managing partner, to inform Gladstone of his resignation. Gladstone later testified that Atchison earned approximately $225,000 annually as an Arthur Young partner before his resignation. ACC records revealed that Atchison's new position came with an annual salary of approximately $930,000.

The close relationship that Atchison developed with Keating before resigning from Arthur Young alarmed congressional investigators. Testimony before the congressional committee disclosed that Atchison, while he was serving as the engagement partner on the Lincoln audit, wrote several letters to banking regula-

---

10. Thomas and Jackson, "Regulators Cite Delays and Phone Bugs," A4.

**EXHIBIT 3
Memorandum from Jack
Atchison to William
Gladstone**

[This memorandum appeared on Arthur Young letterhead.]

TO: Office of Chairman   FROM: Phoenix Office
      William L. Gladstone   Jack D. Atchison
      Hugh Grant, West Regional Office
      Al Boos, Phoenix Office

SUBJECT:

Several weeks ago, Charles H. Keating, Jr., Chairman of American Continental Corporation, asked me to consider joining his company at a senior executive level. Because we were in the process of conducting an audit, I informed Mr. Keating that any discussions regarding future employment would have to await the conclusion of the audit. I also informed Hugh Grant of Mr. Keating's overtures to me.

Knowing Mr. Keating would raise the subject again at the conclusion of the audit, I began to seriously consider the possibility of leaving Arthur Young to join American Continental. Arthur Young has been my professional home for over 24 years, providing a comfortable source of income and rewarding professional environment. My closest personal friends are also my partners. To even consider no longer being a part of Arthur Young was difficult and traumatic, since serving as a partner in Arthur Young has been my single professional goal since 1962.

On April 8 and 11, 1988, I had discussions with Mr. Keating wherein he presented an employment offer which was very rewarding economically and very challenging professionally. His offer addressed all of my economic, job security and position description requirements and concerns. American Continental offers some unique challenges and potential rewards not presently available in Arthur Young. It also presents some risks not present in the Arthur Young environment.

Based on American Continental's offer and my perception of the future there, I have decided to accept their offer and seek to withdraw from the Arthur Young partnership at the earliest possible date. Since American Continental is an SEC client and active issuer of securities requiring registration, and Arthur Young's consent to the use of its report is needed in such filings, an expedited withdrawal arrangement would protect against any real or apparent conflicts of interest between Arthur Young and American Continental.

tors and U.S. senators vigorously supporting the activities of Keating and Lincoln: "Atchison seemed to drop the auditor's traditional stance of independence by repeatedly defending the practices of Lincoln and its corporate parent to Congress and federal regulators. . . . Since when does the outside accountant —the public watchdog—become a proponent of the client's affairs?"[11]

Congressman Gonzalez's committee also questioned Arthur Young representatives regarding Atchison's relationship with the Arthur Young audit team after he joined ACC. The committee was concerned that Atchison may have been in a position to improperly influence the auditors he had supervised just weeks earlier.

CONGRESSMAN LEHMAN: Did anyone at AY have any contact with Mr. Atchison after he left and went to work for Lincoln?

MR. GLADSTONE: Yes, sir.

CONGRESSMAN LEHMAN: In the course of the audit?

MR. GLADSTONE: Yes.

CONGRESSMAN LEHMAN: So he went from one side of the table to the other for $700,000 more?

---

11. Berg, "Lapses by Lincoln's Auditors," D1, D6.

MR. GLADSTONE: That is what happened.

CONGRESSMAN LEHMAN: And he—just tell me what his role was in the audits . . . when he was on the other side of the table.

MR. GLADSTONE: He was a senior vice-president for American Continental when he joined them in May 1988.

CONGRESSMAN LEHMAN: Did the job he had there have anything to do with interfacing with the auditors?

MR. GLADSTONE: To some extent, yes.

CONGRESSMAN LEHMAN: What does "to some extent" mean?

MR. GLADSTONE: On major accounting issues that were discussed in the Form 8-K, we did have conversations with Jack Atchison.

CONGRESSMAN LEHMAN: So he was the person Mr. Keating had to interface with you in major decisions?

MR. GLADSTONE: Him, and other officers of American Continental.

During the summer of 1988, the relationship between Lincoln's executives and the Arthur Young audit team gradually soured. Janice Vincent, who became the Lincoln engagement partner following Atchison's resignation, testified that disagreements arose with client management that summer over the accounting treatment applied to several large real estate transactions. The most serious disagreement involved a proposed exchange of assets between Lincoln and another corporation—a transaction for which Lincoln intended to record a $50 million profit. Lincoln management insisted that the exchange involved dissimilar assets. Vincent, on the other hand, stubbornly maintained that the transaction involved the exchange of similar assets and, consequently, that the gain on the transaction could not be recognized. During the congressional hearings, Vincent described how this dispute and related disputes eventually led to the resignation of Arthur Young as Lincoln's auditor.

> These disagreements created an adversarial relationship between members of Arthur Young's audit team and American Continental officials, which resulted in Mr. Keating requesting a meeting with Bill Gladstone. . . . While in New York at that meeting, Mr. Keating turned to me at one point and said, "Lady, you have just lost a job." That did not happen. Rather, he had lost an accounting firm.

Following Arthur Young's resignation in October 1988, Keating retained Touche Ross to audit Lincoln's 1988 financial statements. Touche Ross became ensnared, along with Arthur Andersen and Arthur Young, in the web of litigation following Lincoln's collapse. Purchasers of the ACC bonds sold in Lincoln's branches named Touche Ross as a defendant in a large class-action lawsuit. The suit alleged that had Touche Ross not accepted Lincoln as an audit client, ACC's ability to sell the bonds would have been diminished significantly.

CRITICISM OF ARTHUR YOUNG FOLLOWING LINCOLN'S COLLAPSE

Both Arthur Young and its successor, Ernst & Young, were criticized for the former's role in the Lincoln Savings and Loan debacle. One of the most common criticisms was that Arthur Young too readily accepted documentary evidence provided by Lincoln employees to corroborate the savings and loan's real estate transactions. During the congressional hearings into the collapse of Lincoln, William Gladstone commented on the appraisals that Arthur Young obtained to support these transactions: "All appraisals of land [owned by Lincoln] were done by appraisers hired by the company, and we had to rely on them." Certainly, these appraisals were relevant evidence to be used in auditing Lincoln's real estate transactions. However, appraisals obtained by Arthur Young from independent third parties would have been just as relevant and less subject to bias.[12]

Among Arthur Young's most vocal critics during the congressional hearings was the newly appointed SEC commissioner, Richard Breeden. Commissioner Breeden berated Arthur Young for allegedly failing to cooperate with an SEC investigation into Lincoln's financial affairs.

COMMISSIONER BREEDEN: We subpoenaed the accountants [Arthur Young] to provide all of their work papers and their back-up.

CONGRESSMAN HUBBARD: Do you know if they were forthcoming and helpful in helping you resolve some of these questions, or helping the SEC resolve some of these questions?

COMMISSIONER BREEDEN: No. I would characterize them as very unhelpful, very unforthcoming, and very resistant to cooperate in any way, shape or form.

Earlier, Commissioner Breeden had testified that many of the subpoenaed documents that Arthur Young eventually produced were illegible or obscured: "The firm [Arthur Young] ultimately, after much discussion, produced legible copies of the documents, but not before the Commission [SEC] was forced to prepare court enforcement requests to overcome Arthur Young's uncooperative stance. Unfortunately, a substantial amount of staff time and resources was devoted unnecessarily to overcoming this resistance to the Commission's subpoenas."

When given an opportunity to respond to Commissioner Breeden's charges, William Gladstone maintained that the delays in providing the SEC with the requested documents were not intentional: "We did not stonewall the SEC. There are Arizona state privilege statutes and ethics rules which prohibit our producing our work papers without a client consent. . . . I also take issue with the allegation that we obliterated some papers. . . . The SEC itself requires a confidentiality stamp on all papers on which confidentiality was requested."

The most stinging criticism of Arthur Young during the congressional hearings stemmed from the Kenneth Leventhal & Company investigation of the accounting treatment applied to Lincoln's major real estate transactions. Although the Leventhal report served as the basis for much of the criticism directed at Arthur Young, the report did not mention Arthur Young or, in any way, explicitly criticize its Lincoln audits. Nevertheless, since Arthur Young had issued unqualified opinions on Lincoln's financial statements, many parties, including Ernst & Young officials, regarded the Leventhal report as an indictment of the quality of Arthur Young's audits.

The key finding of the Leventhal report was that Lincoln had repeatedly violated the substance-over-form concept by engaging in "accounting-driven" deals

---

12. Quite possibly, Arthur Young did obtain independent appraisals in certain cases, although Gladstone's testimony suggests otherwise.

among related parties to manufacture illusory profits. Ernst & Young representatives contested this conclusion by pointing out that Leventhal reviewed only 15 of the hundreds of real estate transactions that Lincoln engaged in during Arthur Young's tenure. The Ernst & Young representatives were particularly upset that, based upon a review of these 15 transactions, Leventhal implied that none of Lincoln's major real estate transactions were accounted for properly. In Leventhal's defense, a congressman pointed out that the 15 transactions in question were all very large, accounting collectively for one-half of Lincoln's pretax profits during 1986 and 1987.

At times, the debate over the Leventhal report became very heated. William Gladstone maligned the report, stating that it was gratuitous; contained broad, sweeping generalizations; in certain cases was "flatly wrong"; and in his opinion, was unprofessional. In responding to these charges, Congressman Leach questioned the professionalism of Gladstone's firm.

CONGRESSMAN LEACH: [addressing William Gladstone] I am going to be very frank with you, that I am not impressed with the professional ethics of your firm vis-a-vis the United States Congress. Several days ago, my office was contacted by your firm, and asked if we would be interested in questions to ask of Leventhal. We said, "Surely." The questions you provided were of an offensive nature. They were to request of Leventhal how much they were paid, implying that perhaps based upon their payment from the U.S. Government that their decisions as CPA's would be biased. I consider that to be very offensive.

Now, in addition, one of the questions that was suggested I might ask of the Leventhal firm was: Could it be that their firm is biased because a partner in their firm did not make partner in your firm?

I consider that exceedingly unprofessional. Would you care to respond to that?

MR. GLADSTONE: I do not know who contacted you, and I certainly do not know how the questions were raised.

Later in the hearings, the individual who had submitted the questions to Congressman Leach's office was identified as an Ernst & Young employee.

Congressman Leach also took issue with the contention of Ernst & Young representatives that Leventhal's report contained angry and vengeful comments regarding their firm.

CONGRESSMAN LEACH: I read that report very carefully, and I found no angry, vengeful sweeping statements. But I did find a conclusion that Arthur Young had erred rather grievously. In any regard, what we are looking at is an issue that is anything but an accounting kind of debate. One of the techniques of Lincoln vis-a-vis the U.S. government was to attack the opposition. You are employing the same tactics toward Leventhal. . . . I think that is unprofessional, unethical, and, based upon a very careful reading of their statement, irresponsible.

Now, I would like to ask you if you would care to apologize to the Leventhal firm.

MR. GLADSTONE: First, Mr. Leach, I stated in my opening remarks that I believed that their report was general and sweeping and unprofessional, because what I would call unprofessional about it is the statement that looking at 15 transactions, that therefore they would conclude that nothing Lincoln did had the substance—

CONGRESSMAN LEACH: I have carefully read their report, and they note that they have just been allowed to look at 15 transactions. They could not go into more detail, but they were saying that ACC batted 15 for 15, that all 15 transactions were unusual, perplexing, and in their judgment in each case breached ethical standards in terms of generally accepted accounting principles.

Your firm in effect is saying, "We think that there may be some legal liabilities. Therefore, we are going to stonewall, and we are going to defend each and every one of these transactions."

I believe that you are one of the great firms in the history of accounting. But I also believe that big and great people and institutions can sometimes err. And it is better to acknowledge error than to put one's head in the sand.

I think before our committee you have rather righteously done that.

EPILOGUE

Anthony Elliot, a widower and retired accountant in his eighties, was one of thousands of elderly Californians who invested heavily in the junk bonds of Lincoln Savings and Loan's parent company, ACC. In fact, Elliot invested practically all of his life savings, approximately $200,000, in the ACC bonds. Like many of his friends who had also purchased the bonds—which they, along with Elliot, believed were federally insured—Elliot was forced to scrape by each month on his small Social Security check after ACC defaulted on the bonds. On Thanksgiving Day 1990, Elliot slashed his wrists and bled to death in his bathtub. In a suicide note, he remarked that there was "nothing left for me."[13] Elliot's story is just one of many personal tragedies resulting from the Lincoln Savings and Loan scandal.

The estimated losses linked to the demise of Lincoln Savings and Loan eventually rose to $3.4 billion, making it the most costly savings and loan failure in U.S. history. In March 1991, after posting huge losses—approximately $1 billion in 1989 alone—most of Lincoln's remaining assets were sold to another financial institution by the Resolution Trust Corporation, which had been operating the savings and loan for more than a year. One month later, Lincoln's parent company, ACC, filed for protection from its creditors under the federal bankruptcy laws.

In late 1992, Ernst & Young paid $400 million to settle four lawsuits filed against it by the federal government. These suits stemmed from allegedly negligent audits performed by Ernst & Young for four savings and loans, including Lincoln Savings and Loan. In a similar settlement reported in 1993, Arthur Andersen paid $85 million to the federal government to settle lawsuits resulting from the firm's allegedly negligent audits of five savings and loans, including Lincoln. Finally, although Touche Ross served as Lincoln's auditor for only five months, that firm's successor, Deloitte & Touche, paid nearly $8 million to the federal government to settle charges filed against it for its role in the Lincoln debacle.

In April 1991, Ernst & Young agreed to pay the California State Board of Accountancy $1.5 million to settle negligence complaints that the state agency

---

13. M. Connelly, "Victim of S&L Loss Kills Self," *Los Angeles Times*, 29 November 1990, B1.

filed against the firm for Arthur Young's audits of Lincoln. An Ernst & Young spokesman noted that the accounting firm agreed to the settlement to "avoid protracted and costly litigation" and insisted that the settlement did not involve the "admission of any fault by the firm or any partner."[14] In August 1994, Arthur Andersen agreed to pay $1.7 million to the California State Board of Accountancy for its alleged negligent audits of Lincoln. Andersen personnel were also required to perform 10,000 hours of community service. Like Ernst & Young, Andersen denied any wrongdoing when its settlement with the California State Board was announced.

In October 1990, Ernie Garcia pleaded guilty to fraud for his involvement in the Hidden Valley real estate transaction. His plea bargain agreement with federal prosecutors required him to assist them in their investigation of Charles Keating, Jr. In March 1991, the Lincoln executive who oversaw the sale of ACC's junk bonds through Lincoln's branches pleaded guilty to eight state and federal fraud charges that he had misled the investors who purchased those bonds. Two years later, Charles Keating III was sentenced to eight years in prison after being convicted of fraud and conspiracy charges.

In a California jury trial presided over by Judge Lance Ito, Charles Keating, Jr., was convicted in 1991 on 17 counts of securities fraud for his role in marketing ACC's junk bonds. While serving a 10-year prison term for that conviction, Keating was convicted of similar fraud charges in a federal court and sentenced to an additional 12 years in prison.

In April 1996, a federal appeals court overturned Keating's 1991 conviction. The appellate court ruled that Judge Lance Ito gave improper instructions to the jurors who found Keating guilty of securities fraud. Several months later, a U.S. District judge overturned Keating's federal conviction on fraud charges. The judge ruled that several jurors in the federal trial were aware of Keating's earlier conviction on fraud charges in a state court. According to the judge, that knowledge prejudiced the jurors in favor of convicting Keating. For the same reason, the judge overturned the 1993 conviction of Charles Keating III.

With both of his convictions overturned, Charles Keating was released from federal prison in December 1996 after serving four and one-half years. In January 1999, federal prosecutors announced that they would retry the 75-year-old Keating on various fraud charges. Three months later, the federal prosecutors and Keating reached an agreement, an agreement that gave both parties what they wanted most. In federal court, Keating admitted for the first time that he had committed various fraudulent acts while serving as ACC's chief executive. In return, Keating was sentenced to the time he had already served in prison. Even more important to Keating, his plea bargain arrangement required federal prosecutors to drop all charges still outstanding against his son, Charles Keating III.

QUESTIONS

1. Arthur Young was criticized for failing to ensure that the substance-over-form concept was followed by Lincoln in accounting for its large real estate transac-

---

14. "E&Y Pays $1.5M in Lincoln Failure," *Accounting Today*, 13 May 1991, 1, 25.

tions. Briefly describe the substance-over-form concept and exactly what it requires. Which party—a firm's independent auditors or its financial accountants—is primarily responsible for ensuring compliance with that concept? If auditors are not primarily responsible for ensuring compliance with the substance-over-form rule, what are their responsibilities when the rule has been violated by a client?

2. Explain how the acceptance of large, high-risk audit clients for relatively high audit fees may threaten an audit firm's de facto and perceived independence. Under what circumstances should such prospective clients be avoided?

3. How is an auditor's examination affected when a client has engaged in significant related party transactions? What measures would an auditor generally take to determine that such transactions have been properly recorded by a client?

4. Professional standards require auditors to review a client's "control environment." Define *control environment*. What weaknesses, if any, were evident in Lincoln's control environment?

5. What was the significance of Lincoln receiving nonrecourse notes rather than recourse notes as payment or partial payment on many of the properties it sold?

6. *SAS No. 31*, "Evidential Matter," identifies five key management assertions that underlie a set of financial statements. What were the key assertions that Arthur Young should have attempted to substantiate for the Hidden Valley transaction? What procedures should Arthur Young have used for this purpose, and what types of evidence should have been collected?

7. Do you believe that Jack Atchison's close relationship with Lincoln and Charles Keating prior to his leaving Arthur Young was proper? Why or why not? After joining Lincoln's parent company, ACC, should Atchison have been involved in the audits of Lincoln and ACC? Again, support your answer.

8. Does the *AICPA Code of Professional Conduct* discuss the collegial responsibilities of CPA firms? In your opinion, were representatives of either Ernst & Young or Kenneth Leventhal & Company unprofessional in this regard during their congressional testimony?

9. What responsibility does an auditor have to uncover fraud perpetrated by client management? Discuss factors that mitigate this responsibility and factors that compound it. Relate this discussion to Arthur Young's audits of Lincoln.

CASE 1.6
CRAZY EDDIE, INC.

In 1969, Eddie Antar, a 21-year-old high school dropout from Brooklyn, opened a consumer electronics store with 150 square feet of floor space in New York City.[1] Despite this modest beginning, Antar would eventually dominate the retail consumer electronics market in the New York City metropolitan area. By 1987, Antar's firm, Crazy Eddie, Inc., had 43 retail outlets, sales exceeding $350 million, and outstanding stock with a collective market value of $600 million. Antar personally realized more than $70 million from the sale of Crazy Eddie stock during his tenure as the company's chief executive.

A classic rags-to-riches story became a spectacular business failure in the late 1980s when Crazy Eddie collapsed following allegations of extensive financial wrongdoing by Antar and his associates. Shortly after a hostile takeover of the company in November 1987, the firm's new owners discovered that Crazy Eddie's inventory was overstated by more than $65 million. This huge inventory shortage had been concealed from the public in registration statements filed with the Securities and Exchange Commission (SEC). Subsequent investigations by regulatory authorities revealed that Eddie Antar and his subordinates had grossly overstated Crazy Eddie's reported profits throughout its existence.[2]

---

1. This case was co-authored by Carol Knapp, associate professor at the University of Central Oklahoma.

2. The facts of this case were drawn from numerous articles and SEC enforcement releases published over a period of several years. *The New York Times* and *The Wall Street Journal*, in particular, closely followed the colorful saga of Crazy Eddie and its founder, Eddie Antar. One of the more comprehensive investigative reports that documented the history of Crazy Eddie, Inc., is the following article: G. Belsky and P. Furman, "Calculated Madness: The Rise and Fall of Crazy Eddie Antar," *Crain's New York Business*, 5 June 1989, 21–33. That article provided much of the background information regarding Eddie Antar included in this case.

EDDIE ANTAR: THE MAN BEHIND THE LEGEND

Eddie Antar was born into a large, closely knit Syrian family in 1947. After dropping out of high school at the age of sixteen, Antar began peddling television sets in his Brooklyn neighborhood. Within a few years, Antar and one of his cousins scraped together enough cash to open an electronics store near Coney Island. It was at this tiny store that Antar acquired the nickname "Crazy Eddie." When a customer attempted to leave the store empty-handed, Antar would block the store's exit, sometimes locking the door until the individual agreed to buy something—anything. To entice a reluctant customer to make a purchase, Antar first determined which product the customer was considering and then lowered the price until the customer finally capitulated.

Antar became well known in his neighborhood not only for his unusual sales tactics but also his unconventional, if not asocial, behavior. A bodybuilder and fitness fanatic, he typically came to work in his exercise togs, accompanied by a menacing German shepherd. His quick temper caused repeated problems with vendors, competitors, and subordinates. Antar's most distinctive trait was his inability to trust anyone outside of his large extended family. In later years, when he needed someone to serve in an executive capacity in his company, Antar nearly always tapped a family member, although the individual seldom had the appropriate training or experience for the position. Eventually, Antar's father, sister, two brothers, uncle, brother-in-law, and several cousins would assume leadership positions with Crazy Eddie, while more than one dozen other relatives would hold minor positions with the firm.

CRAZY EDDIE'S FORMULA FOR SUCCESS

In the early 1980s, sales in the consumer electronics industry exploded, doubling in the four-year period from 1981 to 1984 alone. As the public's demand for electronic products grew at an ever-increasing pace, Antar converted his Crazy Eddie stores into consumer electronics supermarkets. Antar stocked the shelves of Crazy Eddie's retail outlets with every electronic gadget he could find and with as many different brands of those products as possible. By 1987, the company featured seven product lines. Following are those product lines and the percentage of sales they accounted for in the company's 1987 income statement.

Televisions	53%
Audio and audio systems	15%
Portable and personal electronics	10%
Car stereos	5%
Accessories and tapes	4%
Computers and games	3%
Miscellaneous items—including microwaves, air conditioners, and small appliances	10%
Total	100%

Antar encouraged his salespeople to supplement each store's profits by pressuring customers to buy extended product warranties. Many, if not most, of the repair costs that Crazy Eddie paid under these warranties were recovered by the company from manufacturers that had issued factory warranties on the products. As a result, the company realized a 100 percent profit margin on much of its warranty revenue.

As his firm grew rapidly during the late 1970s and early 1980s, Antar began extracting large price concessions from his suppliers. His ability to purchase electronic products in large quantities and at cut-rate prices enabled him to become a "transhipper," or secondary supplier, of these goods to smaller consumer electronics retailers in the New York City area. Although manufacturers frowned on this practice and often threatened to stop selling to him, Antar continually increased the scale of his transhipping operation.

The most important ingredient in Antar's marketing strategy was large-scale advertising. Antar created an advertising "umbrella" over his company's principal retail market that included the densely populated area within a 150-mile radius of New York City. Antar blanketed this region with raucous, sometimes annoying, but always memorable radio and television commercials. In 1972, Antar hired a local radio personality and part-time actor known as Doctor Jerry to serve as Crazy Eddie's advertising spokesman. Over the 15 years that the bug-eyed Doctor Jerry hawked products for Crazy Eddie, he became more recognizable, according to one survey, than Ed Koch, the longtime mayor of New York City. Doctor Jerry's series of ear-piercing television commercials that featured him screaming "Crazy Eddie—His prices are insane!" brought the company national notoriety when they were parodied by Dan Akroyd on *Saturday Night Live*.

Crazy Eddie's discounting policy served as the focal theme of the company's advertising campaigns. The company promised to refund the difference between the selling price of a product and any lower price for that same item that a customer found within 30 days of the purchase date. Despite the advertising barrage intended to convince the public that Crazy Eddie was a deep-discounter, the company's prices on most products were in line with those of its major competitors. The company's sales staff routinely diverted customers drawn to Crazy Eddie outlets by "advertised specials" to a higher quality and higher profit margin product.

CRAZY EDDIE GOES PUBLIC

In 1983, Antar decided to sell stock in Crazy Eddie to raise capital to finance his aggressive expansion program. The underwriting firm retained by Antar delayed Crazy Eddie's initial public offering for more than one year after discovering that the company's financial records were in disarray. Among other problems uncovered by the underwriter were extensive related party transactions, interest-free loans to employees, and speculative investments unrelated to the company's principal line of business. The underwriting firm was also disturbed to find that nearly all of the company's key executives were members of the Antar family. Certain of these individuals, including Antar's wife and mother, were receiving salaries approaching $100,000 for little or no work.

To prepare for the initial public offering, the underwriter encouraged Antar, Crazy Eddie's chairman of the board and president, to clean up the company's accounting records and financial affairs. The underwriter also urged Antar to hire a chief financial officer (CFO) who had experience with a public company and who was not a member of the Antar family. The underwriter warned Antar that investors would question the competence of the Crazy Eddie's executives who were his relatives. Despite the underwriter's concern, Antar hired his younger brother, Sam E. Antar—who became known within the company as "Sam the CPA" to distinguish him from his father of the same name—to serve as Crazy Eddie's CFO.

The sale of Crazy Eddie's stock to the public was a tremendous success. Because the initial public offering was oversubscribed, the company's underwriter obtained permission from the SEC to sell 200,000 more shares than originally planned. Following the public offering, Antar worked hard to convince the investment community, particularly financial analysts, that his firm was financially strong and well managed. At every opportunity, Antar painted a picture of continued growth and increased market share for Crazy Eddie.

One tactic Antar used to convince financial analysts that the company had a rosy future was to invite them to a store and demonstrate in person his uncanny ability to "close" sales. Such tactics worked to perfection as analysts from the most prominent investment firms wrote glowing reports regarding Crazy Eddie's management team and the company's bright prospects for the future. One analyst wrote, "Crazy Eddie is a disciplined, competently organized firm with a sophisticated management and a well-trained, dedicated staff."[3] Another analyst wrote that Antar is a "brilliant merchant surrounded by a deeply dedicated organization eager to create an important retail business."[4] Because of such reports and continued strong operating results, as reflected by the company's 1984–1987 financial statements shown in Exhibits 1 and 2, the price of Crazy Eddie's stock skyrocketed. Many investors who purchased the company's stock in the initial public offering realized a 1,000 percent increase in the value of their investments.

Crazy Eddie Goes . . . Bust

Despite Crazy Eddie's impressive operating results during the mid-1980s and the company's stock being one of the hottest investments on Wall Street, all was not well within the firm. By 1986, the company was in deep trouble. By the latter part of that year, the boom days had ended for the consumer electronics industry. Although sales of consumer electronics were still increasing, the rate of growth had tapered off considerably compared to the dramatic growth rates realized by the industry during the early 1980s. Additionally, the consumer electronics industry had become saturated with retailers, particularly in major metropolitan areas such as New York City, Crazy Eddie's home base. Increased competition meant smaller profit margins for Crazy Eddie and diminished Antar's ability to extract sweetheart deals from his suppliers.

Besides the problems posed by the increasingly competitive consumer electronics industry, Crazy Eddie faced a corporate meltdown by the late 1980s. The tripling of the company's annual sales volume between 1984 and 1987 and the

3. J.E. Tannenbaum, "How Mounting Woes at Crazy Eddie Sank a Turnaround Effort," *The Wall Street Journal*, 10 July 1989, A1, A4.

4. G. Belsky and P. Furman, "Calculated Madness: The Rise and Fall of Crazy Eddie Antar," *Crain's New York Business*, 5 June 1989, 26.

	March 1, 1987	March 2, 1986	March 3, 1985	May 31, 1984
CRAZY EDDIE, INC. **BALANCE SHEETS (000s omitted)**				
Current assets				
Cash	$ 9,347	$ 13,296	$22,273	$ 1,375
Short-term investments	121,957	26,840	–	–
Receivables	10,846	2,246	2,740	2,604
Merchandise inventories	109,072	59,864	26,543	23,343
Prepaid expenses	10,639	2,363	645	514
Total current assets	261,861	104,609	52,201	27,836
Restricted cash	–	3,356	7,058	–
Due from affiliates	–	–	–	5,739
Property, plant and equipment	26,401	7,172	3,696	1,845
Construction in process	–	6,253	1,154	–
Other assets	6,596	5,560	1,419	1,149
Total assets	$294,858	$126,950	$65,528	$36,569
Current liabilities				
Accounts payable	$ 50,022	$ 51,723	$23,078	$20,106
Notes payable	–	–	–	2,900
Short-term debt	49,571	2,254	423	124
Unearned revenue	3,641	3,696	1,173	764
Accrued expenses	5,593	17,126	8,733	6,078
Total current liabilities	108,827	74,799	33,407	29,972
Long-term debt	8,459	7,701	7,625	46
Convertible subordinated debentures	80,975	–	–	–
Unearned revenue	3,337	1,829	635	327
Stockholders' equity				
Common stock	313	280	134	50
Additional paid-in capital	57,678	17,668	12,298	574
Retained earnings	35,269	24,673	11,429	5,600
Total stockholders' equity	93,260	42,621	23,861	6,224
Total liabilities and stockholders' equity	$294,858	$126,950	$65,528	$36,569

EXHIBIT 1
1984–1987 Balance Sheets of Crazy Eddie

more complex responsibilities associated with managing a public company imposed a huge administrative burden on Crazy Eddie's executives. Complicating matters was the disintegration of Antar's inner circle of relatives, who had served as his principal advisers during the first 15 years of his company's existence. Antar forced many of his relatives to leave the firm after they sided with his former wife in a bitter divorce. Even as Crazy Eddie's internal affairs spiraled into chaos and the firm lurched toward financial disaster, Wall Street touted the company's stock as a "can't miss" investment.

In late 1986, Eddie Antar resigned as company president, although he retained the title of chairman of the board. A few weeks later, he simply dropped out of sight. By that point, Antar had already realized more than $50 million from the sale of Crazy Eddie stock. In the absence of Antar, Crazy Eddie's financial con-

EXHIBIT 2
1984–1987 Income
Statements of Crazy
Eddie

	CRAZY EDDIE, INC. INCOME STATEMENTS (000s omitted)			
	Year Ended March 1, 1987	Year Ended March 2, 1986	Nine Months Ended March 3, 1985	Year Ended May 31, 1984
Net sales	$ 352,523	$ 262,268	$ 136,319	$ 137,285
Cost of goods sold	(272,255)	(194,371)	(103,421)	(106,934)
Gross profit	80,268	67,897	32,898	30,351
Selling, general and administrative expense	(61,341)	(42,975)	(20,508)	(22,560)
Interest and other income	7,403	3,210	1,211	706
Interest expense	(5,233)	(820)	(438)	(522)
Income before taxes	21,097	27,312	13,163	7,975
Pension contribution	(500)	(800)	(600)	—
Income taxes	(10,001)	(13,268)	(6,734)	(4,202)
Net income	$ 10,596	$ 13,244	$ 5,829	$ 3,773
Net income per share	$.34	$.48	$.24	$.18

dition worsened rapidly. Poor operating results reported in early 1987 for the fourth quarter of that fiscal year sent the company's stock price into a tailspin from which it never recovered. In November 1987, a takeover group headed by two prominent financiers gained control of the company. A company-wide physical inventory taken by the new owners disclosed a $65 million shortage of inventory, an amount that easily negated the total profits reported by Crazy Eddie since it went public in 1984. That inventory shortage would eventually plunge Crazy Eddie into bankruptcy and send regulatory authorities in pursuit of Eddie Antar for an explanation.

CHARGES OF ACCOUNTING IRREGULARITIES

Extensive investigations of Crazy Eddie's financial records by the new owners and regulatory authorities culminated in fraud charges being filed against Eddie Antar and his former associates. The SEC alleged that after Crazy Eddie went public in 1984, Antar became preoccupied with the price of his company's stock. Antar realized that Crazy Eddie had to keep posting impressive operating results to maintain the upward trend in the stock's price. An SEC investigation revealed that within the first six months after the company went public, Antar ordered a subordinate to overstate inventory by $2 million, resulting in the firm's gross profit being overstated by the same amount. The following year Antar ordered year-end inventory to be overstated by $9 million and accounts payable to be understated by $3 million. Court records documented that Crazy Eddie employees overstated year-end inventory by preparing inventory count sheets for items that did not exist. To overstate accounts payable, employees prepared bogus debit memos and entered them in the company's accounting records.

As the economic fortunes of Crazy Eddie began to fade in the late 1980s, Antar became more desperate in his efforts to enhance the company's reported revenues and profits. He ordered company employees to include in inventory consigned merchandise and goods being returned to suppliers. Another fraudulent tactic Antar used to overstate inventory involved transhipping transactions, the large volume transactions between Crazy Eddie and many of its smaller competitors.

Antar knew that financial analysts closely monitor the annual percentage change in "same store" sales for retailers. Any decline in this percentage casts doubt on a retailer's future prospects. As the consumer electronics industry became increasingly crowded, the revenues of Crazy Eddie's individual stores began to fall, although the firm's total revenues continued to climb due to new stores being opened each year. To remedy the drop in same store sales, Antar instructed his employees to record selected transhipping transactions as retail sales of individual stores. For instance, suppose that Crazy Eddie sold 100 microwaves costing $180 each to another retailer at a per unit price of $200. The $20,000 in sales would be recorded as retail sales with a normal gross profit margin of 30 to 50 percent—meaning that inventory would not be credited for the total number of microwaves actually sold. This practice killed two birds with the proverbial stone. Same store sales were inflated for selected operating units, and inventory was overstated with a corresponding increase in gross profit from sales.

WHERE WERE THE AUDITORS?

"Where were the auditors?" was a question posed repeatedly by investors, creditors, and other interested parties when the public learned of the Crazy Eddie fraud. Four different accounting firms audited Crazy Eddie's financial statements over its turbulent history. Antar dismissed Crazy Eddie's first accounting firm, a local firm, before he took the company public. The underwriter that managed Crazy Eddie's initial public offering urged Antar to retain a more prestigious accounting firm to increase the public's confidence in the company's financial statements. As a result, Antar retained Main Hurdman to serve as Crazy Eddie's audit firm. Main Hurdman had a nationwide accounting practice with several prominent clients in the consumer electronics industry. In the mid-1980s, Peat Marwick became Crazy Eddie's audit firm when it merged with Main Hurdman. Following the corporate takeover of Crazy Eddie in 1987, the new owners replaced Peat Marwick with Touche Ross.

Much of the criticism triggered by the Crazy Eddie scandal centered on Main Hurdman and its successor, Peat Marwick. Published reports suggest that Main Hurdman charged Crazy Eddie very modest fees for the company's annual audits. In one year, the accounting firm reportedly charged Crazy Eddie only $85,000 for a full-scope independent audit—an audit of a firm that had several hundred million dollars of revenues. A leading critic of major accounting firms alleged that Main Hurdman had "lowballed" to obtain the Crazy Eddie audit, realizing that it could make up for any lost audit revenue by selling the company consulting services.

In one year, Main Hurdman charged only $85,000 to do a complete audit of Crazy Eddie—a business with hundreds of millions of dollars in reported revenues, dozens of retail stores, and two large warehouses. At the very same time that Main Hurdman was charging the bargain basement price of $85,000 for supposedly conducting an audit, its consulting division was charging Crazy Eddie millions of dollars to computerize Crazy Eddie's inventory system.[5]

This same individual questioned Main Hurdman's ability to objectively audit an inventory system that it had effectively developed. Main Hurdman's independence was also questioned because many of Crazy Eddie's accountants were former members of that accounting firm. Critics charge that a company that hires one or more of its former auditors can more easily conceal fraudulent activities during the course of subsequent audits. That is, a former auditor may help his or her new employer undermine subsequent audits. Crazy Eddie's hiring of several of its former auditors was not unusual; auditors often accept positions with former clients when they leave public accounting. Many accounting firms actually arrange such "placements," a practice that has been widely challenged.

> You would think that if an auditor wanted to leave a public accounting firm, he or she would be discouraged from going to work for clients they had audited. Instead, just the opposite is true with big accounting firms encouraging their personnel to work for clients in the apparent belief that it helps cement the accountant-client relationship.[6]

Most of the criticism directed at Crazy Eddie's auditors stemmed from their failure to uncover the huge overstatement of the company's inventory and the related understatement of accounts payable. Third parties who filed suit against the auditors accused them of "aiding and abetting" the fraud by failing to thoroughly investigate numerous suspicious circumstances they discovered. Of particular concern were several reported instances in which the auditors requested client documents, only to be told that those documents had been lost or inadvertently destroyed.

In Peat Marwick and Main Hurdman's defense, Antar and his associates engaged in a large-scale plan to deceive the auditors. For example, after discovering which inventory sites the auditors would be visiting at year-end, Antar shipped sufficient inventory to those stores or warehouses to conceal any shortages. Likewise, Crazy Eddie personnel systematically destroyed incriminating documents to conceal inventory shortages from the auditors. Antar also ordered his employees to "junk" the sophisticated, computer-based inventory system designed by Main Hurdman and to return to the outdated manual inventory system previously used by the company. The absence of a computer-based inventory system made it much more difficult for the auditors to determine exactly how much inventory the firm had at any point in time.

A particularly disturbing aspect of the Crazy Eddie scandal was the involvement of several key accounting employees in the various fraudulent schemes. These parties included the director of the internal audit staff, the acting controller, and the director of accounts payable. Past audit failures demonstrate that a fraud involving the collusion of numerous client executives, particularly key accounting personnel, is extremely difficult for auditors to uncover.

---

5. M.I. Weiss, "Auditors: Be Watchdogs, Not Just Bean Counters," *Accounting Today*, 15 November 1993, 41.

6. *Ibid.*, 42.

EPILOGUE

In June 1989, Crazy Eddie filed a Chapter 11 bankruptcy petition after losing its line of credit. Later that same year, the company closed its remaining stores and liquidated its assets because it could not obtain credit from its vendors. Meanwhile, Eddie Antar was named as a defendant in several lawsuits, including a large civil suit filed by the SEC and a criminal indictment filed by a U.S. district attorney. In January 1990, a federal judge ordered Antar to repatriate $52 million that he had transferred to foreign bank accounts in 1987. The following month, federal marshals began searching for Antar after he failed to appear in federal court. A judge had scheduled a hearing to force Antar to account for the funds transferred to overseas bank accounts. After Antar surrendered to federal marshals, the judge found him in contempt and released him on his own recognizance. Following this court appearance, Antar became a fugitive. For the next two years, Antar eluded federal authorities despite reported sightings of him in Brooklyn, South America, and Jerusalem.

On June 25, 1992, Israeli police arrested Eddie Antar. At the time, he was living in a small town outside Tel Aviv and posing as an Israeli citizen, David Jacob Levi Cohen. On December 31, 1992, Antar's attorney announced that an extradition agreement had been reached with the U.S. Justice Department and Israeli authorities. After being extradited, Antar was convicted in July 1993 on 17 counts of financial fraud including racketeering, conspiracy, and mail fraud. In May 1994, a federal judge sentenced Antar to twelve and one-half years in federal prison and ordered him to pay restitution of $121 million to former stockholders and creditors.

A federal appeals court overturned Antar's fraud conviction in April 1995. The appeals court ruled that the judge who presided over Antar's trial had been biased against him. The appeals court ordered that a new trial be held under a different judge. In May 1996, Antar's attorneys and federal prosecutors arranged a plea bargain agreement to settle the charges outstanding against him. Under the terms of this agreement, Antar pleaded guilty to one federal charge of racketeering and publicly admitted, for the first time, that he had defrauded investors by manipulating his company's accounting records. Following his admission of guilt, one of the prosecuting attorneys commented that "Crazy Eddie wasn't crazy, he was crooked."[7]

In early 1997, Eddie Antar was sentenced to seven years in federal prison. Antar, who had remained in prison since being extradited to the U.S. in 1993, received credit for the time he had already spent in prison. As a result, he was required to serve only two years of the seven-year prison sentence.

Several of Antar's former associates have also been convicted or have pleaded guilty to fraud charges, including Sam E. Antar, Eddie Antar's brother and Crazy Eddie's former CFO. After being released from prison, Sam E. Antar discussed his role in the fraud in speeches made at conferences attended by accountants and fraud examiners. In those speeches, the former CFO revealed that his older brother financed his college degree in accounting because the family needed an expert accountant to help design, manage, and conceal the company's fraudulent

---

7. F.A. McMorris, "Crazy Eddie Inc.'s Antar Admits Guilt in Racketeering Conspiracy," *The Wall Street Journal*, 9 May 1996, B7.

schemes. Sam graduated magna cum laude in accounting and passed the CPA exam in his first attempt. Upon returning to Crazy Eddie, Sam confessed that he became a "cold-blooded thug" and a willing participant in the massive fraud. "I hurt a lot of people. A lot of people lost their life's savings. . . . Accountants had to pay out money for crimes they did not commit, although they were negligent."[8]

In March 1993, a $42 million settlement was announced for dozens of lawsuits filed against Crazy Eddie. Although the contributions of the various defendants to the settlement pool were not disclosed, among those defendants were Peat Marwick and the local accounting firm used by Crazy Eddie before the company went public.

To date, authorities have recovered more than $120 million from the parties involved in the Crazy Eddie fraud. These funds include more than $20 million recouped from Antar's relatives who profited from sales of Crazy Eddie stock. Antar's family was not left penniless by federal authorities. In the late 1990s, Eddie Antar's mother purchased the Crazy Eddie logo and the company's former advertising catch phrase, "Crazy Eddie—His prices are insane!" which had been sold in bankruptcy proceedings years earlier. In early 1998, two of Eddie Antar's nephews, Sam A. Antar and Adam Kuszer, opened a new Crazy Eddie consumer electronics store in Wayne, New Jersey. The family intends to open six to ten Crazy Eddie stores in the New York City area in coming years. A financial analyst with Goldman Sachs suggested that the reincarnated company could be successful. "There is still a tremendous amount of awareness surrounding that name."[9]

QUESTIONS

1. Compute key ratios and other financial measures for Crazy Eddie during the period 1984–1987. Identify and briefly explain the red flags in Crazy Eddie's financial statements that suggested the firm posed a higher-than-normal level of audit risk.

2. Identify specific audit procedures that might have led to the detection of the following accounting irregularities perpetrated by Crazy Eddie personnel: (a) the falsification of inventory count sheets, (b) the bogus debit memos for accounts payable, (c) the recording of transhipping transactions as retail sales, and (d) the inclusion of consigned merchandise in year-end inventory.

3. The retail consumer electronics industry was undergoing rapid and dramatic changes during the 1980s. Discuss how changes in an audit client's industry should affect audit planning decisions. Relate this discussion to Crazy Eddie.

4. Explain what is implied by the term *lowballing* in an audit context. How can this practice potentially affect the quality of independent audit services?

5. Assume that you were a member of the Crazy Eddie audit team in 1986. You were assigned to test the client's year-end inventory cutoff procedures. You se-

---

8. G. Cheney, "How Crazy Was Crazy Eddie?" *Accounting Today*, 26 October–8 November, 1998, 1, 61.

9. L.W. Foderaro, "Crazy Eddie's Returning, Minus 2 Jailed Founders," *The New York Times*, 20 January 1998, B1.

lected 30 invoices entered in the accounting records near year-end: 15 in the few days prior to the client's fiscal year-end and 15 in the first few days of the new year. Assume that client personnel were unable to locate 10 of these invoices. What course of action would have been appropriate at this point and why?

6. Should companies be allowed to hire individuals who formerly served as their independent auditors? Discuss the pros and cons of this practice.

CASE 1.7
PENN SQUARE BANK

At 7:05 p.m. on July 5, 1982, a squad of bank examiners from the Federal Deposit Insurance Corporation (FDIC) locked the doors of the Penn Square Bank of Oklahoma City, Oklahoma. Thus ended the legacy of a small shopping center bank that grew from total assets of $29 million in 1974, when it was acquired by the flamboyant B.P. "Beep" Jennings, to total assets of more than $500 million at the time of its closing. The more than $2 billion in losses suffered by Penn Square, its affiliated banks, uninsured depositors, and the FDIC insurance fund made this bank failure the most costly in U.S. history at the time. A deluge of lawsuits flooded the courts following Penn Square's collapse. Defendants in these lawsuits included Penn Square's former directors and officers, money brokers that funneled huge sums of uninsured deposits into the bank, Penn Square's correspondent banks, and the bank's audit firm, Peat, Marwick, Mitchell & Company.

Peat Marwick became an easy target of third parties who wanted to hold someone responsible for the bank's failure. Among the parties that pointed accusatory fingers in the direction of Peat Marwick was the U.S. House of Representatives. Representative Fernand St Germain chaired the U.S. House Committee on Banking, Finance and Urban Affairs that investigated the Penn Square debacle. In testimony before that committee, a Peat Marwick partner explained that his firm intended its Penn Square audit report only for the bank's directors. The partner implied that external parties had not and should not have relied on Peat Marwick's unqualified opinion issued on Penn Square's 1981 financial statements just three months prior to the bank's demise. The partner's caveat provoked an indignant response from Representative St Germain.

> You are not aware of the fact that the people at Penn Square dealing with brokers gave your reports . . . to people, credit unions, S&Ls around this nation who put enormous sums of money into this institution based on your audit reports, since that was all that

was available. . . . Did it come as a complete and total surprise to you, like the fact that when you get to be 10 years old you find out there is no Santa Claus?[1]

Peat Marwick's relationship with Penn Square Bank spanned only seven months. Not only was this client relationship one of the shortest for Peat Marwick, it also proved to be one of the most costly.

THE HISTORY OF PENN SQUARE

Penn Square Bank was incorporated in 1960 and during its entire 22-year existence was located in a shopping mall in a northwest Oklahoma City neighborhood. For many years, the bank's primary customers were the small businesses in the mall and residents of the surrounding community. The role of the bank changed rapidly after being acquired by Jennings in 1974. Under Jennings' ownership, the bank became caught up in the Oklahoma oil boom of the late 1970s and went on a lending spree to oil and gas speculators—a spree that doubled the bank's assets every two years from 1976 to 1982. When closed by the FDIC, oil and gas loans accounted for over 80 percent of the bank's assets.

Penn Square's explosive growth was engineered primarily by one individual, William Patterson. Jennings hired Patterson as a favor to a family friend shortly after he acquired the bank. Patterson, then in his mid-twenties, was given a job as a loan officer, although he had little experience in the banking industry. Within 18 months, the affable and ambitious Patterson was managing the bank's oil and gas loan portfolio and had become Jennings' protege and most trusted ally. Patterson became well known in the Oklahoma City banking community for his idiosyncracies. His antics included wearing a Mickey Mouse hat while doing business with prospective clients and drinking beer from his cowboy boots at swank Oklahoma City watering holes.

To finance its rapid growth, Penn Square was forced to continually expand its deposit base. The bank lured depositors by offering interest rate premiums on "jumbo" certificates of deposit (CDs). These CDs carried interest rates 25 to 150 basis points above prevailing market rates. Although the bank grew at a phenomenal rate under the guidance of Jennings and Patterson, Penn Square was still only a medium-sized bank when it failed. In terms of total assets, Penn Square ranked at the time as only the seventh largest bank ever closed by the FDIC. The failure of the Oklahoma City bank was noteworthy not because of its size but rather because some of the nation's largest banks had become involved in the speculative oil and gas lending activities of Penn Square's energy division.

In the late 1970s, Penn Square's reputation for financing even the highest risk oil and gas ventures caused the bank to be swamped with loan requests from would-be wildcatters. The bank's limited size prevented it from funding all of these loans. Patterson eventually turned to major metropolitan banks around the country and asked them to "participate" in financing oil and gas ventures. Penn Square arranged the lending syndicates for these ventures and performed all necessary administrative functions, such as obtaining appraisals and engineering es-

---

1. This and all subsequent quotations were taken from the following source: U.S. Congress, House, Committee on Banking, Finance and Urban Affairs; *Penn Square Bank Failure, Part 1* (Washington, D.C.: U.S. Government Printing Office, 1982).

timates of oil reserves. In some cases, Penn Square served strictly as an interme-
diary in these loans. The banks providing the loans in these "100 percent participations" simply paid Penn Square a fee for its services. Seattle First National
Bank, Continental Illinois, Chase Manhattan, and several other large metropolitan banks financed numerous oil and gas ventures with the assistance of Penn
Square. Continental Illinois alone doled out more than $1 billion of such loans.

President Jimmy Carter's energy conservation policies and massive overpro-
duction by the Organization of Petroleum Exporting Countries (OPEC) caused oil
and gas prices to plummet in 1980. Many of the Penn Square-backed exploration
ventures were aimed at recovering oil and gas from the deepest reservoirs. These
reservoirs had not been tapped prior to the 1970s oil boom because low petroleum
prices made it economically unfeasible to extract the oil from them. As the price
of crude oil suddenly dropped several dollars per barrel, these ventures quickly
became unprofitable.

By early 1980, the Office of the Comptroller of the Currency (OCC) had turned
a wary eye in the direction of Penn Square. The bank's large profits, booming loan
volume, and unheard-of growth rates caused the OCC to become suspicious. An
investigation by OCC federal bank examiners uncovered numerous violations of
banking laws by Penn Square, including insufficient liquidity, inadequate capital,
and poor loan documentation. In late 1980, the OCC forced the bank's directors
to sign an "administrative agreement" that required them to take remedial measures to correct these problems. Actions taken by Penn Square in response to the
OCC order included the hiring of a new president, Eldon Beller, a banker with
strong credentials in the Oklahoma City business community. The bank also hired
several other key executive officers with considerable banking experience.
Additionally, Penn Square tightened and codified its loan review and documentation procedures and increased its reserve for loan losses 100 percent over the
previous year.

The measures taken by Penn Square resulted in a more positive evaluation of
the bank by federal bank examiners in the fall of 1981. Shortly after the examiners left the bank, the oil glut worsened, forcing increasing numbers of small exploration companies—the backbone of Penn Square's clientele—out of business.
Faced with the need to attract additional deposits and loan customers to sustain
its rapid growth, Penn Square returned to its former ways. In the last seven
months of its existence, Penn Square loaned more than $1 billion to oil and gas
speculators, by direct loans or indirectly through participation deals, eclipsing
even its own pre-1980 frantic lending pace.

By the time federal examiners returned to Penn Square in the spring of 1982, the
bank's financial condition had deteriorated alarmingly. Penn Square was in such
poor condition in the last few weeks before its closing that the Federal Reserve
was forced to extend the bank several million dollars in emergency loans to keep
it solvent. Finally, in July 1982, the OCC decided that Penn Square was beyond res-
cue and ordered the FDIC to shut down the bank and serve as its receiver.

ARTHUR YOUNG'S DISMISSAL BY PENN SQUARE

The Oklahoma City office of Arthur Young & Company audited Penn Square's
annual financial statements from 1976 through 1980. Beginning with the fiscal
year ending December 31, 1979, Penn Square Bank became a wholly-owned sub-

sidiary of the newly formed bank holding company First Penn Corporation. Nevertheless, the de facto audit client remained Penn Square Bank. For the years ending December 31, 1976, through December 31, 1979, the bank received unqualified opinions from Arthur Young. In 1980, Arthur Young issued a qualified opinion on Penn Square's financial statements (see Exhibit 1). The qualification stated that the auditors were unable to satisfy themselves "as to the adequacy of the reserve for possible loan losses."

During the Penn Square congressional hearings in the fall of 1982, Harold Russell, the managing partner of Arthur Young's Oklahoma City office, discussed the problems his firm encountered during its 1980 Penn Square audit. Russell reported that the bank's loan documentation practices had deteriorated between 1979 and 1980. Arthur Young found that many loans did not have current engineering reports documenting oil reserves. Other loans had engineering reports that did not include an opinion of the engineer or did not list the assumptions used in estimating the reserves. When asked if he discussed these problems with client management, Russell replied affirmatively. He also testified that Jennings was "not pleased" with Arthur Young's decision to qualify its 1980 opinion. Without prior warning, Jennings notified Russell in late November 1981 that Peat Marwick had been retained to audit the bank's 1981 financial statements. Media reports implied that Arthur Young had been dismissed because of its 1980 qualified opinion, a rumor repeatedly denied by Penn Square officials.[2]

EXHIBIT 1
Arthur Young's 1980 Penn Square Audit Opinion

The Board of Directors
First Penn Corporation

We have examined the accompanying balance sheets (company and consolidated) of First Penn Corporation at December 31, 1980 and 1979, and the related statements (company and consolidated) of income, stockholders' equity, and changes in financial position for the years then ended. Except as stated in the following paragraph, our examinations were made in accordance with generally accepted auditing standards and, accordingly, included such tests of the accounting records and such other auditing procedures as we considered necessary in the circumstances.

We were unable to satisfy ourselves as to the adequacy of the reserve for possible loan losses at December 31, 1980, due to the lack of supporting documentation of collateral values of certain loans.

In our opinion, except for the effects of such adjustments, if any, on the 1980 financial statements (company and consolidated) as might have been determined to be necessary had we been able to satisfy ourselves as to the adequacy of the reserve for possible loan losses, the statements mentioned above present fairly the financial position (company and consolidated) of First Penn Corporation at December 31, 1980 and 1979, and the results of operations (company and consolidated) and the changes in financial position (company and consolidated) for the years then ended, in conformity with generally accepted accounting principles applied on a consistent basis during the period.

Arthur Young & Company
March 13, 1981

---

2. Peat Marwick officials testified that their firm made the standard inquiries of Arthur Young required at the time by *SAS No. 7*, "Communications between Predecessor and Successor Auditors." Arthur Young responded to these inquiries by stating that its relationship with Penn Square Bank had been "free of significant problems." However, Arthur Young did bring to Peat Marwick's attention the qualified opinion that it had issued on Penn Square's 1980 financial statements.

Representative St Germain's committee wanted to know why Penn Square selected Peat Marwick as its new auditor following Arthur Young's dismissal. Jim Blanton, the managing partner of Peat Marwick's Oklahoma City office, told the committee that several members of his firm were well acquainted with Penn Square's top executives. Blanton suggested that these relationships likely prompted Penn Square to retain Peat Marwick as its new audit firm in the fall of 1981.

Under further questioning by the committee, Blanton disclosed that several of Peat Marwick's Oklahoma City partners had previously obtained more than $2 million in loans and a $1 million line of credit from Penn Square. These loans presented the audit firm with an independence "problem" that had to be resolved before the bank could be accepted as a client. The agreement reached between the two parties required Penn Square to "fully participate out" the loans and the line of credit to other banks. These participations were intended to be nonrecourse transactions. However, on July 1, 1982—just four days prior to the bank's closing—Peat Marwick learned that Penn Square had repurchased one of the loans. Peat Marwick officials insisted that this repurchase had been done without their knowledge and that it was "completely contrary to our prior understanding with the bank."

PEAT MARWICK'S 1981 AUDIT OF PENN SQUARE

Jim Blanton submitted to the congressional investigative committee a detailed memorandum that discussed, among other items, his firm's 1981 audit of Penn Square. Peat Marwick's 1981 audit focused on the bank's allowance for possible loan losses. Blanton pointed out that Penn Square wrote off $4.8 million in loans in 1981, compared with just slightly more than $600,000 in 1980. Additionally, Blanton noted that the balance of the allowance account on December 31, 1981, was more than twice its balance one year earlier. Nevertheless, Penn Square's allowance for loan losses equaled only 1.5 percent of the bank's total loans at the end of 1981, a modest percentage by industry standards. (Note: Exhibit 2 contains Penn Square's comparative year-end balance sheets for 1980 and 1981, while Exhibit 3 [page 89] presents note 4 to those balance sheets. This note summarized the activity in the allowance for possible loan losses account for 1980 and 1981.)

Blanton reported that during the 1981 audit his firm paid close attention to the $15 million in problem loans that triggered Arthur Young's qualification the previous year. By the end of 1981, Penn Square had repaid many of those loans. For the problem loans still outstanding as of December 31, 1981, Blanton maintained that the concerns raised by Arthur Young had been addressed by the establishment of a credit review department and by other remedial measures taken by the bank. To support this contention, Blanton referred to the OCC's October 1981 report on the bank. That report commended Penn Square's directors for the improvement in the bank's administrative and operating policies.

The results of the 1981 Penn Square audit apparently left little doubt in the minds of the Peat Marwick auditors that the bank's financial statements were fairly stated. Exhibit 4 (page 89) presents the unqualified opinion Peat Marwick issued on Penn Square's 1981 financial statements. According to Peat Marwick's congressional testimony, several senior partners in the firm, including Blanton, reviewed and approved the wording of that opinion.

PENN SQUARE BANK, N.A.
(A Wholly-owned Subsidiary of First Penn Corporation)

| | December 31, | |
Assets	1981	1980
Cash, time deposits and due from banks	$ 87,465,338	$ 59,625,519
Investment securities (note 2):		
U.S. Treasury securities	13,123,075	10,992,420
Obligations of state and political subdivisions	34,362,974	31,334,926
Loans (notes 3 and 4)	277,407,896	203,437,140
Less:		
Unearned discount	2,171,330	1,537,889
Allowance for loan losses	4,141,447	2,004,587
Loans, net	271,095,119	199,894,664
Federal funds sold	53,000,000	16,000,000
Bank premises, property and equipment, net (note 5)	3,877,929	2,481,667
Accrued interest receivable	20,495,932	7,372,553
Other assets (note 9)	1,704,004	762,888
	$485,124,371	$328,464,637

Liabilities and Stockholders' Equity		
Deposits:		
Demand	$232,636,575	$142,624,714
Savings and NOW accounts	18,223,800	13,341,126
Time (note 6)	196,817,006	144,822,794
Total deposits	447,677,381	300,788,634
Loans sold under agreements to repurchase	—	2,795,561
Federal funds purchased	900,000	650,000
Accrued interest and other liabilities (note 9)	4,949,589	3,808,039
Total liabilities	453,526,970	308,042,234
Stockholders' equity:		
Common stock	1,000,000	1,000,000
Surplus	18,000,000	10,500,000
Undivided profits	12,597,401	8,922,403
Total stockholders' equity	31,597,401	20,422,403
Commitments and contingent liabilities (note 12)	—	—
	$485,124,371	$328,464,637

See accompanying notes to financial statements.

Although Blanton's testimony supported Peat Marwick's decision to accept Penn Square's 1981 allowance for possible loan losses, congressional investigators repeatedly questioned the wisdom of that decision. Congressman Doug Barnard noted that Penn Square had reserved a much smaller percentage of specifically identified problem loans than was normal, according to statistics made available by federal bank agencies. In rebuttal, a Peat Marwick partner suggested that loan review "is a highly judgmental area, and there are different rules of thumb used."

The congressional investigators also dissected the "management letter" that Peat Marwick provided to Penn Square's directors upon completion of the audit. That letter criticized several facets of Penn Square's internal controls. The inves-

A summary of transactions in the allowance for possible loan losses is as follows:

	1981	1980
Balance at beginning of year	$2,004,587	$1,002,097
Recoveries credited to the allowance	629,417	212,061
Provision charged to expense	6,343,000	1,407,830
	8,977,004	2,621,988
Less loans charged off	(4,835,557)	(617,401)
Balance at end of year	$4,141,447	$2,004,587

Management's judgment as to the level of future losses on existing loans involves the consideration and related effect of current and anticipated economic conditions on specific borrowers, an evaluation of the existing relationship among loans, examinations by regulatory authorities and management's internal review of the loan portfolio. In determining the collectibility of certain loans, management also considers the fair value of the underlying collateral.

During 1981, the Bank formed a loan review function and adopted a formalized approach to the evaluation and documentation of credit risks within the loan portfolio. The conclusions reached from this systematic analysis of the loans are translated on a quarterly basis to adjustments, if any, which are deemed necessary to maintain the allowance for possible loan losses at an adequate level. Also during 1981, the Bank significantly improved its documentation of the loan files with respect to credit and collateral information.

It should be understood that estimates of future loan losses involve an exercise of judgment. It is the judgment of management that the allowance is adequate at both December 31, 1981 and 1980.

EXHIBIT 3
Note 4 to Penn Square's Comparative Balance Sheets for 1980 and 1981: Allowance for Possible Loan Losses

The Board of Directors and Stockholders
First Penn Corporation

We have examined the consolidated and parent-only financial statements of First Penn Corporation and subsidiaries and the consolidated balance sheet of Penn Square Bank, N.A., and subsidiary as listed in the accompanying index. Our examination was made in accordance with generally accepted auditing standards, and accordingly included such tests of the accounting records and such other auditing procedures as we considered necessary in the circumstances. The financial statements for the year ended December 31, 1980, for First Penn Corporation as listed in the accompanying index, which are included for comparative purposes, were examined by other auditors whose report, dated March 13, 1981, was qualified because they were unable to satisfy themselves as to the adequacy of the allowance for possible loan losses due to the lack of supporting documentation of collateral values of certain loans. As described in note 4 to the accompanying financial statements, the subsidiary bank, during 1981, formalized its approach to the evaluation of credit risks within the loan portfolio and documentation of the loan files with respect to credit and collateral information. The consolidated balance sheet for Penn Square Bank, N.A., and subsidiary as of December 31, 1980, which is included for comparative purposes, was included in the consolidated balance sheet of First Penn Corporation but was not presented separately and, therefore, not covered by the aforementioned auditors' report dated March 13, 1981.

In our opinion, the aforementioned financial statements present fairly the consolidated and parent-only financial position of First Penn Corporation and subsidiaries at December 31, 1981, the results of their operations and the changes in their financial position for the year then ended, and the consolidated financial position of Penn Square Bank, N.A., and subsidiary at December 31, 1981, in conformity with generally accepted accounting principles applied on a basis consistent with that of the preceding year.

Peat, Marwick, Mitchell & Co.
March 19, 1982

EXHIBIT 4
Peat Marwick's 1981 Penn Square Audit Opinion

tigators questioned why these problems had not been mentioned in the audit report. At one point in the hearings, Congressman George Wortley directly asked Blanton whether the bank's internal controls were "adequate."

MR. BLANTON: No, sir. We don't believe they were adequate.

CONGRESSMAN WORTLEY: Well, did you criticize them in the public statement?

MR. BLANTON: No, sir.

CONGRESSMAN WORTLEY: You only criticized them in the management letter?

MR. BLANTON: That is correct.

CONGRESSMAN WORTLEY: Do you think that is fair to the public? And is that a custom of the profession?

MR. BLANTON: I am not sure that I can determine what is fair or unfair to the public. I can say that it is a normal procedure to issue a management letter, and that we do not address in the financial statements or in footnotes all of the problems of a client.

CONGRESSMAN WORTLEY: Well, do you not feel that you have a responsibility to someone other than your client, in this case Penn Square? Is the whole purpose of an audit not to make certain that things are verified and the public is adequately informed of it, and shareholders and investors and depositors?

Finally, the congressional committee scrutinized communications that took place between the Peat Marwick auditors assigned to the Penn Square engagement and the Peat Marwick audit team for Chase Manhattan. Chase Manhattan was one of the large metropolitan banks that participated in many of Penn Square's loan syndicates. The congressional committee questioned whether Chase Manhattan's auditors, after learning of Penn Square's rapidly deteriorating financial condition from their colleagues on the Penn Square audit, passed that information along to Chase's executives. Following the congressional hearings, the FDIC sued Chase Manhattan for improperly withdrawing funds from Penn Square just a few days before the bank's closing.

The Peat Marwick partners testifying before the investigative committee denied that Chase Manhattan had obtained inside information concerning Penn Square's financial condition from Peat Marwick auditors. Congressman Ed Weber pursued this issue by asking Blanton whether independent auditors are required to protect the confidentiality of sensitive information they obtain from clients.

MR. BLANTON: That is correct.

CONGRESSMAN WEBER: And the thing that clouds the issue here is that we may be dealing in an area of civil fraud or actual illegality, and the question is at that point, do you maintain the confidentiality of those potential violations of law from other people who may be affected by that information? [Pause.]

CONGRESSMAN WEBER: Can you answer?

MR. BLANTON: I am thinking. I really do not know the answer to that question. It obviously has been the subject of much debate among accountants.

CONGRESSMAN WEBER: You are in a situation of a conflict of interest. You are representing two clients who have conflicting interests. The interest of one client is to keep the information totally confidential. The interest of the other client, of course, is to be informed.

MR. BLANTON: I think that I can safely say that it is our firm policy that we do not ever discuss the condition of one client with another client.

PENN SQUARE—AN AUDIT FAILURE?

The evidence introduced into the congressional testimony that most damaged the credibility of Peat Marwick's Penn Square audit was an OCC report that labeled the audit "unacceptable." That report, dated March 31, 1982, stated:

> The unqualified opinion [issued by Peat Marwick] was rendered despite the identification of excess collateral exceptions, discovery of incidences where the bank was making payments of principal and interest to the correspondent banks on certain participations without first receiving payment from the borrowers, and acceptance of a reserve for possible loan losses which was deemed inadequate by the examiners during their review of the loan portfolio.

Congressman Weber noted that the spring 1982 OCC audit of Penn Square, which was performed simultaneously with Peat Marwick's audit of the bank, uncovered "serious problems." Unfortunately, the Peat Marwick audit team did not have access to the results of the OCC audit. Although the Peat Marwick auditors identified major problems with Penn Square's financial records and operating policies, they concluded that those problems were not as severe as later documented in the OCC report.

Peat Marwick's testimony during the congressional hearings suggests that the audit firm may have overrelied on the controls Penn Square implemented in 1980 at the insistence of the OCC. As suggested earlier, Penn Square officials soon abandoned those controls in the face of deteriorating economic conditions. Peat Marwick may also have been lulled into a false sense of security by the favorable report issued on Penn Square by the OCC examiners in the fall of 1981.

At least one definitive conclusion can be drawn from analyzing Peat Marwick's 1981 audit of Penn Square: the alleged Penn Square audit failure would not have occurred had oil prices continued their upward surge. As noted by one of the congressional investigators, Penn Square was a "house of cards" built on the assumption of continually escalating oil prices. Because of the Penn Square debacle, audit firms will likely look more warily upon prospective clients whose future operating results are more dependent on external variables than on the decisions of a prudent, disciplined management team.

EPILOGUE

In the spring of 1985, a federal jury acquitted William Patterson on 26 counts of bank fraud in a criminal lawsuit filed against him in Oklahoma City. Three years later, Patterson avoided conviction on 12 similar complaints when a federal judge declared a mistrial in a criminal case filed in Chicago. Finally, in July 1988, in a plea bargain agreement with federal prosecutors, Patterson pleaded guilty to misapplication of bank funds and was sentenced to two years in federal prison. In 1984, a colleague of Patterson's at Penn Square pleaded guilty to bank fraud charges and received a 30-month prison sentence.

Various plaintiffs filed more than $1 billion in civil lawsuits against Peat Marwick for its involvement with Penn Square Bank. Nearly all of those lawsuits were settled privately. The FDIC sued Peat Marwick for $90 million and reportedly collected one-half of that amount from the audit firm in a confidential settlement. The U.S. Justice Department filed suit against 12 Peat Marwick employees or former employees. These indictments accused the 12 individuals of conflict of interest and related offenses. These charges were apparently settled privately as well.

Following the banking and savings and loan crises of the 1980s, the auditing profession took several steps to help auditors develop more effective audit strategies for financial institutions. Among these measures was the publication of a monograph entitled *Auditing the Allowance for Credit Losses of Banks* (New York: AICPA, 1986). This publication outlines steps that auditors can take to corroborate the material accuracy of a client's allowance for credit losses or bad loans. Peat Marwick's 1981 audit of Penn Square, and several other "problem audits" of the 1980s, suggest that the allowance for credit losses easily qualifies as the most problematic account in audits of financial institutions.

QUESTIONS

1. What characteristic of the Penn Square loan portfolio caused the business risk of this bank to be much higher than it would have been otherwise? Which component of audit risk, as discussed in *SAS No. 47*, "Audit Risk and Materiality in Conducting an Audit," is affected by a client's business risk? Demonstrate with a numerical example how a client's business risk influences the audit risk that the company poses for its audit firm.

2. Suppose an audit firm accepts a client that received a qualified opinion from its previous auditor. Does that audit firm's professional responsibilities differ from those it would assume on a more typical audit engagement? Why or why not? What steps have the auditing profession taken to minimize "opinion shopping" by audit clients?

3. Did the Penn Square loans to the Peat Marwick partners present the audit firm with an apparent or de facto independence problem? Defend your answer.

4. What reporting responsibilities, if any, do auditors have when they discover serious weaknesses in a client's internal controls? Should auditors report on the quality or adequacy of a client's internal controls to financial statement users?

5. One of the Peat Marwick partners implied that his firm's audit report was intended only for the benefit of the bank's board of directors. Under common law, were any other parties justified in relying on Peat Marwick's audit report? Penn Square Bank and the holding company of which it was a subsidiary were privately owned. Does this fact change your answer?

6. Would Peat Marwick have violated the profession's ethical standards if its New York City office had informed Chase Manhattan that Penn Square was on the verge of bankruptcy?

7. Peat Marwick was criticized for not warning parties relying on Penn Square's 1981 financial statements that the bank was in danger of failing. Under present auditing standards, what responsibility, if any, do auditors have to forewarn financial statement users of clients in danger of failing?

CASE 1.8
STAR TECHNOLOGIES, INC.

Economic ups and downs are a fact of life for companies in high-tech industries. Take the case of Star Technologies, Inc., a Virginia-based computer manufacturer incorporated in 1981 that went public in 1984.[1] In its early years, Star marketed scientific computers or "supercomputers" for highly specialized uses, including military surveillance and petroleum exploration. Star's operating results gyrated wildly during the 1980s. Exhibit 1 presents Star's key financial data for the five-year period 1985–1989. Notice that in 1985 Star reported a net loss exceeding $8 million on revenues of $21.2 million. The following year's results were even worse. In 1987, Star's revenues vaulted to $44 million, allowing the company to earn an after-tax profit of $1.4 million. Two years later, more bad news. Star's revenues fell to $39 million in 1989, resulting in a loss of $4.4 million.

Like many firms in the highly competitive computer industry, Star found itself trapped in a vicious cycle during the 1980s, a cycle that accounted for the large swings in its operating results. Star's 1989 annual report declared that the company was committed to staying "in the forefront of technological innovation" in the computer industry. Because of this commitment, Star's 1989 R&D expenditures consumed 20 percent of its revenues. Unfortunately, rapid changes in technology within the computer industry rendered many of Star's impressive products obsolete shortly after they were introduced. This short product life cycle forced Star's executives to repeatedly "go back to the drawing board" and incur

1. Two enforcement releases issued by the Securities and Exchange Commission (SEC) and various annual reports of Star Technologies, Inc., provided the background facts for this case. The parties involved in this case neither admitted nor denied the SEC's reported findings and conclusions. Unless indicated otherwise, the quotations in this case were drawn from the following source: Securities and Exchange Commission, *Accounting and Auditing Enforcement Release No. 455*, 24 June 1993.

EXHIBIT 1
Selected Financial Data
Reported by Star
Technologies, 1985–1989
(000s omitted)

	1989	1988	1987	1986	1985
Revenue	$39,004	$35,689	$44,050	$ 15,050	$21,298
Operating income	(2,614)	3,830	4,729	(17,946)	(6,983)
Net income	(4,393)	2,218	1,374	(19,971)	(8,092)
Working capital	13,855	13,217	8,621	3,946	22,328
Total assets	31,277	25,025	28,528	35,908	44,957
Total debt	19,796	12,976	16,294	26,134	18,866

heavy R&D expenditures. As history later proved, only a few computer manufacturers could prosper under such conditions. Star Technologies was not among those firms.

A Fallen Star

By the end of fiscal 1989—March 31, 1989, Star faced a financial crisis. Among the company's major products was a computer designed for use in petroleum exploration. Company officials forecasted that Star would sell 29 of the computers during 1989. Because of changes in computer technology and a slowdown in petroleum exploration activities, Star sold only one of these computers during 1989 and had no outstanding sales orders for the product at year-end. Star's poor operating results for 1989 caused the company to violate several covenants of a lending agreement with its principal bank. That bank had extended Star a $5.8 million long-term loan. The debt covenant violations accelerated the maturity date of the loan, making it immediately due and payable at the end of fiscal 1989.

Price Waterhouse audited Star's financial statements throughout the late 1980s. During the fiscal 1989 audit, several contentious issues arose between Price Waterhouse and Star's top executives. Among these issues were the refusal of Star's management to reclassify the $5.8 million bank loan as a current liability, disagreements over the adequacy of Star's reserves for bad debts and inventory obsolescence, and the capitalization of R&D expenditures by the company. Eventually, the company's management and the Price Waterhouse partner who oversaw the 1989 Star audit resolved these issues to their mutual satisfaction, allowing Price Waterhouse to issue an unqualified opinion on Star's 1989 financial statements. Exhibit 2 contains the company's 1988 and 1989 balance sheets. Exhibit 3 (page 96) presents the company's income statements and statements of cash flows for the period 1987–1989.

In January 1990, Price Waterhouse's national office received an anonymous letter alleging that the 1989 audit of Star Technologies was an "audit failure." After a brief investigation, the national office deemed the allegation unfounded. An executive partner in Price Waterhouse's Washington, D.C., office, which had issued the 1989 Star audit opinion, was not satisfied with the national office's investigation and decided to pursue the matter further. Following a lengthy discussion with the individual who served as the audit manager on the 1989 Star audit, the executive partner concluded that the audit had been inadequate and reported this finding to the national office. In early 1990, Price Waterhouse notified Star that it was withdrawing the audit opinion issued on the company's 1989 financial statements. Price Waterhouse also informed Star that those financial statements con-

STAR TECHNOLOGIES, INC. BALANCE SHEETS (000s omitted)		
	March 31,	
	1989	1988
Current assets:		
Cash and equivalents	$ 1,444	$ 1,651
Accounts receivable	5,025	4,063
Inventory	12,962	10,732
Other current assets	1,952	582
Total current assets	21,383	17,028
Property and equipment, net	6,917	5,033
Other assets	2,977	2,964
Total assets	$ 31,277	$ 25,025
Current liabilities:		
Accounts payable	$ 4,739	$ 1,524
Accrued payroll and related benefits	1,156	926
Other accrued liabilities	277	747
Deferred revenue	266	381
Notes payable	1,090	233
Total current liabilities	7,528	3,811
Notes payable, net of current portion	18,706	12,743
Total liabilities	26,234	16,554
Stockholders' equity:		
Convertible preferred stock	2	2
Common stock	161	155
Additional paid-in capital	49,299	48,340
Retained earnings (deficit)	(44,419)	(40,026)
Total stockholders' equity	5,043	8,471
Total liabilities and stockholders' equity	$ 31,277	$ 25,025

EXHIBIT 2
Star Technologies, Inc.,
1988–1989 Balance
Sheets

tained material errors. Although Star's executives initially disagreed with the audit firm's conclusion, they later accepted that decision and issued restated financial statements for 1989.

PRICE WATERHOUSE'S 1989 AUDIT OF STAR TECHNOLOGIES

Clark Childers, an audit partner with Price Waterhouse since 1984, served as the engagement partner on the annual audits of Star's financial statements from 1987 through 1989. Childers' principal subordinate during the 1989 Star audit was Paul Argy, a senior audit manager to be considered for promotion to partner the following year. Argy assumed responsibility for planning and coordinating the 1989 audit, supervising the staff assigned to the engagement, and serving as Price Waterhouse's on-site liaison with Star's executives.

The Star audit proved to be a difficult engagement for Argy. He repeatedly clashed with client management over the accounting and financial reporting issues highlighted in the following sections. During one of those confrontations,

EXHIBIT 3
Star Technologies, Inc., 1987–1989 Income Statements and Statements of Cash Flows

STAR TECHNOLOGIES, INC. CONSOLIDATED STATEMENTS OF OPERATIONS (000s omitted)			
	Year Ended March 31,		
	1989	**1988**	**1987**
Revenue	$39,004	$35,689	$44,050
Costs and expenses:			
Cost of revenue	22,498	17,343	25,437
Research and development	7,945	4,684	5,031
Marketing and sales	8,206	7,363	6,118
General and administrative	2,969	2,469	2,410
Provision for restructuring	—	—	325
Operating income (loss)	(2,614)	3,830	4,729
Interest expense	(1,597)	(1,453)	(1,971)
Other income (expense)	(182)	(93)	(84)
Income (loss) before income taxes and extraordinary items	(4,393)	2,284	2,674
Provision for income taxes	—	(1,286)	(1,230)
Income (loss) before extraordinary items	(4,393)	998	1,444
Extraordinary items:			
Utilization of NOL carryforward	—	1,220	1,230
Provision for stockholder suit settlement	—	—	(1,300)
Net income (loss)	$ (4,393)	$ 2,218	$ 1,374

(continued)

Star's management demanded that Argy be removed from the audit. Childers refused to remove Argy but from that point apparently assumed a larger role in resolving disputes that arose with client officials. Following one particularly heated encounter between Childers and Star management, the company's executives evidently decided to dismiss Price Waterhouse. A subsequent investigation by the Securities and Exchange Commission (SEC) revealed that Star's audit committee interceded and refused to allow Price Waterhouse to be dismissed.

R&D Expenditures

In 1989, Star established a joint R&D effort with Glen Culler & Associates, a small company that developed supercomputers. Star advanced nearly $900,000 to Culler during fiscal 1989. The agreement between the two companies required those funds to be repaid in 10 years and obligated Culler to use the funds to develop a new computer that Star would have an exclusive right to manufacture. Culler pledged all of its assets as collateral for the $900,000 advance. This stipulation of the agreement was inconsequential since Culler had no source of revenue or working capital other than Star, its sole customer; had a negative net worth of nearly $200,000; and had few tangible assets. Finally, the agreement between the two companies granted Star the right to acquire Culler.

Star's management maintained that the $900,000 advanced to Culler during 1989 qualified as a note receivable and included it in "other" assets on Star's 1989 balance sheet. Childers agreed with this decision. As required by Price Waterhouse, a second audit partner reviewed the 1989 Star workpapers before Childers released the audit opinion on the company's financial statements. This

STAR TECHNOLOGIES, INC.
CONSOLIDATED STATEMENTS OF CASH FLOWS (000s omitted)

| | Year Ended March 31, | | |
	1989	1988	1987
Cash flows from (used for) operating activities:			
Net income (loss) before extraordinary items	$(4,393)	$ 998	$ 1,444
Extraordinary items	—	1,220	(70)
Adjustments to reconcile net income to net cash from operating activities:			
Depreciation and amortization	3,758	2,976	3,872
Stock issued for services	—	—	68
(Increase) decrease in accounts receivable	(867)	(896)	174
(Increase) decrease in inventory	(1,094)	4,090	1,689
Increase (decrease) in accounts payable	3,215	(3,241)	2,465
Increase (decrease) in accrued liabilities	(240)	(356)	(370)
Increase (decrease) in deferred revenue	(115)	232	(1,513)
Net cash from operating activities	264	5,023	7,759
Cash flows from (used for) investing activities:			
Deferred software and contract costs	(452)	(893)	—
Capital expenditures and other	(4,654)	(563)	130
Advances to Culler	(800)	—	—
Acquisition of Graphicon	(611)	—	—
Net cash from (used for) investing activities	(6,517)	(1,456)	130
Cash flows from (used for) financing activities:			
(Decrease) increase in notes payable	6,023	(3,318)	(9,840)
Proceeds from stock option exercises	—	873	337
Proceeds from stock issuances	23	—	—
Net cash from (used for) financing activities	6,046	(2,445)	(9,503)
Net increase (decrease) in cash and equivalents	(207)	1,122	(1,614)
Cash and equivalents, beginning of year	1,651	529	2,143
Cash and equivalents, end of year	$ 1,444	$ 1,651	$ 529

**EXHIBIT 3—continued
Star Technologies, Inc.,
1987–1989 Income
Statements and
Statements of Cash
Flows**

partner questioned the decision to report the $900,000 advance to Culler as an asset in Star's 1989 balance sheet and suggested instead writing off the advance as R&D expense in Star's 1989 income statement. The review partner then referred Childers to paragraphs 11 and 12 of *Statement on Financial Accounting Standards No. 2*, "Accounting for Research and Development Costs." Listed next are excerpts from those two paragraphs.

> The costs of services performed by others in connection with the research and development activities of an enterprise, including research and development conducted by others on behalf of the enterprise, shall be included in research and development costs.
>
> If repayment to the enterprise of any loan or advance by the enterprise to the other parties depends solely on the results of the research and development having future economic benefit, the loan or advance shall be accounted for as costs incurred by the enterprise. The costs shall be charged to research and development expense . . .

To further support his position that the $900,000 advance to Culler should be expensed, the review partner cited the description of the agreement between Star and Culler included in the draft of Star's 1989 financial statement footnotes. That description specifically referred to the agreement as a "joint research and development agreement."

After meeting with the review partner, Childers consulted with Star's chief financial officer (CFO). Childers told the CFO that the description of the Star–Culler agreement included in the draft of the financial statement footnotes suggested that the $900,000 advance should be treated as R&D expense by Star.

> Following that conversation, Star's CFO caused all references to the transaction as a research and development agreement to be deleted from the final version of the financial statements. The final version described the agreement as a "working capital agreement."

Childers accepted this revision without referring to the actual contract between the two parties. An inspection of that document would have revealed that the CFO's updated description of the Star–Culler relationship was misleading. The change in the footnote description of the Star–Culler agreement apparently satisfied the review partner, causing him to drop his objection to Star's financial statement treatment of the $900,000 advance to Culler.

During fiscal 1990, Star acquired Culler. While reviewing this transaction, Childers and Argy discovered that Star's 1989 financial statement footnotes had not accurately described the Star–Culler agreement. Childers and Argy contacted Price Waterhouse's national office for advice on this matter. To provide a clear understanding of the Star–Culler agreement, Argy forwarded to the national office copies of relevant documents pertaining to that agreement. After studying those documents, a Price Waterhouse partner in the firm's national office concluded that, at a minimum, $400,000 of the $900,000 advanced to Culler by Star during fiscal 1989 should have been treated as R&D expense by Star.[2]

The national office partner then addressed the issue of whether Star's 1989 financial statements should be restated. The partner asked Childers if an adjustment to write off $400,000 of the Culler receivable to R&D expense would have materially impacted Star's 1989 financial statements. Childers convinced the national partner that such an adjustment would have had an immaterial effect on Star's financial statements. Childers also told the national partner that an adjustment had been proposed during the 1989 audit to write off a portion of the $900,000 Culler receivable to expense. According to Childers, that adjustment had been waived due to its immaterial effect on Star's financial statements. The SEC's subsequent investigation found no evidence of that adjustment in Price Waterhouse's workpapers. Following his interaction with the national partner, Childers instructed a subordinate to include such a proposed adjustment in the 1989 Star workpapers. The subordinate did not comply with Childers' request.

Reserve for Inventory Obsolescence

One of Star's original products was the ST-100 computer. Although a state-of-the-art computer when first marketed in 1982, by 1989 the ST-100 was outmoded. During 1989, Star added $3.5 million to the reserve for inventory obsolescence for its remaining inventory of ST-100s, reducing that inventory to a net book value of $2 million. Argy and other members of the Star engagement team believed that

---

2. The $400,000 amount represented the funds advanced to Culler after Star signed the agreement giving it the right to acquire that company. The national office partner maintained that since Star essentially had de facto control of Culler after the agreement was signed, the funds subsequently advanced to Culler should have been treated as an operating expense by Star.

the ST-100 inventory was still overvalued. Argy recommended an additional $1.5 million write-down for that inventory.

Star's management resisted Argy's suggestion to write the ST-100 inventory down to a net book value of $500,000. The client's executives persuaded Childers that the company would sell ST-100s in the future despite not having any existing orders for that product and despite having sold only one ST-100 during 1989. Star's management also provided Childers with a list of $1 million of spare parts included in the ST-100 inventory that would allegedly be needed by Star to service previously sold ST-100s.

> Childers accepted the $1 million spare parts requirement at face value and failed to perform any procedures or make additional inquiries to support the value. With regard to the remaining $1 million of obsolete ST-100 inventory, Childers agreed, apparently in a compromise with Star's management, to an arbitrary reserve increase of $350,000 without any documentation as to the basis for, or the rationale behind, the adjustment.

Reserve for Bad Debts

Star reported slightly more than $5 million of net accounts receivable at the end of fiscal 1989. Two of Star's largest receivables had been outstanding for more than four years. These receivables, both in litigation at the time, totaled $1,062,000 and resulted from earlier sales of ST-100 computers. Before year-end adjusting entries, Star's allowance for doubtful accounts totaled $673,000. After analyzing Star's receivables, Argy determined that the allowance should be increased by approximately $400,000. That figure roughly equaled the total of the two disputed receivables less the existing balance of the allowance account.

In previous years, Price Waterhouse had reduced any proposed adjustment to the allowance account by the value of the collateral for potentially uncollectible receivables. Since the collateral for the disputed receivables, two ST-100 computers, was minimal, Argy decided that the proposed adjustment for uncollectible receivables should not be reduced.

Childers advised Star's management that he agreed with Argy's analysis of the allowance for doubtful accounts. The client's executives balked at making the $400,000 addition to the allowance and instead referred Childers to the company's attorneys. Those attorneys insisted that the proposed adjustment was excessive. As a compromise, Star's CEO recommended increasing the allowance account $65,000 at the end of fiscal 1989. Childers agreed to that adjustment. The SEC later challenged Childers' decision to accept the modest increase in the allowance account.

> Childers had an inadequate basis to accept the CEO's proposition to increase the bad debt reserve by only $65,000. There was insufficient audit evidence to suggest that the remaining $335,000 of the receivables in question were collectible. In circumstances such as these, opinions of counsel are not dispositive evidence of collectibility.

"Mystery" Assets

During the 1989 Star audit, a Price Waterhouse staff auditor discovered an account entitled "Assets in Process" having a balance of approximately $435,000. When questioned, a Star official initially reported that the assets represented by that account involved computer equipment purchased and placed in service in 1985. Star could not provide invoices or other documentation to support the existence or valuation of these assets, nor were any depreciation records available for the assets.[3] In fact, the client could not locate the assets or describe them in detail to the auditors. Star's CFO claimed that the equipment could not be identified because it had been fully integrated into the company's existing computer facilities.

The staff auditor who uncovered the Assets in Process account noted in the 1989 workpapers that Star depreciated computer equipment over five years and began depreciating such assets in the year they were placed into service. Since the equipment purportedly represented by the account had been placed in service in 1985, the staff auditor reasoned that it should have been fully depreciated by the end of fiscal 1989. Argy agreed with his subordinate's analysis and concluded that the mystery assets should be immediately written off to expense.

When Childers brought the Assets in Process account to the attention of Star's CFO, the CFO refused to accept the proposed adjustment to write off the balance of the account. At this point, the CFO claimed that the assets had actually been placed in service in 1987 rather than 1985, although he could provide no evidence to support that assertion. Instead of accepting the proposed $435,000 adjustment, the CFO offered to record $100,000 of depreciation expense on the assets in 1989 and write off the remaining $335,000 cost of those assets over the following four years. Childers accepted the CFO's proposal.

Classification of Notes Payable

Star's poor operating results for fiscal 1989 resulted in the company violating seven debt covenants included in the loan agreement with its principal bank. These debt covenant violations caused a $5.8 million bank loan to be immediately due and payable, as noted earlier. On June 15, 1989, Price Waterhouse completed the 1989 Star audit; however, Childers refused to issue an audit report on Star's financial statements until the company's bank waived the debt covenant violations. On June 29, 1989, Star faxed Price Waterhouse a waiver obtained two days earlier from its bank.

> The waiver covered only a five-month period, but also stated that it was not the bank's intention to accelerate the loans by virtue of defaults existing at the 1989 fiscal year-end. After reviewing the waiver, the audit senior told Childers that in his opinion the waiver was not adequate to classify the loans as a long-term liability.

Childers disagreed with the audit senior's conclusion. Because the bank stated that it had no intention of making the $5.8 million loan immediately due and payable, Childers believed the loan qualified as a long-term liability. Shortly after receiving the bank waiver, Childers signed the unqualified audit opinion on Star's 1989 financial statements, dating the opinion as of June 15. Star included that opinion in its 1989 10-K filed with the SEC.

WHERE WAS ARGY?

Paul Argy left the Star audit engagement approximately one week before the 1989 audit was completed to begin work on a new assignment in another city. Argy

---

3. Price Waterhouse had identified this account in earlier audits but apparently made no effort to corroborate the given assets' existence or valuation.

returned to Price Waterhouse's Washington, D.C., office on July 10, more than 10 days after Childers issued the unqualified opinion on Star's 1989 financial statements. Upon Argy's return, Childers instructed him to complete his review of the workpapers for the Star audit and to sign off on the "audit summary" for the engagement. A Price Waterhouse policy required the audit manager on an engagement to sign off on the audit summary document after completing his or her review of the workpapers. Argy initially refused to sign off on the Star audit. Argy had contested several of the questionable decisions made by Childers during the 1989 Star audit and believed that the 1989 workpapers contained "materially incorrect" conclusions.

After several confrontations with Childers, Argy capitulated and signed off on the Star workpapers and the audit summary. Although Argy signed those documents on July 14 and 15, 1989, he dated his sign-offs as of June 15, 1989, the date the Star fieldwork had been completed.

EPILOGUE

Price Waterhouse recalled its opinion on Star's 1989 financial statements on March 9, 1990. The following month, the company's management issued financial statements for fiscal 1989 that contained appropriate adjustments for the items discussed earlier. Star's amended 1989 income statement reported a net loss of $7.4 million rather than the $4.4 million loss reported in the company's original 1989 income statement shown in Exhibit 3. On March 28, 1990, Price Waterhouse issued an unqualified audit opinion on Star's restated 1989 financial statements. One week later, Star dismissed Price Waterhouse and retained Coopers & Lybrand as its independent audit firm.

The SEC's investigation of Star's original 1989 financial statements and its 1989 audit culminated in sanctions being imposed on both Star and the two key members of the 1989 audit engagement team. The SEC issued a cease and desist order against Star that prohibited the company from future violations of the federal securities laws. Paul Argy received an 18-month suspension from practicing before the SEC, while Clark Childers received a five-year suspension.[4]

In commenting on Argy's involvement in the 1989 Star audit, the SEC complimented him for recommending that Star make several large and necessary adjustments to its 1989 financial statements.

> Argy acted properly in insisting on material adjustments to Star's financial statements, notwithstanding strong opposition to those proposed adjustments by Star's CFO. He properly recognized and confronted Childers with his belief that the audit conclusions were improper and the audit evidence was insufficient.

The SEC went on to chastise Argy for eventually capitulating and signing off on the 1989 Star audit workpapers when he believed they contained materially incorrect conclusions.

---

4. In 1999, Paul Argy's application to regain his right to practice before the SEC was approved by the federal agency. At the time, Argy was a partner of a small CPA firm, Argy, Wiltse & Robinson. See Securities and Exchange Commission, *Accounting and Auditing Enforcement Release No. 1130*, 22 April 1999.

Instead of signing off on the Star workpapers, the SEC contended that Argy should have dissociated himself from the Star audit. That alternative was available to him since Price Waterhouse had a "disagreement procedure" allowing auditors on an engagement to explicitly dissociate themselves from any decision with which they did not agree. The SEC suggested that Argy may have allowed his desire to be promoted cloud his professional judgment.

> An independent accountant, including an audit manager, cannot excuse his failure to comply with GAAS because of a sense of futility after his proposed approaches to certain accounting issues are repeatedly rejected. . . . The audit manager may encounter pressure to compromise audit standards and may encounter frustration in dealing with partners and clients. The audit manager may also sense that his response to those pressures may adversely affect his opportunity for advancement. However, in fulfilling his responsibilities, the audit manager plays a crucial role in ensuring that an audit report is issued only when the audit was in fact conducted in accordance with GAAS.

In handing Childers a five-year suspension, the SEC affirmed that the audit partner shouldered a greater degree of responsibility for the 1989 Star audit than did his subordinate, Argy. The SEC charged Childers with the following seven specific allegations of misconduct.

1. Failing to ensure that sufficient competent evidential matter was obtained to afford a reasonable basis for his conclusions
2. Failing to exercise due professional care and sufficient professional skepticism in the performance of the audit
3. Failing to assure that the financial statements on which Price Waterhouse issued an unqualified opinion were prepared in accordance with GAAP
4. Responding without an adequate basis to the questions of the second partner reviewer when issues were raised about the agreement with Culler
5. Instructing Argy to sign-off on the audit regardless of Argy's stated disagreement with the conclusions reached by Childers
6. Making misleading statements to the Price Waterhouse national office concerning its investigation of Star's agreement with Culler
7. Instructing a Price Waterhouse audit manager to make inappropriate alterations to workpapers

Star Technologies' financial condition steadily worsened in the years following its unpleasant encounter with the SEC. The company's computer manufacturing operations never became economically viable. By the late 1990s, Standard & Poor's reported that Star's primary line of business was "computer programming services" and that the company had only 20 employees. The company's common stock traded for $.12 per share in late 1999.

QUESTIONS

1. Explain why "industry knowledge" is so important to an audit engagement team. Identify risk factors commonly posed by companies in "high-tech" industries.
2. Review Star Technologies' financial statements included in Exhibits 2 and 3. What changes in Star's financial status between fiscal year-end 1988 and 1989 should have been of concern to the company's independent auditors? How

should these changes have affected key audit planning decisions for the 1989 Star audit?

3. Review Star's statements of cash flows shown in Exhibit 3. What information can auditors obtain from a client's cash flow data that is relevant to the audit plan developed for the client?

4. Refer to *SAS No. 31*, "Evidential Matter." What management assertions did Star violate in its original 1989 financial statements? Explain.

5. Star's bank indicated in the waiver of the debt covenant violations that it did not intend to accelerate the maturity date of the $5.8 million loan. Was that statement a sufficient basis for classifying the loan as a long-term liability rather than as a current liability? Defend your answer.

6. Briefly describe the nature and purpose of the audit review process. Identify any breakdowns that occurred in the audit review process during the 1989 Star audit.

7. How should disagreements between members of an audit engagement team be resolved? What mistakes, if any, were made by Childers and/or Argy in resolving the conflicts that arose between them during the 1989 Star audit?

CASE 1.9
THE FUND OF FUNDS, LTD.

Bernie Cornfeld founded Investors Overseas Services (IOS) in 1956 with an initial investment of $300. Cornfeld, who was 29 years old at the time, recognized that the large contingent of U.S. troops stationed in post-World War II Europe collectively had a huge amount of funds to invest but few investment opportunities. Cornfeld created 11 specialized mutual funds in which members of the U.S. military could invest as little as $25 per month. The most successful of these funds was The Fund of Funds, Ltd., an open-ended mutual fund that initially invested only in U.S.-based mutual funds. This fund's assets eventually approached $500 million.

Cornfeld was born in 1927 in Istanbul, Turkey, and immigrated with his parents to New York three years later. As a young man, Cornfeld became involved in the revolutionary Socialist Youth League and actively campaigned for socialistic political candidates. Trained as a social worker and employed for several years as a New York taxi driver, Cornfeld became disenchanted with politics while in his mid-twenties and turned his attention instead to the world of finance. Five-feet five-inches tall and shy by nature because of a speech impediment, Cornfeld rose from total obscurity at the time he founded IOS to international fame and an estimated net worth of $200 million only a decade later. At the height of IOS's financial success, Cornfeld lived in a castle in France; dated actress Victoria Principal; and could count as friends many international jet-setters, including his best friend, the acclaimed designer Oleg Cassini.

The Securities and Exchange Commission (SEC) disrupted Cornfeld's idyllic lifestyle in the mid-1960s with a lengthy investigation of IOS's financial affairs. As the IOS mutual funds, Fund of Funds in particular, grew dramatically in size during the early 1960s, the SEC became increasingly alarmed. By 1965, IOS transactions often accounted for 5 percent of the daily volume of activity on the New York Stock Exchange. The SEC feared that IOS portfolio managers might eventually be able to manipulate the stock market for their own benefit. Even more troubling to the SEC was the difficulty of imposing regulatory oversight on IOS, since the firm's corporate headquarters was in Geneva, Switzerland. After a two-year investigation, the SEC and Cornfeld reached an agreement. The SEC dropped its investigation of IOS. In exchange, Cornfeld agreed to abide by all SEC regulations and pledged not to allow IOS to obtain a controlling interest in any U.S. company.

A contemporary of Bernie Cornfeld in the international investment community of the 1960s was John McCandish King, a Denver-based speculator in the oil and gas industry. Cornfeld and King were the same age and both rose from obscurity to tremendous wealth in a short period of time. The similarities between the two men stopped there. At six-feet three-inches, the 250-pound King towered over the diminutive Cornfeld. A high school dropout, the brash and often arrogant King was known for his expensive taste in cowboy boots, his 10-gallon cowboy hats, and his 3,000 pairs of cuff links. King's stretch limousine sported a custom-designed sunroof to accommodate his zealous interest in hunting. While still in his twenties, King became renowned for his seemingly innate ability to discover oil. In 1952, King invested $1,500, one-half of his net worth at the time, in an oil-drilling venture in Oklahoma. A string of wildcat wells in that venture allowed him to form King Resources, which soon became one of the nation's largest and most profitable independent oil companies. By the mid-1960s, *Forbes* estimated King's wealth at $300 million, meaning that the towering Texan was well on his way to achieving his personal goal of becoming a billionaire.

In early 1968, Cornfeld decided to diversify Fund of Funds' investment portfolio. A mutual acquaintance arranged a meeting in April 1968 between Cornfeld and King to discuss the possibility of Fund of Funds investing in oil and natural gas properties owned by King Resources. Cornfeld then invited King to make a presentation during a Fund of Funds board of directors meeting in Acapulco, Mexico. Following that presentation, Cornfeld and King reached an agreement. Fund of Funds would establish a natural resources proprietary account (NRPA) for investments in oil and gas properties to be purchased from King Resources. Although the two men never signed a formal contract, the minutes of the Fund of Funds board of directors meeting documented the intended relationship between the two companies:

> The role of King Resources with respect to the contemplated Natural Resources Proprietary Account would be that of a vendor of properties to the proprietary account, with such properties to be sold on an arm's length basis at prices no less favorable to the proprietary account than the prices charged by King to its 200-odd industrial and other purchasers.[1]

A Fund of Funds executive later testified he understood that King Resources would sell natural resource properties to Fund of Funds at cost plus a "reasonable markup" of 7 to 8 percent.

Initially, Cornfeld agreed to purchase $10 million of oil and gas properties from King Resources. By the end of 1969, however, the overbearing King had convinced Fund of Funds' officers to purchase more than $100 million of oil and gas properties from his company. Unfortunately for Fund of Funds' stockholders, King took unfair advantage of the mutual fund's executives, who knew little

---

1. This and all subsequent quotations were taken from the following court opinion: *The Fund of Funds, Limited v. Arthur Andersen & Co.*, 545 F. Supp. 1314 (1982).

about the oil and gas industry. Court records later revealed that King often bought relatively inexpensive oil and gas properties and then immediately sold those properties to Fund of Funds at grossly inflated prices. King unloaded properties on Fund of Funds for as much as 50 times what he had paid for the properties a few days earlier.

Within a few years, falling stock prices and the weight of the poor investments made for Fund of Funds by King forced the mutual fund into bankruptcy. Among the defendants in the tangle of civil lawsuits stemming from Fund of Funds' collapse was Arthur Andersen & Co., the audit firm of both Fund of Funds and King Resources. Arthur Andersen was sued by John Orr, a Touche Ross partner appointed to serve as Fund of Funds' bankruptcy trustee. Orr alleged that Arthur Andersen failed to disclose to the officers of the mutual fund that they were being defrauded by King Resources. When the verdict in the subsequent trial was handed down, Arthur Andersen became the victim of the largest court-ordered judgment ever imposed on a public accounting firm at the time.

Arthur Andersen's Dual Relationship with Fund of Funds and King Resources

Three Arthur Andersen offices were involved in each annual audit of Fund of Funds. The Geneva office coordinated the audits of all the IOS mutual funds and paid particular attention to the Fund of Funds audit, given the size, prominence, and complexity of that fund. The New York City office assumed primary responsibility for the Fund of Funds audit. Finally, Andersen's Denver office performed selected audit procedures each year on the Fund of Funds' NRPA. The Denver office also audited King Resources, which was headquartered in Denver. In fact, the partner in charge of the King Resources audit and the principal manager assigned to that audit supervised the NRPA segment of the Fund of Funds audit.

A central issue in the suit filed against Arthur Andersen by the Fund of Funds' bankruptcy trustee was Andersen's awareness of the excessive prices King Resources charged the mutual fund for oil and gas properties. Arthur Andersen's Fund of Funds workpapers noted that King Resources had "carte blanche authority to buy oil and gas properties" for the NRPA. The Denver office of Arthur Andersen also had complete access to King Resources' accounting data that documented the cost of the properties sold to Fund of Funds and the profit margins on those sales.

A closely related issue was exactly when Arthur Andersen discovered that Fund of Funds was being charged exorbitant prices for oil and gas properties by King Resources. Arthur Andersen issued its audit report on Fund of Funds' 1968 financial statements on February 5, 1969. Plaintiff counsel in the Fund of Funds litigation attempted to establish that Arthur Andersen knew when it prepared its 1968 audit report that King Resources was overcharging Fund of Funds for the oil and gas properties.

A final issue addressed at length in the Fund of Funds civil suit was Arthur Andersen's awareness of, and involvement in, several so-called revaluation transactions arranged by King Resources for Fund of Funds. Because Fund of Funds was an open-ended mutual fund, on a daily basis it revalued its entire portfolio. To compute its net asset value (NAV), Fund of Funds established a market value for each of its investments, including its natural resource properties. This collective market value was then divided by the number of outstanding mutual fund shares to arrive at the NAV. Mutual funds use their NAV to distribute proceeds to shareholders electing to redeem their shares. The illiquid nature of Fund of Funds' NRPA investments complicated the computation of its daily NAV. King Resources periodically sold parcels of natural resource properties owned by Fund of Funds to establish a fair market value for the residual portions of those properties retained by the mutual fund. Alternatively, King Resources would sell a portion of its own equity interest in these properties to establish a fair market value for Fund of Funds' NRPA investments.[2]

Evidence presented during the Fund of Funds trial demonstrated that many of the revaluation transactions arranged by King Resources were fraudulent. In at least two cases, King Resources found a third party that agreed to buy a small portion of either Fund of Funds' or King Resources' interest in an oil and gas property at a price considerably higher than its fair market value. Unknown to Fund of Funds' officials, King Resources made secret "side agreements" with the purchasers of these properties. These side agreements obligated King Resources to compensate the purchasers for any losses they subsequently incurred on these properties. Because of these side agreements, the revaluation transactions were not arm's length transactions and thus not a valid basis for establishing a fair market value for the given properties. King Resources arranged these fraudulent revaluation transactions to convince Fund of Funds' executives that the natural resource investments were profitable. Since these transactions grossly inflated the NAV of Fund of Funds' shares, the investors who redeemed their shares following these transactions profited from them. On the other hand, these transactions adversely affected those investors who retained their mutual fund shares indefinitely.

ARTHUR ANDERSEN'S 1968 AND 1969 AUDITS OF FUND OF FUNDS

Court records in the Fund of Funds trial documented that Arthur Andersen considered the IOS and Fund of Funds audits high-risk engagements. The highest-risk financial statement items in the 1968 and 1969 Fund of Funds audits were the large investments in natural resource properties. During the Fund of Funds trial, plaintiff counsel established that Arthur Andersen had "repeated serious difficulties with King as a client at least since 1961" and had expressed concern regarding several of King's questionable business practices. These prior difficulties with John King placed Arthur Andersen on notice that the Fund of Funds–King Resources transactions needed to be scrutinized closely.

During the 1968 Fund of Funds audit, Arthur Andersen personnel in the Denver office compiled King Resources' sales data for its natural resource properties. These data revealed that King Resources realized much higher gross profit margins on properties sold to Fund of Funds than it did on properties sold to other customers. The accounting firm documented the following gross profit per-

---

2. King Resources retained a 12.5 percent equity interest in most of the natural resource properties it sold to Fund of Funds.

centages for five of the sales made by King Resources to Fund of Funds: 98.7, 98.6, 85.6, 58, and 56.7 percent. These gross profit percentages appeared particularly excessive since most of the properties had been owned only a short time by King Resources before being sold to Fund of Funds. The court reached the following conclusion regarding Arthur Andersen's knowledge of the prices charged Fund of Funds by King Resources: "It is reasonable to find that AA knew what FOF paid for the [natural resource] interests purchased in 1968, that AA knew what King Resources paid for them, and that AA knew King Resources' profits [on these transactions] prior to February 5, 1969, when the FOF audit report was filed."

During the trial in the Fund of Funds case, a lengthy debate ensued regarding the client confidentiality rule. That debate focused on whether the confidentiality rule precluded Arthur Andersen from using the sales data obtained from King Resources to audit Fund of Funds' natural resource investments. Clouding this issue was the close linkage between the Fund of Funds and King Resources audits.

> The NRPA audit was performed by using the records of King Resources, and sometimes AA staffers would work on the King Resources and NRPA audits contemporaneously. Thus, AA's understanding of the ongoing business relationship between FOF and the King group can be determined from documents found in AA files for King Resources or NRPA and from testimony regarding the actual conduct of the audits.

Another critical issue Arthur Andersen faced during the Fund of Funds audits was the validity of the revaluation transactions. In December 1968, John King arranged for Fund of Funds to sell 10 percent of a natural resource property to Fox–Raff, a Seattle brokerage firm audited by Arthur Andersen. This sale allowed Fund of Funds to recognize a $900,000 increase in the value of its investment portfolio. Arthur Andersen questioned this transaction, since Fund of Funds had owned the property a very short time and since there were no new geological data suggesting that the market value of the property had risen. Arthur Andersen also doubted whether the sale of a 10 percent interest in the property justified recognizing an increase in the remaining 90 percent interest retained by Fund of Funds.

In January 1969, Phil Carr, the Arthur Andersen partner in the Denver office responsible for both the King Resources audit and the audit of Fund of Funds' NRPA investments, discovered that the Fox–Raff transaction was not a bona fide sale. King had provided Fox–Raff with the required down payment for the purchase transaction and relieved the brokerage firm of any commitment to pay the balance of the purchase price. Carr passed this information on to John Robinson of the New York City office of Arthur Andersen, the engagement audit partner for Fund of Funds. According to court records, the Fox–Raff transaction was ultimately discussed at the "very highest partnership level" within Arthur Andersen. For undisclosed reasons, the accounting firm chose not to inform Fund of Funds' executives that the Fox–Raff sale was not an arm's length transaction. Arthur Andersen also decided that the revaluation of the Fund of Funds assets due to the Fox–Raff transaction had not materially affected the mutual fund's NAV. Shortly after this latter decision was made, Arthur Andersen issued an unqualified opinion on Fund of Funds' 1968 financial statements. (Because of the complexity of this case, Exhibit 1 provides a glossary of the principal parties involved, as well as a summary of certain of the key events.)

EXHIBIT 1
Key Parties and Events in the Fund of Funds Case

Blakely–Wolcott transaction. A transaction that involved the sale of an oil and gas property by King Resources to a third party in 1966. Arthur Andersen subsequently discovered that John King had negotiated an undisclosed and illicit "side agreement" with the purchaser of the property that invalidated the sale as an arm's length transaction. This discovery was significant because it cast doubt on the integrity of the audit evidence Arthur Andersen collected from John King to support Fund of Funds' 1969 financial statements.

Phil Carr. An Arthur Andersen partner assigned to the firm's Denver office. Carr supervised both the King Resources audit and the audit of Fund of Funds' NRPA.

Bernie Cornfeld. The founder of Investors Overseas Services.

Fox–Raff transaction. A transaction involving the sale of a small portion of an oil and gas property owned by Fund of Funds to a Seattle brokerage firm. John King arranged the transaction to establish a fair market value for the portion of the property retained by Fund of Funds. Arthur Andersen discovered, after the fact, that King had a "side agreement" with the brokerage firm.

Investors Overseas Services (IOS). An investment company founded by Bernie Cornfeld in 1956. One of the many mutual funds managed by IOS was The Fund of Funds, Ltd.

John McCandish King. The founder and principal owner of King Resources.

King Resources. An investment company specializing in natural resource properties. King Resources sold Fund of Funds more than $100 million of oil and gas properties during the late 1960s.

John Mecom. An investor who purchased a small percentage of a large oil and gas property owned by Fund of Funds. This transaction allowed Fund of Funds to increase the value of its residual interest in the property by $119 million.

John Orr. A Touche Ross partner who was appointed the bankruptcy trustee for Fund of Funds.

John Robinson. A New York partner with Arthur Andersen who served as the audit engagement partner for Fund of Funds.

While planning the 1969 Fund of Funds audit, Phil Carr developed a set of guidelines to be used in auditing subsequent revaluation transactions. Two factors prompted Carr to develop these guidelines. First, Carr wanted to avoid a controversy similar to that which arose following the discovery of the non-arm's length nature of the Fox–Raff revaluation transaction. Second, Carr developed these guidelines in reaction to the larger role his audit team would play in the 1969 Fund of Funds audit. Court testimony disclosed that during the 1969 audit Arthur Andersen's Denver office assumed "full audit responsibility for the investment [NRPA] account both as to cost and market value." During the 1968 engagement, Phil Carr had perceived the Denver office's role in the Fund of Funds audit as primarily collecting and compiling information for the New York City audit team regarding the mutual fund's natural resource investments. The higher level of responsibility assigned to his audit team for the risky Fund of Funds audit troubled Carr. Also troubling to him was a stern warning he had been given by the IOS audit engagement partner in Geneva. That partner told Carr that it would not be appropriate simply to disclose the valuation method used by Fund of Funds for its natural resource properties if such disclosure "does not fairly present the facts."

In November 1969, Carr drafted a memo discussing the guidelines Arthur Andersen would follow in reviewing revaluation transactions. The memorandum, reproduced in Exhibit 2, was approved by the regional director of Arthur Andersen's West Coast audit practice and by an executive partner in the firm's

EXHIBIT 2
Arthur Andersen Memo
Dictating Conditions
for Recognizing
Increases in the Value of
Fund of Funds' Natural
Resource Properties

November 7, 1969

Any significant increase in the value of natural resource properties over original cost to FOF must, for audit purposes, be supported by either:

1) An appraisal report rendered by a competent, independent expert, or

2) an arm's length sale of a sufficiently large portion of a property to establish a proportionate value for the portion retained.

Item 2 above is where we currently are not in clear agreement with the client. King Resources Company has been informed by FOF (purportedly Ed Cowett, Executive Vice President) that sale of a 10% interest in a property would be sufficient for FOF's purposes in ascribing a proportionate value to the 90% retained. This procedure was first used at December 31, 1968, when King Resources Company arranged, on behalf of FOF, for the sale of a 10% interest in an oil and gas drilling prospect and certain uranium claims and leases to Fox–Raff, Inc., a Seattle brokerage firm affiliate.

Since our responsibilities here in Denver with respect to the December 31, 1968, FOF audit consisted only of determining the basis on which King Resources determined the valuations (not auditing such values), we discussed this transaction with John Robinson and Nick Constantakis in New York but left any final audit decision up to them. It is our understanding that the King Resources valuations determined by the 10% sale were allowed to stand in the final FOF audit report.

On the question of what constitutes adequate sales data for valuation purposes (i.e., the 10% question), we have proposed the following to King Resources:

1) No unrealized appreciation would be allowed on sales of relatively small percentages of properties to private investors or others who do not have the necessary expertise to determine a realistic fair market value. By "relatively small," we envision approximately 50% as being a minimum level in this type of sale to establish proportionate values for the remaining interests. This would preclude any unrealized appreciation on sales such as the December, 1968, sale to Fox–Raff, Inc. since it could not be reasonably sustained that a brokerage firm has the expertise necessary to evaluate primarily undeveloped resource interests.

2) Appreciation would be allowed if supported by arm's length sales to knowledgeable outside parties. For example, if King Resources sold a 25% interest in the Arctic permits to Texaco or another major oil company, we believe it would be appropriate to ascribe proportionate value to the 75% retained. Just where to draw the line on the percentage has not been clearly established. We feel 10% would be a bare minimum and would like to see a higher number.

Drafted by: Phil Carr, Partner,
Denver Office of AA & Co.

Chicago headquarters. Arthur Andersen gave copies of the memo to a Fund of Funds officer and to executives of King Resources.

In late 1969, King Resources began searching for a third party to purchase a small interest in a large natural resource property in the Arctic that Fund of Funds had previously acquired from King Resources. A revaluation transaction was needed to establish the property's fair market value. King Resources attempted to structure a revaluation transaction that would satisfy the key stipulations included in Phil Carr's memo shown in Exhibit 2. Eventually, King Resources arranged for a sale of slightly less than 10 percent of the Arctic property to John Mecom. Mecom was the principal owner of U.S. Oil of Louisiana, another Arthur Andersen audit client. At the time, Mecom was experiencing serious financial difficulties. In fact, Arthur Andersen's managing partner had met with Mecom and John King in February 1968 to help Mecom resolve his financial problems.

The Arctic revaluation transaction allowed Fund of Funds to recognize a more than 25 percent increase in the value of its total investment portfolio—an increase of approximately $119 million. Unknown to Arthur Andersen, John King had negotiated a side agreement with Mecom, similar to the agreement he had arranged with Fox–Raff the previous year. Because of this side agreement, the Mecom transaction failed to qualify as a valid arm's length sale, and thus was not a proper basis for increasing the value of Fund of Funds' residual interest in the Arctic property.

The impact of the Arctic revaluation transaction on Fund of Funds' investment portfolio alarmed Phil Carr. Carr discussed the transaction with the regional director of Arthur Andersen's West Coast audit practice. He informed the regional director that the Denver office's review of the revaluation transaction alone did not provide sufficient evidence to support the increased market value ascribed to Fund of Funds' investment in the Arctic property. The regional director supported Carr's position. Carr went on to argue that Arthur Andersen's headquarters office in Chicago should assume final responsibility for approving the valuation of Fund of Funds' natural resource investments.

Several executive partners of Arthur Andersen discussed and analyzed the NRPA investments before the accounting firm issued its 1969 Fund of Funds audit opinion. This discussion focused on whether it was possible to reach a firm audit conclusion regarding the fair market value of the investments. The IOS audit engagement partner in Geneva was very concerned with the possibility of Fund of Funds receiving a qualified audit opinion. That individual remarked that a qualification would cause an "explosion" at Fund of Funds. Nevertheless, Arthur Andersen issued the audit report shown in Exhibit 3 on Fund of Funds' 1969 financial statements. In that audit report, Arthur Andersen declined to express an opinion on whether Fund of Funds' NRPA investments were properly valued. (Notice that the opinion paragraph of the audit report includes a "subject to" qualification relating to the proper valuation of the NRPA investments.)

EXHIBIT 3
Arthur Andersen's Audit Opinion on Fund of Funds' 1969 Financial Statements

To the Shareholders and Board of Directors,
The Fund of Funds, Limited:

We have examined the consolidated statements of net assets and investments of The Fund of Funds, Limited (an Ontario, Canada, corporation) and subsidiary as of December 31, 1969, and the related consolidated statements of fund operations and changes in net assets for the year then ended. Our examination was made in accordance with generally accepted auditing standards, and accordingly included such tests of the accounting records and such other auditing procedures as we considered necessary in the circumstances. Investments owned by the Fund at December 31, 1969, were confirmed directly to us by the custodian or brokers. The position of investments sold short was confirmed directly to us by the custodian or brokers. Consistent with past practice, certain investments, in the absence of quoted market prices, have been valued by the Board of Directors as indicated in Note 9. These valuations have been reviewed by us to ascertain that they have been determined on the bases described, but since we are not competent to appraise these investments we do not express an opinion as to such valuations.

In our opinion, subject to the effect of certain investment valuations referred to in the preceding paragraph, the above-mentioned financial statements present fairly the financial position of The Fund of Funds, Limited and subsidiary as of December 31, 1969, and the results of their operations and the changes in their net assets for the year then ended, in conformity with generally accepted accounting principles applied on a basis consistent with that of the preceding year.

Arthur Andersen's review of the 1969 Arctic revaluation transaction became a focal point of the trial in the Fund of Funds civil suit. In evaluating Arthur Andersen's review of that transaction, the judge in the Fund of Funds case focused on Andersen's awareness of what became known as the Blakely–Wolcott transaction—a transaction that accounted for nearly 40 percent of King Resources' 1966 net income. The Blakely–Wolcott transaction involved another sale of an oil and gas property by King Resources in which John King had negotiated an illicit and undisclosed side agreement with the purchaser of the property. Although similar to the Fox–Raff and Mecom transactions, the Blakey–Wolcott deal did not involve Fund of Funds. The audit workpapers for the 1966 King Resources audit documented that Arthur Andersen had questioned the validity of the transaction. In fact, the workpapers noted that the Blakely–Wolcott transaction was a "borderline case of simply writing up property." Nevertheless, Arthur Andersen accepted King Resources' accounting treatment for the transaction. Andersen made this decision only after obtaining a representation letter from John King in which he denied the existence of any side agreements related to the Blakely–Wolcott sale.

In early 1970, before signing off on the 1969 Fund of Funds audit, Arthur Andersen's Denver office uncovered concrete evidence indicating that the Blakely–Wolcott transaction was fraudulent. This discovery impugned the integrity of all of the audit evidence collected from John King and King Resources to support the 1969 Fund of Funds' financial statements. Most important, this discovery cast doubt on the audit evidence used to corroborate the large increase in the fair market value of the Arctic property. Nevertheless, as observed by the judge in the Fund of Funds case, Arthur Andersen still chose to rely heavily on evidence collected from John King and King Resources while completing the 1969 audit.

> AA's audit thus continued after the December 1969 Arctic revaluation and after AA knew about Blakely–Wolcott. AA sought and obtained representation letters from King and [an associate] that the Arctic sale was bona fide. Although AA obtained representation letters from Mecom and [an associate] confirming the terms of the express purchase [Arctic] agreement, no inquiry was made of Mecom concerning side agreements as was made to King Resources.

THE FUND OF FUNDS, LIMITED V. ARTHUR ANDERSEN & CO.: ALLEGATIONS AND COURT RULINGS

In the civil suit filed against Arthur Andersen by the Fund of Funds' bankruptcy trustee, the principal allegation was that Andersen allowed King Resources to defraud Fund of Funds. The trustee argued that Arthur Andersen should have disclosed to Fund of Funds the prices paid by King Resources for properties later sold to the mutual fund. These data, which were obtained by Arthur Andersen during the annual audits of King Resources, would have revealed that Fund of Funds was being charged exorbitant amounts for those oil and gas properties. The trustee also alleged that Arthur Andersen should have disclosed to Fund of Funds its doubts regarding the validity of the Arctic revaluation transaction. According to the trustee, Fund of Funds would not have relied on the Arctic transaction to revalue its investment portfolio if Arthur Andersen had disclosed its concerns regarding the transaction's validity.

Finally, the trustee alleged that Arthur Andersen breached its contractual obligation to disclose to Fund of Funds' officers irregularities [fraud] discovered during the annual audits of the mutual fund. Exhibit 4 presents an excerpt from the engagement letter for the 1968 Fund of Funds audit. As indicated in the final paragraph of that excerpt, Arthur Andersen had agreed to disclose any irregularities discovered during the audit to Fund of Funds' officers.

Arthur Andersen responded to each allegation made by the Fund of Funds' bankruptcy trustee. First, the accounting firm maintained that disclosing to Fund of Funds information obtained during audits of King Resources would have violated the client confidentiality rule.[3] Second, Arthur Andersen insisted that Fund of Funds' board of directors had the primary responsibility for determining whether the Arctic revaluation transaction justified revaluing the mutual fund's remaining equity interest in the Arctic property. In this same vein, Arthur Andersen contended that there was no available evidence prior to that transaction, and very little afterwards, that suggested it was fraudulent. Arthur Andersen also argued that the plaintiff had not proved that the revaluation transaction resulted in a material overstatement of the mutual fund's NAV. Finally, Andersen asserted that none of the transactions or activities discovered during the Fund of Funds audits qualified as irregularities and thus were not subject to being reported to client management.

The presiding judge in the Fund of Funds case ruled that Arthur Andersen knew that King Resources was defrauding the mutual fund. In the judge's opinion, Arthur Andersen had a responsibility to disclose to Fund of Funds the prices that King Resources paid to acquire the oil and gas properties ultimately sold to

EXHIBIT 4
Excerpt from Arthur Andersen's Engagement Letter for 1968 Fund of Funds Audit

Our audit work on companies for which we are responsible will consist of examination of the respective balance sheets and statements of net assets and investments as of December 31, 1968, and the related statements of income, surplus and changes in net assets for the year then ending in order to enable us to express an opinion on the financial position and the results of their operations. These examinations will be made in accordance with generally accepted auditing standards and will include all auditing procedures which we consider necessary in the circumstances. These procedures will include, among other things, review and tests of the accounting procedures and internal controls, tests of documentary evidence supporting the transactions recorded in the accounts and direct confirmation of certain assets and liabilities by correspondence with selected customers, creditors, legal counsel, banks, etc.

While certain types of defalcations and similar irregularities may be disclosed by this kind of an examination, it is not designed for that purpose and will not involve the audit of a sufficiently large portion of the total transactions to afford assurances that any defalcations and irregularities will be uncovered. Generally, primary reliance for such disclosure is placed on a company's system of internal control and effective supervision of its accounts and procedures. *Of course, any irregularities coming to our attention would be reported to you immediately.* [Emphasis added by court.]

---

3. Plaintiff legal counsel argued that Arthur Andersen, at the very least, had a responsibility to resign from the Fund of Funds engagement after discovering that King Resources was charging the mutual fund exorbitant prices for the oil and gas properties. Arthur Andersen's attorneys observed that even if their firm had resigned, Fund of Funds would not have benefited, since its management would still have been unaware of King Resources' pricing structure.

the mutual fund—even though Andersen collected these data during the audits of King Resources. The judge also ruled that Arthur Andersen should have disclosed to Fund of Funds its concerns regarding the Arctic revaluation transaction.

> Moreover, AA knew all the facts which reasonably suggested that the methodology and result of the 1969 Arctic revaluation was a sham and yet AA persisted in the misleading and incomplete disclosures. . . . Although Fund of Funds management bears primary responsibility for business decisions, the auditor must inform the client when the basic terms of business dealings are so confused as to effectively prevent any conclusions as to the client's financial picture.

The judge found that the Arctic revaluation transaction clearly had a material effect on Fund of Funds' NAV and, thus, had a "substantial likelihood" of influencing a reasonable investor. Because the Fund of Funds' trustee sued Arthur Andersen under the Securities Exchange Act of 1934, the trustee had to prove scienter, or intent to deceive, on the part of Arthur Andersen. The judge ruled that Arthur Andersen exhibited such a reckless disregard for the truth that the scienter standard was satisfied.[4]

Regarding the breach of contract allegation, the judge found that Arthur Andersen failed to satisfy its contractual commitment to report irregularities discovered during the Fund of Funds audits to the mutual fund's officers. In particular, the judge ruled that the Arctic revaluation transaction was fraudulent and thus an irregularity that should have been reported to Fund of Funds' management. The judge emphasized three points in making this ruling: (1) Arthur Andersen knew, prior to issuing its audit opinion on the 1969 Fund of Funds' financial statements, that John King had engaged in a similar fraudulent sale in 1966, namely, the Blakely–Wolcott transaction;[5] (2) Arthur Andersen knew that John Mecom did not have the financial wherewithal to buy a 10 percent interest in the Arctic property; and (3) Arthur Andersen failed to ask Mecom whether the Arctic transaction included a side agreement with John King.

Two issues in the Fund of Funds case had particularly important implications for the public accounting profession. The first of these issues concerned the client confidentiality defense asserted by Arthur Andersen. Arthur Andersen insisted that the client confidentiality rule precluded it from disclosing to Fund of Funds' executives the excessive prices King Resources was charging the mutual fund for oil and gas properties. The judge in the Fund of Funds case discredited this argument.

> AA's invocation of the shield of client confidentiality conveniently disregards the fact that King Resources' and [an affiliated firm's] records were used for the NRPA audits and that on numerous occasions AA sought information about the King Resources/FOF relationship from the King group. Assuming that the duty of confidentiality applies in this instance . . . [the auditor] may: (1) strongly encourage one client to make the necessary disclosure; (2) disclose that it has relevant information not available to the other client; or (3) resign from one account. AA did none of these.

---

4. Another important issue in the Fund of Funds case was exactly what standards of conduct governed Arthur Andersen's performance during its audits of the large mutual fund. According to the judge in this case, "GAAS were relevant to but not determinative of AA's duties of inquiry and disclosure."

5. At the time, Arthur Andersen was also aware that the 1968 Fox–Raff revaluation transaction, another transaction arranged by John King, was not legitimate.

A second important issue raised by the Fund of Funds case involved the profession's audit reporting standards. Arthur Andersen's audit report on Fund of Funds' 1969 financial statements contained a "subject to" qualification, as shown in Exhibit 3. The judge ruled that the "subject to" qualification failed to adequately warn financial statement users that Arthur Andersen seriously questioned the valuation of Fund of Funds' NRPA: "The addition of the words 'subject to' in the 1969 FOF Annual Report was neither soon enough nor complete enough to avoid substantial damage to FOF." Several years later, the profession eliminated "subject to" qualifications.

EPILOGUE

Following a two-month trial in the summer of 1981, the Fund of Funds' bankruptcy trustee was awarded an $80.7 million judgment against Arthur Andersen. In July 1982, Judge Charles Stewart, who presided over the trial, reduced that judgment by approximately $10 million. Nevertheless, the huge size of the judgment raised concerns within the profession regarding the economic viability of accounting firms, particularly smaller national firms that might be forced into bankruptcy if required to pay such a large sum. Ironically, the Fund of Funds shareholders, who were the principal victims of the frauds perpetrated by John King, ultimately recovered the majority of their losses. The Arthur Andersen judgment alone allowed them to recoup a significant portion of their original investments in the mutual fund. The shareholders received an even larger payoff following the discovery of oil on the large Arctic property that John King pawned off on the mutual fund in 1969.[6]

John King was convicted and sentenced to prison for the fraudulent transactions he arranged through King Resources. King spent less than two years in prison. Shortly after his release, he suffered a broken neck when he fell from his horse. King died a few months later. Bernie Cornfeld served nearly one year in a Swiss prison after being indicted for securities fraud, although he was never convicted of that charge. In 1970, Cornfeld lost control of IOS to a prominent businessman and financier, Robert Vesco. Approximately three years later, the SEC filed suit against Vesco, charging him with stealing $224 million from the IOS funds. Vesco fled the United States and became one of the most sought-after fugitives in U.S. history. For more than two decades, Vesco lived in Havana under the protection of his friend, Fidel Castro. That friendship apparently ended in 1996 when a Cuban court convicted Vesco of defrauding investors in a venture intended to develop a "wonder" drug effective against cancer. Vesco received a 13-year prison sentence.

After being released from Swiss prison, Bernie Cornfeld spent most of his remaining years in Acapulco. In 1992, Cornfeld resurfaced in the headlines of U.S. newspapers when he unsuccessfully attempted to purchase MGM Studios in Hollywood. During the last few years of his life, Cornfeld squandered his fortune on a string of bad investments. He died in a London hospital of natural causes in

---

6. Following the liquidation of Fund of Funds, its former shareholders received shares of stock in a company that was formed to assume ownership of the Arctic property.

1995. Cornfeld's close friends established a memorial fund to pay his large hospital bill.

QUESTIONS

1. Was it appropriate for Arthur Andersen's Denver office to audit King Resources and to be involved in the audit of Fund of Funds' NRPA investments? Identify the advantages and disadvantages of this arrangement for Arthur Andersen.

2. According to the judge in the Fund of Funds case, Arthur Andersen could have resigned from the Fund of Funds engagement when it discovered the excessive prices being charged the mutual fund by King Resources. Arthur Andersen contended that resigning at that point would not have benefitted Fund of Funds. Do you agree? Why or why not? Does the profession's *Code of Professional Conduct* recommend a course of action in this set of circumstances?

3. During the 1968 Fund of Funds audit, the engagement audit partner decided that the revaluation of the mutual fund's assets following the Fox–Raff transaction did not materially affect its NAV. Do you believe that was an appropriate decision? Defend your answer. What precedent, if any, did that decision establish for future audits of Fund of Funds?

4. Arthur Andersen contended during the Fund of Funds trial that the client's board of directors was primarily responsible for reviewing and eventually approving revaluation transactions. Do you agree with that position? Why did the judge reject this argument?

5. During the 1966 audit of King Resources, Arthur Andersen placed significant reliance on the letter of representations signed by John King. That letter indicated that the Blakely–Wolcott sale was an arm's length transaction. What are the primary objectives an auditor hopes to accomplish by obtaining a letter of representations from client management? How competent is the audit evidence provided by a letter of representations?

6. What additional evidence could Arthur Andersen have obtained to evaluate the legitimacy of the Arctic revaluation transaction?

7. Discuss the general elements of proof a plaintiff must establish when bringing a suit under the Securities Exchange Act of 1934. Briefly discuss the evidence that Fund of Funds' attorneys likely presented to the court to establish each of these elements of proof.

8. The judge in the Fund of Funds case criticized the qualified audit opinion Arthur Andersen issued on Fund of Funds' 1969 financial statements as being "neither soon enough nor complete enough to avoid substantial damage to Fund of Funds." Draft an audit report that would be appropriate for the 1969 Fund of Funds' financial statements, given present audit reporting standards.

Case 1.10
AMRE, Inc.

In the popular movie *The Tin Men* released in 1987, Richard Dreyfus and Danny DeVito portray aluminum siding salesmen during the early 1960s. The two competitors use every means possible to obtain an unfair advantage over each other. Like other aluminum siding salesmen, the key to success for Dreyfus and DeVito is obtaining and vigorously pursuing "leads," or indications of interest from potential customers. Leads are not only a key success factor for home siding companies but also figure prominently in many of these firms' accounting and control systems. Take the case of AMRE, Inc., a firm that for nearly two decades sold home siding and interior refurnishing products such as cabinet countertops. AMRE, short for American Remodeling, began operations in 1980 in Irving, Texas, home of the Dallas Cowboys. Within a few years, the fast-growing firm ranked as the largest company in the home siding industry, an industry historically dominated by small businesses that market their services in one metropolitan area. In 1987, AMRE went public and listed its common stock on the New York Stock Exchange.

AMRE's principal operating expenses were advertising costs incurred to identify potential leads via direct mail and television commercials. Throughout the 1980s, AMRE charged a portion of its advertising costs each year to a deferred expense account. AMRE justified this accounting treatment by maintaining that these advertising costs benefited future periods. Each accounting period, AMRE divided its total advertising costs by the number of new leads generated that period. AMRE then multiplied the resulting "cost per lead" by the total number of "unset leads," that is, new leads that had not yet been pursued, to determine the amount of advertising costs to defer. The firm charged the remaining advertising costs for that period to its advertising expense account.

AMRE created a computer-based "lead bank" during the mid-1980s. When a potential customer contacted AMRE, a clerk collected and then entered information in the lead bank that could be used to develop an appropriate sales pitch for that individual. This information included variables such as age, income, home market value, and length of residency. Data for each sales presentation were also entered in the lead bank. This information allowed AMRE to evaluate each sales-person's performance by computing measures such as sales as a percentage of appointments, cancellation rate, and average dollar sales per appointment. The control functions and data provided by AMRE's computerized lead bank contributed significantly to the company's early success in the intensely competitive home siding industry.

Accounting for "Leads" Leads to Trouble

When AMRE went public in February 1987, the company's top officers issued optimistic revenue and profit projections to financial analysts tracking the firm. (At the time, AMRE's fiscal year ran from May 1 of one year until April 30 of the next. The company's first fiscal year as a public company, fiscal 1988, ended April 30, 1988.) As the end of AMRE's first quarter as a public company approached, July 31, 1987, the net income projected for that quarter earlier in the year was clearly unattainable.

Robert Levin, an AMRE executive and major stockholder, feared that AMRE's stock price would drop sharply if the company failed to reach its forecasted earnings for the first quarter of fiscal 1988. Levin, a CPA since 1972, served as the company's principal financial officer and held the titles of executive vice-president, treasurer, and chief operating officer. To inflate AMRE's net income for the first quarter of fiscal 1988, Levin instructed the company's chief accounting officer, Dennie D. Brown, to overstate the number of unset leads in AMRE's computerized lead bank.[1] Brown, in turn, instructed Walter W. Richardson, the company's vice-president of data processing who had served as AMRE's controller in the early 1980s, to enter fictitious unset leads in the lead bank. Entering the fictitious leads in the lead bank caused a disproportionate amount of AMRE's advertising costs for the first quarter of 1988 to be deferred rather than expensed. This accounting scam allowed AMRE to overstate its pretax income for that quarter by approximately $1 million, or by nearly 50 percent.

Once corporate executives misrepresent their firm's operating results for one accounting period, the temptation to manipulate its operating results in later periods becomes difficult to resist. In the second quarter of fiscal 1988, AMRE's executives again inflated the company's unset leads to understate the firm's advertising expenses.

During the third and fourth quarters of fiscal 1988, AMRE's actual operating results again fell far short of expectations. At this point, Levin decided to expand the scope of the accounting fraud. In addition to overstating unset leads, Levin instructed his subordinates to overstate AMRE's ending inventory for the third and fourth quarters of fiscal 1988. Richardson complied by entering fictitious inventory in AMRE's computerized inventory records and by preparing bogus

---

1. The information reported in this case was drawn principally from a series of enforcement releases issued by the Securities and Exchange Commission (SEC) in the early 1990s. The individuals involved in this case neither admitted nor denied the facts as represented by the SEC.

inventory count sheets that were later submitted to the company's Price Waterhouse auditors.

Levin also instructed AMRE's accounting personnel to overstate the company's revenue for the third and fourth quarters of fiscal 1988. AMRE used the percentage-of-completion method to recognize revenue on unfinished installation jobs at the end of an accounting period. To overstate the revenue booked on unfinished projects at the end of fiscal 1988, AMRE grossly overstated their percentage of completion. In fact, AMRE recognized revenue at the end of fiscal 1988 on customer projects that had not been started.

AMRE reported a pretax income of $12.2 million in its fiscal 1988 financial statements. A subsequent investigation by the Securities and Exchange Commission (SEC) revealed that AMRE's actual pretax income for that year was less than 50 percent of the reported figure. Before AMRE filed its 1988 10-K with the SEC, Levin met with AMRE's chief executive officer and chairman of the board, Steven D. Bedowitz. At this meeting, Levin admitted to Bedowitz for the first time that illicit accounting methods had been used to overstate AMRE's reported profit for 1988. According to the SEC's investigation, Bedowitz "concurred with these efforts to improperly increase AMRE's earnings."[2]

Bedowitz and Levin signed the "Letter to Shareholders" included in AMRE's 1988 annual report. That letter began with the following greeting: "We are proud to announce that fiscal 1988 was another record year for AMRE in both earnings and revenues." In a subsequent AMRE annual report, Levin recalled how he had met Bedowitz in 1981, several years before Levin accepted an executive position with AMRE. At the time, Levin worked for a building materials company that was an AMRE supplier.

> We discovered that we were very much alike. We both had a lot of energy, ambition, and dreams. Our partnership was inevitable.[3]

Price Waterhouse issued an unqualified opinion on AMRE's financial statements for fiscal 1988. Nevertheless, a financial analyst for *The New York Times* questioned the credibility of those financial statements.[4] The analyst pointed out that AMRE's use of the percentage-of-completion accounting method seemed unusual. Businesses typically use the percentage-of-completion method to recognize revenue on projects that take several months, if not years, to complete. AMRE's installation jobs required only a few days to complete. Even more troubling to the analyst was three weeks of "unbilled revenues" AMRE had recognized on unfinished installation jobs near the end of 1988. That figure seemed excessive since AMRE's average time to complete an installation job was one week. The analyst also questioned AMRE's advertising expense figure by pointing out that the company's deferred advertising costs had been rising rapidly. In summary, the analyst bluntly challenged the integrity of AMRE's financial statements.

> To short-sellers, it looks like a classic pattern of inflating revenues and understating expenses, a pattern that often ends in a write-off. Mr. Wesselman [an AMRE spokesper-

2. Securities and Exchange Commission, *Accounting and Auditing Enforcement Release No. 356*, 2 March 1992.

3. AMRE, Inc., 1989 Annual Report, 11.

4. F. Norris, "AMRE Drawing Short Sellers," *The New York Times*, 19 December 1988, D8.

son] said the company's accounting practices were proper and were periodically reviewed with outside auditors.[5]

AMRE's 1989 Fiscal Year

During fiscal 1989, AMRE's top executives continued to misrepresent the firm's reported operating results and financial condition. In addition to the schemes used the prior year, during fiscal 1989 AMRE's executives materially understated the company's accounts payable and materially overstated receivables.

Late in fiscal 1989, AMRE's executives decided to end the accounting fraud. The executives met regularly to discuss how best to terminate the fraud without raising the suspicions of the firm's Price Waterhouse auditors and other parties. One method the executives settled on was to transfer fictitious assets in AMRE's accounting records to the firm's Decks division. That division's principal line of business was building backyard decks on residential homes. Company officials had already decided to eliminate the Decks division. By transferring approximately $3 million of fictitious assets to that division, AMRE "buried" the write-offs of those assets in the discontinued operations section of its 1989 income statement. AMRE booked these write-offs principally during the third quarter of fiscal 1989.

Company executives wrote off approximately $5 million of additional fictitious assets as losses or expenses in the fourth quarter of fiscal 1989 via adjusting entries. These write-offs and those of the previous quarter resulted in AMRE reporting a net loss of nearly $6 million in 1989. Exhibit 1 summarizes key financial data included in AMRE's 1989 annual report for the five-year period 1985–1989.

The Role of AMRE's New CFO in Terminating the Accounting Fraud

In March 1989, near the end of AMRE's fourth quarter of fiscal 1989, AMRE hired Mac M. Martirossian to serve as the company's chief accounting officer. Martirossian, a CPA since 1976, had more than 10 years of public accounting ex-

EXHIBIT 1
Key Financial Data for AMRE, Inc., 1985–1989 (in thousands)

	Year Ended April 30,				
	1989	**1988**	**1987**	**1986**	**1985**
Contract revenues	$183,885	$121,033	$72,187	$39,575	$22,451
Contract costs	64,702	41,369	25,017	15,275	9,259
Gross profit	119,183	79,664	47,170	24,300	13,192
Operating income	1,602	9,983	6,153	1,516	661
Net income	(5,744)	7,298	2,907	878	414
Working capital	11,719	15,307	13,236	40	175
Total assets	50,399	34,113	23,527	7,239	2,471
Stockholders' equity	27,174	23,565	16,895	1,334	456

---

5. *Ibid.*

perience with the Dallas office of Price Waterhouse, which performed AMRE's annual audits. In July 1989, Martirossian assumed the title of chief financial officer (CFO). Levin, who had essentially served as AMRE's CFO for several years, retained the titles of executive vice-president, treasurer, and chief operating officer.

While becoming acquainted with AMRE's accounting system in his first few weeks with the firm, Martirossian discovered numerous accounting entries that lacked adequate documentation. Martirossian immediately began investigating this obvious internal control problem. No doubt, AMRE's top executives realized that the inquisitive accountant would eventually "put two and two together." So, they decided to reveal the fraud to Martirossian. (Recognize that by this point the executives had already begun terminating the fraud.)

The startling confession made by his new colleagues stunned Martirossian. On April 28, 1989, just two days before the end of fiscal 1989, Martirossian called a meeting with the executives involved in the fraud. At this meeting, he insisted that the misstatements remaining in the company's accounting records be immediately corrected. If the corrections were not made, Martirossian threatened to resign.

> Martirossian further stated that he would hold himself responsible for the company's financial statements for periods after fiscal 1989, but that the scheme's participants would be responsible for correcting the misstatements in the periods to which they related, and for addressing any questions [from AMRE's independent auditors and other parties] arising from the corrections.[6]

Bedowitz acquiesced to Martirossian's demand. Initially, the two men decided to correct AMRE's accounting records with a large prior period adjustment. In a matter of days, this plan backfired. Outside directors on AMRE's board became aware of the prior period adjustment and began questioning why it was necessary. At this point, AMRE's executives, including Martirossian, met to consider other alternatives for correcting the company's accounting records. The executives decided that the remaining errors in AMRE's accounting records would be written off against the operating results of the fourth quarter of fiscal 1989 via period-ending adjusting entries, as discussed earlier.

Shortly after the end of fiscal 1989, Martirossian attended several meetings between AMRE's top executives and representatives of Price Waterhouse. At these meetings, the large accounting adjustments made by AMRE during the fourth quarter of fiscal 1989 were discussed. According to the SEC, Martirossian sat silently while other company executives provided false explanations to Price Waterhouse regarding the large adjustments.

The efforts of his colleagues to mislead the Price Waterhouse auditors troubled Martirossian. Before Price Waterhouse completed its 1989 audit of AMRE, Martirossian arranged a confidential meeting at a local hotel with key Price Waterhouse personnel assigned to the AMRE audit. Martirossian had become well acquainted with several of these individuals during the 10 years he worked for Price Waterhouse's Dallas office.

> At this meeting, Martirossian expressed a high level of anxiety regarding the audit, and he specifically stated that a portion of the adjustments "did not pass the smell test." Further, he also posed questions to the auditors that linked seemingly unrelated audit

6. Securities and Exchange Commission, *Accounting and Auditing Enforcement Release No. 394*, 30 June 1992.

issues and events to the adjustments in an attempt to direct the auditors to the undisclosed scheme [accounting fraud].[7]

Although he hinted strongly to the auditors that AMRE's fourth-quarter writeoffs were suspicious, Martirossian never revealed the true nature or purpose of those adjustments. Price Waterhouse ultimately accepted the large fourthquarter adjustments before issuing an unqualified opinion on AMRE's 1989 financial statements.

Following the completion of the 1989 audit, Martirossian signed a letter of representations addressed to Price Waterhouse. This letter indicated that he and other key AMRE executives were not aware of any irregularities that would materially affect the accuracy of the company's financial statements.

During fiscal 1990, Martirossian undertook an extensive effort to improve AMRE's accounting and financial reporting functions. This effort included implementing several measures to strengthen the company's internal control system. Martirossian also searched the company's accounting records for any remaining errors and reviewed the company's accounting policies to ensure that they were being properly applied.

THE FRAUD IS DISCLOSED PUBLICLY

In 1990, the SEC revealed that it was investigating AMRE's financial statements for the previous few years. *The New York Times* article in late 1988 that challenged AMRE's financial data prompted that investigation. In early 1991, AMRE formed a special committee consisting of three outside members of its board to scrutinize the company's financial affairs. Following the report of this committee, AMRE publicly revealed that its financial statements for each year 1987 through 1990, but principally 1988 and 1989, contained material errors. AMRE issued restated financial statements for each of those years. From early 1992 through mid-1994, the SEC issued several enforcement releases disclosing the results of its lengthy investigation of AMRE's accounting fraud.[8]

Each of the AMRE executives who actively participated in the fraud, including Bedowitz, Levin, Brown, and Richardson, agreed to a consent order issued by the SEC. The executives neither admitted nor denied their alleged roles in the fraud but did agree not to violate federal securities laws in the future. Levin and Brown also forfeited proceeds they had received from the sale of AMRE stock while the fraud was in progress. This feature of the agreement required Brown to pay approximately $16,000 to the federal government. Levin paid nearly $1.8 million to the federal government, including a $500,000 fine for violating the provisions of the Insider Trading Sanctions Act.

In November 1991, *The Wall Street Journal* reported that Bedowitz, Levin, and AMRE, Inc., had reached an agreement to settle a large class action lawsuit filed by AMRE's stockholders.[9] This agreement required the two former AMRE exec-

---

7. *Ibid.*

8. AMRE's financial condition continued to deteriorate during the mid-1990s. In 1997, the company ceased operations and filed for involuntary bankruptcy.

9. K. Blumenthal, "AMRE, Ex-Officers Agree to Settlement of Stockholder Lawsuit," *The Wall Street Journal*, 12 November 1991, A13.

utives to contribute approximately $8.8 million to a settlement pool. AMRE, Inc., contributed another $5.9 million to the settlement pool.

Martirossian reached an agreement with the SEC similar to the agreement made by the federal agency with the other AMRE executives. However, the federal agency issued a separate enforcement release describing Martirossian's role in the fraud. The SEC criticized Martirossian for not insisting that proper measures be taken to correct AMRE's accounting records and for not disclosing the fraud to Price Waterhouse.

> Martirossian's non-participation in the original fraudulent scheme cannot justify his actions in turning a blind eye to the methods utilized by AMRE to correct the material misstatements. . . . Although he expressed concern and posed questions to AMRE's auditors in an attempt to expose the existence of the scheme to them, Martirossian's effort to discharge his duty to make accurate and complete disclosure to AMRE's auditors was ineffectual and misleading because he failed to provide the auditors all of the information he possessed.[10]

SEC INVESTIGATES PRICE WATERHOUSE'S 1988 AND 1989 AMRE AUDITS

After the SEC finished dealing with AMRE's executives, the federal agency turned its attention to the company's independent audit firm, Price Waterhouse. The SEC focused on the conduct of two members of the AMRE audit engagement team, Edward J. Smith and Joel E. Reed. Smith served as AMRE's audit engagement partner, while Reed was a senior audit manager assigned to the AMRE audits.

Among the SEC's complaints lodged against Price Waterhouse was that the audit firm failed to properly test AMRE's deferred advertising expenses. Recall that AMRE computed the advertising costs to be deferred for a given accounting period by multiplying the "cost per lead" for that period by the number of "unset leads" at the end of the period. One method AMRE used to inflate its reported profits was to create fictitious unset leads. Staff auditors of Price Waterhouse assigned to the AMRE engagement verified the cost-per-lead computation during the 1988 audit. However, the staff auditors failed to adequately test the number of unset leads reported by AMRE at the end of fiscal 1988. The auditors simply compared the number of unset leads on two client-prepared schedules.

> The audit of the unset leads deferral was flawed because no procedures were performed to verify the integrity of the reports on which the audit relied. In fact, the reports were not supported by underlying data. Although the number of unset leads supposedly had increased during the year by over 200% (from 10,438 to 31,580), the audit relied on AMRE's summary reports.[11]

Price Waterhouse's audit planning memorandum for the 1988 AMRE audit indicated that EDP audit procedures would be used to test the integrity of AMRE's lead bank. AMRE executives involved in the accounting fraud feared that these

---

10. Securities and Exchange Commission, *Accounting and Auditing Enforcement Release No. 394,* 30 June 1992.

11. Securities and Exchange Commission, *Accounting and Auditing Enforcement Release No. 554,* 26 April 1994.

procedures would result in detection of the fictitious leads in the lead bank. These executives persuaded Smith and Reed to bypass the EDP tests.

AMRE also inflated its reported profits by overstating year-end inventory. During fiscal 1988, AMRE's inventory increased by 213 percent, while sales increased 68 percent and inventory purchases increased 66 percent. The 1988 AMRE audit planning memorandum identified the large increase in inventory as a key risk factor. The audit planning memorandum also pointed out that AMRE did not use a perpetual inventory system, meaning that the year-end inventory quantities would be determined by a physical count.

Price Waterhouse's initial audit plan for 1988 called for the observation of the client's physical inventory counts at 11 of 26 inventory sites. The previous year, Price Waterhouse visited nine of 22 inventory sites during the physical counts. Client management complained that the increase in the number of inventory sites to be observed by Price Waterhouse would materially increase the cost of the 1988 audit. AMRE's executives convinced Price Waterhouse to allow AMRE accounting personnel to monitor the physical counts at three of the inventory sites that the auditors had selected for observation. According to the SEC's investigation, AMRE management inflated the year-end inventory of each of the 18 inventory sites not observed at year-end by Price Waterhouse. These inventory sites included the three sites where AMRE accounting personnel observed the physical counts. In total, AMRE overstated its 1988 year-end inventory by $1.4 million.

During the third and fourth quarters of fiscal 1989, AMRE began writing off its fictitious assets. Recall that AMRE's executives concealed several million dollars of such write-offs in the losses booked for the discontinued Decks division. The Price Waterhouse auditors reviewed the large losses stemming from the elimination of AMRE's Decks division during fiscal 1989. However, according to the SEC, the Price Waterhouse auditors accepted the client's explanations for these losses without applying any "meaningful audit procedures" to them.[12]

While writing off fictitious assets during the fourth quarter of 1989, AMRE purged 17,000 bogus unset leads from the computerized lead bank. The average cost of these leads was $108.33, meaning that the total loss related to their write-off exceeded $1.8 million. A Price Waterhouse staff auditor asked an AMRE accountant why the large number of unset leads was being dropped from the lead bank. The accountant responded that the unset leads had been improperly recorded due to an "accounting control weakness." In the audit workpapers, the staff auditor concluded, based on the AMRE accountant's statement, that this "weakness" was an "isolated incident" that did not require further investigation.[13] Smith and Reed concurred with the staff auditor's assessment and did not require any further audit procedures to be applied to the large adjustment.

The SEC also questioned Price Waterhouse's review of the quarterly financial data included in AMRE's 1989 10-K registration statement. Near the end of the 1989 audit, Smith recommended that AMRE disclose in the 10-K the large period-ending accounting adjustments that were largely responsible for the company's net loss for fiscal 1989. AMRE's executives refused. After reconsidering the matter, Smith noted in the audit workpapers that the fourth quarter adjustments did not need to be disclosed separately.

---

12. *Ibid.*

13. *Ibid.*

Smith concluded that the adjustments did not require disclosure because "the quarterly data is not part of the financial statements and the disclosure is informative only . . . the magnitude of the adjustments is not sufficient to cause us to require them to do it."[14]

A key factor that reportedly influenced Smith and Reed's decisions to accept AMRE's questionable accounting treatments was their familiarity with Martirossian, a former colleague of theirs in the Dallas office of Price Waterhouse. According to the SEC, Smith and Reed "relied improperly on his [Martirossian's] unverified representations based upon their prior experience with him and his reputation for integrity within Price Waterhouse."[15]

In an enforcement release issued in April 1994, the SEC concluded that Smith and Reed had failed to comply with generally accepted auditing standards during the 1988 and 1989 AMRE audits. As a result, the SEC prohibited Smith and Reed from being assigned to audits of SEC registrants for nine months.

QUESTIONS

1. Define the terms *ethics* and *professional ethics*. Using the following scale, evaluate the conduct of each individual involved in this case.

```
    -100 . . . . . . . . . . . . . . . . . . . . 0 . . . . . . . . . . . . . . . . . . . . 100
    Highly                                                          Highly
    Unethical                                                       Ethical
```

2. Do you believe that the individuals who behaved unethically in this case were appropriately punished? Defend your answer.

3. Identify the alternative courses of action available to Martirossian when he became aware of the accounting fraud at AMRE. Assume the role of Martirossian. Which of these alternatives would you have chosen? Why?

4. Was AMRE's practice of deferring a portion of its advertising costs in an asset account appropriate? Defend your answer.

5. What key red flags, or audit risk factors, were present during the 1988 and 1989 AMRE audits? Did Price Waterhouse appropriately consider these factors in planning those audits? Why or why not?

6. Was Price Waterhouse justified during the 1988 audit in agreeing to allow client personnel to observe the physical counts at certain inventory sites? To what extent should an audit client be allowed to influence key audit planning decisions?

7. *SAS No. 31*, "Evidential Matter," identifies five management assertions that underlie a set of financial statements. Which of these assertions should have been of most concern to Price Waterhouse regarding the large period-ending adjustments AMRE recorded during the fourth quarter of fiscal 1989?

8. What responsibility do auditors have for quarterly financial information reported in the footnotes to a client's audited financial statements?

---

14. *Ibid.*

15. *Ibid.*

CASE 1.11
GENERAL TECHNOLOGIES GROUP LTD.

Each year, the Securities and Exchange Commission (SEC) issues dozens of *Accounting and Auditing Enforcement Releases (AAERs)*. These releases, which the SEC began issuing in 1982, report major violations of generally accepted accounting principles (GAAP) and/or generally accepted auditing standards (GAAS). In August 1984, Frederick S. Todman & Company, a New York-based accounting firm, found itself the subject of *AAER No. 36*.

In *AAER No. 36*, the SEC charged Todman with "improper professional conduct" during its audits of a large brokerage firm, Bell & Beckwith. From 1977 through 1982, Todman issued unqualified audit opinions on Bell & Beckwith's annual financial statements. The SEC alleged that those audit opinions were "false and misleading" since Bell & Beckwith's financial statements contained material errors resulting from management fraud. Following are the specific charges the SEC leveled against Todman for its audits of Bell & Beckwith.

1. Todman failed to perform the audits with sufficient personnel having adequate technical training and auditing proficiency.
2. The Bell & Beckwith audits were not adequately planned and the staff auditors assigned to the engagements were not properly supervised.
3. A proper study and evaluation of Bell & Beckwith's internal control was not performed during the audits.
4. Todman auditors relied on management representations in the face of records and information evidencing those representations to be false.
5. The workpapers for the Bell & Beckwith audits did not adequately document the procedures performed and the conclusions drawn.

The SEC publicly censured Todman for the deficient Bell & Beckwith audits. Todman was also required to retain an "independent reviewer" to conduct an intensive study of its audit practices and procedures and to implement the recommendations made by the reviewer. Among the reviewer's recommendations was that Todman establish a quality control function. The individual staffing this function would perform a "pre-issuance review" on all Todman audits involving SEC registrants to ensure compliance with GAAS on those engagements. This individual would also approve the assignment of personnel and the issuance of audit reports on all SEC engagements.

ANOTHER "PROBLEM" CLIENT FOR TODMAN

Management fraud ranks among the worst fears of public accounting firms. Because management fraud is a rare phenomenon, most accounting firms have limited experience dealing with one of its principal consequences, namely, fraudulent financial statements. This is especially true of small accounting firms, such as Todman, which had only two practice offices and fewer than 10 partners in the late 1980s. Unfortunately, in a span of less than one decade, Todman experienced two close encounters with fraudulent schemes orchestrated by client executives.

One of Todman's practice offices was located on Long Island in Valley Stream, New York. During the 1980s, Todman audited General Technologies Group Ltd., a company based in nearby Copaigue. General Tech manufactured electrical components including aircraft instruments, postal vending machines, and a variety of electro-mechanical products sold principally to the military. Exhibit 1 summarizes key financial data reported by General Tech over the four-year period 1985–1988. (The company's fiscal year coincided with the calendar year.)

General Tech reported a net income of approximately $500,000 for 1985 on revenues of $11 million. Despite a sizable increase in revenues, 1986 was a poor year financially for General Tech. Preliminary data compiled in early 1987 by the company's accountants indicated that General Tech suffered a net loss of nearly $2 million in 1986. However, that loss was not reported in General Tech's 1986 financial statements, thanks to a fraudulent scheme hatched by the company's top executives.

A FRAUD IS BORN

Three individuals plotted and executed the fraud used to misrepresent General Tech's financial statement data during the late 1980s. Two of these three men were General Tech executives, the company's chief executive officer (CEO) and its vice-president of operations (VPO). The third schemer was an accountant but not

EXHIBIT 1
Selected Financial Data
Reported by General
Technologies, 1985–1988

	1988	1987	1986	1985
Net sales	$11,389,530	$13,638,344	$17,271,738	$10,899,202
Cost of goods sold	5,181,583	7,027,710	12,299,634	6,120,298
Income before income taxes	768,597	907,010	632,051	769,524
Net income	439,867	803,845	177,599	496,424
Total inventories	14,213,658	12,521,206	9,818,797	6,149,137
Work-in-process inventory	11,080,004	9,611,879	6,567,158	3,418,748

an employee of General Tech. General Tech had "outsourced" its principal accounting and financial reporting functions to this latter individual's accounting firm. SEC enforcement releases focusing on the General Tech fraud referred to this individual simply as the company's "Consultant."

Shortly after the close of General Tech's 1986 fiscal year, the company's CEO and Consultant discussed General Tech's poor operating results for that year. After deciding that reporting a loss for 1986 was unacceptable, the two men came up with a plan to dramatically—and fraudulently—improve the company's reported financial data for that year. The fraudulent scheme centered primarily on General Tech's inventory.

At the end of each year, General Tech prepared a Labor Inventory Report (LIR) for its work-in-process inventory, which was historically the largest component of the company's total inventories. The LIR, a computer-generated report, listed each WIP item and its three cost elements: labor, overhead, and materials. This report displayed the quantity, total cost per unit, and total extended cost of each WIP item. Separate computations (extensions) were reported for each cost element. For example, the amount of labor charged to each item was extended by the per unit cost of that labor. The LIR also reported the total cost of the year-end WIP inventory.

General Tech's Consultant instructed the VPO to materially overstate the dollar value of the company's WIP inventory on December 31, 1986. Although initially hesitant, the VPO complied with the Consultant's request when told to do so by General Tech's CEO. To overstate the year-end WIP inventory, the VPO modified the computer program that produced the LIR. This change in the computer program doubled the per unit labor cost charged to each WIP item at the end of 1986. Although the per unit labor cost was doubled by the program, the LIR reported the actual labor cost per unit. Thus, the product of the per unit labor cost and labor quantity listed on the LIR for any given WIP item equaled one-half of the product or extension of those amounts reported on the LIR. The overhead assigned to each WIP item was equal to 164 percent of the labor cost charged to that item. As a result, the overstatement of the labor charges triggered an even larger overstatement of the overhead charged to each WIP item.

The fraudulent inventory scheme understated General Tech's 1986 cost of goods sold by approximately $2,375,000. This understatement of cost of goods sold, when combined with a few smaller errors, converted the company's estimated net loss of nearly $2 million for 1986 into a reported net income of $177,000 for the year. A similar scheme was used to misrepresent General Tech's reported operating results for 1987 and 1988. However, in both of those years, the labor cost assigned to each WIP item was inflated by a factor of four. Of course, quadrupling the assigned labor costs resulted in an even larger overstatement of the overhead charged to WIP items. The net understatement of cost of goods sold for 1987 was approximately $1,373,000, while the comparable figure for 1988 was $1,430,000.[1]

In both 1987 and 1988, General Tech's reported operating results were affected by the fraudulent understatement of cost of goods sold and other irregularities perpetrated by company executives. In 1987, General Tech reported a net income

---

1. The understatements of cost of goods sold for 1987 and 1988 were net amounts. These amounts equaled the difference between the end-of-the-year and beginning-of-the-year overstatement of inventory in each case.

of $804,000, while the company actually experienced a net loss estimated at $2 million. For fiscal 1988, the company reported a net income of $440,000, while suffering an actual loss of more than $8 million.

TODMAN'S 1986 AUDIT OF GENERAL TECH

Alan Kappel, a partner of Frederick S. Todman & Company, served as the audit engagement partner for the 1986 through 1988 audits of General Tech. The audit engagement team for the 1986 audit consisted of Kappel, two Todman staff accountants, and three accountants employed by the accounting firm of General Tech's Consultant. Neither of the two Todman staff accountants was a CPA and only one had previous auditing experience. An SEC investigation revealed that the three employees of General Tech's Consultant created most of the "client-prepared" schedules to which audit tests were applied by themselves and the two Todman staff accountants. The SEC reported that Kappel played a minimal role in the 1986 audit. He apparently did not plan the audit, neglected to supervise the individuals who performed the fieldwork, and reviewed only a limited number of the audit workpapers. An SEC enforcement release harshly criticized Kappel's conduct during the 1986 General Tech audit.

> Kappel relied entirely on the Consultant's employees and the two Todman employees to perform the audit work. . . . The 1986 audit was not planned. No audit plan or audit program was prepared by Kappel or other Todman personnel. Instead, the [auditors] simply divided the work among themselves, with infrequent communication with Kappel. . . . Todman's audit was so deficient that Kappel and Todman failed to discover management's fraudulent conduct even though it would have been readily apparent had proper audit steps been performed.[2]

Kappel reportedly never reviewed the 1986 year-end LIR that was the focal point of the General Tech inventory fraud. However, a Todman staff accountant, apparently on his own initiative, obtained the LIR and applied limited audit procedures to that report. Among these procedures was a test of the clerical accuracy of the materials costs listed on the LIR for selected WIP items. For the items selected for testing, the staff accountant multiplied the quantity of materials charged to each item by the per unit cost of those materials. The staff accountant failed to apply a comparable test to the labor component of the WIP items. If such a test had been performed, the inventory fraud would have been easily detected since the labor extension for each WIP item did not equal the product of the item's labor quantity and per unit labor cost reported on the LIR.

> . . . had the auditors performed an arithmetic test of the extension of labor on the LIR, the test would have revealed labor values equal to one-half of the actual amount reported in the total column of the LIR.

Another audit procedure that would have detected the overstatement of labor assigned to the WIP inventory would have been comparing the LIR to the count sheets prepared during General Tech's year-end physical inventory. These count

---

2. Securities and Exchange Commission, *Accounting and Auditing Enforcement Release No. 552*, 22 April 1994. Unless indicated otherwise, the remaining quotes in this case were taken from this source.

sheets reflected the proper labor charges for each WIP item. A quick comparison of the two records would have revealed that the labor charges reported on the LIR for each WIP item were exactly double the labor charges reported on the count sheets for those items.

During the 1986 audit, one of the two Todman staff accountants assigned to the engagement did find a material inventory error. This error involved the raw materials inventory, not the client's WIP inventory. The auditor discovered that the dollar value of the raw materials inventory in General Tech's accounting records exceeded by $270,000 the dollar value determined by a physical count. Although the auditor documented this difference in the General Tech workpapers, the error was apparently never investigated and General Tech's accounting records were not corrected.

Despite performing limited, and often flawed, audit procedures on General Tech's accounting records, Todman issued an unqualified opinion on the client's 1986 financial statements. That opinion was dated March 27, 1987.

DISMISSAL AND RE-ENGAGEMENT OF TODMAN

Late in 1987, General Tech dismissed Todman as its independent auditor at the insistence of its bank. The company replaced Todman with Cooper, Selvin & Strassberg, another New York-based CPA firm.

Shortly after beginning its 1987 audit of General Tech, Cooper Selvin questioned the accuracy of the company's inventory value, which seemed disproportionately large compared to the 1986 inventory value. After further investigation, the auditors also challenged the large increase in General Tech's inventory between the end of 1985 and the end of 1986. The Cooper Selvin auditors uncovered the apparent source of the large increases in inventory when they reviewed General Tech's year-end LIRs for 1985 through 1987. A comparison of the 1985 and 1986 LIRs revealed that the per unit labor costs charged to inventory items in 1986 were exactly double the comparable charges for 1985. The auditors then discovered that the per unit labor charges for 1987 were quadruple the comparable charges applied to the 1985 year-end WIP inventory. When the Cooper Selvin auditors brought this matter to the client's attention, General Tech's executives fabricated false and implausible explanations for the increased labor charges.

Besides questioning the accuracy of General Tech's inventory valuation, Cooper Selvin raised other important issues with the company's management. For example, Cooper Selvin pointed out that the company failed to accrue certain expenses at the end of 1987. No doubt, General Tech's executives were unhappy with the inquisitive and persistent Cooper Selvin auditors, which likely explains why those executives dismissed the firm before it completed the 1987 audit.

After dismissing Cooper Selvin, General Tech contacted Alan Kappel and began negotiations to re-engage Todman as its independent audit firm. Following discussions with Todman's senior executives, Kappel agreed to replace Cooper Selvin as General Tech's audit firm. During the negotiations with General Tech, Kappel learned that Cooper Selvin had questioned the accuracy of the company's inventory valuation. Nevertheless, neither Kappel, nor any other Todman auditor, discussed this matter with Cooper Selvin personnel. Kappel did obtain copies of the workpapers that Cooper Selvin completed prior to its dismissal.

As required by the SEC, General Tech included information in its 1987 10-K registration statement regarding its auditor changes. Exhibit 2 presents that information. Notice that this disclosure did not specifically reveal Cooper Selvin's concern regarding the valuation of General Tech's inventory.

TODMAN'S 1987 AUDIT OF GENERAL TECH

The SEC charged that Todman's 1987 audit of General Tech was deficient in many respects. In fact, the 1987 audit suffered from the same flaws as the 1986 audit, primarily a lack of planning and supervision.

> The 1987 audit was inadequately planned. Kappel and the other Todman staff never developed an audit plan and no meetings were held with the audit staff prior to beginning work on the 1987 audit. As in the prior year's audit, the Todman audit staff simply divided the work among themselves and began with no direction from Kappel.

Similar to the 1986 audit, employees of the Consultant's accounting firm performed much of the fieldwork on the 1987 audit. Again, these individuals applied unsupervised audit tests to General Tech audit schedules that they had prepared. Several months following the completion of the 1987 audit, Kappel became concerned regarding these individuals' lack of independence. In October 1988, Kappel obtained a letter from General Tech's Consultant. In that letter, the Consultant stated that his accounting firm was independent of General Tech. Kappel also included a memo in the General Tech workpapers asserting that the Consultant's employees were supervised at "all times" by Todman personnel during the 1987 audit.

The SEC's criticism of Todman's 1987 audit of General Tech focused principally on the auditors' failure to detect the obvious errors in the LIR. Kappel knew that Cooper Selvin had discovered mathematical errors in the 1987 year-end LIR. In particular, he knew that Cooper Selvin had identified errors in the per unit costs of WIP inventory items in that accounting record. According to the SEC, had Kappel studied the General Tech workpapers prepared by Cooper Selvin, the fraudulent overstatement of inventory would have been readily apparent.

> Moreover, had Kappel adequately reviewed [Cooper Selvin's] workpapers which he obtained he would have discovered a roadmap clearly delineating the doubling and quadrupling of General Tech's value of the work-in-process inventory.

EXHIBIT 2
Auditor Change Disclosure Included in General Technologies' 1987 10-K

General Tech engaged Cooper, Selvin & Strassberg, Certified Public Accountants ("Cooper Selvin") to audit its 1987 financial statements and to issue their report with respect thereto. Prior to the completion of the audit, it was mutually agreed to terminate Cooper Selvin's engagement and the audit was completed by Frederick S. Todman & Company, Certified Public Accountants ("Todman"). (Todman also audited General Tech's financial statements for the years ended December 31, 1982 through 1986 and issued their reports thereto.) In connection with their engagement, Cooper Selvin advised General Tech management as to what they regarded as weaknesses in internal controls and their concerns about the reliability of management information. These concerns about weaknesses in internal controls and the reliability of management information were addressed by Todman in connection with their audit of the 1987 financial statements and all adjustments which Todman believed necessary were made.

Instead of investigating the alleged errors in General Tech's inventory records, the SEC charged that Kappel "simply accepted" the client's false explanation for those errors.

General Tech's management convinced Kappel that there was a simple explanation why the labor costs charged to the WIP items in the 1987 year-end inventory were twice the comparable labor charges assigned to the WIP items in the 1986 year-end inventory.[3] According to management, the items in the 1987 WIP inventory were 100 percent complete with respect to labor, while the items in the 1986 WIP inventory had been exactly 50 percent complete. The SEC noted that this explanation was farfetched for two reasons. First, it was statistically improbable that each item in the 1986 WIP inventory was exactly 50 percent complete with respect to labor, while each item in the 1987 WIP inventory was 100 percent complete for that cost element. Second, and more important, Kappel and the other Todman auditors never discovered that labor was assigned to a WIP item *only* when 100 percent of the labor charges had been incurred for that item. Thus, no labor charges should have been applied to the 1986 year-end WIP inventory if, as management alleged, each of those items was only 50 percent complete.

Todman completed the 1987 General Tech audit approximately six weeks after being re-engaged as the company's audit firm. On May 3, 1988, Todman issued an unqualified opinion on General Tech's 1987 financial statements.

TODMAN'S 1988 AUDIT OF GENERAL TECH

Most of the problems evident during the 1986 and 1987 General Tech audits resurfaced during Todman's 1988 audit of the company. These problems included an absence of proper audit planning, inadequate supervision of inexperienced personnel assigned to the engagement, and the use of non-independent personnel on the audit.

The SEC's subsequent investigation revealed that Todman's inventory audit procedures during the 1988 audit were even more deficient than the comparable procedures applied in the two prior years. For example, the SEC reported that "no tests whatsoever were performed" on the 1988 year-end LIR. As a result, the Todman auditors once again failed to discover that the client had fraudulently quadrupled the labor costs assigned to the year-end WIP inventory. Additionally, Todman failed to perform a "price test" on a large portion of General Tech's year-end raw materials inventory. A Todman auditor requested purchase invoices to corroborate the per unit prices applied to the quantities of individual raw material inventory items. However, the General Tech personnel who had access to these invoices refused to provide them to the Todman auditor. When the auditor informed Kappel of the client's refusal to produce the invoices, "Kappel failed to take any action" according to the SEC. Thus, Todman never completed the price tests, meaning that the raw materials inventory was included in the client's balance sheet at its "untested" value.

---

3. Recognize that the labor assigned to the 1986 WIP inventory was double the amount that should have been assigned, while the labor charged to the 1987 WIP inventory had been intentionally quadrupled.

On May 5, 1989, Todman issued an unqualified opinion on General Tech's 1988 financial statements. Similar to the 1986 and 1987 audit opinions on General Tech's financial statements, Todman's Valley Stream office issued the 1988 opinion. Several months earlier, the independent reviewer who had examined Todman's audit policies and practices recommended that the accounting firm not allow any audits to be "coordinated" by the Valley Stream office. The reviewer also recommended that no audit opinions be issued by that office since it had "irremediable problems." Todman's partners had agreed to implement the independent reviewer's recommendations. In fact, the 1984 agreement with the SEC that stemmed from Todman's deficient Bell & Beckwith audits mandated that the accounting firm implement the independent reviewer's recommendations.

WHERE WAS TODMAN'S QUALITY CONTROL DIRECTOR?

Todman hired Paul Young as its Quality Control Director in March 1987 at about the time the 1986 audit of General Tech was being completed. Young was not involved in that audit but did have oversight responsibilities for both the 1987 and 1988 General Tech audits.

One of Young's primary responsibilities as Todman's Quality Control Director was completing a "pre-issuance review" for each audit engagement involving an SEC registrant. The purpose of a pre-issuance review was to determine that GAAS had been properly applied on an audit. For example, Young reviewed the audit plan for each SEC client to determine whether the engagement had been adequately planned. Before an audit opinion could be issued by Todman on an SEC registrant's financial statements, the engagement partner was obligated to contact Young and obtain his permission to release the report. Despite his assigned responsibilities, Young had a very limited role in the 1987 General Tech audit. According to the SEC, Young did not complete a pre-issuance review for the engagement, apparently did not review any of the workpapers prepared during that audit, and did not approve the issuance of the audit opinion. In fact, the SEC charged that Young had "no substantive discussions" with Alan Kappel, the audit engagement partner, regarding the 1987 General Tech audit.

The independent reviewer that the SEC required Todman to retain following its deficient Bell & Beckwith audits performed a "follow-up review" of the accounting firm's audit practices and procedures in the fall of 1988. This review was intended to determine whether Todman had implemented the independent reviewer's original recommendations. Apparently in anticipation of the independent reviewer's arrival, Young signed off on certain General Tech workpapers for the 1987 audit to indicate that he had reviewed those workpapers. Young backdated his signatures to suggest that he had examined the workpapers before the completion of the General Tech audit and the issuance of the audit opinion.

The independent reviewer sharply criticized the 1987 General Tech audit. He commented on the inadequate planning of that engagement, the inadequate supervision of the personnel who completed the fieldwork, and the lack of documentation for the audit procedures applied to inventory. Despite Young's apparent review of selected workpapers prepared during the 1987 General Tech audit, the reviewer also criticized the quality control procedures applied to that engagement. In his report to the SEC, the independent reviewer recommended that Todman be required to strengthen its quality control function and the role of its quality control director. That report also stressed the need for Young to approve the issuance of audit opinions on engagements involving SEC registrants.

The independent reviewer's criticism prompted Young to take a much more active role in the 1988 General Tech audit compared with his role in the 1987 audit. Young identified several deficiencies in the 1988 audit while it was in progress and brought these matters to the attention of both Alan Kappel and Irv Weiner, Todman's managing partner. The SEC reported that Kappel failed to address many of the issues raised by Young. When Young informed Weiner that Kappel was "dragging his feet" in responding to quality control issues on the General Tech audit, Weiner complained that Young was "spending too much time" on that engagement.[4]

In early May 1989, Kappel called Young at home and insisted that the audit opinion on General Tech's 1988 financial statements had to be released immediately. Many of the concerns Young had previously raised regarding deficiencies in the 1988 General Tech audit were still unresolved at this point. After obtaining an oral commitment from Kappel to address those matters, Young concurred with Kappel's decision to release the audit opinion. The unresolved issues were not addressed adequately by Kappel, nor did Young determine after the fact whether Kappel had resolved those issues. As noted earlier, Todman's Valley Stream office issued the 1988 General Tech audit opinion. Young realized that Todman had agreed several months earlier not to issue any additional audit opinions from the Valley Stream office.

One of the several SEC enforcement releases that dealt with the General Tech fraud focused exclusively on Paul Young. The SEC severely criticized Young's performance as Todman's quality control director.

> Young failed to perform his quality review function in a professionally responsible manner. Moreover, Young undermined the integrity of the follow-up independent review . . . by misdating documents to create the impression he had reviewed them before Todman's audit report on General Tech's 1987 financial statements. Accordingly, Young's failure to perform properly as quality control director on the 1987 and 1988 audits demonstrates his improper professional conduct.[5]

EPILOGUE

By late 1989, General Tech's executives could no longer conceal the company's true financial condition. General Tech filed for bankruptcy in December 1989 and was liquidated in 1994. Among the lawsuits resulting from the General Tech fraud were civil complaints filed by the SEC against the company's Consultant and its executives who actively participated in the fraud or were aware of the fraud. The SEC charged each of these individuals with defrauding General Tech's investors. Without either admitting or denying the charges, each man agreed to a court order that barred him from engaging in future violations of federal securities laws.

---

4. Securities and Exchange Commission, *Accounting and Auditing Enforcement Release No. 663*, 12 April 1995.

5. *Ibid.*

Alan Kappel, Paul Young, and Irv Weiner also settled charges filed against them by the SEC without admitting or denying the reported facts of the case. Kappel agreed to be permanently banned from practicing before the SEC. The SEC censured both Young and Weiner. In addition, Young was banned for one year from practicing before the SEC, while Weiner received a five-year ban.

On December 31, 1993, Frederick S. Todman & Company disbanded and a new partnership entitled Todman & Co. was formed. Two of the eight partners of Todman & Co. had served as partners of the original Todman firm. In early 1994, the SEC and the new Todman firm agreed to a series of stipulations to ensure that the firm established and maintained an adequate system of quality controls. This agreement included a requirement that Todman retain an independent consultant to review its quality control policies and procedures. All recommendations made by the consultant had to be implemented by Todman within 60 days. Todman also agreed to undergo two follow-up reviews of its quality controls by the independent consultant.

QUESTIONS

1. When auditing a client's inventory, which of the management assertions identified by *SAS No. 31*, "Evidential Matter," is of primary concern to an auditor? Why?

2. General Tech's LIR was a computer-generated report. What steps should auditors take to test the reliability of key accounting software programs of a client?

3. Identify additional audit tests that the Todman auditors could have, and probably should have, applied to General Tech's year-end LIRs.

4. List the generally accepted auditing standards that one or more Todman auditors apparently violated. Briefly indicate how each standard was violated.

5. Do you believe that General Tech's auditor change disclosure shown in Exhibit 2 was sufficient? Are investors, creditors, and other third parties entitled to "full and fair disclosure" regarding auditor changes? Defend your answer.

6. Define "audit quality." Identify three important quality control procedures, other than those mentioned in this case, that audit firms can implement.

7. Briefly describe the SEC's oversight responsibilities for the financial reporting domain. Do you believe the SEC took appropriate measures when dealing with the parties involved in the General Technologies fraud?

CASE 1.12
REGINA COMPANY, INC.

Donald Sheelen was born into a middle-class family in upstate New York in 1946. In high school, the handsome Sheelen was the prototype of the all-American boy, excelling in both academics and athletics. Following graduation, Sheelen attended the University of Dayton, where he was elected president of his senior class and named a Big Man on Campus. After earning an MBA from Syracuse University, Sheelen landed a job with a large Wall Street brokerage firm and then three years later accepted a middle-management position with Johnson & Johnson. At the age of 34, Sheelen was hired by Regina Company, Inc., and placed in charge of the company's marketing department.

Regina was a wholly-owned subsidiary of the large conglomerate General Signal Corporation. Founded in Rathway, New Jersey, in 1892, Regina had originally been a music box manufacturer before entering the floorcare industry in the early 1900s. Throughout most of its existence, Regina was known as a complacent, slow-growth company and was dominated within the floorcare industry by Hoover and Eureka. Regina's corporate image changed quickly after Donald Sheelen signed on with the company.

CORNFLAKES, CELEBRITY, AND CASH FOR DONALD SHEELEN

After becoming company president in 1983, Sheelen announced that he intended to make Regina the industry's dominant firm by the end of the decade. He repeatedly vowed that Regina would "bomb" Hoover, the number one firm in the industry at the time. The exuberant executive even laid a Hoover doormat outside his office so that each day he could "walk over" his company's major rival.[1] Sheelen believed that to challenge Hoover and Eureka, Regina had to expand its product line and dramatically increase its advertising expenditures. Under his leadership, Regina introduced a series of new products, including a portable spa and an upright vacuum cleaner. To promote these and other new products, Sheelen poured millions of dollars into Regina's advertising budget. Eventually, the company's annual advertising expenditures exceeded 20 percent of its annual sales and eclipsed the combined advertising outlays of Hoover and Eureka.

Sheelen became well known both inside and outside the floorcare industry for his so-called cornflake routine that he often performed at trade shows and during news conferences. This routine involved sprinkling crushed cereal on a carpet and then demonstrating that a Regina vacuum cleaner did a much better job of cleaning up the mess than did a Hoover. Sheelen converted this demonstration into a television advertisement and was promptly sued by Hoover, which forced him to cancel the popular commercial. Hoover proved that the commercial was misleading since the Regina vacuum cleaner used in the cornflake caper had an industrial-strength suction not available on the model sold to retail customers.

Regina's board of directors named Sheelen the company's chief executive officer in early 1984. A few months later, he and several other Regina executives bought a majority interest in the company via a leveraged buyout. Sheelen personally invested only $750,000 in the venture but emerged with more than a 50 percent equity interest in Regina, which had total assets approaching $40 million at the time. The following year, Sheelen and his partners took Regina public. Surging sales and profits quickly landed Regina on the "buy" lists of several large brokerage firms and tagged the company's stock as a "can't miss" investment on Wall Street. (Exhibit 1 presents Regina's balance sheets and income statements for 1986 through 1988.) In commenting on the company, one financial analyst noted, "Regina is not only an earnings play but an investment in a skilled management team that has turned the company around."[2]

Within two years after going public, Regina's stock price had soared by nearly 500 percent and analysts expected it to go much higher. Regina's lofty stock price made Sheelen and the company's other principal stockholders millionaires many times over. Sheelen's stock alone had a market value of almost $100 million by 1988.

REGINA'S PROFITS: JUST SO MUCH HOT AIR

Unfortunately, the too-good-to-be-true story of Regina Company was . . . too good to be true. The sparkling sales and earnings figures released by Regina after it went public had been doctored by Sheelen. For the fiscal year ended June 30, 1988, the company actually suffered a multimillion-dollar loss rather than the reported $11 million profit. Instead of a growth company with bright prospects, Regina was a dying company mired in mounting losses.

---

1. J.A. Byrne, "How Don Sheelen Made a Mess That Regina Couldn't Clean Up," *Business Week*, 12 February 1990, 46–50.

2. G.G. Marcal, "Regina Keeps Cleaning Up," *Business Week*, 12 January 1987, 117.

EXHIBIT 1
Regina Company's
1986–1988 Financial
Statements

Regina Company, Inc.
Balance Sheets 1986–1988 (000s omitted)

	1988	June 30, 1987	1986
Current Assets:			
Cash	$ 885	$ 514	$ 63
Receivables (net)	51,076	27,801	14,402
Inventories	39,135	19,577	9,762
Other Current Assets	3,015	1,449	708
Total Current Assets	94,111	49,341	24,935
Property, Plant and Equipment	21,548	14,788	16,383
Other Assets	2,481	1,112	1,884
Total Assets	$118,140	$ 65,241	$43,202
Current Liabilities:			
Short-term Borrowings	$ —	$ —	$ 2,707
Current Portion of Long-term Debt	1,250	900	—
Accounts Payable	13,288	15,072	7,344
Accrued Liabilities	4,710	5,468	3,127
Income Taxes Payable	3,782	2,619	1,554
Total Current Liabilities	23,030	24,059	14,732
Long-term Debt:			
Industrial Revenue Bonds	12,650	13,900	14,800
Mississippi State Debt	1,975	—	—
Bank Debt	47,432	5,941	—
Total Long-term Debt	62,057	19,841	14,800
Deferred Income Taxes	1,881	1,254	685
Stockholders' Equity:			
Common Stock	1	1	1
Additional Paid-in Capital	7,902	7,771	7,774
Retained Earnings	23,269	12,315	5,210
Total Stockholders' Equity	31,172	20,087	12,985
Total Liabilities and Stockholders' Equity	$118,140	$ 65,241	$43,202

(continued)

→ Not a complementary growth rate when compared to growth in sales & revenue

    Regina's financial difficulties stemmed largely from product quality problems. Sheelen and the company's other top executives failed to pay sufficient attention to quality control issues during the manufacturing process for the new products introduced during the mid-1980s. These new products were innovative and less expensive than those of the company's competitors. They were also unreliable, having been rushed to the market without being adequately tested. Customer return rates several times greater than those of Regina's competitors negated the impressive sales figures registered following the introduction of the new products. One major retailer reported a return rate of 50 percent for a Regina vacuum cleaner, while the comparable models of Hoover and Eureka had return rates of less than 1 percent.

    By 1987, Sheelen realized that Regina was in deep trouble. Rather than admitting the problems facing the company, Sheelen chose to conceal them via several

d homogenous
b consideration
Note

**EXHIBIT 1—continued
Regina Company's
1986–1988 Financial
Statements**

Regina Company, Inc. Income Statements 1986–1988 (000s omitted)			
	1988	**June 30, 1987**	**1986**
Net Sales	$181,123	$ 128,234	$76,144
Operating Costs and Expenses:			
Cost of Goods Sold	94,934	70,756	46,213
Selling, Distribution, and Administrative	21,870	14,621	10,366
Advertising	39,992	26,449	8,557
Research and Development	2,423	1,530	1,182
Total Operating Costs and Expenses	159,219	113,356	66,318
Operating Income	21,904	14,878	9,826
Interest Expense	3,189	1,584	1,930
Income Before Income Taxes	18,715	13,294	7,896
Income Tax Expense	7,761	6,189	3,807
Net Income	$ 10,954	$ 7,105	$ 4,089
Earnings per Share	$1.21	$.78	$.46

illicit accounting schemes. In a subsequent investigation, the Securities and Exchange Commission (SEC) charged that inflating Regina's stock price was the prime motive behind these schemes. Colleagues of Sheelen later corroborated this allegation when they testified that he was obsessed with maintaining the company's stock price at a high level: "Nothing fired Sheelen's emotions like the company's stock price. Even a temporary flutter would cause him to rush to the phone to drum up support. He would pick up the phone himself and say, 'Why don't you [a financial analyst] write something to get the stock up?'"[3]

Sheelen began earnestly manipulating Regina's reported operating results during the second quarter of the company's 1988 fiscal year. Regina had posted steady increases in sales and earnings from 1985 through most of 1987. By December 31, 1987, the end of the second quarter of fiscal 1988, Regina's huge sales returns were threatening the company's impressive sales and earnings trends. At that point, Sheelen began establishing target sales and earnings goals that he believed Regina had to reach for the company to sustain "the confidence of the securities markets."[4]

To meet his financial targets for the second quarter of 1988, Sheelen instructed Vincent Golden, Regina's chief financial officer, to understate the company's product returns for that quarter: "With Golden's approval, employees altered Regina's computer system so that products returned by certain large volume customers could be processed through Regina's customer service department but would not be recorded on the company's books." Sheelen and Golden continued to misrepresent Regina's product returns for the final two quarters of fiscal 1988.

---

3. Byrne, "How Don Sheelen Made a Mess," 47.

4. This and all subsequent quotations, unless indicated otherwise, were taken from Securities and Exchange Commission, *Accounting and Auditing Enforcement Release No. 215*, 8 February 1989.

According to the SEC, the company understated its sales returns by at least $13 million for the year.

During the fourth quarter of fiscal 1988, Sheelen realized that slashing recorded sales returns alone would not allow Regina to achieve the sales and earnings goals he had established for that year. With Golden's help, Sheelen came up with several other accounting schemes to ensure that Regina reached his 1988 target sales and earnings figures of approximately $180 million and $1.20 per share, respectively. Sheelen instructed Golden to record bogus sales during the fourth quarter of fiscal 1988: "With Golden's approval, Regina's computer system was programmed to create false invoices in amounts of prior orders from certain large volume customers. Large volume customers were used because Golden and certain members of his staff believed that such customers were less likely than smaller customers to respond to audit confirmations." Golden also made sure that the bogus invoices were not sent to Regina's customers or routed to members of the company's accounting department who were unaware of the earnings manipulation scheme. In total, Golden and his subordinates generated 200 bogus invoices, representing collective sales of more than $5 million.

Another method Sheelen used during 1988 to inflate Regina's revenues involved booking what Golden referred to as "ship-in-place" sales. These items were sales orders that Regina had received but not filled as of June 30, 1988. In fact, some of the orders were not due to be shipped for several weeks following Regina's fiscal year-end. Golden recorded approximately $6 million of ship-in-place sales in the last few days of fiscal 1988. The SEC charged that the recording of these sales blatantly violated generally accepted accounting principles: "The ship-in-place transactions did not qualify for revenue recognition under GAAP because no exchange had taken place, the risks of loss and rights of ownership had not passed from Regina to customers, and there was no substantial business purpose for structuring the transactions as ship-in-place transactions." The last measure Sheelen and Golden used to attain Regina's earnings goal for 1988 was simply to understate the company's cost of goods sold for the fourth quarter by more than $3 million.

In the late summer of 1988, Regina released its fiscal 1988 financial statements. Those statements reported net sales of approximately $181 million and earnings per share of $1.21. In Regina's 1988 annual report, Sheelen boasted of the company's financial performance and suggested that the following year it would produce even better operating results. (Exhibit 2 contains excerpts from Sheelen's 1988 letter to Regina's stockholders.)

On September 15, 1988, Sheelen told a group of financial analysts that Regina would be reporting an increase in sales for the first quarter of fiscal 1989. In fact, Sheelen knew that Regina's sales had declined during that quarter. Over the next few days, Sheelen gradually realized that he could no longer conceal Regina's deteriorating financial condition. On September 20, 1988, he called Golden into his office. The two men decided to reveal that Regina's prior financial statements were materially misstated. Instead of disclosing the true cause of the inaccurate financial statements, Sheelen and Golden elected to blame the errors on computer malfunctions.

After meeting with Golden, Sheelen issued a press release reporting that Regina's sales would be lower than previously forecast for the first quarter of fiscal 1989. The press release also indicated that the company would suffer a loss for that quarter. Sheelen then notified Peat, Marwick, Mitchell & Company,

EXHIBIT 2
Excerpts from Donald Sheelen's 1988 Letter to Regina's Stockholders

> It feels real good to finish Fiscal 1988 and to be thankful that your company achieved its best year ever. I'm sure you can see by looking at the numbers that we have set records in both Sales and Earnings. We are very proud of this, but we are also especially proud of the consistency over the last eight years—Fiscal 1988 was our eighth consecutive year of record Sales and Earnings. . . .
>
> I feel especially good about the significant change in Regina's product mix over the last four years. As early as 1984, virtually 100% of earnings came from one line—Electrikbroom. Now, four years later, we have a broad base with five major lines contributing to our growth. Regina has gone from being the "runt" of the floorcare industry in the United States to being on the verge of taking over the Number 1 spot. . . .
>
> Every year when I look at what our Company has achieved, I ask myself the question what about the future. I have always said to you that there are no guarantees for the future, but my level of confidence has never been greater than today. I feel this way because the number of different programs/products that we are bringing to the market have never been greater. There is no question that we will probably make a few mistakes over the next year—we have in the past—but I also believe that we will set new records in all areas. By the time this report reaches you, we should be on the verge of making public announcements which we believe will very much enhance our growth.

Regina's audit firm, that the company's 1988 financial statements contained errors resulting from glitches in computer processing. Sheelen asked the audit firm to review Regina's accounting records to determine the magnitude of the errors.

The price of Regina's common stock plunged 60 percent by the close of the financial markets on September 21, 1988, as investors reacted to Sheelen's press release. Over the next few days, Sheelen and Golden resigned their positions with Regina and Peat Marwick withdrew the unqualified audit opinion issued several weeks earlier on the company's fiscal 1988 financial statements. In early October, a U.S. attorney initiated a criminal investigation of Regina's financial affairs. During that investigation, Sheelen voluntarily revealed the details of the earnings manipulation schemes used to misrepresent Regina's 1988 operating results.

AFTERMATH OF THE REGINA FRAUD

Donald Sheelen and Vincent Golden pleaded guilty to federal mail and securities fraud charges in February 1989. According to the U.S. attorney who prosecuted the case, the fraudulent scheme bilked investors of more than $100 million. When the company filed for bankruptcy in 1989, its common stock became essentially worthless. In July 1989, a competitor, Electrolux Corporation, acquired Regina. An Israeli company purchased Regina in 1994 and then sold it the following year to Philips Electronics, N.V., a large Dutch firm. Regina ceased operating as a separate entity after being acquired by Philips.

In May 1989, a federal judge sentenced Sheelen to a one-year prison term, a sentence that he served in a halfway house. Golden received a six-month sentence. The federal judge also fined both men and placed them on probation; Sheelen paid a $25,000 fine, while Golden was fined $12,500. According to the judge, the lenient sentences were appropriate because both men had cooperated with authorities investigating the scandal. Before beginning his sentence, Sheelen contacted Regina's new chairman and asked if he could return to the company.

The chairman reportedly responded with a question of his own: "Are you _____ crazy?"[5]

One charge leveled at Sheelen and Golden by the SEC was that the former executives had repeatedly and intentionally misled the company's audit firm, Peat Marwick. As an example, the SEC pointed out that Peat Marwick auditors discovered one of the ship-in-place sales transactions and notified Golden. Golden assured the auditors that no similar transactions had been recorded in Regina's accounting records. In the enforcement release that focused on the Regina scandal, the SEC did not fault Peat Marwick for failing to uncover the massive fraud masterminded by Sheelen and Golden. Nevertheless, several articles in the financial press criticized the audit firm. A Peat Marwick partner responded to such criticism by noting that "We're only human and prefer to trust the people we're auditing."[6]

QUESTIONS

1. Prepare common-sized financial statements for Regina for the period 1986 to 1988. Also, compute key liquidity, solvency, activity, and profitability ratios for 1987 and 1988. Given these data, identify what you believe were the high-risk financial statement line items for the 1988 Regina audit.

2. Identify audit procedures that might have resulted in Peat Marwick's discovering (a) the $5 million of bogus sales recorded by Regina executives during fiscal 1988 and (b) the intentional understatement of the company's sales returns for that same period.

3. Identify and discuss the principal audit objectives associated with the performance of year-end sales cutoff tests. Which of the fraudulent errors in Regina's accounting records would such tests have likely uncovered? Explain.

4. Were the Peat Marwick auditors justified in relying on Golden's assertion that the ship-in-place sales transaction they discovered was an isolated item? If not, what additional audit procedures do you believe Peat Marwick should have performed at that point?

5. As noted in the case, one Peat Marwick partner stated that his firm preferred "to trust the people we're auditing." Should auditors trust their clients? If so, under what circumstances and to what extent?

---

5. Byrne, "How Don Sheelen Made a Mess," 50.

6. L. Berton, "Battle of the Books: Audit Firms Are Hit by More Investor Suits for Not Finding Fraud," *The Wall Street Journal*, 24 January 1989, A1, A12.

Section Two
Audits of High-Risk Accounts

CASE 2.1
DOUGHTIE'S FOODS, INC.

In the late 1970s, William Nashwinter accepted a position as a salesman with Doughtie's Foods, Inc., a publicly owned food products company headquartered in Portsmouth, Virginia.[1] The ambitious young salesman impressed his superiors with his hard work and dedication and was soon promoted to general manager of the Gravins Division of Doughtie's, a promotion that nearly doubled his salary. The Gravins Division was essentially a large warehouse that wholesaled frozen-food products to retail outlets on the East Coast.

Nashwinter quickly discovered that managing a large wholesale operation was much more complicated and stressful than working a sales route. Within a short time after accepting the promotion, Nashwinter found himself being maligned by corporate headquarters for his division's poor performance. After several rounds of scathing criticism for failing to meet what he perceived to be unrealistic profit goals, Nashwinter decided to take matters into his own hands. The young manager began fabricating fictitious inventory on his monthly performance reports to headquarters. By inflating his monthly inventory balance, Nashwinter lowered his division's cost of goods sold and thus increased its gross profit.

Several years later, Nashwinter insisted that he had never intended to continue his scheme indefinitely. Instead, he saw his actions simply as a solution to a short-term problem: "I always had in the back of my mind that the division would make enough legitimate profit one day to justify the fake numbers."[2]

---

1. This case was developed primarily from Securities and Exchange Commission, *Accounting and Auditing Enforcement Release No. 30*, 21 May 1984.

2. R.L. Hudson, "SEC Charges Fudging of Corporate Figures Is a Growing Practice," *The Wall Street Journal*, 2 June 1983, 1, 19.

Unfortunately for Nashwinter, his division's actual operating results continued to be disappointing. With each passing year, Nashwinter had to fabricate larger amounts of fictitious inventory to reach his profit goals. Finally, in 1982, Nashwinter admitted to a superior that he had been filing false inventory reports to corporate headquarters for several years. Doughtie's management immediately fired Nashwinter and retained Price Waterhouse to determine the magnitude of the inventory errors in Gravins' accounting records and their impact on the company's consolidated financial statements. Price Waterhouse's study revealed that Nashwinter's scheme had overstated Doughtie's 1980 consolidated net income by 15 percent, while the company's 1981 net income had been overstated by 39 percent.[3]

Nashwinter used simple methods to misrepresent his division's inventory. In 1980, he inflated Gravins' inventory by including three pages of fictitious inventory items in the count sheets that summarized the results of the division's annual physical inventory. Nashwinter also changed the unit of measure of many inventory items. Rather than reporting 15 single boxes of a given product, for example, Nashwinter changed the inventory sheet so that it reported 15 cases of the product. In 1981, after Doughtie's acquired a computerized inventory system, Nashwinter simply input fictitious inventory items into his division's computerized inventory ledger.

In 1980 and 1981, the CPA firm of Goodman & Company audited Doughtie's. Thomas Wilson of Goodman & Company served as the audit manager on the 1980 audit and as the audit engagement partner the next year, after having been promoted to partner. In both years, Frank Pollard was the audit supervisor assigned to the Doughtie's engagement. Following the disclosure of Nashwinter's scheme to the Securities and Exchange Commission (SEC) by Doughtie's executives, the federal agency began investigating the 1980 and 1981 audits of the food distribution company. The SEC subsequently criticized Wilson and Pollard for their roles in those audits, particularly for their failure to rigorously audit Doughtie's inventory account.

The SEC maintained that Doughtie's inventory should have been considered a high-risk account and thus subject to a higher-than-normal degree of scrutiny by Wilson and Pollard during the 1980 and 1981 audits. First, inventory was the largest line item on the Doughtie's balance sheet, accounting for approximately 40 percent of the company's total assets. Second, Wilson and Pollard were aware of several weaknesses in Doughtie's internal controls for inventory, particularly within the Gravins Division. These weaknesses increased the likelihood of inventory errors. Finally, the SEC noted that Gravins' inventory increased rapidly during 1980 and 1981. The federal agency maintained that Wilson and Pollard should have considered the audit implications of this high growth rate and the closely related implications of the division's abnormally low inventory turnover.

The SEC also criticized Wilson and Pollard for failing to pursue problems that they or their subordinates uncovered during the 1980 and 1981 audits of Gravins' inventory. Following the completion of the physical inventory for Gravins in 1980, Nashwinter forwarded the three fictitious inventory count sheets to Wilson and Pollard. Nashwinter claimed that the Goodman & Company auditors had

---

3. Nashwinter's scheme affected Doughtie's reported earnings for several earlier years, but Price Waterhouse was unable to determine the magnitude of those misstatements.

overlooked the three count sheets. After briefly reviewing these count sheets, Wilson and Pollard added the items on them to Gravins' inventory. Following the division's 1981 physical inventory, the audit senior on the Doughtie's engagement could not reconcile the quantities for numerous items listed on the inventory count sheets with the quantities shown on the computer printout that summarized the details of Gravins' year-end inventory balance. The senior notified Wilson of the problem and wrote Nashwinter a memo asking for an explanation. Wilson failed to follow up on the problem, and Nashwinter never responded to the memo. In his review of the senior's workpapers, Pollard either did not notice the numerous differences between the count sheets and the computer listing of Gravins' inventory or chose not to investigate those differences.

Nashwinter's testimony to the SEC was not complimentary of Goodman & Company's annual audits. Nashwinter testified that he often made up excuses to account for missing or misplaced inventory and that the auditors apparently never double-checked his explanations. He also testified that the auditors were lax when it came time to test count inventory items in Gravins' blast freezer: "A lot of times the auditors didn't want to stay in the freezer. It was too cold."[4]

Epilogue

For their roles in the Doughtie's case, the SEC required Wilson and Pollard to complete several professional education courses. The SEC also required that selected audits supervised by the two men in the future be subjected to peer reviews to determine that the appropriate audit procedures had been performed. Goodman & Company was not sanctioned by the SEC, since Wilson and Pollard had failed to comply with the firm's quality control standards. In 1983, Doughtie's dismissed Goodman & Company and retained Price Waterhouse as its audit firm. In 1999, *The Wall Street Journal* reported that Sysco Corporation purchased Doughtie's Foods for $25.5 million.[5]

To settle the charges filed against him by the SEC, William Nashwinter signed a consent decree in which he neither admitted nor denied the charges but agreed not to violate federal securities laws in the future. At last report, Nashwinter still worked in the food distribution industry.

Questions

1. What are the auditor's primary objectives when he or she observes the client's annual physical inventory? Identify the key audit procedures that an auditor would typically perform during and after the client's physical inventory.

2. What audit procedure or procedures might have prevented Nashwinter from successfully overstating the 1980 year-end inventory of the Gravins Division? What audit procedure or procedures might have prevented Nashwinter from overstating the division's 1981 year-end inventory?

4. Hudson, "Fudging of Corporate Figures," 19.

5. *The Wall Street Journal*, "Sysco to Buy Doughtie's Foods," 18 February 1999, B16.

3. In 1981, Gravins' inventory turnover was approximately one-half that of comparable divisions within the firm. How should this fact have affected the planning for the 1981 audit of Doughtie's? What audit procedures should Wilson and Pollard have performed to investigate Gravins' unusually low inventory turnover rate?

4. Nashwinter was under considerable pressure to improve his division's operating results. Discuss how this fact, if known to the auditors of Doughtie's, should have affected their assessment of audit risk for this client.

CASE 2.2
FLIGHT TRANSPORTATION CORPORATION

In January 1982, Charles Aune picked up his phone and called the Federal Bureau of Investigation (FBI).[1] Aune then proceeded to tell the FBI of a large-scale fraud being perpetrated by his former employer. Until 1981, Aune had worked for Flight Transportation Corporation (FTC), an aviation company based in Eden Prairie, Minnesota. FTC's principal line of business was executive and group air charters. In 1980 and 1981, the rapidly growing company reported revenues of $8 million and $24.8 million, respectively. FTC's dramatic growth caught the attention of investors nationwide. The company's strong operating results were particularly impressive since they were posted in the face of a recession gripping the country. Unfortunately for investors, most of FTC's revenues existed only in the minds of the company's executives. Similarly, several million dollars of assets reported in the company's 1980 and 1981 balance sheets were purely imaginary.

From 1979 through 1982, FTC executives used the company's bogus financial statements to raise more than $32 million of capital in three securities offerings to the public. The executives diverted much of these funds for their personal use. For example, the company's president financed his expensive hobby, collecting vintage cars, by tapping the company's bank accounts. In June 1982, FTC was preparing to sell an additional $24 million of securities. However, a secret six-month investigation by the FBI, prompted by Charles Aune's phone call, resulted in the Securities and Exchange Commission (SEC) shutting down the company's operations. A federal judge then appointed a receiver to take custody of the company's assets.

---

1. Most of the facts of this case and the quotations, unless indicated otherwise, were drawn from the following source: Securities and Exchange Commission, *Accounting and Auditing Enforcement Release No. 81*, 5 December 1985.

Over the next several months, press reports of the FTC fraud shocked investors who had purchased the company's securities on the basis of its impressive financial statements. Almost immediately, the underwriting firms that had managed FTC's securities offerings came under fire. An executive of one of these firms responded to this criticism. "I don't see this as embarrassing to our firm at all. Underwriters aren't auditors."[2] Predictably, the press then turned to FTC's auditors, Fox & Company, for an explanation. John Harrington, a senior partner with Fox & Company, served as the audit engagement partner on the 1980 and 1981 FTC audits. Harrington defended those audits, each of which concluded with an unqualified opinion issued on FTC's financial statements.

> We're not the guardians of the world. It's the con artists who should be punished. Besides, if we go into every client's office with our eyes wide open, saying, "there's a crime in here somewhere," nobody is going to hire us.[3]

Fox's 1980 Audit of FTC

The Minneapolis office of Fox & Company, the thirteenth-largest accounting firm in the nation at the time, acquired FTC as an audit client in March 1980. In prior years, a sole practitioner had audited the company. Besides Harrington, the audit engagement team assigned to the 1980 and 1981 FTC audits included an audit manager, Gregory Arnott, and three staff auditors. Arnott supervised the fieldwork for both audits. The 1980 FTC audit was the first engagement on which Arnott served as an audit manager, since he had been promoted to that position shortly before the audit began. In his previous eight years with Fox & Company, Arnott had worked on only one audit of a public company. Harrington had been a partner with Fox & Company since 1975 and had served for a time as the managing partner of Fox's Minneapolis office. During the early 1980s, Harrington oversaw the auditing practice of the Minneapolis office. He also reviewed and approved each SEC registration statement filed by clients of that office.

Harrington and Arnott met with FTC's top executives in early March 1980 to discuss the 1980 audit. An engagement letter, signed by Harrington and an FTC officer, documented the contractual details of that audit. The two auditors and client executives also discussed the staffing of the audit and timing issues during the March meeting. FTC's fiscal year ended on June 30. The company's president, William Rubin, insisted that the audited financial statements be ready for the printer by early August. Rubin wanted the audit completed quickly to expedite the filing of a registration statement with the SEC. FTC needed the SEC's approval of that registration statement to sell a large block of new securities to the public.

Like most large accounting firms, Fox & Company used a risk assessment questionnaire during the planning phase of each audit to document "special" audit risks. This questionnaire contained several items focusing on high-risk audit factors such as related party transactions. When asked whether FTC had

2. K. Johnson, "How High-flying Numbers Fooled the Experts," *The New York Times*, 29 August 1982, Section 3, 9.

3. *Ibid.*

engaged in any related party transactions during fiscal 1980, FTC officials responded with a blunt "no." However, shortly after the audit fieldwork began, a Fox auditor discovered that most of FTC's revenues stemmed from a contractual arrangement with International Air Systems (IAS), a company owned by William Rubin. Approximately two-thirds of FTC's 1980 consolidated revenues resulted from more than 100 air charters that had been flown on IAS aircraft. To the staff auditor's surprise, he could find almost no documentary support for this $5.2 million of air charter revenues. There were no sales invoices, no entries in the sales journal, and no related expenses recorded for these revenues. The support for the revenues consisted almost entirely of handwritten entries made directly into FTC's general journal. Because of their unusual nature and the lack of documentation, the staff auditor prepared a list of the air charter revenues. He gave this list to Arnott.

Arnott asked FTC's controller to supply the documentation for the air charter revenues. The controller responded that the auditors would have to make arrangements with Rubin to obtain that documentation. Arnott then took the matter to Harrington, who contacted Rubin. After a brief conversation with Harrington, Rubin agreed to provide extensive documentation for the IAS-related revenues. This documentation was to include sales invoices, cash receipts and disbursements records, canceled checks, contracts, and computer runs listing the individual air charters. Despite Rubin's interest in completing the audit as quickly as possible, he repeatedly stonewalled the auditors when they asked for the documentation. Computer malfunctions served as Rubin's most popular excuse for failing to turn over the requested documents to the audit team.

A few days before the projected completion date for the 1980 audit, Rubin finally provided the Fox auditors with evidence to support the suspicious air charter revenues. This evidence consisted of two one-page documents. Exhibit 1 presents the first of these documents, a brief and ambiguous one-page contract between IAS and FTC. The second item, another one-page document, listed the number of charter flights flown for FTC on IAS aircraft and the resulting revenues for FTC. When the auditors balked at accepting this documentation, Rubin took Harrington aside and told him that the air charter revenues were not FTC revenues at all. Instead, these revenues had been produced by IAS, which again, was owned by Rubin. Rubin explained to Harrington that "he was bored, had plenty of money, and wanted to use IAS to help FTC get into the charter business." Consequently, Rubin had "donated" the more than $5 million of IAS air charter revenues to FTC.

A. IAS shall provide FTC with large aircraft (727s and/or DC 8s) for charter to the Cayman Islands and Mexico.

B. All revenues earned by FTC will be recorded by IAS during the term of the agreement and provided to FTC at the conclusion of all flights along with the gross or net profit to be paid. Gross profit will be earned and paid if sufficient volume is attained. If volume is not high enough, only net profit will be paid to FTC.

C. This agreement covers the period from July 1, 1979, through June 30, 1980.

Source: Securities and Exchange Commission, *Accounting and Auditing Enforcement Release No. 81*, 5 December 1985.

EXHIBIT 1
Alleged Contractual Agreement between FTC and IAS

Harrington accepted Rubin's explanation for the IAS revenues booked in FTC's accounting records, an explanation that accounted for FTC's lack of documentation for those transactions. Harrington then explained to Arnott the true nature of the air charter revenues. He also informed Arnott that, in his opinion, no additional evidence would be needed to support those revenues. Arnott disagreed with Harrington initially but then changed his mind after the two men discussed the matter further. Arnott eventually indicated in the 1980 audit workpapers that the $5.2 million of air charter revenues were "appropriately included" in FTC's 1980 financial statements.

During a subsequent SEC investigation, Arnott testified that he never believed sufficient competent audit evidence had been obtained to support the air charter revenues. An SEC representative then questioned Arnott regarding his awareness of Fox's "disagreement procedure." This policy allowed a subordinate member of an audit team to express disagreement with a decision rendered on an audit engagement. Such a disagreement was to be documented in a written memorandum included in the audit workpapers. This memorandum effectively dissociated the subordinate from the given decision. Arnott testified that he was aware of the disagreement procedure but did not take advantage of it for two reasons. First, he realized that as the audit engagement partner Harrington would make the final decision regarding the suspicious air charter revenues. Second, he was worried that his job with Fox & Company might be jeopardized if he followed that procedure.

The SEC also quizzed Harrington regarding his discussion of the air charter revenues with Arnott. Harrington testified that he could not recall Arnott ever disagreeing with the decision that sufficient competent evidence had been collected to support the air charter revenues.

Fox's 1981 Audit of FTC

In July 1980, shortly after the beginning of FTC's 1981 fiscal year, the company established a subsidiary in the Cayman Islands. The reported purpose of this subsidiary was to operate an air charter business. During fiscal 1981, FTC recorded $13 million of nonexistent revenues through FTC Cayman Ltd., its Cayman Islands subsidiary. These revenues accounted for more than one-half of FTC's consolidated revenues for fiscal 1981. FTC's consolidated balance sheet as of June 30, 1981, the final day of the company's 1981 fiscal year, reported more than $6 million of nonexistent receivables, land, and other assets related to FTC Cayman.

In June 1981, Harrington and Arnott met with Rubin and other FTC officers in a planning conference for the 1981 audit. During this meeting, Rubin told Harrington and Arnott that FTC's new Cayman Island subsidiary produced most of FTC's 1981 revenues. Rubin also told the auditors that the documentation for these revenues was in the Cayman Islands but would be brought to Minnesota during the audit. Again, Rubin wanted the audit completed as quickly as possible. The parties agreed to a fieldwork completion date of July 31 and a projected audit report signing date of August 12.

When the 1981 audit began in early July, the only documentation made available to the Fox auditors was a trial balance and a computerized general ledger and general journal. On August 6, one week after the fieldwork was supposed to have been finished and less than one week before the audit report was to be signed, FTC officials gave the auditors the fiscal 1981 bank statements for FTC Cayman. Except for a few other minor items, these bank statements were the only externally prepared documents provided to the Fox auditors to support FTC Cayman's revenues. These bank statements were not obtained directly from the subsidiary's bank but instead were given to the Fox auditors by an FTC employee.

Rubin told Harrington and Arnott that they could verify the subsidiary's revenues by reviewing the deposits reported in its bank statements during fiscal 1981. A member of the audit engagement team did just that. A reconciliation of the revenues reported by FTC Cayman and the deposits reflected in the subsidiary's 1981 bank statements resulted in a small unlocated difference between the two amounts. Given this small difference, the auditors concluded that the subsidiary's 1981 revenues were materially accurate. In fact, the bank statements were forgeries.

The Fox auditors attempted to confirm $3 million of cash that FTC Cayman reportedly had on deposit in the Cayman Islands as of June 30, 1981. Throughout the audit, FTC executives tried to persuade the auditors that obtaining a confirmation for that cash balance would be difficult given the bank secrecy laws in the Cayman Islands. The auditors mailed a confirmation to the subsidiary's Cayman Islands bank using an address supplied by FTC. That confirmation was never returned. Eventually, Harrington agreed to accept a confirmation of the year-end cash balance that an employee of the subsidiary had allegedly obtained from the Cayman Islands bank. The SEC's subsequent investigation revealed that the employee forged the confirmation.

Harrington also arranged to speak with an official of the Cayman Islands bank to obtain an oral confirmation of the subsidiary's year-end cash balance. Rubin invited Harrington to come to his office to receive this confirmation over the telephone. After Rubin placed a call—allegedly to the bank—and had a brief conversation, he handed the telephone receiver to Harrington. The individual at the other end of the line then confirmed that FTC's subsidiary had the reported amount of cash on deposit as of June 30, 1981.

The Fox auditors also attempted to confirm a $2 million receivable of FTC Cayman at the end of fiscal 1981. The auditors mailed a confirmation for this amount to a tour group operator who allegedly organized most of the subsidiary's air charter flights. A confirmation was returned indicating that the receivable did exist in the correct amount. However, the confirmation returned was not the confirmation that had been mailed by the Fox auditors. The returned confirmation was a forgery that contained typographical errors not present in the original confirmation.

EPILOGUE

The SEC investigation of the 1980 and 1981 FTC audits culminated in sanctions imposed on both John Harrington and Gregory Arnott. Harrington was permanently banned from practicing before the SEC. However, the SEC's disciplinary order allowed Harrington to apply for a repeal of this ban after five years. Arnott's right to practice before the SEC was suspended for one year. In commenting on Arnott's role in the FTC audits, the SEC stressed the need for members of an audit engagement team to maintain an independent state of mind even if that means jeopardizing their jobs.

> Arnott engaged in unprofessional conduct by abdicating his role as an independent professional to the audit partner. He properly recognized that the audit evidence was inadequate and took the appropriate step of informing the partner. However, he failed to act on his conviction and caused the workpapers to evidence incorrectly his agreement.

Following a series of highly publicized "problem" audits by Fox & Company, including the 1980 and 1981 FTC audits, the SEC prohibited the firm from accepting new SEC clients for a six-month period beginning in 1983. The SEC also formed an independent committee to review Fox & Company's auditing practice and to recommend changes to improve the firm's quality control procedures. In 1985, Fox & Company merged with Alexander Grant & Company. The newly created firm was named Grant Thornton.

In 1982, the SEC sanctioned William Rubin for his role in the FTC fraud. The SEC permanently enjoined Rubin from further violations of federal securities laws. Eventually, the SEC, other federal agencies, and private plaintiffs recovered more than $45 million from FTC and its executives, including almost $2 million from Rubin. FTC's court-appointed receiver distributed these funds to the company's bondholders, other creditors, and stockholders.

Questions

1. Assume the role of Gregory Arnott during the 1980 FTC audit. Draft a memo to be included in the FTC workpapers that expresses your disagreement with John Harrington's decision that sufficient competent evidence had been collected to support the suspicious air charter revenues.

2. Identify measures accounting firms can adopt to lower the risk that auditors will capitulate to their superiors when technical disagreements arise during an audit.

3. Assume that you were the staff auditor who discovered the bogus air charter revenues during the 1980 audit. What responsibilities did you have regarding those revenues? For example, did you have a responsibility to write a memo dissociating yourself from Harrington's decision to accept those revenues? Make any assumptions you believe are necessary to respond to this question.

4. In your opinion, what additional audit procedures should the Fox auditors have applied to the 1981 FTC Cayman revenues?

5. Identify the flaws in the confirmation procedures applied by the Fox auditors. How did these flaws affect the competence and sufficiency of the audit evidence yielded by these procedures?

6. Besides the related party transactions, what other "special" audit risks existed in the FTC audits? How should these factors have affected the planning decisions for these audits?

7. Identify specific measures audit firms can take to ensure that client-imposed pressure does not adversely affect the quality of an independent audit.

CASE 2.3
J.B. HANAUER & CO.

Pick up the financial statements of a brokerage firm and you will find a balance sheet quite different from the typical corporate balance sheet.[1] Take Quick & Reilly, for example, a large discount broker. In a recent balance sheet, Quick & Reilly reported total assets of almost $2.5 billion. Receivables from customers and other brokerage firms accounted for approximately 95 percent of those assets. Likewise, short-term payables tend to dominate the liability side of a brokerage firm's balance sheet. Quick & Reilly reported $2.3 billion of liabilities, 94 percent of which involved debts to customers and other brokerage firms. Clearly, confirmation procedures for receivables and payables are important audit tests applied to brokerage clients. So it was in the late 1970s and early 1980s for the annual audits of J.B. Hanauer & Co., a brokerage firm headquartered in New Jersey that had several branch offices in south Florida.

Stanley Goldberg supervised the annual audits of J.B. Hanauer & Co. for several years. During his career, Goldberg served as a partner with three different public accounting firms: J.K. Lasser & Co., Touche Ross & Co., and Richard A. Eisner & Co. Goldberg became a partner of Touche Ross following a merger between that firm and J.K. Lasser. When Goldberg left Touche Ross to join Eisner, Hanauer's executives wanted Goldberg to continue supervising their annual audits. As a result, in 1980 these executives dismissed Touche Ross and retained the Eisner firm.

ASSESSMENT OF HANAUER'S INTERNAL CONTROLS

Hanauer's fiscal year ended on March 31. Two to three months prior to that date, Goldberg sent a senior and two or more staff accountants to Hanauer's offices to

---

1. This case was developed primarily from the following source: Securities and Exchange Commission, *Accounting and Auditing Enforcement Release No. 13*, 22 September 1983.

complete the internal control phase of the annual audit. Given the nature of the brokerage business, internal controls are extremely important. The large volume of cash and securities that exchange hands daily dictates that brokerage firms establish extensive and rigorous internal controls over their day-to-day operations.

During each audit of Hanauer, Goldberg's subordinates completed a lengthy internal control questionnaire covering all facets of Hanauer's internal control structure. Among the key issues documented in the internal control workpapers was the unusual scope of job responsibilities assigned to the brokerage firm's sales staff. Exhibit 1 lists some of these responsibilities.

Apparently, Goldberg was uncomfortable with the extensive and unusual degree of authority granted the Hanauer's sales staff. Contributing to his concern was that in 1977 the SEC had censured several of Hanauer's executives and employees, including some salespeople, for engaging in improper securities transactions.[2] Goldberg's doubts regarding the competence and integrity of these latter individuals had been allayed somewhat by Hanauer's response to the SEC's sanctions. In a news release, the firm correctly pointed out that the individuals had not admitted to any of the charges. The news release also stated that the individuals agreed to accept the SEC's penalties to avoid the costs associated with contesting the allegations in court.

Despite several questions regarding the reliability of Hanauer's internal controls, each year that Goldberg supervised the firm's independent audit, he concluded that there were no material weaknesses in its internal control structure. The Securities Exchange Act of 1934 required Goldberg to file reports to this effect with the SEC, since Hanauer was a registered broker-dealer under that federal law.

CUSTOMER ACCOUNT CONFIRMATION PROCEDURES

As suggested earlier, confirmation procedures are a critical audit procedure for brokerage clients. In planning their confirmation procedures each year, Hanauer's auditors identified four groups of customer accounts. The accounts of primary concern involved those with "open" balances at the end of Hanauer's fiscal year. The open accounts with credit balances represented customers to whom Hanauer owed cash at year-end, while the open accounts with debit balances rep-

EXHIBIT 1
Selected Job
Responsibilities of
Hanauer's Sales Staff

- Opened customer accounts and obtained all required personal data such as addresses and credit references.
- Provided requested price quotations to customers.
- Accepted and processed customer purchase orders.
- Mailed or personally delivered customer confirmations.
- Obtained bearer (coupon) bonds from Hanauer's vault and delivered them to customers, often at locations other than Hanauer's offices.
- Received payment for securities from customers in currency, often at locations other than Hanauer's offices.
- Deposited cash received from customers in Hanauer's bank accounts.

---

2. "J.B. Hanauer & Co., Officials Are Censured By SEC for Dealings," *The Wall Street Journal*, 30 September 1977, 4.

resented customers who owed cash to the brokerage firm. In 1978, Goldberg decided to send confirmations to all customers with open balances at year-end. In 1979 and 1980, Goldberg's subordinates mailed confirmations to approximately 50 percent of these customers.

The third group of accounts included those with only securities balances at year-end. For the customers represented by these accounts, Hanauer held securities that had been purchased but not delivered. The fourth group of accounts included those that had neither an open balance nor a securities balance. Many of these accounts were inactive or dormant. Each year, Goldberg instructed his subordinates to mail confirmations to a small, randomly selected sample of these final two groups of accounts.

In 1978, a senior executive of Hanauer asked Goldberg not to send confirmations to certain accounts that had been selected for that purpose. The executive indicated that many of his firm's customers insisted that their account information be kept strictly confidential. When pressed to provide an explanation for this confidentiality, the executive responded that these customers wished to conceal the existence of their brokerage accounts from their spouses. Goldberg agreed not to mail confirmations to certain accounts. Before mailing the confirmations for the 1978 audit, the senior assigned to the Hanauer audit engagement provided a Hanauer accountant with a list of the accounts selected for confirmation. The accountant then individually contacted the salespeople of Hanauer and asked them to check off the accounts that they did not want confirmed. This procedure was repeated during both the 1979 and 1980 Hanauer audits.

Exhibit 2 lists selected data regarding the confirmation procedures applied during the 1978–1980 Hanauer audits. The table in Exhibit 2 indicates the number of accounts selected for confirmation each year, the number of confirmations not mailed at the request of Hanauer personnel, and the dollar value of the unmailed confirmations relative to the total dollar value of all the accounts selected for confirmation.

Goldberg instructed his subordinates to perform alternative audit procedures on those open accounts that the client did not want confirmed. These procedures consisted principally of determining that the year-end account balance was eventually "cleared" by a receipt from the customer or a disbursement to the customer. The auditors also occasionally checked the supporting documentation for these entries, such as canceled checks. During at least one Hanauer audit, Goldberg's subordinates attempted to determine whether there were any discernible differences in the accounts that the client allowed to be confirmed and those that it did not. Apparently, the senior and staff auditors assigned to the engagement performed this procedure on their own initiative. Goldberg's subordinates discovered no such differences, or, alternatively, failed to document such differences in the Hanauer workpapers.

	Number of Accounts Selected for Confirmation	Confirmations Not Mailed at Hanauer's Request	Dollar Value of Unmailed Confirmations as a Percentage of Dollar Value of Accounts Selected for Confirmation
1978	227	45	18%
1979	145	36	25%
1980	216	36	26%

EXHIBIT 2
Selected Account
Confirmation Data,
1978–1980 Audits of
J.B. Hanauer & Co.

At the completion of each Hanauer audit for the period 1978–1980, Goldberg authorized an unqualified audit opinion on the brokerage firm's financial statements. Because Hanauer was a registered broker-dealer under the Securities Exchange Act of 1934, the firm filed these financial statements with the SEC.

MONEY LAUNDERING ALLEGATIONS LEVELED AGAINST HANAUER

In the early 1980s, a series of articles in several major newspapers revealed that J.B. Hanauer & Co. was under investigation by the U.S. Attorney's office, a federal grand jury, the Internal Revenue Service (IRS), and the SEC. The allegations against the firm centered on charges that Hanauer was involved in a "money laundering" operation. According to published reports, many Hanauer customers purchased large blocks of bearer (coupon) bonds under fictitious names. These transactions were made on a cash basis and involved covert exchanges of large bundles of cash between Hanauer representatives and the customers at such locations as restaurants, bars, and airport parking lots.

Under the Currency and Foreign Transactions Reporting Act, brokers, banks, and other financial institutions must report cash transactions exceeding $10,000 to the IRS. Hanauer's employees often avoided this requirement by entering large cash transactions in the accounting records on a piecemeal basis. For example, a $45,000 cash receipt might be entered in $9,000 "chunks" over a period of five days. Likewise, to prevent Hanauer's banks from reporting these transactions to the IRS, the brokerage firm's employees deposited large cash receipts in multiple deposits of less than $10,000.

The cash basis of transacting business provided Hanauer sales staff with the opportunity to take unfair advantage of their customers. In one case, the SEC reported that a Hanauer salesman collected nearly $70,000 from a customer in payment for a purchase of municipal bonds, bonds that cost less than $60,000. The salesman pocketed that difference. To prevent customers from discovering that they had been defrauded, Hanauer's sales representatives routinely destroyed customer transaction confirmations. Because many of the securities Hanauer bought and sold were infrequently traded, customers often could not obtain independent confirmations of the prices the brokerage firm charged them for these securities.

The SEC's investigation also revealed that Hanauer's salespeople routinely ignored the firm's internal control policies regarding the recording of customer account information. Many of the accounts involving the confidential cash transactions were recorded under fictitious names. Additionally, Hanauer's sales staff failed to obtain all required information for many of these accounts. Several accounts established under fictitious names lacked bank references, home and business addresses, and telephone numbers. The SEC pointed out that Hanauer's failure to identify the actual customers with whom it was transacting business posed serious financial risks for the firm. Investors who had access to market price quotations could simply refuse to complete a transaction if the market price of the securities they had purchased, but not yet paid for, dropped significantly in the first few days following the transaction.

JUDGMENT DAY FOR HANAUER AND GOLDBERG

In early 1982, Hanauer's executives settled several charges filed against the firm by the SEC. The federal agency sanctioned 18 of the company's employees and officers, including two executive officers who were barred indefinitely from working in the brokerage industry. Four of these individuals were among those censured by the SEC in 1977. The SEC also fined Hanauer an amount equal to the fraudulent overcharges on the large customer cash transactions. Among other penalties imposed on the firm were restrictions on future expansion and the forfeiture of profits for a four-month period on new customer accounts. Finally, the SEC required Hanauer to retain a new accounting firm and to establish internal controls that would prevent future violations of federal securities laws. In response to published reports of the SEC settlement, Hanauer's president stated that a key factor in the firm's decision to settle the case was avoiding the costs of fighting the charges in court.

Two years following the settlement with the SEC, Hanauer pleaded guilty to criminal charges of failing to comply with the requirements of the Currency and Foreign Transactions Reporting Act. In responding to this settlement, Hanauer's president noted that his firm failed to report the large cash transactions because of clerical oversights. He also insisted that the firm pleaded guilty to the criminal charges to avoid the costs of future litigation.

In September 1983, the SEC sanctioned Stanley Goldberg for his role in the Hanauer case. The SEC charged that Goldberg should have recognized the material weaknesses in his client's internal controls. Additionally, the SEC maintained that Goldberg should have recognized that the client had imposed material scope limitations on its annual audits by not allowing many customer accounts to be confirmed. Goldberg's failure to instruct his subordinates to apply extensive alternative audit procedures to those accounts that the client did not want confirmed particularly disturbed the SEC. Finally, the SEC pointed out that Goldberg never inquired of his subordinates regarding how many confirmations were not mailed at the client's request or the collective dollar value of those accounts. Surprisingly, this information was not compiled in a summary format in the Hanauer audit workpapers.

QUESTIONS

1. Identify internal control risks generally faced by a brokerage firm. Identify specific control risks posed by Hanauer's operations. Did Hanauer's auditors properly investigate these risks and take them into consideration when planning their year-end tests?

2. Identify the audit objectives that Hanauer's auditors hoped to accomplish as a result of their account confirmation procedures. In your response, consider each of the four types of account balances.

3. What additional alternative audit procedures do you believe the Hanauer auditors should have applied to those accounts that the client did not want confirmed?

4. Define a material audit scope limitation in general terms. Do you agree with the SEC that Hanauer's management imposed a material scope limitation on its annual audits?

5. Should an audit client be allowed to "follow" its engagement audit partner to another accounting firm? Discuss the issues raised by auditor changes made for this purpose.

CASE 2.4
BERKSHIRE HATHAWAY, INC.

In 1983, GEICO, a large insurance company, announced plans to purchase several million shares of its outstanding common stock at a price of $60 per share. Among GEICO's largest stockholders was Berkshire Hathaway, Inc., an investment company. Executives of the two companies agreed that Berkshire would tender approximately 350,000 of its GEICO shares in the stock buyback plan, which would allow Berkshire to treat the transaction as a proportionate redemption. In a proportionate redemption, the percentage equity interest of one company (the investor) in a second company (the investee) is maintained at the level that existed immediately before the transaction. For federal taxation purposes, the proceeds received by the investor company in a proportionate redemption are taxed as dividends by applying the effective intercorporate dividend tax rate. In 1983, that tax rate was approximately 6.9 percent.

Berkshire also chose to treat the proceeds received from the redemption of the GEICO stock as dividend income in its 1983 financial statements. Peat, Marwick, Mitchell & Company, Berkshire's audit firm, approved that accounting treatment. In 1984, another company in which Berkshire had a significant equity interest, General Foods, announced a stock buyback plan. Again, Berkshire structured the sale of the stock to General Foods so that the transaction qualified as a proportionate redemption. Berkshire also opted to report the proceeds received from General Foods as dividend income in its 1984 financial statements.

In late 1984, representatives of Peat Marwick told Berkshire executives that the proceeds of the General Foods stock redemption should not be considered dividend income for financial reporting purposes. Instead, Peat Marwick maintained that the transaction should be recorded as a sale of stock with the difference between the selling price and cost reported as a capital gain on Berkshire's income statement. This treatment of the transaction was less favorable for financial reporting purposes than the option preferred by Berkshire since it did not allow the total proceeds received from General Foods to be reported as revenue. Peat Marwick's recommendation annoyed Berkshire's executives. The accounting firm's next decision irritated those executives even more. Peat Marwick insisted that Berkshire restate its 1983 financial statements to reflect the GEICO stock redemption as a sale of stock rather than as a dividend distribution.

Warren Buffett, Berkshire's chief executive officer, discussed the GEICO and General Foods stock redemptions at length in his company's 1984 annual report.[1] Buffett disputed Peat Marwick's contention that the transactions should be treated as sales of stock and not as dividend distributions. He then explained why he eventually agreed to accept the audit firm's position:

> We disagree with [Peat Marwick's] position from both the viewpoint of economic substance and proper accounting. But, to avoid a qualified auditor's opinion, we have adopted Peat Marwick's 1984 view and restated 1983 accordingly. None of this, however, has any effect on intrinsic business value: our ownership interests in GEICO and General Foods, our cash, our taxes, and the market value and tax basis of our holdings all remain the same.[2]

Treating the General Foods transaction as a sale of stock reduced Berkshire's 1984 net income by 8 percent. Applying that accounting treatment to the 1983 GEICO transaction reduced Berkshire's previously reported net income for 1983 by 1 percent.

The Wall Street Journal reported the disagreement between Berkshire executives and Peat Marwick that evolved from the proportionate redemption transactions. When asked to comment on Buffett's criticism of Peat Marwick in his company's 1984 annual report, a Peat Marwick partner simply noted, "It's the client's prerogative to disagree. Our report speaks for itself."[3] Another prerogative of an audit client is to change auditors. In 1985, Berkshire retained Touche Ross & Company to audit its financial statements. As required by the Securities and Exchange Commission, Berkshire filed an 8-K statement with that federal agency to disclose the change in auditors. In that statement, Berkshire reported it was "dissatisfied" with Peat Marwick's inconsistency regarding the proper accounting treatment for stock redemptions.[4]

QUESTIONS

1. Warren Buffett invoked the substance-over-form concept to justify accounting for the GEICO and General Foods transactions as dividend distributions rather

---

1. Warren Buffett gained control of Berkshire Hathaway in the mid-1960s and since that time has become recognized as one of the nation's shrewdest investors. Dubbed the "Oracle of Omaha" for his skill in identifying undervalued and underappreciated stocks, Buffett's name appears annually near the top of the *Forbes 400*. Recently, *Forbes* pegged Buffett's estimated net worth at more than $35 billion.

2. 1984 Annual Report of Berkshire Hathaway, Inc., 3.

3. L. Berton, "Billionaire Investor Loses Recent Battle with Auditor," *The Wall Street Journal*, 26 April 1985, 18.

4. "Berkshire Hathaway Dismisses Its Auditor in Accounting Dispute," *The Wall Street Journal*, 8 July 1985, 21.

than as sales of stock. Buffett pointed out that Berkshire's proportionate interest in those companies' undistributed earnings since it purchased their stock far exceeded the amount of funds Berkshire received in the stock redemptions. Buffett also observed that the Internal Revenue Service considers proportionate redemptions to be equivalent to dividend distributions. Do you agree with Buffett that the substance of each of the proportionate redemptions was a dividend and not a sale of stock? Defend your answer.

2. In deciding how to account for an unusual or unique transaction for financial reporting purposes, should one consider the tax treatment applied to the transaction? Explain.

3. In 1983, Peat Marwick accepted Berkshire's decision to account for the GEICO transaction as a dividend distribution but then decided the following year that both the GEICO and General Foods transactions should be treated as sales of stock. Did Peat Marwick have a right to change its position on the proper accounting treatment for the stock redemptions? What factor or factors may have been responsible for Peat Marwick's decision to change its position regarding these transactions?

CASE 2.5
IFG LEASING

In 1974, Inter-Regional Financial Group, Inc. (IFG), a financial services company based in Minneapolis, purchased a small leasing company located in Great Falls, Montana. The leasing company, renamed IFG Leasing, was a wholly-owned subsidiary of IFG but filed periodic financial statements with the Securities and Exchange Commission (SEC) because it had publicly traded debt securities. IFG Leasing's sole line of business was the writing of "small ticket" leases. Small ticket leases typically have terms of three to five years and involve assets such as farm machinery, office furniture, and construction equipment. IFG Leasing rapidly expanded following its acquisition by IFG. In 1974, IFG Leasing had 30 employees and $20 million in lease receivables, the company's principal asset.[1] Seven years later, IFG Leasing had more than 400 employees in 10 branch offices scattered across the country and nearly $400 million in lease receivables, which represented 35 percent of IFG's consolidated assets.

Most of IFG Leasing's phenomenal growth occurred in the period 1979–1981. In hindsight, that rapid growth appears even more dramatic when one considers that U.S. interest rates reached their all-time high during that period. In December 1980, the prime interest rate peaked at 21.5 percent. At the same time, the effective interest rate charged by IFG Leasing to its customers approached 26 percent.

An aggressive marketing strategy allowed IFG Leasing to grow rapidly during a troubled economic period. Most of IFG Leasing's customers were companies and individuals who could not obtain asset financing from other sources.

---

1. By 1981, lease receivables accounted for 96 percent of IFG Leasing's total assets.

[IFG] Leasing enjoyed rapid growth by effectively becoming a "lender of last resort," lending to lessees who for a variety of reasons could not obtain financing elsewhere. . . . In short, Leasing fueled its growth with a substantial amount of "bad" credit risks.[2]

IFG Leasing experienced a much higher delinquency rate than other small ticket lessors.[3] By late 1981, internal reports indicated that approximately 15 percent of the company's receivables were 90 days or more delinquent. The industry norm was 1.2 percent. IFG Leasing's surging delinquency rate created a severe cash flow problem for the company during the early 1980s. The company used short-term loans to finance purchases of equipment and other assets for its leasing operations. Funds provided by customers' monthly lease payments provided the cash flows to service these loans. As the company's delinquency rate rose steadily, IFG Leasing was forced to obtain emergency cash infusions from its parent company and other IFG subsidiaries. In July 1983, IFG Leasing discontinued leasing equipment and focused its efforts exclusively on collecting outstanding lease receivables.

ACCOUNTING AND CONTROL PROBLEMS AT IFG LEASING

An SEC investigation in 1988 revealed that IFG Leasing concealed its deteriorating financial condition during the early 1980s from its banks and other financial statement users. The SEC discovered that IFG Leasing consistently reported an insufficient allowance for uncollectible lease receivables. Each accounting period, the company debited a fixed percentage of new lease receivables to bad debt expense with an offsetting credit to the allowance for uncollectible lease receivables. In 1981, company officials increased this percentage from 1.5 to 2 percent; the following year, they bumped the estimated bad debt rate up to 3 percent. These percentages proved to be grossly inadequate. The SEC's investigation disclosed that by September 1982, at least 20 percent of the company's receivables was more than 90 days delinquent. Surprisingly, the SEC investigation revealed that no one within the company had been assigned specific responsibility for evaluating the adequacy of the allowance for uncollectible lease receivables.

[IFG] Leasing's CEO testified that he relied on the company's CAO (chief accounting officer) to review the allowance. . . . The CAO testified that he relied on the CEO and the collections department to determine the adequacy of the allowance, and counted on Touche Ross [the company's auditors] to corroborate its adequacy. The collections manager testified that he relied on the CAO to review the adequacy of the allowance. . . .

2. This and all subsequent quotations were taken from Securities and Exchange Commission, *Accounting and Auditing Enforcement Release No. 200*, 23 September 1988.

3. When IFG Leasing recorded a lease, it debited lease receivables for the total amount of the payments to be received from the lessee over the term of the lease and credited the appropriate asset account (less the expected residual value of the asset). In that same entry, the company credited the difference between the aggregate lease payments and the depreciable cost of the leased asset to a deferred income account. IFG Leasing recorded income on the leases at a decreasing rate over the lease term, with a significant amount of the gross profit on each lease "front-ended" shortly after the lease was signed. The SEC later observed that this "front-ending" of lease income was a "very aggressive" accounting method compared with the income recognition methods used by other small-ticket lessors.

IFG [the parent company] senior management testified that they relied on IFG Leasing and Touche Ross to assess the allowance's adequacy.

Besides the obvious control problems related to lease receivables, the SEC identified several other major deficiencies in IFG Leasing's internal controls. For instance, the company had no systematic procedure for repossessing assets from customers who defaulted on lease payments. Many delinquent lessees continued to use leased equipment indefinitely. The SEC's investigation also disclosed that the company's leasing policies were often violated. Personnel in branch offices frequently changed lease terms without obtaining proper authorization. Finally, the SEC suggested that the company's performance-based compensation policies and the dominance of its operations by one individual, its founder and chief executive officer (CEO), contributed to a weak control environment.

As noted earlier, IFG Leasing's rapidly increasing delinquencies on its lease receivables presented major problems for the company in the early 1980s. Many of these problems stemmed from contractual features of its loan agreements. The loan agreements signed by the company when acquiring equipment generally included a clause that made a loan immediately due and payable if the equipment lessee became 90 days or more past due on its payments. Another common clause in IFG Leasing's loan agreements made a loan immediately due and payable if the company's 90-day delinquencies exceeded 6 percent of its total lease receivables.

IFG Leasing included aging summaries for its lease receivables in periodic financial statements filed with the SEC. The company also regularly submitted these summaries to banks and other lenders. To conceal the company's high delinquency rate on its lease receivables, a company executive began altering the aging summaries in 1980. Exhibit 1 lists delinquencies that IFG Leasing reported publicly and the corresponding delinquencies actually reflected by the company's accounting records. The SEC charged that the false aging summaries not only obscured the collectibility of the lease receivables but also caused IFG Leasing's overall financial statements to be misleading: "As a result, investors and creditors had no indication of [IFG] Leasing's critically deteriorating financial condition."

In early 1981, IFG Leasing's chief accounting officer, along with other company officials, brought the misleading aging summaries to the attention of IFG Leasing's CEO. The CEO refused to correct the aging summaries, alleging that the company's accounting system could not be relied upon to generate accurate estimates of delinquent receivables. The CEO reportedly threatened to fire any officer who disclosed the internally generated loan delinquency figures to anyone outside the company.

In September 1982, IFG Leasing's chief accounting officer reported the company's actual receivables delinquencies to IFG headquarters in Minneapolis.

| | Publicly Reported | | Internally Reported | |
Date	90-Day Delinquencies	% of Lease Receivables	90-Day Delinquencies	% of Lease Receivables
Dec. 1980	$ 6,800,000	2.5	$31,000,000	11.5
Dec. 1981	16,200,000	4.3	57,300,000	15.3
Mar. 1982	25,700,000	6.4	63,700,000	15.9
June 1982	31,700,000	7.5	83,400,000	19.5
Sep. 1982	33,900,000	7.7	89,300,000	20.2

EXHIBIT 1
IFG Leasing's Publicly Reported and Internally Reported Delinquent Receivables, 1980–1982

After reviewing the matter, IFG executives forced the subsidiary to record a $17 million increase in its allowance for uncollectible lease receivables. Several months later, IFG ordered the subsidiary to discontinue writing new leases and instead to focus exclusively on collecting lease receivables.

1980 TOUCHE ROSS AUDIT OF IFG LEASING

Touche Ross & Co. served as the independent audit firm of IFG Leasing and its parent company in the early 1980s. During the interim test-of-controls phase of the 1980 audit of IFG Leasing, Touche Ross auditors discovered that the client's aging summaries of lease receivables excluded numerous delinquent accounts. A Touche Ross audit senior brought this matter to the attention of client accounting personnel, who admitted that the summaries did not include certain delinquent accounts. The senior then discussed the misstated aging summaries with an IFG Leasing executive. The two individuals agreed to address this problem after the company's fiscal year-end. According to the SEC, the audit senior never raised this issue again with the client executive.

During the substantive testing phase of the 1980 audit, a junior auditor discovered that many of IFG Leasing's delinquent receivables did not appear in the company's year-end aging summaries. The junior auditor documented these omissions in the 1980 audit workpapers. After completing his review of these workpapers, the audit engagement partner instructed the audit senior to tell the junior auditor to erase all references she had made in the workpapers to the omitted delinquencies. The senior so instructed the junior auditor. "At first hesitant, the junior complied after being assured that Touche would recommend clarifying language reflecting the omissions that would accompany the aging tables appearing on the Form 10-K."

IFG Leasing never corrected its year-end aging summaries, nor did the company discuss the errors in those summaries elsewhere in its 10-K. After the client filed the 10-K with the SEC, the junior auditor discovered that the problems in the aging summaries were not disclosed or "clarified" in the 10-K. The junior auditor later testified that she did not pursue the matter any further at that point because she believed the audit engagement partner had resolved the issue somehow with client officials.

1981 TOUCHE ROSS AUDIT OF IFG LEASING

The SEC harshly criticized Touche Ross's 1981 audit of IFG Leasing. Touche Ross apparently failed to consider several key audit risk factors while planning the 1981 audit. In fact, the federal agency observed that Touche Ross's 1981 audit program "was in large part carried over from prior audits." Following are summaries of the SEC's principal criticisms of the 1981 audit plan that Touche Ross developed for IFG Leasing.

1. Touche Ross failed to test IFG Leasing's internal accounting controls for delinquent accounts. Because the auditors failed to test whether the accounting sys-

tem accurately aged delinquent accounts, they had no way of knowing whether the aging summaries they received from the client were accurate.

2. The Touche Ross audit plan called for testing of only a small proportion (8 percent) of the client's outstanding lease receivables. By focusing almost exclusively on lease receivables that were in excess of $50,000 and 120 days delinquent, Touche Ross overlooked a significant portion of receivables that were uncollectible.

3. Although the audit plan called for a review of the client's write-off policy for bad debts, it failed to require the field auditors to determine whether IFG Leasing actually applied that policy. In fact, the policy was not being applied. IFG Leasing used a "budget" system to write off bad debts. Because management did not want to "wipe out" the balance of the allowance for uncollectible lease receivables, the company limited write-offs of receivables known to be uncollectible to a predetermined maximum amount each accounting period. This budget system resulted at any point in time in a large backlog of uncollectible receivables that had not been charged to the allowance account. IFG Leasing carried many of these uncollectible receivables on its books for several years.

4. Despite the complexity of the IFG Leasing audit and the numerous audit risk factors posed by the client, most of the individuals assigned to the 1981 engagement were unfamiliar with the client and the leasing industry.

During the 1981 IFG Leasing audit, a junior auditor who had no previous experience with the leasing industry was assigned responsibility for auditing the allowance for uncollectible lease receivables. The junior auditor began his audit of the account by obtaining a computer run from the client that allegedly included all receivables that exceeded $50,000 and were more than 120 days delinquent. The auditor did not test the run to determine that it actually included all receivables meeting those criteria—which it did not. Later in the audit, the audit senior supervising this individual performed a limited test to determine whether the run included the client's designated "problem accounts." Problem accounts were a small subset of delinquent receivables, many of which were in litigation or arbitration. When the senior recognized several of these accounts in the computer run, she apparently concluded that it contained all delinquent accounts satisfying the two audit scope conditions. Neither auditor performed further tests of the run's completeness.

Shortly after obtaining the computer run of delinquent receivables, the junior auditor realized that he could not complete the audit procedures on all of those accounts in the time allotted by the audit budget. With the senior's approval, the junior selected 171 of the 264 accounts listed in the delinquency run for testing. The primary audit procedure used by the junior auditor to test the collectibility of the delinquent accounts was discussing them with the client's collections manager. The collections manager generally expressed an optimistic opinion regarding the ultimate collectibility of individual delinquent accounts. However, the SEC later pointed out that the collections manager had little direct knowledge of the ability and/or incentive of delinquent customers to pay their outstanding balances. Instead, the managers of IFG Leasing's branch offices oversaw collection activities for delinquent accounts and thus were the client personnel most familiar with the collectibility of those accounts.

The audit program for the delinquent receivables also required the junior auditor to obtain written representations from the client's attorneys regarding selected problem accounts. The attorneys were asked to comment on losses the company could expect on problem accounts in litigation or in arbitration. Although the attorneys responded to the junior auditor, they did not respond on a timely basis. The earliest response received was March 8, 1982, *nearly two weeks after Touche Ross had issued an unqualified opinion on IFG Leasing's 1981 financial statements.* The attorneys' written responses identified numerous delinquent receivables not included in the computer run obtained by the junior auditor. These accounts were in excess of $50,000 and more than 120 days past due—the two criteria the client had allegedly used in preparing the computer run. In addition, for many of the problem accounts the attorneys provided higher estimates of projected losses than the estimates that had been developed by the junior auditor.

The SEC criticized the method Touche Ross used to arrive at an independent estimate of IFG Leasing's allowance for uncollectible lease receivables. The junior auditor, on his own initiative, established three guidelines for estimating the client's uncollectible receivables. If a delinquent account was in litigation, the junior auditor estimated that the client would eventually recover an amount equal to 50 percent of the cost of the leased asset. Prior experience demonstrated, however, that IFG Leasing seldom recovered more than 20 percent of the original cost of a repossessed asset. Additionally, the junior auditor failed to apply the 50 percent rule consistently. IFG Leasing's collections manager apparently convinced the junior auditor that a recovery percentage substantially greater than 50 percent should be used in many of these cases. If the junior auditor had applied the 50 percent rule consistently, his estimate of the allowance account would have been nearly $600,000 higher.

For delinquent accounts that the given customers had made a verbal commitment to pay, the junior auditor provided for a reserve of 10 percent. The SEC chided Touche Ross for invoking this rule of thumb, "The workpapers indicate no basis to assume that a mere promise to pay from a severely delinquent lessee provides any reliable indication of collectibility." Finally, the junior auditor did not provide any reserve for delinquent accounts on which a payment of any size had been received in the prior 30 days. Again, the SEC took issue with the validity of this criterion. Many of the customers in this latter category were delinquent on their monthly payments by more than one year, although they had made a nominal payment to IFG Leasing during the prior month.

The junior auditor's crude analysis suggested that the allowance for uncollectible receivables was understated by almost $4 million. After reviewing the junior auditor's workpapers, the audit engagement partner informed him that the assumptions he had used in arriving at his estimate were "too conservative." The partner instructed the junior auditor to reach a more "realistic" estimate of the allowance by "re-reviewing" the large delinquent accounts for which a significant reserve had been established. During his further review of these accounts, the junior auditor did not examine any additional documentation regarding their collectibility. Apparently, the only additional audit procedure performed by the junior auditor was another inquiry of the collections manager regarding these accounts. Based upon this cursory audit procedure, the junior auditor significantly reduced his estimated reserves for the given accounts. The SEC noted that the Touche Ross workpapers provided no support for the changes made by the junior auditor in his original estimates: ". . . the workpapers contain no evidence to support the reductions. Thus there is no basis for the junior auditor's statement that his revised estimates were 'more realistic.'"

After adjusting his initial estimate of the allowance account, the junior auditor noted that his figures showed a $1.2 million "cushion" remaining in the client's account balance. That is, after subtracting his estimated bad debt reserve for the receivables included in the delinquency run from the balance of the client's allowance account, more than $1 million remained in that account to provide a reserve for any nondelinquent receivables that might prove to be uncollectible.[4] These nondelinquent accounts totaled more than $340 million, meaning that the remaining allowance provided for a default rate on these receivables of only one-third of 1 percent. The SEC maintained that the Touche Ross auditors should have realized that percentage was much too low. In fact, the true balance of the allowance account was much smaller than reported by the company. As noted earlier, IFG Leasing gradually wrote off against the allowance account a large backlog of delinquent receivables *known to be uncollectible*, a practice not revealed to, or detected by, the Touche Ross auditors.

1982 TOUCHE ROSS AUDIT OF IFG LEASING

In September 1982, the chief accounting officer of IFG Leasing notified IFG executives that the subsidiary had almost $90 million of receivables 90 days or more past due. This revelation shocked the IFG executives. They instructed Touche Ross to begin the 1982 IFG Leasing audit as quickly as possible and to take a "hard look" at the adequacy of the allowance for uncollectible lease receivables. The magnitude of the delinquent accounts also alarmed the engagement audit partner for IFG Leasing. As a result, the audit partner developed a much more intensive audit plan for the allowance account during the 1982 audit compared with the audit plans used for that account in prior years.

The first change made by the audit partner was assigning an auditor with five years experience to the allowance for uncollectible lease receivables. Second, the partner modified the audit scope for testing delinquent lease receivables. He required that each receivable in excess of $50,000 and 90 days or more past due be tested. To arrive at an independent estimate of the allowance account, the estimated uncollectible percentage for the delinquent accounts exceeding $50,000 was applied to the remaining delinquent accounts. In prior audits, the smaller accounts had simply been ignored. Touche Ross also applied an expected bad debt percentage of 2 percent to all nondelinquent accounts. Finally, many of the oversights that occurred during the prior audits of the allowance account were corrected during the 1982 engagement. For instance, the auditors clerically tested the delinquency run to ensure that it was complete and obtained, on a timely basis, representations from the client's attorneys regarding the collectibility of problem accounts.

---

4. The junior auditor's estimate was significantly understated in the first place since millions of dollars of delinquent accounts were not included in the delinquency computer run. The SEC pointed out that the omission of numerous past due receivables from the computer run could have been discovered quite easily by totaling the dollar value of the accounts listed on the run and then subtracting that total from gross lease receivables. This difference would not have agreed with the total of the nondelinquent accounts reported in the company's records.

When the senior auditor assigned to the allowance for uncollectible lease receivables completed her audit procedures, she recommended a large increase in that account. After reviewing her workpapers, the audit engagement partner discussed the allowance with IFG's chief financial officer. These two individuals agreed to increase the allowance by $17 million, an increase much smaller than the adjustment proposed by the senior.[5] The SEC did not contest the adequacy of that adjustment; however, the federal agency insisted that IFG Leasing should have reported the item as a prior period adjustment, since it amounted to the correction of an error made in an earlier year.

> Where, as here, the adjustment to the estimate results from the oversight or misuse of facts that existed at the time the financial statements were prepared, that adjustment must be accounted for as the correction of an error. In attributing the entire $17 million adjustment to 1982, [IFG] Leasing materially understated its 1982 income, overstated its 1981 income, as well as understated its 1981 allowance, all in violation of GAAP.

The SEC also criticized Touche Ross for not challenging the reporting treatment applied to the $17 million adjustment. Touche Ross's workpapers indicated that the adjustment was attributable to events occurring in 1982 rather than to "problems that existed at the end of 1981 that went undetected." The SEC believed this conclusion was highly suspect, given the circumstances. At the very least, the SEC alleged, the Touche Ross auditors had a responsibility to further investigate the possibility that the large adjustment related, at least partially, to years prior to 1982.

EPILOGUE

In June 1983, IFG Leasing recorded an additional $25 million increase in its allowance for uncollectible lease receivables. Three years later, the SEC issued a permanent injunction against IFG, IFG Leasing, and three executives of the companies. This injunction stemmed from the materially false and misleading aging summaries for lease receivables included in registration statements filed with the federal agency. The injunction permanently enjoined the parties from further violations of the reporting and antifraud stipulations of the federal securities laws. Also in 1986, IFG filed suit against Touche Ross, alleging that the CPA firm negligently audited IFG Leasing. No public comment regarding the resolution of that lawsuit could be found. Finally, in 1988, the SEC censured the Touche Ross audit partner who supervised the 1980 through 1982 audits of IFG Leasing.

QUESTIONS

1. Identify alternative accounting methods that IFG Leasing could have used to estimate its allowance for uncollectible lease receivables. Which of these methods would have been preferable, given the circumstances? Was the "budget" system

---

5. The SEC's enforcement release does not disclose the amount of the senior auditor's proposed adjustment. The release simply states that her adjustment "significantly" exceeded the increase in the allowance account eventually agreed to by IFG management.

of writing off uncollectible receivables against the allowance account an acceptable accounting method?

2. The aging tables included in IFG Leasing's 10-K registration statements qualified as "other information," according to the auditing profession's technical standards. What responsibilities do auditors have to attest to the material accuracy of "other information" included in an annual report or registration statement that also contains audited financial statements?

3. Did the junior auditor who discovered the errors in the 1980 aging summaries fulfill her professional responsibility to follow up on the resolution of that problem? Why or why not?

4. Identify the key "inherent risk" factors for the 1980 through 1982 IFG Leasing audits. How should these factors have influenced the nature, extent, and timing of the audit procedures applied by Touche Ross?

5. During the 1981 audit, client representations served as the principal type of evidence collected to support the balance of the allowance account. Identify the limitations of using client representations as audit evidence. Identify the other basic types of audit evidence. Which, if any, of these additional types of audit evidence should the junior auditor have considered collecting during his examination of the allowance account?

6. The time budget for the allowance account significantly restricted the scope of the audit procedures applied to that account during the 1981 audit. Should time budgets be allowed to restrict the scope of independent audits? Why or why not?

7. Identify the factors that determine whether period-ending adjustments, such as the $17 million adjustment made to the allowance account during the 1982 audit, should be treated as prior period adjustments or changes in accounting estimates. Do you agree with the SEC that the $17 million adjustment should have been reported as a prior period adjustment? Explain.

Case 2.6
Giant Stores Corporation

Following the end of World War II, large discount stores began appearing in the major cities of the northeastern United States and then quickly spread across the nation. Numerous mergers among these stores led to the formation of large discount retail chains that could offer even greater discounts to their customers given the huge quantities in which they purchased goods. Discount chains flourished for more than two decades with their low overhead cost structures and deep discount pricing strategies. In the 1970s, discount retailers began seeing their sales drop as many consumers opted for the higher product quality and better service available in major department stores.

Giant Stores Corporation found itself among the many discount retailers that began experiencing financial problems in the early 1970s. Founded in 1959 and headquartered in Chelmsford, Massachusetts, Giant Stores realized dramatic sales growth during the 1960s. By 1972, the company operated 112 retail outlets. In that year, Giant Stores executives faced the unpleasant prospect of reporting a net loss for the first time in the company's history. But, that loss was not reported. By manipulating the company's financial records, Giant Stores executives converted a $2.5 million loss for 1972 into a $1.5 million profit. This dishonesty did not go unpunished. When the accounting chicanery was later revealed, a federal grand jury indicted several of the company's officers on various fraud charges. Four of those officers either pleaded guilty or were convicted of the charges.

Accounts Payable Irregularities

A principal means Giant Stores executives used to misrepresent their company's financial condition was understating amounts owed to suppliers. Exhibit 1 sum-

EXHIBIT 1
**Accounts Payable
Balances Intentionally
Understated by Giant
Stores Executives**

Vendor	Reduction in Accounts Payable Balance	Purported Reason for Reduction
Various	$300,000	Previously unrecorded advertising credits
Millbrook Distributors	257,000	Return of merchandise, volume discounts, and a concession to retain Giant Stores as a customer
Rozefsky, Inc.	130,000	Return of merchandise
Various (referred to as Miller-Lesser overcharges by the SEC)	177,000	Overcharges on earlier invoices
Several health and beauty aid (HBA) manufacturers	162,000	Return of merchandise

marizes the accounts payable that the executives fraudulently understated as of January 29, 1972, the company's 1972 fiscal year-end. That exhibit also reports the reasons given to Touche Ross, the company's audit firm, for the accounting adjustments used to understate the given accounts payable balances.

Advertising Credits

An investigation by the Securities and Exchange Commission (SEC) revealed that Giant Stores' president and treasurer ordered the head of the company's advertising department to generate $300,000 of fictitious advertising credits near the end of fiscal 1972. The advertising manager complied by preparing a 14-page memorandum listing alleged advertising credits granted to Giant Stores by approximately 1,100 of its suppliers. (Note: Recognize that individual payable accounts were debited when these "credits" were recorded.) The number and cumulative dollar amount of the advertising credits surprised the Touche Ross auditors. When questioned by the auditors, client officials claimed that the advertising department had been negligent in recording and collecting the credits over the previous several months.

To test the 14-page listing of advertising credits, Touche Ross mailed confirmations to four of the vendors on the list and asked client personnel to provide supporting documentation for another 20 of the credits. The SEC charged that the audit procedures applied to the advertising credits were inadequate for several reasons. First, according to the SEC, the sample size of 24 items did not provide sufficient evidence to reach a valid conclusion regarding the material accuracy of the cumulative $300,000 of advertising credits. Second, Touche Ross apparently failed to follow up on comments made by vendors who returned the accounts payable confirmations. Many of these comments suggested that the purported credits were in error. Third, the SEC criticized Touche Ross for relying on internal client documentation to corroborate the secondary sample of 20 credits selected for testing. Given the suspicious nature and timing of the advertising credits, the SEC maintained that Touche Ross should have obtained more rigorous and extensive audit evidence to support those items.

Millbrook Distributors

Giant Stores' chairman of the board and the company's vice-president of finance produced 28 fictitious credit memos in early 1972. These credit memos reduced by $257,000 the outstanding balance of Giant Stores' payable to Millbrook Distributors, a major supplier of health and beauty aids. Touche Ross auditors received three different explanations regarding the source of these credit memos. Initially, Giant officials told the auditors that the credit memos were for merchandise returns. Then the auditors were told that the credit memos resulted from volume discounts granted to Giant Stores. Finally, client management insisted that the reduction in the Millbrook payable was a concession Millbrook made to retain Giant Stores as a customer. A Touche Ross staff auditor questioned the credibility of the latter explanation. The payable reduction seemed much too large a price for Millbrook to pay to retain Giant Stores as a customer, given the relatively modest volume of transactions between the two companies.[1]

Touche Ross eventually requested that a Millbrook executive confirm the $257,000 concession granted to Giant Stores. In response to this request, Giant Stores' vice-president of finance placed a telephone call, in the presence of Touche Ross auditors, to an individual who was supposedly Millbrook's president. Following a brief conversation, the vice-president handed the phone to an auditor. The individual on the other end of the line verbally confirmed the concession and agreed to send Touche Ross a written confirmation to that effect.

A few days later, Giant Stores' vice-president of finance notified Touche Ross that Millbrook's president had changed his mind about providing the written confirmation. Millbrook's president was reportedly angry because the confirmation had not been delivered to him personally, as he had requested. At this point, the two staff auditors assigned to investigate the Millbrook credit memos wrote a memorandum, which they included in the Touche Ross workpapers. In this memorandum, the staff auditors questioned the validity of the $257,000 reduction in the Millbrook payable. Despite this memo, the audit engagement partner decided that sufficient evidence had been collected to support the reduced balance of the Millbrook payable and chose not to pursue the matter any further.

Rozefsky, Inc.

Another vendor of Giant Stores in the early 1970s was Rozefsky, Inc. Giant Stores personnel reduced by $130,000 the amount owed to Rozefsky at the end of fiscal 1972 by posting (debiting) 35 false credit memos to the vendor's payable account. Rozefsky allegedly issued these credit memos for goods returned by various retail outlets of Giant Stores. The SEC's subsequent investigation revealed that many of these memos involved stores that did not stock Rozefsky products.

A Touche Ross staff auditor who obtained copies of the Rozefsky credit memos noticed that a felt-tip marker had been used to obscure a typed sentence on each of them. By holding the memos up to a light, the auditor was able to read the obscured sentence: "Do not post until merchandise is received."[2] Ostensibly, this note

1. Giant Stores never contested the actual amount due Millbrook Distributors. The company later paid that amount and the total amounts due other suppliers whose payable balances were intentionally understated.

2. This and all subsequent quotations were taken from Securities and Exchange Commission, *Accounting Series Release No. 153A*, 27 June 1979.

informed a Giant Stores accounting clerk not to reduce the Rozefsky account balance for the invoiced goods until the cost of the goods was credited to that account.

After reviewing the credit memos, the Touche Ross staff auditor called a Rozefsky accountant and inquired regarding the alleged merchandise returns. The accountant reported that none of the goods had been returned by Giant Stores. The staff auditor then informed the Touche Ross audit engagement partner of the memos and his conversation with the vendor's accountant. When told of this matter by the audit partner, Giant Stores' vice-president of finance responded that he spoke with the Rozefsky accountant shortly after the staff auditor contacted that individual. According to the vice-president, the Rozefsky accountant indicated that the staff auditor misinterpreted their conversation regarding the memos. Additionally, the Rozefsky accountant reportedly confirmed to the vice-president that the memos actually were for returned goods. The vice-president insisted that the audit partner not contact the Rozefsky accountant to discuss the matter any further because of "pending litigation" between the two companies. The audit partner ultimately accepted the client's explanation for the credit memos after receiving letters confirming the merchandise returns. These confirmation letters were provided by the managers of the Giant Stores who allegedly ordered and then returned the merchandise in question to Rozefsky.

Miller-Lesser Overcharges

Giant Stores executives instructed two subordinates to prepare a list of several hundred merchandise purchases on which Giant Stores had been supposedly overcharged by suppliers. These overcharges totaled approximately $177,000. Touche Ross audited these overcharges by selecting random line items from the client-prepared list and then confirming the overcharges via telephone calls to the vendors.

> The procedure used in soliciting the fifteen telephone confirmations allowed Giant to communicate with the vendor first and to inform the vendor that Touche Ross would be calling them. Giant then placed a second call to reexplain the nature of the Touche Ross inquiry, after which the telephone was handed to the Touche Ross auditor. Only then was the Touche Ross auditor permitted to speak over the telephone to the vendor.

The results of this confirmation procedure and limited other audit tests persuaded Touche Ross to accept the overcharges as valid reductions to the various payable accounts. The subsequent SEC investigation disclosed that, under similar circumstances, three of Giant Stores' suppliers provided false confirmations to Touche Ross after apparently being convinced to do so by Giant Stores executives.

HBA Credits

A final deliberate understatement of accounts payable involved several large credit memos that Giant Stores had allegedly received from health and beauty aid (HBA) manufacturers. The credit memos indicated that Giant Stores had returned $162,000 of merchandise to these manufacturers. Apparently none of these merchandise returns ever occurred. Similar to the other fictitious entries to Giant Stores' accounts payable, the SEC criticized Touche Ross for failing to adequately investigate these items.

ADDITIONAL SEC CRITICISM OF THE 1972 TOUCHE ROSS AUDIT OF GIANT STORES

Besides criticizing the audit procedures applied to accounts payable, the SEC challenged several other facets of Touche Ross's 1972 audit of Giant Stores. Of particular concern to the SEC was the extent of pressure that Touche Ross allowed Giant Stores executives to impose on members of the audit engagement team: "The audit was conducted under stressful conditions including a request from Giant to Touche Ross to fire [the audit engagement partner], a Giant executive's threat to throw one staff auditor off the premises and profane verbal abuse of a staff auditor from another Giant executive." At one point during the audit, the bullying tactics of Giant Stores executives and the suspicious nature of the large year-end adjustments to accounts payable led one staff auditor to suggest that the client was engaging in, and attempting to cover up, an accounting fraud. The audit engagement partner chose to ignore the staff auditor's speculation.

The SEC also charged that the Touche Ross audit engagement partner and a second partner who assisted in completing the audit were too willing to compromise with client personnel. According to the SEC, the two partners arrived at certain audit judgments "through a trade-off and bargaining process not conducive to appropriate audit decisions." This bargaining process was particularly evident during a meeting between the partners and Giant Stores executives that took place in April 1972, shortly before the completion of the 1972 audit. The purpose of the meeting was to determine the final disposition of several questionable items that the Touche Ross auditors identified during the audit.

> During this meeting, Giant personnel continuously calculated earnings per share on a pocket calculator. When the calculations reached Giant's reduced target earnings of $.83 per share, Giant ceased to be contentious.

COLLAPSE OF GIANT STORES

Giant Stores filed its 10-K statement for the fiscal year ended January 29, 1972, with the SEC on April 28, 1972. The 10-K included an unqualified audit opinion issued by Touche Ross on Giant Stores' financial statements. Later in the year, Giant used those financial statements and the accompanying audit opinion to help sell $3 million of additional stock and to raise $12 million of debt capital.

In an April 1973 press release, the president of Giant Stores disclosed that "bookkeeping errors" might affect the company's reported profit for the prior year. Approximately one month later, Touche Ross withdrew its unqualified opinion on Giant Stores' 1972 financial statements. In August 1973, Giant Stores filed a bankruptcy petition with a federal court in Boston. Two years later, that court declared Giant insolvent and began liquidating the company.

The former president and vice-president of finance of Giant Stores were convicted in 1978 of conspiracy to file false financial statements with the SEC. Prior to those convictions, the former chairman and treasurer of Giant Stores pleaded guilty to similar charges. Each of the four individuals was fined and given jail terms ranging from six to eighteen months.

The SEC issued the final report on its lengthy investigation of the Giant Stores fraud in June 1979. As a result of that investigation, the SEC censured Touche Ross and prohibited the Giant Stores audit engagement partner from practicing before the federal agency for five months. The SEC also required Touche Ross to undergo an extensive review of its operating procedures by a panel of independent experts. Exhibit 2 lists the specific operating procedures of Touche Ross that the SEC instructed the independent panel to review.

QUESTIONS

1. In auditing accounts payable, which of the five management assertions identified by *SAS No. 31*, "Evidential Matter," is of primary concern to an auditor? Why?

2. Auditors often use a "search for unrecorded liabilities" as a year-end substantive test for a client's current liabilities. Briefly explain the nature of the search for unrecorded liabilities. How might this audit procedure have resulted in the detection of the irregularities in Giant Stores' accounts payable?

3. Develop a statistical sampling plan that Touche Ross could have employed to test the material accuracy of the $300,000 total of the 14-page listing of purported advertising credits.

4. Discuss the validity of audit evidence collected via telephone confirmations. Under what general conditions is it permissible for auditors to accept telephone confirmations?

5. How do accounts payable and accounts receivable confirmation procedures differ? Comment on both technical differences and differences in audit objectives between the two audit tests.

EXHIBIT 2
Touche Ross Operating Procedures that the SEC Instructed an Independent Panel to Review

1. Hiring practices for all professionals (partners and employees).
2. Training and continuing education of all professionals.
3. Promotion and compensation of all professionals.
4. Acceptance and retention of clients.
5. Setting and recovering audit engagement fees.
6. Allocation of professional responsibilities within the firm.
7. Professional staffing of offices.
8. Methods of maintaining professional independence.
9. Conduct of audit engagements.
   a. professional staffing and allocation of responsibilities
   b. audit program and workpaper preparation and review
   c. inter-office communications in the case of multi-office engagements
   d. identification and resolution of problems during the course of the audit
   e. independence
   f. review of engagements
   g. availability and application of industry expertise
10. Formulating and communicating firm practices, procedures, and policies to professionals.
11. Procedures for creating and implementing quality controls.
12. Criteria and procedures followed in analyzing potential merger or combination of practice candidates.
13. Adequacy of corrective measures.

6. During the 1972 audit of Giant Stores, differences of opinion arose between the staff auditors assigned to that engagement and the audit engagement partner regarding the material accuracy of certain of the client's outstanding payables. How should such differences of opinion be resolved? Was it appropriate for the staff auditors to include a memorandum in the audit workpapers that questioned the validity of the disputed payables?

CASE 2.7
CAPITALBANC CORPORATION

In 1975, Carlos Cordova and several other investors founded Capital National Bank (CNB) in Bronx, New York.[1] Cordova was appointed the bank's chief executive officer and chairman of the board. Over the next several years, the bank opened five branch offices in the New York City metropolitan area. CNB catered primarily to the banking needs of Hispanic-American and immigrant communities in New York City. In 1986, Cordova and the other owners of CNB formed CapitalBanc Corporation, a publicly owned bank holding company registered with the Securities and Exchange Commission (SEC). Throughout its entire existence, the principal operating entity controlled by CapitalBanc was CNB. Cordova assumed the titles of president, chief executive officer, and chairman of the board of the new bank holding company.

In the fall of 1987, CapitalBanc retained Arthur Andersen & Co. as its independent audit firm. Andersen's first engagement for CapitalBanc was to audit the bank holding company's consolidated financial statements for the fiscal year ending December 31, 1987. Thomas Curtin, an Arthur Andersen partner since 1979, served as the engagement partner for the 1987 CapitalBanc audit. Curtin delegated the responsibility for much of the audit planning to James Lukenda, an audit manager with Arthur Andersen since 1983. Lukenda also supervised the staff auditors assigned to the CapitalBanc engagement.

On December 29, 1987, several Arthur Andersen staff auditors accompanied members of CNB's internal audit staff to the bank's 177th Street Branch. The Arthur Andersen auditors intended to observe and participate in a surprise count of the branch's cash funds by the internal auditors. Related audit objectives in-

---

1. The facts of this case were drawn from the 1987 annual report of CapitalBanc Corporation and the following source: Securities and Exchange Commission, *Accounting and Auditing Enforcement Release No. 458*, 28 June 1993.

cluded testing CNB's compliance with certain control procedures and evaluating the competence of the bank's internal audit staff.

The accounting personnel at each CNB branch maintained a "vault general ledger proof sheet" that reconciled the cash on hand to the balance of the branch's general ledger cash account. During the surprise cash count at the 177th Street Branch, the Arthur Andersen auditors discovered a $2.7 million reconciling item listed on the branch's proof sheet. That amount equaled 61 percent of the branch's general ledger cash balance and 45 percent of the branch's total cash funds that were supposed to be available on the date of the surprise count. When the staff auditors asked to count the $2.7 million of cash represented by the reconciling item, bank employees told them that Cordova had segregated those funds in a locked cabinet within the bank's main vault. Three keys were required to unlock the cabinet. Cordova, who was out of the country at the time, maintained custody of one of those keys.

Stymied temporarily, one of the staff auditors telephoned Lukenda. The staff auditor relayed to Lukenda the information regarding the $2.7 million of segregated cash. After considering the matter and discussing it with Curtin, Lukenda instructed the staff auditor to count the cash upon Cordova's return. Lukenda also reportedly told the staff auditor that it would not be necessary to place audit seals on the doors of the cabinet or to secure it in any other way given the three-key security system used by the branch. Following the telephone conversation with Lukenda, the staff auditor advised bank personnel that Arthur Andersen auditors would count the cash on the date Cordova returned from his trip.

CNB's practice of segregating a large amount of cash in the locked cabinet was clearly not a normal banking procedure. In a subsequent investigation, the SEC commented on this practice.

> It is an unusual circumstance for a substantial portion of a bank's cash to be inaccessible for an extended period of time. It is also unusual for a substantial portion of a bank's assets not to be invested and earning interest for an extended period of time.[2]

In early January 1988, an employee of the 177th Street Branch notified Arthur Andersen that Cordova would return on January 14. On that date, the Arthur Andersen staff auditors arrived at the branch to complete their count of the cash funds. Cordova opened the locked cabinet in the main vault in the presence of the staff auditors. The auditors then proceeded to count the $2.7 million that had not been counted on December 29, 1987. All of the cash was present. None of the other cash funds of the 177th Street Branch or other CNB branches was counted by the Arthur Andersen auditors on January 14, 1988.

After counting the segregated cash, the staff auditors asked Cordova why he kept those funds in the locked cabinet. Cordova replied that a customer who cashed a large certificate of deposit insisted on having the funds available on demand at all times. According to Cordova, the customer intended to use the funds to buy foreign currencies when market conditions became favorable. The volatility of the foreign currency market dictated that the customer have immediate access to the funds on a daily basis.

Near the completion of the 1987 CapitalBanc audit, Lukenda reviewed the workpaper that documented Cordova's explanation for the $2.7 million of segre-

---

2. Securities and Exchange Commission, *Accounting and Auditing Enforcement Release No. 458,* 28 June 1993.

gated cash. Lukenda then discussed that explanation with Curtin. After considering the matter, Curtin instructed Lukenda to have the staff auditors confirm that there was an offsetting liability to the given customer in CNB's accounting records equal to the amount of the segregated funds. The staff auditors obtained the documentation for this liability directly from CNB personnel. This information was not confirmed with the customer or independently verified by the auditors in any other way. The staff auditors also did not obtain documentation confirming that the customer had cashed a large certificate of deposit. Finally, the staff auditors neglected to obtain any evidence to corroborate Cordova's assertion regarding the customer's planned use of the funds.

Following the completion of the CapitalBanc audit in March 1988, Arthur Andersen issued an unqualified opinion on the firm's 1987 financial statements. Those financial statements reported a net income of $701,000, total cash funds of $14.1 million, and total assets of $143.2 million. CapitalBanc included the audited financial statements in its 1987 10-K registration statement filed with the SEC.

EPILOGUE

In July 1990, the Office of the Comptroller of the Currency declared CapitalBanc Corporation insolvent and placed it under the control of the Federal Deposit Insurance Corporation (FDIC). The following year, Banco Popular de Puerto Rico purchased the assets of CNB from the FDIC.

In late 1991, Carlos Cordova pleaded guilty to three counts of bank fraud and conspiracy to commit bank fraud. Two of Cordova's associates pleaded guilty to similar charges. Earlier in 1991, Cordova had agreed to an order issued by the SEC that permanently banned him from serving as an officer or director of a public company. A federal investigation of CNB's financial affairs revealed that Cordova misappropriated at least $400,000 of the $2.7 million allegedly stored in the locked cabinet in the 177th Street Branch's main vault. Cordova, with the help of his subordinates, had intentionally concealed this shortage from the Arthur Andersen auditors during the 1987 audit. Cordova secretly returned to the 177th Street Branch on January 9, 1988, and placed cash obtained from other CNB branches in the locked cabinet. As a result, Arthur Andersen's count of the cash in the locked cabinet on January 14, 1988, failed to uncover Cordova's embezzlement.

The description of the three-key security system relayed to the Arthur Andersen auditors by employees of the 177th Street Branch was a subterfuge. The fast-thinking employees conceived that hoax to deter the auditors from gaining access to the locked cabinet on the day of the surprise cash count. Cordova's explanation regarding why he kept the large amount of cash segregated in the locked cabinet was also a fabrication.

In 1993, the SEC reported the results of its investigation of Arthur Andersen's 1987 CapitalBanc audit, an investigation that focused on the audit of the 177th Street Branch's cash funds. In that report, the SEC disclosed the following sanctions imposed on Thomas Curtin and James Lukenda.

> It is hereby ordered, that Respondents [Curtin and Lukenda] are censured and must be
> duly registered and in good standing as certified public accountants in the states in

which they each reside or their principal office is located and they must each become a member of or be associated with a member firm of the SEC Practice Section of the AICPA's Division for CPA Firms as long as they practice before the Commission.[3]

QUESTIONS

1. In auditing cash, which of the five management assertions discussed in *SAS No. 31*, "Evidential Matter," is of primary concern to the auditor? Why?
2. Identify audit procedures that should be applied to cash funds maintained by a client on its business premises.
3. Identify mistakes or oversights made by Arthur Andersen personnel while auditing the cash funds at the 177th Street Branch.

---

3. *Ibid.*

Section Three
Internal Control Issues

CASE 3.1
THE TROLLEY DODGERS

In 1890, the Brooklyn Trolley Dodgers professional baseball team joined the National League. Over the following years, the Dodgers would have considerable difficulty competing with the other baseball teams in the New York City area. Those teams, principal among them the New York Yankees, were much better financed and generally stocked with players of higher caliber. In 1958, after nearly seven decades of mostly frustration on and off the baseball field, the Dodgers shocked the sports world by moving to Los Angeles. Walter O'Malley, the flamboyant owner of the Dodgers, saw an opportunity to introduce professional baseball to the rapidly growing population of the West Coast. More important, O'Malley saw an opportunity to make his team more profitable. As an inducement to the Dodgers, Los Angeles County purchased a goat farm located in Chavez Ravine, an area two miles northwest of downtown Los Angeles, and gave the property to O'Malley for the site of his new baseball stadium.

Since moving to Los Angeles, the Dodgers have been the envy of the baseball world: "In everything from profit to stadium maintenance . . . the Dodgers are the prototype of how a franchise should be run."[1] During the 1980s, the Dodgers reigned as the most profitable franchise in baseball with a pretax profit margin approaching 25 percent in many years. In late 1997, Peter O'Malley, Walter O'Malley's son and the Dodgers' principal owner, sold the franchise for $350 million to media mogul Rupert Murdoch. A spokesman for Murdoch complimented the O'Malley family for the longstanding success of the Dodgers organization. "The O'Malleys have set a gold standard for franchise ownership . . . we will do all in our power to live up to that standard."[2]

---

1. R.J. Harris, "Forkball for Dodgers: Costs Up, Gate Off," *The Wall Street Journal*, 31 August 1990, B1, B4.

2. R. Newhan, "Dodger Sale Heads for Home," *Los Angeles Times*, 5 September 1997, C1, C12.

During an interview before he sold the Dodgers, Peter O'Malley attributed the success of his organization to the experts he had retained in all functional areas: "I don't have to be an expert on taxes, split-fingered fastballs, or labor relations with our ushers. That talent is all available."[3] Edward Campos, a longtime accountant for the Dodgers, was seemingly a perfect example of one of those experts in the Dodgers organization. Campos accepted an entry-level position with the Dodgers as a young man. By 1986, after almost two decades with the club, he had worked his way up the employment hierarchy to become the operations payroll chief.

After taking charge of the Dodgers' payroll department, Campos designed and implemented a new payroll system, a system that reportedly only he fully understood. In fact, Campos controlled the system so completely that he personally filled out the weekly payroll cards for each of the 400 employees of the Dodgers. Campos was known not only for his work ethic but also for his loyalty to the club and its owners: "The Dodgers trusted him, and when he was on vacation, he even came back and did the payroll."[4]

Unfortunately, the Dodgers' trust in Campos was misplaced. Over a period of several years, Campos embezzled several hundred thousand dollars from his employer. According to court records, Campos padded the Dodgers' payroll by adding fictitious employees to various departments in the organization. In addition, Campos routinely inflated the number of hours worked by several employees and then split the resulting overpayments fifty-fifty with those individuals.

The fraudulent scheme came unraveled when Campos became ill with appendicitis, forcing the Dodgers' controller to temporarily assume his responsibilities. While completing the payroll one week, the controller noticed that several employees, including ushers, security guards, and ticket salespeople, were being paid unusually large amounts. In some cases, employees earning $7 an hour received weekly paychecks approaching $2,000. Following a criminal investigation and the filing of charges against Campos and his cohorts, all the individuals involved in the payroll fraud confessed.

A state court sentenced Campos to eight years in prison and required him to make restitution of approximately $132,000 to the Dodgers. Another of the conspirators also received a prison sentence. The remaining individuals involved in the payroll scheme made restitution and were placed on probation.

QUESTIONS

1. Identify the key audit objectives for a client's payroll function. Comment on both objectives related to tests of controls and those related to substantive audit procedures.
2. What internal control weaknesses were evident in the Dodgers' payroll system?
3. Identify audit procedures that might have led to the discovery of the fraudulent scheme masterminded by Campos.

3. Harris, "Forkball for Dodgers," B1.

4. P. Feldman, "7 Accused of Embezzling $332,583 from Dodgers," *Los Angeles Times*, 17 September 1986, Sec. 2, 1, 6.

CASE 3.2
HOWARD STREET JEWELERS, INC.

Lore Levi was worried as she scanned the March 1983 bank statement for the Howard Street Jewelers.[1] For more than four decades, she and her husband, Julius, had owned and operated the small business. Certainly the business had experienced ups and downs before, but now it seemed to be in a downward spiral from which it could not recover. In previous times when sales had slackened, the Levis had survived by cutting costs here and there. But now, despite several measures the Levis had taken to control costs, the business's cash position continued to steadily worsen. If a turnaround did not occur soon, Mrs. Levi feared that she and her husband might be forced to close their store.

Mrs. Levi had a theory regarding the financial problems of Howard Street Jewelers. On more than one occasion, she had wondered whether Betty the cashier, a trusted and reliable employee for nearly 20 years, might be stealing from the cash register. To Mrs. Levi, it was a logical assumption. Besides working as a part-time sales clerk, Betty handled all of the cash that came into the business and maintained the cash receipts and sales records. If anybody had an opportunity to steal from the business, it was Betty.

Reluctantly, Mrs. Levi approached her husband about her theory. Mrs. Levi pointed out to Julius that Betty had unrestricted access to the cash receipts of the business. Additionally, over the previous few years, Betty had developed a taste for more expensive clothes and more frequent and costly vacations. Julius quickly dismissed his wife's speculation. To him, the possibility that Betty could be steal-

---

1. Most of the facts of this case were reconstructed from information included in several legal opinions. The following two articles served as additional sources for this case: *Securities Regulation and Law Report*, "Accounting & Disclosure: Accounting Briefs," Vol. 23, No. 21 (24 May 1991), 814; *Securities Regulation and Law Report*, "Accounting & Disclosure: Accounting Briefs," Vol. 24, No. 19 (8 May 1992), 708.

ing from the business seemed preposterous. A frustrated Mrs. Levi then raised the subject with her son, Alvin, who worked side by side with his parents in the family business. Alvin responded similarly to his father and warned his mother that she was becoming paranoid.

Near the end of each year, the Levis met with their accountant to discuss various matters, principally taxation issues. The Levis placed considerable trust in the CPA who served as their accountant; for almost 40 years he had given them solid, professional advice on a wide range of accounting and business matters. When Mrs. Levi confided to the accountant about her suspicions regarding Betty the cashier, he listened intently and then commented that he had noticed occasional shortages in the cash receipts records that seemed larger than normal for a small retail business. Despite Julius's protestations that Betty could not be responsible for any cash shortages, the accountant encouraged the Levis to closely monitor her work.

Embezzlements are often discovered by luck rather than by design. So it was with the Howard Street Jewelers. In the spring of 1985, a customer approached the cash register and told Alvin Levi that she wanted to make a payment on a lay-away item. Alvin, who was working the cash register because it was Betty's day off, searched the file of lay-away sales tickets and the daily sales records but found no trace of the customer's lay-away purchase. Finally, he apologized and asked the customer to return the next day when Betty would be back at work.

The following day, Alvin told Betty that he was unable to find the lay-away sales ticket. Betty expressed surprise and said she would search for the ticket herself. Within a few minutes, Betty approached Alvin, waving the sales ticket in her hand. Alvin was stumped. He had searched the lay-away sales file several times and simply could not accept Betty's explanation that the missing ticket had been there all along. Suspicious, as well, was the fact that the sale had not been recorded in the sales records—a simple oversight, Betty had explained. As Alvin returned to his work, a troubling and sickening sensation settled into the pit of his stomach. Over the next several weeks, Alvin studied the daily sales and cash receipts records. He soon realized that his mother had been right all along. Betty, the trusted, reliable, longtime cashier of the Howard Street Jewelers, was stealing from the business. The estimated embezzlement loss suffered by Howard Street Jewelers over the term of Betty's employment approached $350,000.

QUESTIONS

1. Identify the internal control concepts that the Levis overlooked or ignored.
2. When Mrs. Levi informed the CPA of her suspicions regarding Betty, what responsibilities, if any, did the CPA have to pursue this matter? In addition to preparing tax returns for Howard Street Jewelers, alternately assume that the CPA (a) *audited* the business's annual financial statements, (b) *reviewed* the annual financial statements, and (c) *compiled* the annual financial statements.
3. Assume that you have a small CPA firm and have been contacted by a husband and wife, Robby and Sharon White, who are in the final stages of negotiating to purchase a local jewelry store. Robby will prepare jewelry settings, size jewelry for customers, and perform related tasks, while Sharon will be the head sales-clerk. The Whites intend to retain four of the current employees of the jewelry

store—two salesclerks, a cashier, and a college student who cleans the store, runs errands, and does various other odd jobs. They inform you that the average inventory of the jewelry store is $100,000 and that annual sales average $400,000, 30 percent of which occur in the six weeks prior to Christmas.

The Whites are interested in retaining you as their accountant should they purchase the store. They know little about accounting and have no prior experience as business owners. They would require assistance in establishing an accounting system, monthly financial statements for internal use, annual financial statements to be submitted to their banker, and all necessary tax returns. Robby and Sharon are particularly concerned with control issues, given the dollar value of inventory that will be on hand in the store and the significant amount of cash that will be processed daily.

You see this as an excellent opportunity to acquire a good client. However, you have not had a chance to prepare for your meeting with the Whites because they came in without an appointment. You do not want to ask them to come back later, since that may encourage them to check out your competitor across the street.

Required: Provide the Whites with an overview of the key internal control issues they will face in operating a jewelry store. In your overview, identify at least five control activities you believe they should implement if they acquire the store. You have never had a jewelry store as a client but you have several small retail clients. Attempt to impress the Whites with your understanding of internal control issues for small retail businesses.

CASE 3.3
E.F. HUTTON
& COMPANY, INC.

Edward F. Hutton was born into a poor family in New York City in 1876. Fatherless at the age of ten and lacking a high school education, Hutton drifted from one job to another in New York City's financial district until his mid-twenties. Hutton's personal fortunes took a sudden turn for the better when he married the daughter of a well-to-do broker. In 1904, with the financial backing of his father-in-law, Hutton founded a small brokerage firm, E.F. Hutton & Company, Inc. Ever the opportunist, Hutton recognized the growth potential for his industry in California and opened a San Francisco office of his firm in 1905. E.F. Hutton & Co. was the first brokerage with operations on both coasts and the first to have a private telegraph wire connecting New York City and San Francisco. With this communications link, Hutton's firm had the ability to complete bi-coastal securities transactions in a matter of three minutes.

The devastating San Francisco earthquake of 1906 contributed heavily to the early financial success of E.F. Hutton & Co. Hutton's direct telegraph line to New York City was one of the few, possibly the only, communication linkages to the East Coast immediately following the 1906 quake. Because no other Wall Street brokerage firms were aware of the earthquake for several hours, the Hutton firm was able to use that short period of time to pile up large trading profits for itself and its customers. E.F. Hutton & Co. cultivated and rewarded such ingenuity over its entire existence. Top management disdained bureaucratic policies, centralized decision making, and organizational charts, all of which they believed stifled employee creativity. Instead, Hutton's management encouraged subordinates to exercise their own judgment and to be innovative, particularly when it came to increasing their employer's profitability. Ironically, the firm's laissez-faire management style ultimately proved to be its undoing.

E.F. Hutton & Co. grew and prospered over the first three-quarters of the twentieth century. By the 1970s, Hutton ranked as the second largest brokerage firm in

199

the nation and enjoyed the industry's highest return on stockholders' equity. But then, disaster struck. In the spring of 1985, the brokerage firm pleaded guilty to 2,000 counts of mail and wire fraud. The fallout from this scandal eventually drove Hutton to the brink of insolvency before it was bought out in 1988 by Shearson Lehman Brothers, one of its major competitors.

The mail and wire fraud indictment filed against Hutton culminated an intensive, two-year investigation by the U.S. Justice Department. Federal prosecutors charged Hutton with defrauding numerous banks with which it did business. These charges stemmed from a complex cash management system that the brokerage firm used to run up huge negative balances in its operating bank accounts. The enormous cash overdrafts were essentially interest-free loans from Hutton's banks. The banks extending these "loans" either failed to uncover Hutton's scheme or were coerced into ignoring it by Hutton officials. In any case, the cash overdrafts allowed Hutton's branch managers to earn abnormally large amounts of interest profits, 10 percent of which went directly to the managers in the form of an annual bonus.

The disclosure of the Hutton scheme and the firm's subsequent guilty plea shocked the nation's financial community and the federal government. Justice Department officials alleged that Hutton's cash management practices, if used by a large number of corporations, would have threatened the nation's entire banking system. That allegation prompted a lengthy investigation of the Hutton scandal by the Subcommittee on Crime of the U.S. House of Representatives Committee on the Judiciary. Exactly who was responsible for the massive Hutton fraud and how it went undetected for so long were the key questions addressed by the subcommittee. Of particular interest to Congress was the failure of the Justice Department to indict any Hutton officer or employee on fraud charges. Instead, the plea bargain agreement with the Justice Department simply allowed Hutton, as a firm, to plead guilty to the fraud charges, pay a multimillion-dollar fine, and make millions of dollars in restitution to the affected banks.

The Subcommittee on Crime was frustrated repeatedly in its efforts to determine which Hutton officer or branch manager conceived the abusive cash management practices. Hutton's free-spirited corporate culture and loosely organized structure made it impossible to pinpoint responsibility for the fraud. Gradually, the objective of the congressional inquiry evolved from determining who was responsible for the fraudulent scheme to determining who was aware of the scheme yet failed to notify federal authorities. The focus of the investigation eventually settled on Hutton's independent auditors, Arthur Andersen & Company. Evidence presented before the investigative subcommittee demonstrated that Arthur Andersen auditors questioned the legality of Hutton's cash management scheme years before the Justice Department began its probe. The subcommittee grilled Arthur Andersen representatives to determine why the accounting firm failed to take affirmative steps to convince Hutton officials to discontinue the fraudulent cash management methods.

OVERVIEW OF HUTTON'S CASH MANAGEMENT SYSTEM

Cash management became a popular topic in the late 1970s in corporate boardrooms and MBA programs. Corporate managers came to realize that electronic technology provided them with the means to manage cash balances efficiently and profitably. Over the past two decades, cash management models, similar to the economic order quantity model for inventory, have become widely used by large corporations. A key component of these models is the management of bank float. A company benefits by decreasing the length of time that its in-transit deposits are "floating" through the banking system. Likewise, increasing bank float for disbursement checks also benefits a company.

Aggressive cash management is particularly important in the cash-intensive brokerage industry. To expedite the clearing of customers' checks, brokerage firms commonly open bank accounts in the communities in which their retail offices are located. Conversely, to delay the clearing of their checks, brokerage firms establish disbursement accounts at banks far removed from their retail offices. In fact, a consulting company specializing in cash management markets an optical scanning device that reads ZIP Codes on vendor invoices. This device then determines which disbursement bank of a given company would maximize the amount of time required for the invoice payment to clear the banking system.

Most cash management methods, including those just described, are clearly legal. However, "innovative" companies, such as E.F. Hutton, have been known to develop cash management methods that abuse the banking system. In the early 1980s, Bank of America discovered that its electronic scanning equipment rejected a disproportionately large percentage of Hutton's checks. On average, Bank of America experienced a 1 percent rejection rate for checks, but the rejection rate for Hutton's checks approached 50 percent. The rejection of a check by a bank's electronic scanner forces bank personnel to process the check manually, which adds, often significantly, to the time required for the check to clear. Methods that can be used to cause a check to be rejected for automatic processing include tampering with the micro-encoding line (such as stapling the check at that point), bending the corners, and smearing a small quantity of a foreign substance on the check's surface—petroleum jelly is apparently the foreign substance of choice among tamperers. When Bank of America brought the check-clearing problem to E.F. Hutton's attention, the brokerage firm's top management avoided any legal action by quickly resolving the problem to the satisfaction of the large bank.

The Justice Department's investigation of Hutton's cash management practices focused principally on the brokerage firm's drawdown system. This system, originally developed with the cooperation and participation of several of Hutton's banks, allowed the firm to minimize cash balances in noninterest-bearing collection accounts maintained by its retail branches. With the help of a complex equation, each retail office estimated by 1 P.M. of each business day the dollar amount of customer remittances that would be available at the end of that day in its collection account. These funds were then transferred by wire out of the collection account and into an interest-bearing regional clearing account.

Gradually, over a several-year period, many of Hutton's branch managers began abusing the drawdown system. Because the managers received 10 percent of the interest profits of their branch as a year-end bonus, they had an incentive to draw down excessive amounts in their collection accounts. In one case, Hutton's drawdown equation indicated that $70,000 would be available for withdrawal at the end of a certain branch's business day. Instead of transferring that amount, the branch manager transferred approximately $7 million to his regional clearing account. This practice resulted in huge cash overdrafts in the local

Hutton bank accounts—overdrafts that in a few cases exceeded the entire capital of the affected banks.

Among the key questions posed by the congressional subcommittee was why banks allowed Hutton to overdraw its collection accounts. Congressional testimony revealed that some of Hutton's banks simply treated the cash overdrafts as a cost of doing business with the huge and prestigious brokerage firm. However, the Justice Department's earlier investigation had also revealed that many of Hutton's smaller banks were not aware that they were the victims of a systematic effort by Hutton branch managers to obtain interest-free funds. This finding resulted in fraud charges being filed against Hutton. In fact, when federal authorities exposed the Hutton scheme, many of its banks immediately demanded restitution.[1]

Although the overdrafts at the branch level were typically quite modest, when accumulated for all of Hutton's branches, the total reached a staggering one-half billion dollars by the end of 1983. The collective impact of Hutton's cash management practices on its income statement was also dramatic. In 1981, interest profits accounted for almost three-fourths of the net income of the firm's retail brokerage division, an abnormally high percentage for the brokerage industry.

ARTHUR ANDERSEN'S INVOLVEMENT IN HUTTON'S CASH MANAGEMENT PRACTICES

As the congressional investigation of the Hutton scandal progressed, Arthur Andersen found itself the focus of mounting criticism from the media, particularly the business press. This criticism stemmed from the perception that Andersen could have easily brought Hutton's abusive cash management practices to a sudden and complete halt. Ironically, this perception resulted largely from testimony of Hutton's executives before the congressional subcommittee. These executives successfully channeled much of the subcommittee's hostility toward Arthur Andersen. During the subcommittee's hearings, one congressman remarked to Arthur Andersen officials: "Management at E.F. Hutton suggest that you were the culprits . . . that these practices weren't brought to their attention."[2] In fact, Arthur Andersen auditors discovered the overdrafts and questioned Hutton officials regarding their legality.

Exhibit 1 contains a memo included in Arthur Andersen's workpapers for the 1979 Hutton audit. This memo describes a meeting between Arthur Andersen personnel and several Hutton officials in which the brokerage firm's cash management practices were discussed. During that meeting, Joel Miller, the engagement audit partner, requested that Tom Rae, a Hutton executive vice-president

---

1. The Justice Department also discovered that Hutton engaged in practices known as "chaining" and "crisscrossing" to create bank float. Hutton used these methods, like the drawdown system, to manufacture short-term, interest-free loans. For a discussion of these methods, see B. Donnelly, "Cash Management: Where Do You Draw the Line?" *Institutional Investor*, September 1985, 69–79.

2. This and all subsequent quotations, unless indicated otherwise, were taken from U.S. Congress, House, Committee on the Judiciary, *E.F. Hutton Mail and Wire Fraud Case, Part 2* (Washington, D.C.: U.S. Government Printing Office, 1986).

NEW YORK OFFICE
MARCH 7, 1980

MEMORANDUM FOR THE FILES

RE: E.F. HUTTON MONEY MANAGEMENT PROCEDURES

On March 5, 1980, representatives of AA & Co. and E.F. Hutton met to discuss the client's procedures in the area of "money management." Present in attendance were Joel Miller, Louis Lynn, Pat Gallagher, John Tesoro and Ted Chambers of AA & Co. and Thomas Rae, Michael Casteliano and Larry Volpe of E.F. Hutton. The purpose of the meeting was to obtain a greater understanding of the client's cash management procedures, whereby efforts are made by the firm to pay down bank loans and, thus, reduce interest expense. In addition, the meeting was also intended to discuss the company procedure of writing checks even though the balance per books is zero or negative. This is particularly relevant in light of the recent TI Industries lawsuit where the firm was found criminally at fault for writing checks in excess of book and bank balances.

Bill Sullivan explained Hutton's procedure with eleven different banks (client is presently exploring the possibility of using five more banks) where checks are drawn on these banks even though the balance per book would not cover the amount of the checks. Mr. Sullivan pointed out that in each of these banks Hutton has deposited funds which, even though they are legally segregated and cannot be used by the bank to cover shortages in Hutton's general account, are treated as "offsets" by the banks under a "global approach" which allows Hutton to overdraw its balances. In addition, Hutton has put up as collateral available customer securities to "cover" the various banks' uncollected funds. These funds result in deposits made by Hutton via check which have not cleared (normal clearing period is one day).

Similarly, the company also has a "check payable" or "zero balance" checking agreement with the Bank of America for payment to vendors and for using dividend payments to customers. Under this agreement, the Company writes checks overdrawing book balances, but maintains a zero or small deposit balance with the bank. This procedure is possible, according to William Sullivan, because the bank, each business day at 1 P.M., notifies the Company as to the required federal funds deposit to cover checks clearing the bank that day. The bank does not require any collateral for this particular arrangement.

The client maintains that the key to engaging in such transactions is that Hutton has the "means" to make ultimate payment. In other words, in the normal course of business the settlement of transactions will result in actual cash balances being deposited in the banks and, as a result, the balances per bank are rarely, if ever, overdrawn. Mr. Rae stated that the fact Hutton has the "means" to pay, precludes any possible illegalities in processing these transactions. Mr. Sullivan further pointed out that Hutton has always been "above board" in its dealings with the banks and that the banks are fully aware of the nature of these transactions (i.e., drawing checks on the account even though Hutton's records do not reflect a book cash balance large enough to cover the check at the time it is drawn). He also stated that several banks (Chase Manhattan, for example) have requested Hutton actually increase the scope of these activities.

After the discussion of the procedures employed and their legality, Joel Miller, AA & Co., engagement partner, requested that Tom Rae render a written legal opinion stating that Hutton's activities in this area don't present any potential legal problems. Mr. Rae declined to render such an opinion, stating that the banks are fully cognizant of Hutton's procedures, that this is an accepted banking practice and that there is no question as to the propriety of such transactions, again making reference to the means of payment principle. After Tom Rae declined to issue an opinion on this matter, Bill Sullivan offered to call one of the banks Hutton uses, Morgan Guaranty, and ask them what the banks would do if a company were to issue checks with no book balances. Joel Miller then stated that he would discuss the matter with other partners at AA & Co. whose clients include major money center banks to ascertain what the banks' point of view is regarding these transactions.

Louis T. Lynn

John Tesoro

EXHIBIT 1
Arthur Andersen
Workpaper Memo
Regarding E.F. Hutton's
Cash Management
Practices—1979 Audit

responsible for legal affairs, provide Arthur Andersen with a written opinion affirming the legality of Hutton's drawdown system. Rae refused to provide such an opinion, maintaining that the system was obviously legal. Rae insisted that Hutton's banks were fully aware of the nature of the drawdown system (a contention that proved to be untrue) and that Hutton's ability to pay any overdrafts precluded them from being illegal. Hutton officials repeatedly used this ability-to-pay, or "means," argument when responding to questions posed by Arthur Andersen auditors regarding the legality of the drawdown system.

The party testifying before the congressional subcommittee who was most critical of Arthur Andersen was Abraham Briloff, an accounting professor at Baruch College, City University of New York. Briloff castigated Arthur Andersen for failing to pursue the overdrafting problem once it was uncovered.

> Where has Arthur Andersen failed? . . . At the outset and most importantly, they failed to follow through on what they absolutely saw and understood, as early as 1980, as to what was going on. They questioned counsel, and counsel said, "Go away, we're too busy to respond." It is my view that had AA *really* fulfilled its responsibilities under the circumstances, the money-management excesses would have been stopped dead no later than 1980 or 1981.

Briloff was particularly alarmed that Arthur Andersen personnel failed to discuss the legality of the cash management practices with other parties following the meeting described in the workpaper memo reproduced in Exhibit 1.

> Note the concluding paragraph of AA's March 7, 1980, memorandum in which the firm agreed to undertake some "homework." Note that it was going to inquire of its banking partners regarding prevailing practice. Did AA fulfill that assignment? If so, what contemporaneous documents are in its files describing its pursuits, and the results therefrom? If it was to turn out that AA did nothing to verify the glib responses from the Hutton people, then I maintain that the firm has failed to follow through in a most material respect. . . . [Arthur Andersen was] extremely naive if they accepted as the last word the word of house counsel who was there to protect his own neck, his own turf.

Briloff maintained that Arthur Andersen, at the very least, had a responsibility to obtain an independent legal opinion regarding the legality of Hutton's cash management practices. Representatives of Arthur Andersen subsequently disputed Briloff's contention before the congressional subcommittee.

In fact, Arthur Andersen did not complete the follow-up procedures discussed in the 1980 memo. To explain why these procedures were not completed, Joel Miller, the audit engagement partner, was called to testify before the subcommittee.

CONGRESSMAN HUGHES: Mr. Miller, what did you do after the meeting that took place on March 7, to check the accuracy of what was related to you?

MR. MILLER: Well, after the meeting, sir, I reflected on the entire meeting; the fact that I had a hundred bank confirmations with no exceptions noted . . . the fact that I found no evidence of checks bouncing, I found no unusual fees being charged by the banks to Hutton . . .

CONGRESSMAN HUGHES: That's not my question. My question is: what did you do after the meeting? Because, frankly, to your credit, you did see that there were some problems . . . Did you ever get to the bank's point of view on the system?

MR. MILLER: No, sir.

CONGRESSMAN HUGHES: Well, here's what you say, "Joel Miller then stated that he would discuss the matter with other partners at AA & Co. whose clients include major money-center banks, to ascertain what the banks' point of view is regarding these transactions."

MR. MILLER: Sir, I had a hundred confirmations from the banks. When I got back to my office and reflected on the entire meeting, I concluded that none of the banks had notified me of any problems—

CONGRESSMAN HUGHES: So you didn't follow through.

MR. MILLER: Well, I followed through in that I reflected on the entire problem and I concluded I would stick by the opinion that I believe Mr. Rae gave me.

The congressional testimony also revealed that Arthur Andersen raised the overdrafting issue with Hutton's audit committee. However, Briloff pointed out that the Hutton audit committee was ineffectual. The audit committee consisted of three individuals, including actress Dina Merrill, granddaughter of Edward F. Hutton. These three individuals had little understanding or appreciation of complex accounting and auditing issues. Two business journalists who wrote a definitive history of the brokerage firm's downfall noted that the audit committee met at most only once or twice per year and was treated as "something of a joke"[3] by top management.

The lack of a strong audit committee provided further evidence of what one congressman described as an environment of "plausible deniability" within the Hutton firm. Hutton's officers allegedly created this environment to insulate themselves from responsibility for the malfeasance of their subordinates.

> We have fixed our posteriors to these chairs, now, for weeks in a row, and the only thing we're getting out of witnesses is "Well, don't look at me, look at the other guy. You know, I didn't know, I didn't ask a question, I didn't hear it, I wasn't there when it happened." Everything is built on plausible deniability—construct the situation, the scenario, so everybody can deny they were a part of it, and yet the thing goes on merrily down the road. And nobody but nobody is ever involved.

Briloff argued that Hutton's weak control environment made it incumbent on Arthur Andersen auditors to take their concerns regarding the aggressive cash management practices to the very top level of the corporate hierarchy. By doing so, Arthur Andersen would have forced Hutton's top management to either eliminate the fraudulent practices or go on record in defense of them.

A final issue that Arthur Andersen representatives were asked to address by the congressional subcommittee involved the disclosure of Hutton's cash overdrafts in its periodic financial statements. Briloff and Representative Hughes, the chairman of the subcommittee, maintained that Hutton's financial statement disclosure for the overdrafts was inadequate. Exhibit 2 contains a memo included in Arthur Andersen's workpapers for the 1981 Hutton audit. That memo discusses the fact that regulatory authorities questioned the legality of Hutton's cash

---

3. D.S. Carpenter, and J. Feloni, *The Fall of the House of Hutton* (New York: Harper & Row, 1989), 117.

**EXHIBIT 2
Arthur Andersen
Workpaper Memo
Regarding E.F. Hutton's
Cash Management
Practices—1981 Audit**

NEW YORK OFFICE
FEBRUARY 25, 1982

MEMORANDUM FOR THE FILES

RE: TRANSFERS OF FUNDS

On February 25, 1982, Joel Miller and John Tesoro met with Tom Lynch (Executive V.P.), Tom Rae (Executive V.P., Legal), and Loren Schechter (Senior V.P., Legal) as well as Irwin Schneiderman of Cahill, Gordon & Reindel [the latter firm was Hutton's outside legal counsel] to discuss a situation concerning Hutton's policy of transferring cash balances between banks as well as "drawing down" cash from Hutton's branches to regional headquarters and finally to New York. It was brought to the attention of Hutton management that checks drawn on a bank in upstate New York had "bounced" as a result of "drawing down" balances for which subsequent deposits had not been made by the time such checks cleared. In addition, it was also brought to Hutton's attention by the New York State Banking Regulators that a significant amount of transfers took place between Manufacturers Hanover Trust and Chemical Bank in late December and January.

Concerning the first issue, Tom Rae stated that overdraft situations at the local bank should never have occurred and that the personnel responsible have been notified as to Company policy concerning drawdown procedures at the local bank level. Mr. Rae stated that the bank involved desires to continue doing business with EFH and did not seek to charge Hutton interest on the overdrawn balances (in answer to Joel Miller's question).

As far as the second issue is concerned, the Banking Regulators and the Federal Reserve Board expressed concern over the controls of Manufacturers Hanover concerning transferring of large balances when, in fact, there may not be sufficient funds to cover these transfers (i.e., from a credit risk point of view). Additionally, the Fed also apparently expressed concern over "creating float" as opposed to taking advantage of the float inherent in the banking system. We were assured of the fact that no action has been brought against Hutton nor unasserted claims, and in fact, the banks have not "lost" in the sense that EFH leaves money on deposit in the normal course of business (albeit *not* formal compensating balance arrangements).

Messrs. Schneiderman and Rae went on to state that Hutton is not regulated by the Fed or the New York State Banking Regulators and that this was more of a banking issue. They stated, however, that it was possible the SEC could have been notified of such occurrences. The major concern of management was potential negative publicity if the media were informed.

Concerning the financial statements, based upon our discussion, we concluded that no disclosure was warranted as promulgated by FASB Statement No. 5 and that the financial statements have a liability caption entitled "Drafts & Checks Payable," which is far in excess of "Cash." This clearly illustrates the fact that checks have been written for amounts in excess of bank balances. This very topic was addressed in our 1979 examination where we concluded, after conferring with Tom Rae, that an entity does not have a legal problem with such a "drawdown" or transfer procedure as long as it has the *intention* and means to make payment as EFH has done in the past. Additionally, Tom Rae stated that as a result of the aforementioned transaction, no customer of Hutton was disadvantaged. Messrs. Lynch, Rae, Schechter, and Schneiderman were of the opinion that there were no claims asserted or unasserted, that EFH would suffer no financial loss, and that the only exposure might be unfavorable publicity.

John Tesoro

Joel Miller

management practices. The memo concludes with Arthur Andersen's rationale for accepting Hutton's financial statement disclosure for the cash overdrafts. Arthur Andersen agreed with Hutton management that "Drafts & Checks Payable" was a sufficiently descriptive caption for the overdrafts on Hutton's balance sheet. The accounting firm also agreed that despite the concern of regulatory authorities, no contingent liability disclosures for the overdrafts were necessary under *FASB Statement No. 5*, "Accounting for Contingencies."

Contrary to Arthur Andersen's position, Briloff argued that the overdrafts should have been listed explicitly as "Cash Overdrafts" in Hutton's annual balance sheets. Briloff also insisted that Hutton's financial statement footnotes should have disclosed that the overdrafts provided a source of interest-free loans for the brokerage firm. Finally, Briloff contended that Hutton's footnotes should have revealed that the brokerage firm used customer securities as collateral for the overdrafts. This disclosure would have alerted Hutton's customers that their investments were at risk if Hutton became insolvent. Representative Hughes agreed with Briloff that Hutton's financial statements misled third parties regarding the overdrafts.

> I'm not sure that I would be put on notice as to what was taking place by reading "drafts and checks payable." If you [addressing Arthur Andersen personnel] had described it as "overdrafts" I would know. The average person knows what an overdraft is. I don't think that you have fairly and honestly provided the information that would be needed for somebody reading that to understand what was going on.

Representative Hughes was also dismayed by Hutton's failure to disclose in its financial statements the Justice Department's ongoing investigation from 1982 through 1984. Exhibit 3 contains the contingent liabilities footnote included in Hutton's 1984 financial statements. Hutton released those financial statements approximately one month prior to pleading guilty to the 2,000 counts of mail and wire fraud. The plea bargain agreement obligated the brokerage firm to pay millions of dollars in fines and restitution to the victimized banks. Hughes questioned Briloff regarding the adequacy of the footnote disclosure shown in Exhibit 3.

CONGRESSMAN HUGHES: In your opinion, was this disclosure adequate, given that it was a little more than a month before Hutton pleaded guilty to 2,000 counts of mail and wire fraud, that obviously, at this time, Andersen was on notice of the ongoing grand jury investigation, and, in fact, had been subpoenaed?

PROFESSOR BRILOFF: This disclosure was very much like a bikini bathing suit, what it revealed was interesting, what it concealed was vital.

AUDITORS AND THE PUBLIC INTEREST

The congressional investigation of the E.F. Hutton scandal was another installment in a series of public relations disasters for the public accounting profession. *The Wall Street Journal* and other national newspapers reported blow by blow the daily verbal attacks of the congressional subcommittee on Arthur Andersen for its role in the debacle and the related criticism of the independent audit function as

The company and its subsidiaries are defendants in legal actions relating to its securities, commodities, investment banking, insurance and leasing businesses. Certainly these actions purport to be brought on behalf of various classes of claimants and seek damages of material [*sic*] for indeterminate amounts. In the opinion of management, these actions will not result in any material, adverse effect on the consolidated financial position of the company.

EXHIBIT 3
E.F. Hutton's Contingent Liabilities Footnote in its 1984 10-K

a whole. Representative Mazzoli leveled some of the most serious charges against the profession.

> Maybe some of the newer practitioners of accountancy have lost sight of the traditions and the lofty history of the profession because they walk into firms now that are groveling for money just like the most mercantile of companies. Maybe they are incapable of having this high fiduciary standard that we, at least in my generation, grew up with in law, and accountancy, and medicine.

Representative Hughes also tongue lashed the public accounting profession throughout the Hutton hearings. He admonished the profession to encourage auditors to serve the public interest rather than focusing on serving the interests of their clients.

> As the U.S. Supreme Court recently noted, by certifying the public reports that collectively depict a corporation's financial statements, the independent auditor assumes a public responsibility transcending any employment relationship with the client. The public watchdog function demands that the accountant maintain total independence from the client at all times and requires complete fidelity to the public trust.

QUESTIONS

1. *SAS No. 47*, "Audit Risk and Materiality in Conducting an Audit," discusses the key components of audit risk that an auditor faces on any given engagement. Which components of audit risk were affected by the incentive compensation scheme that Hutton had established for its branch managers? Which audit risk elements did the "plausible deniability" nature of Hutton's corporate culture affect? How should each of these factors have influenced Arthur Andersen's audits of E.F. Hutton?

2. In your opinion, did Arthur Andersen have a responsibility to obtain an independent legal opinion regarding the legality of Hutton's cash management practices as suggested by Professor Briloff?

3. *SAS No. 31*, "Evidential Matter," identifies five key management assertions that underlie a set of financial statements. In the Hutton case, which of these assertions was most subject to question? Explain.

4. Representative Hughes maintained that "the average person" may have been misled by Hutton's financial statement disclosures regarding the massive cash overdrafts. Should companies make their financial statements understandable to "the average person"? Or, should companies direct their financial statements to individuals who have considerable knowledge of accounting and financial reporting issues?

5. Hutton's 1984 financial statements did not disclose the plea bargain agreement with the Justice Department announced shortly after the release of those statements. Does *FASB Statement No. 5*, "Accounting for Contingencies," mandate disclosure of the terms of such an agreement and the expected financial statement impact? Defend your answer.

CASE 3.4
SAKS FIFTH AVENUE

Attracting customers and closing sales are challenges that face all retailers rang-ing from a Piggly Wiggly grocery in a small southern town to the Giorgio Armani boutique nestled among the elegant shops lining Rodeo Drive in Beverly Hills. Besides the never-ending need to produce revenues, retailers wrestle daily with many other challenges and problems that pose serious threats to their operations. Theft of cash and inventory by employees historically ranks as one of the most common threats to retail operations. Increasing numbers of employee lawsuits, lawsuits predicated on sexual harassment, racial discrimination, and related charges, also jeopardize the financial health of many retailers. Effective internal controls rank as the most reliable deterrent to losses stemming from employee theft and lawsuits. Saks Fifth Avenue, an upscale merchandiser based in New York, learned that lesson firsthand in the late 1990s.

PROMOTIONS, PAY RAISES, AND PILFERING

In late 1993, Joseph Fierro accepted a part-time sales position with a Saks Fifth Avenue store in New York City.[1] Fierro was assigned to the Men's Polo Department of that store, a department supervised by Robert Perley. Fierro's hard work and ingenuity produced sizable sales and impressed his superior. Within a few months, Perley hired Fierro as a full-time salesperson at an annual salary of $30,000. A few months later, Perley created a special position for Fierro, "Clothing Specialist," so that he could give his star employee a 20 percent raise.

---

1. The facts and quotations appearing in this case were drawn from the following legal opin-ion: *Fierro v. Saks Fifth Avenue*, 13 F. Supp. 2d 481 (1998).

By early 1996, Fierro's annual salary had risen to $46,000 on the strength of strong performance appraisals consistently given to him by Perley.

In late August 1996, Joseph Fierro purchased a shirt from another department of the Saks store in which he worked. To obtain an employee discount for the shirt, a discount that he was not entitled to receive, Fierro forged two signatures on a document used to authorize employee sales discounts. The signatures he forged were those of Robert Perley and Donna Ruffman, a co-worker. Fierro also entered the transaction in one of his department's electronic cash registers using Ms. Ruffman's employee identification number. The illicit discount saved Fierro $9.85.

Approximately one week later, two auditors from Saks' Loss Prevention Department reviewed the August transactions entered in the electronic cash registers of the Men's Polo Department. The auditors noticed the employee sales transaction entered by Ms. Ruffman. After examining the documentation for that transaction, they suspected that someone had forged the authorization signatures for the related discount. The auditors questioned several employees in the department regarding the transaction, including Joseph Fierro. Fierro initially denied that he had entered the transaction in his department's cash register. When the auditors suggested that they could easily determine who initiated the transaction, Fierro recanted. He admitted originating the transaction and forging the signatures of both Perley and Ms. Ruffman. In a written statement, Fierro later apologized for the incident.

> I realize it was wrong to do this. I exercised poor judgment and I am truthfully sorry for what I did. I realize that something like this is wrong and it will never happen again.

After being questioned by the Loss Prevention auditors, Fierro returned to his department and discussed the matter with Perley. Perley told Fierro that he had no influence on the Loss Prevention Department's decisions but pledged to help him in any way he could. Perley later testified that he telephoned both the Loss Prevention Department and the Human Resources Department and appealed to them not to terminate Fierro.

On September 13, 1996, two representatives of Saks' Human Resources Department notified Fierro that he was being dismissed for violating company policy. They referred Fierro to the Saks' employee handbook that lists specific examples of prohibited employee conduct. Listed next is the preface to that section of the employee handbook. "The following list of prohibited conduct represents essential guidelines that are so fundamental to Saks Fifth Avenue's operations that such violations must result in immediate dismissal." Saks charged Fierro with engaging in the following three acts that mandated the dismissal of an employee.

1. Theft of Saks Fifth Avenue or another associate's merchandise, property, or services;
5. Forging a signature;
28. Ringing a transaction under another associate's number or on a dummy date line when doing so results in an unauthorized or unwarranted benefit to the associate ringing the transaction.

Saks' Human Resources Department conducted an exit interview with Fierro on the date he was terminated. During this interview, Fierro again apologized for the poor judgment he had exercised. He also expressed disbelief that an "exceptional employee" could be fired for such a "trivial transgression."

He Called Me Buttafuoco!

After losing his job at Saks Fifth Avenue, Fierro searched for employment in the New York City area. Among the jobs he applied for was a position with a financial services company. This company insisted on contacting Fierro's former employers. Before the prospective employer contacted Saks, Fierro called a Saks' employee in the Human Resources Department who had conducted his exit interview. This individual had allegedly indicated during the exit interview that the reason Fierro was dismissed would not be disclosed to prospective employers. However, when Fierro telephoned this individual, she informed him that if asked, she would reveal the circumstances that led to his dismissal.

Shortly after Fierro's telephone conversation with the human resources employee, he filed a discrimination lawsuit against Saks Fifth Avenue with the Equal Employment Opportunity Commission (EEOC). Fierro filed the lawsuit pursuant to Title VII of the Civil Rights Act of 1964 and the New York Human Rights Law. In his lawsuit, Fierro claimed that he was subjected to a "hostile work environment" during his employment with Saks. Fierro also claimed that Robert Perley, his supervisor, discriminated against him because of his Italian-American heritage and that Perley fired him in retaliation for his decision to stand up to that discriminatory treatment.

Fierro predicated his charge of discriminatory treatment upon insensitive remarks allegedly made to him by Perley. He claimed that Perley referred to him on occasion by a three-letter term commonly used as a slur against Italian-Americans.[2] Fierro also alleged that Perley occasionally called him "Joey Buttafuoco."[3] Finally, Perley allegedly made an insensitive racial remark alluding to Fierro's Hispanic wife. Fierro testified that after Perley made the latter remark, he approached his supervisor and told him that the remark was unacceptable. At that point, according to Fierro, Perley "commenced a plan to terminate him."

Fierro maintained that the discriminatory remarks allegedly made to him by Perley caused him to have low personal esteem and severely damaged his career. Those remarks also reportedly caused him to suffer "permanent psychological damage." Fierro insisted that he was haunted by images of the three-letter slur that Perley had used in referring to him: ". . . every time I look in the mirror I see those three letters above my head and it really hurts."

District Court Settles Fierro's Lawsuit

Federal district judge Charles Brieant presided over Fierro's lawsuit against Saks Fifth Avenue. Judge Brieant quickly rejected Fierro's claim that Perley discriminated against him. The judge also dismissed the related allegation that Saks fired

---

2. Perley testified that he was of English, Irish, and Scandinavian descent.

3. Joey Buttafuoco rose—or plunged—to infamy in the early 1990s for a highly publicized affair with an underage woman who later attempted to murder his wife. For several months, the travails of Buttafuoco provided headline material for the tabloids and were the source of countless jokes for late night comedians.

Fierro for "standing up" to Perley's discriminatory treatment. Evidence presented by both Fierro and Saks suggested that rather than discriminating against Fierro, Perley considered him a valued employee and gave him glowing job performance appraisals. The evidence reviewed by Judge Brieant also suggested that Perley was not involved in Fierro's dismissal. That decision apparently was made by the Human Resources Department with considerable input from the Loss Prevention Department. In fact, as noted earlier, Perley made two telephone calls to intercede on Fierro's behalf.

Judge Brieant concluded that Saks' dismissal of Fierro was not a discriminatory action but simply a consistent application of the company's zero tolerance policy for employee theft. The judge admitted that the theft loss Saks suffered was "relatively trivial." But, he went on to note that retailers have a "strong business interest in deterring employee pilfering." Neither the Civil Rights Act of 1964, nor the New York Human Rights Law, the judge observed, prohibit employers from being "overly rigid or even harsh" in punishing employee theft. Saks' employment records demonstrated that the company consistently punished employee theft with the harsh measure of termination. For example, Saks immediately dismissed a former co-worker of Fierro who was caught "booking credits to his own account."

Judge Brieant considered more seriously Fierro's claim that he was subjected to a hostile work environment. The judge invoked the following definition of a hostile work environment.

> A hostile work environment exists when the workplace is permeated with discriminatory intimidation, ridicule, and insult, that is sufficiently severe or pervasive to alter the conditions of the victim's employment.

An employer can assert several defenses in an employee lawsuit alleging a hostile work environment. Among the most credible defenses, Judge Brieant noted, is the existence of an explicit anti-harassment policy. Saks had such a policy during Fierro's employment. The company also had a related complaint procedure allowing employees to file a grievance against a superior or co-worker for engaging in "hostile" behavior. Judge Brieant noted that Fierro never filed a grievance against Perley or his co-workers during his three years with Saks. When asked why he did not take such action, Fierro testified that "I was afraid of repercussions. If you start to conflict with your manager, before you know it it's not a very pleasant outcome." Judge Brieant found Fierro's inaction unsatisfactory.

> At some point, employees must be required to accept responsibility for alerting their employers to the possibility of harassment. Without such a requirement, it is difficult to see how Title VII's deterrent purposes are to be served, or how employers can possibly avoid liability in Title VII cases. Put simply, an employer cannot combat harassment of which it is unaware.

Fierro presented evidence supporting his contention that references to individuals' racial background, sexual orientation, and religious affiliation were common in his former department. However, his former co-workers testified that they intended such references to be humorous or self-deprecating. Perley denied participating "in this intended humor" by his subordinates. After reviewing the evidence presented in Fierro's lawsuit, Judge Brieant observed that Perley's department "did not adhere to the highest standards of decorum."[4] Nevertheless, he suggested that the department's work environment was not hostile but "merely offensive."

> Conduct that is merely offensive and not severe enough to create an objectively hostile or abusive work environment—an environment that a reasonable person would find hostile or abusive—is beyond Title VII's purview. Thus for racist comments, slurs, and jokes to constitute a hostile work environment, there must be more than a few isolated incidents of racial enmity, meaning that instead of sporadic racial slurs, there must be a steady barrage of opprobrious racial comments.

In July 1998, Judge Brieant dismissed Fierro's allegation that he was subjected to a hostile work environment at Saks Fifth Avenue. The judge noted that Fierro did not make such a claim during his employment with Saks or during his exit interview. Instead, that allegation and the related discrimination charges apparently originated near the time Saks refused to give Fierro a "clean" employment reference. Judge Brieant concluded that the timing of Fierro's allegations and Saks' refusal to provide the employment reference was "hardly a coincidence."

Questions

1. In your opinion, was Saks' zero tolerance policy for employee theft reasonable? Was the policy likely cost-effective? Defend your answers.
2. Did Saks' anti-harassment policy and the related complaint procedure qualify as internal controls? Explain.
3. Identify five control procedures that you would commonly find in a men's clothing department of a major department store. Identify the control objective associated with each of these procedures.
4. Should a company's independent auditors be concerned with whether or not a client provides a non-hostile work environment for its employees? If your answer is "yes," identify the specific audit issues that would be relevant in this context.

---

4. Despite this observation, Judge Brieant complimented Perley for a department that "had an enviable record of diversity." The department included "men and women of African-American, Hispanic, Irish, Jewish, and Italian descent, as well as homosexuals."

CASE 3.5
TRITON ENERGY LTD.

Bill Lee dominated Triton Energy's operations for almost three decades. Named Triton's chief executive officer (CEO) in 1966, Lee retired in the mid-1990s after leading the Dallas-based oil and gas exploration firm through three turbulent decades. During Lee's tenure, Triton discovered large oil and gas deposits in several remote sites scattered around the globe. Although adept at finding oil, Triton's small size hampered the company's efforts to exploit its oil and gas properties. Major oil firms, large metropolitan banks, and other well heeled investors often refused to participate in the development of promising oil and gas properties discovered by Triton. Why? Because they were unnerved by Bill Lee's reputation as a run-and-gun, devil-may-care "wildcatter."

To compensate for Triton's limited access to deep-pocketed financiers, Lee resorted to less conventional strategies to achieve his firm's financial objectives. In the early 1980s, Triton struck oil in northwestern France at a site overlooked by many major oil firms. To expedite its drilling efforts and to get a "jump" on competitors that began snapping up leases on nearby properties, Triton formed an alliance with the state-owned petroleum firm, Compagnie Francaise des Petroles. This partnership proved very beneficial for Triton since it gave the firm ready access to the governmental agency that regulated France's petroleum industry. A business journalist commented on Triton's political skills as a key factor in its successful French venture.

> Triton's success is due not just to sound geology but also to good politics. It has established a close relationship with the all-powerful French energy administration, which issues all new drilling permits.[1]

---

1. P. Kemezis and W. Glasgall, "A Texas Wildcatter Cashes In On French Oil," *Business Week*, 13 May 1985, 106–107.

Triton's policy of working closely with governmental agencies and bureaucrats landed the company in trouble with U.S. authorities during the 1990s. Charges that Triton bribed foreign officials to obtain favorable treatment from governmental agencies led to investigations of the company's overseas operations by the U.S. Justice Department and the Securities and Exchange Commission (SEC). These investigations centered on alleged violations of the Foreign Corrupt Practices Act of 1977, including the accounting and internal control stipulations of that federal statute.

A BRIEF HISTORY OF A TEXAS WILDCATTER

L.R. Wiley founded Triton Energy Corporation, the predecessor of Triton Energy Ltd., in 1962. At the time, industry analysts estimated that there were approximately 30,000 businesses involved in oil and gas exploration, most of which were small "Mom and Pop," or simply "Pop," operations. The volatile ups and downs of the petroleum industry dramatically thinned the ranks of oil and gas producers during the 1960s and 1970s. The oil bust of the 1980s wiped out most of the surviving firms in the industry. Less than 20 significant "independent" oil and gas producers remained in business by 1985.[2] Triton Energy was one of those firms.

Bill Lee joined Triton in the early 1960s and was promoted to CEO in 1966. Under Lee, Triton competed in the rough-and-tumble business of oil and gas exploration by employing a rough-and-tumble business strategy. Lee recognized that the large domestic oil firms in the U.S. had already identified the prime drilling sites in this country. So, Lee decided that Triton should focus its exploration efforts in other oil-producing countries, particularly in regions of those countries largely overlooked by "Big Oil." During Lee's tenure with Triton, the company launched exploration ventures in Argentina, Australia, Canada, Columbia, France, Indonesia, Malaysia, New Zealand, and Thailand.

In the early 1970s, Triton discovered a large oil and gas field in the Gulf of Thailand. Recurring disagreements and confrontations with the Thai government stymied Triton from developing that field for more than 10 years. Lee's experience with the Thai government taught him an important lesson: If Triton's exploration ventures were to be successful in foreign countries, the company had to foster good relationships with key governmental officials in those countries. As noted earlier, Lee applied this strategy well in working with French governmental officials in the 1980s after discovering a large oil reservoir near Paris.

Lee created Triton Indonesia, Inc., a wholly-owned subsidiary of Triton Energy, to develop an oil field that the company acquired in Indonesia in 1988. This oil field, located on the island of Sumatra and known as the Enim Field, belonged to a Dutch firm in the 1930s. At the time, Sumatra was a protectorate of the Netherlands. When the Japanese invaded Indonesia during World War II, retreating Dutch soldiers dynamited the Enim Field to render it useless to Japan. Over the next four decades, the dense jungles of Sumatra reclaimed the oil field. In the mid-1980s, Lee learned of the potential oil reserves still buried in the Enim

---

2. The dominant companies in the oil and gas industry include such firms as Exxon, Texaco, and Phillips Petroleum. These firms are often referred to as the "majors" or simply as "Big Oil."

Field. A small Canadian company owned the drilling rights for those reserves. Triton wrested control of the drilling rights from that company in a protracted legal battle. After investing several million dollars and several years of hard work in the Enim Field, Triton began pumping thousands of barrels each day from the long dormant oil reservoir.

Triton's strategy of working closely with officials of the Indonesian government contributed greatly to the success of the Enim Field project. To strengthen Triton's ties to those officials, the company hired a French citizen, Roland Siouffi, as a consultant. Siouffi, who had resided in Indonesia for nearly three decades, served as Triton's liaison with Indonesian tax authorities and with governmental agencies that oversaw the country's oil and gas industry.

In 1991, Triton struck black gold again, this time in Columbia. Several large firms had drilled exploratory wells in the foothills of the Andes Mountains that stretch across Columbia. Those wells came up dry. Nevertheless, geological reports convinced Lee and other Triton executives that the region contained large but well hidden oil reservoirs. Lee and his colleagues were right. In 1991, Triton pinpointed huge oil and gas deposits trapped in complex geological structures lying beneath the Columbian jungles. These reservoirs were the largest discovered in the western hemisphere since the 1968 Prudhoe Bay discovery in Alaska. Again, Triton established close working relationships with governmental officials, this time in Columbia, to develop the new oil field.

On the strength of Triton's Indonesian and Columbian oil strikes, the company's stock skied from a few dollars per share in the late 1980s to more than $50 per share in 1991.[3] Triton's common stock ranked as one of the 10 best performing stocks on the New York Stock Exchange in 1991. Despite the company's obvious knack for finding oil, many Wall Street analysts refused to recommend Triton's common stock. Rumors of bribing foreign officials, allegations of creative accounting methods, and other corporate wrongdoings soured these analysts on Triton. One Wall Street portfolio manager succinctly summed up his view of Triton. "Bill Lee is not a guy I'd like to see running an oil company I had invested in."[4]

The allegations of abusive management practices and creative accounting caught up with Triton in the mid-1990s. Those allegations prompted the U.S. Justice Department and the SEC to probe Triton's ties to government officials in foreign countries. These investigations focused on the relationships that Triton executives cultivated with Indonesian officials during the development of the Enim Field.

The central issue addressed by U.S. authorities while investigating Triton was whether the company had violated a seldom-enforced federal statute, the Foreign Corrupt Practices Act of 1977 (FCPA). The FCPA was a by-product of the scandal-ridden Watergate era of the 1970s. During the Watergate investigations, the Office of the Special Prosecutor uncovered numerous bribes, kickbacks, and other payments made by U.S. corporations to officials of foreign governments to initiate or maintain business relationships. Widespread public disapproval compelled Congress to pass the FCPA, which criminalizes such payments. The FCPA also requires U.S. companies to maintain internal control systems that provide reasonable assurance of discovering illicit foreign payments.

---

3. D. Galant, "The Home Runs of 1991," *Institutional Investor*, March 1992, 51-56.

4. T. Mack, "Lucky Bill Lee," *Forbes*, 14 October 1991, 50.

The accounting provisions [of the FCPA] were enacted by Congress along with the antibribery provisions because Congress concluded that almost all bribery of foreign officials by American corporations was covered up in the corporations' books and that the requirement for accurate records and adequate internal controls would deter bribery.[5]

Exhibit 1 summarizes the FCPA's key antibribery and internal control requirements.

INDONESIAN CHARGES

Triton Energy's former controller sued the company in 1991, claiming that he had been fired in 1989 after refusing to sign off on the company's 10-K registration statement. The controller refused to sign off on the 1989 10-K because it failed to disclose "bribery, kickbacks and payments to government officials, customs officials, auditors, inspectors and other persons in positions of responsibility in Indonesia, Columbia, and Argentina."[6] The controller acknowledged that Triton's

EXHIBIT 1
Key Provisions of Foreign
Corrupt Practices Act

Antibribery Provisions:

Section 30 (A) of the Securities Exchange Act, the antibribery provision of the FCPA, prohibits any issuer . . . or any officer, director, employee, or agent of an issuer from making use of instruments or interstate commerce corruptly to pay, offer to pay, promise to pay, or to authorize the payment of any money, gift, or promise to give, anything of value to any foreign official for purposes of influencing any act or decision of such foreign official in his official capacity, or inducing such foreign official to do or omit to do any act in violation of the lawful duty of such official, or inducing such foreign official to use his influence with a foreign government or instrumentality thereof to affect or influence any act or decision of such government or instrumentality, in order to assist such issuer in obtaining or retaining business for or with, or directing business to, any person.

Recordkeeping and Internal Control Provisions:

Section 13(b)(2) of the Securities Exchange Act is comprised of two accounting provisions referred to as the "books and records" and "internal controls" provisions. These accounting provisions were enacted as part of the FCPA to strengthen the accuracy of records and to "promote the reliability and completeness of financial information that issuers are required to file with the Commission or disseminate to investors pursuant to the Securities Exchange Act." Section 13(b)(2)(A) requires issuers to make and keep books, records, and accounts that accurately and fairly reflect the transactions and dispositions of their assets. Section 13(b)(2)(B) requires issuers to devise and maintain a system of internal accounting controls sufficient to provide reasonable assurances that, among other things, transactions are executed in accordance with management's general or specific authorization and that transactions are recorded as necessary to permit presentation of financial statements in conformity with GAAP and to maintain accountability for assets.

Source: Securities and Exchange Commission, *Accounting and Auditing Enforcement Release No. 889*, 27 February 1997.

---

5. This quotation and the remaining quotations in this case, unless indicated otherwise, were drawn from the following source: Securities and Exchange Commission, *Accounting and Auditing Enforcement Release No. 889*, 27 February 1997.

6. A. Zipser, "Crude Grab?" *Barron's*, 25 May 1992, 15.

senior management had not authorized the payments but insisted that the FCPA required such payments to be disclosed in the company's 10-K. Before the case went to trial, Triton officials dismissed the charges, suggesting that they were "totally without merit."[7] During the trial, considerable evidence surfaced supporting the controller's allegations. A memo written by Triton's former internal audit director contained the most damaging of this evidence.

In late 1989, Triton management sent the company's new internal audit director to review and report on Triton Indonesia's operations. Upon returning, the internal audit director filed a lengthy memorandum with several Triton executives, including the company's president and at least two key vice-presidents. Exhibit 2 presents selected excerpts from that memo. The memo documented extensive wrongdoing by employees and officials of Triton Indonesia. At one point, the frustrated internal audit director complained that the subsidiary's accounting records were so misleading it was impossible "to tell a real transaction from one that has been faked."[8] After reading the memo, the alarmed Triton executives ordered that all copies be collected and destroyed. Despite these instructions, one copy of the memo survived and became a key exhibit in the lawsuit filed against Triton by its former controller.

Another former Triton accountant also corroborated many of the former controller's allegations. This individual, who had previously served as a Price Waterhouse auditor, joined Triton Indonesia's accounting staff in early 1989. Almost immediately, the accountant discovered serious internal control deficiencies in the subsidiary's operations. Inadequate segregation of key accounting and control responsibilities created an environment in which individuals could easily perpetrate and then conceal fraudulent transactions. The accountant's most serious charge regarding his former employer involved an admission made by his superior. The superior told the accountant that auditors from Pertamina, the state-owned Indonesian oil firm, had been "bought" by Triton. Among other responsibilities, these auditors regularly reviewed Triton Indonesia's tax records.

> I understood the words 'buy the audit' to mean bribe Pertamina auditors. To me, it represented an illegal transaction, the proposal of an illegal transaction.[9]

EXHIBIT 2
Selected Excerpts from Internal Audit Memo Regarding Operations of Triton Indonesia

"In Indonesia, I found myself in a country of state supported corruption."

"I was told that we pay between $1,000 and $1,900 per month just to get our invoice to Pertamina [the state-owned Indonesian oil company] paid."

"We must pay people in customs in order to get our equipment off the dock so that it can be used in operations."

"What is worse, and this is extremely confidential, is that we paid the auditors in order to have their audit exceptions taken care of. . . . This part is particularly bad to me. I had hoped that at least the Indonesian auditors were honest."

Source: A. Zipser, "Crude Grab?" *Barron's*, 25 May 1992, 12–15.

7. Mack, "Lucky Bill Lee," 50.

8. A. Zipser, "Trials of Triton," *Barron's*, 26 July 1993, 14–15.

9. Zipser, "Crude Grab?" *Barron's*, 13.

Co-workers reportedly shunned the accountant after he objected to such conduct. A few weeks later, the accountant resigned. Because he was concerned that his brief tenure with Triton Indonesia might blight his professional career, the accountant filed a 37-page report with the U.S. embassy in Indonesia. That report documented questionable transactions, events, and circumstances he had encountered during his employment with Triton Indonesia. In the report, the accountant described his former superiors as "unprincipled, unethical liars."[10]

Peat Marwick served as Triton Energy's audit firm over a span of more than two decades beginning in 1969. During the planning phase for the 1991 audit, Peat Marwick learned of the memorandum written by Triton's former internal audit director. A Peat Marwick auditor questioned client management concerning the unlawful activities allegedly documented in that memo. Company officials convinced Peat Marwick that all copies of the memo had been destroyed. A Triton executive then prepared a memo responding to Peat Marwick's inquiries. This second memo omitted many key details of questionable activities documented by the internal audit director. At a subsequent meeting with Peat Marwick representatives, Triton management directly refuted the principal allegation reportedly included in the internal audit memo. Several Triton officials told Peat Marwick that there was no evidence Triton Indonesia officers or employees had bribed Indonesian auditors.[11]

In the summer of 1992, the jury that heard the lawsuit filed by Triton's former controller ruled in his favor and awarded him a $124 million judgment. That judgment ranks as one of the largest wrongful termination awards ever handed down by a U.S. court.[12] Following the trial, the surviving copy of the memo written by Triton's former internal audit director became a road map for the SEC to follow in investigating Triton's abusive management and accounting practices.

RESULTS OF SEC INVESTIGATION

For the right to develop the Enim Field, Triton Indonesia negotiated a contract with the Indonesian government. This contract made the nation's state-owned oil company, Pertamina, a partner in the project. The agreement gave the Triton subsidiary operational and financial control over the joint venture but allowed Pertamina to review and override all important decisions involving the project. Another feature of the agreement required Triton Indonesia to transport oil recovered from the Enim Field through Pertamina's pipelines. Finally, the agreement obligated Triton Indonesia to pay significant taxes to the Indonesian government based upon the Enim Field's production.

Two Indonesian audit teams periodically examined Triton Indonesia's accounting and tax records. Pertamina auditors reviewed the accounting records to

---

10. *Ibid.*, 14.

11. In 1992, Triton Energy retained Price Waterhouse to serve as its audit firm, replacing Peat Marwick.

12. The judgment was subsequently reduced in a private, out-of-court settlement involving the former controller, Triton, and Triton's insurer. The former controller received approximately $10 million from Triton and an undisclosed additional sum from Triton's insurer. Shortly before the jury verdict was announced, the former controller had offered to settle the case for $5 million.

ensure that the Triton subsidiary complied with its contractual obligations to
Pertamina. Auditors from the Indonesian Ministry of Finance and Pertamina auditors inspected the tax records to ensure that the proper taxes were being paid to
the Indonesian government. The Ministry of Finance auditors were known as
the "BPKP" auditors since they worked for the agency's audit branch, Badan
Pengawasan Keuangan Dan Pembangunan.

Pertamina and BPKP auditors concluded a joint tax audit of a Triton Indonesia
operating unit in May 1989. The audit revealed that the unit owed approximately
$618,000 of additional taxes. Of this total, $385,000 involved additional taxes
levied by Pertamina auditors, while the remaining $233,000 were additional taxes
assessed by BPKP auditors. Two officers of Triton Indonesia discussed this matter with Roland Siouffi, the long time Indonesian resident hired the year before to
serve as a liaison with government officials. Siouffi then met with two key members of the Pertamina audit team. Apparently, Siouffi negotiated to pay these
two individuals $160,000 to eliminate the additional tax assessment of $385,000
proposed by the Pertamina auditors. In August 1989, Triton Indonesia paid
$165,000 to a company controlled by Siouffi. A few weeks later, that company
paid $120,000 and $40,000, respectively, to the two Pertamina auditors. Triton
Indonesia's controller prepared false documentation for the payment made to
Siouffi's company. The documentation indicated that the payment was for seis-
mic data purchased for the Enim Field.

In August 1989, a BPKP auditor notified Triton Indonesia that it still owed
$233,000 of taxes. An executive of Triton Indonesia discussed this matter with
Siouffi. After meeting with the BPKP auditor, Siouffi told Triton Indonesia's management that in exchange for $20,000 the auditor would reduce the $233,000 tax
bill to $155,000. Triton Indonesia processed a $22,500 payment to another company controlled by Siouffi, who then paid the BPKP auditor $20,000.[13] Triton
Indonesia's controller prepared false documentation indicating that the payment
to Siouffi's company was for equipment repairs at the Enim Field made by
Siouffi's employees. Following the payments made to the Pertamina and BPKP
auditors by Siouffi, Triton Indonesia received letters from the two audit teams indicating that they had resolved the issues raised during the tax audit.

Throughout 1989 and 1990, Triton Indonesia continued to channel illicit "facil-
itating payments" to various government officials through Roland Siouffi. Triton
Indonesia fabricated false documentation to "sanitize" each payment for accounting purposes. The SEC identified $450,000 of such payments improperly
recorded in Triton Indonesia's accounting records.

Triton Indonesia officers periodically briefed key members of Triton Energy's
management regarding the illicit payoffs funneled through Siouffi. In these brief-
ings, the Triton Energy officers also learned of the false accounting entries and
documentation prepared to conceal the true nature of the payments.

> The Triton Energy officers expressed concern about such practices which they had nei-
> ther directed nor authorized, but failed to require Triton Indonesia to discontinue those
> practices.

At one point, a Triton Indonesia officer directly told Triton Energy's president that
illicit payments were being made to Siouffi. The president responded "that he

---

13. Triton Indonesia apparently paid Siouffi a "commission" for each illicit payment he funneled to government officials. In this case, the commission was $2,500.

had worked in another foreign country and understood that such things had to be done in certain environments."[14]

SEC Sends a Message

In 1997, the SEC climaxed a four-year investigation of Triton Indonesia and its parent company by issuing a series of enforcement releases. Those releases charged Triton and its executives with violating the antibribery, accounting, and control requirements of the FCPA. Without admitting or denying these charges, six officers of Triton Energy and Triton Indonesia signed consent decrees that prohibited them from violating federal securities laws in the future. The consent decrees also imposed a $300,000 fine on Triton Energy and fines of $35,000 and $50,000 on two former Triton Indonesia officers. Exhibit 3 presents the footnote appended to Triton Energy's 1996 financial statements that described the company's settlement with the SEC.

Although Triton Energy did not authorize the illicit payments and the bogus accounting for the payments, the SEC sharply criticized two executives who were aware of the practices and allowed them to continue unchecked.

> . . . the senior management of Triton Energy, ____ and ____, simply acknowledged the existence of such practices and treated them as a cost of doing business in a foreign jurisdiction. The toleration of such practices is inimical to a fair business environment and undermines public confidence in the integrity of public corporations.

The SEC publicly conceded that it intended the Triton case to send a "message" to corporate managers. SEC officials noted that the case "underscored the responsibilities of corporate management in the area of foreign payments"[15] and impressed upon U.S. companies that "it's not O.K. to pay bribes as long as you don't get caught."[16]

EXHIBIT 3
Triton Energy's
Disclosure of SEC
Settlement in 1996
Financial Statement
Footnotes

> In February 1997, the Company and the Securities and Exchange Commission ("SEC") concluded a settlement of the SEC's investigation of possible violations of the Foreign Corrupt Practices Act in connection with Triton Indonesia, Inc.'s former operations in Indonesia. The investigation was settled on a "consent decree" basis in which the Company neither admitted nor denied charges made by the SEC that the Company violated the Securities Exchange Act of 1934 when Triton Indonesia, Inc. made certain payments in 1989 and 1990 to a consultant advising Triton Indonesia, Inc. on its relations with the Indonesian state oil company and tax authority, misbooked the payments and failed to maintain adequate internal controls. Under the terms of the settlement, the Company's subsidiary, TEC, was permanently enjoined from future violations of the books and records and internal control provisions of the Securities Exchange Act of 1934 and paid a civil monetary penalty of $300,000. In 1996, the Company was advised that the Department of Justice had concluded a parallel inquiry without taking any action.

---

14. Apparently, the attention drawn to the illicit payments by the lawsuit filed by Triton Energy's former controller caused Triton Indonesia to stop making those payments.

15. *Securities Regulation and Law Report*, "SEC Official Predicts More FCPA Cases in Near Future," 2 May 1997, 607.

16. L. Eaton, "Triton Energy Settles Indonesia Bribery Case for $300,000," *The New York Times*, 28 February 1997, D2.

Prior to the Triton case, more than 10 years had elapsed since the SEC had filed FCPA charges against a public company. During the late 1990s, frequent allegations of illicit foreign payments by U.S. corporations prompted the SEC to initiate several FCPA investigations. The SEC attributes the apparent increase in such payments to the increasingly global nature of U.S. corporations.[17] Each year, additional U.S. companies attempt to establish footholds in emerging markets. Funneling illicit payments to officials of foreign countries is often the most effective method of breaking down entry barriers to those markets.

The growing sophistication of illicit foreign payment schemes complicates the SEC's efforts to more rigorously enforce the FCPA. In fact, critics of the FCPA suggest that it is practically unenforceable except in the most blatant cases. As one journalist noted, the days of "bulky cash payments in large sealed envelopes" are long past.

> Now the bribes, kickbacks, and 'facilitating payments,' such as those described in Triton Energy's internal memorandum, more often get channeled through expensive 'consultants,' dummy charities, and construction projects that never seem to materialize.[18]

Many corporate executives have lobbied against enforcement of the FCPA. These executives maintain that the federal law places U.S. multinational companies at a significant competitive disadvantage to other multinational firms. A member of President Clinton's administration supported this point of view when he observed that the U.S. is the only country that has "criminalized bribery of foreign officials."[19]

EPILOGUE

Bill Lee was never directly implicated in the Indonesian payments scandal and retired as Triton Energy's CEO in January 1993. The SEC sanctioned the Triton executives involved in that scandal. All of those executives subsequently resigned their positions with the company. Thomas Finck, who came to Triton after the Indonesian scandal, replaced Lee as Triton's CEO. In 1996, a journalist noted that Triton's new CEO seemed to be employing some of his predecessor's "old tricks."[20] One of Finck's first major decisions was to reorganize Triton Energy as a subsidiary of an offshore holding company headquartered in the Cayman Islands. Finck reported that moving Triton's headquarters to the Cayman Islands would significantly reduce the company's tax burden. Critics placed a different spin on the decision. They suggested that the company's desire "to avoid scrutiny under the U.S. Foreign Corrupt Practices Act"[21] likely motivated the move to the Caymans.

---

17. *Securities Regulation and Law Report*, "SEC Official Predicts More FCPA Cases in Near Future," 2 May 1997, 607.

18. A. Zipser, "A Rarely Enforced Law," *Barron's*, 25 May 1992, 14.

19. *Ibid.*

20. A. Zipser, "New Management, Old Tricks as Oil Firm Heads for Caymans," *Barron's*, 25 March 1996, 10.

21. *Ibid.*

Triton Energy sold its Indonesian subsidiary in 1996 but under Finck continued its high-risk strategy of searching for obscure and overlooked oil fields across the globe. Depressed oil prices caused the value of Triton's sizable oil reserves to fall dramatically during the 1990s, leaving the company in a financial lurch in early 1998. Company officials announced that Triton was for sale and retained an investment banking firm to find a potential buyer. When a buyer could not be found, Triton announced plans to restructure its operations and to continue as an independent entity. That announcement caused Triton's stock to plummet to $20 per share, its lowest level in several years, and prompted Thomas Finck to resign as the company's CEO.

QUESTIONS

1. Identify the key factors that complicate the audit of a multinational company.

2. Identify specific control activities that Triton Energy could have implemented for Triton Indonesia and its other foreign subsidiaries to minimize the likelihood of illicit payments to government officials. Would these control activities have been cost effective?

3. Does an audit firm of a multinational company have a responsibility to apply audit procedures intended to determine whether the client has complied with the FCPA? Defend your answer.

4. If a company employs a high-risk business strategy, does that necessarily increase the inherent risk and control risk components of audit risk for the company? Explain.

5. What responsibility, if any, does an accountant of a public company have when he or she discovers that the company has violated a law? How does the accountant's position on the company's employment hierarchy affect that responsibility, if at all? What responsibility does an auditor of a public company have if he or she discovers illegal acts by the client? Does the auditor's position on his firm's employment hierarchy affect this responsibility?

6. If the citizens of certain foreign countries believe that the payment of bribes is an acceptable business practice, is it appropriate for U.S. companies to challenge that belief when doing business in those countries? Defend your answer.

7. The SEC reported that the sanctions imposed on Triton Energy were meant to send a "message" to corporate managers. Should the SEC and other regulatory authorities selectively prosecute companies, organizations, or individuals to encourage compliance with legal or professional standards? Defend your answer.

CASE 3.6
GOODNER BROTHERS, INC.

"Woody, that's $2,400 you owe me. Okay? We're straight on that?"

"Yeah, yeah. I got you."

"And, you'll pay me back by next Friday?"

"Al. I said I'd pay you back by Friday, didn't I?

"Just checkin'."

Borrowing money from a friend can strain even the strongest relationship. When the borrowed money will soon be plunked down on a blackjack table, the impact on the friendship can be devastating.

Woody Robinson and Al Hunt were sitting side by side at a blackjack table in Tunica, Mississippi. The two long time friends and their wives were spending their summer vacations together as they had several times. After three days loitering in the casinos that line the banks of the Mississippi River 20 miles south of Memphis, Woody found himself hitting up his friend for loans. By the end of the vacation, Woody owed Al nearly $5,000. The question facing Woody was how he was going to repay his friend.[1]

TWO PALS NAMED WOODY AND AL

Woodrow Wilson Robinson and Albert Leroy Hunt lived and worked in Huntington, West Virginia, a city of 60,000 tucked in the westernmost corner of

---

1. The central facts of this case were drawn from a legal opinion written in the 1990s. The names of the actual parties involved in the case and the relevant locations have been changed. Additionally, certain of the factual circumstances reported in this case are fictionalized accounts of background material disclosed in the legal opinion.

the state. The blue-collar city sits on the south bank of the Ohio River. Ohio is less than one mile away across the river, while Kentucky can be reached with a 10-minute drive westward on Interstate 64. Woody and Al were born six days apart in a small hospital in eastern Kentucky, were best friends throughout grade school and high school, and roomed together for four years at college. In the fall of 1990, a few months after they graduated with business management degrees, each served as the other's best man at their respective weddings.

Following graduation, Al went to work for Curcio's Auto Supply on the western outskirts of Huntington, a business owned by his future father-in-law. Curcio's sold lawnmowers, bicycles, and automotive parts and supplies including tires and batteries, the business's two largest revenue producers. Curcio's also installed the automotive parts it sold, provided oil and lube service, and performed small engine repairs.

Within weeks of going to work for Curcio's, Al helped Woody land a job with a large tire wholesaler that was Curcio's largest supplier. Goodner Brothers, Inc., sold tires of all types and sizes from 14 locations scattered from southern New York to northwestern South Carolina and from central Ohio to the Delaware shore. Goodner concentrated its operations in mid-sized cities such as Huntington, West Virginia; Lynchburg, Virginia; Harrisburg, Pennsylvania; and Youngstown, Ohio, home to the company's headquarters. Founded in 1969 by two brothers, T.J. and Ross Goodner, two decades later Goodner Brothers' annual sales approached $40 million. The Goodner family dominated the company's operations. In 1990, T.J. served as the company's president, while Ross was the chief operating officer. Four second-generation Goodners also held key positions in the company.

Goodner purchased tires from several large manufacturers and then wholesaled those tires to retail auto supply stores and other retailers that had auto supply departments. Goodner's customers included Sears, Wal-Mart, Kmart, and dozens of smaller retail chains. The company also purchased discontinued tires from manufacturers, large retailers, and other wholesalers and then resold those tires at cut-rate prices to school districts, municipalities, and companies with small fleets of automobiles.

Goodner Brothers hired Woody to work as a sales representative for its Huntington location. Woody sold tires to more than 80 customers in his sales region that stretched from the west side of Huntington into eastern Kentucky and north into Ohio. Woody, who worked strictly on a commission basis, was an effective and successful salesman. Unfortunately, a bad habit that Woody acquired during his college days gradually developed into a severe problem. By the mid-1990s, a gambling obsession threatened to wreck the young salesman's career and personal life.

Woody bet on any and all types of sporting events, including baseball and football games, horse races, and boxing matches. He also spent hundreds of dollars each month buying lottery tickets and lost increasingly large sums on frequent gambling excursions with his friend Al. By the summer of 1996 when Woody, Al, and their wives visited Tunica, Mississippi, Woody's financial condition was desperate. He owed more than $50,000 to various bookies with whom he placed illicit bets, was falling behind on his mortgage payments, and had "maxed out" several credit cards. Worst of all, two bookies to whom Woody owed several thousand dollars were demanding payment and had begun making menacing remarks alluding to his wife, Rachelle.

WOODY FINDS A SOLUTION

Upon returning to Huntington in early July 1996, Woody struck upon an idea to bail him out of his financial problems: he decided to begin stealing from his employer, Goodner Brothers. Other than a few traffic tickets, Woody had never been in trouble with law enforcement authorities. Yet, in Woody's mind, he had no other reasonable alternatives. At this point, resorting to stealing seemed the lesser of two evils.

One reason Woody decided to steal from his employer was the ease with which it could be done. After several years with Goodner, Woody was very familiar with the company's sloppy accounting practices and lax control over its inventory and other assets. Goodner's executives preached one dominant theme to their sales staff: "Volume, volume, volume." Goodner achieved its ambitious sales goals by undercutting competitors' prices. The company's dominant market share in the geographical region it served came at a high price. Goodner's gross profit margin averaged 17.4 percent, considerably below the mean gross profit margin of 24.1 percent for comparable tire wholesalers. To compensate for its low gross profit margin, Goodner scrimped on operating expenses, including expenditures on internal control measures.

The company staffed each of its 14 sales outlets with a skeletal crew of 10 to 12 employees. A sales manager supervised the other employees at each outlet and also worked a sales district. The remaining staff typically included two sales representatives, a receptionist who doubled as a secretary, a bookkeeper, and five to seven employees who delivered tires and worked in the unit's inventory warehouse. Goodner's Huntington location had two storage areas, a small warehouse adjacent to the sales office and a larger storage area two miles away that previously housed a discount grocery store. Other than padlocks, Goodner provided little security for its tire inventory, which typically ranged from $300,000 to $700,000 for each sales outlet.

Instead of an extensive system of internal controls, T.J. and Ross Goodner relied heavily on the honesty and integrity of the employees they hired. Central to the company's employment policy was never to hire someone unless that individual could provide three strong references, preferably from reputable individuals with some connection to Goodner Brothers. Besides following up on employment references, Goodner Brothers obtained thorough background checks on prospective employees from local detective agencies. For more than two decades, Goodner's employment strategy had served the company well. Less than 10 of several hundred individuals employed by the company had been terminated for stealing or other misuse of company assets or facilities.

Each Goodner sales outlet maintained a computerized accounting system. The system typically consisted of an "off-the-shelf" general ledger package intended for a small retail business and a hodgepodge of assorted accounting documents. Besides the Huntington facility's bookkeeper, the unit's sales manager and two sales representatives had unrestricted access to the accounting system. Since the large volume of sales and purchase transactions often swamped the bookkeeper, sales representatives frequently entered transactions directly into the system. The sales reps routinely accessed, reviewed, and updated their customers' accounts. Rather than completing purchase orders, sales orders, credit memos, and other accounting documents on a timely basis, the sales reps commonly jotted the details of a transaction on a piece of scrap paper. The sales reps eventually passed these "source documents" on to the bookkeeper or used them to enter transaction data directly into the accounting system.

Sales reps and the sales manager jointly executed the credit function for each Goodner sales outlet. Initial sales to new customers required the approval of the sales manager, while the credit worthiness of existing clients was monitored by the appropriate sales rep. Sales reps had direct access to the inventory storage areas. During heavy sales periods, sales reps often loaded and delivered customer orders themselves.

Each sales office took a year-end physical inventory to bring its perpetual inventory records into agreement with the amount of inventory actually on hand. One concession that T.J. and Ross Goodner made to the policy of relying on their employees' honesty was mandating one intra-year inventory count for each sales office. Goodner's management used these inventories, which were taken by the company's two-person internal audit staff, to monitor inventory shrinkage at each sales outlet. Historically, Goodner's inventory shrinkage significantly exceeded the industry norm. The company often purchased large shipments of "seconds" from manufacturers. Tires included in these lots had minor defects that prevented them from being sold to retailers. Upon inspection, some of these tires could not be sold on a wholesale basis either. Periodically, these tires were dropped off at a tire disposal facility. A sales office's accounting records were not adjusted for these "throw-aways" until the year-end physical inventory was taken.

SELLING TIRES ON THE SLY

Within a few days after Woody hatched his plan to pay off his gambling debts, he visited the remote storage site for the Huntington sales office. Woody rummaged through its dimly lit and cluttered interior searching for individual lots of tires that apparently had been collecting dust for several months. After finding several stacks of tires satisfying that requirement, Woody jotted down their specifications in a small notebook. For each lot, Woody listed customers who could potentially find some use for the given tires.

Later that same day, Woody made his first "sale." A local plumbing supplies dealer needed tires for his small fleet of vehicles. Woody convinced the business's owner that Goodner was attempting to "move" some old inventory. That inventory would be sold on a cash basis and at prices significantly below Goodner's cost. The owner agreed to purchase two dozen of the tires. After delivering the tires in his large pickup, Woody received a cash payment of $900 directly from the customer.

Over the next several months, Woody routinely stole inventory and kept the proceeds. Woody concealed the thefts in various ways. In some cases, he would charge merchandise that he had sold for his own benefit to the accounts of large volume customers. Woody preferred this technique since it allowed him to reduce the inventory balance in the Huntington facility's accounting records. When customers complained to him for being charged for merchandise they had not purchased, Woody simply apologized and corrected their account balances. If the customers paid the illicit charges, they unknowingly helped Woody sustain his fraudulent scheme.

Goodner's customers frequently returned tires for various reasons. Woody completed credit memos for sales transactions voided by his customers, but instead of returning the tires to Goodner's inventory, he often sold them and kept the proceeds. Goodner occasionally consigned tires to large retailers for promotional sales events. When the consignees returned the unsold tires to Goodner, Woody would routinely sell some of the tires to other customers for cash. Finally, Woody began offering to take "throw-aways" to the tire disposal facility in nearby Shoals, West Virginia, a task typically assigned to a sales outlet's delivery workers. Not surprisingly, most of the tires that Woody carted off for disposal were not defective.

The ease with which he could steal tires made Woody increasingly bold. In late 1996, Woody offered to sell Al Hunt tires he had allegedly purchased from a manufacturer. By this time, Al owned and operated Curcio's Tires. Woody told Al that he discovered the manufacturer was disposing of its inventory of discontinued tires and decided to buy them himself. When Al asked whether such "self-dealing" violated Goodner company policy, Woody replied, "It's none of their business what I do in my spare time. Why should I let them know about this great deal that I stumbled upon?"

At first reluctant, Al eventually agreed to purchase several dozen tires from his good friend. No doubt, the incredibly low prices at which Woody was selling the tires made the decision much easier. At those prices, Al realized he would earn a sizable profit on the tires. Over the next 12 months, Woody continued to sell "closeout" tires to his friend. After one such purchase, Al called the manufacturer from whom Woody had reportedly purchased the tires. Al had become suspicious of the frequency of the closeout sales and the bargain basement prices at which Woody purchased the tires. When he called the manufacturer, a sales rep told Al that his company had only one closeout sale each year. The sales rep also informed Al that his company sold closeout merchandise directly to wholesalers, never to individuals or retail establishments.

The next time Al spoke to Woody, he mentioned matter-of-factly that he had contacted Woody's primary supplier of closeout tires. Al then told his friend that a sales rep for the company indicated that such merchandise was only sold to wholesalers.

"So, what's the point, Al?"

"Well, I just found it kind of strange that, uh, that . . ."

"C'mon, get to the point, Al."

"Well, Woody, I was just wondering where you're getting these tires that you're selling."

"Do you want to know, Al? Do you really want to know, buddy? I'll tell you if you want to know," Woody replied angrily.

After a lengthy pause, Al shrugged his shoulders and told his friend to "Just forget it." Despite his suspicion, Al continued to buy tires from Woody. He never again asked his friend where he was obtaining the tires.

INTERNAL AUDITORS DISCOVER INVENTORY SHORTAGE

On December 31, 1996, the employees of Goodner's Huntington location met to take a physical inventory. The employees treated the annual event as a prelude to their New Year's Eve party. Counting typically began around noon and was finished within three hours. The employees worked in teams of three. Two members of each team climbed and crawled over the large stacks of tires and shouted out their counts to the third member who recorded the counts on pre-formatted count sheets.

Woody arranged to work with two delivery workers who were relatively unfamiliar with Goodner's inventory since they had been hired only a few weeks earlier. Woody made sure that his team was one of the two count teams assigned to the remote storage facility. Most of the inventory he had stolen over the previous six months had been taken from that site. Woody estimated that he had stolen approximately $45,000 of inventory from the remote storage facility, which represented about 10 percent of the site's book inventory. By maintaining the count sheets for his team, Woody could easily inflate the quantities for the tire lots that he and his team members counted.

After the counting was completed at the remote storage facility, Woody offered to take the count sheets for both count teams to the sales office where the total inventory would be compiled. On the way to the sales office, he stopped in a vacant parking lot to review the count sheets. Woody quickly determined that the apparent shortage remaining at the remote site was approximately $20,000. He reduced that shortage to less than $10,000 by altering the count sheets prepared by the other count team.

When the year-end inventory was tallied for Goodner's Huntington location, the difference between the physical inventory and the book inventory was $12,000, or 2.1 percent. That percentage exceeded the historical shrinkage rate of approximately 1.6 percent for Goodner's sales offices. But, Felix Garcia, the sales manager for the Huntington sales office, did not believe that the 1996 shrinkage was excessive. As it turned out, neither did the accounting personnel and internal auditors at Goodner's corporate headquarters.

Woody continued "ripping off" Goodner throughout 1997. By mid-year, Woody was selling most of the tires he stole to his friend, Al Hunt. On one occasion, Woody warned Al not to sell the tires too cheaply. Woody had become concerned that Curcio's modest prices and its increasing sales volume might spark the curiosity and envy of other Huntington tire retailers.

In October 1997, Goodner's internal audit team arrived to count the Huntington location's inventory. Although company policy dictated that the internal auditors count the inventory of each Goodner sales outlet annually, the average interval between the internal audit inventory counts typically ranged from 15 to 20 months. The internal auditors had last counted the Huntington location's inventory in May 1996, two months before Woody Robinson began stealing tires. Woody was unaware that the internal auditors periodically counted the entire inventory of each Goodner operating unit. Instead, he understood that the internal auditors only did a few test counts during their infrequent visits to the Huntington sales office.

After completing their inventory counts, the two internal auditors arrived at an inventory value of $498,000. A quick check of the Huntington inventory accounting records revealed a book inventory of $639,000. The auditors had never encountered such a large difference between the physical and book inventory totals. Unsure what to do at this point, the auditors eventually decided to take the matter directly to Felix Garcia, the Huntington sales manager. The size of the inventory shortage shocked Garcia. He insisted that the auditors must have overlooked some inventory. Garcia, the two internal auditors, and three delivery workers spent the following day recounting the entire inventory. The resulting physical inventory value was $496,000, $2,000 less than the original value arrived at by the auditors.

Following the second physical inventory, the two internal auditors and Garcia met at a local restaurant to review the Huntington unit's inventory records. No glaring trends were evident in those records to either Garcia or the auditors. Garcia admitted to the auditors that the long hours required "just to keep the tires coming and going" left him little time to monitor his unit's accounting records. When pressed by the auditors to provide possible explanations for the inventory shortage, Garcia erupted. "Listen. Like I just said, my job is simple. My job is selling tires. I sell as many tires as I can, as quickly as I can. I let you guys and those other suits up in Youngstown track the numbers."

The following day, the senior internal auditor called his immediate superior, Goodner's chief financial officer (CFO). The size of the inventory shortage alarmed the CFO. Immediately, the CFO suspected that the inventory shortage was linked to the Huntington unit's downward trend in monthly profits over the past two years. Through 1995, the Huntington sales office consistently ranked as Goodner's second or third most profitable sales outlet. Over the past 18 months, the unit's slumping profits caused it to fall to the bottom one-third of the company's sales outlets in terms of profit margin percentage. Tacking on the large inventory shortage would cause the Huntington location to be Goodner's least profitable sales office over the previous year and one-half.

After discussing the matter with T.J. and Ross Goodner, the CFO contacted the company's independent audit firm and arranged for the firm to investigate the inventory shortage. The Goodners agreed with the CFO that Felix Garcia should be suspended with pay until the investigation was concluded. Garcia's lack of a reasonable explanation for the missing inventory and the anger he directed at the internal auditors prompted the executives to conclude that he was likely responsible for the inventory shortage.

Within a few days, four auditors from Goodner's independent audit firm arrived at the Huntington sales office. Goodner's audit firm was a regional CPA firm with six offices, all in Ohio. Goodner obtained an annual audit of its financial statements because one was demanded by the New York bank that provided the company with a line of credit. Goodner's independent auditors had never paid much attention to the internal controls of the client's sales offices. Instead, they performed a "balance sheet" audit that emphasized corroborating Goodner's year-end assets and liabilities.

During their investigation of the missing inventory, the auditors were appalled by the Huntington unit's lax and often nonexistent controls. The extensive control weaknesses complicated their efforts to identify the source of the inventory shortage. Nevertheless, after several days, the auditors' suspicions began settling on Woody Robinson. A file of customer complaints that Felix Garcia kept in his desk revealed that over the past year an unusually large number of customer complaints had been filed against Woody. During that time, 14 of his customers had protested charges included on their monthly statements. Only two customers serviced by the other sales rep had filed similar complaints during that time frame.

When questioned by the auditors, Garcia conceded that he had not discussed the customer complaints with Woody or the other sales rep. In fact, Garcia was unaware that a disproportionate number of the complaints had been filed against Woody. When Garcia received a customer complaint, he simply passed it on to the appropriate sales rep and allowed that individual to deal with the matter. He maintained a file of the customer complaints only because he had been told to do so by the previous sales manager whom he had replaced three years earlier.

After the independent auditors collected other incriminating evidence against Woody, they arranged for a meeting with him. Also attending that meeting were Goodner's CFO and Felix Garcia. When the auditors produced the incriminating evidence, Woody disclaimed any knowledge of, or responsibility for, the inventory shortage. Woody's denial provoked an immediate and indignant response from Goodner's CFO. "Listen Robinson, you may have fooled the people you've been working with, but you're not fooling me. You'd better spill the beans right now, or else." At this point, Woody stood, announced that he was retaining an attorney, and walked out of the meeting.

EPILOGUE

Goodner Brothers filed a criminal complaint against Woody Robinson two weeks after he refused to discuss the inventory shortage at the Huntington sales office. A few weeks later, Woody's attorney reached a plea bargain agreement with the local district attorney. Woody received a five-year sentence for grand larceny, four years of which were suspended. He eventually served seven months of that sentence in a minimum-security prison. A condition of the plea bargain agreement required Woody to provide a full and candid written summary of the fraudulent scheme that he had perpetrated on his employer.

Woody's confession implicated Al Hunt in his theft scheme. Over the 15 months that Woody had stolen from Goodner, he had "fenced" more than one-half of the stolen inventory through Curcio's Tires. Although the district attorney questioned Al Hunt extensively, he decided not to file criminal charges against him.[2]

Goodner Brothers filed a $185,000 insurance claim to recoup the losses stemming from Woody Robinson's malfeasance. The company's insurer eventually paid Goodner $130,000, which equaled the theft losses that Goodner could document. After settling the claim, the insurance company sued Curcio's Tires and Al Hunt to recover the $98,000 windfall that Curcio's allegedly realized due to Al Hunt's involvement in the theft ring. The case went to federal district court where a judge ordered Hunt to pay $64,000 to Goodner's insurer. Al Hunt then sued Woody Robinson to recover that judgment. The presiding judge, who also had presided over the earlier case, quickly dismissed Al Hunt's lawsuit. According to the judge, Al Hunt's complicity in the fraudulent scheme voided his right to recover the $64,000 judgment from his former friend.

---

2. Ironically, Woody's confession also implicated his wife, Rachelle. Woody revealed to authorities that Rachelle typically deposited the large checks written to him by Al Hunt. The authorities reasoned that Rachelle must have been aware of Woody's fraudulent scheme and thus an accessory to his crime. However, Woody testified that he told his wife the checks were for gambling losses owed to him by Al. After interrogating Rachelle at length, the authorities decided not to prosecute her.

QUESTIONS

1. List what you believe should have been the three to five key internal control objectives for Goodner's Huntington sales office.

2. List the key internal control weaknesses that were evident in the Huntington unit's operations.

3. Develop one or more control policies or procedures to alleviate the control weaknesses you identified in responding to Question 2.

4. Besides Woody Robinson, what other parties were at least partially responsible for the inventory losses Goodner suffered? Defend your answer.

CASE 3.7
TROBERG STORES

"Checker needed up front."

Kirby Jacobson placed a final can on the shelf in front of him and then turned and headed for the checkout stand at the front of the store. Kirby worked for Troberg Stores, a chain of small grocery stores located in a cluster of small towns in northern Minnesota. After graduating from high school in 1980, Kirby accepted a job as a stocker with Troberg's Sixth Street store in his hometown. Fifteen years later, Kirby had risen to the position of assistant store manager.

Although technically a management position, Kirby's job required him to be a jack-of-all-trades for the Sixth Street store. He worked as a stocker and checker when needed, prepared purchase orders for three departments, closed the store several days per week, and trained new employees. Kirby was a quiet and introverted individual who was known for his punctuality and work ethic. Coworkers always called Kirby first if they needed someone to fill in for them.

"I'll help you over here at register three, Ma'am," Kirby said politely to a young woman nearly hidden behind an overloaded shopping cart. The Sixth Street store had four checkout stands. During the day, the store's three full-time cashiers staffed checkout stands one through three. Kirby, the two other assistant store managers, the produce manager, and the dairy manager served as relief checkers. Relief checkers typically manned register four. On this afternoon in early May 1995, Kirby opened checkout stand number three because the cash register in checkout stand four was being repaired. Violet Rahal, the cashier assigned to register three, had taken her lunch break a few minutes earlier at 1 P.M.

After checking out several customers, Kirby closed register three and resumed his stocking duties. Thirty minutes later, Violet Rahal returned from her lunch break. Because she noticed that several items at her work station had been rearranged, Violet asked Roma Charboneau, the cashier at register two, if someone used register three during her lunch break. Roma replied that Kirby had checked out several customers at register three. Violet then counted her cash till. Then, she counted it again. Each time, she arrived at the same total. Her cash till was short by $210. Violet immediately reported the shortage to Angelo Velotti, the store manager.[1]

WHO STOLE THE CASH?

Cash shortages had been a recurring problem for Troberg's Sixth Street store. Over the previous 12 months, Angelo Velotti had reported four cash shortages, each exceeding $200, to the owner of Troberg Stores, Elliott Paulsen. The cash shortage Violet Rahal discovered was the first that could be tracked to a specific cash register and a specific time of day.

When Violet reported the missing $210 to Velotti, the frustrated store manager slammed his fist on his desk. "What is going on here?" he shouted.

"I counted my till when I left for lunch. Just like I always do," Violet responded timidly. "Then, when I got back—"

"Violet, I'm not accusing you. But this has to stop."

A shaken Violet regained her composure and continued. "When I got back, I noticed that someone had been using register three. Roma said that it was Kirby."

"Kirby," Velotti muttered under his breath in disgust.

"So, I counted my till. Twice. Each time, I came up short by $210."

"Stay here, Violet. I'm getting to the bottom of this right now."

Velotti marched to aisle four where Kirby was stocking and brusquely told the assistant store manager to come to his office. When Kirby asked why, Velotti snapped, "You'll find out soon enough."

Velotti's frustration stemmed from mounting pressure that Paulsen was applying on him to tighten the internal controls of the Sixth Street store. Each time Velotti reported a cash shortage, Paulsen exploded. "We're barely making ends meet as it is!" Paulsen had bellowed on the previous occasion Velotti reported an apparent theft of cash.

Increasing competition from nationwide grocery chains had been slicing away at Troberg's revenues and profits for several years. Residents of the small towns in which Troberg's stores were located often decided to drive to larger metropolitan areas to take advantage of the lower prices and greater variety of merchandise offered by the large grocery chains. By the spring of 1995, Troberg's gross profit percentage hovered at an anemic 10 percent, meaning that the Sixth Street store needed to produce $2,000 of revenues to replace the gross profit lost due to a $200 theft. The gross profit percentage for comparable grocery chains ranged from 18 to 25 percent.

At the same time Paulsen was demanding that Velotti eliminate the Sixth Street store's theft losses, he was slashing the store's operating budget. During the past year, Velotti had trimmed the store's payroll from 30 to 24 employees. Velotti realized that reducing the store's staff during each work shift and assigning more job responsibilities to each employee provided dishonest subordinates a greater

---

1. This case was developed from a legal opinion written in the late 1990s. The names of the actual parties involved in the case and the case setting have been changed. In addition, certain of the factual circumstances reported in this case are fictionalized accounts of the facts disclosed in the legal opinion.

opportunity to take advantage of the business. But, when he tried to make that argument to Paulsen, the owner refused to listen. "Doesn't matter how many or how few employees you have since honesty is a part of everybody's job description," Paulsen had once barked at Velotti.

After returning to his office with Kirby Jacobson in tow, Angelo Velotti told Violet and Kirby that he was calling the local police department. Velotti asked the police department to immediately dispatch an officer to the Sixth Street store to investigate the apparent theft. Next, Velotti telephoned Elliott Paulsen. As expected, the unpleasant news detonated Paulsen's notoriously quick temper.

A few weeks earlier, Paulsen and Velotti had spent several hours studying the previous four thefts of cash at the Sixth Street store. Three of those shortages had been discovered at the end of the day when an assistant store manager prepared the daily cash deposit. On each of those occasions, the assistant store manager who discovered the cash shortage had been Kirby Jacobson. The fourth shortage occurred at register four one busy Saturday afternoon. Kirby had worked as a relief checker during the shift in which that cash shortage arose, along with three other individuals. Since the exact time that the cash shortage occurred could not be pinpointed, the shortage could not be traced to a specific individual.

Paulsen and Velotti concluded that Kirby's connection with the four thefts was not a coincidence. The two men later testified that their investigation caused them to "lose trust and confidence" in Kirby, although they had never previously questioned his integrity. They also testified that prior to the May 1995 theft they had discussed changing Kirby's job responsibilities so that he would not have access to the store's cash.

Elliott Paulsen, who lived in a nearby community, and Officer Jessica Burnett arrived at the Sixth Street store within one hour after Violet Rahal discovered the $210 cash shortage. Officer Burnett first spoke privately with Paulsen. The owner told the police officer about the Sixth Street store's rash of cash thefts over the previous 12 months and Kirby's link to each of those thefts. Officer Burnett then interviewed the Troberg employees on the scene, including Velotti. Although Roma Charboneau reported seeing three "suspicious characters" milling around the candy counter near register three while it was unattended, Officer Burnett quickly concluded that the theft was likely an "inside job." The officer then decided that Kirby Jacobson and Violet Rahal should take polygraph examinations.

Officer Burnett followed the required procedures to administer polygraph examinations in the case of a suspected employee theft. The Employee Polygraph Protection Act (EPPA), a federal statute enacted by Congress in 1988, dictates the procedures to be followed in such circumstances. First, Officer Burnett obtained the permission of Elliott Paulsen, the victim of the crime, to conduct the polygraph examinations. Next, the officer met with the two suspects, Kirby Jacobson and Violet Rahal. Officer Burnett advised the two employees that they were not required to take a polygraph test. When she was certain that Jacobson and Rahal understood their legal rights, the officer asked each of them to take a polygraph test at a later date.

TRUTH AND CONSEQUENCES

Both Kirby and Violet agreed to submit to a polygraph examination regarding their involvement in, or knowledge of, the May 1995 theft at Troberg's Sixth Street store. Kirby later testified that he consented to take the polygraph because he believed it was the only way to "clear his name." At the time, Kirby was unaware that Elliott Paulsen and Angelo Velotti suspected he was responsible for all five thefts at the Sixth Street store. When Kirby agreed to take a polygraph test, Paulsen and Velotti decided that they would await the outcome of that test before making a final decision regarding his employment status.

In early June 1995, the state Department of Criminal Investigation administered polygraph tests to Kirby Jacobson and Violet Rahal. Violet easily "passed" the test. The polygrapher reported finding no signs of undue anxiety or other inappropriate physiological responses in Violet's polygraph results.[2] Analysis of Kirby's polygraph printout revealed indications of emotional distress and deception, suggesting that he was not being truthful regarding his alleged lack of involvement in the theft. After reviewing the polygraph results, Officer Burnett told Elliott Paulsen that she believed Kirby had stolen the $210. Despite that belief, the officer declined to file criminal charges against Jacobson. She informed Paulsen that there was insufficient evidence to prove beyond a reasonable doubt that Kirby had stolen the cash.

Shortly after receiving the polygraph results, Paulsen met with Velotti. The two men decided not to dismiss Kirby. They later testified that they chose not to fire Kirby because he had been a valued employee of the Sixth Street store for so many years. Instead, they chose to demote him from assistant store manager to stocker, the lowest employment position at the Sixth Street store and the first job Kirby held at the store 15 years earlier. They also decided to forbid Kirby from handling any cash in the store. Despite the demotion, Paulsen and Velotti did not reduce Kirby's salary or his other employment benefits.

The day following his meeting with Paulsen, Velotti called Kirby into his office. Velotti notified Kirby of his demotion and informed him that he would never again be considered for a managerial position with the company. Shocked by the news, Kirby did not question Velotti regarding the decision but instead quietly walked out of the office. A few days later, Velotti, who had remained angry at Kirby since the May 1995 theft, privately told Kirby that he would "never forget" the incident. Velotti also told Kirby he should consider accepting another employment opportunity if one became available.

The weeks following Kirby's demotion were very unpleasant for him. Kirby later testified that the demotion "devastated and humiliated" him. Worst of all was the treatment he received from the management personnel in the store. His former peers openly gossiped about his alleged involvement in the May 1995 theft and made jokes regarding his demotion. Kirby soon found his work environment intolerable and resigned his job with the Sixth Street store. After leaving Troberg Stores, Kirby lapsed into a depression and eventually sought psychological counseling.

---

2. The legal opinion from which this case was developed provided the following description of a polygraph. "The basic theory underlying the polygraph is that a subject's honesty, dishonesty, or guilty knowledge can be judged from those physical responses that are scientifically related to emotional upset. . . . The tension associated with the inner conflict of choosing between willful dishonesty and truthfulness is presumed to be measurable by recording changes in inherent body functions. The polygraph does not measure whether the subject is either lying or telling the truth. Rather it merely records the physiological changes that occur as the subject responds to a series of questions requiring simple 'yes' or 'no' answers."

KIRBY FIGHTS BACK

Two years following his resignation, Kirby Jacobson filed a civil complaint against Troberg Stores, Elliott Paulsen, and Angelo Velotti. Kirby's lawsuit charged that during and following the investigation of the May 1995 theft, Troberg Stores violated his civil rights under the EPPA. Kirby's lawsuit contained the following specific allegations:

(1) Troberg Stores caused him to take the polygraph examination;
(2) Troberg improperly used the polygraph results;
(3) Troberg disciplined him on the basis of the polygraph results; and
(4) he was constructively discharged by Troberg based on the polygraph results.

The federal judge who presided over Kirby's lawsuit found that few legal cases had been filed by individuals under the EPPA since it was passed in 1988. To provide a sound basis for his opinion in the case, the judge reviewed the history of the polygraph and dissected the requirements of, and legislative rationale underlying, the EPPA.

The polygraph was invented in the late 1920s. During the latter part of the twentieth century, businesses began routinely using polygraph examinations to screen new employees, to investigate apparent theft and embezzlement by employees, and for related purposes. The absence of statutory guidelines for, and restrictions on the use of, polygraph examinations resulted in many employers abusing polygraph tests, including using them to justify discriminatory employment practices. To remedy such abusive practices, Congress passed the EPPA.

Exhibit 1 presents a key excerpt from the EPPA. That passage seemingly eliminates the use of polygraph tests for employment purposes within the private sector. However, a subsequent section of the EPPA allows employers under certain restrictive conditions to request an employee to submit to a polygraph examination. Exhibit 2 presents this exception, referred to as the "ongoing investigation exemption."[3] Since Troberg Stores failed to follow all the steps outlined in Exhibit 2, the federal judge overseeing Kirby's lawsuit ruled that the company could not invoke the ongoing investigation exemption to the EPPA in preparing a defense to Kirby's charges.

Except as provided in Sections 2006 and 2007 of this title, it shall be unlawful for any employer engaged in or affecting commerce or in the production of goods for commerce—
 	
 (1) directly or indirectly, to require, request, suggest, or cause any employee or prospective employee to take or submit to any lie detector test;
 (2) to use, accept, refer to, or inquire concerning the results of any lie detector test of any employee or prospective employee;
 (3) to discharge, discipline, discriminate against in any manner, or deny employment or promotion to, or threaten to take any action against—
   (a) any employee or prospective employee who refuses, declines, or fails to take or submit to any lie detector test, or
   (b) any employee or prospective employee on the basis of the results of any lie detector test.

EXHIBIT 1
Key Excerpt from
Employee Polygraph
Protection Act

---

3. Even if an employer invokes the ongoing investigation exemption to the EPPA, the employer may not rely exclusively on polygraph results to make an adverse employment decision regarding an employee suspected of theft.

**EXHIBIT 2
"Ongoing Investigation
Exemption" Included in
Employee Polygraph
Protection Act**

Subject to Sections 2006 and 2009 of this title, this chapter shall not prohibit an employer from requesting an employee to submit to a polygraph test if

(1) the test is administered in connection with an ongoing investigation involving economic loss or injury to the employer's business, such as theft, embezzlement, misappropriation, or an act of unlawful industrial espionage or sabotage;

(2) the employee had access to the property that is the subject of the investigation;

(3) the employer had a reasonable suspicion that the employee was involved in the incident or activity under investigation; and

(4) the employer executes a statement, provided to the examinee before the test, that
  (a) sets forth with particularity the specific incident or activity being investigated and the basis for testing particular employees,
  (b) is signed by a person (other than a polygraph examiner) authorized to legally bind the employer,
  (c) is retained by the employer for at least 3 years, and
  (d) contains at a minimum
    (i) an identification of the specific economic loss or injury to the business of the employer,
    (ii) a statement indicating that the employee had access to the property that is the subject of the investigation, and
    (iii) a statement describing the basis of the employer's reasonable suspicion that the employee was involved in the incident or activity under investigation.

. . . the EPPA contemplates the situation in which [Troberg Stores] found itself with [Kirby Jacobson] and provides explicit instructions as to how [Troberg Stores] could have protected its business and acted in response to results of a polygraph test that implicated its employee in the store theft. [Troberg Stores], however, had to comply with all of the requirements specified in Sections 2006 and 2007 in order to invoke use of the ongoing investigation exemption.

In his legal opinion, the federal judge responded to each allegation that Kirby Jacobson filed against Troberg Stores. Regarding the first allegation, the judge ruled that the company had not required or effectively caused Kirby to take the polygraph examination. Instead, the judge ruled that Officer Burnett, on her own initiative, requested Kirby to take the polygraph test. The judge found in favor of Kirby on the remaining three allegations. First, the judge ruled that Troberg Stores and its management improperly used the polygraph results in evaluating Kirby's employment status. Second, evidence presented by Kirby's legal counsel clearly demonstrated that Paulsen and Velotti relied on the polygraph results in deciding to demote Kirby. Finally, the judge agreed that Kirby faced an intolerable work environment following his demotion, which effectively forced him to resign his job. Since Troberg Stores and its management were ultimately responsible for creating the hostile work environment, the judge ruled that the company had constructively discharged Kirby.

The federal judge awarded Kirby Jacobson approximately $40,000 in damages from Troberg Stores and its management. Included in those damages were $15,000 for "emotional distress" inflicted on Kirby by his former employer and approximately $25,000 for lost wages and employment benefits.

In awarding the judgment to Kirby Jacobson, the judge acknowledged that Kirby "may well have committed the theft from the cash register." The judge then went on to point out that Troberg Stores bungled two opportunities to dismiss Kirby. First, the company could have dismissed Kirby immediately following the May 1995 theft. Circumstantial evidence collected by Paulsen and Velotti clearly implicated Kirby in the previous thefts at the Sixth Street store. According to the judge, the additional suspicion cast on Kirby's integrity by the May 1995 theft provided Troberg Stores sufficient justification to fire him with little risk of any legal repercussions. Second, Troberg Stores could have taken advantage of the "ongoing investigation exemption" of the EPPA. That option was available to the company since Paulsen and Velotti initiated an investigation of the previous thefts at the Sixth Street store prior to the May 1995 incident. By invoking this exemption to the EPPA, the company could have used the polygraph test results, along with the other available incriminating evidence, to dismiss Kirby, again with little risk of any legal reprisal.[4]

QUESTIONS

1. The management of Troberg Stores was unfamiliar with the EPPA. Should a business's internal control process address its need to comply with all relevant state and federal statutes? Or, is such compliance beyond the scope of an entity's internal control process? Defend your answer.

2. The legal opinion on which this case was based did not elaborate on the internal controls Troberg Stores had in place for its cash processing activities. Visit a local grocery store and unobtrusively observe one or more checkout stands. Develop a list of policies and procedures apparently used by the store to maintain control over its checkout stand operations. For each of these items, identify the apparent control objective.

3. What types of duties should typically be segregated or separated across employees of a small business? What measures can a small business implement if adequate segregation of duties is not economically feasible?

4. What ethical responsibilities does a business's managers and owners have when they suspect an employee of theft? Should such ethical considerations be integrated into a business's internal control policies and procedures? Explain.

5. Do you believe the EPPA improperly limits retail businesses' ability to investigate and prosecute potential incidents of employee theft? Defend your answer. Identify other laws and regulations that have potential control implications for retail businesses.

---

4. Troberg's financial problems worsened following Kirby Jacobson's resignation. In the late 1990s, a large competitor purchased all of Troberg's stores.

SECTION FOUR
ETHICAL RESPONSIBILITIES OF ACCOUNTANTS

CASE 4.1
CREVE COUER PIZZA, INC.

Imagine this scenario. A few years after graduating from the University of Arizona, Morehouse College, or Penn State University with an accounting degree, you find yourself working as an audit senior with an international accounting firm. Your best friend, Rick, who you have known since kindergarten, is a special agent with the Internal Revenue Service (IRS). Over lunch one day, Rick mentions the IRS's informant program.

"You know, Jess, you could pick up a few hundred dollars here and there working as a controlled informant for us. In fact, if you would feed us information regarding one or two of those large corporate clients of yours, you could make a bundle."

"That's funny, Rick. Real funny. Me, a double agent, spying on my clients for the IRS? Have you ever heard of the confidentiality rule?"

Sound farfetched? Not really. Since 1939, the IRS has operated an informant program. Most individuals who participate in this program provide information on a one-time basis; however, the IRS also retains hundreds of "controlled informants" who work in tandem with one or more IRS special agents on a continuing basis. Controlled informants provide the IRS with incriminating evidence regarding individuals and businesses suspected of cheating on their taxes. In the early 1990s, the IRS revealed that more than 40 of these controlled informants were CPAs.

Now consider this scenario. You, the audit senior, are again having lunch with your friend Rick, the IRS special agent. Rick knows that the IRS is investigating you for large deductions taken in recent years on your federal income tax returns for a questionable tax shelter scheme. The additional tax assessments and fines you face significantly exceed your net worth. Your legal costs alone will be several thousand dollars. To date, you have been successful in concealing the IRS investigation from your spouse, other family members, and your employer, but that will not be possible much longer.

"Jess, I know this investigation is really worrying you. But, I can get you out of this whole mess. I talked to my supervisor. She and three other agents are working on a case involving one of your audit clients. I can't tell you which one right now. If you agree to work with them as a controlled informant and provide them with information that you can easily get your hands on, they will close the case on you. You will be off the hook. No questions. No fines or additional taxes. Case closed . . . permanently."

"Rick, come on, I can't do that. What if my firm finds out? I'd lose my job. I would probably lose my certificate."

"Yeah, but face these facts. If the IRS proves its case against you, you are going to lose your job and your certificate . . . and probably a whole lot more. Maybe even your marriage. Think about it, Jess. Realistically, the agency is looking at a maximum recovery of $50,000 or so from you. But if you cooperate with my supervisor, she can probably squeeze 20 or 30 million out of your client."

"You're sure they would let me off . . . free and clear?"

"Yes. Free and clear. Come on, Jess, we need you. More important, you need us. Plus, think of it this way. You made one mistake by becoming involved in that phony tax shelter scam. But, your client has been ripping off the government, big time, for years. You would be doing a public service by turning in these crooks."

Returning to reality, consider the case of James Checksfield. In 1981, Checksfield, a Missouri CPA, became a controlled informant for the IRS. The IRS special agent who recruited Checksfield had been his close friend for several years and knew that Checksfield was under investigation by the IRS. Reportedly, Checksfield owed back taxes of nearly $30,000 because of his failure to file federal income tax returns from 1974 through 1977. At the same time the IRS recruited Checksfield, the federal agency was also investigating a Missouri-based company, Creve Couer Pizza, Inc. The IRS believed that the owner of this chain of pizza restaurants was "skimming receipts" from his business—that is, failing to report on his federal income tax returns the total sales revenue of his eight restaurants. Checksfield had served as Creve Couer's CPA for several years, although both the IRS and Checksfield denied that he was recruited specifically to provide information regarding that company.

From 1982 through 1985, Checksfield funneled information to the IRS regarding Creve Couer Pizza. Based upon this information, federal prosecutors filed a six-count indictment against the owner of that business in 1989. This indictment charged the owner with under-reporting his taxable income by several hundred thousand dollars. The owner faced fines of nearly $1 million and a prison term of up to 24 years if convicted of the charges. Meanwhile, the IRS dropped its case against Checksfield. Both the IRS and Checksfield maintained that there was no connection between the decision to drop the case against him and his decision to provide the IRS with information regarding Creve Couer Pizza.

Following the indictment filed against the owner of Creve Couer Pizza, the owner's attorneys subpoenaed the information that the IRS had used to build its case against him. As a result, the owner discovered the role played by his long time friend and accountant in the IRS investigation. Quite naturally, the owner was very upset. "What my accountant did to me was very mean and devious. He sat here in my home with me and my family. He was like a member of the family. On the other hand, he was working against me."[1] In another interview, the owner commented, "A client has the right to feel he's getting undivided loyalty from his accountant."[2] Contributing to the owner's anger was the fact that he paid more than $50,000 in fees for accounting and taxation services to Checksfield during the time the CPA was working undercover for the IRS.

The print and electronic media reported the case of the "singing CPA" nationwide, prompting extensive criticism of the IRS. More important, the case caused many clients of CPAs to doubt whether they could trust their accountants to protect the confidentiality of sensitive financial information. When questioned concerning the matter, the IRS expressed no remorse for using Checksfield to gather incriminating evidence regarding the owner of Creve Couer Pizza. An IRS representative also rejected the contention that communications between accountants and their clients should be "privileged" under federal law similar to communications between attorneys and their clients.

> The IRS says the claim of a privileged [accountant-client] relationship is nonsense. "To the contrary," says Edward Federico of the IRS's criminal-investigation division in St. Louis, "the accountant has a moral and legal obligation to turn over information."[3]

The accounting profession was appalled by the Checksfield case and tried to minimize the damage it had done to the public's trust in CPAs. In particular, the profession condemned the actions of the IRS.

> Rarely has there been such a case of prosecutorial zeal that violated rudimentary standards of decency . . . turning the client-accountant relationship into a secret tool for government agents is an abominable practice. It demeans the service. It erodes trust in the accounting profession.[4]

EPILOGUE

In August 1990, the Missouri State Board of Accountancy revoked James Checksfield's CPA license for violating a state law that prohibits CPAs from disclosing confidential client information without the client's permission. In November 1991, the U.S. Justice Department suddenly announced that it was dropping the tax evasion charges against the owner of Creve Couer Pizza, although pretrial arguments had already been presented for the case. The Justice Department had little to say regarding its decision. Legal experts speculated that federal prosecutors dropped the charges because the judge hearing the case was expected to disallow the evidence the IRS collected with the assistance of Checksfield.

Despite the negative publicity produced by the Creve Couer case, the IRS continues to use accountants both in public accounting and private industry as informants. *Forbes* magazine recently reported a case in which a disgruntled

1. "Accountant Spies on Client for IRS," *Kansas City Star*, 18 March 1992, 2.

2. "The Case of the Singing CPA," *Newsweek*, 17 July 1989, 41.

3. *Ibid.*

4. "IRS Oversteps With CPA Stoolies," *Accounting Today*, 6 January 1992, 22.

controller of a retail electronics chain got even with his boss.[5] Shortly before leaving the firm, the controller copied accounting and tax records documenting a large scale tax fraud perpetrated by the chain's owner. Thanks to this information, the IRS collected a nearly $7 million fine from the owner and sent him to jail for 10 months. The former controller received a significant but undisclosed "finder's fee" from the IRS for his "cooperation."

QUESTIONS

1. Do CPAs who provide accounting, taxation, and related services to small businesses have a professional responsibility to serve as the "moral conscience" of those clients? Explain.

2. In a 1984 opinion handed down by the U.S. Supreme Court, Chief Justice Warren Burger noted that "the independent auditor assumes a public responsibility transcending any employment relationship with the client." If this is true, do auditors have a moral or professional responsibility to turn in clients who are cheating on their taxes or violating other laws?

3. Assume that you were Jess in the second hypothetical scenario presented in this case. How would you respond to your friend's suggestion that you become a controlled informant for the IRS? Identify the parties that would be affected by your decision and the obligations you would have to each.

4. In your opinion, should communications between accountants and their clients be "privileged"? Defend your answer.

5. J. Novack, "Boomerang," *Forbes*, 7 July 1997, 42–43.

CASE 4.2
LAUREL VALLEY ESTATES

In 1978, two California businessmen, Claude Trout and Harry Moore, formed a real estate development company, which they named Laurel Valley Estates.[1] The partnership agreement signed by Trout and Moore stated that the two partners would make equal capital contributions to the new firm and would share equally in its profits. Trout's initial capital contribution was a 400-acre parcel of undivided land appraised at $640,000; Moore contributed an equal amount of cash. From 1978 through the end of 1981, Trout supervised the subdivision of the 400-acre property into residential lots and the addition of improvements. During that same period, Moore negotiated with several construction companies to build expensive tract homes on the property.

Near the end of 1981, Moore became restless with the slow progress being made in developing the Laurel Valley property. Moore questioned whether Trout was properly managing the partnership's dwindling cash funds and whether those funds would be depleted before the completion of the project. To allay his concern regarding Laurel Valley's financial status, Moore decided to retain Newby & Company, an accounting firm that he had employed in previous business ventures, to review the partnership's books. After learning of Moore's decision, Trout told Moore that he had no objection to Newby & Company's reviewing the partnership's accounting records. In fact, Trout offered to engage Newby & Company as the partnership's permanent accounting firm. Moore accepted Trout's offer. A few days later, Trout notified Douglas & Michaels, the partnership's accounting firm since its inception in 1978, of the decision to switch to Newby & Company.

---

1. This case was developed from a legal opinion written in the 1980s. The names of the actual parties involved in the case have been changed. In addition, certain of the factual circumstances reported in this case are fictionalized accounts of the actual facts disclosed in the legal opinion.

In early December 1981, Jay Kent Newby, a staff accountant with Newby & Company and the son of the firm's founder, arrived at the Laurel Valley offices to review the partnership's books. Newby asked Trout for a listing of all tangible assets held in the partnership's name, as well as the partnership's general ledger, cash receipts and cash disbursements journals, and check register.

Late in the afternoon of his second day on the Laurel Valley engagement, a visibly upset Newby stormed into Trout's office, interrupting a conversation between Trout and his secretary. Newby told Trout that he had uncovered major problems in the partnership's financial records. The property that Trout contributed to the partnership was listed as an asset in the firm's general ledger; however, Trout had never transferred the legal title of that property to Laurel Valley Estates. Newby then charged that over the past three years, Trout had squandered most of the cash invested in the partnership by Moore. According to Newby, Trout had paid exorbitant amounts to contractors he had retained to develop the Laurel Valley property. Newby also implied that many of the contractors were close friends or relatives of Trout. Newby concluded his tirade by informing Trout, in the presence of Trout's secretary, that the partnership's records were fraudulent, that Trout owed hundreds of thousands of dollars to the partnership, and that Trout "could be looking at jail."

Newby's allegations stunned Claude Trout. After regaining his composure, Trout offered to deed the Laurel Valley property to the partnership. Newby snapped that "it was too late" to do that. Within minutes, Newby had packed his briefcase and was on his way out the door when Trout stopped him. "What can I do to clear this up?" Trout asked. After a brief pause, Newby replied sarcastically, "Pray."

Early the next morning, Harry Moore telephoned Trout and asked that he drive to Sacramento to meet with him, Jay Kent Newby, and Newby's father in the accounting firm's office. Trout agreed to make the short trip to Sacramento. Jay Kent Newby presided over the meeting that afternoon among the four men. Newby reported that he had devised a plan for resolving the situation without any legal action being taken against Trout. Because Trout was obviously "crooked and dishonest," Newby suggested that Moore be allowed to withdraw immediately from the partnership. Newby's plan called for Trout to return Moore's initial cash investment in the partnership and to pay Moore interest on his investment for the prior three years. When Trout asked Moore if that was what he wanted, Moore, who had yet to speak during the meeting, nodded affirmatively.

Trout agreed to the settlement arranged by Jay Kent Newby and then apologized for the mistake he had made. He insisted he had been unaware of the need to transfer the title of the 400-acre property to the partnership. Additionally, Trout maintained that he had made every effort to conserve the funds committed to the partnership by Moore. Within two weeks, Trout borrowed approximately $900,000 to liquidate Moore's ownership interest in Laurel Valley Estates.

Following the dissolution of the partnership, Trout lost interest in completing the development of the Laurel Valley property and sold it, incurring a large loss. Over the following several months, Trout's health deteriorated, and he was eventually forced to seek psychiatric help. Trout attributed his physical and mental deterioration to the dissolution of his partnership with Moore and to Jay Kent Newby's allegation that he was "crooked and dishonest."

In late 1982, Trout told Jim Hardy, a partner of Laurel Valley Estates' original accounting firm, of the problem that led to the breakup of his partnership with

Moore. Hardy immediately informed Trout that state law did not require him to deed the Laurel Valley property to the partnership. According to Hardy, the stated intentions of partners dictate whether personal assets of individual partners have been contributed to the partnership. Because the Trout and Moore partnership agreement clearly specified that Trout's initial capital contribution would be the 400-acre property, that property was legally a partnership asset although the title remained in Trout's name. In fact, Hardy had researched that specific question when he set up the books for Laurel Valley Estates shortly after the partnership's formation in 1978.

Trout was livid after learning that he had not been required to transfer the title of the 400-acre property to Laurel Valley Estates, as Jay Kent Newby had insisted. Trout immediately sued Newby & Company, charging the accounting firm with professional malpractice, fraud, and the intentional infliction of emotional distress. The judge who presided over the initial hearing in the case decided there was no basis for any of the charges and dismissed Trout's suit. A few days later, Claude Trout died of a heart attack.

Several months following Trout's death, the executor of his estate appealed the dismissal of the lawsuit against Newby & Company. The appellate court ruled that considerable evidence existed supporting Trout's allegation of professional malpractice by Newby & Company but agreed with the lower court's decision to dismiss the charges of fraud and infliction of emotional distress. The appellate judge who wrote the legal opinion in the case stated that Jay Kent Newby should have researched more thoroughly the legal question regarding Trout's initial capital contribution to the partnership before rendering any professional advice to Trout. The judge also ruled that a jury trial should decide whether the accounting firm's actions caused Trout's damages. Finally, the judge observed that although Newby & Company could not be sued for the intentional infliction of emotional distress because of legal technicalities, plaintiff counsel might be able to prove that Jay Kent Newby had slandered Trout.

A few days before the trial was to begin in the civil lawsuit involving Newby & Company and Trout's executor, the accounting firm offered to make a sizable payment to Trout's estate to settle the case. Trout's executor accepted the offer only after Newby & Company's partners extended a personal apology to members of the Trout family for the unfortunate incident involving Jay Kent Newby and Claude Trout.

QUESTIONS

1. What professional responsibilities did Jay Kent Newby fail to fulfill in his interaction with Claude Trout? Identify specific ethical rules and other professional standards that he violated. Would your answer be affected by the fact that Newby was not a CPA at the time? Given this additional fact, what other parties, if any, violated one or more of the public accounting profession's ethical rules or standards?
2. The controversy in this case focused on the legal question of whether Trout was required to deed the 400-acre property to the partnership. Are auditors required to be competent in such legal matters? If you had been in Jay Kent Newby's position, what would you have done when you discovered that the property had not been deeded to the partnership?

3. Trout was technically a client of Newby & Company when that firm reviewed the partnership's accounting records in late 1981. When Trout sued Newby & Company for professional malpractice, he filed a tort action against the accounting firm. Identify the general elements of proof that a client must establish when suing an accounting firm for professional malpractice. What other type of lawsuit could Trout have filed against Newby & Company, given that he was in privity with the accounting firm?

CASE 4.3
SUZETTE WASHINGTON, ACCOUNTING MAJOR

Suzette Washington financed her college education by working as an inventory clerk for Bertolini's, a clothing store chain located in the southeastern United States.[1] Bertolini's caters primarily to fashion-conscious young men and women. The company's stores carry a wide range of clothing including casual wear, business suits, and accessories. The Bertolini's store for which Suzette worked is located a few blocks from the campus of the large state university that she attended. Except for management personnel, most of Bertolini's employees are college students. Suzette's best friend and roommate, Paula Kaye, worked for Bertolini's as a sales clerk. Paula majored in marketing, while Suzette was an accounting major.

During Suzette's senior year in college, Bertolini's began experiencing abnormally high inventory shrinkage in the store's three departments that stocked men's apparel. Suzette's supervisor, an assistant store manager, confided in her that he believed one or more of the sales clerks might be stealing merchandise. Over lunch one day in the student union, Suzette casually mentioned the inventory problem to Paula. Paula quickly changed the subject by asking Suzette about her plans for the weekend.

"Paula, rewind for just a second. Do you know something that I don't?"

"Huh? What do you mean?"

"Missing inventory . . . shrinkage . . . theft?"

After a few awkward moments, Paula stopped eating and looked squarely into her friend's eyes. "Suzette, I don't know if it's true, but I've heard a rumor that Alex and Matt are stealing a few things each week. Polo shirts, silk ties, jeans.

1. This case was developed from information provided by a former college student who is now a CPA employed with an accounting firm. The names, location, and certain other background facts have been changed.

Occasionally, they take something expensive, like a hand-knit sweater or sports jacket."

"How are they doing it?"

"I've heard—and don't repeat any of this now—I've heard that a couple of times per week, Alex stashes one or two items at the bottom of the trash container beneath the number two cash register. Then Matt, you know he empties the trash every night in the dumpster out in the alley, takes the items out and puts them in his car."

"Paula, we can't let them get away with this. We have to tell someone."

"No 'we' aren't. Remember, this is just a rumor. I don't know that it's true. If you tell a manager, there will be questions. And more questions. Maybe the police will be brought in. You know that eventually someone's going to find out who told. And then . . . slashed tires . . . phone calls in the middle of the night."

"So, don't get involved? Don't do anything? Just let those guys keep stealing?"

"Suze, you work in inventory. You know the markup they put on those clothes. They expect to lose a few things here and there to employees."

"Maybe the markup wouldn't be so high if theft wasn't a problem."

Now, there was no doubt in Paula's mind that Suzette was going to report the alleged theft scheme to management. "Two months, Suze. Two months till we graduate. Can you wait till then to spill the beans? Then we can move out-of-state before our cars are spray-painted."

One week following Suzette and Paula's conversation, a Bertolini's store manager received an anonymous typed message that revealed the two-person theft ring rumored to be operating within the store. Bertolini's immediately retained a private detective. Over a four-week period, the detective documented $500 of merchandise thefts by Alex and Matt. After Bertolini's notified the police, the local district attorney filed criminal charges against the two young men. A plea bargain agreement arranged by their attorneys resulted in suspended prison sentences for Alex and Matt. The terms of that agreement included making restitution to Bertolini's, completing several hundred hours of community service, and a lengthy period of probation.

QUESTIONS

1. What would you do if you found yourself in a situation similar to that faced by Suzette in this case?

2. Do you believe that it was appropriate for Suzette to report the alleged theft ring to a store manager? Would it have been unethical for Suzette *not* to report the rumored theft ring?

3. Accounting majors are preparing to enter a profession recognized as having one of the strongest and most rigorously enforced ethical codes. Given this fact, do you believe that accounting majors have a greater responsibility than other business majors to behave ethically?

4. Briefly discuss internal control activities that might have prevented the theft losses suffered by Bertolini's.

CASE 4.4
ROCKY MOUNT UNDERGARMENT COMPANY, INC.

Employees involved in the accounting and control functions of organizations often face ethical dilemmas. Typically, at some point in each of these dilemmas an employee must decide whether he or she will "do the right thing." Consider the huge scandal involving Equity Funding Corporation of America in the early 1970s. In that scandal, dozens of the life insurance company's employees actively participated in a fraudulent scheme intended to grossly overstate Equity Funding's revenues and profits. These employees routinely prepared phony insurance applications, invoices, and other fake documents to conceal the fraud masterminded by the firm's top executives. When questioned by a reporter following the disclosure of the fraud, one of Equity Funding's employees meekly observed, "I simply lacked the courage to do what was right."[1]

In early 1986, several employees of Rocky Mount Undergarment Co., Inc. (RMUC), came face to face with an ethical dilemma. RMUC, a North Carolina-based company, manufactured undergarments and other apparel products. Approximately one-half of the company's annual sales were to three large merchandisers: Kmart (29 percent), Wal-Mart (11 percent), and Sears (9 percent). RMUC employed nearly 1,300 workers in its production facilities and another 40 individuals in its administrative functions. Between 1981 and 1984, RMUC realized steady growth in revenues and profits. In 1981, RMUC reported a net income of $378,000 on net sales of $17.9 million. Three years later, the company reported a net income of $1.5 million on net sales of $32 million.

Unfortunately, RMUC failed to sustain its impressive profit trend in 1985 as reflected by the financial data presented for the firm in Exhibit 1. Disproportion-

---

1. H. Anderson, "12 More Ex-Equity Officials Get Jail, Fine or Probation," *Los Angeles Times*, 25 March 1975, Section 3, 9 & 11.

EXHIBIT 1
RMUC, Inc., Selected
Financial Data, 1981–1985

RMUC, Inc. Selected Financial Data, 1981–1985 (000s omitted)					
	1985	1984	1983	1982	1981
Net sales	$39,505	$32,167	$25,697	$21,063	$17,851
Cost of sales	32,415	24,199	19,700	16,590	14,358
Selling, general & administrative expenses	5,791	4,523	3,405	2,694	2,454
Net income	452	1,529	1,153	756	378
Total assets	24,808	14,745	11,134	6,916	5,529
Stockholders' equity	11,263	6,999	3,510	3,469	2,714
Current assets	20,924	12,678	9,648	5,779	4,639
Accounts receivable	7,115	4,725	3,734	2,608	1,290
Inventory	12,158	7,507	5,694	2,869	3,045
Current liabilities	7,302	6,999	3,510	3,469	2,714

ately high production costs cut sharply into the company's profit margin during that year. These high production costs resulted from cost overruns on several large customer orders and from significant training and other start-up costs linked to the opening of a new factory.

A subsequent investigation by the Securities and Exchange Commission (SEC) revealed that two RMUC executives, the company's senior executive and another high-ranking officer, refused to allow the firm to report its actual net income of $452,000 for 1985. To inflate the company's 1985 net income, these executives instructed three RMUC employees to overstate the firm's year-end inventory and thereby understate its cost of goods sold. Initially, the employees were reluctant to participate in the scheme. The two executives warned the employees that unless they cooperated, the company might "cease operations and dismiss its employees."[2] After much prodding, the three employees capitulated and began systematically overstating the firm's 1985 year-end inventory.

> Following [the two executives'] specific instructions, the three RMUC employees inflated quantity figures on selected count sheets by adding numerals to the accurate quantity figures per item which had been previously recorded thereon during the physical inventory count. The three RMUC employees then multiplied the inflated quantity figures per item on the count sheets by the actual unit cost per item and recorded the resulting false and inflated cost figures on the count sheets.

While the three employees were overstating RMUC's inventory, the two company executives who concocted the scheme periodically telephoned them to check on their progress. At one point, the employees indicated that they were unwilling to continue falsifying RMUC's year-end inventory quantities. Additional coaxing and cajoling by the two executives convinced the employees to resume their fraudulent activities. Eventually, the employees "manufactured" more than $900,000 of bogus inventory. After RMUC's senior executive reviewed and approved the falsified inventory count sheets, the count sheets were forwarded to the company's independent audit firm.

To further overstate RMUC's December 31, 1985, inventory, the company's senior executive instructed another RMUC employee to obtain a false confirmation

---

2. This and all subsequent quotes were taken from Securities and Exchange Commission, *Accounting and Auditing Enforcement Release No. 212*, 9 January 1989.

letter from Stretchlon Industries, Inc. Stretchlon supplied RMUC with most of the elastic needed in its manufacturing processes. At the time, RMUC had an agreement to purchase 50 percent of Stretchlon's common stock at net book value. On December 31, 1985, Stretchlon had in its possession only a nominal amount of RMUC inventory. Nevertheless, a Stretchlon executive agreed to supply a confirmation letter to RMUC's independent auditors indicating that his firm held approximately $165,000 of RMUC inventory at the end of 1985. As a condition for providing the confirmation, the Stretchlon executive insisted that RMUC prepare and forward to him a false shipping document to corroborate the existence of the fictitious inventory. After receiving this shipping document, the Stretchlon executive signed the false confirmation and mailed it to RMUC's independent audit firm.

The fraudulent schemes engineered by RMUC's executives overstated the firm's December 31, 1985, inventory by approximately $1,076,000. Instead of reporting inventory of $12,158,000, in its original December 31, 1985, balance sheet, RMUC reported inventory of $13,234,000. The overstatement of inventory boosted RMUC's reported net income for 1985 to $1,059,000, which was more than $600,000 higher than the actual figure.

Near the completion of the 1985 audit, RMUC's auditors asked the company's senior executive to sign a letter of representations. Among other items, this letter indicated that the executive was not aware of any irregularities [fraud] involving the company's financial statements. The letter also stated that RMUC's financial statements fairly reflected its financial condition as of the end of 1985 and its operating results for that year. Shortly after receiving the signed letter of representations, RMUC's audit firm issued an unqualified opinion on the firm's 1985 financial statements.

Following the SEC's discovery of the fraudulent misrepresentations in RMUC's 1985 financial statements, the federal agency filed civil charges against the firm's two executives involved in the fraud. The SEC eventually settled these charges by obtaining a court order that prohibited the executives from engaging in any further violations of federal securities laws. RMUC also issued corrected financial statements for 1985. Exhibit 2 presents a footnote included in those financial statements. That footnote describes the inventory-related misstatements in the company's original 1985 financial statements.

QUESTIONS

1. Did the overstatement of RMUC's inventory at the end of 1985 materially affect the company's reported financial data for that year? Defend your answer.

2. What audit procedures might have prevented or detected the overstatements of RMUC's inventory quantities at the end of 1985?

EXHIBIT 2
Footnote Disclosure of RMUC's Inventory Fraud

Subsequent to the issuance of its financial statements for the year ended December 31, 1985, the Company determined that inventory as reported was misstated. The accompanying financial statements have been restated to reflect correction of such misstatement. The significant effects of restatement were to reduce inventories $1,076,000, increase cost of sales $1,140,000, increase selling, general and administrative expenses $40,000, and reduce net income $607,000 from the amounts previously reported.

3. How did RMUC's buyout option for Stretchlon affect the quality of the evidence provided by the inventory confirmation letter, if at all? Explain.

4. Refer to Exhibit 2. In your view, did the footnote included in that exhibit adequately describe the misrepresentations in RMUC's original financial statements for 1985? Why or why not?

5. How would you have reacted if you had been one of the employees pressured by RMUC's executives to misrepresent the company's 1985 year-end inventory? Before responding, identify the alternative courses of action that would have been available to you.

CASE 4.5
OAK INDUSTRIES, INC.

Oak Industries began operations in the early 1930s as a manufacturer of car radio components. The California-based company struggled financially through its first few years but managed to emerge from the Depression, unlike many of its competitors. In the late 1960s, Oak expanded into the cable television industry. Technological innovations developed by the company heavily contributed to the tremendous growth of that industry during the past few decades. In 1977, Oak began marketing subscription television services. Within four years, Oak ranked as the largest operator of subscription television systems in the United States. Oak's subscription television subsidiary also generated the majority of the company's annual revenues by the early 1980s.

OAK'S "RAINY DAY RESERVES"

Exhibit 1 presents selected financial data for Oak Industries for the period 1978–1981. Oak established new sales and profit records each successive year during this period. In fact, in both 1980 and 1981 the company's *actual* net income eclipsed the figure reported by the company. In 1980, Oak's top executives became concerned that the company could not indefinitely sustain its impressive growth rate in annual profits. To help the company maintain this trend, the executives began creating reserves that could be used to boost Oak's reported profits in later years.

> To report a smooth upward earnings trend and to provide a "cushion" of profits to be used in periods of lower actual earnings, Oak implemented a policy during 1980 and

EXHIBIT 1
Oak Industries, Inc.,
Selected Financial Data,
1978–1981

Oak Industries, Inc. Selected Financial Data, 1978–1981				
	1981	**1980**	**1979**	**1978**
Net sales*	$507,119	$385,586	$281,348	$192,181
Gross profit	168,437	125,163	86,060	51,402
Net income	30,350	20,082	11,170	4,850
Earnings per share	2.23	1.85	1.36	.72

*Net sales, gross profit, and net income are expressed in thousands of dollars

Source: Oak Industries, Inc., 1982 Form 10-K filed with the Securities and Exchange Commission.

1981 of establishing unneeded reserves to be released (reversed) in later periods, if needed.[1]

These "rainy day reserves" included overstatements of the company's allowances for inventory obsolescence and uncollectible receivables.

Unfortunately, Oak needed to "dip" into its rainy day reserves much sooner than expected. In 1981, Oak established subscription television operations in the Dallas-Fort Worth and Phoenix metropolitan areas. Almost immediately, the company began encountering major financial problems in these new operations due principally to unexpectedly low sales. Based upon its sales forecasts for these two new market areas, Oak had stockpiled a large quantity of television decoder boxes. Because of the significant shortfall in subscribers, much of this inventory was not needed. To make matters worse, rapid technological changes soon rendered the excess inventory obsolete. Oak also had an unusually high rate of sales returns for a new model of a decoder box that it sold to new subscribers. Quality control problems in Oak's manufacturing processes caused this model to be unreliable. Finally, Oak experienced a higher than normal rate of uncollectible receivables in the Dallas-Fort Worth and Phoenix market areas.

REVERSAL OF THE RAINY DAY RESERVES

In the first quarter of fiscal 1982, Oak's senior executives instructed the company's financial officers to "release" several million dollars of the reserves established during 1980 and 1981. The reversal of these reserves significantly reduced the company's reported expenses. If the reserves had not been reversed, the company's net income for the first quarter of 1982 would have been nearly 50 percent lower than the reported figure of $7.5 million. Reversing the reserves allowed the company to sustain its smooth upward earnings trend during the first quarter of 1982. Oak's top executives proudly noted in the company's financial report for the first three months of 1982 that "First quarter sales and net income were greater than in any first quarter in the Company's history."

---

1. Securities and Exchange Commission, *Accounting and Auditing Enforcement Release No. 63,* 25 June 1985.

As fiscal 1982 progressed, Oak's financial problems worsened. At year-end, the management of Oak's subscription television subsidiary notified corporate headquarters of $40 million of asset write-offs and increases in loss reserves needed for that subsidiary. Oak's senior executives realized that if they booked the $40 million of additional expenses, the company's consolidated income statement for 1982 would reflect a large loss. Instead of reporting that loss, the executives decided to report earnings per share of $.25 for 1982, which translated to a net income of approximately $4.1 million.

To "manufacture" the desired net income for fiscal 1982, Oak's senior executives turned to the company's chief financial officer (CFO), who oversaw the company's accounting department. The senior executives instructed the CFO to take the necessary steps to reach the target earnings figure. In response to that directive, the CFO asked the firm's controller to determine the portion of the subscription television subsidiary's $40 million of unrecorded expenses that could be booked if the company were to report earnings per share of $.25 for 1982. After the controller arrived at this figure, the CFO instructed him to arbitrarily allocate that amount between the company's bad debt and inventory obsolescence reserves. The controller complied, resulting in Oak reporting the management-mandated $.25 earnings per share for 1982.

SEC INVESTIGATION FOCUSES ON OAK'S CONTROLLER

The SEC investigation that uncovered the illicit accounting methods used by Oak Industries in the early 1980s focused on the firm's controller. Particularly disturbing to the SEC were the controller's impressive credentials. In addition to being a CPA, the controller had an extensive accounting background, including several years of experience with Arthur Andersen & Co., Oak's independent audit firm.

The SEC discovered that Oak's controller often questioned his superiors' judgment, at least initially, when they instructed him to misrepresent the company's financial data. For example, the controller recommended disclosing in Oak's financial statements for the first quarter of 1982 that the company had reversed several million dollars of the illicit rainy day reserves. When the firm's senior executives rejected the controller's recommendation, he relented and subsequently helped prepare the misleading financial statements for the first quarter of 1982.

Later in 1982, Oak's controller received a series of memos from the CFO of the firm's subscription television subsidiary. Among other financial problems being experienced by that unit, these memos notified the controller that the subsidiary's inventory obsolescence reserve was significantly understated. At the end of the fourth quarter of 1982, the subsidiary's CFO reported that his unit's inventory should be written down by nearly $10 million. Nevertheless, according to the SEC, the controller "accepted senior management's judgment and failed to take steps necessary to cause Oak to record the necessary reserves."[2]

---

2. This and subsequent quotations, unless indicated otherwise, are taken from Securities and Exchange Commission, *Accounting and Auditing Enforcement Release No. 93,* 26 March 1986.

The SEC also reported that Oak's controller knew that key accounting documents were being withheld from the company's independent auditors, Arthur Andersen & Co. Oak often prepared two sets of loss exposure analyses: one set to be used for internal decision-making purposes and another set to be forwarded to Arthur Andersen. The loss exposure analyses given to the independent auditors understated the severity of Oak's inventory obsolescence and bad debt problems. During Oak's 1982 audit, the firm's controller received a memorandum written by one of the company's internal auditors. This memorandum suggested that the independent auditors be given an "edited version" of an earlier memo that analyzed the status of Oak's reserve (allowance) for uncollectible receivables. This edited version of the earlier memo significantly understated Oak's estimated uncollectible receivables at the end of 1982.

> We [the internal audit staff] would like to issue the edited version of the . . . memo to Arthur Andersen to avoid any additional suspicions on their part as to the content. We believe the revised memo has been toned down sufficiently to be issued to them.

The controller apparently did not prevent the internal audit staff from forwarding the misleading memo to the independent auditors. As a result, Oak's independent auditors received an inaccurate analysis of the year-end status of the client's uncollectible receivables.

Near the end of Arthur Andersen's 1982 audit of Oak Industries, the company's controller signed a letter of representations addressed to the audit firm. Among other assertions, this letter indicated that company officials had provided all of Oak's financial records and related information to Arthur Andersen. The letter of representations also stated that Oak's financial statements had been prepared in accordance with GAAP.

EPILOGUE

In June 1985 and March 1986, the SEC issued enforcement releases documenting Oak Industries' abusive accounting and financial reporting practices. These releases also reported the sanctions imposed on the company and its executives involved in the fraudulent scheme. The SEC permanently banned Oak's chief executive officer from serving as an officer or director of a publicly owned firm. Four other Oak officers, including its CFO and controller, settled charges filed against them by agreeing not to violate federal securities laws in the future. The terms of the agreement also required Oak to establish an audit committee that would assume an active role in the company's accounting and financial reporting function. In early 1985, Oak voluntarily reissued its financial statements for 1982 and 1983. Collectively, these financial statements reduced Oak's previously reported net income for those years by approximately $44 million, or $2.70 per share. The company also disclosed in early 1985 that it would be discontinuing its subscription television operations.

One of the SEC's enforcement releases in the Oak Industries case focused exclusively on the firm's controller. In this release, the SEC noted that the controller clearly was not a "primary decision-maker" within the firm or a member of its senior management. As a result, the controller was not directly responsible for the company's earnings manipulation scheme. Nevertheless, the SEC maintained that the controller neglected his professional responsibilities when he became aware of that scheme. This was true despite the controller often challenging his superiors' questionable decisions.

> Although [the controller] may have made the appropriate recommendations to his corporate supervisors, when those recommendations were rejected, [he] acted as the "good soldier," implementing their directions which he knew or should have known were improper.

The SEC's refusal to recognize the "good soldier" defense as a valid justification for questionable conduct by mid-level corporate executives was debated by the business press. Most parties who commented on this issue supported the SEC's position. However, one individual warned, "It's unrealistic to place a burden on mid-level [corporate] managers to discharge obligations that they're not in a position to discharge."[3]

Often complicating the role of a corporate controller is the fact that his or her immediate superior lacks an accounting background. This was true in the Oak Industries case. Oak's controller was a CPA, but his immediate superior, the company's CFO, was not. The chief accountant of the SEC's enforcement division at the time, Robert Sack, observed that "added pressure" is often placed on a controller when his or her superior is not a CPA.[4] Sack recommended that in such cases a controller develop a relationship with the firm's board of directors, legal counsel, and independent auditors. These parties can serve as useful allies for the controller if his or her superior makes unreasonable demands at some point regarding accounting or financial reporting issues.

QUESTIONS

1. Is it unethical for a company to intentionally understate its earnings? Why or why not?

2. Should auditors be equally concerned with potential understatements and potential overstatements of a client's revenues and expenses? Identify audit techniques that may be particularly helpful in uncovering understatements of revenues and overstatements of expenses.

3. Place yourself in the position of Oak's controller when the company's senior executives rejected his recommendation to disclose the reversal of the rainy day reserves. What would you have done at that point?

4. What responsibilities does a company's controller and other accounting employees have when interacting with the firm's independent auditors? Do these responsibilities conflict with other job-related responsibilities of a company's accounting employees? Explain.

5. Should the SEC and other regulatory bodies hold corporate accountants who are CPAs to a higher standard of conduct than corporate accountants who are not CPAs? Defend your answer.

---

3. K. Victor, "Tough-Minded SEC Takes Aim At Corporate 'Good Soldiers'," *Legal Times*, 7 April 1986, 1.

4. *Securities Regulation and Law Reports*, "Internationalization Raising Questions on SEC Disclosure System, Peters Says," 12 December 1986, 1773.

CASE 4.6
F&C INTERNATIONAL, INC.

Alex Fries emigrated to the United States from Germany in the early nineteenth century.[1] The excitement and opportunities promised by the western frontier fascinated thousands of new Americans, including the young German who followed his dreams and the Ohio River west to Cincinnati. A chemist by training, Fries began working in the booming distillery industry of southern Ohio and northern Kentucky. Fries' background suited him well for an important need of distilleries, namely, developing flavors to make their often "sour" products more appealing to the public. Alex Fries eventually established his own flavor company. Thanks largely to Fries, Cincinnati became the home of the small but important flavor industry in the United States. By late in the twentieth century, the flavor industry's annual revenues approached $5 billion.

Alex Fries' success in the flavor industry became a family affair. Two of his grandsons created their own flavor company, Fries & Fries, in the early 1900s. Several decades later, another descendant of Alex Fries, Jon Fries, served as the president and CEO of F&C International, Inc., a flavor company whose common stock traded on the NASDAQ exchange. F&C International, also based in Cincinnati, reigned for a time during the 1980s as Ohio's fastest-growing corporation. Sadly, the legacy of the Fries family in the flavor industry came to a distasteful end in the early 1990s.

---

1. The facts of this case were developed from several SEC enforcement releases and a series of articles appearing in the *Cincinnati Enquirer*. The key parties in this case neither admitted nor denied the facts reported by the SEC. Those parties include Jon Fries, Catherine Sprauer, Fletcher Anderson, and Craig Schuster.

THE FRAUD

Jon Fries orchestrated a large-scale financial fraud that proved to be the undoing of F&C International. At least 10 other F&C executives or high-level employees actively participated in the scam or allowed it to continue unchecked out of their inaction. The methods used by Fries and his cohorts were not unique or even innovative. Fries realized that the most effective strategy for embellishing his company's periodic operating results was to inflate revenues and overstate period-ending inventories. Throughout the early 1990s, F&C systematically overstated sales revenues by backdating valid sales transactions, by shipping customers product they had not ordered, and by recording bogus sales transactions. To overstate inventory, F&C personnel filled barrels with water and then labeled those barrels as containing high-concentrate flavor products. The company also neglected to write off defective goods, included waste products from manufacturing processes in inventory, and entered nonexistent inventory in the accounting records. Company officials used F&C's misleading financial statements to sell equity securities and to obtain significant bank financing.

Fraudulent schemes complicate every day operating decisions for a company's executives. F&C's executives struggled to develop appropriate sales and inventory management strategies since the company's accounting records were unreliable. To help remedy this problem, F&C created an imaginary warehouse, Warehouse Q.

> Warehouse Q became the accounting repository for product returned by customers for being below specification, unuseable or nonexistent items, and items that could not be found in the actual warehouses.[2]

Another baffling problem that faced Fries and his confederates was concealing the company's fraudulent activities from F&C's independent auditors. The executives continually plotted to divert their auditors' attention from suspicious transactions and circumstances uncovered during the annual audits. Subversive measures taken by the executives included creating false documents, mislabeling inventory counted by the auditors, and undercutting subordinates' attempts to expose the fraud.

Eventually, the size and complexity of F&C's fraud caused the scheme to unravel. Allegations that the company's financial statements contained material irregularities triggered an investigation by the Securities and Exchange Commission (SEC). The investigation revealed that F&C overstated its cumulative pretax earnings during the early 1990s by approximately $8 million. The company understated its pretax net loss for fiscal 1992 alone by nearly 140 percent, or $3.8 million.

THE DIVISION CONTROLLER

Catherine Sprauer accepted an accounting position with F&C International in July 1992, shortly after the June 30 close of the company's 1992 fiscal year.

---

2. Securities and Exchange Commission, *Accounting and Auditing Enforcement Release No. 605*, 28 September 1994. All subsequent quotations are taken from this source.

Sprauer, a CPA and 28 years old at the time, drafted the Management's Discussion and Analysis (MD&A) section of F&C's 1992 10-K registration statement. In October 1992, Sprauer became the controller of F&C's Flavor Division. Following that promotion, Sprauer continued to help prepare the MD&A sections of F&C's periodic financial reports submitted to the SEC.

In early January 1993, an F&C employee told Sprauer that he saw company employees filling inventory barrels with water in the final few days of June 1992. This individual also advised Sprauer that he had documentation linking two F&C executives to that incident, which was apparently intended to overstate the company's year-end inventory for fiscal 1992. According to the SEC, Sprauer abruptly ended the conversation with this employee and did not discuss his allegations with anyone.

Later that same day, another F&C employee approached Sprauer and confessed that he was involved in the episode recounted to her earlier in the day. This individual told Sprauer that he had acted under the direct instructions of Jon Fries. The employee then attempted to hand Sprauer a listing of inventory items affected by the fraud. Sprauer refused to accept the list. The persistent employee apparently placed the list in Sprauer's correspondence file. The document detailed approximately $350,000 of nonexistent inventory in F&C's accounting records. Sprauer reportedly never showed the list of bogus inventory to her superiors, to other F&C accountants, or to the company's independent auditors. However, she subsequently warned F&C's chief operating officer (COO), Fletcher Anderson, that the company had "significant inventory problems."

THE CHIEF OPERATING OFFICER

Fletcher Anderson became the COO of F&C International in September 1992 and joined the company's board of directors a few days later. On March 23, 1993, Anderson succeeded Jon Fries as F&C's president and CEO. During the fall of 1992, Anderson stumbled across several suspicious transactions in F&C's accounting records. In late September 1992, Anderson discovered sales shipments made before the given customers had placed purchase orders with F&C. He also learned that other sales shipments had been delivered to F&C warehouses rather than to customers. Finally, in early October 1992, Anderson uncovered a forged bill of lading for a customer shipment. The bill of lading had been altered to change the reported month of shipment from October to September. Each of these errors inflated F&C's reported earnings for the first quarter of fiscal 1993, which ended September 30, 1992.

More direct evidence that F&C's financial data were being systematically distorted came to Anderson's attention during the second quarter of 1993. In November, a subordinate told Anderson that some of the company's inventory of flavor concentrate was simply water labeled as concentrate. The following month, Anderson learned of Warehouse Q and that at least $1.5 million of the inventory "stored" in that warehouse could not be located or was defective.

Catherine Sprauer submitted her resignation to Fletcher Anderson in late January 1993. Among the reasons Sprauer gave for her resignation were serious doubts regarding the reliability of the company's inventory records. Anderson insisted that Sprauer not tell him why she believed those records were unreliable.

Reportedly, Anderson wanted to avoid testifying regarding Sprauer's concerns in any subsequent litigation.

In February 1993, shortly before Anderson replaced Jon Fries as F&C's top executive, an F&C cost accountant warned him that the company had an inventory problem "in the magnitude of $3-4 million." Anderson later told the SEC that although the cost accountant had access to F&C's inventory records and its actual inventory, he believed the accountant was overstating the severity of the company's inventory problem.

THE CHIEF FINANCIAL OFFICER

Craig Schuster served as the chief financial officer (CFO) of F&C International during the early 1990s. As F&C's CFO, Schuster oversaw the preparation of and signed the company's registration statements filed with the SEC, including the company's 10-K reports for fiscal 1991 and 1992. Throughout 1992, Schuster became aware of various problems in F&C's accounting records, most notably the existence of Warehouse Q. In March 1992, Schuster learned that his subordinates could not locate many items listed in F&C's perpetual inventory records. A few months later, Schuster discovered that customer shipments were being backdated in an apparent attempt to recognize sales revenue prematurely. Finally, in late 1992, Schuster determined that approximately $1 million of F&C's work-in-process inventory was classified as finished goods.

On December 17, 1992, a frustrated Schuster prepared and forwarded to Fletcher Anderson a 23-page list of $1.5 million of inventory allegedly stored in Warehouse Q. The memo apparently revealed that the inventory could not be located or was defective. The SEC's enforcement releases focusing on the F&C fraud failed to indicate how or whether Anderson responded to Schuster's memo.

Because he supervised the preparation of F&C's financial reports filed with the SEC, Schuster knew that those reports did not comment on the company's inventory problems. On January 1, 1993, Craig Schuster resigned as the CFO of F&C International. The final F&C registration statement Schuster signed was the company's 10-Q for the first quarter of fiscal 1993, which ended September 30, 1992.

THE REST OF THE STORY

In a September 28, 1994, enforcement release, the SEC criticized Catherine Sprauer, Fletcher Anderson, and Craig Schuster for failing to ensure that F&C's financial reports "filed with the Commission and disseminated to the investing public were accurate." The federal agency also chastised the three individuals for not disclosing in F&C's financial reports "significant accounting problems of which they were aware." Finally, the SEC chided Anderson and Schuster for not establishing adequate internal controls to provide for the proper recognition of revenue and the proper valuation of inventory. In an agreement reached with the SEC to settle the allegations pending against them, the three former F&C executives pledged to "permanently cease and desist" from committing or causing violations of federal securities laws.

A second enforcement release issued by the SEC on September 28, 1994, contained a series of allegations directed at Jon Fries and seven other senior F&C executives. The SEC charged that these executives were primarily responsible for F&C's fraudulent earnings scheme. To settle these charges, each executive pledged not to violate federal securities laws in the future. The settlement agreement permanently banned Jon Fries from serving as an officer or director of a public company. Several of the individuals also agreed to forfeit proceeds received from earlier sales of F&C securities. Fries relinquished more than $2 million he had realized from the sale of F&C securities. Finally, the SEC imposed civil fines on four of these executives that ranged from $11,500 to $20,000.

F&C International filed for bankruptcy in April 1993 shortly after the fraud became public. The following year, a competitor purchased F&C's remaining assets. In March 1995, Jon Fries began serving a 15-month sentence in a federal prison for his role in the F&C fraud.

QUESTIONS

1. Jon Fries (CEO), Fletcher Anderson (COO), Craig Schuster (CFO), and Catherine Sprauer (division controller) were the four central figures in this case. Identify the key responsibilities associated with the professional roles these individuals occupied. Briefly describe the type and extent of interaction each of these individuals likely had with F&C's independent auditors.

2. Using the scale shown next, evaluate the conduct of the four key individuals discussed in this case. Be prepared to defend your answers.

```
   -100 . . . . . . . . . . . . . . . . . . . . 0 . . . . . . . . . . . . . . . . . . . . 100
   Highly                                                              Highly
   Unethical                                                           Ethical
```

3. For a moment, step into the shoes of Catherine Sprauer. What would you have done during and following each of the confrontations she had with the two employees who approached her during January 1993 alleging fraud?

4. Craig Schuster resigned as F&C's CFO on January 1, 1993. Apparently, Schuster did not reveal to any third parties the concerns he had regarding F&C's accounting records and previous financial statements. In your opinion, did Schuster have a responsibility to inform someone of those concerns following his resignation? Defend your answer.

5. Assume that you, rather than Fletcher Anderson, were F&C's COO in December 1992. What would you have done upon receiving the list of Warehouse Q inventory from Craig Schuster?

CASE 4.7
ACCUHEALTH, INC.

One morning in early 1990, William Makadok opened the door to the office occupied by one of his colleagues, a fellow officer of Accuhealth, Inc.[1] Scattered across the individual's desk were large piles of cash and several empty envelopes. Makadok quickly closed the door and returned to his office. Later that day, Makadok observed the officer casually distributing the envelopes, bulging with cash, to executives and senior employees of Accuhealth.

The two scenes just described startled Makadok. Those scenes added to, if not confirmed, Makadok's suspicion that Accuhealth's top executives were embezzling cash from the company. A few weeks earlier, Makadok had discovered a suspicious alteration to a weekly "cash report sheet" prepared for one of Accuhealth's retail drug stores. Each Accuhealth store reported its weekly cash sales to headquarters on this document. On the altered cash report sheet the original cash sales figure had been crossed out and replaced with a lower figure. The difference between the two amounts had been reported on a line item labeled "Office."

William Makadok had been hired in the summer of 1989 to serve as a vice-president and the chief accounting officer of Accuhealth, a New York-based firm that operated a chain of drug stores and a home healthcare business. The strong indications that his fellow executives were involved in a large-scale and well-organized embezzlement scheme deeply troubled the CPA. In his early fifties at the time, Makadok had more than two decades of professional experience, including several years in public accounting. Never before in his career had

---

1. The facts reported in this case were taken from several enforcement releases issued by the Securities and Exchange Commission, various annual reports of Accuhealth, Inc., and numerous newspaper articles.

Makadok encountered a fraudulent scheme apparently masterminded by a company's top executives. The situation posed a simple question for William Makadok: What would he do?

ACCUHEALTH: A BRIEF HISTORY

Stanley Lepelstat founded Leroy Pharmacies in 1981. Lepelstat, who had more than two decades of work experience with retail drug store chains before he established his own firm, took Leroy Pharmacies public in 1988 and then changed its name to Accuhealth, Inc., two years later. Initially, the company owned and operated a small chain of retail stores that sold prescription drugs, cosmetics, small kitchen appliances, and related merchandise. Lepelstat added a home healthcare line of business to his firm in 1987. In this new line of business, Accuhealth sold and rented home medical equipment and provided in-home infusion (intravenous) therapy for the critically ill. Exhibit 1 summarizes key financial data of Accuhealth for the period 1987–1991.

During the 1980s and early 1990s, Lepelstat, his family, and a few close friends dominated the day-to-day operations of Leroy Pharmacies and its successor, Accuhealth, Inc. Lepelstat served as the firm's president, chief executive officer, and chairman of the board, while his wife, Sheila, was the company's personnel director and held the titles of vice-president, secretary, and treasurer. The Lepelstats' son, Lawrence, joined the firm in 1990 and was placed in charge of its home healthcare subsidiary. Both Lawrence and his mother sat on Accuhealth's board of directors. Another Lepelstat also served on the company's board of directors in the early 1990s. Mark Lepelstat, Lawrence's brother, was appointed to the board of directors although he was not an employee or otherwise involved with Accuhealth. Other members of the board of directors included several long time associates of Stanley Lepelstat who held executive positions with the company.

Accuhealth's 1991 annual report disclosed that the company's top executives had modest compensation packages. The average salary of Accuhealth's seven top executives, which included the two senior Lepelstats, averaged only $51,000. Those seven executives easily controlled the bulk of Accuhealth's outstanding common stock. The senior Lepelstats, alone, owned more than 53 percent of the company's common stock.

IN"ACCU"RATE FINANCIAL STATEMENTS

In 1993, law enforcement agencies, including the Securities and Exchange Commission (SEC), began investigating rumors that Accuhealth's officers were

EXHIBIT 1
Selected Financial Data Reported by Accuhealth, 1987–1991 (000s omitted)

	1991	1990	1989	1988	1987
Net sales	$35,152	$33,797	$32,747	$27,677	$23,207
Gross profit	10,988	10,350	9,576	7,944	6,756
Net income	301	(783)	(96)	441	466
Total assets	12,139	12,033	12,147	8,860	6,892
Total liabilities	9,349	9,590	8,950	5,720	6,680

engaging in a massive fraud. The SEC's investigation revealed that Stanley Lepelstat had directed a systematic cash-skimming operation within his business since its inception in 1981. Lepelstat and his colleagues embezzled funds primarily from cash sales of two of the company's retail drug stores. Each week, a company official called an accounting clerk at one of those two drug stores to specify the amount of cash to be forwarded to corporate headquarters.

> The store manager segregated the cash and bundled it separately in a paper bag for pickup by either Miszke [a senior pharmacist with Accuhealth] or an officer. The diverted cash was then taken to the company headquarters where Miszke and/or an officer would divide it up and put it into plain white envelopes for distribution. . . . No particular effort was made to conceal the distribution.[2]

A store manager typically recorded the amount of cash embezzled each week from his or her store on the given store's cash report sheet. The manager listed the funds on a line labeled "Office," as William Makadok eventually discovered.[3] At headquarters, the sales and cash receipts recorded for the store was the net figure, that is, the actual weekly sales less the embezzled funds. Accuhealth officials kept meticulous records on an electronic spreadsheet documenting the funds embezzled each week and the weekly cash payments made to individuals within the firm. Stanley Lepelstat reviewed a weekly printout of these cash payments. The company's chief financial officer (CFO) also received a monthly report of the cash receipts stolen from individual stores. Most likely, Accuhealth's officers used the embezzlement data to arrive at compensation adjustments (pay raises) for given employees and to determine the "true" profitability of stores affected by the cash-skimming scheme.

Regulatory authorities estimated that Accuhealth's senior management embezzled between $500,000 and $900,000 annually from 1986 through 1992.[4] The cash-skimming operation negatively impacted Accuhealth's apparent profitability since it reduced the company's reported sales. Beginning in 1989, senior management decided to correct this "problem." Inflating year-end inventory ranks among the easiest methods to intentionally overstate profits in a retail environment. From 1989 through 1992, Accuhealth executives ordered subordinates to fraudulently increase the company's year-end pharmaceuticals inventory. The employees responsible for counting pharmaceuticals at retail stores simply overstated the quantities of selected items on inventory count sheets for stores where the counting procedures were not observed by the company's independent auditors. According to the SEC, Stanley Lepelstat also ordered subordinates to double-count certain high-priced inventory items maintained in Accuhealth's warehouse. One of these subordinates was George Miszke, Accuhealth's senior pharmacist who also participated in the cash-skimming operation.

---

2. Securities and Exchange Commission, *Accounting and Auditing Enforcement Release No. 589*, 8 September 1994.

3. In some cases, the store manager subtracted the embezzled funds from the sum of the daily cash receipts. That is, the actual sum of the daily cash receipts amounts would exceed the weekly total listed at the bottom of the cash report sheet by the amount of the embezzled funds. This method concealed embezzled funds more effectively from the company's independent auditors.

4. For certain periods, the actual amount of embezzled funds could not be determined since Accuhealth personnel destroyed the relevant documents for those periods.

> After those drugs were counted in the company's warehouse, Miszke, under orders from the CEO [Stanley Lepelstat], transported them at night or over the weekend to drugstores where they were included in inventory and counted again. This surreptitious inventory movement was possible because the physical inventory counts were conducted over several days.[5]

Numerous Accuhealth officers and employees knew of the company's fraudulent schemes and/or participated in them. These individuals apparently had a nonchalant attitude toward the schemes, treating them as just another company policy or procedure. This nonchalant attitude did not prevail when it came to concealing the frauds from the company's independent auditors. Besides the flagrant efforts to conceal the inventory irregularities just described, Accuhealth personnel repeatedly and systematically misled the auditors when they raised questions regarding accounts affected by the fraudulent schemes.

WILLIAM MAKADOK REVISITED

When we left William Makadok, he faced an unpleasant dilemma: what to do given the nearly irrefutable evidence that his employer was engaging in an extensive financial fraud. After considering his options, Makadok decided to avoid the issue.

> Makadok did not take any steps to investigate any of these incidents nor did he bring them to the attention of Accuhealth's independent auditors. He consciously avoided undertaking any effort that would confirm any doubts or concerns caused by his observations.[6]

Makadok made another important decision after stumbling across the evidence of Accuhealth's fraudulent schemes during mid-1990. The chief accountant resolved not to sign off on Accuhealth's 1990 10-K, which would be prepared for the company's fiscal year ending December 31, 1990. True to his conviction, Makadok resigned his position with Accuhealth one month before the company filed its 1990 10-K with the SEC. When Accuhealth's independent auditors learned of Makadok's resignation, they wanted to know why he was leaving the company. Makadok did not reply candidly to the auditors. Instead, he told them that his decision to leave Accuhealth "was motivated purely by another employment opportunity."

Although Makadok did not sign off on Accuhealth's 1990 10-K, he did prepare and sign off on the company's financial reports filed with the SEC for the second and third quarters of 1990. Those quarterly financial reports, similar to Accuhealth's annual financial reports, misrepresented the company's operating results and financial condition. The SEC subsequently revealed that company officials stole more than $200,000 of cash receipts during each of those quarters.

An important focus of the SEC's investigation of Accuhealth was the conduct of its key accounting personnel, including William Makadok. In examining

---

5. Securities and Exchange Commission, *Accounting and Auditing Enforcement Release No. 589*, 8 September 1994.

6. Securities and Exchange Commission, *Accounting and Auditing Enforcement Release No. 588*, 8 September 1994.

Makadok's conduct, a central issue addressed by the SEC was whether he violated Rule 10b-5 of the Securities Exchange Act of 1934. That rule prohibits an individual from making material misstatements in, or omitting material information from, a registration statement filed under the 1934 Act that would cause the document to be misleading to purchasers or sellers of the relevant securities.

In 1984, the U.S. Supreme Court established a major precedent relevant to Rule 10b-5 when it handed down a decision in the *Ernst & Ernst v. Hochfelder et al.* case.[7] Under the Hochfelder ruling, scienter must be present for an individual to violate Rule 10b-5—scienter being "a mental state embracing intent to deceive, manipulate or defraud." Many court decisions subsequent to Hochfelder have held that the scienter requirement is met if an individual acts with "reckless disregard for the truth." That is, although the individual did not have a conscious intent to deceive third parties, he or she recklessly allowed material representations to be included in a registration statement filed under the 1934 Act without obtaining a reasonable basis for determining whether those representations were true. In recent years, the SEC has generally adopted recklessness as the benchmark for determining whether a given individual has violated Rule 10b-5.

In deciding if Makadok breached Rule 10b-5, the SEC first addressed the issue of whether the misrepresentations in Accuhealth's quarterly financial reports that he prepared qualified as "material facts." Earlier court rulings had established the following definition of a material fact in the context of the 1934 Act: "A fact is material if there is a substantial likelihood that a reasonable investor would consider the information to be important."[8] The SEC ruled that the embezzlement scheme Makadok unintentionally discovered was clearly a material fact that would have been of interest to a "reasonable investor" in Accuhealth's common stock.

The second issue faced by the SEC in deciding whether Makadok violated Rule 10b-5 was whether he, at a minimum, acted recklessly in signing off on Accuhealth's 1990 quarterly financial reports. The SEC correctly observed that Makadok "did not actively participate in the fraud or benefit from it financially." Nevertheless, the federal agency maintained that his conduct qualified as reckless.

> Makadok signed two form 10-Qs that contained materially false financial information. Makadok signed these reports in reckless disregard of whether the information contained in them was materially misstated. By engaging in such conduct, Makadok directly violated Section 10(b) of the Exchange Act and Rule 10b-5 promulgated thereunder.[9]

EPILOGUE

In February 1993, the SEC publicly announced that it was investigating Accuhealth's internal accounting practices. Arthur Andersen, Accuhealth's audit firm, withdrew its opinion on the company's most recent financial statements a

---

7. Exhibit 1 in Case 8.5, *First Securities Company of Chicago*, contains Rule 10b-5. That case also includes a discussion of the Supreme Court ruling in the *Ernst & Ernst v. Hochfelder et al.* case.

8. *Basic, Inc. v. Levinson*, 485 U.S. 224 (1988), 231–232.

9. Securities and Exchange Commission, *Accounting and Auditing Enforcement Release No. 588*, 8 September 1994.

few days later. Trading in Accuhealth's common stock was also suspended following the SEC's announcement and several of the company's directors resigned, including Stanley and Sheila Lepelstat.

The SEC wrapped up its lengthy investigation of Accuhealth's financial affairs in mid-1994 and published the key findings of that investigation in a series of enforcement releases over the next several months. William Makadok received a three-year suspension from practicing before the SEC. Other parties sanctioned included Stanley and Sheila Lepelstat and George Miszke. Several of Accuhealth's former executives, including Stanley Lepelstat, were permanently barred from serving as an officer or director of any public company. The SEC also ordered Stanley Lepelstat to surrender $100,000 of profits that he had realized from selling Accuhealth common stock during the embezzlement scheme. Lepelstat later pleaded guilty to fraud charges filed against him in a U.S. district court.

In October 1994, Accuhealth settled legal claims against several of its former executives that stemmed from the cash-skimming scheme. Stanley Lepelstat agreed to the cancellation of a $600,000 note receivable from Accuhealth. Stanley Lepelstat, Sheila Lepelstat, and several other former Accuhealth executives also agreed to return to the company the Accuhealth common stock they owned. Accuhealth received more than 300,000 shares of common stock as a result of this restitution agreement.

In 1994, Accuhealth sold its retail drug stores to focus exclusively on the home healthcare line of business. In May of that year, Accuhealth hired a new president and chief executive officer to oversee its day-to-day operations. That individual, Glenn Davis, was a former audit partner with Coopers & Lybrand, one of the Big Six accounting firms and Accuhealth's auditor prior to 1990. In an interview with *The New York Times*, Mr. Davis reported that he was "looking for something more entrepreneurial and meaningful" when he accepted his new position.[10]

QUESTIONS

1. Identify the parties who had a stake in, or would be affected by, the outcome of the ethical dilemma faced by William Makadok in 1990. What obligation, if any, did Makadok have to each of these parties?

2. Place yourself in William Makadok's position. Would you have responded differently than he did to the difficult circumstances he faced? Explain.

3. The SEC did not criticize Accuhealth's independent auditors in the various enforcement releases issued concerning the company's fraudulent schemes. Under what general circumstances should auditors *not* be held at least partially responsible for such schemes? Defend your answer.

4. What specific audit procedures might have led to the detection of Accuhealth's fraudulent cash and inventory schemes?

5. The "control environment" is generally considered the most important component of any organization's internal control process. Defend that generalization. Use examples from this case to support your answer.

---

10. D. Martin, "Making House Calls," *The New York Times*, 18 September 1994, 4.

SECTION FIVE
ETHICAL RESPONSIBILITIES
OF INDEPENDENT AUDITORS

CASE 5.1
CARDILLO TRAVEL
SYSTEMS, INC.

If virtue is not its own reward, I don't know any other stipend attached to it.

Lord Byron

ACT 1

Russell Smith knew why he had been summoned to the office of A. Walter Rognlien, the 74-year-old chairman of the board and chief executive officer of Smith's employer, Cardillo Travel Systems, Inc.[1] Just two days earlier, Cardillo's in-house attorney, Raymond Riley, had requested that Smith, the company's controller, sign an affidavit regarding the nature of a transaction Rognlien had negotiated with United Airlines. The affidavit stated that the transaction involved a $203,000 payment by United Airlines to Cardillo but failed to disclose why the payment was being made or for what specific purpose the funds would be used. The affidavit included a statement indicating that Cardillo's stockholders' equity exceeded $3 million, a statement that Smith knew to be incorrect. Smith also knew that Cardillo was involved in a lawsuit and that a court injunction issued in the case required the company to maintain stockholders' equity of at least $3 million. Because of the blatant misrepresentation in the affidavit concerning Cardillo's stockholders' equity and a sense of uneasiness regarding United Airlines' payment to Cardillo, Smith had refused to sign the affidavit.

---

1. The events discussed in this case were reconstructed principally from information included in Securities and Exchange Commission, *Accounting and Auditing Enforcement Release No. 143,* 4 August 1987. All quotations appearing in this case were taken from that document.

When Smith stepped into Rognlien's office on that day in May 1985, he found not only Rognlien but also Riley and two other Cardillo executives. One of the other executives was Esther Lawrence, the firm's energetic 44-year-old president and chief operating officer and Rognlien's wife and confidante. Lawrence, a long time employee, assumed control of Cardillo's day-to-day operations in 1984. Rognlien's two sons by a previous marriage left the company in the early 1980s following a power struggle with Lawrence and their father.

As Smith sat waiting for the meeting to begin, his apprehension mounted. Although Cardillo had a long and proud history, in recent years the company had begun experiencing serious financial problems. Founded in 1935 and purchased in 1956 by Rognlien, Cardillo ranked as the fourth-largest travel agency in the nation and the first to be listed on a national stock exchange. Cardillo's annual revenues steadily increased after Rognlien acquired the company, approaching $100 million by 1984. Unfortunately, the company's operating expenses increased more rapidly. An aggressive franchising strategy implemented by Rognlien contributed heavily to the company's poor operating results. In 1984 alone that strategy more than doubled the number of travel agency franchises operated by Rognlien. Under the leadership of Rognlien and Lawrence, Cardillo posted collective losses of nearly $1.5 million between 1982 and 1984.

Shortly after the meeting began, the overbearing and volatile Rognlien demanded that Smith sign the affidavit. When Smith steadfastly refused, Rognlien showed him the first page of an unsigned agreement between United Airlines and Cardillo. Rognlien then explained that the $203,000 payment was intended to cover expenses incurred by Cardillo in changing from American Airlines' Sabre computer reservation system to United Airlines' Apollo system. Although the payment was intended to reimburse Cardillo for those expenses and was refundable to United Airlines if not spent, Rognlien wanted Smith to record the payment immediately as revenue.

Not surprisingly, Rognlien's suggested treatment of the United Airlines payment would allow Cardillo to meet the $3 million minimum stockholders' equity threshold established by the court order outstanding against the company. Without hesitation, Smith informed Rognlien that recognizing the United Airlines payment as revenue would be improper. At that point, "Rognlien told Smith that he was incompetent and unprofessional because he refused to book the United payment as income. Rognlien further told Smith that Cardillo did not need a controller like Smith who would not do what was expected of him."

ACT 2

In November 1985, Helen Shepherd, the audit partner supervising the 1985 audit of Cardillo by Touche Ross, stumbled across information in the client's files regarding the agreement Rognlien negotiated with United Airlines earlier that year. When Shepherd asked her subordinates about this agreement, one of them told her of a $203,000 adjusting entry Cardillo recorded in late June, an entry apparently linked to the United Airlines–Cardillo agreement. The entry, which Esther Lawrence approved, follows:

Dr Receivables—United Airlines	$203,210	
Cr Travel Commissions and Fees		$203,210

Shepherd's subordinates discovered the adjusting entry during their second-quarter review of Cardillo's 10-Q statement. When asked, Lawrence had told the auditors the entry involved commissions earned by Cardillo from United Airlines during the second quarter. The auditors accepted Lawrence's explanation without attempting to corroborate it with other audit evidence.

After discussing the adjusting entry with her subordinates, Shepherd questioned Lawrence. Lawrence insisted that the adjusting entry had been properly recorded. Shepherd then requested that Lawrence ask United Airlines to provide Touche Ross with a confirmation verifying the key stipulations of the agreement with Cardillo. Shepherd's concern regarding the adjusting entry stemmed from information she had reviewed in the client's files that pertained to the United Airlines agreement. That information suggested the United Airlines payment to Cardillo was refundable under certain conditions and thus not recognizable immediately as revenue.

Shortly after the meeting between Shepherd and Lawrence, Walter Rognlien contacted the audit partner. Like Lawrence, Rognlien maintained that the $203,000 amount had been properly recorded as commission revenue during the second quarter. Rognlien also told Shepherd that the disputed amount, which United Airlines paid to Cardillo during the third quarter of 1985, was not refundable to United Airlines under any circumstances. After some prodding by Shepherd, Rognlien agreed to allow her to request a confirmation from United Airlines concerning certain features of the agreement.

On December 17, 1985, Shepherd received the requested confirmation from United Airlines. The confirmation stated that the disputed amount was refundable through 1990 if certain stipulations of the contractual agreement between the two parties were not fulfilled.[2] After receiving the confirmation, Shepherd called Rognlien and asked him to explain the obvious difference of opinion between United Airlines and Cardillo regarding the terms of their agreement. Rognlien told Shepherd that he had a secret arrangement with the chairman of the board of United Airlines: "Rognlien claimed that pursuant to this confidential business arrangement, the $203,210 would never have to be repaid to United. Shepherd asked Rognlien for permission to contact United's chairman to confirm the confidential business arrangement. Rognlien refused. In fact, as Rognlien knew, no such agreement existed."

A few days following Shepherd's conversation with Rognlien, she advised William Kaye, Cardillo's vice-president of finance, that the $203,000 amount could not be recognized as revenue until the contractual agreement with United Airlines expired in 1990. Kaye refused to make the appropriate adjusting entry, explaining that Lawrence had insisted that the payment from United Airlines be credited to a revenue account. On December 30, 1985, Rognlien called Shepherd and told her that he was terminating Cardillo's relationship with Touche Ross.

In early February 1986, Cardillo filed an 8-K statement with the Securities and Exchange Commission (SEC) notifying that agency of the company's change in

---

2. Shepherd apparently never learned that the $203,000 payment was intended to reimburse Cardillo for expenses incurred switching to United Airlines' reservation system. As a result, she focused almost exclusively on the question of when Cardillo should recognize the United Airlines' payment as revenue. If she had been aware of the true nature of the payment, she almost certainly would have been even more adamant regarding the impropriety of the $203,000 adjusting entry.

auditors. SEC regulations required Cardillo to disclose in the 8-K statement any disagreements involving technical accounting, auditing, or financial reporting issues with its former auditor. The 8-K, signed by Lawrence, indicated that no such disagreements preceded Cardillo's decision to dismiss Touche Ross. SEC regulations also required Touche Ross to draft a letter commenting on the existence of any disagreements with Cardillo. This letter had to be filed as an exhibit to the 8-K statement. In Touche Ross's exhibit letter, Shepherd discussed the dispute involving the United Airlines payment to Cardillo. Shepherd disclosed that the improper accounting treatment given that transaction resulted in misrepresented financial statements for Cardillo for the six months ended June 30, 1985, and the nine months ended September 30, 1985.

In late February 1986, Raymond Riley, Cardillo's legal counsel, wrote Shepherd and insisted that she had misinterpreted the United Airlines–Cardillo transaction in the Touche Ross exhibit letter filed with the company's 8-K. Riley also informed Shepherd that Cardillo would not pay the $17,500 invoice that Touche Ross had submitted to his company. This invoice was for professional services Touche Ross had rendered prior to being dismissed by Rognlien.

ACT 3

On January 21, 1986, Cardillo retained KMG Main Hurdman (KMG) to replace Touche Ross as its independent audit firm. KMG soon addressed the accounting treatment Cardillo applied to the United Airlines payment. When KMG personnel discussed the payment with Rognlien, he informed them of the alleged secret agreement with United Airlines that superseded the written contractual agreement. According to Rognlien, the secret agreement precluded United Airlines from demanding a refund of the $203,000 payment under any circumstances. KMG refused to accept this explanation. Roger Shlonsky, the KMG audit partner responsible for the Cardillo engagement, told Rognlien that the payment would have to be recognized as revenue on a pro rata basis over the five-year period of the agreement with United Airlines.[3]

In early 1986, Cardillo began experiencing severe liquidity problems. These problems worsened a few months later when a judge imposed a $685,000 judgment on Cardillo to resolve a civil suit filed against the company. Following the judge's ruling, Raymond Riley alerted Rognlien and Lawrence that the adverse judgment qualified as a "material event" and thus had to be reported to the SEC in a form 8-K filing. In the memorandum he sent to his superiors, Riley discussed the serious implications of not disclosing the settlement to the SEC: "My primary concern by not releasing such report and information is that the officers and directors of Cardillo may be subject to violation of rule 10b-5 of the SEC rules by failing to disclose information that may be material to a potential investor."

Within 10 days of receiving Riley's memorandum, Rognlien sold 100,000 shares of Cardillo stock in the open market. Two weeks later, Lawrence issued a press release disclosing for the first time the adverse legal settlement. However,

---

3. Cardillo executives also successfully concealed from the KMG auditors the fact that the United Airlines payment was simply an advance to cover installation expenses for the new reservation system.

Lawrence failed to disclose the amount of the settlement or that Cardillo remained viable only because Rognlien had invested in the company the proceeds from the sale of the 100,000 shares of stock. Additionally, Lawrence's press release underestimated the firm's expected loss for 1985 by approximately 300 percent.

Following Lawrence's press release, Roger Shlonsky met with Rognlien and Lawrence. Shlonsky informed them that the press release grossly understated Cardillo's estimated loss for fiscal 1985. Shortly after that meeting, KMG resigned as Cardillo's independent audit firm.

EPILOGUE

In May 1987, the creditors of Cardillo Travel Systems, Inc., forced the company into involuntary bankruptcy proceedings. Later that same year, the SEC concluded a lengthy investigation of the firm. The SEC found that Rognlien, Lawrence, and Kaye had violated several provisions of the federal securities laws. These violations included making false representations to outside auditors, failing to maintain accurate financial records, and failing to file prompt financial reports with the SEC. In addition, the federal agency charged Rognlien with violating the insider trading provisions of the federal securities laws. As a result of these findings, the SEC imposed permanent injunctions on each of the three individuals. The SEC also attempted to recover from Rognlien the $237,000 he received from selling the 100,000 shares of Cardillo stock in April 1986. In January 1989, the two parties resolved this matter when Rognlien agreed to pay the SEC $60,000.

QUESTIONS

1. Identify the accountants in this case who faced ethical dilemmas. Also identify the parties who would be potentially affected by the outcome of each of these ethical dilemmas. What responsibility did the accountant in each case owe to these parties? Did the accountants fulfill these responsibilities?

2. Describe the procedures an auditor should perform during a review of a client's quarterly financial statements. In your opinion, did the Touche Ross auditors who discovered the $203,000 adjusting entry during their 1985 second-quarter review take all appropriate steps to corroborate that entry? Should the auditors have immediately informed the audit partner, Helen Shepherd, of the entry?

3. In reviewing the United Airlines–Cardillo agreement, Shepherd collected evidence that supported the $203,000 adjusting entry as booked and evidence that suggested the entry was recorded improperly. Identify each of these items of evidence. What characteristics of audit evidence do the profession's technical standards suggest auditors should consider? Analyze the audit evidence that Shepherd collected regarding the disputed entry in terms of these characteristics.

4. What are the principal objectives of the SEC's rules that require 8-K statements to be filed when public companies change auditors? Did Shepherd violate the client confidentiality rule when she discussed the United Airlines–Cardillo transaction in the exhibit letter she filed with Cardillo's 8-K auditor change statement?

In your opinion, did Shepherd have a responsibility to disclose to Cardillo executives the information she intended to include in the exhibit letter?

5. Do the profession's technical standards explicitly require auditors to evaluate the integrity of a prospective client's key executives? Identify the specific measures auditors can use to assess the integrity of a prospective client's executives.

Case 5.2
The PTL Club

Jim and Tammy Bakker founded the PTL (Praise the Lord) Club, a religious broadcasting organization, in 1974. A little more than one decade later, the PTL Club claimed more than 500,000 members and boasted annual revenues of almost $130 million. Bakker and his close associates came under intense scrutiny in 1987 following a revelation that they used PTL funds to pay a former church secretary to remain silent concerning a brief liaison between herself and Bakker. That disclosure triggered a series of investigations of PTL's finances. Key agencies involved in those investigations included the Internal Revenue Service, the Federal Bureau of Investigation, and the U.S. Postal Service. In March 1987, Bakker resigned as PTL's chairman. Two years later, a federal jury convicted him of fraud and conspiracy charges. A federal judge then fined Bakker $500,000 and sentenced him to 45 years in prison.[1]

The Bakker scandal spurred a nationwide debate focusing on the issue of whether the financial affairs of religious broadcasting companies should be subject to regulatory oversight. The investigations of PTL revealed that Bakker and his associates received huge salaries and bonuses from funds raised via the organization's televised appeals. In 1986, PTL paid the Bakkers almost $2 million. During the first three months of 1987, while PTL struggled to cope with severe cash flow problems, the couple received $640,000. Critics also chastised the

---

1. In early 1991, a federal appeals court upheld Bakker's conviction on the fraud and conspiracy charges but voided Bakker's 45-year sentence, as well as the $500,000 fine, and ordered that a new sentencing hearing be held. According to the appeals court, the trial judge who imposed the lengthy sentence on Bakker may have allowed his personal religious predispositions to influence his sentencing decision. Following the re-sentencing hearing in August 1991, Bakker received an 18-year sentence. In 1994, Bakker was paroled after serving nearly five years in federal prison.

Bakkers for their flamboyant lifestyle. Tammy Bakker decorated PTL's executive suites in Fort Mill, South Carolina, in opulent style, including gold-plated bathroom fixtures and extravagant chandeliers. The Bakkers enjoyed a rambling Palm Springs ranch house on their many trips to the West Coast, a $600,000 condominium in Highland Beach, Florida, and a fleet of luxury automobiles, including Rolls-Royces.

Before 1987, Jim Bakker's critics persistently called for more extensive financial disclosures by PTL. Bakker resisted such demands. He repeatedly insisted that such disclosures were not necessary, since PTL maintained strong financial controls. In addition, Bakker often reminded his critics that PTL "had excellent accountants and that it had external audits by reputable [CPA] firms."[2] The subsequent investigations of PTL revealed that the organization's internal controls were extremely weak, and nonexistent in many cases. Investigators found that Bakker's subordinates issued paychecks to individuals not employed by PTL and paid large sums to consultants who never provided any services to the organization. Additionally, investigators could not find documentation for millions of dollars of construction costs recorded in PTL's accounting records.

One of the most troubling weaknesses uncovered in PTL's accounting system involved a secret payroll account used to disburse funds to Bakker and his closest aides. This account was so secretive that the organization's chief financial officer was not informed of the expenses funneled through it, while PTL's board of directors was totally unaware of its existence. Surprisingly, during the mid-1980s a partner of Laventhol & Horwath, PTL's independent audit firm, maintained the secret payroll account, including overseeing the preparation of the checks issued on that account.[3] Even more surprisingly, that same partner also supervised PTL's annual audits.

Laventhol was widely criticized for its role in the PTL scandal and eventually named as a co-defendant in a $757 million class action lawsuit filed by PTL contributors. The suit alleged that Laventhol assisted Bakker in misrepresenting PTL's financial condition and facilitated Bakker's efforts to embezzle millions of dollars from PTL through the secret payroll account. Among several other parties named as co-defendants in the lawsuit were Bakker and PTL's former audit firm, Deloitte, Haskins & Sells. PTL dismissed Deloitte as its audit firm in 1985 for undisclosed reasons and then retained Laventhol as its new audit firm.

Laventhol's decision to accept PTL as a client was apparently linked to an aggressive marketing strategy adopted by the firm in the late 1970s. From 1980 to 1986 alone, Laventhol's nationwide revenues increased 300 percent. This phenomenal growth resulted in part from Laventhol's acceptance of high-risk audit clients that other audit firms hesitated or refused to consider as clients. A former Laventhol employee bluntly observed that the firm "took too many risky clients like PTL—a strategy that, ironically, accountants often advise their clients to avoid."[4] Critics charged that the large fees Laventhol received from PTL influenced the accounting firm's decisions regarding that client. In the civil lawsuit

---

2. L. Berton, "Laventhol & Horwath Beset by Litigation, Runs into Hard Times," *The Wall Street Journal*, 17 May 1990, A1, A10.

3. Although Laventhol prepared the checks written on this account, the accounting firm forwarded the checks to a PTL executive to be signed.

4. Berton, "Laventhol & Horwath Beset by Litigation," A1.

that named Laventhol as a co-defendant, the plaintiffs maintained that the CPA firm permitted the questionable payments from the secret payroll account "because PTL was the largest client for its [Laventhol's] Charlotte office."[5]

In the fall of 1990, Laventhol, the seventh-largest CPA firm in the United States at the time, filed for bankruptcy. Attorneys for PTL's contributors subsequently dropped the accounting firm as a co-defendant in the $757 million class action lawsuit.[6] Two months later, the jury hearing that case rendered a $130 million judgment against Jim Bakker to be paid to the plaintiffs. The jury ruled that Deloitte & Touche, the successor firm of Deloitte, Haskins & Sells, was not guilty of any malfeasance in the case. In commenting on the jury's verdict, a Deloitte official noted that the suit was "a well-financed and well-executed attempt to recover enormous damages from an innocent accounting firm for the alleged wrongdoing of others."[7,8]

QUESTIONS

1. Identify the ethical questions raised by the maintenance of PTL's secret payroll account by the Laventhol partner. Does the fact that PTL was a private organization not registered with the Securities and Exchange Commission affect the propriety of the partner's actions? Explain.

2. What procedures should an audit firm perform before accepting an audit client, particularly a high-risk client such as PTL?

3. Briefly define the so-called "deep pockets theory" as it relates to the litigation problems of large public accounting firms in recent years. What measures can these firms take to protect themselves from large class action lawsuits predicated upon false or largely unfounded allegations?

---

5. M. Isikoff and A. Harris, "PTL Contributors Sue Ministry's Accounting Firms," *Washington Post*, 19 November 1987, C10, C16.

6. Laventhol's partners and former partners did not escape financial responsibility for the firm's role in the PTL scandal. In a subsequent bankruptcy plan approved in 1992 by the U.S. Bankruptcy Court of New York, Laventhol's partners and former partners contributed approximately $47 million to a settlement pool to liquidate outstanding claims against Laventhol. This pool was to be divided among Laventhol's creditors and several parties that had sued the firm including PTL's contributors. Individual payments made by Laventhol partners to this settlement pool reportedly ranged as high as $700,000.

7. "Deloitte Victorious in PTL Case," *Public Accounting Report*, 31 January 1991, 5.

8. An excellent and comprehensive summary of the accounting and auditing issues involved in the PTL scandal can be found in *Anatomy of A Fraud* (New York: Wiley, 1993), by Gary Tidwell.

CASE 5.3
PHILLIPS PETROLEUM COMPANY

Bill Grant sat in the middle of a large jail cell with 12 other inmates as the long October night dragged on.[1] To pass the time, Grant and several other inmates played cards and talked about their hopes of being reunited with their families. The accommodations of the Tulsa County Jail were not unlike those of most jails: unkempt, dimly lit, and 12 beds for 13 inmates. What made this scene unusual was not the less-than-glamorous, overcrowded condition of the jail cell, but rather the presence of Grant, an audit partner with Arthur Young & Company, an international accounting firm.

On October 6, 1975, Bill Grant, at the time the managing partner of Arthur Young's Tulsa office, appeared at a hearing in a Tulsa federal courthouse. Judge Allen Barrow presided over that hearing. Judge Barrow ordered Grant to produce certain audit workpapers previously subpoenaed by a federal grand jury. These workpapers pertained to Phillips Petroleum Company, the largest audit client of Arthur Young's Tulsa office. When Grant respectfully denied Judge Barrow's request, the federal magistrate cited him for civil contempt. The court bailiff then handcuffed Grant and led him away to jail. Apparently, the judge hoped that an overnight stay in a crowded jail cell would convince Grant to change his mind.

---

1. The facts of this case were drawn principally from the following articles: "Arthur Young Aide Cited for Contempt and Jailed in Tulsa," *The Wall Street Journal*, 8 October 1975, 10; F. Andrews, "Arthur Young Faces Test on Protecting Client Audit Secrets," *The Wall Street Journal*, 14 October 1975, 23; "Arthur Young & Co. Gives Grand Jury Data On Phillips Petroleum," *The Wall Street Journal*, 15 October 1975, 28; "Pleas by Phillips Petroleum Filed On U.S. Charges," *The Wall Street Journal*, 23 November 1977, 2.

The federal grand jury's interest in the Arthur Young workpapers stemmed from an ongoing investigation of Phillips. That investigation focused on possible tax fraud related to a secret, multimillion-dollar fund that Phillips' executives had established to make political contributions. One contribution made from the secret fund, which Phillips maintained in a Swiss bank account, was an illegal donation of $100,000 to what became known during the Watergate era as CREEP—the Committee to Reelect the President (Richard Nixon). Under the terms of an earlier plea bargain agreement with Watergate special prosecutor Archibald Cox, Phillips' chairman of the board had admitted to the $100,000 contribution to Nixon's 1972 reelection campaign and pleaded guilty to one misdemeanor.[2] Following that plea bargain agreement, another federal prosecutor filed a seven-count indictment against Phillips. This indictment charged that Phillips filed false federal tax returns by failing to report interest revenue earned on the secret Swiss bank account.

Prior to Bill Grant's appearance before Judge Barrow, Arthur Young turned over to the federal grand jury approximately 12,000 pages of workpapers prepared during earlier audits of Phillips. Arthur Young refused to give the grand jury several workpapers relating to two key items: (1) certain tax accruals made by Phillips and (2) attorneys' letters obtained by Arthur Young from Phillips' law firms. Among other topics, these latter documents discussed various "unasserted claims" involving Phillips that were known to Phillips' attorneys. Apparently, the federal grand jury believed that the contested workpapers would provide important insight on the allegations pending against Phillips.

Arthur Young declined to provide the contested workpapers to the grand jury on the grounds that they contained confidential information that, if disclosed, would be potentially damaging to Phillips. Tax accrual audit workpapers, for example, typically contain an audit firm's analysis of tax-related decisions made by their clients. Access to such workpapers would make it much easier for the Internal Revenue Service (IRS) to "build a case" against a given company.

Judge Barrow released Bill Grant from the Tulsa County Jail on October 7, 1975, but ordered Grant to make an appearance the following week in his courtroom. If Grant again refused to produce the workpapers subpoenaed by the grand jury, he faced a criminal contempt citation and a 17-month jail term. During the week between Grant's two court appearances, Arthur Young's attorneys worked out a compromise with Judge Barrow. Under the terms of this agreement, Arthur Young turned over copies of the requested tax accrual workpapers to Judge Barrow. However, all matters other than those specifically identified by the subpoena were masked in the copies of those workpapers given to the grand jury. Judge Barrow also granted Arthur Young the right to contest any subsequent court order to provide the original "unmasked" tax accrual workpapers to the grand jury.

Judge Barrow did not relent regarding the attorneys' letters. He ordered Arthur Young to provide copies of those letters to the grand jury. Phillips filed a motion to appeal this order but that appeal was denied.

---

2. Phillips' chairman also revealed that he delivered $50,000 to Nixon in a New York City apartment during the 1968 presidential campaign in which Nixon eventually defeated Senator Hubert Humphrey.

EPILOGUE

The Watergate-related problems of Phillips Petroleum continued to plague the company for two years following the resolution of the dispute involving the Arthur Young workpapers. In early 1976, Phillips' executives temporarily turned over control of the company to its outside directors. This decision followed the filing of a large class action lawsuit against Phillips, a lawsuit prompted by the charges of illegal campaign contributions. In November 1977, Phillips settled these charges by pleading guilty of conspiring to make illegal campaign contributions, pleading no contest to four related tax evasion charges, and paying a fine of $30,000.

Ironically, Arthur Young's tax accrual workpapers for another audit client, the large oil company Amerada Hess, triggered another major litigation case. The central issue in this latter case was whether the IRS had the right to review copies of auditors' tax accrual workpapers. In 1984, the Supreme Court decided the case by unanimously ruling that the IRS has the right to review tax accrual workpapers prepared during an independent audit.

QUESTIONS

1. Was Bill Grant justified in refusing to provide the requested workpapers to the grand jury? Defend your answer.

2. What responsibility, if any, does a public accounting firm have to its partners and employees when they are subpoenaed to testify regarding a client?

3. Briefly discuss the purpose of "attorneys' letters" obtained during an audit. If attorneys realize that these documents can be routinely subpoenaed, how will this realization likely affect the quality of the audit evidence provided by attorneys' letters?

4. Do you believe that auditors' knowledge that tax accrual audit workpapers can be obtained by the IRS affects the documentation included in those workpapers? Explain.

5. Suppose that Arthur Young discovered during its 1973 Phillips audit the illegal campaign contribution made to President Nixon's 1972 reelection campaign. How should this discovery have affected the remainder of the audit, if at all?

CASE 5.4
MARINER CORPORATION

In 1984, the principal owners of Florida-based Diversified Electronic Components, Inc. (Dielco) decided to sell their company.[1] Dielco's owners turned to the public accounting firm of Arthur Young & Company to help them find a buyer. The agreement between the two parties called for Arthur Young to be compensated on a contingent fee basis for its services. If Arthur Young located a buyer for Dielco, the accounting firm would receive a fee equal to a predetermined percentage of the sales price.

Arthur Young prepared a "selling memorandum" describing Dielco and distributed this document to potential buyers of the company. Among the parties to whom Arthur Young sent a copy of the selling memorandum was Mariner Corporation. Mariner's owners immediately expressed an interest in acquiring Dielco and subsequently signed a contractual letter of intent to purchase the company. Before closing the deal, Mariner insisted on an audit of Dielco's financial statements. If the audit established that Dielco's net worth (stockholders' equity) equaled or exceeded a predetermined figure, the deal would be consummated at the purchase price stated in the letter of intent. Mariner would have no obligation to purchase Dielco if the audit revealed a net worth less than the required minimum amount.

Mariner's executives engaged Arthur Young to audit Dielco's financial statements. Despite having received the selling memorandum directly from Arthur Young, Mariner's executives were unaware that Dielco's owners had retained Arthur Young to find a buyer for their firm. Mariner's management was also

1. The facts of this case and the quotations appearing within it were drawn from the following legal opinion: *Arthur Young & Company v. Mariner Corporation*, 630 So. 2d 1199 (Fla. App. 4 Dist., 1994).

unaware that Arthur Young stood to receive a substantial fee from Dielco's owners if the deal was closed, a fee contingent on the sales price obtained for the company.

Arthur Young audited Dielco's financial statements as requested by Mariner. The results of the audit suggested that Dielco's net worth exceeded the minimum amount Mariner had established for closing the deal. Following Arthur Young's audit, Mariner purchased Dielco in April 1985. Shortly thereafter, Dielco's former owners paid Arthur Young for its services.

The acquisition of Dielco proved to be a poor business decision for Mariner. Almost immediately, Dielco began experiencing severe financial problems. Eventually, those problems forced Dielco to file for bankruptcy.

As Dielco's financial condition was deteriorating, Mariner's executives learned that Arthur Young had been retained by Dielco's former owners to find a buyer for their company. Mariner's executives also discovered how Dielco's former owners compensated Arthur Young for its services. These discoveries and Dielco's filing for bankruptcy prompted Mariner to sue Arthur Young. Mariner predicated this lawsuit on two primary allegations. First, Mariner charged that the contingent fee received by Arthur Young impaired the firm's independence while auditing Dielco. Mariner's officers claimed that if they had known of the contingent fee arrangement, they would not have relied on Arthur Young's audit in deciding to acquire Dielco. Second, Mariner charged that flaws in Arthur Young's audit resulted in the accounting firm failing to discover the overstatement of Dielco's net worth.

After a lengthy trial in a Florida state court, a jury ruled in Mariner's favor and awarded the company damages of $1.3 million. Arthur Young immediately appealed the verdict. During the appeal, Arthur Young first maintained that it was not liable for Mariner's damages because of language included in the Florida statute under which Mariner's attorneys filed the lawsuit. Surprisingly, that Florida law specifically exempts accounting firms from liability "when rendering services in connection with the regular practice of accounting." The appellate court quickly rejected Arthur Young's contention by pointing out that "the brokerage services provided by Arthur Young were not connected to the regular practice of its profession but were a brand new endeavor for it."

The principal issue contested during the appeal was whether Arthur Young served as an "agent of the seller" while performing its services for Dielco. Under the applicable state law, Arthur Young had to qualify as an agent of the seller (Dielco) to be held liable to Mariner. That law defines an agent as a "salesman" and then goes on to provide a definition of that term.

> "Salesman" means any natural person, other than a dealer, employed, appointed, or authorized by a dealer or issuer to sell securities in any manner or act as an investment adviser as defined in this section.

Arthur Young maintained that it did not qualify as an agent of Dielco in arranging the sale of the company and thus was not liable to Mariner. Not surprisingly, Mariner strenuously argued just the reverse during the appeal. The appellate court agreed with Mariner.

> There was substantial evidence that AY was acting as the agent of the seller in securing the sale of Dielco. The accounting firm signed an agreement to prepare a selling memorandum, contact potential buyers, assist in the negotiation of the sale, and "represent

your [Dielco's] interests." For their services, they were to be paid a contingent fee based on the amount of the selling price due on the closing of a sale. They were acting as any broker acts in a sale.

QUESTIONS

1. Ignoring the profession's past and present ethical rules, do you believe that Arthur Young behaved ethically during its interaction with Mariner Corporation? Defend your answer.

2. Identify the present ethical rules that govern the receipt of contingent fees by public accounting firms. If these rules had been in effect during the mid-1980s, would Arthur Young have violated them in this case?

3. Identify the pros and cons of accounting firms rendering services similar to those that Arthur Young provided to Dielco. What risks and opportunities do offering such services pose for accounting firms?

CASE 5.5
KOGER PROPERTIES, INC.

Becoming a partner with one of the large international accounting firms easily ranks among the most popular career goals of accounting majors.[1] Michael Goodbread staked out that career goal nearly three decades ago. After graduating from college, Goodbread made the first step toward reaching his objective when he accepted an entry-level position with Touche Ross & Company. In February 1973, Goodbread received his CPA license in the state of Florida after passing the CPA exam. Eight years later, the partners of Touche Ross selected Goodbread to join their ranks. In December 1989, Goodbread accomplished his career goal a second time by becoming a partner of Deloitte & Touche, the firm formed by the merger of Deloitte, Haskins & Sells and Touche Ross. Before the merger, Goodbread served as an audit partner in the Jacksonville, Florida, office of Touche Ross. Goodbread assumed an identical position with the newly formed Jacksonville office of Deloitte & Touche following the merger.

The six-digit salaries earned by partners of large international accounting firms provide them ample discretionary funds for investment purposes. Like many investors, Goodbread often considered local companies when making investment decisions. One local firm that caught Goodbread's attention during the late 1980s was Koger Properties, Inc., a real estate development company headquartered in Jacksonville. Koger's "claim to fame" was originating the concept of an office park. According to a Koger annual report, the company opened the first office park in 1957 in Jacksonville. By the early 1990s, Koger operated nearly 40 office parks in two dozen metropolitan areas scattered across the southern United States.

---

1. The events discussed in this case were reconstructed principally from information included in Securities and Exchange Commission, *Accounting and Auditing Enforcement Release No. 861*, 10 December 1996.

In December 1988, Goodbread purchased 400 shares of Koger's common stock at a price of $26 per share. At the time, Koger had approximately 25 million shares of common stock outstanding.

Following the December 1989 merger creating Deloitte & Touche, one of Goodbread's first assignments with his new firm was supervising the audit of Koger Properties for its fiscal year ending March 31, 1990. Koger had previously been an audit client of Deloitte, Haskins & Sells. In his role as audit engagement partner, Goodbread oversaw all facets of the Koger audit. On February 21, 1990, Goodbread signed the "audit planning memorandum" that laid out the general strategy Deloitte & Touche intended to follow in completing the Koger audit. Several months later, on June 27, 1990, Goodbread signed the "audit report record" for the Koger engagement. The signing of that document by the audit engagement partner formally completes a Deloitte & Touche audit.

Goodbread dated the unqualified opinion issued on Koger's 1990 financial statements as of June 11, 1990. Almost exactly one month earlier, on May 10, 1990, Goodbread sold the 400 shares of Koger stock that he had owned since December 1988. Goodbread sold the stock at a price of $20.75 per share.

The Securities and Exchange Commission (SEC) eventually learned that Goodbread held an ownership interest in Koger Properties while he supervised the company's 1990 audit. The SEC charged that Goodbread's ownership interest in Koger violated the federal agency's independence rules, the *Code of Professional Conduct* of the American Institute of Certified Public Accountants (AICPA), and generally accepted auditing standards. Most important, the SEC charged that Goodbread caused Deloitte & Touche to issue an improper opinion on Koger's 1990 financial statements. Instead of the unqualified opinion Deloitte & Touche issued on those financial statements, the SEC maintained that a disclaimer of opinion was required given the circumstances. Following its investigation of the matter, the SEC publicly censured Goodbread.

The embarrassing revelation of Michael Goodbread's ownership interest in Koger Properties marked the beginning of a long series of problems that Deloitte & Touche encountered with that audit client. In September 1991, Koger filed for bankruptcy. A short time earlier, Koger's stockholders had filed a large class action lawsuit against Deloitte & Touche. The suit alleged that the 1989 Koger audit performed by Deloitte, Haskins & Sells and the 1990 Koger audit performed by Deloitte & Touche were deficient. Those deficient audits allegedly contributed to the subsequent decline in Koger's stock price.

A federal jury agreed with the Koger stockholders and ordered Deloitte to pay the plaintiffs $81.3 million to compensate them for damages suffered because of the 1989 and 1990 audits. In July 1997, the U.S. Court of Appeals reversed the lower court's ruling and voided the huge judgment awarded to Koger's stockholders. The appellate court ruled that the stockholders failed to prove that any errors made by Deloitte during the 1989 and 1990 Koger audits caused the losses they later incurred.[2]

Another of the "megafirms" created by a merger of two large international accounting firms encountered an independence problem similar to that experienced by Deloitte & Touche in the Koger Properties case. However, Pricewaterhouse-Coopers' "problem" was much more severe and embarrassing. In 1999, that firm

---

2. *Securities Regulation and Law Report*, "Investors' 10b-5 Claims Against Deloitte Fail in CA for Lack of Loss Causation," 18 July 1997, 1018.

CASE 5.5 KOGER PROPERTIES, INC.

agreed to be censured by the SEC for dozens of alleged violations of the profession's independence rules.

> Without admitting or denying wrongdoing, PricewaterhouseCoopers has agreed to be censured by federal regulators over a dispute that ownership of client stock had compromised its independence as an auditor. The Big Five firm agreed to pay $2.5 million to establish education programs for the profession designed to improve auditor compliance. . . . The Securities and Exchange Commission claims it turned up 70 instances from 1996 to 1998 in which some of the partners and managers of the firm purchased client stock.[3]

The problems experienced by Deloitte & Touche and PricewaterhouseCoopers apparently stem from unfamiliarity with the profession's auditor independence rules. In the late 1990s, a top SEC official revealed that personnel from the large international accounting firms frequently contact the federal agency to inquire of its most basic ethical rules for independent auditors. According to this official, these inquiries commonly include questions regarding "such fundamental issues as the prohibition against owning stock in companies they audit."[4]

QUESTIONS

1. The SEC charged that Goodbread violated its independence rules, the *AICPA Code of Professional Conduct*, and generally accepted auditing standards. Explain the SEC's rationale in making each of those allegations.

2. In your opinion, did Goodbread's equity interest in Koger likely qualify as a "material" investment for him? Was the materiality of that investment a relevant issue in this case? Explain.

3. Given that Goodbread purchased stock of Koger Properties in 1988, under what conditions, if any, could he have later served as the audit engagement partner for that company?

4. During much of the nineteenth century in Great Britain, independent auditors were not only allowed to have an equity interest in their clients but were required to invest in their clients in certain circumstances. Explain the rationale likely underlying that rule. Would such a rule "make sense" in today's business environment in the U.S.? Defend your answer.

---

3. *Accounting Today*, "PwC Censured for Owning Client Stock," 8–21 February 1999, 3.

4. E. MacDonald, "Levitt Says Wave of Accounting Mergers Could Affect Independence of Auditors," *The Wall Street Journal*, 21 October 1997, A2 & A4.

CASE 5.6
AMERICAN FUEL & SUPPLY COMPANY, INC.

Consider this scenario. You are the audit manager responsible for supervising the fieldwork for a major audit client. After hundreds of hours of hard work, the audit is successfully completed, the client receives a clean opinion, and you and your colleagues go on to your next assignments. Now, the bad news. Several months later, you discover that the client's financial statements contain a material error, an error not revealed by the audit. What should you do at this point? What will you do? An audit manager with Touche Ross faced these difficult circumstances in 1986.

In the mid-1980s, Wisconsin-based American Fuel & Supply Company, Inc., (AFS) was a wholesale distributor of automotive supplies, lawn and garden supplies, and related products.[1] AFS's president and sole shareholder directed the company's day-to-day operations. AFS purchased merchandise from several vendors. One of the company's largest suppliers was Chevron Chemical Company, a division of Chevron Corporation. Products that AFS purchased from Chevron included insecticides and weedkillers bearing the Ortho brand label.

AFS prepared comparative financial statements for its fiscal year ending December 31, 1985. An unqualified audit opinion accompanied those financial statements, an opinion issued by Touche Ross and dated February 28, 1986. AFS distributed 100 copies of the financial statements, principally to creditors such as Chevron Chemical.

Several months following the completion of the 1985 AFS audit, Touche Ross personnel discovered that the company's 1985 financial statements contained a material error. AFS had billed certain of its customers twice for merchandise they had purchased. This error caused the company's 1985 revenues to be overstated

---

1. The principal facts of this case and the quotations appearing within it were drawn from the following legal opinion: *Chevron Chemical v. Deloitte & Touche*, 483 N.W. 2d 314 (Wis. App. 1992).

by nearly $1 million. More important, the error had converted the net loss actually suffered by AFS that year to a reported net income. Chevron Chemical and other creditors of AFS later testified that they relied on the erroneous financial statements in deciding to continue extending credit to the company.

During August and September 1986, members of the AFS audit engagement team wrestled with the question of what they should do, given the dilemma they faced. A central figure in these deliberations was James Wagner, the audit manager who had supervised the fieldwork on the 1985 AFS audit. In late August 1986, Wagner bluntly summarized the situation for his superiors: "there is a set of financial statements out being used by [AFS's] vendors and lenders that has an error in it." Two weeks later, Wagner, a Touche Ross audit partner, and the accounting firm's assistant legal counsel held a conference call to discuss the matter. During this conference call, these individuals agreed on the course of action Touche Ross would take to resolve the matter.

> . . . unless AFS notified its creditors and vendors of the existence of the error in the financial statements, Touche would withdraw their opinion and give notice to its creditors and vendors whom they knew were relying upon the financial statements that their opinion had been withdrawn.

Following the conference call, Touche Ross representatives met with AFS officials. Touche Ross unsuccessfully tried to persuade AFS's management to recall the company's 1985 financial statements. Touche Ross then advised the client that it intended to withdraw the audit report issued on those financial statements and to contact all parties known to be relying on that report. Touche Ross indicated that it would inform these parties that they should no longer rely on the withdrawn audit opinion.

A few days later, Touche Ross personnel met again with AFS's management. The company's legal counsel also attended this meeting. AFS's attorney insisted that Touche Ross would violate the confidentiality of its contractual relationship with AFS by withdrawing its audit opinion and notifying third parties of that decision. The client's attorney then threatened legal action against Touche Ross if the accounting firm carried through on its planned course of action.

Eventually, AFS and Touche Ross hammered out a compromise. This compromise permitted Touche Ross to notify AFS's sole secured creditor (lender) that the firm's audit opinion on AFS's 1985 financial statements had been withdrawn. However, Touche Ross could not notify AFS's unsecured creditors of its decision to withdraw the audit report. These unsecured creditors included Chevron Chemical and AFS's other suppliers.

James Wagner believed the compromise was unacceptable. In a confidential memo apparently intended for his superiors, Wagner stated that Touche Ross had an obligation to the other parties relying on the audit opinion issued on AFS's 1985 financial statements. Wagner suggested that Touche Ross should "send a letter to the vendors or creditors that we know have received the financial statements telling them that . . . the opinion should no longer be relied upon."

EPILOGUE

AFS filed for bankruptcy in April 1987. The company's president filed for personal bankruptcy approximately two years later. In early 1989, Chevron Chemical sued Touche Ross, alleging that the accounting firm negligently audited AFS's 1985 financial statements. Chevron Chemical also maintained that Touche Ross had a responsibility to notify it after learning of the error in AFS's 1985 financial statements. A Wisconsin state court rejected the allegation that Touche Ross negligently audited AFS in 1985. However, that court ruled and a Wisconsin state appellate court later agreed that Touche Ross "was negligent as a matter of law in failing to notify plaintiff [Chevron Chemical] of the withdrawal of their opinion." The original state court awarded damages of $1.6 million to Chevron Chemical.

QUESTIONS

1. A major focus of the lawsuit Chevron Chemical filed against Touche Ross was the auditing profession's rules regarding the "subsequent discovery of facts existing at the date of the auditor's report." Those rules distinguish between situations in which a client cooperates with the auditor in making all necessary disclosures and situations involving uncooperative clients. Briefly summarize the differing responsibilities that auditors have in those two sets of circumstances.

2. Given your previous answer, do you believe that Touche Ross complied with the applicable professional standards after learning of the error in AFS's 1985 financial statements? Explain.

3. Do you agree with the assertion of AFS's legal counsel that Touche Ross would have violated the profession's client confidentiality rule by withdrawing its 1985 audit opinion and notifying all relevant third parties of that decision? Why or why not?

4. Suppose that Touche Ross had resigned as AFS's auditor following the completion of the 1985 audit but prior to the discovery of the error in the 1985 financial statements. What responsibility, if any, would Touche Ross have had when it learned of the error in AFS's 1985 financial statements?

CASE 5.7
MALLON RESOURCES
CORPORATION

At some point in their careers, every public accountant reaches that crossroads where they must answer the important question: Should I stay in public accounting or should I accept a job offer in the "outside" world? Duane Knight, a CPA employed by the Denver-based accounting firm of Hein + Associates (HA), reached that point in his career in February 1994.[1] Knight graduated with an accounting degree from Colorado State University in 1983 and accepted a job three years later with HA. By 1994, Knight had risen to the position of audit manager, one step from becoming a partner with his firm. On February 15, 1994, George Mallon, the president and chief executive officer of Mallon Resources Corporation, telephoned Knight. Mallon asked Knight if he would be interested in becoming the treasurer and principal accounting officer of Mallon Resources, a publicly owned company that operated a gold mine and owned several large oil and gas properties.

Knight was well acquainted with Mallon Resources since HA had served as the company's audit firm for several years. In fact, Knight had been assigned to the audit engagement team for that client since 1991. In February 1994 when George Mallon contacted him, Knight was supervising the fieldwork on the audit of Mallon Resources for its fiscal year ended December 31, 1993.

Following his conversation with George Mallon, Knight became concerned that he had an "independence problem." This concern caused Knight to discuss the matter with a fellow audit manager at HA. After reviewing the applicable professional standards, the two men concluded that Knight indeed had an inde-

---

1. Most of the facts presented in this case and all of the quotations appearing within it were taken from Securities and Exchange Commission, *Accounting and Auditing Enforcement Release No. 798*, 2 July 1996.

pendence problem. However, Knight did not immediately bring this matter to the attention of his superiors at HA.

George Mallon formally offered Knight the position of treasurer and chief accounting officer of Mallon Resources on February 17, 1994. Knight promptly notified a senior HA audit partner of the job offer. The two men decided that Knight should dissociate himself from the Mallon Resources audit while the job offer was pending. One week later, on February 24, 1994, Knight accepted the job offer extended by George Mallon. Knight immediately informed his superiors at HA of his decision and that he would terminate his position with the accounting firm on March 31 and assume his new position with Mallon Resources on April 1. Within the next few days, HA assigned another audit manager to oversee the Mallon Resources audit. Despite the decision to remove Knight from the Mallon Resources audit, he continued to be involved in that engagement during his last few weeks of employment with HA.

Knight's involvement in the Mallon Resources audit after February 24, 1994, included developing several "prepared-by-client" schedules for the company. Among these schedules were analyses of Mallon Resources' tax deferrals. HA audited these schedules and filed them in the Mallon Resources workpapers. Knight also prepared unaudited exhibits included in the 1993 10-K registration statement that Mallon Resources submitted to the Securities and Exchange Commission (SEC). Knight's former subordinates on the HA engagement team reviewed these exhibits. Finally, during March 1994 Knight spent considerable time in the Mallon Resources corporate offices. At least some of this time he spent working on matters related to the company's 1993 audit. For example, on March 28, Knight reviewed the Management's Discussion and Analysis (MD&A) section that accompanied Mallon Resources' 1993 audited financial statements. He also discussed the content of the MD&A section with the company's legal counsel.

Clarence Hein contacted Knight on March 29, 1994, two days before Knight formally joined Mallon Resources. Hein, HA's managing partner, served as the audit engagement partner for the Mallon Resources audit. Hein asked Knight to review several important and unresolved issues on the audit, which was nearing completion. Eventually, Hein arranged a conference call with SEC personnel to discuss one of those issues. Knight, Hein, and the new audit manager assigned to the Mallon Resources audit participated in that conference call. During the telephone conversation, Knight was identified simply as a "future Mallon employee."

> Although Hein knew that Knight was still a Hein + Associates employee, he told Knight that he should represent Mallon's perspective in the telephone call with the [SEC] staff.

Following the conference call, Hein asked Knight to write a memo on behalf of Mallon Resources that documented the resolution of the issue discussed with the SEC. Two weeks later, after Knight had begun working for Mallon Resources, he sent the memorandum to Hein. The memo was then included in the workpaper file for the 1993 Mallon Resources audit.

Mallon Resources filed its 1993 10-K with the SEC on April 4, 1994. The 10-K contained the company's audited financial statements for 1993 and HA's unqualified audit opinion on those statements. During the first two weeks of April, Knight, now an employee of Mallon Resources, continued to work on assignments for HA. Knight eventually billed HA for 55 hours of work he performed as an "independent contractor" for the accounting firm during those two weeks.

In June 1994, the SEC began investigating Duane Knight's relationship with HA and Mallon Resources during the company's 1993 audit. The SEC questioned Knight's status after reviewing documents Mallon Resources had submitted to the federal agency. Those documents suggested that Knight had served in dual and conflicting roles during the 1993 Mallon Resources audit. (Note: Exhibit 1 contains a timeline that summarizes the key events in this case.)

December 31, 1993	1993 fiscal year of Mallon Resources ends.	
January 1994	Duane Knight, an audit manager with Hein + Associates (HA), is assigned to the 1993 Mallon Resources audit. The audit engagement partner is Clarence Hein, HA's managing partner. Knight drafts an audit planning memorandum, the audit budget, and the client engagement letter.	
January 27, 1994	Representatives of HA and Mallon Resources sign the audit engagement letter.	
Early February 1994	Knight supervises fieldwork on the Mallon Resources audit.	
February 15, 1994	George Mallon, president and CEO of Mallon Resources, telephones Knight. The two men discuss Knight becoming Mallon Resources' treasurer and principal accounting officer.	
February 15, 1994	Following his conversation with Mallon, Knight tells another HA audit manager that he may have an "independence problem." After reviewing the AICPA's professional standards, the two audit managers conclude that Knight does have an independence problem. Knight does not immediately inform his superiors at HA of his telephone conversation with George Mallon.	
February 17, 1994	Knight receives a written offer of employment from Mallon. Knight informs a senior audit partner with HA of the offer. The two men agree that Knight cannot work on the Mallon Resources audit while the offer is pending.	
February 24, 1994	Knight accepts the employment offer from Mallon and agrees to a start date of April 1, 1994. Knight informs his superiors at HA of his decision.	
Late February, 1994	Another audit manager is assigned to the Mallon Resources audit to replace Knight.	
February 24– March 28, 1994	Knight, who is still employed by HA, drafts several "prepared-by-client" schedules analyzing Mallon Resources' tax deferrals. These schedules are then audited by HA and included in the 1993 workpapers for the Mallon Resources engagement. Knight also prepares unaudited exhibits included in Mallon Resources' 1993 10-K registration statement. HA auditors review these exhibits.	
March 28, 1994	Knight discusses the content of the MD&A section of Mallon Resources' 1993 annual report with the company's general counsel.	
March 29, 1994	Clarence Hein asks Knight to review several important accounting and auditing issues that remain unresolved on the Mallon Resources audit. Knight, Hein, and the new audit manager assigned to the Mallon Resources audit conduct a telephone conference call with the SEC to discuss one of those issues. During this conference call, Knight is identified simply as a "future Mallon employee."	
March 30, 1994	Hein asks Knight to write a memorandum documenting Mallon Resources' position regarding the accounting issue discussed with the SEC.	

EXHIBIT 1
Timeline, Mallon Resources Case

(continued)

**EXHIBIT 1—continued
Timeline, Mallon
Resources Case**

April 1, 1994	Knight formally becomes an employee of Mallon Resources.
April 4, 1994	Mallon Resources files its 1993 10-K with the SEC. The 10-K includes an unqualified audit opinion issued by HA on the company's 1993 financial statements.
April 14, 1994	Knight sends the memo that Hein requested on March 30 to HA. That memo is included in the workpapers for the 1993 Mallon Resources audit.
April 15, 1994	Knight sends a bill to HA for 55 hours of work he performed for the firm as an "independent contractor" during the first two weeks of April.
Mid-June 1994	Documents submitted by Mallon Resources to the SEC raise questions in the minds of SEC personnel regarding Knight's relationship with HA and Mallon Resources during the company's 1993 audit.
June 21, 1994	The SEC begins a formal inquiry regarding the relationships between and among Knight, HA, and Mallon Resources during the company's 1993 audit.
July 5, 1994	HA informs the SEC that Knight left the firm on April 15 to begin his employment with Mallon Resources. HA also informs the SEC that Knight did not work on the 1993 Mallon Resources audit following his February 15 telephone conversation with George Mallon.
July 11, 1994	The SEC requests additional information from HA regarding Knight's involvement with the 1993 Mallon Resources audit. HA acknowledges that Knight actually began working for Mallon Resources on April 1 but that he continued to perform limited work for HA through April 15. Clarence Hein reveals that Knight participated, at Hein's request, in the March 29 conference call with the SEC.
July 15, 1994	Knight confirms to the SEC that he participated in the March 29 conference call.
July 20, 1994	The SEC notifies Mallon Resources that HA was not independent during its 1993 audit of the company. Thus, Mallon Resources must retain another accounting firm to audit the financial statements included in its 1993 10-K.
August 1, 1994	Knight, Hein, HA's legal counsel, and Mallon Resources' legal counsel meet with SEC representatives. At this meeting, the SEC is told that other than Knight's participation in the March 29 conference call he had no significant involvement in the preparation or audit of Mallon Resources' 1993 financial statements following February 15.
August 2, 1994	The SEC interviews the audit manager who replaced Knight on the 1993 Mallon Resources audit. This individual reveals that Knight prepared certain schedules for Mallon Resources in late March that were then audited by HA and included in the Mallon Resources workpaper file.
December 5, 1994	Mallon Resources submits an amended 10-K for 1993 to the SEC. That 10-K includes an unqualified audit opinion issued by Price Waterhouse.
July 2, 1996	The SEC issues an enforcement release that announces sanctions imposed on Duane Knight and Hein + Associates for their conduct during the 1993 audit of Mallon Resources.

On July 5, in response to an SEC inquiry, HA informed the agency that Knight had left the firm on April 15 to begin his employment with Mallon Resources. HA also informed the SEC that Knight did not work on the 1993 audit of Mallon Resources following his February 15 conversation with George Mallon. On July 11, in response to a second SEC inquiry, HA disclosed that Knight actually began employment with Mallon Resources on April 1. HA also disclosed that Knight continued to perform limited work for the accounting firm through April 15. This latter work reportedly did not involve the Mallon Resources engagement. Finally, HA revealed that Knight participated in the March 29 conference call at the request of Clarence Hein. Knight also independently confirmed to the SEC that he had been involved in the March 29 conference call.

On July 20, the SEC notified Mallon Resources that its 1993 10-K registration statement was deficient. The SEC ruled that HA was not independent of Mallon Resources and thus the company had not met its obligation to obtain an independent audit opinion on its 1993 financial statements. Following this ruling, Mallon Resources dismissed HA and retained Price Waterhouse as its new audit firm. In early December 1994, Mallon Resources submitted an amended 1993 10-K to the SEC. An unqualified audit opinion issued by Price Waterhouse accompanied the financial statements in that 10-K.

SEC representatives met with Knight, Hein, HA's legal counsel, and Mallon Resources' legal counsel on August 1. At that meeting, the SEC representatives were told that, other than the March 29 conference call, Knight had no substantive involvement with the preparation or audit of Mallon Resources' 1993 financial statements following February 15. The next day, August 2, the SEC interviewed the audit manager who replaced Knight on the Mallon Resources audit. This individual contradicted the information the SEC obtained the previous day by testifying that Knight prepared certain schedules "on behalf of" Mallon Resources during March 1994. This audit manager also revealed that HA had audited those schedules and included them in the client's 1993 audit workpaper file.

Without admitting or denying the facts of this case as reported by the SEC, Knight and HA agreed to sanctions imposed on them by the federal agency. Those sanctions included a public censure of Knight and his former employer. The SEC also required HA to retain an independent reviewer. This individual would study HA's quality controls for safeguarding the firm's independence on audit engagements and make recommendations for improvements in those controls. The settlement agreement between HA and the SEC obligated the accounting firm to implement the independent reviewer's recommendations.

In the enforcement release that announced the sanctions imposed on Knight and HA, the SEC stressed the critical importance of auditor independence to the investing and lending public. The federal agency noted that auditors "must avoid even an appearance of impropriety" to assure that the public has confidence in audited financial statements. Later in the enforcement release, the SEC explained its rationale for disqualifying the 1993 audit opinion that HA issued on Mallon Resources' financial statements.

> When an auditor accepts employment with an issuer, any work subsequently performed by the auditor taints the entire audit, regardless of the nature of that work. Knight's participation in the audit tainted the entire auditing process thereby requiring a re-audit of Mallon's financial statements.

QUESTIONS

1. Define auditor independence. Why is independence often referred to as the cornerstone of the auditing profession?

2. Identify the specific violations of the profession's ethical rules by the parties involved in this case. Relying on the timeline included in Exhibit 1, indicate when each of these violations occurred.

3. Do you agree with the SEC that Knight's conduct following his acceptance of the job offer from George Mallon "tainted" the entire 1993 audit of Mallon Resources? Why or why not?

4. Should auditors be allowed to become employees of their former clients? Defend your answer. What problems does this practice pose for (a) the auditing profession, (b) audit firms, and (c) audit clients?

SECTION SIX
PROFESSIONAL ROLES

CASE 6.1
LEIGH ANN WALKER, STAFF ACCOUNTANT

Leigh Ann Walker graduated from a major state university in the spring of 1989 with a bachelor's degree in accounting.[1] During her college career, Walker earned a 3.9 grade point average and participated in many extracurricular activities, including several student business organizations. Her closest friends often teased her about the busy schedule she maintained and the fact that she was, at times, a little too "intense." During the fall of 1988, Walker interviewed with several public accounting firms and large corporations and received six job offers. After considering those offers, she decided to accept an entry-level position on the auditing staff of a "Big Six" accounting firm. Walker was not sure whether she wanted to pursue a partnership position with her new employer. But, she believed that the training programs the firm provided and the breadth of experience she would receive from a wide array of client assignments would get her career off to a fast start.

Walker spent the first two weeks on her new job at her firm's regional audit staff training school. On returning to her local office in early June 1989, she was assigned to work on the audit of Saint Andrew's Hospital, a large sectarian hospital with a June 30 fiscal year-end. Walker's immediate superior on the Saint Andrew's engagement was Jackie Vaughn, a third-year senior. On her first day on the Saint Andrew's audit, Walker learned that she would audit the hospital's cash accounts and assist with accounts receivable. Walker was excited about her first client assignment and pleased that she would be working for Vaughn. Vaughn

1. This case is based upon a true set of facts; however, the names of the parties involved have been changed. An employee of a job placement firm provided much of the information incorporated in this case. This firm had been retained by the student identified in this case as Leigh Ann Walker.

SECTION SIX   PROFESSIONAL ROLES

had a reputation as a demanding supervisor who typically brought her engagements in under budget. She was also known for having an excellent rapport with her clients, a thorough knowledge of technical standards, and for being fair and straightforward with her subordinates.

Like many newly hired staff auditors, Walker was apprehensive about her new job. She understood the purpose of independent audits and was familiar with the work performed by auditors but doubted that her two-week staff-training seminar and one auditing course had adequately prepared her for her new work role. After being assigned to work under Vaughn's supervision, Walker was relieved. She sensed that although Vaughn was demanding, the senior would be patient and understanding with a new staff auditor. More importantly, she believed that she could learn a great deal from working closely with Vaughn. Walker resolved that she would work hard to impress Vaughn and had hopes that the senior would mentor her through the first few years of her career.

Early in Walker's second week on the Saint Andrew's engagement, Jackie Vaughn casually asked over lunch one day whether she had taken the CPA examination in May. After a brief pause, Walker replied that she had not but planned to study intensively for the exam during the next five months and then take it in November. Vaughn indicated that was a good strategy and offered to lend Walker a set of CPA review manuals—an offer Walker declined. In fact, Walker had returned to her home state during the first week of May and sat for the CPA exam. Fear of failure, or, rather, fear of admitting failure, caused Walker to decide not to tell her co-workers that she had taken the exam. She realized that most of her peers would not pass all sections of the exam on their first attempt. Nevertheless, Walker wanted to avoid the embarrassment of admitting throughout the remainder of her career that she had not been a "first timer."

Walker continued to work on the Saint Andrew's engagement throughout the summer. She completed the cash audit within budget, thoroughly documenting her work. Vaughn was pleased with Walker's work and frequently complimented and encouraged her. As the engagement was winding down in early August, Walker received her grades on the CPA exam in the mail one Friday evening. To her surprise, she had passed all parts of the exam. She hurriedly called Vaughn to tell her the good news and was disappointed by her senior's less-than-enthusiastic response. Oddly, Vaughn seemed irritated if not disturbed by Walker's call. Walker then recalled having earlier told Vaughn that she had not taken the exam in May. Walker immediately apologized and explained why she had chosen not to disclose that she had taken the exam. Following her explanation, Vaughn still seemed annoyed, so Walker decided to drop the subject and pursue it later in person.

The following week, Vaughn spent Monday through Wednesday with another client, while Walker and the other staff assigned to the Saint Andrew's engagement continued to wrap up the hospital audit. On Wednesday morning, Walker received a call from Don Roberts, the office managing partner and Saint Andrew's audit engagement partner. Roberts asked Walker to meet with him late that afternoon in his office. She assumed that Roberts simply wanted to congratulate her on passing the CPA exam.

The usually upbeat Roberts was somber when Walker stepped into his office that afternoon. After she was seated, Roberts informed her that he had spoken with Jackie Vaughn several times during the past few days and that he had consulted with the three other audit partners in the office regarding a situation involving Walker. Roberts explained that Vaughn was very concerned about Walker's having lied to her regarding the CPA exam. Vaughn told Roberts that she did not want Walker assigned to any future engagements of hers, since she could not trust Walker to be truthful. Vaughn had also suggested that Walker be dismissed from the firm because of the lack of integrity that she had demonstrated.

After a brief silence, Roberts told a stunned Walker that he and the other audit partners agreed with Vaughn. He informed Walker that she would be given 60 days to find another job. Roberts also told Walker that he and the other partners would not disclose that she had been "counseled out" of the firm if contacted by employers interested in hiring her.

QUESTIONS

1. In your opinion, did Vaughn overreact to Walker's admission that she had been untruthful regarding the CPA exam? If so, how would you have dealt with the situation if you had been in Vaughn's position? How would you have dealt with the situation if you had been in Roberts' position?

2. Vaughn obviously questioned Walker's personal integrity. Is it possible that one can fulfill the responsibilities of a professional role while lacking personal integrity? Why or why not?

CASE 6.2
BILL DeBurger,
In-Charge Accountant

"Bill, will you have that inventory memo done by this afternoon?"

"Yeah, Sam, it's coming along. I should have it done by five, or so."

"Make it three . . . or so. Okay, Bub?"

Bill responded with a smile and a nod. He had a good relationship with Sam Hakes, the partner supervising the audit of Marcelle Stores.[1]

Bill DeBurger was an in-charge accountant who had 18 months experience with his employer, a large national accounting firm. Bill's firm used the title "in-charge" for the employment position between staff accountant and audit senior. Other titles used by accounting firms for this position include "advanced staff" and "semisenior." Typically, Bill's firm promoted individuals to in-charge after one year. An additional one to two years experience and successful completion of the CPA exam were usually required before promotion to audit senior. The title "in-charge" was a misnomer, at least in Bill's mind. None of the in-charges he knew had ever been placed in-charge of an audit, even a small audit. Based upon Bill's experience, an in-charge was someone a senior or manager expected to work with little or no supervision. "Here's the audit program for payables. Go spend the next five weeks completing the 12 program steps . . . and don't bother me," seemed to be the prevailing attitude in making work assignments to in-charges.

As he turned back to the legal pad in front of him, Bill forced himself to think of Marcelle Stores' inventory—all $50 million of it. Bill's task was to summarize in a two-page memo 900 hours of work that he, two staff accountants, and five internal auditors had done over the past two months. Not included in the 900

---

1. A former public accountant who is now a college instructor provided the key background facts presented in this case. The names and certain other background facts have been changed.

hours was the time spent on eight inventory observations performed by other offices of Bill's firm. Marcelle Stores was a regional chain of 112 specialty stores that featured a broad range of products for do-it-yourself interior decorators. The company's most recent fiscal year had been a difficult one. A poor economy, increasing competition, and higher supplier prices had slashed Marcelle's profit to the bone over the past 12 months. The previous year, the company posted a profit of slightly less than $8 million; for the year just completed, the company's pre-audit net income hovered at an anemic $500,000.

Inventory was the focal point of each audit of Marcelle's financial statements. This year, inventory was doubly important. Any material overstatement discovered in the inventory account would convert a poor year profit-wise for Marcelle into a disastrous year in which the company posted its first-ever loss.

Facing Bill on the small table that served as his makeshift desk were two stacks of workpapers, each two feet tall. Those workpapers summarized the results of extensive price tests, inventory observation procedures, year-end cutoff tests, an analysis of the reserve for inventory obsolescence, and various other audit procedures. Bill's task was to assimilate all of this audit evidence into a conclusion regarding Marcelle's inventory. Bill realized that Sam Hakes expected that conclusion to include the key catch phrase "presented fairly, in all material respects, in conformity with generally accepted accounting principles."

As Bill attempted to outline the inventory memo, he gradually admitted to himself that he had no idea whether Marcelle's inventory dollar value was materially accurate. The workpaper summarizing the individual errors discovered in the inventory account reflected a net overstatement of only $72,000. That amount was not material even in reference to Marcelle's unusually small net income. However, Bill realized that the $72,000 figure was little better than a guess. The client's allowance for inventory obsolescence particularly troubled Bill. He had heard a rumor that Marcelle intended to discontinue two of the 14 sales departments in its stores. If that were true, the inventory in those departments would have to be sold at deep discounts. The collective dollar value of those two departments' inventory approached $6 million, while the client's allowance for inventory obsolescence had a year-end balance of only $225,000. Earlier in the audit, Bill had asked Sam about the rumored closing of the two departments. The typically easygoing partner had replied with a terse "Don't worry about it."

Bill always took his work assignments seriously and wanted to do a professional job in completing them. He believed that independent audits served an extremely important role in a free market economy. Bill was often annoyed that certain of his colleagues did not share his view. Some of his co-workers seemed to have an attitude of "Just get the work done." These individuals stressed form over substance: "Tic and tie, make the workpapers look good, and don't be too concerned with the results. A clean opinion is going to be issued no matter what you find."

Finally, Bill made a decision. He was not going to sign off on the inventory account regardless of the consequences. He did not know whether the inventory account balance was materially accurate, and he was not going to write a memo indicating otherwise. Moments later, Bill walked into the client office being used by Sam Hakes and closed the door behind him.

"What's up?" Sam asked as he flipped through a workpaper file.

"Sam, I've decided that I can't sign off on the inventory account," Bill blurted out.

"What?" was Sam's stunned, one-word reply.

Bill stalled for a few moments to bolster his courage as he fidgeted with his tie. "Well . . . like I said, I'm not signing off on the inventory account."

"Why?" By this point, a disturbing crimson shade had already engulfed Sam's ears and was creeping slowly across his face.

"Sam . . . I just don't think I can sign off. I mean, I'm just not sure whether the inventory number is right."

"You're not *sure*?" After a brief pause, Sam continued, this time pronouncing each of his words with a deliberate and sarcastic tone. "You mean to tell me that you spent almost 1,000 hours on that account, and you're not *sure* whether the general ledger number is right?"

"Well . . . yeah. Ya know, it's just tough to . . . to reach a conclusion, ya know, on an account that large."

Sam leaned back in his chair and cleared his throat before speaking. "Mr. DeBurger, I want you to go back into that room of yours and close the door. Then you sit down at that table and write a nice, neat, very precise and to-the-point inventory memo. And hear this: I'm not telling you what to include in that memo. But, you're going to write that memo, and you're going to have it on my desk in two hours. Understood?" Sam's face was entirely crimson as he completed his short speech.

"Uh, okay," Bill replied.

Bill returned to the small conference room that had served as his work area for the past two months. He sat in his chair and stared at the pictures of his two-year-old twins, Lesley and Kelly, which he had taped to the wall above the phone. After a few minutes, he picked up his pencil, leaned forward, and began outlining the inventory memo.

QUESTIONS

1. What conclusion do you believe Bill DeBurger reached in his inventory memo? Put yourself in his position. What conclusion would you have expressed in the inventory memo? Why?

2. Would you have dealt with your uncertainty regarding the inventory account differently than Bill did? For example, would you have used a different approach to raise the subject with Sam Hakes?

3. Evaluate Sam Hakes' response to Bill's statement that he was unable to sign off on the inventory account. In your view, did Sam deal with the situation appropriately? Was Sam's approach "professional"? Explain.

4. Is it appropriate for relatively inexperienced auditors to be assigned the primary responsibility for such critical accounts as Marcelle Stores' inventory? Explain.

CASE 6.3
SARAH RUSSELL, STAFF ACCOUNTANT

Sarah Russell grew up in a small town in the flatlands of western Kansas, where she was born.[1] In high school, she was homecoming queen, valedictorian of her graduating class, starting guard on her basketball team for two years, and a candy striper (volunteer) at the local hospital. Since her parents had attended the University of Kansas, Sarah was off to Lawrence at age 18. After spending her freshman year posting straight A's in 30 hours of college courses, Sarah settled on accounting as her major after seriously considering journalism, pre-law, and finance. Although Sarah had yet to take any courses in accounting, she had been impressed by a presentation that a female partner of a large accounting firm had made at a career fair. Sarah was excited by the challenges and opportunities presented by public accounting, as described by the partner. Here was a field in which she could learn a great deal in a short period of time and advance rapidly to a position where she had important responsibilities. Plus, public accounting provided a wide range of career paths. If she really enjoyed public accounting, she could pursue a partnership position with a large accounting firm. Then again, she might "hang out her shingle" in her hometown, see the world on the internal audit staff of a large corporation, or return to college after a couple of years of real-world experience to earn an MBA.

Sarah completed the tough accounting courses at the University of Kansas with only two small blemishes on her transcript—B's in individual and corporate taxation. During the fall semester of her senior year, Sarah accepted a position as

---

1. This case was authored by Carol Knapp, an associate professor at the University of Central Oklahoma. This case is based upon experiences related by a young woman previously employed by a large accounting firm. The names of the individuals involved in this case and other background facts, such as locations, have been changed.

a staff accountant with a Big Eight accounting firm. Sarah considered staying in her home state but decided instead to request an assignment in her new employer's Chicago office. She believed that exposure to big-city life would allow her to arrive at a more informed decision when it was time to make a long-term commitment to a career path and a lifestyle.

During her first year on the job, Sarah served on six audit engagements. Her clients included a pipeline company, a religious foundation, and a professional sports team. She worked hard on those assignments and earned impressive performance appraisals from each of her immediate supervisors. Somehow Sarah also squeezed a CPA review course into her hectic schedule that first year. And she was glad she did. She was among the few rookies in her large office to pass the CPA exam in one attempt. With that barrier out of the way, Sarah focused her energy on being promoted to audit senior as quickly as possible.

Several individuals were particularly supportive of Sarah during her first year, including R.J. Bell, an audit partner. Bell was 40 years old and had been a partner for eight years. According to the office grapevine, he was in line to become the new office managing partner within the next year or so. Bell tried to get to know the new staff accountants assigned to the audit staff and to help them adjust to their jobs in any way he could. Several times during the year, Bell invited small groups of staff accountants to his home to have dinner with him and his family. Recognizing that Sarah was new to Chicago, he made a special effort to include her in such social gatherings and to give her complimentary tickets to cultural and sporting events. When Sarah's old car from college died, Bell arranged for her to obtain a loan from a local bank. Sarah appreciated Bell's help and guidance. She considered the firm to be very lucky to have an audit partner so supportive of staff accountants.

Shortly after her first anniversary with the firm, Sarah received a telephone call from Bell at home one Saturday afternoon. At first, Sarah thought there must be a client emergency that required her assistance, but Bell did not bring up any client business during the conversation. Instead, he told Sarah that he had just called to chat. Sarah felt mildly uncomfortable with the situation but spoke with Bell for a few minutes before making up an excuse to get off the phone.

The following day, Sarah, an avid jogger, had just completed a four-mile run on her regular jogging trail in a city park when Bell pulled up as she was walking toward her car. "Hi, Sarah. How was your run?" Bell asked nonchalantly. "I was just driving by and thought you might like to get a Coke after your workout."

As Sarah approached Bell's car she felt awkward but tried to act natural, as if his unexpected appearance was only a coincidence. "Thanks, R.J. But, I really need to get back to my apartment. I've got several errands to run and phone calls to make."

"You sure? I'm buying."

"Yeah, I'd better get home."

"Well, okay."

Over the next several weeks, Bell made a concerted effort to develop a personal relationship with Sarah. Eventually, Bell, who was known for working long hours, was calling her nearly every evening from his office just "to chat." Once or twice per week, he invited her to get a drink with him after work. On a couple of occasions, she accepted, hoping that by doing so he would stop asking her. No such luck. Finally, she began avoiding him in the office and stopped answering her home phone when she thought it was him calling. Twice, Bell dropped by her apartment in the evening. Panic-stricken both times, Sarah refused to answer the door, hoping he would quickly decide that she was not home.

Bell's persistence caused Sarah to feel increasing levels of stress and powerlessness. She did not know what to do or to whom she could turn. She was reluctant to discuss the matter with her friends in the office since she did not want to start a rumor mill. Embarrassment prevented her from discussing the matter with her parents or other family members. Worst of all, Sarah began wondering whether she had somehow encouraged Bell's behavior. She racked her brain to recall each time that she had spoken or met with him during her first year on the job. She could not remember saying anything that could have been misconstrued by him. But, maybe she had inadvertently said something that had given him the wrong impression. Maybe he had mistaken the sense of respect and admiration she had for him as affection. Maybe she had asked him an inappropriate question. Maybe . . .

EPILOGUE

After more than six weeks of enduring Bell's advances, Sarah mustered the courage to make an appointment with him during office hours one Friday afternoon. When Sarah informed Bell that she wanted to keep their relationship on a strictly professional level, he failed to respond for several awkward moments. Finally, he remarked that Sarah must have misinterpreted his actions in recent weeks. He was simply trying to make her feel more comfortable with her job. "I go out of my way to be as friendly and sociable with as many members of the audit staff as I can." Bell then told Sarah that, given the circumstances, he would see to it that she was not assigned to any of his engagements in the future. After a few moments of silence, he tersely asked, "Is there anything else I can do for you, Miss Russell?" Sarah shook her head softly and then got up and left his office.

Sarah had no further contact or conversations with Bell following that Friday afternoon meeting in his office. A few months later, she decided to return to Kansas to be closer to her family. At last report, Sarah was the chief financial officer of a small manufacturing company headquartered in her home state.

QUESTIONS

1. In your opinion, how should Sarah have handled this matter? Identify the factors that Sarah should have considered in dealing with the situation. Also, identify the professional and personal responsibilities of Sarah, R.J. Bell, and other relevant individuals in this matter.
2. What were the costs and potential costs to Sarah's employer in this case? How should accounting firms attempt to prevent these types of situations from occurring? Assume that rather than speaking to Bell, Sarah told the office managing partner of the problem she faced. How should the office managing partner have responded to the situation?
3. This case took place in the early 1980s. Do you think this type of situation could occur now? Explain.

CASE 6.4
TOMMY O'CONNELL, AUDIT SENIOR

Tommy O'Connell had been a senior with a Big Five accounting firm for less than one month when he was assigned to the audit engagement for the Altamesa Manufacturing Company.[1] Tommy worked out of his firm's Fort Worth, Texas, office, while Altamesa was headquartered in Amarillo, the "capital" of the Texas Panhandle. The young senior realized that being assigned to the tough Altamesa engagement signaled that Jack Morrison, the Altamesa audit partner and the office managing partner, regarded his work highly. Serving as the audit senior on the Altamesa job would allow Tommy to become better acquainted with Morrison. Despite the challenges and opportunities posed by the new assignment, Tommy did not look forward to spending three months in Amarillo, a five-hour drive from Fort Worth. This would be his first assignment outside Fort Worth since his marriage six months earlier. He dreaded breaking the news to his wife, Suzie, who often complained about the long hours his job required.

Altamesa manufactured steel girders used in the construction and renovation of bridges in West Texas, New Mexico, Colorado, and Oklahoma. The company's business was very cyclical and linked closely to the funding available to municipalities in Altamesa's four-state market area. To learn more about the company and its personnel, Tommy arranged to have lunch with Emily Williams, the audit senior on the Altamesa job the two previous years. According to Emily, Altamesa's management took aggressive positions regarding year-end expense accruals and revenue recognition. The company used the percentage-of-completion method to recognize revenue, since its sales contracts extended over two to five

---

1. The facts of this case were reconstructed from an actual series of events. Names and certain background information have been changed to conceal the identities of the individuals involved in the case.

years. Emily recounted several disputes with the company's chief accountant regarding the estimated stage of completion of jobs in progress. In an effort to "front-load" as much of the profit on jobs as possible, the chief accountant typically insisted that jobs were further along than they actually were.

Speaking with Emily made Tommy even more apprehensive about tackling the Altamesa engagement. But, he realized that the job gave him an excellent chance to strengthen his fast-track image within his office. To reach his goal of being promoted to manager by his fifth year with the firm, Tommy needed to prove himself on difficult assignments such as the Altamesa engagement.

AN UNPLEASANT SURPRISE FOR TOMMY

It was late May, just two weeks before Tommy would be leaving for Amarillo to begin the Altamesa audit—the company had a June 30 fiscal year-end. Tommy, Jack Morrison, and an audit manager were having lunch at the Cattleman's Restaurant in the "Cowtown" district of north Fort Worth.

"Tommy, I've decided to send Carl with you out to Amarillo. Is that okay?" asked Jack Morrison.

"Uhh . . . sure, Jack. Yeah, that'll be fine," Tommy replied.

"Of all people," Tommy thought to himself, "he would send Carl Wilmeth to Amarillo with me." Carl was a staff accountant with only a few months' experience, having been hired in the middle of the just-completed busy season. Other than being auditors and approximately the same age, the two young men had little in common. Tommy was from Lockettville, a small town in rural West Texas, while Carl had been raised in the exclusive Highland Park community of north central Dallas. Texas Tech, a large state-supported university, was Tommy's alma mater. Carl had earned his accounting degree from a small private college in the East.

Tommy did not appreciate Carl's cocky attitude, and his lack of experience made him a questionable choice for the Altamesa engagement in Tommy's mind. As he tried to choke down the rest of his prime rib, Tommy recalled the complaints he had heard about Carl's job performance. Over the past three months, Carl had worked on two audits. In both cases, he had performed admirably—too admirably, in fact, coming in well under budget on his assigned tasks. On one engagement, Carl completed an assignment in less than 60 hours when the audit budget allotted 100 hours; the previous year, 110 hours had been required to complete that same task. Both seniors who had supervised Carl suspected that he had not completed all of his assigned audit procedures, although he signed off on those procedures on the audit program. The tasks assigned to Carl had been large-scale tests of transactions that involved checking invoices, receiving reports, purchase orders, and other documents for various attributes. Given the nature of the tests, the seniors would have had difficulty confirming their suspicions.

"BOSS" TOMMY

Six weeks later, in early July, the Altamesa audit was in full swing. Carl had just finished his third assigned task on the job, in record time, of course. "Boss, here's that disbursements file. Anything else you want me to do this afternoon? Since I'm way ahead of schedule, maybe I should take off and work on my tan out on the golf course."

"No, Carl. I think we have plenty to keep you busy right here." Tommy was agitated but he tried not to let it show. "Why don't you pull out the contracts file and then talk to Ed Grady in the sales office. Get copies of any new contracts or proposals over the past year and put them in the contracts file."

At this point, Tommy simply did not have time to review Carl's cash disbursements workpapers. He was too busy trying to untangle Altamesa's complex method of allocating overhead costs to jobs in process. Later that afternoon, he had an appointment to meet with the chief accountant and a production superintendent to discuss the status of a large job. Tommy and the chief accountant had already butted heads on two occasions regarding a job's stage of completion. Emily had been right: The chief accountant clearly meant to recognize profit on in-progress jobs as quickly as possible. With four decades of experience, Scrooge—a nickname Emily had pinned on the chief accountant—obviously considered the young auditors a nuisance and did not appreciate their probing questions. Each time Tommy asked him a question regarding an important issue, the chief accountant registered his disgust by pursing his lips and running his hand through his thinning hair. He then responded with a rambling, convoluted answer intended to confuse rather than inform.

To comprehend Altamesa's accounting decisions for its long-term contracts, Tommy spent several hours of nonchargeable time each night in his motel room flipping through copies of job order worksheets and contracts. Occasionally, he referred to prior-year workpapers, his firm's policy and procedures manual, and even his tattered cost accounting textbook from his college days. Carl spent most of his evenings in the motel's club being taught the Texas Two-step and Cotton-eyed Joe by several new friends he had acquired.

During July and August, Tommy and Carl worked 50 to 60 hours per week on the Altamesa engagement. Several times Tommy wondered to himself whether it was worthwhile to work so hard to earn recognition as a "superstar" senior. He was also increasingly concerned about the impact of his fast-track strategy on his marriage. When he tried to explain to Suzie that the long hours and travel would pay off when he eventually made partner, she was unimpressed. "Who cares if you make partner. I just want to spend more time with my husband," was her stock reply.

TO TELL OR NOT TO TELL

Finally, late August rolled around and the Altamesa job was almost complete. Jack Morrison had been in Amarillo for the past three days combing through the Altamesa workpapers. Nothing seemed to escape Morrison's eagle eye. Tommy had worked 12 hours per day since Morrison had arrived, tracking down missing invoices, checking on late confirmations, and tying up dozens of other loose ends. Carl was already back in Fort Worth, probably working on his golf swing. Morrison had allowed Carl to leave two days earlier after he finished clearing the review comments in Carl's files.

"Tommy, I have to admit that I was a little concerned about sending a light senior out to run this audit. But, by golly, you have done a great job." Morrison did not look up as he continued to sign off on the workpapers spread before him on Altamesa's conference table. "You know, this kid Carl does super work. I've never seen cleaner, more organized workpapers from a staff accountant."

Tommy grimaced as he sat next to Morrison at the conference table. "Yeah, right. They should look clean, since he didn't do half of what he signed off on," Tommy thought to himself. Here was his opportunity. For the past several weeks, Tommy had planned to sit down with Morrison and talk to him regarding Carl's job performance. But now he was reluctant to do so. How do you tell a partner that you suspect much of the work he is reviewing may not have been done? Besides, Tommy realized that as Carl's immediate supervisor, he was responsible for that work. Tommy knew that he was facing a no-win situation. He leaned back in his chair and remained silent, hoping that Morrison would hurry through the last few workpaper files so they could make it back to Fort Worth by midnight.

EPILOGUE

Tommy never informed Jack Morrison of his suspicions regarding Carl's work. Thankfully, no problems—of a legal nature—ever arose on the jobs to which Carl was assigned. After passing the CPA exam in his first attempt, Carl left the accounting firm and enrolled in a prestigious MBA program. At last report, Carl was a junior executive with a large investment banking firm. Tommy reached his goal of being promoted to audit manager within five years. One year later, he decided that he was not cut out to be a partner and resigned from the firm to accept a position in private industry.

QUESTIONS

1. Compare and contrast the professional roles of an audit senior and a staff accountant. In your analysis, consider the different responsibilities assigned to each role, the job-related stresses that individuals in the two roles face, and how each role contributes to the successful completion of an audit engagement. Which of these two roles is (a) more important and (b) more stressful? Defend your choices.
2. Assume that you are Tommy O'Connell and have learned that Carl Wilmeth will be working for you on the Altamesa audit engagement. Would you handle this situation any differently than Tommy did? Explain.
3. Again, assume that you are Tommy. Carl is badgering you for something to do midway through the Altamesa job. You suspect that he is not completing all of his assigned procedures, but at the time you are wrestling with an important and contentious accounting issue. What would you do at this point? What could you do to confirm your suspicions that Carl is not completing his assignments?
4. Now, assume that Jack Morrison is reviewing the Altamesa workpapers. To date, you (Tommy) have said nothing to Morrison about your suspicions regarding Carl. Do you have a professional responsibility to raise this matter now with Morrison? Explain.

5. Assume that at some point Tommy did discuss Carl's questionable work performance with Morrison. Tommy could not prove that Carl was failing to complete his assigned tasks. Tommy's only evidence in this regard was the fact that Carl had come in significantly under budget on every major task assigned to him over a period of several months. If you were Jack Morrison, how would you have handled this matter?

CASE 6.5
AVIS LOVE, STAFF ACCOUNTANT

"Oh no, not Store 51," Avis Love moaned under her breath. For the third time, Avis compared the dates listed in the cash receipts journal with the corresponding dates on the bank deposit slips. Avis shook her head softly and leaned back in her chair. There was no doubt in her mind now. Mo Rappele had definitely held open Store 51's cash receipts journal at the end of October.[1]

Avis Love was a staff accountant with the Atlanta office of a large, international accounting firm. Several months earlier, Avis had graduated with an accounting degree from the University of Alabama at Birmingham. Although she did not plan to pursue a career in public accounting, Avis had accepted one of the several offers she received from major accounting firms. The 22-year-old wanted to take a two- or three-year "vacation" from college, while at the same time accumulating a bankroll to finance three years of law school. Avis intended to practice law with a major firm for a few years and then return to her hometown in eastern Alabama and set up her own practice.

For the past few weeks, Avis had been assigned to the audit engagement for Lowell, Inc., a public company that operated nearly 100 retail sporting goods stores scattered across the South. Avis was just completing a year-end cash receipts cutoff test for a sample of 20 Lowell stores. The audit procedures she performed included preparing a list of the cash receipts reported in each of these stores' accounting records during the last five days of Lowell's fiscal year, which ended October 31. She had then obtained the relevant bank statements for each of the stores to determine whether the cash receipts had been deposited on a

---

1. The key facts of this case were developed from an actual series of events. Names, locations, and certain other background information have been changed to conceal the identities of the individuals involved in the case.

timely basis. For three of the stores in her sample, the deposit dates for the cash receipts ranged from three to seven days following the dates the receipts were entered in the cash receipts journal. The individual store managers had apparently backdated cash receipts for the first several days of the new fiscal year, making it appear that the receipts occurred in the fiscal year presently under audit by Avis's firm.

Avis quickly realized that the objective of the store managers was not to overstate their units' year-end cash balances. Instead, the managers intended to inflate their recorded sales. Before Avis began the cutoff test, Meredith Miller, the senior assigned to the Lowell audit and Avis's immediate superior, advised her that there was a higher than normal risk of cash receipts and sales cutoff errors for Lowell this year. The end of Lowell's fiscal year coincided with the end of a three-month sales promotion. This campaign to boost Lowell's sagging sales included bonuses for store managers who exceeded their quarterly sales quota. This was the first time that Lowell had run such a campaign and it was a modest success. Fourth quarter sales for the fiscal year just ended topped the corresponding sales for the previous fiscal year by 6 percent.

When Avis uncovered the first case of backdated cash receipts, she had felt a noticeable surge of excitement. In several months of tracing down invoices and receiving reports, ticking and tying, and performing other mundane tests, the young accountant had occasionally found isolated errors in client accounting records. But, this was different. This was fraud.

Avis had a much different reaction when she uncovered the second case of backdated cash receipts. She suddenly realized that the results of her cutoff test would have "real world" implications for several parties, principally the store managers involved in the scheme. During the past few months, Avis had visited six of Lowell's retail stores to perform various interim tests of controls and to observe physical inventory procedures. The typical store manager was in his or her early thirties, married, with one or two small children. Because Lowell's employees were underpaid, the stores were chronically understaffed, meaning that the store managers worked extremely long hours to earn their modest salaries.

No doubt, the store managers who backdated sales to increase their bonuses would be fired immediately. Clay Shamblin, Lowell's chief executive officer (CEO), was a hard-nosed businessman known for his punctuality, honesty, and work ethic. Shamblin exhibited little patience with subordinates who did not display those same traits.

When Avis came to the last store in her sample, she had hesitated. She realized that Mo Rappele managed Store 51. Three weeks earlier, Avis had spent a long Saturday afternoon observing the physical inventory at Store 51 on the outskirts of Atlanta. Although the Lowell store managers were generally courteous and accommodating, Mo had gone out of his way to help Avis complete her tasks. Mo allowed Avis to use his own desk in the store's cramped office, shared a pizza with her during an afternoon break, and introduced her to his wife and two small children who dropped by the store during the afternoon.

"Mo, what a stupid thing to do," Avis thought to herself after reviewing the workpapers for the cutoff tests a final time. "And for just a few extra dollars." Mo had apparently backdated cash receipts for only the first two days of the new year. According to Avis's calculations, the backdated sales increased Mo's year-end bonus by slightly more than $100. From the standpoint of Lowell, Inc., the backdated sales for Mo's store clearly had an immaterial impact on the company's operating results for the year just ended.

After putting away the workpapers for the cutoff test, a thought dawned on Avis. The Lowell audit program required her to perform cash receipts cutoff tests for 20 stores . . . any 20 stores she selected. Why not just drop Store 51 from her sample and replace it with Store 52 or 53 or whatever?

EPILOGUE

Avis brooded over the results of her cutoff test the remainder of that day at work and most of that evening. The following day, she gave the workpaper file to Meredith Miller. Avis reluctantly told Meredith about the backdated cash receipts and sales she had discovered in three stores: Store 12, Store 24, and Store 51. Meredith congratulated Avis on her thorough work and told her that Clay Shamblin would be very interested in her findings.

A few days later, Shamblin called Avis into his office and warmly thanked her for uncovering the backdated sales. The CEO told her that the company's internal auditors tested the year-end cash receipts and sales cutoff for the remaining 72 stores and identified seven additional store managers who had tampered with their stores' accounting records. As Avis was leaving the CEO's office, he thanked her once more and assured her that the store managers involved in the scam had been fired and would "be looking for a new line of work . . . in another part of the country."

QUESTIONS

1. Identify the parties potentially affected by the outcome of the ethical dilemma faced by Avis Love. What obligation, if any, did Avis have to each of these parties?

2. Would it have been appropriate for Avis to substitute another store for Store 51 after she discovered the cutoff errors in that store's accounting records? Defend your answer.

3. Does the *AICPA Code of Professional Conduct* prohibit auditors from developing friendships with client personnel? If not, what measures can auditors take to prevent such friendships from interfering with the performance of their professional responsibilities?

4. Identify the key audit objectives associated with year-end cash receipts and sales cutoff tests.

5. What method would you have recommended that Avis or her colleagues use in assessing whether the cutoff errors she discovered had a material impact on Lowell's year-end financial statements? Identify the factors or benchmarks that should have been considered in making this assessment.

CASE 6.6
CHARLES TOLLISON,
AUDIT MANAGER

"No, that's okay, Bea. I'll write that memo this weekend and send it to Mr. Fielder. You go on home."[1]

"Are your sure, Chuck? I don't mind staying a while longer."

"Thanks, Bea, but you've already put in too much overtime this week."

After he sent his secretary home, Charles Tollison spent several minutes shuffling through the audit workpapers and correspondence stacked on his desk trying to decide what work he would take home over the weekend. Finally, only one decision remained. Tollison couldn't decide whether to take the inventory file with him. Compulsive by nature, Tollison knew that if he took the inventory file home, he would have to complete his review of that file, which would increase his weekend workload from six hours to more than 12 hours. As he stewed over his decision, Tollison stepped to the window of his office and idly watched the rush hour traffic on the downtown streets several stories below.

It was nearly six-thirty on a Friday evening in early August. Charles Tollison, an audit manager for a large international accounting firm, had suffered through a tough week. His largest audit client was negotiating to buy a smaller competitor. For the past two months, Tollison had supervised the fieldwork on an intensive acquisition audit of the competitor's accounting records. The client's CEO suspected that the competitor's executives had embellished their firm's financial data in anticipation of the proposed buyout. Since the client was overextending itself financially to acquire the other firm, the CEO wanted to be sure that firm's financial data were reliable. The CEO's principal concern was the valuation of the competitor's inventory, which accounted for 45 percent of its total assets.

---

1. This case was developed from information obtained from a CPA employed for many years with a large international accounting firm.

The client's CEO had requested that Tollison be assigned to the acquisition audit because she respected Tollison and the quality of his work. Normally, an audit manager spends little time "in the trenches" supervising day-to-day audit procedures. However, because of the nature of this engagement, Tollison had felt it necessary to spend week after week working elbow to elbow with his subordinates for 10 hours per day, six and seven days per week, poring over the accounting records of the takeover candidate.

As Tollison stared at the gridlocked streets below, he was very relieved that the acquisition audit was almost complete. After he tied up a few loose ends in the inventory file, he would turn the workpapers over to the audit engagement partner for a final review.

Tollison's tough week had been highlighted by several contentious meetings with client personnel, a missed birthday party for his eight-year-old daughter, and an early breakfast Thursday morning with his office managing partner, Walker Linton. Over that breakfast, Linton notified Tollison that he had been passed over for promotion to partner—for the second year in a row. The news had been difficult for Tollison to accept. For more than 13 years, Tollison had been a hardworking and dedicated employee of the large accounting firm. He had never turned down a difficult assignment, never complained about the long hours his work required, and made countless personal sacrifices, the most recent being the missed birthday party. After informing Tollison of the bad news, Linton had encouraged him to stay with the firm. Linton promised that the following year he would vigorously campaign for Tollison's promotion including "calling in all favors" owed to him by partners in other offices. Despite the promise, Tollison realized that he had only a minimal chance of being promoted to partner the following year. Very seldom were two-time "losers" ticketed for promotion by the firm's Partner Selection Committee.

Although he had been hoping for the best, Tollison had not expected a favorable report from the Partner Selection Committee. In recent weeks, he had gradually admitted to himself that he simply did not have the profile for which the committee was searching. Tollison was not a rainmaker like his friend and fellow audit manager, Craig Allen, whose name appeared on the roster of new partners to be formally announced the following week. Allen was a member of several important civic organizations and had a network of well-connected friends at the local country club. These connections had served Allen well, allowing him to steer several new clients to the firm in recent years.

Instead of a rainmaker, Tollison was a technician. If someone in the office had a difficult accounting or auditing issue to resolve, that individual went first to Tollison, not to one of the office's six audit partners. When a new client posed complex technical issues, the audit engagement partner nearly always requested that Tollison be assigned to the job. One reason Tollison was a perfect choice for difficult engagements was that he "micro-managed" his jobs, that is, he insisted on being involved in every aspect of an audit. Tollison's management style often resulted in him "busting" time budgets for audits, although he seldom missed an important deadline. To avoid missing deadlines when a job was nearing completion, Tollison and the subordinates assigned to his engagements would work excessive overtime, including long weekend stints.

Finally, Tollison turned away from his window and slumped into his chair. As he sat there, he tried to drive away the bitterness that he was feeling. "If Jim hadn't left the firm, maybe I wouldn't be in this predicament," Tollison thought to himself. Three years earlier, Jim Berkey, an audit partner and Tollison's closest friend within the firm, had resigned to become the chief financial officer of a large client. Following Berkey's resignation, Tollison had no one within the firm to sponsor him through the tedious and political partner selection process. Instead, Tollison had been "lost in the shuffle" with the dozens of other hardworking, technically-inclined audit managers within the firm who aspired to a partnership position.

Near the end of breakfast Thursday morning, Walker Linton had mentioned to Tollison the possibility that he could remain with the firm in a senior manager position. In recent years, Tollison's firm had relaxed its "up or out" promotion policy. Tollison wasn't sure he wanted to remain with the firm as a manager with no possibility of being promoted to partner. Granted, there were clearly advantages associated with becoming a permanent senior manager. For example, no equity interest in the firm meant not absorbing any portion of future litigation losses suffered by the firm. On the other hand, accepting an appointment as a permanent senior manager in Tollison's mind seemed equivalent to having "career failure" stenciled on his office door.

Ten minutes till seven, time to leave. Tollison left the inventory file lying on his desk as he closed his bulging briefcase and then stepped toward the door of his office. After flipping off the light switch, Tollison paused momentarily. He then grudgingly turned and stepped back to his desk, picked up the inventory file, and tucked it under his arm.

QUESTIONS

1. Do you believe Charles Tollison was qualified for a partnership position with his firm? Explain.

2. Did Tollison's firm treat him "fairly"? Why or why not?

3. Identify the criteria you believe large international accounting firms should use when evaluating individuals for promotion to partner. In your opinion, which of these criteria should be most heavily weighted by these firms? Should smaller accounting firms establish different criteria for evaluating individuals for promotion to partner? Explain.

4. Discuss the advantages and disadvantages of the "up or out" promotion policy followed by many accounting firms.

SECTION SEVEN
PROFESSIONAL ISSUES

CASE 7.1
HOPKINS V. PRICE WATERHOUSE

In 1978, at the age of 34, Ann Hopkins faced a dilemma that a growing number of professional women are being forced to confront. Hopkins had to make a difficult choice involving her family and her career. Although comfortable with her position at Touche Ross & Company, for whom she had worked several years, Hopkins realized that either she or her husband, also a Touche Ross employee, had to leave the firm because of its nepotism rules. Otherwise, neither would be considered for promotion to partner. Hopkins chose to make the personal sacrifice. She resigned from Touche Ross and within a few days accepted a position in the consulting division of Price Waterhouse.

Four years later, Hopkins was nominated for promotion to partner with Price Waterhouse, the oldest and, arguably, most prestigious of the Big Eight public accounting firms. Eighty-eight individuals were nominated for promotion to partner that year with Price Waterhouse. Hopkins, a senior manager in the firm's Washington, D.C., office, was the only woman in that group. Hopkins stood out from the other nominees in another respect. She had generated the most business for Price Waterhouse of all the partner candidates. Over the previous four years, clients obtained by Hopkins yielded $40 million of revenues for Price Waterhouse. Because client development skills generally rank as the most important criterion in partnership promotion decisions, Hopkins appeared to be a shoo-in for promotion.

Strengthening Hopkins' case even more was the unanimous and strong backing her nomination received from the seven partners in the Washington, D.C., office. The extent of home office support for a candidate's nomination was another key factor Price Waterhouse considered in evaluating individuals for promotion to partner.

Much to her surprise, Hopkins was not awarded a partnership position. Instead, the senior manager was told that she would be considered for promotion the following year. A few months later, Hopkins was surprised again when her office managing partner informed her that she was no longer considered a viable candidate for promotion to partner. The firm's top executives did invite her to remain with Price Waterhouse in a nonpartner capacity. Disenchanted and somewhat bitter, Hopkins resigned from Price Waterhouse in January 1984 and accepted a position with the World Bank in Washington, D.C. Eventually, nagging uncertainty regarding her failure to make partner caused Hopkins to file a civil lawsuit against Price Waterhouse.

PRIOR CRITICISM OF PERSONNEL PRACTICES OF BIG EIGHT FIRMS

The lawsuit Ann Hopkins filed against Price Waterhouse drew attention to an issue simmering within the public accounting profession for years. During a 1976 investigation of the profession by a U.S. Senate subcommittee, several parties charged that Big Eight firms' personnel practices discriminated against females and minorities.[1] At one point during its hearings, the Senate subcommittee requested each of the Big Eight firms to disclose the average compensation of their partners and the number of females and nonwhite males in their partner ranks. This request evoked uncooperative responses from several of the Big Eight firms. Exhibit 1 presents two of these responses. Exhibit 2 (page 344) contains a letter that Senator Lee Metcalf, chairman of the investigative subcommittee, wrote to Ernst & Ernst after that firm questioned the Senate's authority to investigate the personnel practices of private partnerships. Eventually, six of the Big Eight firms provided the requested information regarding the number of females and minority males among their partners. Collectively, these firms had seven female partners and four partners who were African-American males out of a total of more than 3,500 partners.

The criticism leveled at the personnel practices of Big Eight firms by the 1976 Senate investigation spurred academic researchers and investigative reporters to begin monitoring the progress of women and minorities within Big Eight firms.[2] By the late 1980s, when the Hopkins suit against Price Waterhouse was working its way through the courts, neither group had made significant inroads into the top hierarchy of the Big Eight firms. For instance, in 1988, women held approximately 3.5 percent of the partnership positions with Big Eight firms, although these firms had been hiring women in considerable numbers since the mid-1970s.[3]

---

1. U.S. Congress, Senate Subcommittee on Reports, Accounting and Management of the Committee on Government Operations, *The Accounting Establishment* (Washington, D.C.: U.S. Government Printing Office, 1977).

2. See the following sources: D. Rankin, "More Women Moving into Public Accounting, but Few to the Top," *The New York Times*, 17 December 1977, 18; E. Berg, "The Big Eight: Still a Male Bastion," *The New York Times*, 12 July 1988, D1; K. Rankin, "Minorities Seek Truce with Big 8," *Accounting Today*, 11 September 1989, 6.

3. Berg, "The Big Eight," D1; "Women Comprise Half of 1986-87 Graduates," *Public Accounting Report*, 1 February 1988, 7.

EXHIBIT 1
Selected Responses to U.S. Senate Request for Information Regarding Big Eight Firms' Personnel Practices

June 11, 1976

The Honorable Lee Metcalf, Chairman
Subcommittee on Reports, Accounting,
    and Management
Committee on Government Operations
United States Senate
Washington, D.C. 20510

Dear Senator Metcalf:

I acknowledge receipt of your letter of June 7, 1976. As you know, this firm has responded and in considerable detail to the Committee's earlier requests. However, we consider the information sought in this letter to exceed the scope of the Committee's investigative authority. Moreover, the information sought includes data proprietary to this firm and its individual members. As a result, we respectfully decline to provide the requested data.

Very truly yours,

Russell E. Palmer
Managing Partner and
Chief Executive Officer
Touche Ross & Company

June 30, 1976

The Honorable Lee Metcalf, Chairman
Subcommittee on Reports, Accounting,
    and Management
United States Senate
Washington, D.C. 20510

Dear Senator Metcalf:

This will acknowledge your letter of June 7 which was received during the period I was away from my office.

We find it difficult to understand why the compensation of our partners is a matter of valid interest to a subcommittee of the Committee on Government Operations. We are even more perplexed with the suggestion that this could be a matter of importance in an assessment of our professional performance.

Along with these reservations we also confess to a deep-rooted belief that members of a private partnership have a right to maintain privacy over such matters if they wish to do so. Therefore, absent an understanding of its justification, we respectfully decline to furnish the compensation information you have requested.

Two partners (.5% of the total number of our partners) are female. None of our partners are blacks.

Yours very truly,

William S. Kanaga
Arthur Young & Company

Continued concern regarding the progress of women and minorities within Big Eight firms focused considerable attention on Ann Hopkins' civil suit against Price Waterhouse. Although the Hopkins case provides only anecdotal evidence regarding the personnel practices of large, international accounting firms, it is

EXHIBIT 2
U.S. Senate Response to Ernst & Ernst's Reluctance to Provide Requested Personnel Information

June 28, 1976

Mr. R.T. Baker
Managing Partner
Ernst & Ernst
Union Commerce Building
Cleveland, Ohio 64115

Dear Mr. Baker:

In your letter of June 24, you question the authority of this subcommittee to request information from your firm on various subjects. You note that our authority is primarily directed to the accounting practices of Federal departments and agencies.

Our requests for information from your firm are based on the unusual and substantial relationship which has developed between certain Federal agencies and influential segments of the accounting profession. This relationship has led to official recognition by Federal agencies of judgments on binding standards which have been made entirely within the private sector. The Securities and Exchange Commission has even formalized its acceptance of private decision-making through Accounting Series Release 150. The Moss amendment to the Energy Policy and Conservation Act also contemplates Federal recognition of private decisions on the manner of uniform accounting to be developed for the oil and gas industry.

The substantial reliance by Federal agencies upon decisions made in the private sector represents a significant delegation of the statutory authority vested in those agencies. This arrangement involves important decisions affecting the policies of the Federal government and other segments of our society.

Decisions made by Federal agencies are subject to review by Congress and the public. Much progress has been made both in Congress and the Federal government in opening the processes of decision-making to public scrutiny. The public has a right to know the identity and interests of those who act under the public's authority to determine the directions which this nation shall take.

When public decision-making authority is delegated to the private sector, the public has an even greater interest in knowing who is directing important national policies. As you are well aware, little information is available to Congress or the public concerning the activities of accounting firms. That is why it is necessary for this subcommittee to request information on various activities of accounting firms.

Your firm is substantially involved in the private decision-making process which develops accounting standards that are recognized by Federal agencies. The information which has so far been requested by this subcommittee is only a small fraction of the information that is publicly available regarding the identity and interests of Federal officials, or even major corporate officials. Yet, the decision-making area in which your firm is involved influences public policy as much or more than do many companies for which the requested information is publicly available.

This subcommittee has a responsibility to ensure that Federal accounting practices are responsive to the public interest. We must be informed on matters which are relevant to Federal accounting practices. That is why your firm has been requested to provide information to this subcommittee.

Very truly yours,

Lee Metcalf, Chairman
Subcommittee on Reports,
    Accounting, and Management

noteworthy for several reasons. First, the case yielded revealing insights into the partnership selection process employed by large accounting firms. Second, the case pointed to the need to rid performance appraisal methods of gender-based criteria in all disciplines, including professional fields. Finally, *Hopkins v. Price Waterhouse* stimulated discussion of measures that professional firms could take to facilitate the career success of their female employees.

PRICE WATERHOUSE'S CONSIDERATION OF ANN HOPKINS FOR PROMOTION TO PARTNER

During the 1980s, the partners of Price Waterhouse nominated each year senior managers whom they considered to be viable partner candidates. Price Waterhouse's admissions committee collected these nominations and then provided a list of the nominees to each partner in the firm. The admissions committee invited partners to provide either a "long form" or "short form" evaluation of the individual candidates. Typically, a partner well acquainted with a nominee provided a long form evaluation. Partners having had little or no contact with a given nominee submitted a short form evaluation or no evaluation at all. Both forms required the partners to assess the partnership potential of the nominees on several scaled dimensions, including client development abilities, interpersonal skills, and technical expertise. After responding to the scaled items, the partners indicated whether the given individual should be promoted, whether he or she should be denied promotion, or whether the promotion decision should be deferred for one or more years. The partners also provided a brief written explanation documenting the key reasons for their overall recommendation for each candidate.

After studying and summarizing the evaluations, the admissions committee prepared three lists of candidates: those recommended for admission to partnership, those not recommended for promotion, and a final list of candidates who received a "hold" recommendation. These latter candidates typically included individuals having partner potential but also one or more weaknesses that needed to be remedied before they were considered again for promotion. The admissions committee submitted its recommendations to the firm's policy board, which reviewed them and selected the final slate of candidates to be voted on by the entire partnership.[4]

The admissions committee received 32 evaluation forms commenting on Ann Hopkins' nomination for partner. Thirteen partners submitted positive recommendations, eight recommended she not be promoted, three suggested she be held over for consideration the following year, and eight did not include a recommendation in their evaluation forms. The most common criticism of Hopkins by partners who recommended she not be promoted was that she had poor interpersonal skills and an abrasive personality. These individuals criticized her for being too demanding of her subordinates, for using profanity, and for being generally harsh and overly aggressive. Two partners used gender-specific terms when commenting on Hopkins. One partner referred to her as "macho," while another observed that "she may have overcompensated for being a woman."[5]

---

4. This description of Price Waterhouse's partnership selection process was summarized from information presented in the 1985 court opinion *Hopkins v. Price Waterhouse*, 618 F. Supp. 1109 (D.C.D.C. 1985).

5. This and all subsequent quotations were taken from *Hopkins v. Price Waterhouse*.

After reviewing Hopkins' evaluations, the admissions committee recommended that she be held over for consideration, a recommendation accepted by the policy board. The admissions committee apparently decided that her interpersonal skills needed to be strengthened to allow her to function effectively as a partner. To improve her chances of promotion the following year, Hopkins agreed to undergo a "Quality Control Review" to identify specific aspects of her job-related skills needing improvement. Several partners indicated they would give her opportunities to demonstrate that she was remedying the deficiencies in her interpersonal skills. These partners never followed through on their commitments. Four months after Hopkins completed the Quality Control Review, her office managing partner informed her that she would not be nominated for partner that year. Hopkins was also told that she probably would never be considered again for promotion to partner.

Ann Hopkins' Civil Suit against Price Waterhouse

Ann Hopkins learned of the "hold" recommendation given to her nomination for partner in mid-1983. At that time, her office managing partner discussed with her some of the reservations partners expressed regarding her nomination. In particular, he told Hopkins that several partners believed her appearance and interpersonal manner were overtly masculine and that these traits caused her to be less appealing as a partner candidate. The office managing partner suggested that she could improve her chances for promotion if she would "walk more femininely, wear make-up, have her hair styled, and wear jewelry." Following her resignation from Price Waterhouse, Hopkins recalled these suggestions and began to question why she was denied promotion to partner. She speculated that Price Waterhouse denied her promotion not because she was unqualified to be a partner with the firm but, rather, because existing partners perceived she was unqualified to be a *female* partner. Eventually, Hopkins concluded that Price Waterhouse applied different standards for promoting females and males to partner. This issue became the focal point of the civil trial in the *Hopkins v. Price Waterhouse* case. The specific allegations that Hopkins brought against Price Waterhouse follow:

1. The criticisms of her interpersonal skills were fabricated by the Price Waterhouse partners.
2. Even if the criticisms of her interpersonal skills were valid, Price Waterhouse had promoted male candidates to partner having similar deficiencies in their interpersonal skills.
3. The criticisms of her interpersonal skills resulted from sexual stereotyping by Price Waterhouse partners.
4. Price Waterhouse's partnership selection process did not discount the sexually discriminatory comments made regarding her candidacy.

The judge who presided over the civil trial dismissed Hopkins' first allegation. According to the judge, the defense counsel clearly proved that Hopkins did have poor interpersonal skills, particularly when dealing with subordinates. The judge ruled that Price Waterhouse was well within its rights to deny an individual a partnership position who did not possess adequate interpersonal skills. However, the judge then pointed to court testimony documenting that Price Waterhouse previously promoted to partner male candidates described as "crude, abrasive, and overbearing." These comments were very similar to criticisms of Hopkins' interpersonal skills made during the partner selection process. A review of the firm's past promotion decisions also revealed that two earlier female partner candidates may have been denied admission to the partnership for reasons identical to those that cost Hopkins her promotion. Evaluation comments made for those candidates criticized them for acting like "Ma Barker" or for trying to be "one of the boys."

An earlier legal case established the precedent that an employer who evaluates a woman with an aggressive or abrasive personality differently than a man with similar personality traits is guilty of sex discrimination. After reviewing all of the evidence presented during the trial, the judge ruled that Price Waterhouse had evaluated Hopkins as a candidate for becoming a female partner rather than simply a partner with the firm.

> [Female] candidates were viewed favorably if partners believed they maintained their femininity while becoming effective professional managers. To be identified as a "women's liber" was regarded as a negative comment. Nothing was done to discourage sexually biased evaluations. One partner repeatedly commented that he could not consider any woman seriously as a partnership candidate and believed that women were not capable of functioning as senior managers—yet the firm took no action to discourage his comments and recorded his vote in the overall summary of the evaluations.

Although Hopkins was found to have been the victim of sex discrimination, the judge deemed that the discrimination was not overt or intentional. In fact, Hopkins freely admitted during the trial that she never perceived she was being discriminated against because of her gender while employed with Price Waterhouse. Instead, sexually discriminatory attitudes latent within the culture of Price Waterhouse victimized Hopkins' candidacy for partner. That is, the partners who made the sexually biased remarks regarding Hopkins were unaware that they evaluated her unfairly relative to male candidates for partner. Nevertheless, the judge ruled that Price Waterhouse perpetuated an evaluation system that allowed sexual stereotypes to undermine the promotion opportunities of female employees.

> There is no direct evidence of any determined purpose to maliciously discriminate against women but plaintiff appears to have been a victim of "omissive and subtle" discriminations created by a system that made evaluations based on "outmoded" attitudes. . . . Price Waterhouse should have been aware that women being evaluated by male partners might well be victims of discriminatory stereotypes. Yet the firm made no efforts . . . to discourage comments tainted by sexism or to determine whether they were influenced by stereotypes.

EPILOGUE

In May 1990, six years after Ann Hopkins filed suit against Price Waterhouse, a federal judge ordered the firm to pay her $400,000 of compensatory damages. More important, the judge ordered the CPA firm to offer Hopkins a partnership position. During a party to celebrate the court decision, Hopkins maintained that she had no reservations joining a firm that had unfairly rejected her for partnership seven years earlier. She also joked with her male co-workers at the World Bank regarding several less-than-complimentary remarks made regarding her during the trial. In particular, she questioned the assertion of one Price Waterhouse partner that she needed to enroll in charm school. Moments later, Hopkins took a long and noisy slug of champagne—straight from the bottle.

Growing numbers of women have obtained partnership positions with the large international accounting firms since the resolution of the *Hopkins* case. But, women still remain significantly underrepresented in the partnership ranks of those firms. By 1998, only one Big Five accounting firm reported that more than 10 percent of its partners were women.[6] That firm, Deloitte & Touche, had 212 women partners, representing 11 percent of its total partners. Fifteen years earlier, less than 1 percent of Deloitte's partners were women. Deloitte may have more women partners than its competitors because of a program the firm established in 1993 entitled Men and Women as Colleagues. Increasing the retention of female employees ranks as the primary objective of this program. Specific policies implemented by Deloitte in this program include career mentoring and flex-time work scheduling. Deloitte's ambitious goal is to have approximately equal numbers of men and women at all employment ranks within the next decade.

Since the early 1990s, a committee of the AICPA has closely tracked and reported upon the progress of women in accounting firms of all sizes, ranging from the Big Five firms to small local firms. That committee, the Women and Family Issues Executive Committee (WFIEC), periodically performs a nationwide survey to collect data regarding women in public accounting. In 1999, two professors who have served on the WFIEC, Professor Mary Doucet and Professor Karen Hooks, reported the results of the most recent WFIEC survey.[7] The survey results generally confirm that the proportion of women occupying the upper ranks of accounting firms of all sizes is growing steadily . . . but slowly.

Professors Doucet and Hooks urge women to be proactive in managing their careers. The two professors recommend that women public accountants adopt the following five-point strategy to move forward and *upward* in their careers.

1. Act like an executive from Day One of your employment.
2. Find a mentor.
3. When barriers to promotion or career success arise, immediately discuss the relevant issues or problems with the appropriate superiors.
4. Don't adopt a negative attitude. Expect to be promoted, expect to succeed.
5. Be prepared to negotiate when promotion and other employment opportunities arise. Make your case in a professional but forceful manner.

QUESTIONS

1. Do public accounting firms have a responsibility to facilitate the career success of female employees? Why or why not? In addition to the measures mentioned

6. M. Groves, "Some Firms Look Through Glass Ceiling to See Ways of Tapping Women's Talent," *Los Angeles Times*, 12 July 1998, D5.

7. M. Doucet and K. Hooks, "Toward an Equal Future," *Journal of Accountancy*, June 1999, 71–76.

in this case, identify policies and strategies accounting firms could implement to increase the retention rate of female employees.

2. In business circles, one frequently hears references to the "old boy network." Many women in professional firms complain that their gender precludes them from becoming a member of the old boy network within their firm. Define, in your own terms, what is meant by the phrase *old boy network*. Should professional firms attempt to break down these networks?

3. Suppose that an audit client objects to a given auditor because of his or her gender or race. Identify the alternative courses of action the auditor's employer should consider taking in such a case. Which of these alternatives do you believe the accounting firm should take? Defend your answer.

4. The nepotism rules of many professional firms pose a major inconvenience for married couples who work for, or would like to work for, these firms. Discuss the costs and benefits of these rules in a public accounting setting. In practice, do you believe these rules are equally fair (or unfair) to both sexes?

5. Several of the large public accounting firms asked to provide information to the U.S. Senate during the 1976 investigation of the accounting profession claimed that the request was an invasion of their privacy. Do you agree or disagree with these firms' view? Why? Even if such disclosures are considered an invasion of privacy, are they justified from a public interest perspective?

CASE 7.2
WHEN AUDITORS
BECOME LOBBYISTS

In the early 1990s, an avalanche of controversy blindsided the Financial Accounting Standards Board (FASB). This controversy stemmed from a proposed accounting rule calling for corporations to recognize compensation expense for certain stock options when they were granted to executives and employees. Shortly after the FASB circulated the proposal in an exposure draft, hundreds of letters flooded the rule-making body. Most of those letters sharply criticized the proposed change in accounting for stock options.

Even Congress and the President of the United States voiced opinions on the proposed stock option accounting rule. In early 1994, the Senate passed a resolution by a vote of 88-9 urging the FASB to drop the proposed standard. Two senators who seldom agree on important policy matters joined together to lead the debate against the proposal. Senator Barbara Boxer, a liberal Democrat from California, criticized the FASB for "pursuing an abstract theory" that will "damage the growth potential of many companies."[1] On the other side of the aisle, Senator Phil Gramm, a staunch Republican from Texas, bluntly observed, "The bottom line here is that this is a stupid proposal."[2] President Clinton expressed his concern that the stock option accounting standard might "undermine the competitiveness" of many of the nation's most important industries.[3]

By far, the most vocal critics of the FASB's stock option proposal were business executives of large public companies—the individuals who stood to lose the most

---

1. K. Rankin, "Congress Rips FASB on Stock Options," *Accounting Today*, 1 November 1993, 1, 33.

2. *Ibid.*

3. C. Harlan, "Accounting Proposal Stirs Unusual Uproar in Executive Suites," *The Wall Street Journal*, 7 March 1994, A1, A8.

if the standard were adopted. The 200-member Business Roundtable, composed of chief executive officers of large public companies, waged a public relations war against the FASB's efforts to overhaul accounting for stock options. These individuals realized that the new standard would likely cause many companies to stop issuing stock options, which for many years had been a lucrative source of income for corporate executives. The FASB's proposal so incensed the top executive of one computer firm that he suggested disbanding the rule-making body.

> The arrogant, out-of-touch FASB bureaucracy should simply close its doors and stop damaging corporate America for the sake of accounting principles.[4]

Numerous editorials in the business press criticized the proposed stock option rule. For example, an editorial in *Forbes* referred to the stock option proposal as "FASB's Folly."[5] The editorial noted that the proposed accounting rule ranked as one of the FASB's "most asinine, destructive proposals ever" and then added that "the idea is utterly illogical."[6]

Many prominent members of the accounting profession became involved in the controversy swirling around the proposed stock option rule. Eventually, the debate within the profession took on a nasty tone. Charges that certain accounting firms were lobbying against the proposal to appease their large audit clients were met with angry rebuttals. Nevertheless, these charges raised anew important issues that have faced the accounting profession over the past two decades. Among these issues is whether accounting firms undermine the integrity and credibility of the independent audit function when they lobby on behalf of controversial positions supported by their audit clients. A related question is whether the authority for issuing accounting rules should remain in the private sector or be assumed by a governmental agency.

STOCK OPTIONS AS COMPENSATION EXPENSE

Companies often include stock options as a component of their compensation plan for key executives and employees. In 1978, the financially troubled Chrysler Corporation wanted to hire Lee Iacocca as its chief executive, an individual who had enjoyed a successful career as a top executive of Ford Motor Company. Chrysler offered Iacocca a $1 annual salary and 400,000 stock options. The stock options gave Iacocca the right to purchase 400,000 shares of Chrysler common stock at a predetermined exercise price over a several-year period. If Iacocca succeeded in turning around Chrysler, the company's stock price would likely rise well above the exercise price of his stock options. He could then cash in those options by purchasing Chrysler's stock at the exercise price and reselling it at the higher market price. Within a few years, Iacocca masterminded one of the most celebrated corporate turnarounds in U.S. history. Iacocca was rewarded for that turnaround when he pocketed a $40 million profit on his stock options.

---

4. T.J. Rodgers, "New FASB Rule Is Ill-Conceived," *Business Credit*, June 1994, 20–21.

5. "FASB's Folly," *Forbes*, 31 January 1994, 26.

6. *Ibid.*

In recent years, executive stock option grants have become an important corporate strategy for newly formed companies. Compensatory stock option plans are particularly prevalent among emerging companies in high-technology industries, including the computer industry and the biotechnology industry. Newly formed companies in these industries typically cannot afford to pay the large salaries commanded by the executives they want to hire. As a result, these companies often use the "Chrysler" strategy to attract these individuals.

In 1972, the Accounting Principles Board, the FASB's predecessor, issued *APB Opinion No. 25*, "Accounting for Stock Issued to Employees." Under *APB No. 25*, companies are generally not required to recognize compensation expense when they issue stock options to executives and employees if those options have an exercise price equal to or higher than the stock's market price on the date the options are granted. The FASB decided that this "nonaccounting" approach for out-of-the-money stock options was unreasonable and decided to change it. The FASB's position was very simple. Although stock options may have an exercise price equal to or above the current market price of a company's stock on the date granted, they still have an economic value on that date. This economic value arises from the opportunity the holders of the options may have to purchase the company's common stock at less than market value at some point over the term of the options. The FASB maintained that this economic value is a component of an entity's compensation expense and should be recognized as such in its accounting records.

One of the more difficult issues addressed by the FASB's stock option proposal was how companies should determine the economic or fair value of out-of-the-money stock options when they are granted. The FASB suggested that companies use option-pricing models for this purpose. Such models have long been employed by sophisticated investors to determine the economic value of publicly traded stock options. To compute the economic value of a stock option using an option-pricing model, several assumptions must be made. For example, the future volatility of the underlying common stock must be estimated. Small changes in these assumptions can result in wide fluctuations in the estimated value of a stock option.

CRITICISM OF FASB'S PROPOSED STOCK OPTION RULE

Opponents of the FASB's proposed change in accounting for stock options advanced two key arguments for rejecting the proposal, including the difficulty of establishing a reasonable estimate of stock options' economic value. The primary argument used to counter the FASB's proposal was that it would create financial problems for thousands of companies, particularly "start-up" companies.

Critics of the FASB's proposal maintained that because most new companies initially have minimal earnings, they could not offer stock options to executives they wanted to hire if the value of these options had to be expensed immediately. As a result, these companies would have difficulty attracting highly qualified personnel for their key management positions. Carrying this argument to its logical conclusion, fewer new companies would be formed if the FASB's proposal was adopted. The resulting implications for the national economy, according to an editorial in *Forbes*, would be dire. *Forbes* pointed out that in the mid-1980s, newly formed companies accounted for 14 million of the nearly 19 million new jobs created nationwide.[7] A federal official denounced the FASB for stubbornly ignoring these negative economic consequences when considering the proposed stock option standard.

> Faced with these arguments, the FASB's rebuttal is simple: When it comes to accounting principles, economic consequences be damned; the truth will set investors free.[8]

Big Six accounting firms, both individually and jointly, also publicly registered strong disagreement with the stock option proposal. In commenting on the proposal, an Ernst & Young partner noted, "Why introduce an extremely subjective measure into financial statements?"[9] An 11-page analysis of the proposed rule by Arthur Andersen & Co. contained the following summary observation:

> We believe it is in the best interests of the public, the financial community, and the FASB itself for the Board to address those issues that have a significant impact on improving the relevance and usefulness of financial reporting. In our view, employers' accounting for stock options and other stock compensation does not meet that test.[10]

Coopers & Lybrand studied the proposal's potential impact on the earnings of 700 companies that issue stock options.[11] This study demonstrated that the proposed accounting rule would have a large negative impact on corporate earnings, particularly the earnings of new companies. In July 1994, the Big Six firms banded together and sent a joint letter to the FASB. In that letter, these firms strongly encouraged the FASB to drop the stock option proposal from its agenda.[12]

SUPPORT FOR FASB's STOCK OPTION PROPOSAL

Supporters of the new accounting standard for stock options maintained that it was needed to recognize a very material expense of corporations that was going unrecorded. These same parties charged that the arguments used by opponents of the proposed standard were flimsy, at best. The proposal's defenders rejected the contention that compensation expense associated with newly issued stock options should not be booked simply because it is difficult to estimate. Warren Buffett, a billionaire investor and frequent critic of the FASB, noted that "It is both silly and cynical to say that an important item of cost should not be recognized simply because it can't be quantified with pinpoint accuracy."[13]

---

7. *Ibid.*

8. J.C. Beese, "A Rule That Stunts Growth," *The Wall Street Journal*, 8 February 1994, A18.

9. R. Khalaf, "If It Ain't Broke . . .," *Forbes*, 12 April 1993, 100.

10. Arthur Andersen & Co., *Arthur Andersen Accounting News Briefs*, "FASB Exposure Draft 'Accounting for Stock-based Compensation,'" August 1993, 8.

11. M.S. Akresh and J. Fuersich, "Stock Options: Accounting, Valuation, and Management Issues," *Management Accounting*, March 1994, 51–53.

12. P.B.W. Miller, "Ethics and Stock Options—An Update," *In The Public Interest*, Newsletter of The Public Interest Section of the American Accounting Association, October 1994, 3.

13. Harlan, "Accounting Proposal Stirs Unusual Uproar," A8.

The economic consequences argument articulated by opponents of the stock option proposal was derided by many parties who defended the proposal. The FASB's vice-chairman, James Leisenring, insisted that the FASB had no mandate or responsibility to consider the economic consequences of new accounting standards such as their impact on job creation in the economy.[14] Likewise, Professor Paul Pacter of the University of Connecticut argued that the FASB must maintain a neutral attitude regarding the economic impact of new accounting standards.

> Accounting standards seek to measure and report faithfully the economic events and transactions that have taken place. This objective applies equally to events and transactions that are favorable to the business and those that are unfavorable. Accounting standards are not and should not be designed to obscure or distort reality. If the reality is that stock options have value and are intended to motivate employees and to compensate them for their services, accounting should reflect that reality.[15]

Supporters of the FASB's stock option proposal pointed to the fiasco in the savings and loan industry during the 1980s as a reminder of what can happen when economic considerations are allowed to dictate the choice of accounting methods. Regulatory authorities, including Congress, believed that the savings and loan industry's severe financial problems at the time would be short-lived. To mask the "temporary" bankrupt status of hundreds of insolvent savings and loans, Congress mandated that they be allowed to use accounting methods that overstated their assets and reported profits. This decision proved disastrous. Executives of many insolvent savings and loans made increasingly speculative investments, hoping to return them to a profitable condition. As a result, the losses of these savings and loans piled up at an ever-increasing rate. Finally, in the late 1980s when the savings and loan crisis threatened the health of the national economy, the federal government stepped in and spent several hundred billion dollars to bail out the industry.

Dennis Beresford, the chairman of the FASB and target of much of the criticism directed toward the stock option proposal, balked at the suggestion that his organization consider the economic consequences of new accounting rules. Beresford noted that the business community had often argued against new accounting standards because of their supposed negative economic consequences. In many of these cases, Beresford maintained, business executives simply wanted to avoid economic reality by not accounting for certain expenses. *The New York Times*, which strongly supported the stock option proposal, reinforced that point of view.

> For both pensions and post-retirement health benefits, companies resisted accounting reforms. . . . But when corporate boards were finally forced to look at reasonable estimates of the costs, companies began to control these costs.[16]

Several parties alleged that the economic consequences argument used by business executives to denounce the FASB's stock option proposal served simply

---

14. Rankin, "Congress Rips FASB," 33.

15. P. Pacter, "FASB's Stock Option Proposal: Correcting A Serious Flaw," *CPA Journal*, March 1994, 60–61.

16. F. Norris, "In Accounting, Truth Can Be Very Scary," *The New York Times*, 11 April 1993, Section 3, 1.

as a smoke screen to conceal their true motive in criticizing the proposal. For many years, corporate executives had been reaping windfall profits from the exercise of stock options, a job "perk" they did not want to see fall by the wayside because of the proposed accounting rule. Consider just two examples of enormous profits realized by corporate officers as a result of stock option grants. In 1992, two top executives of U.S. Surgical Corporation realized more than $80 million by cashing in stock options granted to them in prior years.[17] Topping that figure was a nearly $400 million profit on stock options realized by a Walt Disney Company executive in 1997.[18]

Of the hundreds of letters received by the FASB regarding the stock option proposal, one was a tongue-in-cheek correspondence from Mr. Beauregard T. Greede, the chairman of Sillicorp, Inc. Mr. Greede was quite upset with the FASB's suggestion that his firm record the expense associated with the stock options he had been granted.

> Do you think my handpicked board of directors would have awarded me options on a gazillion shares of Sillicorp stock if they'd had to tell the stockholders what the options were worth? And expense 'em![19]

A financial analyst who supported the FASB's stock option proposal provided a more direct point of view on this matter.

> To me, it doesn't make sense that you can give stock options to executives and not call it compensation. If it's compensation, it has to be accounted for. Right now, the companies have a free ride and they don't want to give it up. And that's what the uproar is about.[20]

The Debate Over Stock Options Turns Nasty

As the controversy over the stock option proposal escalated, the debate within the accounting profession became sidetracked. Instead of focusing on the soundness of the FASB's stock option proposal, accountants began debating whether accounting firms should lobby the FASB on proposed new standards. This debate centered on the Big Six accounting firms. Recall that in July 1994 the Big Six firms in a joint letter asked the FASB to drop the stock option proposal. An accounting professor questioned the motives of the Big Six firms in submitting this letter to the FASB.

> This letter is dreadful in several respects. Its arguments are strictly political and advance the interests of corporate management. . . . When I weigh this letter on the ethics scales, I find it wanting. The economic world is waiting for and needs responsible behavior and more complete financial statements, but these people advocate the opposite.[21]

---

17. L. Berton and J.S. Lublin, "Executives Say Accounting Idea Is Poorly Timed," *The Wall Street Journal*, 4 December 1992, B1, B12.

18. "Eisner Uses Stock Option to Sell Shares," *The Norman Transcript*, 4 December 1997, 24.

19. G.M. Kang, "Hands Off My Stock Pile," *Business Week*, 12 April 1993, 28–30.

20. G.A. Cheney, "Stock Option Quest Sparks Questions About FASB's Future," *Accounting Today*, 10 October 1994, 10, 12.

21. Miller, "Ethics and Stock Options," 3.

Walter Schuetze, the Chief Accountant of the Securities and Exchange Commission (SEC), was the most prominent member of the profession to criticize the Big Six accounting firms' lobbying efforts against the stock option proposal. Schuetze pointed out that representatives of these firms initially supported the proposal when it appeared on the FASB's agenda in 1984. He suggested that the firms changed their position "in response to fear of losing clients or other forms of retaliation."[22] A former Big Six partner and former member of the FASB, Schuetze went on to suggest that the Big Six's lobbying efforts against the stock option proposal called into question the independence of these firms.

> If public companies are pressuring their outside auditors . . . to take particular positions on financial accounting and reporting issues and outside auditors are subordinating their views to those of their clients, can the outside auditor community continue to claim to be independent?[23]

Schuetze's criticism of Big Six accounting firms did not go unanswered. An editorial in the bimonthly publication *Accounting Today* chastised Schuetze for his disapproving remarks regarding the Big Six firms. The editorial noted that Schuetze was "unnecessarily shrill" in his criticism and suggested that he did the profession "a disservice by his intemperate remarks."[24] Philip Chenok, president of the American Institute of Certified Public Accountants, also berated Schuetze for his criticism of the dominant firms in the accounting profession. Chenok said he found it "offensive and inappropriate for the Chief Accountant of the SEC to suggest a loss of independence [by the major accounting firms] over the stock option matter."[25]

INVITING GOVERNMENT INTERVENTION?

In criticizing Big Six firms for becoming "cheerleaders"[26] for their audit clients in the campaign against the stock option proposal, Walter Schuetze warned these firms that they might be damaging their own interests. Schuetze noted that such lobbying efforts could serve as an invitation for regulatory authorities "to regulate more heavily, and more directly, the auditing profession in particular and financial accounting and reporting in general."[27]

Schuetze's warning was not unfounded. During a 1970s investigation of the accounting profession, the U.S. Senate assailed the large accounting firms that dominate the profession.[28] Among the specific charges leveled at these firms was that

---

22. "Schuetze Wary Over CPA Independence on Stock Option Proposal," *Journal of Accountancy*, March 1994, 9–10.

23. *Ibid.*

24. "No Option Left," *Accounting Today*, 7 February 1994, 3.

25. "Accountants Are Chided Over Stock-Option Stance," *The Wall Street Journal*, 12 January 1994, A5.

26. *Ibid.*

27. "Schuetze Wary Over CPA Independence," 10.

28. U.S. Congress, Senate Subcommittee on Reports, Accounting and Management of the Committee on Government Operations, *The Accounting Establishment* (Washington, D.C.: U.S. Government Printing Office, 1977).

they routinely lobbied rule-making bodies to adopt accounting rules benefitting their largest audit clients. Like Schuetze, the Senate suggested that such lobbying efforts cast doubt on these firms' independence. Although never seriously considered, one recommendation spawned by the Senate's investigation was the creation of a federal agency to assume responsibility for the independent audit function.

A more credible recommendation that stemmed from the 1970s Senate investigation of the accounting profession was the creation of a federal agency to establish accounting standards. The heated controversy over the FASB's stock option proposal raised again the possibility of intervention in the profession's rule-making processes by the federal government. A former Chief Accountant of the SEC, John Burton, questioned whether the FASB could survive given the mounting pressure exerted on it by the business community.[29] In recent years, two members of the FASB, both former partners of Big Six accounting firms, have resigned. In each case, these individuals cited as reasons for their resignation the pressure exerted on them by corporate interests opposed to one or more of the FASB's proposals.

The Big Six accounting firms oppose the federal government assuming a direct role in the establishment of accounting standards. However, when these firms criticize a proposed standard, they risk further undercutting the FASB's authority and hastening its demise. As the controversy over the stock option proposal became very heated, the large accounting firms carefully focused their criticism specifically on that proposal. While criticizing the stock option proposal, these firms expressed support for retaining the FASB as the principal rule-making authority for the accounting profession.

> We believe that setting financial accounting standards should remain in the private sector. We oppose direct involvement by Congress in establishing financial accounting standards. The current arrangements under which the FASB establishes financial accounting standards subject to oversight by the SEC generally work well.[30]

EPILOGUE

In late 1994, the FASB rescinded its controversial stock option proposal. In its place, the FASB issued *Statement of Financial Accounting Standards No. 123*, "Accounting for Stock-Based Compensation," which became effective for fiscal years beginning after December 15, 1995. *SFAS No. 123 encourages* companies to recognize compensation expense for compensatory stock options that have an exercise price higher than the stock price on the grant date. However, this "fair value" method of accounting for stock options is not mandatory. Companies are permitted to simply disclose in their financial statement footnotes the compensation expense for newly-issued, out-of-the-money compensatory stock options. Apparently, most companies choose this disclosure option. Microsoft is one of these companies. For the first year *SFAS No. 123* was in effect, Microsoft's finan-

29. L. Berton, "FASB Finds That Criticism Increases Difficulty of Finding New Member," *The Wall Street Journal*, 18 January 1991, B3.

30. Arthur Andersen & Co., "FASB Exposure Draft," 8.

cial statement footnotes revealed that the company's pre-tax earnings would have been reduced by $570 million, or 17 percent, if compensation expense had been recorded for compensatory stock options it issued that year.

The adoption of *SFAS No. 123* failed to placate those parties who insisted that companies should book compensation expense for out-of-the-money compensatory stock options. Once more, Warren Buffett, the billionaire investor, ranked among the most vocal of these critics. In the spring of 1999, Buffett chided the accounting profession for *SFAS No. 123's* "outrageous" accounting treatment for such options.

> In effect, accounting principles offer management a choice: Pay employees in one form and count the cost, or pay them in another form and ignore the cost. Small wonder then that the use of options has mushroomed. . . . Whatever the merits of options may be, their accounting treatment is outrageous.[31]

Dennis Beresford retired as the FASB chairman in 1997 and accepted a faculty position with the University of Georgia. Shortly before leaving the FASB, Beresford made the following comments regarding the stock option controversy.

> In recent months, I have heard personally from a number of individual auditors and corporate executives who told me that they were embarrassed about how the issue was handled. Sure, they differed with the FASB's position on expensing options. But they felt that the efforts to discredit the Board may have ended up discrediting the whole profession. After all, the definition of a professional is someone who acts more in the public interest than in his or her own self interest.[32]

Walter Schuetze retired from his position as Chief Accountant of the SEC shortly following the resolution of the stock option controversy. In October 1997, Schuetze surprised the business world by returning to the SEC, this time as the Chief Accountant of the agency's powerful Enforcement Division. A prominent Wall Street investment banker observed that Schuetze's return to the SEC would not be looked upon fondly by many parties.

> Walter will probably strike fear in the hearts of a lot of people in public accounting and the corporate world. When he retired, many people at public accounting firms and in businesses were glad to see him go.[33]

In 1997, the FASB found itself entangled in another controversy over a proposed accounting rule. The proposal mandated that companies report certain financial derivatives at fair market value in their balance sheets. At the time, the chairman of the SEC estimated that corporations had $23 trillion of financial derivatives that went unreported in their periodic financial statements. Many corporate executives bitterly protested the proposed new rule. No doubt, much of this criticism stemmed from the large losses that the rule would cause many corporations to recognize. Several members of Congress and federal regulators, including Alan Greenspan, chairman of the Federal Reserve, also challenged the proposed rule. The new chairman of the FASB, Edmund Jenkins, vowed that, un-

---

31. *1998 Annual Report*, Berkshire Hathaway, Inc., 13–14.

32. D.R. Beresford, "What Did We Learn from the Stock Compensation Project," *Accounting Horizons*, June 1996, 125–130.

33. E. MacDonald, "SEC Names Accounting-Industry Critic to a Top Enforcement Post at Agency," *The Wall Street Journal*, 10 October 1997, B9.

like the FASB's compromise on the proposed stock option rule, the FASB would not rescind or modify the proposed standard for financial derivatives. He also warned the accounting profession that if federal authorities vetoed the proposed derivatives rule, the FASB might be disbanded. "If the FASB were humbled a second time, its loss of credibility might spur the Securities and Exchange Commission to take over the job."[34]

In June 1998, the FASB adopted the controversial derivatives rule. By that time, the estimated dollar value of financial derivatives approached $65 trillion, nearly triple the estimated figure reported by the SEC's chairman in 1997.[35] One year later, the FASB postponed for a second time the new standard's effective date after more than 100 large companies insisted that they needed more time to implement the rule.

QUESTIONS

1. Identify the principal advantages and disadvantages of having the rule-making bodies in the accounting profession controlled by the private sector rather than the federal government.

2. Large accounting firms are among the parties most knowledgeable of accounting theory and the pragmatic or everyday problems of applying accounting standards. As such, these firms are well positioned to evaluate the soundness of proposed accounting rules. Should rule-making bodies make use of the expertise and insight of these firms when considering proposed accounting standards? Why or why not? If so, explain how this could be done while minimizing the risk that these firms would antagonize their clients or, conversely, be seen as catering to the economic interests of their clients.

3. Assume that you are the managing partner of an office of a large accounting firm. The chief executive officer of your office's largest client has contacted you and asked that you write a letter to the FASB, on behalf of your firm, criticizing a new accounting rule being considered by the FASB. What should you do at this point?

4. Should the FASB consider the economic consequences of proposed accounting standards when deciding whether to adopt these standards? Explain. Identify the key issues or factors the FASB should consider when deliberating on proposed accounting rules.

---

34. R. Lowenstein, "Corporate America Bullies FASB, Part II," *The Wall Street Journal*, 11 September 1997, C1.

35. E. MacDonald, "FASB Approves Controversial Derivatives Rule," *The Wall Street Journal*, 21 June 1998, A3.

CASE 7.3
MAURICE STANS, CPA

On March 7, 1972, Maurice Stans telephoned an old friend, Walter Hanson. The two accountants had known each other for decades. Both men had worked their way up the career ladder of a major international accounting firm. Walter Hanson served as the senior partner of Peat Marwick Mitchell & Co., one of the Big Eight accounting firms. Stans had worked with Arthur Andersen, another Big Eight firm, before becoming an executive partner with Alexander Grant & Co., the nation's ninth largest accounting firm at the time. In the mid-1950s, Stans served as the president of the American Institute of Certified Public Accountants (AICPA) before leaving public accounting to join the Eisenhower Administration.

Stans' first political appointment was to the post of Deputy Postmaster General. Later, President Eisenhower appointed him director of the Bureau of the Budget. In that position, he earned the distinction of authoring a balanced federal budget, the last such federal budget for several decades. During his service in the Eisenhower Administration, Stans became a close friend of Vice-President Richard Nixon. In 1968, he agreed to serve as the finance chairperson for Nixon's presidential campaign. In that capacity, Stans directed the campaign's fund raising efforts. Following Nixon's election, Stans accepted an appointment as Secretary of Commerce in the new administration. When President Nixon decided to run for reelection in 1972, Stans resigned his cabinet post and became the finance chairperson for the reelection campaign.

Stans was as an aggressive and effective fund raiser. In 1972, he raised $60.2 million for President Nixon's reelection campaign, a staggering figure at the time for a presidential campaign. During the subsequent Watergate hearings, congressional investigators questioned whether Stans knew that some of the funds he raised were used for illicit purposes.

One witness testified that he had questioned Stans about $50,000 which seemed to be going to some doubtful purpose. Stans responded: "I don't want to know and you don't want to know."[1]

One successful fund-raising technique Stans employed was establishing contribution quotas for major firms in selected industries. For example, Stans reportedly established a contribution quota of $400,000 for every major oil company.[2] The contribution quota for each of the Big Eight accounting firms was reportedly $100,000.

The March 7, 1972, telephone conversation between Stans and Walter Hanson of Peat Marwick focused on that firm's contribution quota to President Nixon's reelection campaign. Hanson was apparently distraught by Stans' insistence that Peat Marwick partners contribute to the reelection campaign. Hanson suggested that any effort by Stans to encourage the firm's partners to contribute to a particular political party or candidate would violate a federal statute. That law, the Hatch Act, prohibits the solicitation of campaign contributions from federal contractors. Since Peat Marwick had several large contracts with the federal government, Hanson maintained that his firm clearly qualified as a government contractor. Stans allegedly rebuffed Hanson by telling him "Don't worry about that statute. The fact that you're a government contractor is all the more reason for you to give."[3] Stans also reportedly informed Hanson that any contributions made by Peat Marwick partners before April 7, 1972, would be kept confidential. Because of a new federal statute, political contributions made following that date would have to be reported publicly.

In November 1973, the *Washington Post* pointed out that one month before Stans' telephone conversation with Hanson in March 1972, Peat Marwick had been indicted on fraud charges. The Securities and Exchange Commission (SEC), a federal agency, filed the charges, which stemmed from Peat Marwick's audits of the National Student Marketing Corporation (NSMC).[4] This disclosure caused many parties to question whether the resolution of the fraud charges would be linked to how generously Peat Marwick's partners contributed to President Nixon's reelection campaign. When the *Washington Post* article was published, Stans and John N. Mitchell, former Attorney General under President Nixon, faced a federal indictment for allegedly obstructing an SEC criminal prosecution. That prosecution focused on Robert Vesco, a prominent corporate executive, who contributed $200,000 to President Nixon's 1972 campaign.

Published reports suggest that several Big Eight firms contributed heavily to President Nixon's 1972 campaign.[5] Peat Marwick was apparently not one of those firms. In 1975, Peat Marwick and the SEC reached an agreement to settle the fraud charges filed against the accounting firm related to its NSMC audits. The

1. *The Guardian*, "A Suitcase Full of Dollars," 23 April 1998, 18.

2. J. Abramson and T. Petzinger, "Big Political Donors Find Ways Around Watergate Reforms," *The Wall Street Journal*, 11 June 1992, A1 & A12.

3. M. Mintz, "Republican Pressure For Funds Probed," *Washington Post*, 2 November 1973, A1 & A8.

4. *Op. cit.* See the National Student Marketing Corporation case (Case 8.7) included in this text.

5. *Op. cit.*

agreement banned Peat Marwick from accepting any SEC registrants as new audit clients for a six-month period. This sanction was among the harshest ever imposed by the SEC on an accounting firm. Peat Marwick also agreed to undergo a thorough review of its audit practices by a committee jointly named by the firm and the SEC.

On April 28, 1974, a federal jury found Maurice Stans and John Mitchell innocent of all nine federal charges filed against them in connection with Robert Vesco's $200,000 contribution to President Nixon's 1972 campaign. Shortly following that verdict, the federal prosecutor appointed to investigate the Watergate scandal launched an intensive probe into Stans' activities during the 1972 presidential campaign. On October 24, 1974, *CBS News* reported that "Stans is under investigation . . . [for] bribery, extortion, knowingly accepting illegal contributions, sale of ambassadorships, and failure to disclose contributions."[6] After an exhaustive investigation, the Watergate prosecutor dropped all of the major charges against Stans. However, Stans did plead guilty to five misdemeanor violations of campaign financing laws. The only sanction imposed on Stans was a $5,000 fine. Despite this relatively small fine, Stans paid a heavy price emotionally and financially fighting the charges filed against him in the two cases. In total, Stans incurred legal expenses exceeding $1 million defending himself from those charges.

Stans' troubles did not end with the resolution of his litigation problems. In 1973, an accounting professor, Abraham Briloff, filed an ethics complaint against Stans with the AICPA. The AICPA subsequently charged Stans with engaging in an act discreditable to the accounting profession. This charge ensued from Stans' guilty plea to the five misdemeanor violations of campaign financing laws. Of all the personal crises that Stans faced during the early 1970s, he found the AICPA's action the most troubling. This ". . . final and most heartsearing blow was from the accounting profession in which and for which I had worked thousands of hours over more than 25 years."[7]

An important characteristic of a profession is self-regulation, including the disciplining of its members.[8] A profession that does not discipline its members invites criticism by external parties and potential intervention by governmental authorities. Similar to many professional organizations, the AICPA has been criticized in recent years for allegedly failing to penalize members who violate its rules of practice or ethical standards. Such criticism was forthcoming in 1976 when the AICPA Trial Board ruled that Maurice Stans had not engaged in an act discreditable to the accounting profession by violating campaign financing laws.[9] Stans, who held a CPA license in New York state, was eventually censured by the New York State Board of Accountancy. That penalty was the minimum punishment that could be imposed by the state agency.

6. M. Stans, *The Terrors of Justice* (New York: Everest House Publishers, 1978), 365.

7. *Ibid.*, 383.

8. M.B. Armstrong and J.I. Vincent, "Public Accounting: A Profession at a Crossroads," *Accounting Horizons*, March 1988, 94–98.

9. U.S. Congress, Senate Subcommittee on Reports, Accounting and Management of the Committee on Government Operations, *The Accounting Establishment* (Washington, D.C.: U.S. Government Printing Office, 1977), 126.

EPILOGUE

Maurice Stans spent the last two decades of his life attempting to clear his name of the stigma resulting from his involvement in the Watergate crisis. In the early 1990s, as the 20-year anniversary of the scandal neared, Stans wrote more than two-dozen major metropolitan newspapers asking them to not refer to him as a Watergate "conspirator" or to use similar characterizations. He also published two books that defended his role in President Nixon's administrations and election campaigns. In all his writings, Stans remained steadfastly loyal to President Nixon. Stans' loyalty was surprising to most Watergate historians since the infamous White House tapes revealed that President Nixon and his top aides discussed a plan "to make Stans scapegoat for the whole disaster."[10] Stans, a member of the Accounting Hall of Fame, died in 1998 at the age of 90.

QUESTIONS

1. Assume that the *AICPA Code of Professional Conduct* that exists today was in force in the early 1970s. Do you believe that Maurice Stans would have been found guilty of engaging in an act discreditable to the accounting profession? Defend your answer.

2. Do you believe Professor Briloff behaved properly (ethically) in filing the complaint against Stans with the AICPA? Under what general conditions, if any, should CPAs file complaints with oversight bodies regarding alleged misconduct by fellow CPAs?

3. Briefly describe the roles and responsibilities of the AICPA and state boards of accountancy in regulating the accounting profession. Indicate how those roles and responsibilities overlap and how they differ.

---

10. *The Guardian*, "A Suitcase Full of Dollars," 18.

CASE 7.4
SCOTT FANE, CPA

Like most young professionals, earning a reasonable livelihood ranked as a top priority for Scott Fane, a CPA specializing in taxation services who relocated to Florida in the mid-1980s. To practice as a CPA in Florida, Scott registered with the Florida Board of Accountancy, which regulates the public accounting profession within the state of Florida. Scott soon butted heads with that state agency. A protracted legal battle ensued. In 1993, the young CPA and the Florida Board of Accountancy finally settled their differences in the hallowed chambers of the U.S. Supreme Court.

SEARCHING FOR CLIENTS IN THE SUNSHINE STATE

Scott Fane moved to Florida from New Jersey in 1985 with the hope that Florida's robust economy would help him quickly establish a thriving accounting practice. In New Jersey, Scott relied on direct solicitation to identify and pursue potential clients. Many businesses depend on direct mail, telephone calls, and in-person visitations to identify potential customers. Historically, professions frown upon the use of direct solicitation by their members to obtain new clients. Threatening gestures by the Federal Trade Commission (FTC) in the 1970s persuaded the American Institute of Certified Public Accountants (AICPA) to eliminate its ban on direct solicitation by AICPA members. Most state boards quickly fell in line with the AICPA and repealed their bans on direct solicitation, including the New Jersey state board. Among the holdouts that continued to prohibit direct solicitation was the Florida state board.

After moving to Florida, Scott targeted his practice development efforts on individuals and small businesses. Most of these potential customers had an ongoing relationship with a CPA. In New Jersey, Scott overcame that problem by contacting potential clients directly and offering to provide them services at fees lower than those charged by their existing CPAs. Florida's ban on direct solicitation effectively undermined that strategy.[1]

> The rule . . . presented a serious obstacle, because most businesses are willing to rely for advice on the accountants or CPA's already serving them. In Fane's experience, persuading a business to sever its existing accounting relations or alter them to include a new CPA on particular assignments requires the new CPA to contact the business and explain the advantages of a change.[2]

In 1990, frustration drove Scott to sue the Florida Board of Accountancy in a U.S. District Court. Scott charged that the state agency's ban on direct solicitation was unconstitutional. Specifically, Scott alleged that the rule violated his First Amendment rights to freedom of speech.

SCOTT SCORES TWICE IN THE LOWER COURTS

In district court, the Florida Board of Accountancy presented a vigorous defense to Fane's allegation. First, the state board maintained that the ban on direct solicitation shielded users of accounting services from zealous, "overreaching" CPAs. Second, the state board claimed that the ban safeguarded auditors' independence, the cornerstone of the independent audit function. To bolster these arguments, the state board called on one of its former chairmen.

The former state board chairman testified that CPAs who solicit clients are "obviously in need of business and may be willing to bend the rules."[3] Thus, the ban on direct solicitation allegedly prevented CPAs from falling prey to their own economic (greedy) impulses. The former chairman also testified that clients obtained via direct solicitation efforts would have considerable leverage on their CPAs. A client might use this leverage to extract concessions from a newly-retained accountant. In the context of independent audits such concessions might ultimately result in improper audit opinions and, more important, in suboptimal decisions by financial statement users relying on those opinions.

The district court judge rejected the arguments made by the Florida Board of Accountancy and its former chairman. Although those arguments seemed reasonable, the judge observed that the state board provided no concrete evidence to corroborate its claims.

> . . . the defendant has failed to demonstrate a causal relationship between in-person, direct, uninvited solicitation, and accountant misconduct. Similarly, the defendant has failed to prove any harm to third parties as a result of the alleged misconduct.[4]

In September 1990, the district court judge ruled in Scott Fane's favor in his lawsuit against the Florida Board of Accountancy. The state board immediately

---

1. Florida defined "direct solicitation" as all uninvited in-person visits or conversations or telephone calls to a specific potential client.

2. *Edenfield v. Fane*, 113 S.Ct. 1792 (1993).

3. *Ibid.*

4. *Fane v. Edenfield*, 945 F.2d 1514 (1990).

appealed that ruling to the U.S. Court of Appeals. In a two-to-one decision, the appellate court sustained the district court judge's ruling. The two appellate judges who supported that decision held that the Florida state board failed to prove there existed a "substantial need" for the ban on direct solicitation. Appellate Judge Edmondson filed a strong dissent to the majority opinion. Judge Edmondson observed that the federal government has historically allowed states significant leeway in regulating the professionals they license. Given this long-standing precedent, the judge believed that any doubt in the case should be resolved in favor of the state board's position.

Judge Edmondson also agreed with the state board's contention that direct solicitation potentially jeopardized CPAs' integrity and credibility. He noted that direct solicitation might provoke individual CPAs to engage in "fraud, undue influence, intimidation, overreaching, and other forms of vexatious conduct."[5] The other two appellate judges suggested that severe sanctions for such conduct served as an effective deterrent. Judge Edmondson disagreed, pointing out that direct solicitation efforts are, by definition, private in nature. How then could state boards monitor these efforts and discourage abusive solicitation practices?

Finally, Judge Edmondson pointed out that Florida "cloaked" CPAs practicing within its boundaries in an "aura of competence" that had the potential to intimidate or "overawe" prospective clients. As a result, Florida had a right and responsibility to take vigorous measures to protect the public from unethical CPAs. In Judge Edmondson's opinion, Florida was attempting to do just that by banning direct solicitation.

> Even if I personally questioned that the Florida rule is necessary for an ordered CPA profession, it would not be my place to second guess state officials about the state rule's wisdom or effectiveness. What is important for me is that reasonable people, such as those that I expect comprise the Florida Board of Accountancy, could think that the rule against in-person solicitation of clients functions to assure greater competence of CPA's, more reasoned selection of CPA's by lay people, and the accuracy of audit statements upon which the public relies.[6]

Dissatisfaction with the appellate court's decision and Judge Edmondson's strong defense of its point-of-view prompted the Florida Board of Accountancy to appeal the Scott Fane case to the U.S. Supreme Court. The focal issue of the case, commercial speech, happened to be a topic of considerable interest to the Supreme Court in the early 1990s. Not surprisingly, then, the Fane case survived the rigorous review process for cases appealed to the Supreme Court and was placed on the high court's 1992–1993 docket.

SCOTT TAKES HIS CASE TO THE U.S. SUPREME COURT

The Supreme Court heard arguments in the Scott Fane case in December 1992 and released its ruling four months later. In that opinion, the Supreme Court stressed the importance of commercial speech, which is defined as "expression related exclusively to the economic interests of the speaker and audience." Prior to the

---

5. *Fane v. Edenfield*, 507 U.S. 761 (1991).

6. *Ibid.*

twentieth century, state and federal courts did not consider commercial speech to be protected by the First Amendment that guarantees freedom of speech for U.S. citizens. During the latter decades of the twentieth century, the federal courts, including the U.S. Supreme Court, gradually extended First Amendment protection to commercial speech.

As a general rule, federal courts protect commercial speech from governmental restraint as long as it is truthful and not misleading. The Supreme Court reaffirmed that principle in the Scott Fane case.

> The commercial marketplace, like other spheres of social and cultural life, provides a forum where ideas and information flourish. Some of the ideas and information are vital, some of slight worth. But the general rule is that the speaker and the audience, not the government, assess the value of the information presented.[7]

Justice Kennedy, who wrote the majority opinion in the case, observed that a governmental agency seeking to restrict commercial speech generally has two responsibilities. First, the agency must establish that the given commercial speech poses serious harms to the public. Second, the agency must demonstrate that the restrictions it intends to impose on the commercial speech alleviates those harms to a material degree.

In the Fane case, Justice Kennedy maintained that the Florida Board of Accountancy failed to prove that direct solicitation poses a serious threat to the consumers of accounting services. Justice Kennedy noted that the state board did not offer any evidence that Fane's direct solicitation efforts in New Jersey had been damaging to his customers or potential customers. Likewise, he quickly dismissed the suggestion by the former chairman of the Florida state board that CPAs who engage in direct solicitation are more likely than other CPAs to capitulate to audit clients and thus jeopardize the integrity of the independent audit function.

> It appears from the literature that a business executive who wishes to obtain a favorable but unjustified audit opinion from a CPA would be less likely to turn to a stranger who has solicited him than to pressure his existing CPA, with whom he has an ongoing, personal relation and over whom he may also have some financial leverage.[8]

Eight of the nine Supreme Court justices voted to uphold the two previous rulings in Scott Fane's case, which effectively eliminated Florida's ban on direct solicitation. In summarizing the majority's view, Justice Kennedy observed that Florida's ban on direct solicitation did not accomplish its intended objective and actually had negative consequences for Florida citizens.

> In denying CPA's and their clients the considerable advantages of solicitation in the commercial context, Florida's law threatens societal interests in broad access to complete and accurate commercial information that the First Amendment is designed to safeguard.[9]

Justice O'Connor filed a dissenting opinion in the Scott Fane case that closely paralleled many of the arguments made previously by Judge Edmondson of the U.S. Court of Appeals. Justice O'Connor argued that individual states should be

---

7. *Edenfield v. Fane*, 113 S.Ct. 1792 (1993).

8. *Ibid.*

9. *Ibid.*

allowed to prohibit commercial speech inconsistent with a profession's public image, although that speech is not directly harmful to the parties to whom it is intended. In Justice O'Connor's view, the recent trend toward allowing professions to become more commercial has had a subtle but adverse impact on professions. "Commercialization has an incremental, indirect, yet profound effect on professional culture, as lawyers know all too well."[10]

EPILOGUE

Scott Fane's legal action against the Florida Board of Accountancy was the first of three major lawsuits the state agency faced in the 1990s. While Fane's case was working its way through the federal courts, the Florida board charged another CPA, Richard Rampell, with violating its ban on direct solicitation. Rampell immediately sued the state board. Similar to Fane, Rampell maintained that the board's ban on direct solicitation was unconstitutional. He made the same allegation concerning the board's rule that banned competitive bidding for attestation engagements. At the time, Florida was the only state that prohibited CPAs from seeking attest clients on a competitive bidding basis. The Florida Supreme Court eventually settled Rampell's lawsuit.

When the U.S. Supreme Court ruled in Scott Fane's favor in April 1993, the Florida Supreme Court pronounced that the Florida Board of Accountancy's ban on direct solicitation was no longer enforceable and dropped that issue from Richard Rampell's case. In July 1993, the Florida Supreme Court ruled in favor of Rampell on the other charge he filed against the Florida Board of Accountancy. This ruling effectively eliminated the board's ban on competitive bidding for attest engagements.

> By prohibiting CPA's from competitive bidding, the Department [Board of Accountancy] restricts economic expression constituting commercial speech. . . . The Department may regulate the profession of accountancy in an attempt to assure quality audits, but its regulations may not restrict economic expression protected by the First Amendment.[11]

In April 1994, the U.S. Supreme Court resolved the third major case filed against the Florida Board of Accountancy in the early 1990s. This case also centered on the issue of commercial speech. In 1992, the Florida board charged Silvia Ibanez, a Florida CPA, with false, deceptive, and misleading advertising. During the 1980s, Ibanez had worked as a public accountant for two major accounting firms. After obtaining a law degree and the Certified Financial Planner (CFP) professional designation, Ibanez established her own law firm. Although she was practicing law, Ibanez included the CPA and CFP designations in the yellow pages listing of her law firm and on her business cards. The young attorney believed those designations enhanced her credibility in the eyes of potential clients.

The Florida Board of Accountancy charged that Ibanez's use of her CPA designation misled the public by suggesting that she was practicing public accounting,

---

10. *Ibid.*

11. *Department of Professional Regulation, Board of Accountancy v. Richard Rampell*, 621 So.2d 426 (Fla. 1993).

which she was not. Additionally, the state board charged that Ibanez's use of the CFP designation violated an ethical rule prohibiting Florida CPAs from using a specialty designation not specifically approved by the board. The Supreme Court ruled in favor of Ibanez on both charges. In support of that decision, the high court referred to its ruling the previous year in the Fane case. Once again, the Supreme Court made clear that it generally will not condone governmental restraint of commercial speech. By finding in Ibanez's favor, the high court overturned the reprimand the Florida state board had imposed on her.

> The reprimand . . . is incompatible with . . . the First Amendment, because the board has not demonstrated with sufficient specificity that any member of the public could have been misled by the attorney's constitutionally protected commercial speech . . . for (1) as long as the attorney holds an active CPA license from the board, consumers cannot be misled by her truthful representation to that effect; and (2) the board's justification for disciplining the attorney for using the CFP designation is not more persuasive, where the board has failed to point to any harm to the public from such designation that is potentially real, not purely hypothetical.[12]

QUESTIONS

1. Review the "rules" presently included in the *AICPA Code of Professional Conduct*. In your opinion, do any of these rules improperly limit accountants' commercial speech?

2. How may an ethical code create economic barriers of entry to a profession? Explain.

3. How may competitive bidding affect the independent audit function? Identify the potential impact on individual audit engagements and the long-range implications for the public accounting profession.

4. In a professional services context, "lowballing" refers to the practice of underpricing one's competition to obtain clients. Identify the advantages and disadvantages of lowballing within the public accounting profession. Also identify the parties who benefit from this practice and the parties it harms.

5. Comment on the advantages and disadvantages of professions being regulated at the state, rather than federal, level.

6. In the Scott Fane opinion, Justice O'Connor alluded to "incremental commercialization" within professions. Identify examples of incremental commercialization within the public accounting profession in recent years. How, if at all, has an increasing emphasis on the commercial aspects of public accounting affected the profession?

---

12. *Ibanez v. Florida Department of Business and Professional Regulation, Board of Accountancy*, 114 S.Ct. 2084 (1994).

CASE 7.5
BARRINGER RESOURCES, INC.

Accounting firms face some degree of litigation risk each time they agree to perform an independent audit. Negligence easily ranks as the most common complaint in lawsuits filed against auditors. Failure to apply confirmation procedures properly, overlooking a material misstatement of inventory, and simply relying too heavily on client representations are allegations frequently found in lawsuits naming auditors as defendants.

Although negligence claims underlie most auditing-related lawsuits, in recent years plaintiff legal counsel have developed many unconventional theories to motivate lawsuits against auditors. Consider a litigation case involving BDO Seidman, an international accounting firm. A retired corporate executive charged that BDO Seidman had defamed him. How? By issuing an unqualified audit opinion on his former employer's financial statements.

TWO DECADES OF UPS AND
DOWNS FOR BARRINGER RESOURCES

Anthony Rene Barringer fought for the British army as a teenager during World War II. Following the war, Barringer, who had a fascination with rocks and minerals from an early age, enrolled in London's Imperial College of Science and Technology. Seven years later, after earning a doctorate in economic geology, Barringer emigrated to Canada to accept a job as an exploration geologist with a mining firm. Restless and inquisitive by nature, Barringer planned to eventually establish his own company so that he would have more freedom to pursue innovative exploration techniques he had developed. In 1961, Barringer finally struck out on his own.

Always intrigued by new ideas and untested concepts, Tony Barringer had difficulty focusing his company's resources on one or even a few lines of business. Nevertheless, his firm's principal line of business involved developing technology useful to mining companies, particularly instruments to track down sizable mineral deposits. Barringer relocated to the United States in the 1960s and incorporated his company under the name of Barringer Resources, Inc. (BRI), in 1967. New Jersey served as the company's headquarters, although BRI's operations were scattered across the western United States and Canada.

The dramatic ups and downs of the volatile mining industry threatened the existence of Tony Barringer's small company for the first two decades of its existence. BRI's operating results gyrated wildly from year to year during that time frame. In 1983, the company posted a net income of $815,000 but the next year suffered a net loss topping $1.5 million. Following another bad year in 1985, BRI rebounded with a $2.5 million profit in 1986. Two years later, the company reported a net loss of $2.3 million. By the end of fiscal 1988, BRI's audited balance sheet listed total assets of $4.3 million, an accumulated retained earnings deficit of $4.2 million, and a meager net worth of $127,000.

Contributing significantly to BRI's financial problems in the late 1980s were the company's efforts to develop a new line of detection instruments and equipment. Tony Barringer initiated those efforts after realizing that the mining instruments and technology patented by his company could be used as weapons in modern society's battle against two key antagonists: terrorism and illicit drug trafficking. In the late 1980s, Barringer poured large amounts of capital into developing detection equipment for explosives and illicit drugs. Those efforts yielded few tangible results, in terms of either reliable products or financial rewards for BRI.

Good-Bye to Tony Barringer

Coopers & Lybrand served as BRI's independent audit firm throughout the 1980s. By late in the decade, Coopers began expressing serious doubts regarding BRI's going concern status. Coopers' audit opinion on BRI's 1987 financial statements included a "subject to" qualification that referred to the company's cash flow problems. During 1988, BRI sought equity financing from external investors to remedy those problems. The only major infusion of cash obtained by the company during the year was $250,000 of equity capital contributed by Investment Partners of America (IPA), a limited partnership.

The IPA investment did not reverse BRI's fortunes. Coopers issued an unqualified opinion on the company's 1988 financial statements. However, that opinion contained a fourth paragraph commenting on BRI's precarious financial status, including several debt covenant violations. Exhibit 1 presents the fourth paragraph of BRI's 1988 audit report.

During 1989, BRI's board of directors implemented a plan to salvage the company from pending bankruptcy. First, the board restructured BRI's operations. This restructuring plan included a spin-off of the company's research laboratories to a separate firm, Barringer Laboratories, Inc. Second, Tony Barringer was replaced as BRI's president and CEO, although he remained the company's largest stockholder. Barringer's severance agreement with BRI contained a clause that made him a "scientific consultant" for the firm. This agreement also included a non-compete clause prohibiting Barringer from establishing a business that ri-

These financial statements have been prepared in accordance with accounting principles applicable to a going concern. Accordingly, they do not give effect to adjustments which would be necessary should the Company be required to realize on its assets and liquidate its liabilities in other than the normal course of business. As described in note 2, the Company has experienced cash flow problems and as at March 24, 1989 is in violation of covenants on certain debt. The Company is presently seeking additional equity financing to improve its working capital or, alternatively, may be required to liquidate certain assets to meet its liabilities as they are due.

EXHIBIT 1
Fourth Paragraph of Coopers & Lybrand's Audit Opinion on BRI's 1988 Financial Statements

valed BRI. BRI's board retained Frank Abella, IPA's primary owner and managing general partner, to serve as its new CEO and vice-chairman of the board of directors. BRI signed a management agreement with IPA. This agreement required BRI to pay IPA $120,000 annually for Abella's services and granted IPA 100,000 shares of BRI common stock.

Shortly after completing the restructuring plan, BRI dismissed its longtime audit firm, Coopers & Lybrand, and retained BDO Seidman. BRI dismissed Coopers on January 4, 1990, four days following the end of the company's 1989 fiscal year. BDO Seidman was engaged the following day. Two months later, BDO Seidman issued the unqualified opinion shown in Exhibit 2 on BRI's 1989 financial statements. Those financial statements reported a net loss exceeding $500,000, which increased BRI's accumulated retained earnings deficit to more than $5 million.

THE EARLY NINETIES BRING MORE BAD NEWS FOR BRI

BRI's disappointing financial results continued in 1990. In 1989, the company realized a loss from continuing operations of $227,000. The following year, that fig-

REPORT OF INDEPENDENT CERTIFIED PUBLIC ACCOUNTANTS

We have audited the accompanying consolidated balance sheet of Barringer Resources, Inc. as of December 31, 1989, and the related consolidated statements of operations, shareholders' equity, and cash flows for the year then ended. These financial statements are the responsibility of the Company's management. Our responsibility is to express an opinion on these financial statements based on our audit.

We conducted our audit in accordance with generally accepted auditing standards. Those standards require that we plan and perform the audit to obtain reasonable assurance about whether the financial statements are free of material misstatement. An audit also includes assessing the accounting estimates made by management, as well as evaluating the overall financial statement presentation. We believe that our audit provides a reasonable basis for our opinion.

In our opinion, the consolidated financial statements referred to above present fairly, in all material respects, the financial position of Barringer Resources, Inc. at December 31, 1989, and the results of its operations and its cash flows for the year then ended in conformity with generally accepted accounting principles.

BDO Seidman
[signed]

New York, New York
March 9, 1990

EXHIBIT 2
BDO Seidman's Audit Opinion on BRI's 1989 Financial Statements

ure ballooned to a loss of $2.2 million. In July 1990, BRI's board of directors suddenly dismissed Frank Abella as the company's CEO and terminated the management agreement with IPA. Two months later, an unhappy Abella resigned from BRI's board after complaining that his authority had been undermined.

Exhibit 3 presents a footnote disclosing Abella's dismissal that accompanied BRI's 1990 financial statements. Notice that the footnote indicated Abella had been "terminated for cause" by the board of directors. The footnote goes on to suggest that Abella was threatening to sue BRI. Among the few slivers of good news for BRI during 1990 was the unqualified audit opinion BDO Seidman issued on its financial statements.

Unfortunately, 1991 was even harsher to BRI than 1990.[1] BRI's loss from continuing operations rose to $3.3 million in 1991, up 50 percent from the previous year. A flurry of litigation also plagued the company during 1991. A former BRI employee named the company a co-defendant in a sexual harassment lawsuit filed against a former BRI executive. In another lawsuit, BRI alleged that its founder and former CEO, Tony Barringer, had violated the non-compete agreement made with the company upon his retirement. An unhappy Barringer soon lodged a counterclaim against his former firm. Frank Abella also filed a lawsuit against BRI in 1991. Abella charged that BRI defamed him by reporting in its 1990 financial statement footnotes that he had been "terminated for cause" by the company's board of directors.

Abella's lawsuit named not only BRI as a defendant, but the company's audit firm, BDO Seidman, as well. The former CEO alleged that BDO Seidman defamed him by allowing BRI to include the "terminated for cause" statement in its 1990 financial statement footnotes. The accounting firm allegedly compounded its error by validating the accuracy of that statement with an unqualified audit opinion on BRI's 1990 financial statements. Abella maintained that BDO Seidman had a professional responsibility to insist that the allegedly defamatory statement be redacted (edited) from the footnotes.

ABELLA V. BDO SEIDMAN

Judge John Boyle of the Superior Court of New Jersey presided over Frank Abella's defamation lawsuit. Judge Boyle dealt first with the defamation claim

EXHIBIT 3
BRI's 1990 Financial Statement Footnote that Disclosed the Termination of Frank Abella

> Effective July 18, 1990, Frank J. Abella, Jr., Managing Partner of Investment Partners of America ("IPA"), was terminated for cause by the Board of Directors of the Company [Barringer Resources] as Vice Chairman and Chief Executive Officer of the Company. As a result, the management agreement between the Company and IPA was terminated. Mr. Abella and/or IPA may institute legal proceedings to recover the balance of the payments which would have been due under the agreement with IPA of approximately $180,000. The Company believes it has meritorious defenses to any claims against the Company made by Mr. Abella and/or IPA and intends to defend against any such claim and to assert counterclaims.

---

1. BRI's board of directors changed the company's name to Barringer Technologies, Inc., during 1991. For clarity purposes, the company's former name is used throughout most of the remainder of this case.

filed against BDO Seidman by Abella, handing down his final judgment on that issue in June 1992.

Generally, the plaintiff in a defamation suit must establish four elements of proof:

1. the defendant made a false and defamatory statement concerning the plaintiff,
2. the defendant published that statement,
3. the defendant was at least negligent in making and publishing the statement, and
4. the plaintiff was harmed by the statement.

Judge Boyle accepted Abella's contention that the "terminated for cause" statement in BRI's 1990 financial statement footnotes was potentially defamatory. However, the judge questioned Abella's assertion that BDO Seidman was involved in "publishing" that statement.

> In order to impose liability for publication, the statement must have been made by the defendant either directly or through some agency relationship . . . [BDO Seidman auditors] are not officers or employees or general agents of the Company. They are auditors. No more, no less.[2]

The judge went on to observe that BRI's executives made the "terminated for cause" statement, meaning that the responsibility for the accuracy of that statement rested solely with those individuals. BDO Seidman's principal responsibility regarding the Abella matter, according to Judge Boyle, was to ensure that the readers of BRI's 1990 financial statements were informed of the loss contingency posed by Abella's dismissal. The judge noted that if BRI had not disclosed that contingency, BDO Seidman would likely have been precluded from issuing an unqualified opinion on the company's financial statements. Judge Boyle also correctly observed that auditors do not have the requisite skills to render judgments regarding the reliability of "published" assertions made by their clients that concern pending legal matters. Instead, auditors generally rely on client legal counsel to corroborate a client's financial disclosures concerning pending litigation.

> While it is within the scope of defendants' duties to verify that the event in question in fact occurred or that a contingency in fact existed, it is not within the scope of defendants' duties to act as the judge or jury to ascertain whether there truly was cause for termination.[3]

For the previous reasons, Judge Boyle ruled that BDO Seidman had not published the "terminated for cause" statement on which Abella based his legal claim against the accounting firm. He also ruled that the accounting firm did not have a responsibility to insist that BRI remove the statement from the 1990 financial statement footnotes. These rulings caused Judge Boyle to issue a summary judgment in favor of BDO Seidman in the case. Nevertheless, Judge Boyle chose to address two additional issues in his *Abella v. BDO Seidman* opinion.

Although a moot point given his ruling that BDO Seidman had not published the potentially defamatory statement, the judge noted that he could find no evidence of negligence by BDO Seidman during the 1990 BRI audit. The judge then made a ruling that could serve as an important precedent in future cases involv-

---

2. *Abella v. Barringer Resources, Inc.*, 260 NJ Super. 92 (1992).

3. *Ibid.*

ing defamation suits against auditors. According to Judge Boyle, even if Abella's legal counsel had established all four elements of proof necessary to create a *prima facie* case of defamation, he still would have ruled in BDO Seidman's favor. In certain contexts, the judge observed, auditors should be entitled to a "qualified" or "conditional" privilege to publish statements that may be potentially defamatory. To support his position, the judge referred to a section of the *Restatement of Torts*, a legal compendium relied on heavily in many jurisdictions.

> This qualified or conditional privilege is based on the public policy that it is essential that true information be given whenever it is reasonably necessary for the protection of one's own interests, the interests of third persons, or certain interests of the public.[4]

To date, at least two other state courts have ruled that auditors have a qualified or conditional privilege to publish potentially defamatory statements.

EPILOGUE

BRI eventually resolved the litigation problems it faced in the early 1990s. In November 1992, a Colorado state court dismissed the sexual harassment lawsuit that named the company as a co-defendant. The following month, BRI's board settled the pending lawsuits involving Tony Barringer. Finally, in December 1993, BRI and Frank Abella settled the defamation lawsuit he filed against the company in 1991. A key feature of that settlement was a grant of 45,000 shares of BRI common stock to Abella.

The latter part of the 1990s also witnessed a significant improvement in the operating results of BRI's successor, Barringer Technologies, Inc. In 1992, the company reported a net loss of nearly $2 million on revenues of $8.7 million. Five years later, Barringer Technologies reported a net income of nearly $6 million on revenues of $23 million. The company's newfound financial success stemmed largely from the explosives and drug detection projects initiated years earlier by Tony Barringer. After several years of development and field testing, those projects yielded highly reliable and cost-efficient technology at a time when the demand for such technology, unfortunately, was increasing dramatically. By 1997, Barringer Technologies reigned as the world's leading producer of high-sensitivity equipment used to detect trace amounts of explosives and illegal drugs. The company's past and present customers include the U.S. Drug Enforcement Agency, the Federal Bureau of Investigation, the U.S. Coast Guard, and major international airports scattered across the globe. During the mid-1990s, the company's stock traded for as low as $.25 per share. A few years later, the stock surged to $16 per share on the strength of its new product line.

And what about Tony Barringer? By the late 1990s, Barringer, in his seventies at the time, had lost interest in bomb and drug detection projects and instead had returned to his first love, searching for minerals. The *Rocky Mountain News* reported in 1996 that Barringer was planning an expedition into the desolate and unfriendly mountain ranges of Nevada to search for gold.[5] Barringer was also de-

---

4. *Ibid.*

5. A. Jeter, "Golden Firm's Gear Used in TWA Probe; Bomb-detection Device Sends Stock Soaring," *Rocky Mountain News*, 5 August 1996, 10A.

veloping equipment to "sniff out" mineral deposits while being transported in low-flying aircraft.

QUESTIONS

1. In his *Abella v. BDO Seidman* opinion, Judge Boyle observed that auditors do not "formulate or endorse or communicate" their clients' representations. Do you agree with this statement? Explain.

2. Judge Boyle ruled that in certain contexts auditors have a "qualified privilege" to publish potentially defamatory statements. Develop a hypothetical scenario involving such a context—other than the one discussed in this case.

3. Identify specific audit procedures that the BDO Seidman auditors could have applied to each of BRI's pending legal cases at the end of 1991.

4. In less than two years, BRI had three CEOs: Tony Barringer, Frank Abella, and the individual who succeeded Abella. What risks does significant turnover in client management pose for auditors? How should these risks affect key planning decisions for audit engagements?

5. Coopers & Lybrand issued a "subject to" qualified opinion on BRI's 1987 financial statements. The following year, Coopers issued an unqualified opinion on BRI's financial statements. That opinion included a fourth paragraph discussing the company's going concern status. BDO Seidman issued a standard unqualified opinion on BRI's 1989 financial statements. Discuss the factors that likely accounted for the dissimilar audit opinions issued on BRI's 1987–1989 financial statements.

CASE 7.6

NATIONAL MEDICAL TRANSPORTATION NETWORK

San Diego-based National Medical Transportation Network (MedTrans) eventually became the largest ambulance services provider in the United States. Reaching that pinnacle was not an easy journey. In early 1992, MedTrans encountered cash flow problems that prompted the company's two owners to search for external financing. The co-owners located a company willing to invest $10 million in MedTrans. During negotiations with that company, MedTrans's auditor, Deloitte & Touche, uncovered problems in its client's accounting records. Those problems prevented Deloitte from issuing an unqualified opinion on MedTrans's 1992 financial statements. After several unpleasant confrontations with MedTrans's chief executive officer, Deloitte resigned as the company's audit firm.

Following Deloitte's resignation, the $10 million investment deal collapsed. Within a few months, MedTrans's two owners sold their firm to a large corporation. Unhappy with Deloitte's lack of "cooperation," MedTrans's former owners sued Deloitte to recover the sizable loss they incurred on the sale of their company. Among other charges, the former owners alleged that Deloitte acted negligently by "withdrawing prematurely" from the 1992 MedTrans audit engagement.

No doubt, Deloitte's legal counsel confidently tackled the MedTrans lawsuit. The allegation that Deloitte negligently withdrew from the 1992 MedTrans audit engagement seemed implausible since the client had adamantly refused to make several large and necessary adjustments to its 1992 financial statements. Threatening comments made to Deloitte auditors by one of MedTrans's co-owners provided even stronger justification for the audit firm's resignation. Imagine then the shock and disbelief of Deloitte's attorneys when the jury that heard the lawsuit agreed with MedTrans's former owners and imposed a multimillion-dollar judgment on the prominent accounting firm.

MedTrans Seeks Help

MedTrans's two principal officers, Roberts and Morgan, served as the company's chief executive officer (CEO) and president, respectively, and each owned 50 percent of MedTrans's common stock. Deloitte audited the company's annual financial statements each year from 1988 through 1991—MedTrans's fiscal year ended March 31. Apparently, Deloitte encountered few problems during those audits and issued an unqualified opinion each year on MedTrans's financial statements.

By the late spring of 1992, MedTrans needed cash, and quickly. The company owed $2 million of payroll taxes and faced a $12 million repayment to its primary lender, which had suddenly and unceremoniously "yanked" MedTrans's line of credit. Making matters worse, MedTrans's chief financial officer (CFO) unexpectedly resigned in early June 1992. That resignation triggered a crisis between MedTrans and the company's audit firm. Deloitte was nearing completion of its 1992 MedTrans audit and had asked the CFO to sign a letter of representations indicating that the company's financial statements were materially accurate. The CFO told Gordon Johns, the Deloitte audit engagement partner, that he could not sign the letter of representations since he did not believe MedTrans's financial statements were reliable. A few days later, the CFO met with Johns to discuss the situation.

> At the meeting, Ensz [the CFO] alerted Johns to four or five matters relevant to the audit. Ensz said that upon informing Roberts [the CEO] that those matters were not properly entered in MedTrans's journals, Roberts told Ensz to leave the journals as they were and 'let's see' if the auditors 'find it.' Questioning Roberts's character for honesty because of some things Roberts advocated in presenting financial information, Ensz also stated he lacked faith in the integrity of Roberts and MedTrans's financial statements.[1]

The CFO's unsettling allegations caused Deloitte to approach the remainder of the 1992 MedTrans audit with extreme caution. By the end of June 1992, the Deloitte auditors concluded that their client's financial statements contained material errors. Those financial statements reported a net income of nearly $2 million for fiscal 1992, while Deloitte's audit suggested that MedTrans had suffered a loss of approximately $500,000. A large increase in MedTrans's allowance for bad debts proposed by Deloitte accounted for most of the difference between those two figures.

During June and July 1992, Roberts negotiated with William Blair & Company to obtain the additional capital needed by MedTrans. In exchange for a $10 million investment in MedTrans, Roberts and Morgan offered Blair a 50 percent ownership interest in the company. While mulling over this offer, Blair's executives reviewed MedTrans's unaudited financial statements for 1992. Based largely upon the $2 million profit reported in those financial statements, Blair forecasted

---

1. This and all subsequent quotations were taken from the following court opinion: *National Medical Transportation Network v. Deloitte & Touche*, 62 Cal. App. 4th 412 (1998).

that MedTrans's annual earnings would top $6 million by 1995. On July 27, Blair's executives tentatively agreed to invest in MedTrans. The agreement was contingent on MedTrans receiving an unqualified audit opinion on its 1992 financial statements.

Roberts's negotiations with Blair were periodically disrupted by an ongoing quarrel with Gordon Johns. Roberts and Johns feuded throughout the summer of 1992 over the large increase in the company's allowance for bad debts that Deloitte believed was necessary. During a July 9 meeting, Roberts warned Johns that MedTrans's audited financial statements would have a significant impact on whether the Blair transaction was consummated.

> A very focused Roberts vocally and explicitly emphasized the importance of MedTrans's pre-tax earnings because of the potential that Blair might invest in the company. . . . Johns [then] presented Roberts with about $2.5 million in suggested adjustments involving the accounts receivable reserve account. Roberts told Johns: "You better not propose any adjustment that will _____ my deal or you'll be sorry."

Shortly after the July 9 meeting, Johns contacted an executive Deloitte partner in the firm's New York headquarters. The executive partner told Johns that "we should not be associated with companies that threaten us." Unless Roberts accepted the proposed adjustments, the executive partner recommended that Johns resign from the engagement. Johns told the executive partner that before raising the issue again with Roberts, he wanted to give him some time to analyze MedTrans's bad debt reserve and to reconsider the need for the proposed adjustments. On July 30, Roberts and Johns met again. During this meeting, Roberts reminded Johns of the impact Deloitte's audit would have on the proposed Blair deal. Roberts also gave Johns a memorandum prepared by MedTrans's personnel that presented a more favorable analysis of the company's bad debt reserve than the analysis developed by Deloitte.

Roberts and Johns met a final time on August 13, 1992, to discuss Deloitte's audit and the pending Blair transaction. At this meeting, Johns presented a memorandum containing a new set of proposed adjustments to MedTrans's 1992 financial statements. Collectively, these adjustments would have reduced MedTrans's pre-audit net income even more than the adjustments originally proposed by Deloitte.

> During Johns's presentation, Roberts rose, threw down the memorandum and said very angrily: "You are finished." Although Johns thought he had been fired, Roberts told Johns not to construe the situation that way. However, after MedTrans's successive rejections of proposed adjustments to its unaudited financial statements, Johns believed the parties' mutually exclusive views of those statements indicated there was no longer a basis for a relationship. Thus, Johns told Roberts that if defendants had not been fired, he was resigning. Roberts told Johns that "you're going to finish this regardless, under court order or otherwise." Johns believed such threat destroyed any ability to continue as an independent auditor. Johns also believed resignation was necessary because MedTrans bullied Deloitte's personnel and defendants were put at risk by MedTrans's lack of commitment to financial statements accurately depicting the difficulties the company experienced in fiscal 1992.

Deloitte formally resigned from the MedTrans engagement shortly after the August 13 meeting between Johns and Roberts. Four days later, Roberts sent a letter to Deloitte reminding the firm that its resignation would have serious repercussions for the pending Blair deal. Roberts also insisted once more that Deloitte complete the 1992 audit. Deloitte refused to be swayed and remained MedTrans's "former" auditor.

DESPERATELY SEEKING A REPLACEMENT AUDITOR

William Blair & Company learned of Deloitte's resignation in mid-August 1992. On August 25, a Blair representative told Roberts that his firm was indefinitely postponing the planned investment in MedTrans and would not reconsider that decision until MedTrans obtained an independent audit opinion on its 1992 financial statements. The Blair official suggested that MedTrans retain Blair & Company's audit firm, Ernst & Young. Roberts immediately contacted Ernst & Young. Within a few days, Roberts sent Deloitte a letter authorizing the firm to "discuss freely with E&Y the audit history of MedTrans with Deloitte, the details of Deloitte's proposed audit of MedTrans for fiscal 1992 and the facts and circumstances of Deloitte's withdrawal/resignation/disengagement as MedTrans's auditor."

Gordon Johns met with representatives of Ernst & Young on September 3, 1992. During that meeting, Johns explained why Deloitte had resigned from the MedTrans engagement. Johns also revealed that he questioned the integrity of MedTrans's senior executives. Despite the information obtained from Johns, E&Y agreed to audit MedTrans's 1992 financial statements.

Roberts concluded during late September that Blair was unlikely to invest in MedTrans regardless of the outcome of E&Y's audit. At that point, Roberts began searching for another potential investor to bail MedTrans out of the financial crisis it faced. Within a few days, a company contacted by Roberts, American Medical Response, Inc. (AMR), expressed interest in acquiring MedTrans. Like MedTrans, AMR's principal line of business was providing ambulance services. When AMR executives recommended that MedTrans retain Peat Marwick, AMR's audit firm, to audit its 1992 financial statements, Roberts dismissed E&Y and contacted Peat Marwick. Roberts also contacted Deloitte and authorized the firm to discuss with Peat Marwick the circumstances surrounding its resignation from the MedTrans audit. After communicating with Deloitte, the San Diego office of Peat Marwick agreed to audit MedTrans's 1992 financial statements. One week after accepting the engagement, Peat Marwick resigned. Subsequent testimony revealed that a "directive" sent by Peat Marwick's headquarters office to the firm's San Diego office prompted that resignation. Peat Marwick's refusal to audit MedTrans apparently quelled AMR's interest in the company.

MedTrans finally retained another audit firm in late October 1992. This firm, identified only as "Silberman" in court transcripts, served as MedTrans's auditor during the mid-1980s. Before accepting the engagement, Silberman discussed with Deloitte the circumstances surrounding its resignation as MedTrans's auditor. In December 1992, Silberman issued an unqualified opinion on MedTrans's 1992 financial statements. Before issuing that opinion, Silberman persuaded MedTrans to accept the large adjustments proposed by Deloitte. MedTrans's 1992 income statement reported a loss of $480,000, which was approximately the figure Deloitte had arrived at several months earlier.

Laidlaw Medical Transportation, Inc., purchased MedTrans in June 1993. Roberts and Morgan netted $3 million from the sale of their company. Under

Laidlaw's ownership, MedTrans soon became the largest provider of ambulance services in the nation.

MEDTRANS SUES DELOITTE

In August 1993, Roberts and Morgan sued Deloitte on behalf of their former company. The principal allegations against Deloitte centered on charges of professional negligence and breach of contract. Roberts and Morgan charged that Deloitte's malfeasance caused Blair not to consummate the $10 million investment deal arranged by Roberts. MedTrans's former co-owners requested damages equal to the difference between the amount they received from the sale of MedTrans and the amount the company allegedly would have been worth had Blair invested in the firm. The lawsuit was tried before a jury in a California state court in July 1995.

MedTrans's legal counsel succinctly summed up the key allegations against Deloitte in the following statement.

> What is the negligence that we contend occurred? What is the breach that we contend occurred? Very simply: they [Deloitte] contracted over a course of years, and in connection with the year of 1992, to perform an audit and to render an opinion, they did neither, and walked away after getting payment for such services.

Deloitte's defense team rebutted these allegations by insisting that the accounting firm had a right to resign from the 1992 audit when it "lost faith in the honesty of MedTrans's senior management." A CPA retained by Deloitte to serve as an expert witness testified that the firm was obligated to resign from the engagement after its independence was "compromised by Roberts's threats."

After a short trial, Judge Philip Sharp instructed the jurors on the legal matters they should consider during their deliberations. The jurors reached their decision quickly, ruling in favor of MedTrans on all key issues raised during the trial. The jury ruled that Deloitte acted negligently and breached its contractual obligations to MedTrans when it withdrew from the 1992 audit engagement. Additionally, the jury ruled that Deloitte "negligently interfered" with and "disrupted" Med-Trans's economic relationships with Blair, Ernst & Young, and Peat Marwick. This latter ruling stemmed from charges that Deloitte made defamatory statements to E&Y and Peat Marwick concerning the integrity of MedTrans's former executives. Deloitte allegedly made these statements during the predecessor-successor auditor communications with those two firms following its resignation as MedTrans's auditor. After issuing their rulings on the specific complaints filed against Deloitte, the jurors awarded MedTrans's former owners a $9.9 million judgment against the accounting firm.

DELOITTE APPEALS JURY VERDICT

Deloitte quickly appealed the jury's verdict. The accounting firm insisted that the trial judge erred when he instructed the jury prior to its deliberations. Included in Judge Sharp's instructions to the jury was the following statement concerning an auditor's right to resign from an engagement.

Once an accountant has undertaken to serve a client, the employment and duty as an accountant continues until ended by consent or request of the client or the accountant withdraws from the employment, if it does not unduly jeopardize the interest of the client, after giving the client reasonable opportunity to employ another accountant or the matter for which the person [accountant] was employed has been concluded.

These instructions, Deloitte maintained, gave the jury only one alternative, namely, deciding the case in MedTrans's favor. The accounting firm argued that the phrase "if it [auditor's resignation] does not unduly jeopardize the interest of the client" implies that an auditor must consider the economic impact on a client before resigning. Deloitte demonstrated during the appeal that professional auditing standards do not require auditors to consider the potential economic impact on a client of a resignation decision. The jury instructions also suggested that an auditor must give a client "reasonable opportunity" to retain another audit firm before resigning. Again, Deloitte established that professional standards do not impose such a responsibility on independent auditors.

Deloitte argued before the appellate court that an accounting firm may resign from an audit engagement whenever it has "good cause" to do so. The firm also insisted that "good cause" in this context must be defined in reference to the professional standards of the auditing discipline. Deloitte then identified three reasons why it had good cause to resign from the 1992 MedTrans audit: MedTrans management's refusal to cooperate fully with the auditors, the auditors' loss of confidence in client management's integrity, and the threats that Roberts made to Johns. Deloitte claimed that Roberts's threats, alone, provided sufficient justification to resign since those threats undermined its independence. MedTrans's attorneys agreed that auditors could resign when they had "good cause" to do so but attempted to persuade the appellate court to apply a more general, legalistic interpretation to that phrase that was independent of professional auditing standards.

Strengthening Deloitte's good cause argument was a "friend of the court" filing submitted by the American Institute of Certified Public Accountants (AICPA). In that filing, the AICPA reiterated Deloitte's assertion that Roberts's threats undermined the audit firm's independence. The AICPA noted that an auditor must decide as a "matter of professional judgment" whether he is independent. "An auditor's independence may be impaired whenever the member and the member's client company or its management are in threatened or actual positions of material adverse interests by reason of threatened or actual litigation." The AICPA went on to observe that "an auditor who believes independence has been impaired is forbidden from issuing an audit opinion."

After briefly contesting Deloitte's contention that it had "good cause" to resign from the 1992 audit, MedTrans's legal counsel adopted a second strategy during the appeal. MedTrans's attorneys argued that Deloitte forfeited its right to file an appeal predicated on the allegedly prejudicial jury instructions since the accounting firm had not offered the trial judge any alternate jury instructions. In fact, Deloitte initially challenged the jury instructions written by Judge Sharp. At that point, Judge Sharp offered to consider alternate instructions developed by Deloitte's legal counsel; however, the accounting firm never submitted revised jury instructions for the judge's consideration. Despite Deloitte's apparent oversight, the appellate court ruled that Deloitte did not forfeit its right to challenge the impact of Judge Sharp's jury instructions on the jury's verdict.

... where as here, the trial court gives a jury instruction which is prejudicially erroneous as given, i.e., which is an incorrect statement of law, the party harmed by the instruction need not have objected to the instruction or proposed a correct instruction of his own in order to preserve the right to complain of the erroneous instruction on appeal.

Jury Verdict Overturned

In early 1998, the California Court of Appeal overturned the jury's verdict in the *MedTrans v. Deloitte* civil case. The appellate court ruled that Judge Sharp's instructions predisposed the jury to rule in MedTrans's favor.

After overturning the jury's verdict, the appellate court addressed each of the major allegations made against Deloitte by MedTrans in the original trial. First, the appellate court rejected MedTrans's contention that Deloitte acted negligently when it withdrew from the 1992 audit. The court agreed with Deloitte that the auditing profession's standards are the primary authoritative source in this context. Applying those standards, the appellate court ruled that Deloitte clearly had a reasonable basis for resigning from the 1992 audit. Second, the appellate court discredited the breach of contract allegation lodged against Deloitte. Recall that MedTrans's management pressured Deloitte to issue an unqualified opinion on the company's original 1992 financial statements. The appellate court ruled that "Deloitte cannot be held liable to MedTrans in breach of contract for having declined to issue a false 'unqualified' audit report." The court also rejected Med-Trans's claim that Deloitte's failure to issue an audit opinion of any kind constituted breach of contract. Finally, the appellate court dismissed MedTrans's assertion that Deloitte's communications with the company's successor auditors were defamatory.

> Defamation is an intentional tort. In any event, as discussed, the record contained ample evidence that defendants' communications with potential successor auditors about their reasons for resigning from their engagement with MedTrans complied with applicable professional standards requiring open communication with potential successor auditors and were consistent with MedTrans's written authorizations requesting defendants to speak freely with those potential successor auditors.

Questions

1. Following his resignation, MedTrans's former CFO met with Gordon Johns, the Deloitte audit engagement partner. Did the CFO have a responsibility to inform Johns of the errors in MedTrans's 1992 financial statements? Defend your answer.
2. What courses of action were available to Johns following his meeting with MedTrans's former CFO? Which of those options would you have selected? Why?
3. How did the threats Roberts made to Johns impair Deloitte's independence? The AICPA maintained that an audit firm is "forbidden" from issuing an audit opinion when it believes its independence has been impaired. Identify three circumstances, unrelated to this case, that would threaten an audit firm's independence.

4. Did Deloitte have a responsibility to be totally candid with MedTrans's prospective successor auditors? Explain. Under present auditing standards, what questions should a prospective successor auditor pose to a predecessor auditor?

5. The jury in the *MedTrans v. Deloitte* lawsuit ruled that the accounting firm negligently resigned from the 1992 audit, breached its contract with the client, and made defamatory statements regarding MedTrans's former executives during the predecessor-successor auditor communications. The appellate court reversed these rulings. Provide an example of each alleged type of misconduct for which an audit firm likely *would be* held legally responsible.

CASE 7.7
STEPHEN GRAY, CPA

During the mid-1980s, Stephen W. Gray owned and operated a small CPA firm in Columbia, Mississippi.[1] Located in south central Mississippi near the banks of the Pearl River, Columbia's population of 5,000 provided Gray with only a modest client base and limited potential for revenue growth. In 1987, Gray struck upon an idea to expand his practice.

For several years, Gray had offered financial planning services to his clients. After developing a financial plan for a customer, Gray referred the individual to a securities broker. The broker then purchased the appropriate investments for the customer. After obtaining a broker's license in June 1987, Gray became affiliated with a Texas-based investment firm, H.D. Vest Investment Securities, Inc., and began offering brokerage services to his clients.

Gray took several steps to protect the integrity of his CPA status after he began providing brokerage services. To safeguard his independence on attest engagements, he refused to provide brokerage services to clients for whom he performed audits and other attestation services. Gray also adopted a strict policy of informing clients that he would earn commissions on securities trades they placed through him. Finally, to make his customers and the general public aware of his dual professional roles, he prominently displayed his broker's license within his office.

Gray realized that accepting commissions technically violated the ethical code of the Mississippi State Board of Public Accountancy. Since 1973, the state agency had vigorously enforced a ban on the receipt of commissions by CPAs. This ban

---

1. Most of the facts and all of the quotations appearing in this case were drawn from the following legal opinion: *Mississippi State Board of Public Accountancy, et al. v. Stephen W. Gray, CPA,* 674 So. 2d 1252 (1996).

included commissions received exclusively from non-attest clients. When he applied for a broker's license in 1987, Gray was also keenly aware of an ongoing conflict between the Federal Trade Commission (FTC) and the American Institute of Certified Public Accountants (AICPA). That conflict involved the FTC's efforts to force the AICPA to allow its members to accept commissions from non-attest clients. The FTC prevailed in 1988 when the AICPA's ruling council voted 191 to 5 to allow members to accept commissions for certain services provided to non-attest clients.[2] Rule 503 of the *AICPA Code of Professional Conduct*, shown in Exhibit 1, expresses the AICPA's present stance regarding the receipt of commissions by its members.

In late 1990, a CPA alerted the Mississippi State Board of Public Accountancy that he had evidence Stephen Gray was accepting commissions in exchange for brokerage services. The CPA stumbled across this evidence while providing accounting services to a former client of Gray. Following a brief investigation, the state board charged Gray with violating its ban against accepting commissions. At an April 19, 1991, hearing before the state agency, Gray acknowledged that he had accepted commissions from non-attest clients. Gray then maintained that the state board exceeded its statutory authority when it adopted the ban on commissions. He also argued that the rule was not in the public interest.

EXHIBIT 1
Rule 503 of the *AICPA Code of Professional Conduct*

Rule 503—Commissions and Referral Fees

A. Prohibited commissions

A member in public practice shall not for a commission recommend or refer to a client any product or service, or for a commission recommend or refer any product or service to be supplied by a client, or receive a commission, when the member or the member's firm also performs for that client

(a) an audit or review of a financial statement; or

(b) a compilation of a financial statement when the member expects, or reasonably might expect, that a third party will use the financial statement and the member's compilation report does not disclose a lack of independence; or

(c) an examination of prospective financial information.

This prohibition applies during the period in which the member is engaged to perform any of the services listed above and the period covered by any historical financial statements involved in such listed services.

B. Disclosure of permitted commissions

A member in public practice who is not prohibited from performing services for or receiving a commission and who is paid or expects to be paid a commission shall disclose that fact to any person or entity to whom the member recommends or refers a product or service to which the commission relates.

C. Referral fees

Any member who accepts a referral fee for recommending or referring any service of a CPA to any person or entity or who pays a referral fee to obtain a client shall disclose such acceptance or payment to the client.

---

2. L. Berton, "Nation's Accountants Vote to End Bans Against Certain Fees and Commissions," *The Wall Street Journal*, 31 August 1988, 33.

The Mississippi state board patiently listened to Gray's arguments. One month later, the board voted to revoke Gray's CPA certificate and his license to practice. Gray immediately appealed that decision, an appeal heard by the Marion County Circuit Court. During the lengthy appeals process, Gray retained both his CPA certificate and license to practice.

In reviewing the state board's decision, the circuit court placed considerable weight on the AICPA rule that allowed CPAs to receive commissions from non-attest clients. The court noted that 46 state boards of accountancy, including the Mississippi state board, prohibited CPAs from receiving such commissions. But then, the court went on to observe that it was even more impressive "that the national association of all CPAs specifically allows for the receipt of commissions."

The circuit court also questioned whether the ban on receiving commissions improperly infringed on CPAs' ability to earn a livelihood. CPAs who ply their trade in the more remote areas of the state, the court observed, were particularly subject to being harmed by this rule. The circuit court proposed a control procedure to mitigate conflicts of interest that might arise from allowing CPAs to accept commissions for non-attest services. This procedure would require CPAs to file a report with the state board disclosing the non-attest services they provided on a commission basis. These reports would also require disclosure of the relationship, if any, between the non-attest and attest services offered by a CPA.

On January 16, 1992, the Marion County Circuit Court released its ruling on Stephen Gray's appeal. That ruling overturned the state board's revocation of Gray's CPA certificate and license to practice. According to the circuit court, the state board's action was "too extreme a remedy for the facts and circumstances of this case."

The Mississippi State Board of Public Accountancy appealed the circuit court's reversal of its decision to the Supreme Court of Mississippi. Under Mississippi state law, the key issue that a state court must consider in reviewing a state agency's decision is whether that decision was arbitrary and capricious. After studying the case, the supreme court concluded that the circuit court never raised the issue of whether the state board's decision was arbitrary and capricious. Instead, the circuit court simply substituted its judgment for that of the state board in overturning the latter's decision. The supreme court ruled that the circuit court's failure to fulfill its judicial mandate invalidated the reversal of the state board's decision.

To bring closure to the Gray case, the Supreme Court of Mississippi decided to tackle the question itself of whether the state board's decision qualified as arbitrary and capricious. First, the supreme court reviewed the legislative authority granted the state board. An excerpt from the relevant state statute follows:

> The Mississippi State Board of Public Accountancy is hereby authorized with the following powers and duties: to adopt and enforce such rules and regulations concerning certified public accountant examinee and licensee qualifications and practices as the board considers necessary to maintain the highest standard of proficiency in the profession of certified public accounting and for protection of the public interest.

Later sections of this statute grant the state board authority to promulgate accounting, auditing, and ethical standards for CPAs. These standards include the following rule that Stephen Gray violated.

> A licensee shall not pay a commission to obtain a client nor shall he accept a commission for a referral to a client of products or services of others. This rule shall not pro-

hibit payments for the purchase of all, or a material part of, an accounting practice or retirement payments to individuals formerly engaged in the practice of public accounting or payments to their heirs and estates.

The supreme court eventually pared the issue of whether the state board's decision was arbitrary and capricious to a more specific question. That question was whether the board's ban on commissions qualified as arbitrary and capricious. After a thorough review of the matter, the supreme court ruled that the ban on commissions was an appropriate professional standard for the board to adopt and enforce. In reaching this decision, the supreme court referred to the *United States v. Arthur Young & Co.* opinion handed down in 1984 by the U.S. Supreme Court.[3] In that opinion, the Supreme Court observed that CPAs have a responsibility to maintain complete fidelity to the public interest at all times. Allowing CPAs to accept commissions could potentially cause them to place their own economic interests over their responsibilities to the public, reasoned the Mississippi Supreme Court. More to the point, the supreme court questioned Gray's ability to retain his independence and objectivity while offering services on a commission basis to non-attest clients.

> Gray's dual role as a certified public accountant and a registered representative of the H.D. Vest firm creates a potential conflict of interest and raises questions of independence and objectivity with regard to whether his investment advice is motivated by the client's tax needs or the commissions those investments might generate.

In May 1996, the Supreme Court of Mississippi issued its decision in the Gray case. The supreme court reversed the circuit court's decision and thereby reinstated the state board's evocation of Stephen Gray's CPA certificate and license.

> The Mississippi State Board of Public Accountancy was acting within its regulatory power when it revoked Gray's license. There is substantial evidence in the record to support the decision, which was not arbitrary or capricious or in violation of Gray's rights. In conclusion, we find that the circuit court improperly substituted its own judgment for that of the Board. Accordingly, we reverse the order of the circuit court and reinstate the Board's decision.

EPILOGUE

In 1996, the Mississippi State Board of Public Accountancy dropped its ban on the receipt of commissions from non-attest clients. The board effectively adopted Rule 503 of the *AICPA Code of Professional Conduct* shown in Exhibit 1.[4] By the late 1990s, nearly 30 states allowed CPAs to receive commissions from non-attest clients.[5]

As noted earlier, Stephen Gray retained his CPA certificate and license to practice while his appeal of the state board's decision worked its way through the judicial system. Following the Mississippi Supreme Court's ruling in the Gray case,

3. *United States v. Arthur Young & Co.*, 104 S. Ct. 1495 (1984).

4. The complete ethical code of the Mississippi State Board of Public Accountancy can be found at that organization's Web site, *msbpa.state.ms.us*.

5. *Public Accounting Report*, "21 States Hold Out On Commissions," 31 March 1998, 5.

the state board reconsidered its original decision to revoke Gray's CPA certificate and license to practice. Instead of enforcing that decision, the state board required Gray's accounting practice to undergo one year of supervisory review. Gray successfully completed that review and is presently a CPA in good standing with the Mississippi State Board of Public Accountancy.

QUESTIONS

1. Why do professions adopt ethical codes for their members? What factors cause professions to change these codes over time?

2. In your opinion, did the Mississippi State Board of Public Accountancy make an appropriate decision when it eventually chose not to enforce the revocation of Stephen Gray's CPA certificate and license to practice? Defend your answer.

3. Suppose that a CPA's spouse holds a broker's license. Would the CPA violate Rule 503 of the *AICPA Code of Professional Conduct* if the spouse provides brokerage services on a commission basis to an attest client of the CPA?

4. Compare and contrast the oversight roles within the accounting profession of state boards of public accountancy and the AICPA. What is the role of "state societies" of CPAs in the accounting profession?

Section Eight
Classic Litigation Cases

O chicken
strip salad

CASE 8.1

FRED STERN & COMPANY, INC.
(*ULTRAMARES CORPORATION v. TOUCHE ET AL.*)

In the business world of the Roaring Twenties, the scams and schemes of flimflam artists and confidence men were legendary. The absence of a strong regulatory system at the federal level to police the securities markets—the Securities and Exchange Commission was not established until 1934—aided, if not encouraged, financial frauds of all types. In all likelihood, the majority of individuals involved in business during the 1920s were scrupulously honest. Nevertheless, the culture of that decade bred a disproportionate number of opportunists who adopted an "anything goes" approach to transacting business. An example of a company in which this self-serving attitude apparently prevailed was Fred Stern & Company, Inc. During the mid-1920s, Stern's executives duped three of the company's creditors out of several hundred thousand dollars.

Based in New York City, Stern imported rubber, a raw material demanded in huge quantities by many industries in the early twentieth century. During the 1920s alone, industrial demand for rubber in the United States more than tripled. The nature of the rubber importation trade required large amounts of working capital. Because Stern was chronically short of working capital, the company relied heavily on banks and other lenders to finance its day-to-day operations.

In March 1924, Stern sought a $100,000 loan from Ultramares Corporation, a finance company whose primary line of business was factoring receivables. Before considering the loan request, Ultramares asked Stern's management for an audited balance sheet. Stern had been audited a few months earlier by Touche, Niven & Company, a prominent accounting firm based in London and New York City. Touche had served as Stern's independent auditor since 1920. Exhibit 1 presents the unqualified opinion Touche issued on Stern's December 31, 1923, balance sheet. Stern's management obtained from Touche 32 serially numbered copies of the audit report. Touche knew that Stern intended to use the audit re-

EXHIBIT 1
Touche, Niven &
Company's Audit Opinion
on Stern's December 31,
1923, Balance Sheet

February 26, 1924

Touche, Niven & Co.
Public Accountants
Eighty Maiden Lane,
New York

Certificate of Auditors

We have examined the accounts of Fred Stern & Co., Inc., for the year ended December 31, 1923, and hereby certify that the annexed balance sheet is in accordance therewith and with the information and explanations given us. We further certify that, subject to provision for federal taxes on income, the said statement in our opinion, presents a true and correct view of the financial condition of Fred Stern & Co., Inc., as at December 31, 1923.

ports to obtain external debt financing but was unaware of the specific banks or finance companies that might receive the audit reports.

After reviewing Stern's audited balance sheet—which reported assets of more than $2.5 million and a net worth of approximately $1 million—and the accompanying audit report, Ultramares granted the $100,000 loan requested by the company. Ultramares later extended two more loans to Stern totaling $65,000. During the same time frame, Stern obtained more than $300,000 in loans from two local banks after providing them with copies of the December 31, 1923, balance sheet and accompanying audit report.

Unfortunately for Ultramares and the two banks that extended loans to Stern, the company was declared bankrupt in January 1925. Subsequent courtroom testimony revealed that the company had been hopelessly insolvent at the end of 1923 when its audited balance sheet reported a net worth of $1 million. An accountant with Stern, identified only as Romberg in court records, concealed Stern's bankrupt status from the Touche auditors. Romberg masked Stern's true financial condition by making several false entries in the company's accounting records. The largest of these entries involved a debit of more than $700,000 to accounts receivable and an offsetting credit to sales.

Following Stern's bankruptcy, Ultramares sued Touche to recover the $165,000 loaned to Stern. Ultramares alleged that the audit firm had been both fraudulent and negligent in auditing Stern's financial records. *The New York Times* noted that the negligence claim in the Ultramares suit was "novel" and would likely serve as a major "test case" for third parties hoping to recover losses from audit firms.[1] The novel aspect of the negligence claim stemmed from the absence of a contractual relationship between Touche and Ultramares. Touche's contract to audit Stern's December 31, 1923, balance sheet was made solely with Stern's management. At the time, a well-entrenched legal doctrine dictated that only a party in privity with another—that is, having an explicit contractual agreement with another—could recover damages resulting from the other party's negligence.

Another interesting facet of the Ultramares lawsuit involved the founder of Touche, Niven & Company, Sir George Alexander Touche. George Touche, who served for two years as the sheriff of London during World War I, merged his accounting practice in the early 1900s with that of a young Scottish accountant, John B. Niven, who had immigrated to New York City. The new firm prospered,

---

1. "Damages Refused for Error in Audit," *The New York Times*, 27 June 1929, 50.

and George Touche, who was knighted in 1917 by King George V, eventually became one of the most respected leaders of the emerging public accounting profession. John Niven also became influential within the profession. Ironically, Niven was serving as the president of the American Institute of Accountants, the predecessor of the AICPA, when Fred Stern & Company was declared insolvent. An issue posed by the Ultramares lawsuit was whether George Touche and his fellow partners who were not involved in the Stern audit could be held personally liable for any malfeasance by the Touche auditors assigned to the Stern engagement. Ultramares raised that issue by naming each of the Touche partners as co-defendants.

ULTRAMARES CORPORATION V. TOUCHE ET AL.: A PROTRACTED LEGAL BATTLE

The Ultramares civil suit against Touche was tried before a jury in a New York state court. Ultramares' principal allegation was that the Touche auditors should have easily discovered the $700,000 overstatement of receivables in Stern's December 31, 1923, balance sheet. That error, if corrected, would have slashed Stern's reported net worth by nearly 70 percent and considerably lessened the likelihood that Ultramares would have extended the company a sizable loan.

A young man by the name of Siess performed most of the field work on the Stern audit. When Siess arrived at Stern's office to begin the audit in early February 1924, he discovered that the company's general ledger had not been posted since the prior April. He spent the next few days posting entries from the client's journals to its general ledger. After Siess completed that task, Stern's accounts receivable totaled approximately $644,000. Stern's accountant, Romberg, obtained the general ledger the day before Siess intended to prepare a trial balance of the company's accounts. After reviewing the ledger, Romberg booked an entry debiting receivables and crediting sales for approximately $706,000. Beside the entry in the receivables account, he entered a number cross-referencing the recorded amount to the company's sales journal.

The following day, Romberg notified Siess of the entry he had recorded in the general ledger. Romberg told Siess that the entry represented Stern's December sales that had been inadvertently omitted from the accounting records. Without questioning Romberg's explanation for the large entry, Siess included the $706,000 in the receivables balance. In fact, the receivables did not exist, the corresponding sales never occurred. To support the entry, Romberg or one of his subordinates hastily prepared 17 bogus sales invoices.

In subsequent testimony, Siess initially reported that he could not recall whether he reviewed any of the 17 invoices allegedly representing Stern's December sales. Plaintiff counsel then demonstrated that "a mere glance" at the invoices would have revealed that they were forged. The invoices lacked shipping numbers, customer order numbers, and other pertinent information. Following this revelation, Siess admitted that he had not examined any of the invoices.[2] Touche's attorneys attempted to justify this oversight by pointing out that audits involve "testing and sampling" rather than an examination of entire

2. *Ultramares Corporation v. Touche et al.*, 255 N.Y. 170, 174 N.E. 441 (1930), 449.

accounting populations.[3] Thus, it was not surprising or unusual, the attorneys argued, that none of the fictitious December sales invoices were among the more than 200 invoices examined during the Stern audit.

The court ruled that auditing on a sample basis is appropriate in most cases. But, given the suspicious nature of the large December sales entry recorded by Romberg, the court concluded that Touche should have specifically reviewed the December sales invoices.

> Verification by test and sample was very likely a sufficient audit as to accounts regularly entered upon the books in the usual course of business. . . . [However], the defendants were put on their guard by the circumstances touching the December accounts receivable to scrutinize with special care.[4]

Ultramares' attorneys noted during the trial that Touche had even more reason than just the suspicious nature of Romberg's December sales entry to question the integrity of the large year-end increase in receivables. While auditing the company's inventory, Touche auditors discovered several errors that collectively caused the inventory account to be overstated by more than $300,000, an overstatement of 90 percent. The auditors also uncovered large errors in Stern's accounts payable and discovered that the company had improperly pledged the same assets as collateral for several bank loans. Given the extent and nature of the problems revealed by the Touche audit, the court ruled that the accounting firm should have been particularly skeptical of the client's accounting records. This should have been the case, the court observed, even though Touche had not encountered any reason in previous audits to question the integrity of Stern's management.

> No doubt the extent to which inquiry must be pressed beyond appearances is a question of judgment, as to which opinions will often differ. No doubt the wisdom that is born after the event will engender suspicion and distrust when old acquaintance and good repute may have silenced doubt at the beginning.[5]

The jury in the *Ultramares* case dismissed the fraud charge against Touche. The jurors ruled that the company's attorneys failed to establish that the audit firm had intentionally deceived Ultramares—intentional deceit being a necessary condition for fraud. Regarding the negligence charge, the jury ruled in favor of Ultramares and ordered Touche to pay the company damages of $186,000.

The judge who presided over the *Ultramares* case overturned the jury's ruling on the negligence charge. In explaining his decision, the judge acknowledged that Ultramares' attorneys clearly established that Touche had been negligent during its 1923 audit of Stern. Nevertheless, the judge ruled that the jury had overlooked the long-standing legal doctrine that only a party in privity could sue and recover damages resulting from a defendant's negligence.

> Negligence is not actionable unless there is a breach of duty owing by defendants to the plaintiff. To hold that the defendants' duty extended to not only Stern but to all persons to whom Stern might exhibit the balance sheet, and who would act in reliance thereon, would compel the defendants to assume a potential liability to practically the entire world.[6]

---

3. *Ibid.*, 449.

4. *Ibid.*

5. *Ibid.*, 444.

6. "Damages Refused for Error in Audit," *The New York Times*, 27 June 1929, 50.

Ultramares' attorneys quickly appealed the trial judge's decision. The appellate division of the New York Supreme Court reviewed the case. In a 3 to 2 vote, the appellate division decided that the trial judge erred in reversing the jury's verdict on the negligence charge. As appellate Justice McAvoy noted, the key question in the case centered on whether Touche had a duty to Ultramares "in the absence of a direct contractual relation."[7] Justice McAvoy concluded that Touche did have an obligation to Ultramares, and to other parties relying on Stern's financial statements, although the accounting firm's contract was expressly and exclusively with Stern.

> One cannot issue an unqualified statement [audit opinion] . . . and then disclaim responsibility for his work. Banks and merchants, to the knowledge of these defendants, require certified balance sheets from independent accountants, and upon these audits they make their loans. Thus, the duty arises to these banks and merchants of an exercise of reasonable care in the making and uttering of certified balance sheets.[8]

Justice McAvoy and two of his colleagues were unwavering in their opinion that Touche had a legal obligation to Ultramares. Nevertheless, the remaining two judges on the appellate panel were just as strongly persuaded that no such obligation existed. In the dissenting opinion, Justice Finch maintained that holding Touche responsible to a third party that subsequently relied upon the Stern financial statements was patently unfair to the accounting firm.

> If the plaintiff [Ultramares] had inquired of the accountants whether they might rely upon the certificate in making a loan, then the accountants would have had the opportunity to gauge their responsibility and risk, and determine with knowledge how thorough their verification of the account should be before assuming the responsibility of making the certificate run to the plaintiff.[9]

Following the appellate division's ruling in the *Ultramares* case, Touche's attorneys appealed the decision to the next highest court in the New York state judicial system, the court of appeals. That court ultimately handed down the final ruling in the lengthy judicial history of the case. The chief justice of New York's court of appeals, Benjamin Cardozo, was a nationally recognized legal scholar whose opinions were given great weight by other courts. Justice Cardozo and his six associate justices ruled unanimously that the judge who presided over the Ultramares trial had properly reversed the jury's decision on the negligence claim. Justice Cardozo reiterated the arguments made by Justice Finch. He maintained that it would be unfair to hold Touche legally responsible to a third party, unknown to Touche when its audit was performed, that happened to obtain and rely upon Stern's audited balance sheet. However, Justice Cardozo went on to suggest that had Ultramares been clearly designated as a beneficiary of the Stern–Touche contract, his ruling would have been different.

Unfortunately for the accounting profession, Justice Cardozo's opinion did not end with his commentary on the negligence question in the *Ultramares* case. After resolving that issue, he sharply criticized Touche's audit of Stern. The judge implied that Ultramares might have been successful in suing Touche on the basis of gross negligence: "Negligence or blindness, even when not equivalent to

---

7. *Ultramares Corporation v. Touche et al.*, 229 App. Div. 581, 243 N.Y.S. 179 (1930), 181.

8. *Ibid.*, 182.

9. *Ibid.*, 186.

fraud, is none the less evidence to sustain an inference of fraud. . . . At least this is so if the negligence is gross . . . [in the Ultramares case] a jury might find that . . . [the Touche auditors] closed their eyes to the obvious, and blindly gave assent."[10]

THE *ULTRAMARES* DECISION: IMPLICATIONS FOR THE PUBLIC ACCOUNTING PROFESSION

In retrospect, the *Ultramares* decision had two principal implications for the public accounting profession. First, Judge Cardozo's opinion established the precedent that certain direct beneficiaries of an audit, generally referred to as primary beneficiaries, are entitled to recover damages from a negligent auditor. Subsequent to the *Ultramares* ruling, very few plaintiffs were successful in establishing themselves as primary beneficiaries of an audit.[11] Consequently, this "expansion" of the auditor's legal exposure proved to be fairly insignificant.

The second key implication of the *Ultramares* case was that it provided a new strategy for plaintiff counsel to use in suing auditors on behalf of nonprivity parties. Following the *Ultramares* ruling, attorneys representing such plaintiffs began predicating lawsuits against auditors on allegations of gross negligence. Before that ruling, nonprivity third parties faced the heavy burden of proving fraud if they wanted to recover losses resulting from auditor malfeasance. Because establishing gross negligence is much easier than proving intent to defraud, the *Ultramares* decision significantly increased auditors' legal exposure to nonprivity third parties.

A secondary issue addressed by Justice Cardozo in the *Ultramares* case was whether Sir George Touche and his fellow partners who had no direct connection with the Stern engagement could be held liable for the inadequate Stern audit. This issue was moot regarding the negligence allegation since that charge had already been dismissed. The issue was still pertinent to the fraud charge. Justice Cardozo ruled that Ultramares was entitled to a re-trial to determine whether Touche's negligence was severe enough to infer fraudulent conduct or gross negligence.[12] Justice Cardozo, in no uncertain terms, ruled that all of Touche's partners were legally responsible for the actions of the firm's employees during the Stern audit, since those employees served as agents of the partners.

EPILOGUE

In the years following the *Ultramares* case, the legal exposure of public accountants to third-party financial statement users was gradually extended. The first

---

10. *Ultramares Corporation v. Touche et al.*, 255 N.Y. 170, 174 N.E. 441 (1930), 449.

11. Decades later, the *Credit Alliance* case established several restrictive conditions that third parties must satisfy to qualify as primary beneficiaries. See: *Credit Alliance Corporation v. Arthur Andersen & Company*, 483 N.E. 2d 110 (N.Y. 1985).

12. For whatever reason, Ultramares chose not to file an amended lawsuit against Touche predicated upon an allegation of gross negligence.

extension came on the heels of the *Ultramares* case with the passage of the Securities Act of 1933. That federal statute imposed on auditors a very significant legal obligation to initial purchasers of new securities marketed on an interstate basis.

Under the 1933 Act, plaintiffs do not have to prove fraud, gross negligence, or even negligence on the part of auditors. Essentially, plaintiffs must only establish that they suffered investment losses and that the relevant financial statements contain material errors or omissions. If a plaintiff establishes those elements of proof, the defendant accounting firm assumes the burden of proving that its employees were "duly diligent" in performing the audit.[13] To sustain a due diligence defense, an accounting firm must show that following a "reasonable investigation," it had "reasonable ground to believe and did believe" that the audited financial statements were materially accurate. Federal courts have not been receptive to the due diligence defense if the plaintiffs have clearly established that the financial statements in question contain material errors.

Auditors' legal exposure has also expanded under the common law over the past several decades. In 1965, the American Law Institute issued *Restatement of Torts*, a legal compendium relied on heavily in many jurisdictions. This source suggests that "foreseen" beneficiaries, in addition to primary beneficiaries, should have a right to recover damages from negligent auditors.[14] Foreseen beneficiaries are members of a limited group or class of third-party financial statement users. Auditors are typically aware of this distinct group of potential financial statement users but unaware of the specific individuals or entities who make up that group.

The 1983 *Rosenblum* ruling went beyond the boundary established by the *Restatement of Torts*. That judicial ruling suggested that even "reasonably foreseeable" or "ordinary" third-party financial statement users should be allowed to recover damages from negligent auditors.[15] Reasonably foreseeable third parties include a much larger population of potential financial statement users than "foreseen" third parties. The most liberal definition of reasonably foreseeable third parties includes individual investors who happen to obtain a copy of audited financial statements and make a decision based upon them.

QUESTIONS

1. Observers of the accounting profession suggest that many courts attempt to "socialize" investment losses by extending auditors' liability to third-party financial statement users. Discuss the benefits and costs of such a policy to public ac-

---

13. Accounting firms have other defenses available to them when sued under the Securities Act of 1933. These defenses include, among others, expiration of the statute of limitations, establishing that the plaintiff knew the relevant financial statements were misleading when he or she purchased the securities, and proving that the plaintiff's damages were not caused by the misleading financial statements.

14. American Law Institute, *Restatement of the Law, Second: Torts* (Philadelphia: American Law Institute, 1965).

15. *H. Rosenblum, Inc. v. Adler*, 461 A. 2d 138 (N.J. 1983).

counting firms, audit clients, and third-party financial statement users, such as investors and creditors. In your view, should the courts have the authority to socialize investment losses? If not, who should determine how investment losses are distributed in our society?

2. Auditors' legal responsibilities differ significantly under the Securities Exchange Act of 1934 and the Securities Act of 1933. Briefly point out these differences and comment on why they exist. Also comment on how auditors' litigation risks differ under the common law and the 1934 Act.

3. The current standard audit report differs significantly from the version issued during the 1920s. Identify the key differences in the two reports and discuss the forces that accounted for the evolution of the audit report into its present form.

4. Why was it common in the 1920s for companies to have only an audited balance sheet prepared for distribution to external third parties? Comment on the factors that over a period of several decades resulted in the adoption of the financial statement package that most companies presently provide to external third parties.

5. When assessing audit risk, should auditors consider the type and number of third parties that may ultimately rely on the client's financial statements? Refer to *SAS No. 47*, "Materiality and Audit Risk in Conducting an Audit," before responding. Should auditors insist that audit engagement letters identify the third parties to whom the client intends to distribute the audited financial statements? Would this practice eliminate auditors' legal liability to nonprivity parties not mentioned in engagement letters?

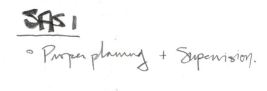

CASE 8.2
BarChris Construction Corporation

Christie Vitolo and Leborio Pugliese became business partners in 1946 when they pooled their resources to form a small construction company in New York City. Initially, Vitolo managed the partnership's financial affairs, while Pugliese supervised the company's construction projects. As the company grew in size, Vitolo's limited understanding of financial management and accounting matters convinced him to hire an accountant, Leonard Russo, to oversee the company's financial functions. Russo was given the title of executive vice-president. A few years later, Vitolo and Pugliese hired two employees of Peat, Marwick, Mitchell & Company, their accounting firm, to serve as the company's controller and treasurer. In 1955, the two partners incorporated their business, forming what later became known as BarChris Construction Corporation. Four years later, they took the company public by selling 560,000 shares of common stock at $3 per share. That stock traded on the American Stock Exchange.

Construction of bowling alleys was BarChris's principal line of business. Bowling as a recreational sport received a tremendous boost in 1952 with the introduction of automatic pin-setting machines in the United States. Over the following decade, the demand for bowling alleys grew at a phenomenal rate. Throughout that time frame, two companies, AMF and Brunswick, constructed most of the hundreds of new bowling alleys scattered across the country. Although much smaller than AMF and Brunswick, BarChris ranked as the third-largest builder of bowling alleys in the United States by 1960. In 1956, BarChris reported sales of $800,000. Four years later, the company's revenues exceeded $9 million, while its net income approached $750,000. In a *Wall Street Journal* article in early 1961, Leonard Russo predicted $15 million of sales for BarChris that year and a profit of $1.2 million.

BarChris built bowling alleys principally for syndicates of small investors. On the date a construction contract was signed, the investment syndicate advanced a small down payment on the bowling alley to BarChris. The investors gave BarChris a promissory note for the balance of the purchase price, a note to be paid off in several annual installments. In 1960, BarChris began engaging in sale and leaseback arrangements with finance companies. In such transactions, BarChris constructed a bowling alley and then sold it to a finance company. The finance company immediately leased the alley to a BarChris subsidiary, which then operated the alley.

Both sales techniques required BarChris to incur large cash expenditures for construction costs before receiving any significant payments from the eventual purchaser of an alley. As a result, the company constantly searched for external financing to bankroll its construction projects. In May 1961, to provide much-needed working capital, BarChris sold $1,740,000 of bonds to the general public under an S-1 registration statement filed with the Securities and Exchange Commission (SEC).[1]

Unfortunately for BarChris and its competitors, the construction market for bowling alleys collapsed in the early 1960s. The sudden decline in new construction projects and another working capital shortage posed a severe financial crisis for BarChris in 1962. BarChris's financial problems worsened during the year after several of the syndicates that had purchased the company's bowling alleys defaulted on their promissory notes. BarChris took control of these bowling alleys and the burden of overseeing their day-to-day operations. In late 1962, after missing interest payments on its outstanding bonds, BarChris filed for protection under Chapter 11 of the federal bankruptcy code.

BONDHOLDERS SUE FOR RECOVERY OF THEIR INVESTMENTS

Following BarChris's bankruptcy filing, the company's bondholders filed a class action lawsuit to recover their investments. Among the defendants named in this lawsuit were the executive officers of BarChris, the company's investment broker, and its accounting firm, Peat Marwick. This lawsuit was noteworthy for the public accounting profession because it was among the first major litigation cases involving independent auditors filed under the Securities Act of 1933, which regulates the sale of new securities.[2] The *BarChris* case provided important insights on the nature and extent of auditors' legal liability under that federal statute. The opinion handed down by the presiding judge in the *BarChris* case focused on the following three issues relevant to Peat Marwick:

1. Did the 1961 S-1 registration statement prepared by BarChris for the purpose of selling the $1.7 million of bonds contain false representations?

---

1. Companies must file an S-1 registration statement with the SEC when they offer new securities for sale to the general public.

2. One study found fewer than two civil suits filed annually under the Securities Act of 1933 during the first few decades it was in effect. During the 1960s and 1970s, the number of such lawsuits increased dramatically. Plaintiff counsel came to recognize that huge judgments could potentially be obtained in class action suits filed against third parties, such as auditors and investment brokers, associated with S-1 registration statements.

2. If the registration statement contained false representations, were they "material"?

3. Did the defendants satisfy their due diligence obligation to review the registration statement to determine whether it was free of material false representations?

Judge McLean, the federal judge who wrote the *BarChris* opinion, demonstrated a masterful understanding of the accounting and auditing issues implicit in each of these questions. As a result, the *BarChris* opinion has been relied upon heavily by judges hearing cases filed under the federal securities laws that involve independent auditors.

ISSUE 1: WERE THERE FALSE REPRESENTATIONS IN THE BARCHRIS S-1 REGISTRATION STATEMENT?

BarChris's 1961 S-1 registration statement contained annual financial statements for 1958 through 1960. Peat Marwick issued unqualified opinions on those financial statements. The registration statement also included financial statements for the first quarter of 1961. Peat Marwick performed what is commonly known as an S-1 review rather than a full-scope audit on the first quarter financial statements for 1961. In evaluating Peat Marwick's conduct in the *BarChris* case, Judge McLean focused principally on the firm's 1960 BarChris audit. Apparently, the judge concluded that prospective investors concentrated on BarChris's audited financial statements for 1960 when reviewing the company's S-1 registration statement.

Exhibit 1 lists the key errors Judge McLean identified in BarChris's 1960 financial statements.[3] The errors in BarChris's sales, net operating income, and earnings per share stemmed principally from two sources. Plaintiffs in the *BarChris* case alleged that the company improperly applied the percentage-of-completion method in accounting for profit recognized on bowling alley construction projects. In fact, the plaintiffs insisted that the completed contract method should have been used for those projects. They argued that there was too much uncertainty involved in the projects to reasonably estimate the profit each would produce. Judge McLean disagreed. The judge ruled that the percentage-of-completion method was the proper accounting technique to use under the circumstances. However, the judge also concluded that the estimated stage of completion of two of the jobs in progress on December 31, 1960, had been overly optimistic. By overstating those jobs' stage of completion, BarChris improperly "front-ended" much of the profit on the projects.

A sale and leaseback transaction was the second major source of the errors in BarChris's 1960 operating results. This transaction involved BarChris's Heavenly Lanes construction project in East Haven, Connecticut. At the time, accounting standards allowed the total gain on sale and leaseback transactions to be reported in the accounting period in which the transaction occurred.[4] Although permissi-

---

3. Although not discussed in this case, Judge McLean identified similar errors in BarChris's unaudited financial statements for the first quarter of 1961.

4. In 1960, accounting standards only required that "the principal details of any important sale-and-leaseback transaction" be disclosed in the financial statements.

EXHIBIT 1
Key Errors Noted in 1960
BarChris Financial
Statements by Judge
McLean

(handwritten: Imaterial)

A. Sales:
Per S-1 Statement	$9,165,320
Correct Figure	8,511,420
Overstatement	$ 653,900
% Overstatement	7.7%

(handwritten: Imaterial)

B. Net Operating Income:
Per S-1 Statement	$1,742,801
Correct Figure	1,496,196
Overstatement	$ 246,605
% Overstatement	16.5%

(handwritten: Imaterial)

C. Earnings per Share:
Per S-1 Statement	$.75
Correct Figure	.65
Overstatement	$.10
% Overstatement	15.3%

D. Current Assets:
Per S-1 Statement	$4,524,021
Correct Figure	3,914,332
Overstatement	$ 609,689
% Overstatement	15.6%

E. Current Ratio:
Per S-1 Statement	1.9
Correct Figure	1.6
% Overstatement	18.8%

F. Contingent Liabilities:
Per S-1 Statement	$4,719,835
Correct Figure	5,095,630
Understatement	$ (375,795)
% Understatement	7.4%

(handwritten left margin: Material B/S — Not stk but bond investor. not material since, SHolders → deemed not important. Using quality.)

ble under generally accepted accounting principles, Judge McLean ruled that this accounting treatment was improper for the Heavenly Lanes sale and leaseback, which was actually an intercompany transaction. The judge observed that the Heavenly Lanes transaction was not a valid sale but simply a "mechanism" BarChris used to finance the completion of that project.[5]

As shown in Exhibit 1, Judge McLean ruled that BarChris overstated its current assets and current ratio at the end of 1960. The liquidity problems BarChris experienced throughout its existence focused considerable attention during the class action lawsuit on how the company's misstated financial data affected its key liquidity measures. A bank transfer of approximately $145,000 to BarChris from one of its unconsolidated subsidiaries in late December 1960 especially troubled Judge McLean. A stipulation of this transaction, arranged by Leonard Russo, required the cash to be returned to the BarChris subsidiary by January 16, 1961. In analyzing this bank transfer, Judge McLean made the following remarks:

---

5. BarChris sold the Heavenly Lanes property to a finance company, which then leased the property to a BarChris subsidiary. However, the terms of the "sale" left BarChris the de facto owner of the property.

... to treat it [the $145,000] as cash on hand without some explanation of the temporary character of the deposit was misleading. The incident is important for the light that it sheds upon BarChris's business practices. This has a bearing upon the credibility of some of BarChris's officers and the weight to be given to their testimony in other respects.[6]

In addition to ruling that BarChris's 1960 year-end cash balance was overstated, Judge McLean also concluded that the company overstated its December 31, 1960, accounts and notes receivable balances. The judge ruled that a $50,000 reserve should have been established at the end of 1960 for a receivable that appeared unlikely to be collected. He also maintained that a receivable from a subsidiary should not have been included in the BarChris balance sheet. In his judgment, that receivable clearly qualified as an intercompany item.

BarChris often discounted with finance companies notes receivable from its customers. The finance companies withheld a certain percentage of the proceeds of these discounted notes as reserves to cover expenses incurred to collect delinquent notes. When a customer paid off a note on its due date, the given finance company remitted the reserve to BarChris. For financial statement purposes, BarChris reported these reserves as current assets due from the finance companies. Judge McLean ruled that reporting the total amount of the reserves as a current asset misled users of BarChris's financial statements for two reasons. First, BarChris forfeited reserves for those notes on which customers defaulted. Second, for notes on which customers did not default, several years often elapsed from the date a note was discounted until the date BarChris received the reserve deducted from the note's proceeds.

The final substantive error Judge McLean identified in the 1960 BarChris financial statements involved the company's contingent liabilities. Most of these contingencies stemmed from the notes receivable that BarChris discounted with finance companies. As indicated in Exhibit 1, the judge ruled that the company understated contingent liabilities by approximately $375,000 in its 1960 financial statements.

ISSUE 2: WERE THE FALSE REPRESENTATIONS IN THE BARCHRIS S-1 REGISTRATION STATEMENT "MATERIAL"?

After identifying the errors in BarChris's 1960 audited financial statements, Judge McLean next addressed the issue of whether those errors were material. For an independent auditor to be held civilly liable under the Securities Act of 1933, the errors that the auditor failed to detect and/or report in a client's financial statements must qualify as material errors. At the time, the SEC's regulations defined the concept of materiality as follows: "The term 'material', when used to qualify a requirement for the furnishing of information as to any subject, limits the information required to those matters as to which an average prudent investor ought reasonably to be informed before purchasing the security registered."

6. This and all subsequent quotations were taken from the following legal opinion: *Escott v. BarChris Construction Corporation*, 283 F. Supp. 643 (1968).

In analyzing the errors that affected BarChris's 1960 income statement, Judge McLean posed the following question: Would these errors have deterred the average prudent investor from purchasing the company's bonds? (Again, these errors are the first three items listed in Exhibit 1.) Judge McLean ruled in each case that the errors were not sufficiently large to have discouraged a prudent investor from purchasing the bonds. In explaining his decision, the judge noted that investment advisory services considered the BarChris bonds "speculative" securities. As a result, prospective investors were unlikely to have been deterred by what he characterized as "comparatively minor errors" in BarChris's reported sales and earnings figures for 1960.

Judge McLean also ruled that the $375,000 understatement of BarChris's contingent liabilities as of December 31, 1960, was not material. On that date, the company reported total assets of $6,101,085. Relative to that total, Judge McLean observed that either the reported or actual contingent liabilities would have been considered a "huge amount" by prospective investors. "If they [investors] were willing to buy the debentures in the face of this information, as they obviously were, I doubt that they would have been deterred if they had been told that the contingent liabilities were actually $375,000 higher."

Finally, Judge McLean held that the overstatement of BarChris's current assets and the consequent overstatement of its current ratio as of December 31, 1960, qualified as material errors. As Exhibit 1 indicates, in percentage terms, there was only a small difference between the overstatement of the current ratio, which Judge McLean ruled to be a material error, and the overstatement of the company's earnings per share, which he ruled as immaterial. The judge reasoned that prospective bondholders would be much more concerned by an overstatement of a company's key liquidity measures than by an overstatement of its earnings. BarChris's history of liquidity problems and its significant working capital needs focused disproportionate attention on its liquidity measures.

ISSUE 3: DID PEAT MARWICK SATISFY ITS DUE DILIGENCE OBLIGATION IN REVIEWING THE S-1 REGISTRATION STATEMENT?

Peat Marwick's key defense strategy in the BarChris civil suit was to invoke the so-called due diligence defense. The Securities Act of 1933 defines this defense as follows:

> After reasonable investigation [the defendant] had reasonable ground to believe and did believe, at the time such part of the registration statement became effective, that the statements therein were true and that there was no omission to state a material fact required to be stated therein or necessary to make the statements therein not misleading.

To sustain a due diligence defense, Peat Marwick needed to establish that its auditors made a "reasonable investigation" of BarChris's S-1 statement and that this investigation caused them to conclude that the financial data in the statement were materially accurate. In assessing Peat Marwick's due diligence defense, Judge McLean focused on the firm's 1960 audit and its subsequent S-1 review performed during the spring of 1961.

The senior auditor assigned to the BarChris engagements in 1960 and 1961 was a young man named Berardi. Judge McLean questioned the choice of Berardi to serve as the senior auditor on the complex BarChris audit. Berardi was not a CPA at the time, had no prior experience with the client's industry, and had just recently been promoted to senior.

After scrutinizing the Peat Marwick workpapers, Judge McLean concluded that Berardi never realized that the Heavenly Lanes sale and leaseback was an intercompany transaction. The audit manager assigned to the BarChris engagement apparently did discover that the transaction was an intercompany item. This individual made the following review comment on one of Berardi's workpapers: ". . . the profit on this job [Heavenly Lanes] should be eliminated as its ownership is within the affiliated group." In response to this review comment, Berardi added the following notation on a workpaper concerning the Heavenly Lanes project: "Properties sold to others by affiliates." As Judge McLean observed, this vague note suggests that Berardi believed the property had been sold to an external third party. If this were the case, Judge McLean argued, Berardi should have taken the appropriate steps to corroborate this sale—which he apparently did not.

Judge McLean ruled that Berardi could not be held responsible for failing to discover that the $145,000 transferred to BarChris by its unconsolidated subsidiary was required to be returned shortly after year-end. As noted by the judge, Russo failed to notify Berardi or the other Peat Marwick auditors that the funds had to be returned. The judge went on to observe that "it would not be reasonable to require Berardi to examine all of BarChris's correspondence when he had no reason to suspect any irregularity." Judge McLean did criticize Berardi for not questioning the balance sheet classification of the reserves due to BarChris from finance companies. The judge believed that Berardi should have recognized that most of those reserves would not be released within one year and thus did not qualify as current assets.

Judge McLean reserved his most severe criticism of Berardi for the senior's S-1 review during the spring of 1961. The legal opinion in the *BarChris* case provided the following description of an S-1 review:

> The purpose of reviewing events subsequent to the date of a certified balance sheet (referred to as an S-1 review when made with reference to a registration statement) is to ascertain whether any material change has occurred in the company's financial position which should be disclosed in order to prevent the balance sheet figures from being misleading.

Exhibit 2 contains a partial list of the audit procedures assigned to Berardi during the S-1 review. Judge McLean specifically noted that the S-1 audit program conformed with generally accepted auditing standards. However, the judge ruled that Berardi failed to satisfactorily perform the audit procedures included in that program.[7]

> He devoted a little over two days to it [the S-1 review], a total of 20 1/2 hours. He did not discover any of the errors or omissions pertaining to the state of affairs in 1961 which I have previously discussed at length. . . . he got answers [from management]

7. Largely as a result of the *BarChris* case, the accounting profession adopted more definitive guidelines for auditors to follow when reviewing important events occurring subsequent to a client's balance sheet date.

EXHIBIT 2
Partial Audit Program
Used by Peat Marwick
during 1961 S-1 Review

1. Review minutes of stockholders, directors, and committee [meetings].
2. Review latest interim financial statements and compare with corresponding statements of preceding year. Inquire regarding significant variations and changes.
4. Review the more important financial records and inquire regarding material transactions not in the ordinary course of business and any other significant items.
6. Inquire as to changes in material contracts.
10. Inquire as to any significant bad debts or accounts in dispute for which provision has not been made.
14. Inquire as to newly discovered liabilities . . . direct or contingent.

which he considered satisfactory, and he did nothing to verify them. . . . as far as results were concerned, his S-1 review was useless.

Following his thorough study of Peat Marwick's audit workpapers, Judge McLean ruled that the audit firm had failed to establish its due diligence defense.[8] The judge reached a similar conclusion regarding the other key defendants in the case. Before Judge McLean could award a financial judgment to the plaintiffs in the *BarChris* case, the parties to the civil suit reached an out-of-court settlement. The terms of that settlement were not publicly disclosed.

QUESTIONS

1. Are the completed contract and percentage-of-completion methods mutually acceptable alternatives in accounting for long-term construction projects? If not, specify the conditions under which each method should be used.

2. *SAS No. 31*, "Evidential Matter," identifies five key management assertions that underlie a set of financial statements. Which of these assertions was violated by the year-end transfer of $145,000 to BarChris by its unconsolidated subsidiary? Suppose that Peat Marwick had prepared and audited a year-end bank transfer schedule for fiscal 1960. Would this audit procedure have likely revealed the improper $145,000 transaction? Why or why not? What other audit procedures might have led to the discovery of this improper year-end bank transfer?

3. Should the accounting profession adopt quantitative materiality guidelines for use by auditors and accountants? Discuss the advantages and disadvantages of such guidelines from an auditor's perspective.

4. Identify the key differences in auditors' potential legal liability under the Securities Act of 1933 and the Securities Exchange Act of 1934.

5. In 1961, accounting standards allowed companies to immediately recognize the total gain on a sale and leaseback transaction. Shortly after the *BarChris* case, the accounting profession disallowed that accounting treatment for sale and leaseback transactions. Should auditors allow clients to use any accounting method for a given transaction as long as the method chosen is not expressly prohibited by professional standards? Defend your answer.

---

8. As noted earlier, two of BarChris's financial executives were former Peat Marwick employees. Reportedly, the Peat Marwick auditors assigned to the BarChris engagement relied on those individuals to inform them of major problems and issues facing the company. This reliance was apparently not justified, since the two executives failed to inform the auditors of several important accounting and financial reporting issues confronting BarChris.

CASE 8.3
1136 TENANTS CORPORATION

For most of his life, New York City businessman I. Jerome Riker was a powerful man with an extensive network of influential friends and business associates. Probably the most influential of Riker's friends was Roy M. Cohn. Cohn served as the prosecuting attorney in the Julius and Ethel Rosenberg espionage trial following World War II. Cohn later worked as the chief legal counsel for Senator Joseph McCarthy during the infamous McCarthy hearings of the mid-1950s in the U.S. Senate. One of the most important power brokers of his time, Cohn had close personal ties to numerous government officials, including J. Edgar Hoover and, years later, Ronald Reagan. Riker benefited greatly from his friendship with Cohn. Cohn steered business deals Riker's way and, for a time, was a co-owner with Riker of American Funding Corporation, a large finance company.

Riker's principal business interests were in the real estate industry. From 1926 through 1965, he served as president of Riker & Company, one of the largest real estate investment companies in New York City. Riker & Co. managed some of the most expensive and exclusive residential properties in the United States, the elegant cooperative apartment buildings that line Park Avenue and Fifth Avenue on the upper east side of Manhattan Island. Besides being prominent in the inner circles of the Manhattan business and civic communities, Riker counted as friends many of the socialites who inhabited the posh Hamptons communities of Long Island. In fact, Riker's most prized real estate property was the glitzy Bath and Tennis Club of Westhampton, Long Island. Riker both managed that property and was its principal stockholder.

During the early 1960s, Riker began embezzling cash from the trust funds of several of the cooperatives his firm managed. Riker used this cash to finance a wide array of capital improvement projects at the Westhampton club. In March 1965, the New York State Supreme Court ordered Riker & Company to cease operations, charging that the firm had been commingling its funds with those of its clients. Three months later, prosecutors indicted Riker on 13 counts of grand larceny. The criminal indictment alleged that Riker stole nearly $1 million from the trust funds of cooperatives previously managed by his firm.

In November 1965, Riker pleaded guilty to the charges filed against him. Judge Gerald Culkin of the New York State Supreme Court gave Riker a suspended sentence and indefinite probation. Judge Culkin defended the light sentence by explaining that Riker had paid back approximately $20,000 of the stolen funds. Riker had intended to repay all the stolen funds, Judge Culkin noted, but had been prevented from doing so by a series of poor investments.

One of the cooperatives from which Riker embezzled funds was the 1136 Tenants Corporation, located at 1136 Fifth Avenue on Manhattan. Riker admitted stealing approximately $130,000 from that cooperative's trust funds. Because they were unable to recover the stolen funds from Riker, the tenants filed a civil suit against Max Rothenberg & Company, the accounting firm that had prepared the cooperative's annual financial statements and tax returns. The principal allegation leveled at the accounting firm was that it should have discovered, and reported to the tenants, Riker's embezzlement from the cooperative's trust funds.

The trial and subsequent appeals in the *1136 Tenants* case focused on the contractual agreement between the tenants and Max Rothenberg & Company. This contract was never reduced to writing. Instead, the contract was simply an oral agreement between a partner of the accounting firm and I. Jerome Riker. The plaintiffs alleged that Riker, their agent, retained the accounting firm to audit the trust funds of 1136 Tenants Corporation and to prepare its annual tax returns. The accounting firm disputed this contention. Rothenberg & Co. maintained that, other than the preparation of tax returns, the oral agreement with Riker was simply to perform so-called write-up, or bookkeeping, services for the cooperative. The courts found that the oral agreement between Riker and the Rothenberg firm, in fact, had been for the performance of write-up services rather than an audit.

> The affidavits and examination before trial . . . show that the plaintiff orally employed defendant firm of accountants to "write up" its books from statements and facts submitted from time to time to the defendant by plaintiff's managing agent, Riker; and defendant made periodic reports thereof in regular accounting form to the plaintiff and its shareholders.[1]

To conceal his embezzlement from the tenants' trust funds, Riker routinely recorded bogus transactions in the cooperative's accounting records. He also occasionally forged accounting documents to authenticate these transactions. As noted by the court, Rothenberg & Co. relied on the information supplied to them by Riker to prepare annual financial statements for the 1136 Tenants Corporation. The accounting firm freely admitted that had it audited the cooperative's trust funds, the irregularities perpetrated by Riker would almost certainly have been uncovered.

Although Rothenberg & Co. had agreed to provide only write-up services to the 1136 Tenants Corporation, the court ruled that the firm had a professional obligation to inform the tenants of certain "suspicious" matters it uncovered. The

---

1. This and all subsequent quotations were taken from the following legal opinion: *1136 Tenants Corporation v. Max Rothenberg & Company*, 277 New York Supp., 2d 996 (1967).

court was referring principally to a workpaper entitled "Missing Invoices" that an accountant with the Rothenberg firm prepared while compiling financial statements for 1136 Tenants. This workpaper detailed more than $44,000 of expenses, expenses for which the accountant could find no supporting documentation. As established by the plaintiffs, Riker fabricated these expenses to extract cash from the cooperative's trust funds.

Also damaging to the Rothenberg firm during the trial was an admission by one of its partners that the annual 1136 Tenants engagements involved more than the provision of write-up services. The partner testified that his subordinates reviewed bank statements and other documentary evidence during these engagements. Apparently, the Rothenberg accountants reviewed these documents to corroborate the financial data in the accounting records maintained for the cooperative's trust funds.

The plaintiffs' legal counsel also established that the tenants had some justification for believing that the Rothenberg firm was providing more than just write-up services. For instance, an income statement compiled for the cooperative by Rothenberg personnel included an expense item labeled simply "Audit." Even more important, the court ruled that the accounting firm failed to issue a definitive disclaimer of opinion on the cooperative's annual financial statements. The absence of such a disclaimer prevented the tenants from determining whether those financial statements had been subjected to a full-scope audit.

The original court that heard the *1136 Tenants* case ruled in favor of the plaintiffs, awarding them a judgment exceeding $230,000. This judgment startled the accounting profession, since the Rothenberg firm received an annual fee of only $600 for the services provided to the tenants. A New York appellate court upheld the judgment against the accounting firm by a 3 to 2 margin. The two judges who voted to repeal the lower court's decision believed that Rothenberg & Co. made a good faith effort to inform the tenants that the cooperative's financial statements had not been audited. The other three appellate judges focused on the conduct of Rothenberg & Co. that had created ambiguity regarding the nature of the services provided to the 1136 Tenants Corporation. This ambiguity, when coupled with the suspicious circumstances uncovered by the accounting firm but not disclosed to the tenants, swayed these three judges to vote in favor of upholding the lower court's decision.

QUESTIONS

1. The court decisions handed down in the *1136 Tenants* case suggest that accountants have a responsibility to precisely specify to their clients the type of professional service to be provided during an engagement. Identify the current technical standards that focus on this issue. What are the principal requirements of these standards? Do the standards require that a written engagement letter be obtained by an accounting firm providing professional services to a client?
2. What steps should CPAs take when they discover financial irregularities during a compilation engagement? Are CPAs required to inform client management when they discover irregularities during such an engagement? If so, briefly summarize the nature of the communications that a CPA should make to the client in this context.

3. In recent years, the product line of services that accounting firms provide has expanded significantly. Identify the principal auditing and auditing-related services that accountants provide, and briefly compare and contrast these services.

4. Recent academic research suggests that the expanding product line of auditing and auditing-related services that accounting firms offer to their clients may be confusing to the users of financial statements. What measures could the profession adopt to eliminate or reduce this confusion? Would these measures, if in place at the time, have limited the legal exposure of Rothenberg & Co. in the *1136 Tenants* case?

CASE 8.4
YALE EXPRESS SYSTEM, INC.

Irving Goldberg joined the accounting department of Republic Carloading & Distributing Company during World War II. Nearly two decades later, Republic's top management rewarded Goldberg's hard work and dedication by promoting him to treasurer of the company. Republic's principal line of business was freight forwarding. The company consolidated partial railroad carloads of freight shipments into full carloads and then forwarded the individual items of freight to their ultimate destinations. In May 1963, Goldberg became an employee of Yale Express System, Inc., when that company acquired Republic. Yale Express, a publicly owned company, was much smaller than Republic and engaged principally in short-haul trucking at the time. Benjamin Eskow founded Yale Express in 1938. Twenty-five years later, the Eskow family still effectively controlled Yale Express. Family members owned 61 percent of Yale Express's outstanding stock and occupied key management positions with the company.

THE TRIALS AND TRIBULATIONS OF IRVING GOLDBERG

After the takeover of Republic by Yale Express, Goldberg remained the treasurer of Republic, which was operated as a wholly owned subsidiary of its new parent company. Within a few months, Yale Express executives began pressuring Goldberg to manipulate Republic's reported operating results. Fred Mackensen, Yale Express's administrative vice-president and an individual instrumental in arranging the takeover of Republic, applied most of this pressure to Goldberg. In a subsequent trial, Goldberg testified that Mackensen wanted to report a profit of $250,000 for Republic during September 1963. Goldberg's figures indicated that the company had posted a small loss during that period. Three months later, Mackensen was upset when Goldberg told him that Republic suffered a net loss of $900,000 for its fiscal year ending December 31, 1963. According to Goldberg, Mackensen would not accept Republic's operating results until the loss had been reduced significantly.

Goldberg testified that he and Mackensen repeatedly butted heads over Republic's accounting methods. The most heated of these disagreements involved Goldberg's method of estimating Republic's unrecorded transportation expenses at the end of each fiscal year. The railroads and trucking companies Republic dealt with were slow to submit invoices for their services, which forced Goldberg to estimate the amount of such expenses to accrue each year-end. Historically, Republic incurred approximately $.84 of transportation charges for each $1 of earned revenue. Mackensen decided that the accrual rate should be only $.78 per $1 of revenue for fiscal 1963. According to Goldberg's analysis, this change overstated Republic's net operating results for 1963 by approximately $1 million. Although Goldberg knew that Republic's financial statements were misstated, he signed a report filed by the company with the Interstate Commerce Commission (ICC) indicating that the statements were accurate. When asked to explain why he vouched for the accuracy of the erroneous financial statements, Goldberg replied that when he signed the ICC report, he was not "responsible mentally."[1]

In April 1964, Goldberg took a voluntary leave of absence from Republic. Since January of that year, he had been under psychiatric care and had been taking sedatives to cope with the heavy stress imposed on him by his superiors. When he returned to Republic in May 1964, Goldberg learned that he had been demoted to a clerk's position, chief of disbursements. Shortly thereafter, he discovered two large adjusting entries posted to Republic's accounting records during his absence. These entries, initialed by Mackensen, reduced Republic's transportation expenses for the first quarter of 1964 by $600,000. At this point, Goldberg went to the board of directors of Yale Express and reported that Republic's operating results were being grossly misrepresented.

Following Goldberg's allegation, Yale Express's board of directors retained Peat Marwick, the company's audit firm, to analyze Republic's transportation expenses. The results of the Peat Marwick study supported Goldberg's claim. Nevertheless, following the completion of that study, the president of the company asked Goldberg to resign. Goldberg refused, stating that his personal financial situation prevented him from resigning. A few months later, Mackensen fired Goldberg. Mackensen justified the dismissal by maintaining that Goldberg's position was no longer needed by the company.

GERALD ESKOW: AMBITION LEADS TO CONVICTION

Gerald Eskow served as the president and chief executive of Yale Express in 1963. Eskow, known for his single-minded dedication to the company and his willingness to work extremely long hours, was the 39-year-old son of the company's

---

1. "Former Official of Unit of Yale Express Claims Mental Irresponsibility," *The Wall Street Journal*, 14 October 1968, 8.

founder. The younger Eskow was proud of his father and the fact that the senior Eskow, in just two decades, transformed a small trucking business into a very profitable public company recognized for its excellent customer service. His father's success motivated Gerald Eskow to add to the prestige of the family name and to the family fortune. He told friends and associates that he intended to build Yale Express into one of the largest transportation companies in the nation. That ambition prompted him to approve the acquisition of Republic Carloading & Distributing Company in the spring of 1963. In hindsight, the purchase of Republic, which was more than twice as large as Yale Express and in deteriorating financial condition at the time, proved to be a poor decision for both Yale Express and Gerald Eskow.

Subsequent court testimony suggested that Gerald Eskow was not aware, at least initially, of the measures taken by Fred Mackensen to misrepresent Republic's operating results. Court records document that Mackensen concealed Republic's operating losses from Eskow by ordering subordinates to falsify Republic's accounting records. In fact, Mackensen's subordinates maintained a "black book" that documented the differences between Republic's actual and publicly reported operating results.[2]

The U.S. Attorney who prosecuted Yale Express's top executives for criminal fraud alleged that by mid-1964, Eskow knew that Republic's operating results were being materially misrepresented. The prosecutor also charged that Eskow realized by then that Republic's deteriorating financial condition threatened the viability of Yale Express. Later that same year, Yale Express used financial statements drawn from its falsified accounting records to obtain a multimillion-dollar loan. Using those bogus financial statements for that purpose eventually proved to be the downfall of both Mackensen and Eskow. The company's consolidated financial statements reported a profit of approximately $1.5 million for the first nine months of 1964, when the company actually lost nearly $2 million.

By March 1965, Yale Express could no longer conceal its severe financial problems. Company executives publicly revealed that Yale Express's operating results for its two previous fiscal years had been misrepresented. Instead of the $1.1 million profit reported in 1963, company officials admitted that Yale Express suffered a loss for that year of more than $1.2 million. At the same time, the executives disclosed that Yale Express lost approximately $3 million during 1964 despite the large profit previously reported for the first nine months of that year. These disclosures spurred stockholders to file a large class action lawsuit against Yale Express's officers and its accounting firm, Peat Marwick. The disclosures also triggered a series of investigations of the company's financial affairs by the Securities and Exchange Commission (SEC), the ICC, and a federal grand jury. In May 1965, to stave off creditors, Yale Express's board of directors filed a bankruptcy petition for the company under Chapter 10 of the Federal Bankruptcy Act.

Following Yale Express's bankruptcy filing, Gerald Eskow called a news conference to criticize the company's directors for authorizing that decision. Eskow insisted that the bankruptcy filing had been too hasty and suggested that the company's reported losses were overstated. Several months later, Eskow announced that he and other members of his family had donated 800,000 shares of Yale Express stock, representing nearly 75 percent of the family's holdings, to the

2. "Two Former Officials of Yale Express Plan to Appeal Convictions," *The Wall Street Journal*, 7 November 1968, 28.

company's employees. Eskow hoped that the dramatic gesture would serve as an incentive for the employees to return the company to a profitable position. "If our good intentions of giving unsolicited gifts are not enough of an impetus to awaken those employees who have given less than their best, or who have stolen time, money or freight from this company, then our noble venture will have been wasted."[3]

In 1967, a federal grand jury indicted Gerald Eskow, Fred Mackensen, and Yale Express's former chief accounting officer on various criminal fraud charges. The grand jury charged that the executives knowingly used false financial statements to raise debt capital for Yale Express in late 1964 and submitted false financial statements to the SEC. In August 1968, Eskow attempted to shift responsibility for the fraudulent financial statements to Peat Marwick. Eskow filed a $20 million civil lawsuit against Peat Marwick that accused the audit firm of concealing Yale Express's true financial condition from company executives.

> In Mr. Eskow's complaint is an allegation that a Peat Marwick staffer on or about August 21, 1964, prepared a "cash flow" workpaper that "advised and alerted" Peat Marwick and the other defendants that Yale Express's "alleged profit" of $717,000 in the first half of 1964 . . . "was false, misleading and fraudulent" and, instead, a loss of $1,615,000 had been sustained. But Peat Marwick "did nothing to correct these errors or to advise (Mr. Eskow) or third parties thereof."[4]

Peat Marwick quickly responded to Eskow's allegation. The accounting firm claimed that Eskow simply wanted to damage the credibility of the Peat Marwick auditors expected to testify against him.[5]

Following a three-week trial, a federal court convicted Eskow and Mackensen in November 1968 on 32 counts of fraud. A federal judge fined Eskow $15,500 and gave him a one-year suspended sentence. The judge fined Mackensen $4,650. Mackensen also received a nine-month suspended sentence. Still professing his innocence, Eskow appealed the conviction. In June 1970, the U.S. Supreme Court rejected his appeal and ruled that the conviction would stand.

Peat Marwick: Auditor, Consultant . . . Defendant

Yale Express retained Peat Marwick in early 1964 to audit its 1963 financial statements. Irving Goldberg testified that the audit firm initially contested Yale Express's 1963 year-end accrual for transportation expenses. According to Goldberg, Peat Marwick believed that the Republic subsidiary had understated its accrued transportation charges by nearly $2 million. Goldberg reported that after Republic increased the balance of the accrued transportation expenses account by $975,000 with a year-end adjusting entry, Peat Marwick stopped questioning that account. Under cross-examination, Goldberg was asked if he told Peat Marwick that the 1963 consolidated financial statements of Yale Express

3. D. Dworsky, "Yale Truckers Get Pep Talk and Gift," *The New York Times*, 24 December 1966, 25, 32.

4. "Yale Express System Former President Sues Auditor, Peat Marwick," *The Wall Street Journal*, 23 August 1968, 4.

5. No public comment on the resolution of Eskow's civil suit against Peat Marwick could be found. Most likely, the suit was settled out of court for no damages or only nominal damages.

were materially misstated, even after the posting of the large audit adjustment. Goldberg replied, "I did not. I couldn't have cared less."[6] Goldberg also admitted that he never brought to Peat Marwick's attention the adjusting entries approved by Mackensen in the spring of 1964. Recall that those adjusting entries materially reduced Republic's transportation expenses for the first quarter of that year.

Peat Marwick issued an unqualified audit opinion on Yale Express's 1963 financial statements on March 31, 1964. On April 9, 1964, Yale Express released its 1963 annual report to its stockholders. Approximately two and one-half months later, the company filed its annual 10-K statement with the SEC.

Following the completion of the 1963 audit, Yale Express's board of directors engaged Peat Marwick to complete a "special studies" consulting project. The board instructed Peat Marwick to investigate Goldberg's allegation that the company's financial data were being misrepresented. Peat Marwick assigned 35 auditors to pore over the transportation invoices received and/or paid by Yale Express during the first five months of 1964. The results of this investigation convinced Peat Marwick that Yale Express materially understated its 1963 accrual for transportation expenses. Exactly when in 1964 Peat Marwick reached this conclusion was later disputed in court. Stockholders who sued Peat Marwick alleged that the firm knew the accrual was understated prior to June 29, 1964, the date Yale Express filed its 1963 10-K with the SEC. Peat Marwick maintained that it did not realize the accrual was understated until after the 10-K had been filed.

A severe liquidity crisis in late 1964 forced Yale Express to seek immediate external financing. The company prepared interim financial statements drawn from its accounting records for the first nine months of 1964 and "widely circulated" these statements in an effort to raise additional capital. Among other parties, Yale Express supplied the interim financial statements to a syndicate of eight insurance companies in a successful attempt to obtain a large loan. These unaudited financial statements were not corrected for the errors discovered by Peat Marwick during its special studies project.

In early November 1964, Robert Conroy, the Peat Marwick partner who supervised the annual audits of Yale Express, met with Eskow and Mackensen in a Wall Street restaurant. According to sworn statements of Eskow and Mackensen, Conroy told the two Yale Express executives that the results of the Peat Marwick special studies project *should not* be considered when compiling the interim financial statements for the first nine months of 1964. Instead, Conroy allegedly recommended that those financial statements be prepared directly from Yale Express's accounting records. At this point, those records had not been adjusted for the significant understatement of transportation expenses discovered by Peat Marwick. Conroy reportedly informed Eskow and Mackensen that those financial statements would be consistent with the prior year's annual report. He also added that any errors in the interim statements would be "picked up" by the year-end Peat Marwick audit.[7]

In an affidavit submitted to the court hearing the class action lawsuit filed by Yale Express's stockholders, Conroy disputed much of Eskow and Mackensen's testimony. Conroy maintained that he repeatedly warned the Yale Express executives that financial statements drawn from the company's unadjusted accounting

---

6. "Former Official of Unit of Yale Express," 8.

7. *Fischer v. Kletz*, 206 F. Supp. 180 (1967), 196.

Do we have to observe client confidentiality?

records would be materially in error. He also testified that the decision to circulate those erroneous financial statements to external parties was made strictly by Yale Express management.

In a preliminary hearing in the Yale Express class action lawsuit, the presiding judge focused on three key issues regarding Peat Marwick's conduct during its tenure with Yale Express. The first of these issues was whether Peat Marwick, after completing the special studies project, had an obligation to inform third parties that Yale Express's transportation expenses and accrued liabilities were significantly understated in its 1963 audited financial statements. In discussing this point, the judge made the following comments.

> The elements of good faith and common honesty which govern the businessman presumably should also apply to the independent public accountant. . . . the common law has long required that a person who has made a representation must correct that representation if it becomes false and if he knows people are relying on it.[8]

The SEC filed a legal brief with the court hearing the Yale Express lawsuit. The federal agency maintained that if an audit firm discovers that an opinion on a client's financial statements is incorrect because of previously undetected errors, the firm has a responsibility to inform third parties of those errors. Following the Yale Express case, the AICPA adopted *Statement on Auditing Procedures No. 41*, "Subsequent Discovery of Facts Existing at the Date of the Auditor's Report." This standard requires auditors to inform financial statement users of undisclosed material errors in financial statements that they have previously audited if client management refuses to do so.[9]

The second key issue involving Peat Marwick in the Yale Express class action lawsuit was whether the CPA firm should have alerted third parties that Yale Express's interim 1964 financial statements contained material errors. On this point, the judge ruled that since Peat Marwick had not contracted to audit those financial statements, the firm had no responsibility to inform third parties of the errors in the statements. That is, while performing the special studies project during which it discovered the errors in the 1964 interim financial statements, Peat Marwick served strictly as a consultant to Yale Express, not as an independent auditor.

The final issue concerning Peat Marwick in the Yale Express litigation was whether the CPA firm aided and abetted the client's fraudulent actions. This issue stemmed from the allegation that Peat Marwick's Robert Conroy suggested that Yale Express's uncorrected financial statements for the first nine months of 1964 be provided to external third parties. In the preliminary opinion handed down in the case, the presiding judge noted that the conflicting testimony on this issue would have to be resolved in court. Since the case was eventually settled out of court, a final judgment on this point was never rendered.

According to published reports, Peat Marwick contributed $650,000 to the settlement pool established by the defendants in the Yale Express class action lawsuit. Ironically, the reorganization plan subsequently approved by the bankruptcy judge for Yale Express left Peat Marwick the company's largest share-

---

8. *Ibid.*, 186, 188.

9. This requirement is an exception to the ethical rule that prohibits auditors from disclosing confidential client information to third parties without first obtaining permission to do so from the client.

holder. Professional fees owed to Peat Marwick by Yale Express caused the audit firm to be the largest unsecured general creditor in the bankruptcy hearing. The bankruptcy court awarded Peat Marwick approximately 12 percent of the new Yale Express common stock issued following the company's reorganization.

QUESTIONS

1. Identify the alternative courses of action available to Goldberg in late 1963 when Mackensen pressured him to manipulate Republic's reported operating results. Which of these alternatives would have been most appropriate for him to choose under the circumstances? Why? Assume Goldberg was a CPA. How would this additional fact affect your answer, if at all?

2. Do you believe Goldberg had a responsibility to inform Peat Marwick that Yale Express's 1963 and interim 1964 financial statements were materially misstated? Why or why not?

3. A fundamental element of internal control is the "control environment." Discuss the factors that affected the control environment at Yale Express. How should these factors have influenced Peat Marwick's audits of the company?

4. What audit risk factors arising subsequent to Yale Express's acquisition of Republic should have been considered by Peat Marwick during the planning phase for the 1963 Yale Express audit?

5. Technically, Peat Marwick served as a consultant, not as an independent auditor, during the special studies project. Discuss the ethical issues that may arise when an audit firm provides both consulting and auditing services to a client, particularly issues stemming from the obligation of CPAs to protect the confidentiality of client financial records. Identify consulting services that audit firms are not allowed to provide to audit clients.

6. Identify the specific legal courses of action, under the common law and statutory law, that the Yale Express stockholders could have taken against Peat Marwick. In each case, identify the elements of proof that the stockholders needed to establish to prevail against Peat Marwick.

7. Why did the AICPA react so quickly and affirmatively to the position expressed by the SEC in the legal brief filed in the Yale Express class action lawsuit? Does the SEC have direct or indirect influence on rule-making processes within the auditing domain?

CASE 8.5

FIRST SECURITIES COMPANY OF CHICAGO (*ERNST & ERNST V. HOCHFELDER ET AL.*)

Ladislas Nay immigrated to the United States from Hungary in 1921 at the age of 18. The opportunities offered by his new land excited the industrious young immigrant and he promised himself that he would make the most of them. Shortly after arriving in the United States, Nay made his way to Chicago and found employment in the booming securities industry with a small brokerage firm. For the next several years, Nay worked long and hard hours learning the brokerage business. Unfortunately for Nay, the Great Depression hit the securities industry particularly hard. Young stockbrokers like himself were the first to be released by their firms when personnel cuts were necessary. During the bleak 1930s, Nay, who by this time had Americanized his first name to Leston, endured several job changes and two failed marriages. In 1942, as World War II began to pull the United States out of the Depression, Nay landed a permanent job with the brokerage firm of Ryan-Nichols & Company.

Within two years of joining Ryan-Nichols, Nay was promoted to president. He eventually became the firm's principal stockholder, accumulating more than 90 percent of its outstanding common stock. In 1945, Nay renamed his firm First Securities Company of Chicago. Nay's firm also successfully applied for membership in the Midwest Stock Exchange that year. Over the next two decades, Nay's career and personal life flourished. His family settled into the upper-class neighborhood of Hyde Park, near the University of Chicago. Nay and his wife, Elizabeth, participated in a wide range of community affairs, including serving on several prominent civic boards. Nay made numerous friends among the faculty and staff of the University of Chicago. In fact, many of his best customers were associated with the prestigious school.

Nay's personal attention to the financial needs of his customers earned him their respect and admiration. One of his customers described him as a kind and considerate man, much "like an old-fashioned English solicitor who took care of a family's affairs."[1] His conservative investment strategies particularly appealed to his retired clients and those nearing retirement. Nay offered many of these customers an opportunity to invest in a lucrative fund that he personally managed. This fund was not an asset of First Securities, nor were any other First Securities personnel aware it existed. Nay referred to this fund as the "escrow syndicate." Nay loaned funds invested in the escrow syndicate to blue-chip companies that developed sudden and unexpected working capital shortages. These companies paid interest rates well above the prevailing market rates. Individuals who invested in the escrow syndicate earned 7 to 12 percent on their investments, considerably more than the interest rates paid at the time by banks on savings accounts.

One of Nay's closest friends, Arnold Schueren, entrusted him with more than $400,000 over three decades and granted him a power of attorney to make investment decisions regarding those funds. Nay invested a large portion of Schueren's savings in the escrow syndicate. Another individual who relied heavily on Nay for investment advice was the widow of a close associate of the famed University of Chicago scientist Enrico Fermi. This woman later testified that Nay managed her family's investments for many years but did not offer her the opportunity to invest in the escrow syndicate until after her husband's death. Nay told her that he only offered this investment opportunity to his "nearest and dearest friends."[2] Following the death of another of his customers, Norman Moyer, Nay convinced Moyer's widow to invest her husband's estate of $90,000 in the escrow syndicate. In total, 17 of Nay's friends and/or their widows invested substantial sums in the escrow syndicate.

DR. JEKYLL AND MR. HYDE: A TRAGIC ENDING

On the morning of June 4, 1968, Leston Nay drove to St. Luke's Hospital in Chicago to pick up his wife, who had fallen and broken her hip the prior week. Earlier that morning, Nay telephoned his secretary to tell her that he would not be in the office that day because he had a stomach virus. Shortly before noon, as his wife, who was still on crutches, made her way to the kitchen of their apartment, Nay retrieved his 12-gauge shotgun and shot her in the upper back from close range. Nay then laid a suicide note on a dressing table in his bedroom, sat down on his bed, put the muzzle of the gun in his mouth, and pulled the trigger.

News of the murder-suicide shocked the Nays' friends and associates. These same people were shocked again when the Chicago police released the contents of Nay's suicide note. The note revealed that the kindly stockbroker led a Dr. Jekyll–Mr. Hyde existence for decades. In the note addressed "To whom it may concern," Nay admitted stealing from his customers for more than 30 years. The escrow syndicate in which his closest friends had invested did not exist—police speculated that Nay lost the investors' funds in the stock market. Nay successfully concealed the missing funds for as long as he did because he periodically

---

1. J.M. Johnston, "How Broker Worked $1 Million Swindle," *Chicago Daily News*, 13 December 1968, 42, 43.

2. *Ibid.*

mailed the investors' checks for interest supposedly earned by the escrow syndi-cate. These periodic interest payments deterred the victims of the scam from questioning the safety of their investments.

In the suicide note, Nay displayed some remorse when he referred to the 80-year-old Mrs. Moyer who was penniless as a result of his actions. He also ex-plained why he had decided to take his life. After Arnold Schueren died in 1967, the executor of his estate demanded that Nay return Schueren's investment in the escrow syndicate. Nay indicated in the suicide note that he "stalled" as long as he could but that the executor would not be put off any longer. So, he took his life. Most likely, Nay murdered his wife to "save" her from the shame she would feel when his fraudulent scheme, of which she was apparently unaware, was disclosed.

DEFRAUDED CUSTOMERS SUE TO RECOVER THEIR INVESTMENTS

The investors in Nay's escrow syndicate filed civil lawsuits against several parties in an effort to recover their collective investments of more than $1 million. Initially, the investors sued the Midwest Stock Exchange. In that suit, the investors alleged that the stock exchange failed to adequately investigate Nay's background before admitting his firm to membership. According to the investors, a more thor-ough investigation might have revealed that Nay had a history, although well concealed, of unscrupulous business practices. The investors suggested that the discovery of Nay's past unethical conduct would have forced the exchange to deny his firm's membership application and possibly prevented him from engag-ing in the escrow syndicate fraud. The court hearing the suit quickly dismissed the investors' claims, concluding that the stock exchange sufficiently investigated Nay's background before approving his firm's membership application.

Nay's 17 escrow participants or their estates also sued First Securities Company of Chicago. The court ruled that the brokerage firm had clearly facili-tated Nay's fraudulent activities. But, since the brokerage firm was bankrupt, the escrow investors found themselves thwarted again.

Finally, Nay's former customers filed suit against Ernst & Ernst, the account-ing firm that audited First Securities Company for more than two decades. The lawsuit alleged that Ernst & Ernst's negligence prevented the firm from detecting what became known throughout the lengthy judicial history of the *First Securities* case as Nay's "mail rule." According to the plaintiffs' legal counsel: "Nay had for-bidden anyone other than himself to open mail addressed to him, and in his ab-sence all such mail was simply allowed to pile up on his desk, even if it was addressed to First Securities for his attention."[3] Nay's mail rule allowed him to conceal the escrow syndicate scam from his subordinates at First Securities and from the brokerage's independent auditors. Had Ernst & Ernst discovered the mail rule, the plaintiffs alleged, a subsequent investigation would have been war-ranted. Such an investigation would have led to the discovery and eventual ter-mination of Nay's escrow investment scam.

3. *Securities and Exchange Commission v. First Securities Company of Chicago*, 463 F.2d 981 (1972), 985.

Handwritten margin notes:

o Neither public nor did they expect their audit to be seen by 3rd parties.

o Did send confirmations to customers (negative)

o No one ever asked "what don't my escrow ow?"

o went to the supreme ct — b/t the rule of law.

ERNST & ERNST V. HOCHFELDER ET AL.

The defrauded investors filed their lawsuit against Ernst & Ernst under the Securities Exchange Act of 1934. That federal statute does not expressly provide civil remedies to stockholders of companies registered with the Securities and Exchange Commission (SEC). However, since the adoption of the 1934 Act, federal courts have allowed stockholders to use the statute as a basis for civil suits against company officers, investment brokers, auditors, and other parties associated with false financial statements filed with the SEC. Most of these suits allege one or more violations of Rule 10b-5 of the 1934 Act, shown in Exhibit 1.

In the *First Securities* case, the plaintiffs charged that Ernst & Ernst's alleged negligence in failing to discover Nay's mail rule constituted a violation of Rule 10b-5.

> The premise [of the investors' suit] was that Ernst & Ernst had failed to utilize "appropriate auditing procedures" in its audits of First Securities. . . . Respondents [investors] contended that if Ernst & Ernst had conducted a proper audit, it would have discovered this "mail rule." The existence of the rule then would have been disclosed to the Exchange [Midwest Stock Exchange] and to the Commission [SEC] by Ernst & Ernst as an irregular procedure that prevented an effective audit.[4]

To support their claim that the mail rule qualified as a critical internal control weakness having important audit implications, the escrow investors submitted affidavits from three expert witnesses with impressive credentials in the accounting profession. Exhibit 2 lists a portion of one of these affidavits.

The federal district court that initially presided over the *Hochfelder et al. v. Ernst & Ernst* case quickly dismissed the lawsuit.[5] This court deemed that there was no substantive evidence to support the allegation that Ernst & Ernst had negligently audited First Securities. When the investors appealed this decision, the U.S. court of appeals reversed the lower court decision and ordered that the case go to trial. In its decision, the appeals court ruled that sufficient doubt existed regarding the negligence claim against Ernst & Ernst to have the case heard. The appeals court also suggested that if the plaintiffs established negligence on the part of Ernst & Ernst, the accounting firm could be held civilly liable to the defrauded investors under Rule 10b-5 of the 1934 Act.

EXHIBIT 1
Rule 10b-5 of the Securities Exchange Act of 1934

Employment of manipulative and deceptive devices. It shall be unlawful for any person, directly or indirectly, by the use of any means or instrumentality of interstate commerce, or of the mails or of any facility of any national securities exchange,

(a) To employ any device, scheme, or artifice to defraud,
(b) To make any untrue statement of a material fact or to omit to state a material fact necessary in order to make the statements made, in the light of the circumstances under which they were made, not misleading, or
(c) To engage in any act, practice, or course of business which operates or would operate as a fraud or deceit upon any person, in connection with the purchase or sale of any security.

4. *Ernst & Ernst v. Hochfelder et al.*, 425 U.S. 185 (1976), 190.

5. *Hochfelder et al. v. Ernst & Ernst*, 503 F.2d 1100 (1974). (One of the investors defrauded by Nay was Olga Hochfelder.)

Expert Witness No. 3:

If I had discovered in making an audit of a security brokerage business that its president had established an office rule that mail addressed to him at the business address, or to the company for his attention should not be opened by anyone but him, even in his absence; and that whenever he was away from the office such mail would remain unopened and pile up on his desk I would have to raise the question whether such rule or practice could possibly have been instituted for the purpose of preventing discovery of irregularities of whatever nature; would, as a minimum, have to undertake additional audit procedures to independently establish a negative answer to the latter question; also failing such an answer either withdraw from the engagement or decline to express an opinion on the financial statements of the enterprise.

EXHIBIT 2
Excerpt from Expert Witness Testimony Regarding Nay's Mail Rule

Before the *Hochfelder* case went to trial in federal district court, Ernst & Ernst appealed the ruling of the U.S. court of appeals to the U.S. Supreme Court. Ernst & Ernst argued before the Supreme Court that the negligence allegation of the escrow investors was insufficient, even if proved, to constitute a violation of Rule 10b-5. This issue had surfaced in many previous civil cases filed under the Securities Exchange Act of 1934. In these earlier cases, the federal courts had generally ruled or suggested that negligence constituted a violation of Rule 10b-5. That is, fraud or gross negligence, either of which is much more difficult for a plaintiff to prove than ordinary negligence, did not have to be established for a defendant to be held civilly liable to a plaintiff under Rule 10b-5. Ernst & Ernst contested these rulings by arguing that Rule 10b-5, as worded, could not be construed to encompass negligent behavior. Given the long-standing controversy surrounding this issue, the Supreme Court decided to rule on the issue in the *Hochfelder* case. This ruling would then establish a precedent for future lawsuits filed under Rule 10b-5.

Before the Supreme Court heard Ernst & Ernst's appeal, the SEC filed a legal brief with the Court. This brief supported the defrauded investors' argument that Rule 10b-5 encompassed both fraudulent and negligent conduct. The SEC pointed out that the end result of investors' acting on false financial statements is the same whether the errors in the statements result from fraud or negligence. Because a central purpose of the federal securities laws is to ensure that investors receive reliable information, the SEC argued that the ambiguity in Rule 10b-5 should be resolved in favor of investors.

Surprisingly, the bulk of the Supreme Court's opinion in the *Hochfelder* case responded to the SEC's legal brief rather than the arguments of the defrauded investors or those of Ernst & Ernst. The Court rejected the SEC's largely philosophical argument and instead focused on the question of whether the authors of Rule 10b-5 intended it to encompass both negligent and fraudulent behavior. In addressing this issue, the Court reviewed the legislative history of the 1934 Act and did a painstaking analysis of the semantics of Rule 10b-5.

The Supreme Court eventually concluded that the key signal to the underlying meaning of Rule 10b-5 was the term *manipulative*. As shown in Exhibit 1, the heading of the rule clearly indicates that it pertains to "manipulative and deceptive" devices. According to the Court, negligence on the part of independent auditors or other parties associated with false financial statements could not be construed as manipulative behavior. The Court suggested that in most cases for behavior to qualify as manipulative, intent to deceive—the legal term being *scienter*—had to be present.

When a statute speaks so specifically in terms of manipulation and deception, and of implementing devices and contrivances—the commonly understood terminology of intentional wrongdoing—and when its history reflects no more expansive intent, we are quite unwilling to extend the scope of the statute to negligent conduct.[6,7]

Two of the nine Supreme Court justices dissented to the *Hochfelder* decision, while one justice abstained. In disagreeing with the majority decision, Justice Harry Blackmun sided with the view expressed by the SEC. He noted that although the decision was probably consistent with the semantics of the Securities Exchange Act of 1934, the decision clashed with the underlying intent of that important federal statute. He wrote, "It seems to me that an investor can be victimized just as much by negligent conduct as by positive deception, and that it is not logical to drive a wedge between the two, saying that Congress clearly intended the one but certainly not the other."[8] Justice Blackmun went on to comment on the "critical importance" of the independent auditor's role and the ultimate responsibility of the auditor to serve the "public interest."[9] Given this societal mandate, Justice Blackmun argued, negligent auditors should be held accountable to investors who rely to their detriment on false financial statements.

AN UNRESOLVED ISSUE

At first reading, the Supreme Court's *Hochfelder* opinion appeared to establish, once and for all, the culpability standard for defining Rule 10b-5 violations. Unfortunately, the opinion is not as precise or definitive as it first appeared. A footnote to the opinion suggests that in certain cases, scienter, or intent to deceive, may not be a necessary element of proof for a plaintiff to establish in a civil suit alleging a Rule 10b-5 violation. The Court noted that some jurisdictions equate scienter with willful or reckless disregard for the truth or, more simply, "recklessness."[10] When engaging in reckless behavior, a party does not actually possess conscious intent to deceive; that is, scienter is not present. For whatever reason, the Court specifically refused to rule on the question of whether reckless behavior would be considered equivalent to scienter and thus constitute a violation of Rule 10b-5. This omission prompted subsequent plaintiffs to predicate alleged Rule 10b-5 violations by independent auditors on reckless behavior, since that type of professional misconduct is much easier to prove than actual scienter.

---

6. *Ernst & Ernst v. Hochfelder et al.*, 214.

7. A particularly troublesome issue for the Supreme Court to resolve was the underlying meaning of Subsection b of Rule 10b-5. Subsections a and c of that rule refer explicitly to fraud, implying that negligence is not a severe enough form of misconduct to constitute a violation of Rule 10b-5. However, Subsection b contains no explicit reference to fraudulent conduct. The SEC construed this omission to suggest that Subsection b covers both fraudulent and negligent misconduct. The Supreme Court rejected this argument, maintaining instead that the explicit references to fraud in Subsections a and c signaled that fraudulent conduct was the implied, although unstated, culpability standard in Subsection b as well.

8. *Ernst & Ernst v. Hochfelder et al.*, 216.

9. *Ibid.*, 218.

10. *Ibid.*, 194.

Epilogue

Congressional critics of the decision in the *Hochfelder* case argued that the alleged "flaw" in Rule 10b-5 should be corrected legislatively. In late 1978, legislators introduced a bill in the U.S. House of Representatives to hold negligent auditors civilly liable to investors who relied on false financial statements filed with the SEC. Fortunately for independent auditors, Congress rejected that bill.

Questions

1. Under present technical standards, to whom, if anyone, would auditors be required to disclose a company policy similar to Nay's mail rule discovered during an audit? Would this disclosure, if required at the time, have likely resulted in Nay discontinuing the mail rule?

2. Ernst & Ernst argued that the mail rule was not relevant to its audits of First Securities since that rule only involved personal transactions of Nay and the escrow investors. Do you agree? Why or why not?

3. Define *negligence* as that term has been used in legal cases involving independent auditors. What is the key distinction between negligence and fraud? Between recklessness and fraud? For all three types of professional misconduct, provide an example of such behavior in an audit context.

4. Assume that the investors defrauded by Nay could have filed their lawsuit against Ernst & Ernst under the Securities Act of 1933. How, if at all, do you believe the outcome of their suit would have been affected?

5. Assume that the jurisdiction in which the *Hochfelder* case was filed invoked the legal precedent established by the *Rusch Factors* case. Given this assumption, would the defrauded investors have been successful in pursuing a negligence claim against Ernst & Ernst under the common law? Why or why not?

CASE 8.6
EQUITY FUNDING
CORPORATION OF AMERICA

In 1960, four partners founded Equity Funding Corporation of America, each assuming an equal ownership interest in the firm. Two of the partners soon resigned, leaving the small company to Stanley Goldblum, who held the title of president, and Michael Riordan, who served as chairman of the board. Equity Funding's principal line of business was selling life insurance policies and "funding programs" that merged life insurance and mutual funds into one financial package for investors. Developing creative financial investments was a hallmark of Equity Funding throughout its existence. After going public in 1964, Equity Funding quickly gained a nationwide reputation as one of the most innovative companies in the ultraconservative life insurance industry.

TRAGEDY THEN TRIUMPH AT EQUITY FUNDING

In January 1969, Michael Riordan died in a mudslide that destroyed his home in the exclusive Brentwood suburb of Los Angeles. Goldblum was immediately appointed chairman of the board. One of Goldblum's first decisions in his new role was naming Fred Levin, a company employee since 1967, as executive vice-president in charge of life insurance operations. Equity Funding's revenues and earnings increased dramatically under the aggressive, growth-oriented management policies of Goldblum and Levin.

By 1972, Equity Funding ranked as one of the 10 largest life insurance companies in the United States and easily qualified as the fastest-growing company in the industry. At the time, Equity Funding's assets totaled approximately $500 million, compared with assets of only $9 million when the company went public

431

eight years earlier. During that same period, the company's pretax earnings surged from $620,000 to $26 million. In late 1972, security analysts for the financial services and insurance industries chose Equity Funding's common stock, out of several hundred stocks in those industries, as their most popular investment recommendation.

The skyrocketing price of Equity Funding's common stock in the early 1970s made both Goldblum and Levin fabulously wealthy and allowed them to join the innermost circle of Los Angeles's celebrity social circuit. The fortune and notoriety achieved by these men was particularly impressive since both came from modest backgrounds. Before joining Equity Funding, Levin, who earned a law degree from Chicago's DePaul University, worked briefly for the state agency that oversaw Illinois's insurance industry. Levin's quick wit, his charming humor, and, most important, his ruthless nature quickly endeared him to Goldblum. Reportedly, Goldblum's chief lieutenant had no qualms about humiliating employees publicly or "firing them on the spot" when he saw fit.

Levin recognized the benefits of having a network of powerful friends and business associates. When he became embroiled in legal problems in the early 1970s, Levin retained one such friend, Edmund Brown, an attorney and former governor of California, to represent him. Levin's wit made him much in demand as a speaker at meetings of insurance executives and financial analysts across the country. At one such meeting in January 1973, he summarized Equity Funding's management philosophy: "We're conservative in our financial management. . . . We are innovative in product development . . . and we are very traditional in our conviction that by serving the public's real needs, we will continue to grow in accordance to the objectives we set for ourselves."[1]

In many ways, Goldblum was a striking contrast to Levin. He disliked wining and dining business associates and instead preferred spending long hours working out on weights. In the early 1970s, Goldblum's personal fortune topped $30 million, an astonishing figure given that only a decade earlier the college dropout worked in a meat-packing plant. Besides attaining tremendous wealth, Goldblum became widely respected within his profession and held several important positions in professional and business organizations. One of those positions involved chairing the ethics committee of the Los Angeles branch of the National Association of Securities Dealers. Former associates recalled that Goldblum vigorously enforced that organization's code of ethics: "He was harsh on transgressors . . . [and gave] substantially stiffer penalties than had been anticipated."[2]

THE HOUSE OF CARDS COLLAPSES

In the spring of 1973, Equity Funding collapsed in a period of a few weeks when a former employee exposed a massive financial fraud within the company. Many parties familiar with the prominent company dismissed the incredible revelations as unfounded lies and gross distortions being spread by a disgruntled former employee. The individual charged, and federal and state investigators soon con-

1. L.J. Seidler, F. Andrews, and M.J. Epstein, *The Equity Funding Papers: The Anatomy of a Fraud* (New York: Wiley, 1977), 55.

2. R.L. Dirks and L. Gross, *The Great Wall Street Scandal* (New York: McGraw-Hill, 1974), 36.

firmed, that most of Equity Funding's life insurance policies were bogus. A lengthy audit by Touche Ross, requested by Equity Funding's court-appointed bankruptcy trustee, disclosed that the company had generated more than $2 billion of fictitious insurance policies in less than one decade. Equity Funding sold most of these bogus policies to reinsurance companies.[3] Goldblum and other company executives camouflaged these policies by regularly holding midnight "file-stuffing" parties. During these often festive and raucous sessions, the conspirators produced reams of supporting documentation for the thousands of nonexistent policies allegedly purchased from Equity Funding.

The Equity Funding fraud, like most financial frauds, began modestly. Before taking their company public in 1964, Goldblum and Riordan worried that potential investors would not be impressed by the firm's reported earnings. To correct this "problem," Goldblum decided that Equity Funding was entitled to rebates or kickbacks from the brokers through whom the company's sales force purchased mutual fund shares. (These mutual fund shares were one component of the "funding programs" that Equity Funding sold to the general public.) Goldblum referred to these rebates, which were purely illusionary, as reciprocal income, or reciprocals. The reciprocals boosted Equity Funding's 1964 net income to the level that Goldblum thought the company should have reached during that fiscal year. According to one account of this scheme, "Goldblum supplied [a subordinate] with an inflated earnings per share figure—attributing the overstatement to reciprocals. [The subordinate] was instructed to make whatever increases were necessary to support the inflated earnings per share figure."[4]

In subsequent years, the reciprocal income had to be supplemented with other fraudulent amounts to achieve Goldblum's predetermined earnings targets. In truth, Equity Funding was never profitable. Before imploding in the spring of 1973, the company was technically insolvent, although Goldblum had just issued a press release reporting record earnings for 1972. In that same press release, the brassy Goldblum boasted that Equity Funding increased the dollar value of its outstanding life insurance policies by nearly 50 percent over the previous 12 months.

One of the most alarming features of the huge Equity Funding fraud was the number of individuals who knew of its existence. Dozens of individuals, both Equity Funding employees and external third parties, helped perpetuate and conceal the company's fraudulent schemes. Eventually, federal prosecutors convicted or obtained guilty pleas from 22 individuals associated with the company, including three of the company's independent auditors. As many as 50 additional Equity Funding employees, primarily clerical personnel, participated directly or indirectly in the fraud. Prosecutors chose not to bring criminal charges against these individuals.

The numerous books and articles documenting the life insurance industry's most infamous scandal suggest that Goldblum and Levin gradually and deliberately induced their co-conspirators to become involved in the fraud.[5] More often

3. Life insurance companies often sell a portion of their outstanding policies to reinsurance companies. This practice effectively dilutes the business risk associated with selling life insurance.

4. A.I. Briloff, *More Debits Than Credits* (New York: Harper & Row, 1976), 323–324.

5. The Equity Funding scandal provided the story line for a major movie produced in 1976 by a British film company. *The Billion Dollar Bubble* starred eventual Academy Award winner James Woods, Christopher Guest, and several other notable actors.

than not, the two executives persuaded subordinates to join the conspiracy by offering them large salaries, stock rights, or exorbitant expense accounts.[6]

Goldblum and other company executives who masterminded the fraud reaped their largest financial benefits from the sale of Equity Funding stock. Goldblum alone realized more than $5 million from the sale of Equity Funding common stock. In fact, maintaining the company's stock price was the key motive underlying Goldblum's fraudulent activities. During 1972, several of the Equity Funding co-conspirators met with Goldblum and pleaded with him to report modest earnings for the next several years. They argued that by doing so the company would have an opportunity to stop the fraudulent practices and become a totally legitimate operation. Goldblum rebuffed his subordinates. He pointed out that if reported earnings did not increase each year, the company's stock price would fall.

One of the seamiest anecdotes from the annals of Equity Funding, and one that graphically portrays the company's amoral culture, came to be known as the Cookie Jar Caper. Several lower-level Equity Funding employees devised an ingenious scheme to pad their bank accounts. These individuals "killed off" fictitious policyholders who had "purchased" Equity Funding life insurance policies, policies subsequently sold by Equity Funding to reinsurance companies. The employees then diverted to themselves the payments made by the reinsurance companies to the beneficiaries of the allegedly deceased policyholders. When Goldblum and Levin discovered this scheme, they ordered the individuals involved to continue it on a much larger scale but to channel the beneficiary payments to Equity Funding's corporate bank accounts.

The numerous insurance examiners and independent auditors who reviewed and reported on Equity Funding's financial records over more than a decade were often victimized by the criminal mischief of the company's executives. At one point, Levin ordered the Equity Funding offices used by state insurance examiners to be bugged so that he would know the specific questions or issues they were addressing.

Three independent auditors involved for several years in the annual audits of Equity Funding were eventually convicted of complicity in the fraudulent scheme. However, most of Equity Funding's independent auditors were unaware of the huge fraud. Equity Funding executives went to great lengths to conceal their fraudulent activities from these individuals. As an example, on the pretense of lunch at an elegant and busy local restaurant, company officers rushed several auditors out of their office, hoping that they would leave their files unlocked. The auditors unwittingly cooperated. Equity Funding clerks then spent the lunch hour copying the insurance policy numbers randomly selected by the auditors for testing. With those numbers in hand, client executives were able to ensure that the selected files were totally "clean."[7]

---

6. Many of these individuals expressed remorse when they testified regarding their involvement in the massive fraud. For example, one reported, "I simply lacked the courage to do what was right." (H. Anderson, "12 More Ex-Equity Officials Get Jail, Fine or Probation," *Los Angeles Times*, 25 March 1975, section 3, 9 & 11.)

7. The various public accounting firms unfortunate enough to have been associated with Equity Funding at some point in its existence collectively paid $44 million to settle the civil lawsuits filed against them following the company's collapse.

THE AFTERMATH OF EQUITY FUNDING

Equity Funding stockholders and those of companies that Equity Funding defrauded suffered losses of hundreds of millions of dollars. The disclosure of the Equity Funding scandal rocked all of Wall Street, dropping the collective market value of publicly owned stocks by more than $15 billion within one week. In comparison, Goldblum, Levin, and their co-conspirators paid a seemingly modest price for their transgressions. Goldblum eventually served four years in the Terminal Island federal prison in Long Beach, California, while Levin spent two and one-half years in that facility.

At his sentencing hearing, a contrite Levin pleaded for leniency: "Someday when this nightmare is over, I will conduct myself in a highly ethical manner, which hopefully will repay for some of the crimes and fraud I committed."[8] Within a few years after his release from prison, Levin was living in Beverly Hills and serving as the president of a small plastics company. In 1984, prosecutors indicted him for embezzling $250,000 from the company's pension fund. Among the more than two dozen other fraud charges listed in the indictment against Levin were several that involved preparing forged invoices and other documents to support fictitious transactions recorded by his company.

Goldblum also returned to the business world after his release from federal prison. In 1984, he was elected president and chief executive officer (CEO) of a small company that operates a chain of medical care clinics. Goldblum remarked that he hoped to "put the company on a sound financial basis" and eventually "build it into a more substantive venture."[9] Ironically, Goldblum's new company was audited at the time by Seidman & Seidman, the accounting firm that had served as Equity Funding's independent auditor during its final year of existence. Shortly after Goldblum joined the company, Seidman & Seidman resigned as its audit firm, forfeiting a $40,000 annual audit fee in the process.

In 1987, Goldblum stepped down as the CEO of the company he joined in 1984. Goldblum soon accepted a position as controller of a similar but much larger firm, Primedex Corporation. In the mid-1990s, Goldblum found himself in the headlines again, this time as an alleged participant in the largest workers' compensation fraud in California history. State prosecutors contend that Goldblum and two fellow officers of Primedex bilked the state of California and several other parties out of millions of dollars.

> Prosecutors charged that the defendants defrauded insurance companies and employers by, among other things, charging for medical services that were never provided, providing illegal kickbacks to doctors and chiropractors, and submitting ghostwritten medical reports.[10]

In February 1999, Goldblum appeared in a southern California court in his ongoing effort to win an acquittal in the workers' comp fraud case. After the court

---

8. H. Anderson, "Goldblum Gets 8-Year Term in Equity Scandal," *Los Angeles Times*, 18 March 1975, section 3, 8 & 9.

9. S.J. Sansweet, "Man Who Presided over Massive Fraud Picked to Head Firm," *The Wall Street Journal*, 7 September 1984, 7.

10. S. Silverstein, "New Charges Added in Workers' Comp Case," *Los Angeles Times*, 1 June 1996, D7.

hearing, police arrested Goldblum and led him away in handcuffs. Goldblum's arrest stemmed from charges unrelated to the workers' comp scam. Months earlier, a southern California bank loaned Goldblum $150,000. Goldblum pledged as collateral for that loan several hundred thousand dollars of securities, securities that the bank later discovered were essentially worthless.[11]

QUESTIONS

1. Is it necessary or appropriate for independent auditors to trust client executives? If so, to what extent should auditors trust client management?

2. When evaluating the integrity of a prospective client's executives, what types of information should auditors obtain and from what sources would they generally collect this information?

3. In your view, was it appropriate for Seidman & Seidman to resign as the audit firm of the company that chose Goldblum as its new president and CEO? Under what conditions is it appropriate for a professional firm, such as a CPA firm, to choose not to provide professional services to a company or individual requesting such services?

---

11. J. Gaw, "Man Arrested in Alleged Scam of O.C. Lender," *Los Angeles Times*, 17 February 1999, C1.

CASE 8.7

NATIONAL STUDENT MARKETING CORPORATION

Anthony Natelli was frustrated. For several days, Natelli had been working fran-tically on a 112-page proxy statement for one of his audit clients, National Student Marketing Corporation (NSMC). It was 2:00 a.m. on August 15, 1969, and Natelli was sitting in the New York City offices of Pandick Press, a financial printing firm. Natelli was waiting for the most recent version of the proxy statement to come off the presses. Three days of little sleep and constant run-ins with NSMC's executives had left Natelli's nerves frayed. Natelli, an audit partner with the Washington, D.C., office of Peat, Marwick, Mitchell & Co., flew to New York City three days earlier with NSMC's chief executive officer (CEO), Cortes Randell, and financial vice-president, Bernard Kurek. Randell had insisted at the last minute that Natelli and the audit supervisor on the NSMC engagement, Joseph Scansaroli, accompany him to New York on his private jet, Snoopy. Since NSMC was an important audit client, Natelli agreed to the hastily arranged trip, al-though he had other work piling up on his desk.

NSMC was in the final stages of closing a deal to acquire an insurance com-pany, Interstate National Corporation. Before the deal could be finalized, the proxy statement had to be submitted to the two firms' stockholders. The proxy statement contained NSMC's financial statements for the nine-month period end-ing May 31, 1969, and restated financial data for NSMC's 1968 fiscal year that had ended on August 31, 1968. The latter data were included in a footnote to the nine-month financial statements.

Finally, around 3:15 a.m., the new version of the proxy statement was printed. With Randell by his side, Natelli studied the financial statements and accompa-nying footnotes included in the proxy statement. The key issue that concerned Natelli in the financial statements was the accounting treatment for a large "com-mitment" that NSMC had recently obtained from the Pontiac Division of General

Motors. NSMC was a leading firm in the small but rapidly growing campus promotions industry. Through a network of 700 campus representatives, NSMC distributed promotional materials for several large companies. Among the products NSMC promoted were automobiles, airline packages for spring break vacations, mini-refrigerators, and even dating services.

When NSMC received a "commitment" from a client to carry out a promotional campaign, the company immediately recognized the majority of the gross profit on the project. Often, these so-called commitments involved no more than a tentative oral agreement made by NSMC with a prospective client. Natelli had clashed repeatedly with Randell regarding the aggressive accounting treatment applied to the commitments. Over the past year, many of NSMC's clients had canceled commitments before making any payments to NSMC. Since NSMC had no legal recourse against clients in such circumstances, the unbilled receivables previously booked by the company for these commitments had to be written off to expense.

After poring over the proxy statement, Natelli reached a decision, a decision his client would not like. Natelli told Randell that NSMC would have to remove from the proxy financial statements the revenue and unbilled receivable related to the $1.2 million Pontiac commitment. Natelli believed that the letter documenting that commitment left too many "outs" for Pontiac. In the past, Natelli had allowed Randell to book revenue related to similar flimsy commitments. But no more. Enough was enough.

ELIZABETH GEDRA, MEET ANTHONY NATELLI

Elizabeth Gedra was frustrated. Each day, she filed into a New York City federal courtroom and then sat there for hours being peppered with unfamiliar terms such as "prior period adjustments," "deferred tax credits," and "percentage-of-completion accounting method." Gedra's frustration stemmed from her doubts that she was qualified to render a decision in the criminal fraud case that she and 11 other New York City jurors were hearing. Finally, in early November 1974, during the second week of the trial, Gedra made a decision, a decision that the judge presiding over the trial would not like. Gedra told the court clerk that she wanted to be excused from the jury. In her view, it would be best for everyone involved if one of the three alternate jurors took her place. Surely, one of those individuals was better qualified to decide the fate of the two well-dressed, well-mannered, and very articulate defendants that she observed each day from her seat in the jury box. The two men, Anthony Natelli and his friend and former subordinate, Joseph Scansaroli, faced prison terms and large fines if convicted of the fraud charges pending against them.

NSMC, THE EARLY YEARS

Cortes Randell was an engineer by training but an entrepreneur at heart. During the mid-1960s, Randell recognized that the large and growing population of college students across the country was a market largely neglected by major companies. Developing cost-effective marketing methods to reach college students posed a major problem for these companies. To solve this problem—and to become his own boss—Randell created National Student Marketing Corporation. Because he lacked a strong background in business, Randell offered key positions in his new company to several of his friends who majored in business at his alma mater, the University of Virginia.

Randell and his cohorts designed a business plan to consolidate the marketing efforts of companies that sold products and services to college students scattered across the nation. NSMC offered such companies customized promotional campaigns carried out by its far-flung and loosely organized network of campus representatives. These promotional campaigns involved plastering college campuses with posters and distributing inexpensive novelty items. Initially, clients compensated NSMC based upon the number of responses to the promotional materials. However, Randell soon began offering promotional services to prospective clients primarily on a fixed-fee basis.

NSMC's revenues grew briskly during its first few years. In 1968, Randell took the company public to finance an aggressive expansion plan he had adopted. Randell's expansion strategy involved acquiring businesses that marketed products and services to college students, products and services that NSMC would then promote on college campuses. Randell quickly acquired more than 20 companies. In exchange for these companies, Randell issued their former owners NSMC common stock. Convincing these individuals to accept NSMC stock for their companies was not a difficult task since the stock reigned as one of the "hottest" investments on Wall Street. NSMC's stock initially sold for $6 per share in April 1968; in less than two years, the stock—adjusted for a stock split—traded at $144 per share. Randell and NSMC's other major stockholders profited handsomely from this huge increase in the company's stock price. In 1969 alone, Randell realized a profit of $3 million from the sale of NSMC stock.

Shortly after taking NSMC public in 1968, the company's audit firm, Arthur Andersen & Co., resigned. Arthur Andersen reportedly resigned because the firm questioned the reliability of information being supplied to it by NSMC's executives. Following Arthur Andersen's resignation, Randell approached Peat, Marwick, Mitchell & Co. about serving as NSMC's audit firm. Before accepting the engagement, Peat Marwick contacted Arthur Andersen. Peat Marwick asked Andersen whether there was any reason it should not accept NSMC as an audit client. Peat Marwick did not ask Arthur Andersen why it resigned as NSMC's auditor nor whether Arthur Andersen had any concerns regarding the integrity of NSMC's management. Arthur Andersen's brief response to Peat Marwick's inquiry indicated that it was not aware of any reason why Peat Marwick should not accept NSMC as a client.[1] Peat Marwick accepted NSMC as an audit client in August 1968.

The first engagement performed by Peat Marwick for NSMC was an audit of the company's financial statements for the fiscal year ended August 31, 1968. The following summer, the accounting firm helped NSMC prepare the proxy statement required for the acquisition of Interstate National Corporation. Peat

---

1. The information regarding Peat Marwick's inquiry of Arthur Andersen was taken from the following source: Securities and Exchange Commission, *Accounting Series Release No. 173*, 2 July 1975.

Marwick reviewed the financial statements included in the proxy statement and later issued a "comfort" letter concerning the proxy statement to Interstate's board of directors.

Anthony Natelli was the audit partner assigned to oversee the NSMC engagements. At the time, Natelli and Cortes Randell were both 32 years old. The similarities between the two men did not end there. Both men were energetic, self-assured, and seemingly headed for very successful careers in business. Natelli managed the Washington, D.C., office of the nation's largest public accounting firm, a prestigious position with a prestigious firm. Randell was a multimillionaire and CEO of a profitable new company that had caught the attention of Wall Street and investors across the nation. The young executive directed NSMC's operations from a lavish suite of offices overlooking Park Avenue on New York's Manhattan Island.

PEAT MARWICK'S 1968 AUDIT OF NSMC

Anthony Natelli and Cortes Randell began bickering over accounting and financial reporting issues shortly after Peat Marwick signed on as NSMC's audit firm. In September 1968, early in Peat Marwick's 1968 audit of NSMC, Randell met with Natelli to discuss the accounting treatment applied to the fixed-fee promotional projects. Bernard Kurek, NSMC's financial vice-president who oversaw the firm's accounting department, and Joseph Scansaroli, Natelli's principal assistant on the NSMC audit, also attended this meeting. NSMC recorded revenue on a fixed-fee promotional project when it obtained a commitment from a client. Randell defended this accounting treatment by pointing out that NSMC's account representatives expended most of the time and effort required on a promotional project before receiving a commitment from a client. Natelli believed this accounting treatment was too aggressive. The audit partner insisted that NSMC use the percentage-of-completion accounting method to recognize gross profit on the fixed-fee promotional projects. Randell eventually acquiesced and NSMC began using this accounting method for its fiscal year ending August 31, 1968.

> After considering alternative methods of accounting, Natelli concluded that he would use a percentage-of-completion approach to the recognition of income on these commitments, pursuant to which the company would accrue that percentage of gross income and related costs on a client's "commitment" that was equal to the proportion of the time spent by the account executive on the project before August 31, 1968, to the total time it was estimated he would have to spend to complete the project.[2]

Natelli's insistence that NSMC apply the percentage-of-completion accounting method to the fixed-fee promotional projects had little impact on the company's reported profits. Why? Because Peat Marwick found that account representatives spent the large majority of time required on a project before obtaining a commitment from the client—as Randell had previously asserted.

In late September 1968, Kurek gave the auditors a list of $1.7 million of commitments allegedly obtained by NSMC earlier that summer. Randell had instructed Kurek to book the revenue on these commitments via adjusting entries

---

2. *United States v. Natelli*, 527 F.2d 311 (1975), 315.

as of August 31, 1968, the final day of NSMC's 1968 fiscal year. These commitments disturbed Natelli for three reasons. First, the commitments were strictly oral. Second, shortly before Kurek provided the list of these commitments to Peat Marwick, Natelli had given Randell some bad news: NSMC had incurred a pre-audit net loss of $232,000 for fiscal 1968. Natelli knew that Randell closely monitored NSMC's stock price and that Randell realized that the stock would plummet if the company reported disappointing results for 1968. The $1.7 million of new commitments would convert NSMC's pre-audit net loss to a net income of $388,000 for 1968, double the profit reported by NSMC the previous year.

Finally, Natelli was troubled by Randell's demand that Peat Marwick not mail written confirmations to the clients from whom NSMC had obtained the $1.7 million of new commitments. Randell suggested that the confirmations might upset the new clients since all of the details of the promotional projects had not been finalized. If Peat Marwick contacted the clients, some of the clients might even cancel the deals. In lieu of sending written confirmations, Randell arranged to have Scansaroli confirm certain of the commitments via telephone conversations with the clients. Eventually, Natelli decided to allow NSMC to record the $1.7 million of new commitments as of August 31, 1968. The Peat Marwick auditors also accepted the stage of completion estimates provided by NSMC for these projects. These estimates indicated that most of the time required on these projects by NSMC personnel had been spent by August 31, 1968. As a result, NSMC booked the majority of the gross profit on these projects in fiscal 1968.

After completing the 1968 audit, Natelli notified Randell that in the future Peat Marwick would allow NSMC to book revenue only on projects backed by a written commitment. In response to this directive, Randell had a subordinate prepare a form letter to formally document each future commitment obtained by NSMC.

On November 14, 1968, Peat Marwick issued an unqualified opinion on NSMC's 1968 financial statements. During late 1968 and 1969, NSMC acquired seven companies via stock swaps. NSMC used its 1968 financial statements to help close these deals.

Peat Marwick's Association With NSMC's 1969 Proxy Statement

Cortes Randell believed that the acquisition of Interstate National Corporation was critical to the future financial success of NSMC. Interstate would provide NSMC with the ability to market a wide range of insurance services to college students through its network of campus sales representatives. Randell projected that NSMC would earn sizable profits from this new line of business. During the summer of 1969, Randell offered Interstate's stockholders one share of NSMC stock for every two shares of Interstate stock they held. To close the deal, the always impatient Randell raised the ante to two shares of NSMC stock for every three shares of Interstate stock. Interstate's board of directors tentatively accepted the latter offer, contingent on the approval of each company's stockholders. This approval would be obtained via the preparation and distribution of a proxy statement to the firms' stockholders.

Because he wanted to quickly close the deal to acquire Interstate, Randell urged Kurek to hurriedly complete the proxy statement. The NSMC financial statements included in the proxy statement covered the nine-month period from September 1, 1968, through May 31, 1969. The proxy statement also contained re-stated earnings data for NSMC for fiscal 1968. These latter data reflected the "pooled" 1968 earnings of NSMC and the seven companies acquired by NSMC during the first nine months of fiscal 1969.

Peat Marwick did not audit NSMC's financial statements for the nine-month period ending May 31, 1969, that were included in the proxy statement. But, the accounting firm helped prepare those financial statements and reviewed them when they were completed. Likewise, Peat Marwick did not update its audit of NSMC's 1968 financial statements, although it did review the restated 1968 earn-ings data incorporated in NSMC's proxy statement. In both cases, the relevant technical pronouncement at the time, *Statement on Auditing Standards No. 1*, dic-tated that Peat Marwick was "associated" with the given financial data. Under *SAS No. 1*, an auditor associated with a client's financial statement data had a re-sponsibility to insist on revision of that data if he or she discovered it was mate-rially in error.

Natelli and Scansaroli faced two important issues during their review of the fi-nancial data included in NSMC's 1969 proxy statement. The first issue involved NSMC's restated earnings data for 1968. During the first few months of 1969, most of the $1.7 million of commitments recorded at the end of fiscal 1968 had been canceled by NSMC's clients, forcing the company to write off the related re-ceivables. The revenues recognized on these commitments accounted for more than 20 percent of NSMC's 1968 revenues. If these revenues had not been recorded in fiscal 1968, the company's net income for that year would have been more than 50 percent lower than the reported figure.

The embarrassing situation faced by Natelli and NSMC's executives was whether to disclose in the proxy statement that the company's 1968 earnings had been materially inflated by the commitments subsequently canceled in 1969. Ultimately, that disclosure was not made in the proxy statement. Instead, NSMC's revised earnings data for 1968—revised for the canceled commitments—were simply merged with the 1968 earnings data of the companies NSMC ac-quired during the first nine months of fiscal 1969. NSMC included these merged earnings data in a vaguely worded footnote appended to its financial statements for the first nine months of 1969. This footnote made no reference to the impact of the canceled commitments on NSMC's previously reported net income for 1968. According to subsequent testimony, Natelli eliminated narrative disclo-sures initially included in the footnote that would have alerted readers to the can-celed commitments and their impact on NSMC's 1968 net income.

A federal judge later ruled that NSMC's failure to disclose in the proxy state-ment the material overstatement of its 1968 net income violated *Accounting Principles Board Opinion No. 9*, "Reporting the Results of Operations."[3] Under *APB No. 9*, the overstatement should have been corrected with a prior period ad-justment in NSMC's subsequent financial statements accompanied by adequate disclosure of the impact on the previous period's net income. This same judge chastised Natelli and Scansaroli for not insisting on disclosure of the overstated 1968 earnings in the proxy statement. "A simple desire to right the wrong that had been perpetrated on the stockholders and others by the false audited finan-

---

3. *United States v. Natelli*, 317.

cial statement should have dictated that course."[4]   A federal prosecutor put it more bluntly. "They [Natelli and Scansaroli] took every penny of the losses, and they tucked them away where nobody would ever find them."[5]

The second important issue faced by Natelli and Scansaroli in their review of NSMC's proxy statement centered on the $1.2 million commitment from the Pontiac Division of General Motors. Randell allegedly obtained this commitment a few months earlier during the spring of 1969. The CEO wanted to include the revenue on that commitment in NSMC's proxy financial statements for the first nine months of fiscal 1969. As noted earlier, after reviewing a draft of the proxy statement on August 15, 1969, Natelli demanded that the revenue (and unbilled receivable) related to the Pontiac commitment be backed out of the company's financial statements. Natelli made this decision after reviewing the letter documenting the Pontiac commitment. In Natelli's view, the "commitment" made by Pontiac was not legally binding and thus not a sufficient basis for recognizing revenue in NSMC's accounting records.

Randell attempted to change Natelli's mind regarding the Pontiac commitment. When he realized that Natelli would not reconsider, Randell privately contacted an NSMC sales representative. Within a few hours, that representative delivered a copy of a commitment letter to Randell from Eastern Airlines. The Eastern Airlines commitment had allegedly been obtained by the sales representative before May 31, 1969, the cutoff date for the proxy financial statements. This commitment was of approximately the same size as the Pontiac commitment that Natelli had rejected. After much cajoling by Randell, Natelli agreed to allow most of the gross profit on the Eastern Airlines commitment to be included in the proxy financial statements. Again, a court subsequently questioned this decision by Natelli.

> The Eastern contract was a matter for deep suspicion because it was substituted so rapidly for the Pontiac contract to which Natelli had objected, and which had, itself, been produced after the end of the fiscal period, though dated earlier. It was still another unbilled commitment produced by Marketing [NSMC] after the close of the fiscal period. Its spectacular appearance, as Natelli himself noted at the time, made its replacement of the Pontiac contract "weird."[6]

Thanks largely to the gross profit booked on the Eastern Airlines commitment, NSMC reported a net income of approximately $700,000 for the first nine months of fiscal 1969 in the proxy income statement. On October 31, 1969, the boards of directors of Interstate and NSMC met and consummated the merger of the two companies. The stock market enthusiastically received the news of the merger. Within two months, NSMC's stock reached its all-time (split-adjusted) high of approximately $144 per share. Shortly after Peat Marwick completed the proxy statement engagement in October 1969, Joseph Scansaroli resigned from the firm to become NSMC's assistant controller.

After completing the review of NSMC's proxy statement in the fall of 1969, Peat Marwick initiated a comfort letter engagement for the company. NSMC intended to provide the comfort letter developed by Peat Marwick to Interstate's

4. *United States v. Natelli*, 319.

5. *The Wall Street Journal*, "National Student Case Alleging Stock Fraud By CPAs Goes to Jury," 14 November 1974, 26.

6. *United States v. Natelli*, 320.

board of directors. Natelli and his subordinates completed the comfort letter engagement in early November 1969. In the comfort letter, Peat Marwick informed Interstate's directors that NSMC's unaudited financial statements in the just-issued proxy statement required significant adjustments. These adjustments stemmed from unbilled receivables recorded by NSMC during the first nine months of fiscal 1969. In the last three months of fiscal 1969, the commitments from which these unbilled receivables arose had been canceled by NSMC's clients. According to the comfort letter, NSMC should have reported a net loss of approximately $80,000 for the first nine months of 1969, instead of the reported net income of $700,000. Peat Marwick recommended in an addendum to the comfort letter that Interstate's and NSMC's stockholders be provided with corrected financial data for the nine-month period covered by the financial statements in NSMC's proxy statement.

Interstate's board of directors received the final version of Peat Marwick's comfort letter a few days *following* the consummation of the NSMC–Interstate merger. Given the startling revelations in the comfort letter, Interstate's board discussed "undoing" the merger. After several days, the Interstate directors decided this option was not feasible.[7] As a result, the troubling revelations in Peat Marwick's comfort letter were not passed on to the former Interstate stockholders, NSMC's stockholders, the general public, or the SEC.

CRIMINAL CHARGES FILED AGAINST NATELLI AND SCANSAROLI

NSMC never collected the unbilled receivable resulting from the suspicious Eastern Airlines commitment that Randell hurriedly obtained when the 1969 proxy statement was being prepared. In February 1970, NSMC wrote off the total amount of that receivable to expense. NSMC also wrote off a large amount of similar unbilled receivables in the first few months of 1970. These write-offs caused many financial analysts to question the health of the company in articles published in the financial press. In turn, these articles caused the price of NSMC's common stock to tumble and prompted the SEC to launch an intensive investigation of the company's financial affairs. Later in 1970, angry stockholders filed a class action lawsuit against NSMC's executives, Peat Marwick, and other parties associated with the company. This lawsuit documented stock market losses of more than $100 million suffered by NSMC's current and former stockholders.

In January 1974, a federal grand jury indicted Cortes Randell, Bernard Kurek, and two other high-ranking NSMC officials on numerous criminal fraud charges. All four individuals subsequently pleaded guilty to one or more of these charges. Randell pleaded guilty to four criminal charges including fraudulently misrepresenting NSMC's financial condition and operating results in the 1969 proxy statement. Randell received the most severe sentence of the four NSMC executives, an

7. Recognize that at this point the Interstate directors were NSMC stockholders. These individuals had benefited significantly from the merger and continued to benefit afterwards given the post-merger increase in the price of NSMC's stock.

18-month prison term and a $40,000 fine. He ultimately served eight months in federal prison. In his guilty plea, Randell confessed to altering or concealing key features of commitment letters obtained by NSMC, including those obtained from the Pontiac Division of General Motors and Eastern Airlines. For example, Randell admitted that he had changed a letter received from Pontiac to make it read as a formal commitment letter.

One count of the federal indictment named Anthony Natelli and Joseph Scansaroli. The federal indictment alleged that Natelli and Scansaroli "willfully and knowingly made and caused to be made false and misleading statements with respect to material facts"[8] in NSMC's 1969 proxy statement. More specifically, the indictment leveled two allegations against each auditor. First, the grand jury charged that Natelli and Scansaroli helped NSMC officials misrepresent the company's 1968 earnings in the proxy statement. This allegation stemmed from the vaguely worded financial statement footnote in the proxy statement that reported NSMC's restated 1968 earnings data. Second, the indictment charged the two men with allowing NSMC to materially overstate its revenues and profit in the unaudited nine-month income statement included in the proxy statement. These overstatements resulted principally from the large Eastern Airlines commitment that eventually proved worthless.

Franklin Velie, the assistant U.S. attorney assigned to prosecute Natelli and Scansaroli, suggested that the charges against the two men were straightforward. "This is a simple case . . . the two Peat Marwick auditors made a bad mistake (which isn't a crime) and then buried it (which is a crime)."[9] Velie went on to observe that "People who read those financial statements were cheated. The proxy statement gave no hint of what the two auditors knew—that NSMC was a losing proposition."[10]

Peat Marwick staunchly defended both Natelli and Scansaroli in a press release following their indictment.

> This is the first time the victims of a crime have been indicted along with its perpetrators. We believe the allegation of criminality against these two professionals is unjustified, unsupported, and unprecedented. Messrs. Natelli and Scansaroli wholly and categorically deny the charge against them, and we fully support them.[11]

Peat Marwick's press release went on to report that Scansaroli "passed" a polygraph examination regarding his alleged involvement in the NSMC fraud.

The criminal indictment filed against Natelli and Scansaroli was seen as an important test case by federal prosecutors and the accounting profession. At issue was whether independent auditors could be held responsible for financial fraud perpetrated by their clients. The importance of the pending case was magnified in early 1974 when the federal government failed to obtain convictions against two Arthur Andersen auditors accused of fraud in the Four Seasons scandal.

---

8. *United States v. Natelli*, 314.

9. F. Andrews, "Fraud Trial of Peat Marwick Attracts Anxious Attention of Other Accountants," *The Wall Street Journal*, 29 October 1974, 44.

10. *Ibid.*

11. D. McClintick, "Peat Marwick Partner Indicted Over Proxy Data," *The Wall Street Journal*, 18 January 1974, 4.

JUDGE TYLER, MEET FRANKLIN VELIE

Judge Harold Tyler was frustrated. Over the past few days, Judge Tyler, the federal judge presiding over the trial of Anthony Natelli and Joseph Scansaroli, had witnessed increasingly hostile tactics by the two teams of opposing lawyers in the case. The defendants' lawyers shrilly objected to practically every major point raised by the prosecuting attorneys. Even more annoying to Judge Tyler was the condescending way he was treated by Assistant U.S. Attorney Franklin Velie, head of the prosecution team. Also distracting were the complaints of a juror, Elizabeth Gedra, who wanted to be dismissed from the jury. Ms. Gedra claimed that she could not understand the charges against the two defendants given the technical accounting jargon constantly bandied about by the attorneys on both sides. Then, there were the inflammatory remarks regarding the trial that appeared in *The Wall Street Journal*. Those remarks, made by a high-ranking SEC official, suggested that the case against Natelli and Scansaroli was "open and shut." Defense counsel maintained that since the jurors were not sequestered, they might have read the comments, although they had been instructed to avoid all media reports regarding the trial. Given the prejudicial nature of the remarks, defense counsel insisted on an immediate mistrial.

As the trial progressed, the patient but strong-willed Judge Tyler increasingly asserted his authority over the proceedings. Judge Tyler eventually convinced Ms. Gedra to remain on the jury. Regarding the prejudicial remarks reported in *The Wall Street Journal*, Judge Tyler decided that he would rule on the defendants' motion for a mistrial following the announcement of the jury's decision. Judge Tyler also forcefully imposed his will on the two teams of opposing attorneys by demanding that they treat each other and himself with more respect. At one point, Judge Tyler angrily warned U.S. Attorney Velie that he objected to being treated like a "country bumpkin."[12]

Since Natelli and Scansaroli faced the same charges, they were tried simultaneously, although they were represented by different legal counsel. Bernard Kurek served as the key prosecution witness against the two men. In tedious detail, a contrite Kurek recalled the key circumstances and events pertinent to the allegations pending against Natelli and Scansaroli. Kurek's recollections generally supported the prosecution's assertion that Natelli and Scansaroli "knowingly and willfully" participated in the NSMC fraud masterminded by Randell. Nevertheless, some of Kurek's testimony proved favorable to Natelli and Scansaroli. For example, Kurek revealed that the two defendants were repeatedly angered and frustrated by Randell's refusal to provide adequate documentation for NSMC's large commitments.

Following Kurek's testimony, the prosecution paraded to the witness stand one-by-one the junior auditors assigned to the NSMC engagements. The prosecution attempted to establish with the junior auditors' testimony that Natelli never believed the Eastern Airlines commitment was authentic. That strategy backfired. Initially, the testimony of one junior auditor supported the prosecution's claim. However, under withering cross-examination by the defendants' legal counsel, this individual contradicted himself on several key points. Natelli's

12. F. Andrews, "National Student Marketing Trial Jolted By 2 Developments That Hurt U.S. Case," *The Wall Street Journal*, 4 November 1971, 7.

and Scansaroli's attorneys then took the offensive. In succession, the attorneys pointedly asked each junior auditor whether Natelli or Scansaroli had ever asked them to do anything improper or dishonest on the NSMC engagements. Each junior auditor firmly replied that neither defendant had done so.

A strong piece of evidence introduced by the prosecution was a report developed by Touche Ross & Co., another Big Eight accounting firm. This report criticized key decisions made by Peat Marwick on the NSMC engagements. A major focus of the Touche Ross report was Natelli's decision to allow NSMC to use the percentage-of-completion accounting method to recognize revenue on the fixed-fee promotional projects. The Touche Ross report correctly pointed out that the commitments were generally cancelable by NSMC's clients. Additionally, Touche Ross noted that there was typically little or no evidence indicating that the large promotional projects could be successfully completed by NSMC's poorly organized network of campus representatives. Given these two factors, Touche Ross suggested that the percentage-of-completion accounting method should not have been applied to the promotional projects. Instead, Touche Ross believed the completed-contract method would have been more appropriate. In fact, NSMC began applying the completed-contract method to its projects shortly after the SEC launched an investigation of the company's accounting and financial reporting practices in 1970.

To raise reasonable doubt regarding the guilt of their clients, Natelli's and Scansaroli's attorneys attempted to establish that the two auditors lacked a motive for their alleged wrongdoing. The defense attorneys continually reminded the jury that neither man benefited financially from NSMC's fraudulent financial statements. This was not true of the other four defendants who had already pleaded guilty. Absent such an economic motive, the defense lawyers maintained that it was unreasonable to conclude that the two individuals knowingly participated in the fraud.

To counter this assertion, the prosecution once again relied on Bernard Kurek's testimony. Each man allegedly told Kurek that he might lose his CPA certificate if the overstated revenues and profit in NSMC's audited financial statements for 1968 were publicly revealed. According to the prosecution, this concern established that both men had a motive to participate in the fraud. More to the point, the two auditors had an incentive to misrepresent NSMC's financial data in the 1969 proxy statement to conceal the mistakes they made during the 1968 NSMC audit. Later, both Natelli and Scansaroli testified that they did not recall discussing the possible loss of their CPA certificate with Kurek.

When Natelli and Scansaroli testified, they both admitted to having made mistakes during the NSMC engagements. For example, Natelli freely admitted that he failed to obtain sufficient documentation for the Eastern Airlines commitment. When Scansaroli took the witness stand, he confessed that he had been "far too easily satisfied"[13] during the NSMC engagements.

Velie questioned Scansaroli at length regarding the audit procedures applied to NSMC's large commitments. A key issue in this line of questioning was the rigor of the telephone confirmation procedures Scansaroli had used in lieu of written confirmations. (Recall that Cortes Randell had insisted that Peat Marwick not mail written confirmations to certain of NSMC's clients.) Scansaroli's testimony

---

13. F. Andrews, "National Student Defendant Concedes He Was 'Too Easily Satisfied' in Audit," *The Wall Street Journal*, 11 November 1974, 10.

suggested that the telephone confirmation procedures were very lax. He admitted obtaining, unintentionally, one of the telephone confirmations from an employee of an NSMC affiliate instead of from an employee of the given NSMC client.[14] Likewise, Velie got Scansaroli to admit that he had not checked NSMC's estimates of completion on several large promotional projects.[15] These estimates were critical since they allowed NSMC to justify recognizing most of the revenue on a project when a commitment was obtained.

After the scathing attack on Scansaroli's integrity and competence by Velie, Scansaroli's attorneys restored his credibility somewhat by introducing into evidence a memo he wrote in January 1970. Scansaroli wrote this memo while employed as NSMC's assistant controller, a position in which he was Kurek's principal subordinate. In the memo, Scansaroli criticized NSMC's aggressive accounting methods and threatened to quit if the company did not strengthen its accounting and financial reporting practices.

THE VERDICT

Following lengthy summations presented by the opposing attorneys, Judge Tyler spent more than 90 minutes instructing the seven-woman, five-man jury that would decide the fate of Anthony Natelli and Joseph Scansaroli. On the first day of deliberations, the jury foreman requested that Judge Tyler explain the meaning of the key phrases "material" and "knowing and willful conduct" included in the federal indictment. On the second day of deliberations, the jury requested that testimony regarding the Pontiac and Eastern Airlines commitments be reread to them.

During the afternoon of the second day of deliberations, the jury foreman sent a message to Judge Tyler. That message indicated the jury was hopelessly deadlocked and would be unable to reach a unanimous verdict as required by law. Judge Tyler brought the jury back into the courtroom and instructed them to continue their deliberations. During this meeting with Judge Tyler, the jury foreman once again requested that the meaning of the terms "material" and "knowing and willful conduct" be explained to the jury. At this point, Judge Tyler added clarifying language to his original instructions to the jury. Judge Tyler advised the jurors that they could infer "knowing and willful conduct" by a defendant if he had "deliberately closed his eyes to the obvious or recklessly stated as fact matters of which he was ignorant."[16]

---

14. The results of the earlier SEC investigation revealed that NSMC employees actually performed some of the telephone confirmations.

15. A Peat Marwick representative had previously informed the SEC that the firm had reviewed and tested NSMC's percentage-of-completion estimates. However, the Peat Marwick auditors apparently failed to document these procedures in their workpapers. The SEC had also questioned NSMC's account representatives regarding Peat Marwick's requests for percentage-of-completion estimates on promotional projects. One account representative testified that he believed Peat Marwick was requesting estimates of the likelihood that the company would obtain binding commitments from given clients.

16. F. Andrews, "Two Auditors Are Convicted Of Stock Fraud," *The Wall Street Journal*, 15 November 1974, 8.

Approximately two hours following the meeting with Judge Tyler, the jury foreman notified him that the jury had reached a decision. A short time later, the packed courtroom waited in silence as the foreman read the verdict for both defendants: "Guilty." Reporters noted that neither Natelli nor Scansaroli showed any reaction to the reading of the verdict. However, members of their families and representatives of Peat Marwick present in the courtroom reacted emotionally when the verdict was announced. Outside the courtroom, Walter Hanson, senior partner of Peat Marwick, commented on the jury's decision.

> We are shocked at the verdict and will fully support Messrs. Natelli and Scansaroli in their appeal. We believe the jury didn't understand the complicated accounting and disclosure questions in the case, as indeed one juror stated to the court midway through the trial.[17]

Within minutes of the conviction of Natelli and Scansaroli, Judge Tyler ruled on the objection that the two men's attorneys had lodged during the trial regarding the prejudicial remarks printed in *The Wall Street Journal*. Judge Tyler reported that he had found no evidence that any juror had read or been told of those remarks. As a result, he denied the defendants' request for a mistrial.

EPILOGUE

In December 1974, Judge Tyler sentenced Anthony Natelli to 60 days in prison and fined him $10,000. Joseph Scansaroli received a 10-day prison sentence and a fine of $2,500. During the sentencing hearing, Judge Tyler observed that the "accounting profession, like the legal profession, frequently failed to understand its public responsibility."[18]

Both Natelli and Scansaroli appealed their convictions. In July 1975, a federal appeals court upheld the criminal conviction of Anthony Natelli. In refusing to overturn the conviction, the federal appeals court responded to a series of arguments made by Natelli. The appeals court quickly rejected Natelli's assertion that the errors in the financial statements included in NSMC's 1969 proxy statement were immaterial. Natelli also maintained that he was not responsible for verifying the Eastern Airlines commitment since Peat Marwick had not been retained to audit the financial statements in NSMC's 1969 proxy statement. Again, the appeals court quickly rejected this argument. The appeals court cited language from the relevant auditing standards at the time that confirmed Natelli and the other Peat Marwick auditors had been "associated" with those unaudited financial statements. Given this fact, the court noted that Natelli had a responsibility not to allow questionable earnings figures to be included in those financial statements. The court went on to observe that auditors' responsibilities are not limited to the requirements specifically imposed on them by professional standards.

> The issue on this appeal is not what an auditor is generally under a duty to do with respect to an unaudited statement, but what these defendants had a duty to do in these unusual and highly suspicious circumstances.[19]

---

17. *Ibid.*

18. A. Lubash, "Stock Defrauder Fined and Jailed," *The New York Times*, 28 December 1974, 31.

19. *United States v. Natelli*, 323.

Although the federal appeals court upheld the conviction of Anthony Natelli, that same court overturned the conviction of Joseph Scansaroli. The appeals court ruled that the jury had erred when it found Scansaroli guilty on both allegations included in the sole count of the federal indictment naming him and Natelli. According to the appeals court, Scansaroli had not been a party to the decision to allow NSMC to substitute the Eastern Airlines commitment for the Pontiac commitment in the proxy financial statements. Instead, the court ruled that Natelli alone made that decision. Since a defendant must be found guilty on all allegations included in each count of an indictment, the appeals court voided Scansaroli's conviction. The court then ordered a retrial of Scansaroli on the sole charge that he helped prepare the misleading financial statement footnote included in the 1969 proxy statement. Prosecutors chose not to retry Scansaroli.

Anthony Natelli appealed his conviction to the U.S. Supreme Court. In October 1977, the Supreme Court refused to hear Natelli's appeal, meaning that his conviction would stand.

The large class action lawsuit filed in 1970 by NSMC's stockholders that named Peat Marwick as a co-defendant was still pending in 1981. Peat Marwick had long contended that it was not liable to NSMC's stockholders for the losses they suffered on their investments in NSMC. A Supreme Court ruling in late 1981 undermined the technicality on which Peat Marwick had based its claim. The following year, Peat Marwick agreed to pay approximately $6.4 million to settle the class action lawsuit.

In July 1975, the SEC issued a lengthy enforcement release discussing the agency's investigation of audit or audit-related engagements performed by Peat Marwick for five clients. Included in these engagements were Peat Marwick's 1968 audit of NSMC and the accounting firm's review of NSMC's 1969 proxy statement. To settle complaints filed by the SEC linked to these engagements, Peat Marwick agreed to have an independent committee perform an extensive review of its audit policies and procedures. Peat Marwick also consented to an SEC order that prohibited the firm from accepting any new SEC clients for a six-month period in late 1975.

Despite NSMC's legal and financial troubles, the company managed to survive for more than a decade following the financial shenanigans of Cortes Randell. At one point, the common stock of the company sold for only $.06 per share, considerably below its record high of $144 per share in late 1969. In 1981, NSMC was liquidated following the sale of its only remaining business segment, Interstate National Corporation, to Fireman's Fund Insurance Company.

QUESTIONS

1. Identify quality control procedures for accounting firms that might have resulted in Peat Marwick avoiding the problems it experienced on the NSMC engagements. Do accounting firms presently employ these procedures?

2. Do you believe that Arthur Andersen had a professional or moral responsibility to inform Peat Marwick why it resigned as NSMC's audit firm? Defend your answer. (Recognize that *SAS No. 84*, "Communications between Predecessor and Successor Auditors," was not in effect in the late 1960s.)

3. Identify the key audit risk factors that Peat Marwick faced during the 1968 NSMC audit. What measures could Peat Marwick have taken to control or minimize the audit risk posed by these factors?

4. Briefly describe the key responsibilities a CPA assumes, under existing professional standards, when he or she is "associated" with unaudited financial data.

5. What factor or factors may explain why Touche Ross reached a different conclusion than Peat Marwick regarding the appropriate accounting treatment for NSMC's fixed-fee promotional projects?

6. In your opinion, did Peat Marwick satisfy its responsibilities on the 1969 comfort letter engagement? Defend your answer. Briefly describe auditors' primary responsibilities, under present professional standards, when they are retained to issue a comfort letter.

7. During the trial of Natelli and Scansaroli, several junior auditors assigned to the NSMC engagements were called to testify for the prosecution. What ethical standards are relevant for auditors in such circumstances?

8. Do you believe the criminal penalties imposed on the individuals involved in the NSMC case were fair? Why or why not?

9. The federal appeals court that reviewed the convictions of Natelli and Scansaroli noted that auditors' professional responsibilities are not necessarily defined by existing professional standards. What implication does this ruling have for practicing auditors?

INDEX